Compilers' Note

The *Atlas of the People's Republic of China* is now being published in English for the first time. The Chinese *pinyin* edition on which it is based was published in June 198 3.

The maps have be en organized into two sets: administrative divisions and topography. In the fir st set, a table of facts or short article appears on the back of each map. Basic information is provided on population, area, climate, topography, major p roducts, and administrative setup. In general, the atlas shows China's admin istrative establishment as of December 1987. Population figures, unless other wise specified, are from 1986. Where possible, recent changes have been in cluded, such as the establishment of Hainan Province in early 1988 and the 1 988 figure for Hong Kong's population.

The second part c f the atlas is an index of place names, to aid readers in locating the map posi tions of those places. After the index are a pronunciation table for Chinese *pin yin* and a conversion table for English equivalents for some geographic terms in *pinyin*.

ATLAS
OF THE PEOPLE'S REPUBLIC OF
CHINA

FOREIGN LANGUAGES PRESS
CHINA CARTOGRAPHIC PUBLISHING HOUSE

1989

BEIJING, CHINA

Managing Editor: *Sun Xiudong*
Cartographic Examiner: *Gu Lifen*

Examiner: *Lu Yongsen* and *Fan Yi*

English Text
Editor: *Yang Dan*

Cover Designer: *Cai Rong*

First Edition 1989

ISBN 0-8351-2319-7
ISBN 7-119-00560-X

Copyright 1989 by Foreign Languages Press, Beijing, China
China Cartographic Publishing House, Beijing, China

Published by Foreign Languages Press
24 Baiwanzhuang Road, Beijing, China
and China Cartographic Publishing House
3 Baizhifang Xijie, Beijing, China

Distributed by China International Book Trading Corporation
(Guoji Shudian), P.O. Box 399, Beijing, China

Printed in the People's Republic of China

CONTENTS

Index to Place Names

LEGEND

	Cities with Populations of over One Million	International Boundary
	Cities with Populations of 300,000 to One Million	Undefined International Boundary
	Cities with Populations of 100,000 to 300,000	Boundary of Province, Autonomous Region, and Municipality under the Central Government
	Towns with Populations of 50,000 to 100,000	Regional Boundary
	Towns with Populations of 10,000 to 50,000	Coastline
	Towns and Villages with Populations under 10,000	Sandbank
★ BEIJING	Capital	Coral Reefs
● Changsha	Seat of the People's Government of Province, Autonomous Region and Municipality Directly under the Central Government	Freshwater Lake
	Seat of the People's Government of Prefecture Level *	Salt Lake
● Zunyi	Seat of the People's Government of City	Seasonal Lake
● Fangshan	Seat of the People's Government of County Level	Shifting Lake
Nankou	Township	River, Stream
MANILA	Capital of Foreign Country	Seasonal River
	Railway	Shifting River
	Highway	Underground River
	Track	Dry Bed
	Canal	Waterfall
300(560)	Shipping Route and Distance: Nautical Mile (Kilometre)	Well
	Shipping Terminal	Spring
	Port	Hot Spring

* Administrative Divisions at Prefecture Level Include Prefectures, Autonomous Prefectures Leagues.

	Irrigation Canal		_184†_	Mountain Peak (m)
	Reservoir		☆	Volcano
	Flood Storage Area		✕	Pass
	Swamp, Saline		⊓⊔⊓⊔	the Great Wall
	Desert		∴	Historic Site

TOPOGRAPHICAL MAPS

BEIJING MANILA	Capital			Desert
Nanjing	Seat of the People's Government of Province, Autonomous Region and Municipality Directly under the Central Government			Crescent Dunes
Yibin	City, County or Town, Village			Undulating Dunes
	Contours			Honeycomb Dunes
	Isobaths			Reg
_1105_	Spot Height (m)			Weathered Monadnock
_3200_	Lake Surface Elevation (m)			Loess Gully
_1894_	Depth of Sea (m)			Dry Bed
	Sandbank, Shoal			Limestone Forest and Sinks
• ⚲ ⚲	Well, Spring, Hot Spring			Snow-Cover, Glacier

SKETCH MAPS OF CITIES

	Streets		⌇	Bridge
	Railway and Station			City Wall
	Park, Greenery		⚊	Pagoda

—→ • |← ←—

GEOGRAPHICAL LOCATION
OF CHINA

1 : 100 000 000

GEOGRAPHICAL

0   1000   200

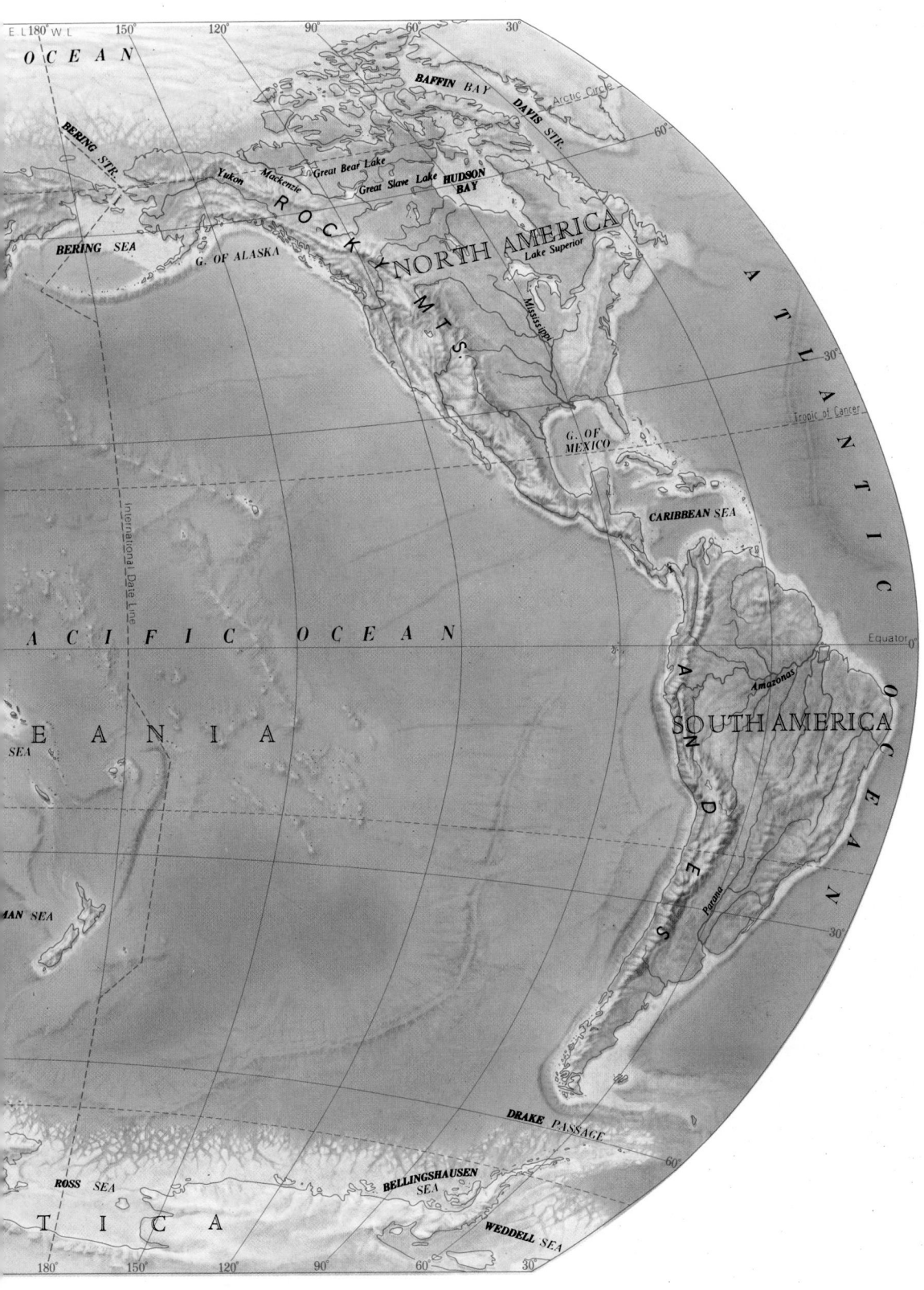

E. L 180° W L   150°   120°   90°   60°   30°

O C E A N

BAFFIN BAY
DAVIS STR.
Arctic Circle
60°

BERING STR.

Yukon   Mackenzie   Great Bear Lake
Great Slave Lake   HUDSON BAY

BERING SEA

G. OF ALASKA

R O C K Y   N O R T H   A M E R I C A

Lake Superior

Mississippi

A T L A N T I C

30°

Tropic of Cancer

G. OF MEXICO

International Date Line

CARIBBEAN SEA

P A C I F I C   O C E A N

A N D E S

Amazonas

Equator   0°

O C E A N I A

SEA

S O U T H   A M E R I C A

Paraná

30°

MAN SEA

DRAKE PASSAGE

60°

ROSS SEA

BELLINGSHAUSEN SEA

T I C A

WEDDELL SEA

180°   150°   120°   90°   60°   30°

00

000   5000   6000 km

The People's Republic of China

The world's third largest country, ranking after the Soviet Union and Canada, China has a land area of about 9.6 million square kilometers, making up 6.5 percent of earth's land mass. Approximately 98 percent of China's land area is located between 20 and 50 north latitude. In climate, the greater part of the country belongs to the temperate zone (i.e., the cold-temperate, temperate, and warm-temperate zones) and the subtropical zone, which respectively account for 45.6 and 26.1 percent of China's land area.

The territory of China extends about 5,200 kilometers from the Pamirs (longitude 73° 40' E) in western Xinjiang Uygur Autonomous Region to the eastern corner of the boundary marker (longitude 135° 5' E) at the confluence of the Heilong and Wusuli Rivers. From north to south, it measures some 5,500 kilometers, stretching from the borderline (latitude 53° 31' N) in the Heilong River north of the town of Mohe to the Zengmu Reef (latitude 4°15' N) at the southernmost tip of the South China Sea Islands. The length of the land boundary is 22,000 kilometers and the mainland coastline, 18,000 kilometers (32,000 kilometers with the coastlines of the 5,000 or more offshore islands included).

China has a vast sea area, its domain extending into the Bohai Sea, the Yellow Sea, the East China Sea, and the South China Sea. Contiguous to each other, the four seas form a northeast-southwest arc covering a total area of 4.78 million square kilometers.

China is bordered by Korea in the northeast; the Soviet Union and Mongolia in the north; Afghanistan, Pakistan, Nepal, Sikkim, Bhutan, and India in the southwest; and Burma, Laos, and Vietnam in the south. Across the seas to the east and southeast it faces Japan, the Philippines, Malaysia, Brunei, and Indonesia.

Administratively, China is divided into three basic levels: provinces (autonomous regions, municipalities directly under the Central Government), counties (cities, banners, special districts, industrial-agricultural district, forest district), and townships (towns). There are twenty-three provinces, five autonomous regions, and three municipalities directly under the Central Government. The administrative units under a province or an autonomous region include prefectures, autonomous prefectures, leagues, cities, counties, autonomous counties, banners, and autonomous banners. Under a county or an autonomous county are townships, nationality townships, and towns. The municipalities directly under the Central Government and large cities are divided into districts and counties, while the autonomous prefectures are divided into counties, autonomous counties, and cities. The autonomous regions, autonomous prefectures, and autonomous counties are all nationality areas.

ADMINISTRATIVE DIVISIONS OF CHINA

1 : 25 000 000

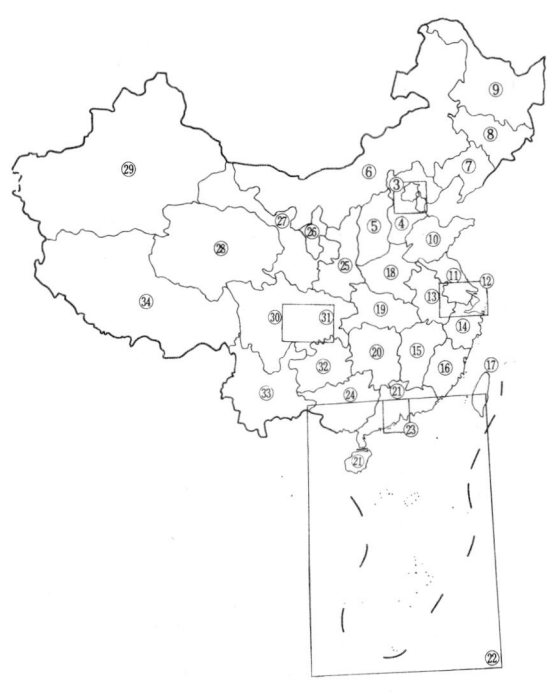

2

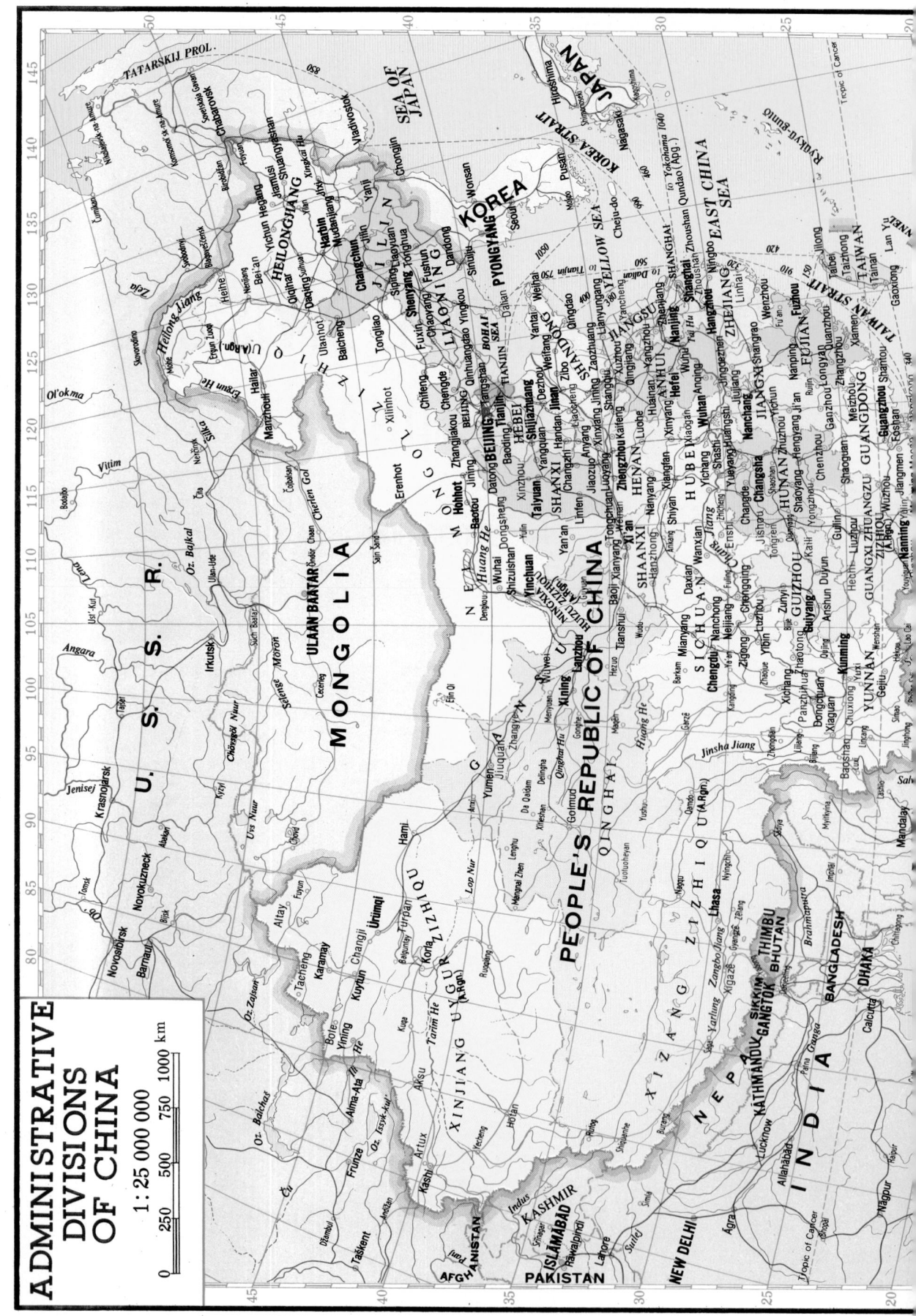

ADMINISTRATIVE
DIVISIONS
OF CHINA

1 : 25 000 000

1000 km
250 500 750
0

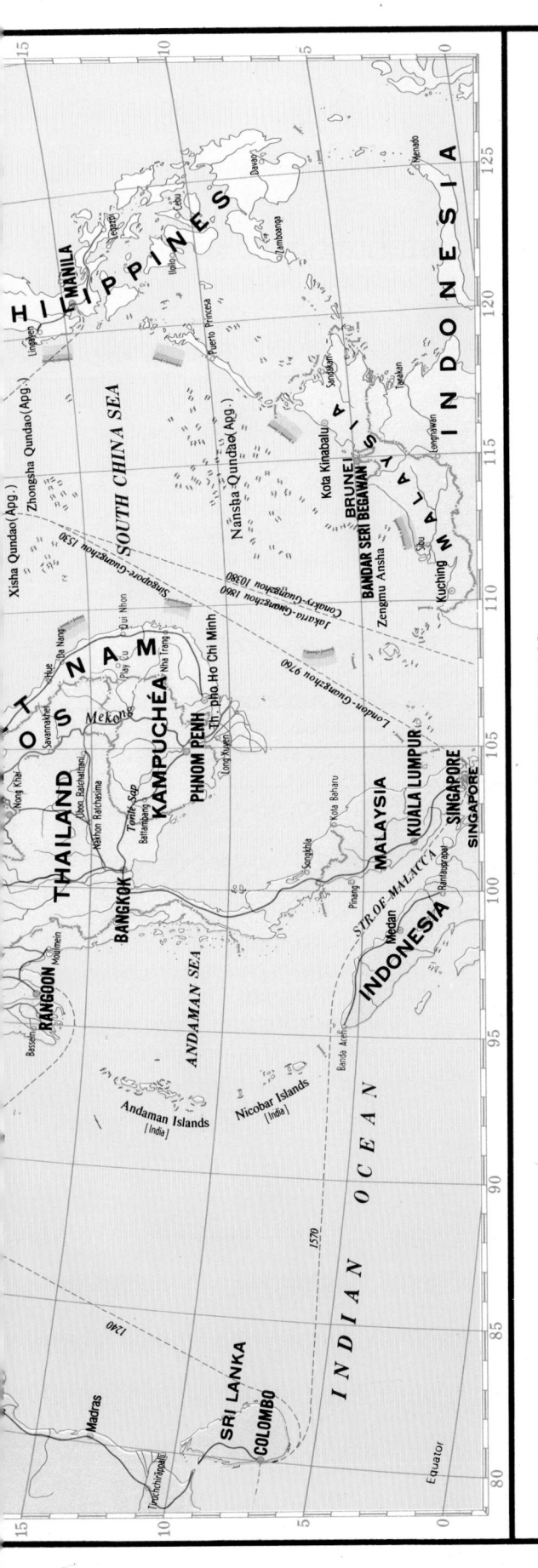

NAMES OF PROVINCES, AUTONOMOUS REGIONS AND MUNICIPALITIES DIRECTLY UNDER THE CENTRAL GOVERNMENT

LEGEND

★	Capital
Xi'an	Seat of the People's Government of Province, Autonomous Region, Municipality Directly under the Central Government Municipality
◉	City
◦	Town
◦	Capital of Foreign Country

FULL NAME	SHORT NAME 1	SHORT NAME 2	ABBREVIATION
Anhui Province	Anhui	Wan	AH
Beijing Municipality	Beijing	Jing	BJ
Fujian Province	Fujian	Min	FJ
Guangdong Province	Guangdong	Yue	GD
Gansu Province	Gansu	Gan	GS
Guangxi Zhuang Autonomous Region	Guangxi	Gui	GX
Guizhou Province	Guizhou	Qian	GZ
Hubei Province	Hubei	E	HB
Hebei Province	Hebei	Ji	HEB
Henan Province	Henan	Yu	HEN
Hainan Province	Hainan	Qiong	HI

FULL NAME	SHORT NAME 1	SHORT NAME 2	ABBREVIATION
Heilongjiang Province	Heilongjiang	Hei	HL
Hunan Province	Hunan	Xiang	HN
Jilin Province	Jilin	Ji	JL
Jiangsu Province	Jiangsu	Su	JS
Jiangxi Province	Jiangxi	Gan	JX
Liaoning Province	Liaoning	Liao	LN
Nei Mongol(Inner Mongolia) Autonomous Region	Nei Mongol		NM
Ningxia Hui Autonomous Region	Ningxia	Ning	NX
Qinghai Province	Qinghai	Qing	QH
Sichuan Province	Sichuan	Chuan	SC

FULL NAME	SHORT NAME 1	SHORT NAME 2	ABBREVIATION
Shandong Province	Shandong	Lu	SD
Shanghai Municipality	Shanghai	Hu	SH
Shaanxi Province	Shaanxi	Shaan	SN
Shanxi Province	Shanxi	Jin	SX
Tianjin Municipality	Tianjin	Jin	TJ
Taiwan Province	Taiwan	Tai	TW
Xinjiang Uygur Autonomous Region	Xinjiang	Xin	XJ
Xizang (Tibet) Autonomous Region	Xizang	Zang	XZ
Yunnan Province	Yunnan	Yun	YN
Zhejiang Province	Zhejiang	Zhe	ZJ

Nationalities and Distribution

China is a country with fifty-six ethnic nationalities. According to the Third National Population Census in 1982, there were 936.7 million Han people, and 67.2 million people of other nationalities. The fifty-five minority nationalities are, from the largest group to the smallest, the Zhuang, Hui, Uygur, Yi, Miao, Manchu, Tibetan, Mongolian, Tujia, Bouyei, Korean, Dong, Yao, Bai, Hani, Kazak, Li, Dai, Lisu, She, Lahu, Va, Shui, Dongxiang, Naxi, Tu, Kirgiz, Qiang, Daur, Jingpo, Mulam, Xibe, Salar, Blang, Gelo, Maonan, Tajik, Pumi, Nu, Achang, Ewenki, Ozbek, Jino, Jing, Deang (Penglong), Yugur, Bonan, Drung, Oroqen, Tatar, Russian, Gaoshan, Hezhen, Moinba, and Lhoba nationalities.

The size of the ethnic groups varies greatly. The Zhuang nationality has 13.4 million people, while the Lhoba, the smallest, has only 1,000 people. Of the 55 minority nationalities, 15 number more than 1 million, 13 more than 100,000, and 7 more than 50,000. Twenty of the ethnic groups have no more than 50,000 people. Furthermore, there are a few ethnic groups in Yunnan and Tibet which are as yet unidentified.

The Han people who can be found across the country are predominant in the Yellow, Yangtze, and Pearl River Valleys and the Songliao Plain of the northeast. Over the course of history, the Han people have established strong ties with other ethnic groups in political, economic, and cultural spheres. The Han nationality plays a leading role in state affairs. The ethnic minorities, though small in population, inhabit 50 to 60 percent of the country's total area. They reside mainly in Inner Mongolia, Xinjiang, Tibet, Guangxi, and Ningxia, as well as in some regions of Heilongjiang, Jilin, Liaoning, Gansu, Qinghai, Sichuan, Yunnan, Guizhou, Guangdong, Hunan, Hebei, Hubei, Fujian, and Taiwan.

As a result of migration, opening of frontier regions, and change of dynasties, the various minorities have intermingled and live in mixed or compact communities. There are more than twenty minorities in Yunnan Province, the province with the most ethnic nationalities in China. People of Korean nationality live in compact communities in Yanbian in Jilin Province, and the Tujia and Miao people live in the western part of Hunan Province. The Li people are prevalent on Hainan Island. In addition, there are about 10 million minority people living in mingled groups in every corner of China, and some concentrated ethnic communities have mixed with Han communities. This pattern of small concentrated communities among larger intermingled groups composed mainly of Han people is typical of China's nationality distribution.

—— 3 ——

BEIJING MUNICIPALITY
TIANJIN MUNICIPALITY

I : I 330 000

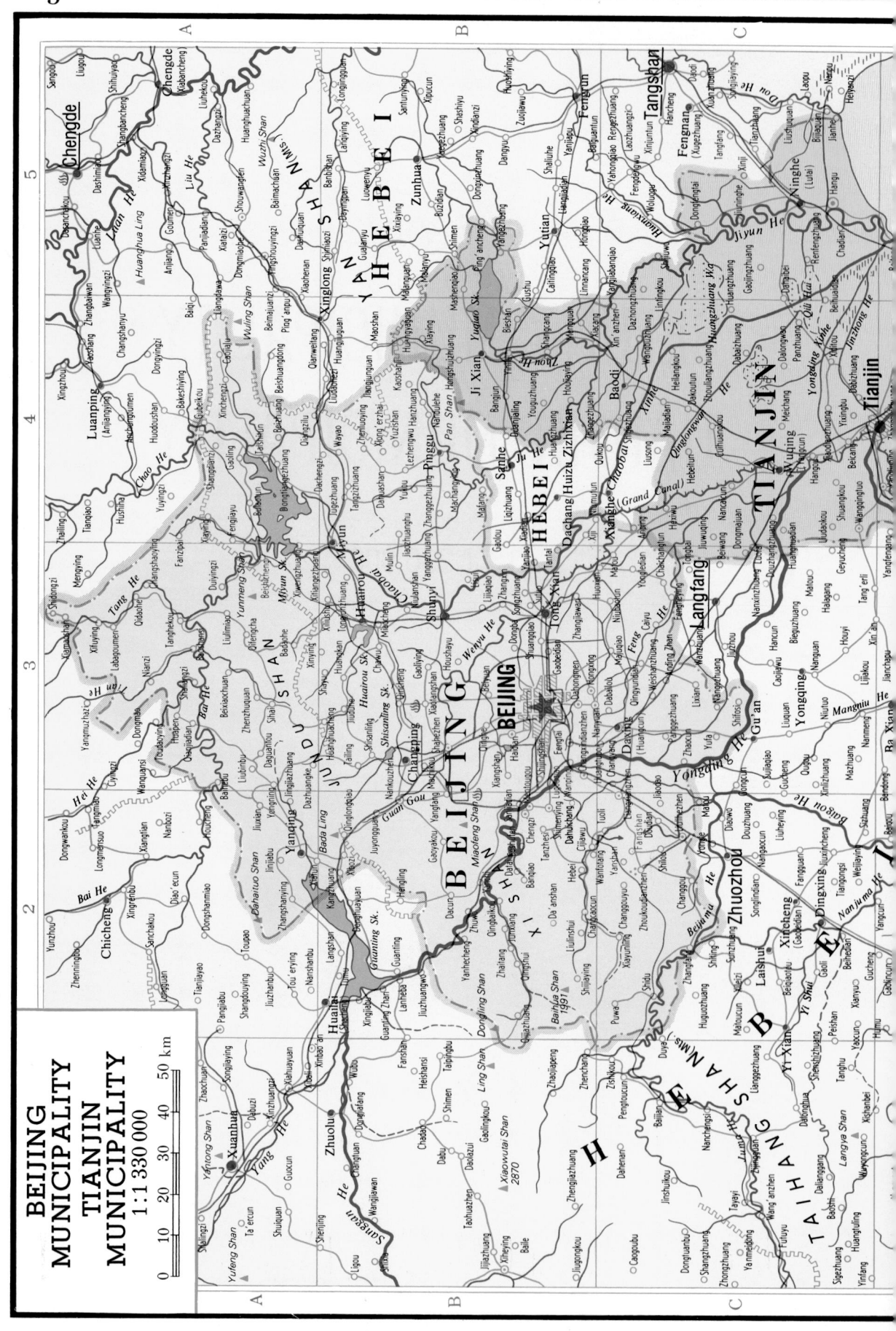

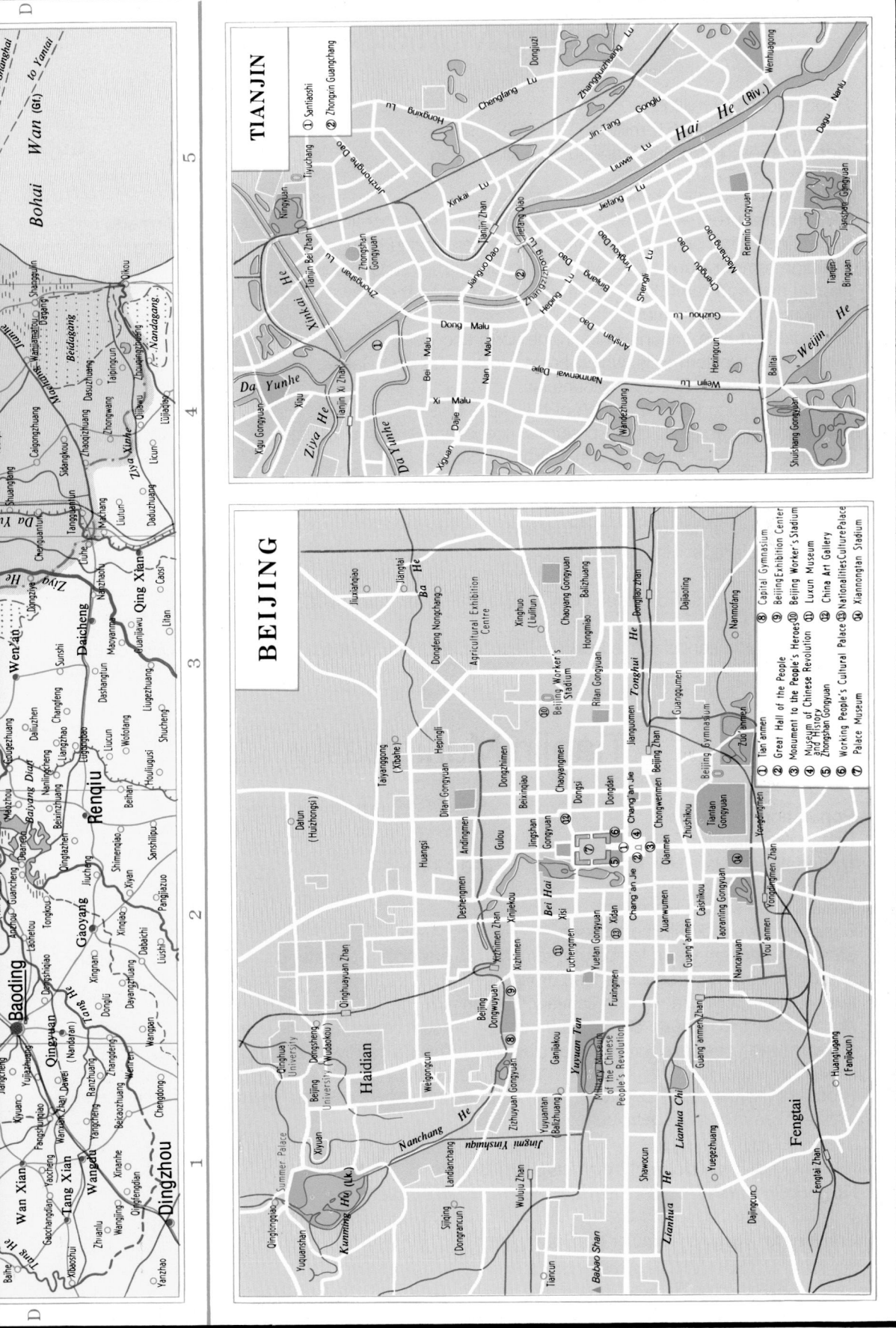

TIANJIN

① Senliaoshi
② Zhongxin Guangchang

Bohai Wan (Gt.)
to Yantai
to Shanghai

Da Yunhe
Xigu Gongyuan
Xigu
Xinkai He
Ziya He
Tianjin Xi Zhan
Da Yunhe
Xiqing
Dajie

Ninghuan
Tiyuchang
Hongqiao Lu
Chengfang Lu
Zhangguozhuang Lu
Dongjuzi
Jin Tang Gonglu
Jintonghe Dao

Hai He (Riv.)
Dagu Nanlu
Wenhuagong
Wenhuagong

Xinkai Lu
Tianjin Bei Zhan
Zhongshan Gongyuan
Jianguo Dao
Jiefang Qiao
Tianjin Zhan
Jiefang Bei Lu
②

Dong Malu
Bei Malu
Xi Malu
Nan Malu

Nanmenwai Dajie
Binjiang Dao
Heping Lu
Shengli Lu
Binjiang Dao
Chang'an Dao
Anshan Dao
Yingkou Dao

Luuwei Lu
Jiefang Lu
Nanjing Lu
Machang Dao
Chengdu Dao

Guizhou Lu
Hexingqun
Weijin He

Renmin Gongyuan
Jianshe Gongyuan
Tiantin
Binguan
Balitai
Shushang Gongyuan

Welin Lu
Weijin Lu

BEIJING

① Tian'anmen
② Great Hall of the People
③ Monument to the People's Heroes
④ Museum of Chinese Revolution and History
⑤ Zhongshan Gongyuan
⑥ Working People's Cultural Palace
⑦ Palace Museum
⑧ Capital Gymnasium
⑨ Beijing Exhibition Center
⑩ Beijing Worker's Stadium
⑪ Luxun Museum
⑫ China Art Gallery
⑬ Nationalities Culture Palace
⑭ Xiannongtan Stadium

Qinglongqiao
Yuquanshan
Summer Palace
Kunming Hu (Lk.)

Qinghua University
Beijing University
Dehsheng (Wudaokou)
Weigongcun
Ganjiakou
Yuyuantan (Balizhuang)
Military Museum of the Chinese People's Revolution
Landianchang
Shijing (Dongrancun)
Wulujiu Zhan
Jingmi Yinshuiqu
Shawicun

Haidian
Nanchang He
Yuyuan Tan
Zizhuyuan gongyuan ⑨
Beijing Dongwuyuan ⑧
Fuxingmen
Fuxingmen

Jiuxiaqiao
Ba He
Jiangtai
Xinghuo (Liufun)
Dongdeng Nongchang
Agricultural Exhibition Centre
Chaoyang Gongyuan
Balizhuang
Hongmiao
Rifan Gongyuan

Datun (Huizhongsi)
Huangsi
Deshengmenwai
Deshengmen
Xizhimen Zhan
Xizhimen
Fuchengmen
Yuetan Gongyuan ⑪
Xidan ⑬

Taiyanggong (Xibahe)
Hepingli
Ditan Gongyuan
Andingmen
Gulou
Jingshan
Bei Hai
Xisi

Dongzhimen
Beixinqiao
Dongsi
Dongdan
⑫
Jianguomen
⑩ Beijing Worker's Stadium
Tonghui He
Dongjiao Zhan
Guangqumen
Dajieoting
Nanmenlang

Chang'an Jie
⑦ ⑥
⑤ ④
③ ①
⑤ Zuo'anmen
Tian'anmen

Chang'an Jie
Qianmen
Taoranting Gongyuan ⑭
Youanmen

Beijing Gymnasium

Chongwenmen Beijing Zhan
Chongwenmen
Zhushikou
Zhushikou
Cashikou
Guang'anmen
Xuanwumen

Tiantan Gongyuan
Yongdingmen
Yongdingmen Zhan

Lianhua Chi
Lianhua He
Yuegezhuang
Dalingcun

Guang'anmen Zhan
Nancaiyuan
Huangkuang (Fanjiacun)
Fengtai Zhan

Fengtai

Babao Shan
Tianlincun

D 5 4 3 2 1

Bohai Wan (Gt.)
Bohai Wan

Beidagang
Nandagang

Qikou
Shanggulin
Banqiao
Dasunzhuang
Dagang
Zhoujiazhuang
Taipingcun
Lüjiaobu
Lüjiaodou

Wanjiamatou
Shangshulin
Sidangkou
Caigongzhuangtun
Zhaoqizhuang
Zhongwang
Licun
Lütun

Xinglongzhuang
Cangzhou
Wen'an
Ziya Yunhe
Tanggujiahun
Jiuhe
Machang
Liutun
Deduzhuang

Ziya He
Daicheng
Qing Xian

Dingwang
Chenguantun
Nazhaok
Caosi
Litan

Dashangtun
Liugezhuang
Shucheng
Shuchengli
Wotolang
Behan
Houliugusi
Nanlingzhuang
Liangzhao
Changfeng
Licun
Liuzhen

Baiyang Diat
Maozhou
Baobei
Qingzhen
Shimenqiao
Senshilipu
Renqiu

Wan Xian
Gaochangdian
Yaocheng
Xiyou
Pangjiazuo
Shuzen
Xiyan
Dabaichi
Wangdu
Jiangzhuang
Yujiazhuang
Fagezhuangdian
Xiyan
Gaoyang
Jiuchang
Tongkou
Laozhentou
Laoshang
Tong He
(Nandan)
Dongjulu
Dayangzhuang
Dongiu
Pangjiazuo
Wangan

Baoding
Qingyuan
Xiaxcheng
Jiangchai
Shangzhuang

Renqiu
Gaoyang
Dingdong

Wumen
Xinhe
Xinanxian
Chengdong
Renzhuang
Zhangdeng
Zhangfuzhuang

Tang He
Xiboshui
Yanzhao
Yanbao
Wangan

Tang Xian
Wangdu
Qingfengdian
Wangling

Dingzhou

Beijing Municipality

Population: 9.8 million
Urban population: 6.6 million
Nationalities: Han, Hui, Manchu, and Mongolian

Area: 16,800 square kilometers
Climatic features: warm-temperate, semi-humid, monsoonal climate; hot, rainy summers; cold, dry winters; short springs and autumns; frequent spring droughts and summer flooding
Average temperature: -7 — -4°C in January, 25 — 26°C in July
Annual average rainfall: 600 mm; over 700 mm on the seaward side of mountains; 75 percent of the rain falls in summer
Physical features: mountainous in the north and west; flatlands in the southeast
Mountains: Western Hills, which belong to the Taihang Range; Jundu Mountain, in the north, which is part of the Yanshan Mountains
Rivers: Yongding River, a branch of the Haihe River
Products: wheat, corn, millet, potatoes, rice, peanuts, soybeans, sesame; cotton, silk cocoons; tobacco; pears, grapes; coal, iron, marble, asbestos
Specialties: Miyun dates, Jingbai pears, Liangxiang chestnuts, Beijing duck

Administrative divisions: 10 districts and 8 counties
Neighboring areas: Hebei Province and Tianjin Municipality

Tourist attractions: Forbidden City, Temple of Heaven, Great Wall, Summer Palace

Comments: the capital of the People's Republic of China, Beijing is a political, economic, cultural, and transportation center.

Tianjin Municipality

Population: 8.2 million
Urban population: 5.8 million
Nationalities: Han, Hui, Korean, Manchu, and Mongolian

Area: 11,000 square kilometers
Coastline: over 100 kilometers long
Climatic features: warm-temperate, semi-humid, monsoonal climate; distinct seasons; occasional summer flooding; frequent spring droughts
Average temperature: -4°C in January, 26°C in July
Annual average rainfall: 550 — 650 mm; 75 percent of the rain falls in summer
Physical features: low-lying alluvial plain along the Haihe River; saline-alkaline soil; faces the Bohai Gulf
Products: wheat, corn, potatoes, sorghum, peanuts, soybeans; cotton, ambary hemp; pears, walnuts; sea products; petroleum, salt

Administrative divisions: 13 districts and 5 counties
Neighboring areas: Hebei Province and Beijing Municipality

Comments: Tianjin is a major port city.

— 4 —

HEBEI PROVINCE

I : 2 330 000

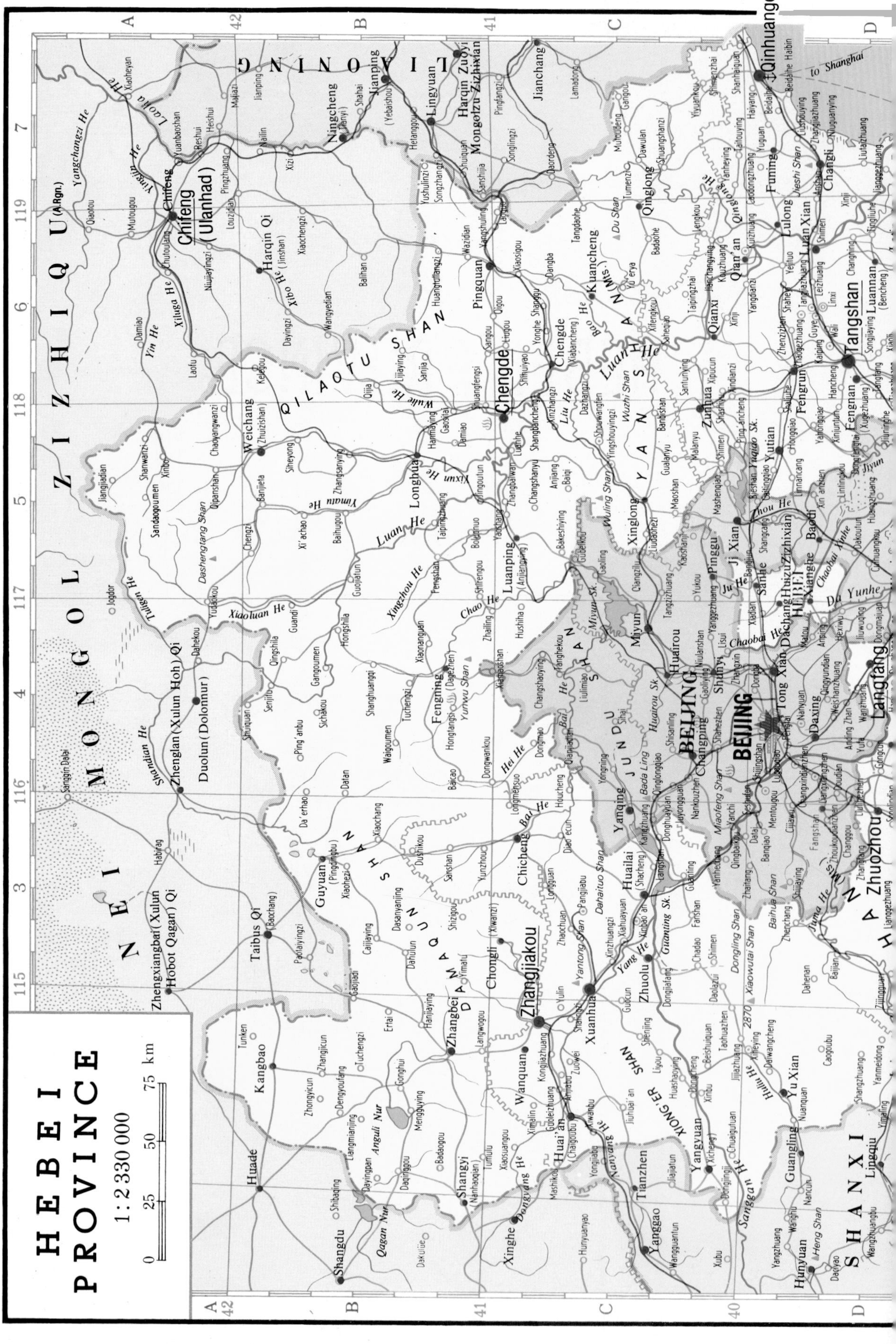

HEBEI PROVINCE

1 : 2 330 000

0 25 50 75 km

LIAONING

NEI MONGOL ZIZHIQU (A.Rgn.)

SHANXI

BEIJING

to Shanghai

Qinhuangdao
Beidaihe

Chifeng (Ulanhad)
Harqin Qi
Ningcheng
Jianping
Lingyuan
Harqin Zuoyi Mongolzu Zizhixian
Jianchang

Weichang (Zhuizishan)
Chengde
Pingquan
Kuancheng
Qinglong
Fuming
Lulong
Luan Xian
Tangshan
Luannan
Qian'an
Fengrun
Zunhua
Yutian
Ji Xian
Ji Xian
Pinggu
Miyun
Huairou
Changping
Shunyi
Tong Xian
Daxing
Langfang
Zhuozhou

Zhangjiakou
Xuanhua
Huailai (Shacheng)
Yanqing
Zhuolu
Yu Xian

Guyuan (Pingdingbu)
Chongli (Xiwanzi)
Chicheng
Fengning

Taibus Qi
Zhangbei
Wanquan
Huai'an
Yangyuan

Kangbao
Huade
Shangyi
Xinghe
Yangyuan
Guangling
Lingqiu
Hunyuan

QILAOTU SHAN
YAN SHAN
JUNDU SHAN
DAMA QUN SHAN
XIONG'ER SHAN

Luan He
Bai He
Chao He
Sanggan He
Yang He

QAGAN NUR
ANGULI NUR

Duolun (Dolonnur)
Zhenglan (Xulun Hoh) Qi
Zhengxiangbai (Xulun Hobot Qagan) Qi

Luoyuan
Yixian

SHANGDU

Xinhe

Chongli

115 116 117 118 119

A B C D

42 41 40 7 6 5 4 3

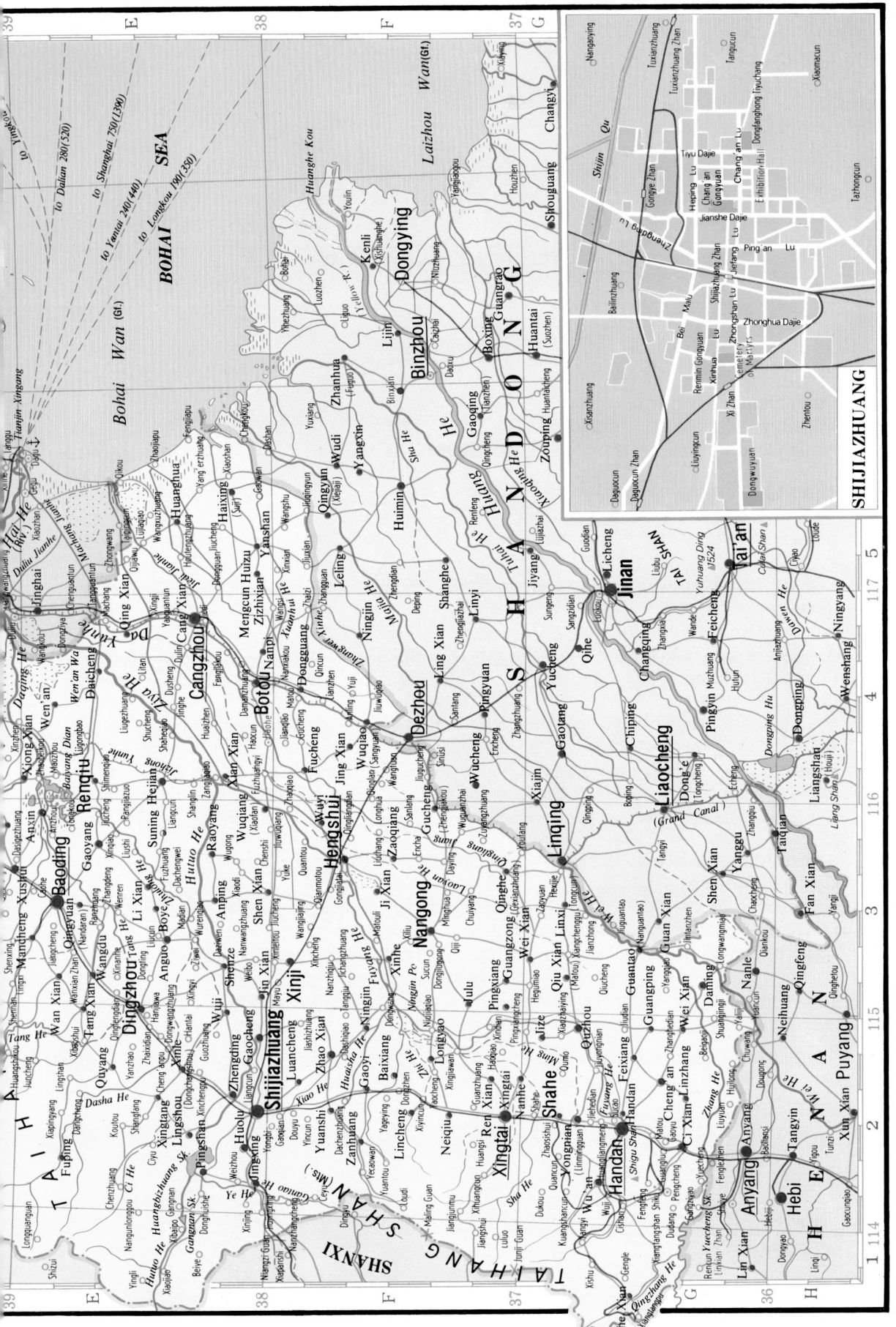

Hebei Province

Population: 56.2 million
Urban population: 20.1 million
Nationalities: Han, Hui, Manchu, Mongolian, and Korean

Area: 190,000 square kilometers
Coastline: 500 kilometers long
Altitude: above 1,000 meters in the mountain areas; under 50 meters on the Hebei Plain in the southeast
Climatic features: temperate continental climate; windy in the spring; hot, rainy summers; dry winters
Average temperature: -14 — -2°C in January, 20 — 27°C in July
Annual average rainfall: 400 — 800 mm, high precipitation on the seaward side of mountains
Physical features: high in the north, northwest, and west; low in the southeast; faces the Bohai Gulf
Mountains: Yanshan Mountains in the north; Taihang Range along the western border
Rivers: Haihe River and tributaries; Luanhe River in the northeast
Products: corn, sorghum, millet, wheat, potatoes, rice, soybeans, peanuts, rape, sesame, mushrooms; cotton, ambary hemp, silk cocoons; tobacco; chestnuts, apricots, grapes, walnuts, dates, persimmons, pears; iron, coal, petroleum, salt

Administrative divisions: 18 cities, 127 counties, and 4 autonomous counties
Capital: Shijiazhuang
Neighboring areas: Beijing and Tianjin Municipalities; Shandong, Henan, Shanxi, and Liaoning Provinces; Inner Mongolia Autonomous Region
Major cities: Shijiazhuang, Tangshan, Handan, Zhangjiakou, Chengde, Qinhuangdao, Baoding

Tourist attractions: Shanhaiguan, the eastern pass of the Great Wall; the imperial summer residence in Chengde; the seaside resort of Beidaihe

SHANXI PROVINCE

1 : 2 000 000

5

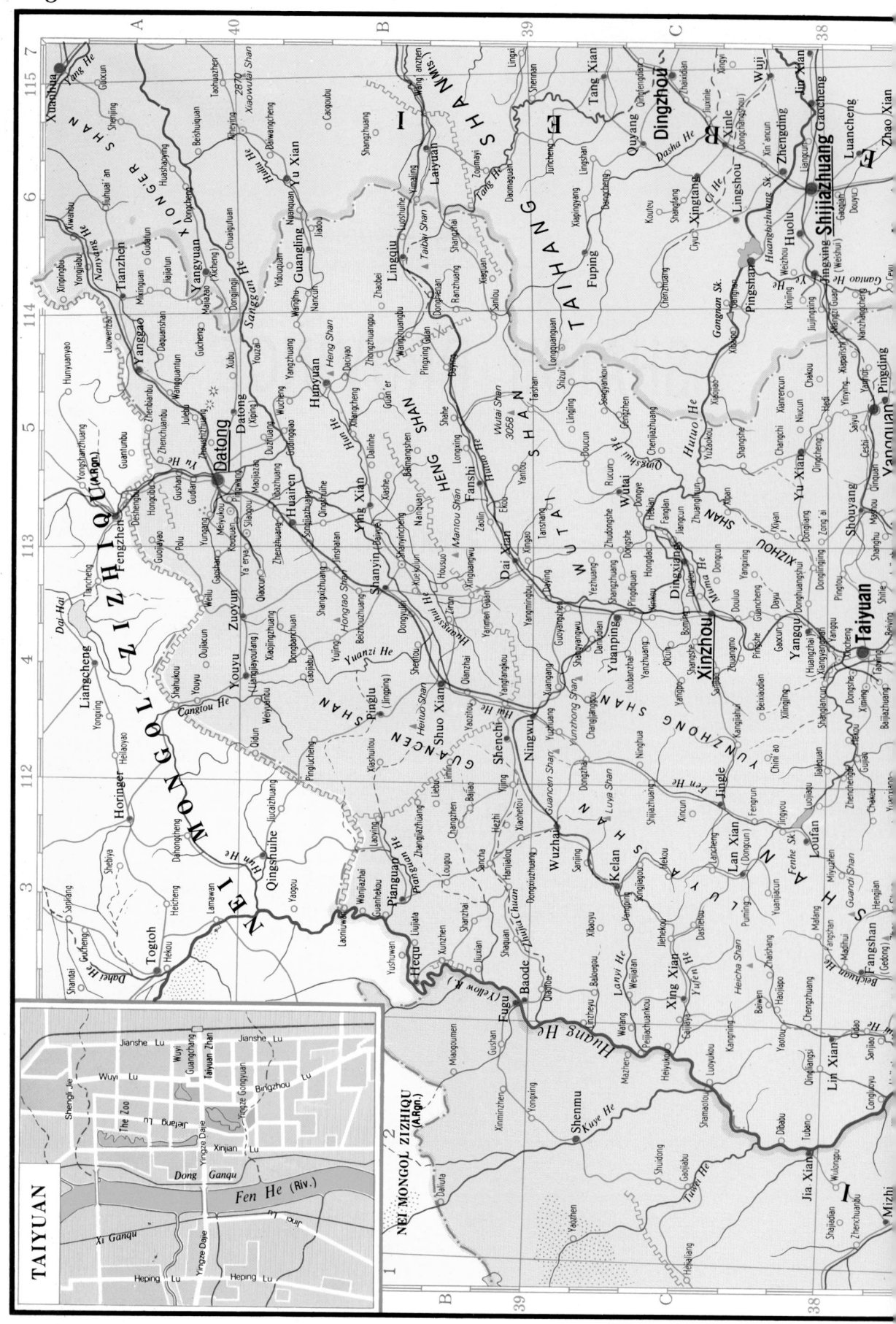

TAIYUAN

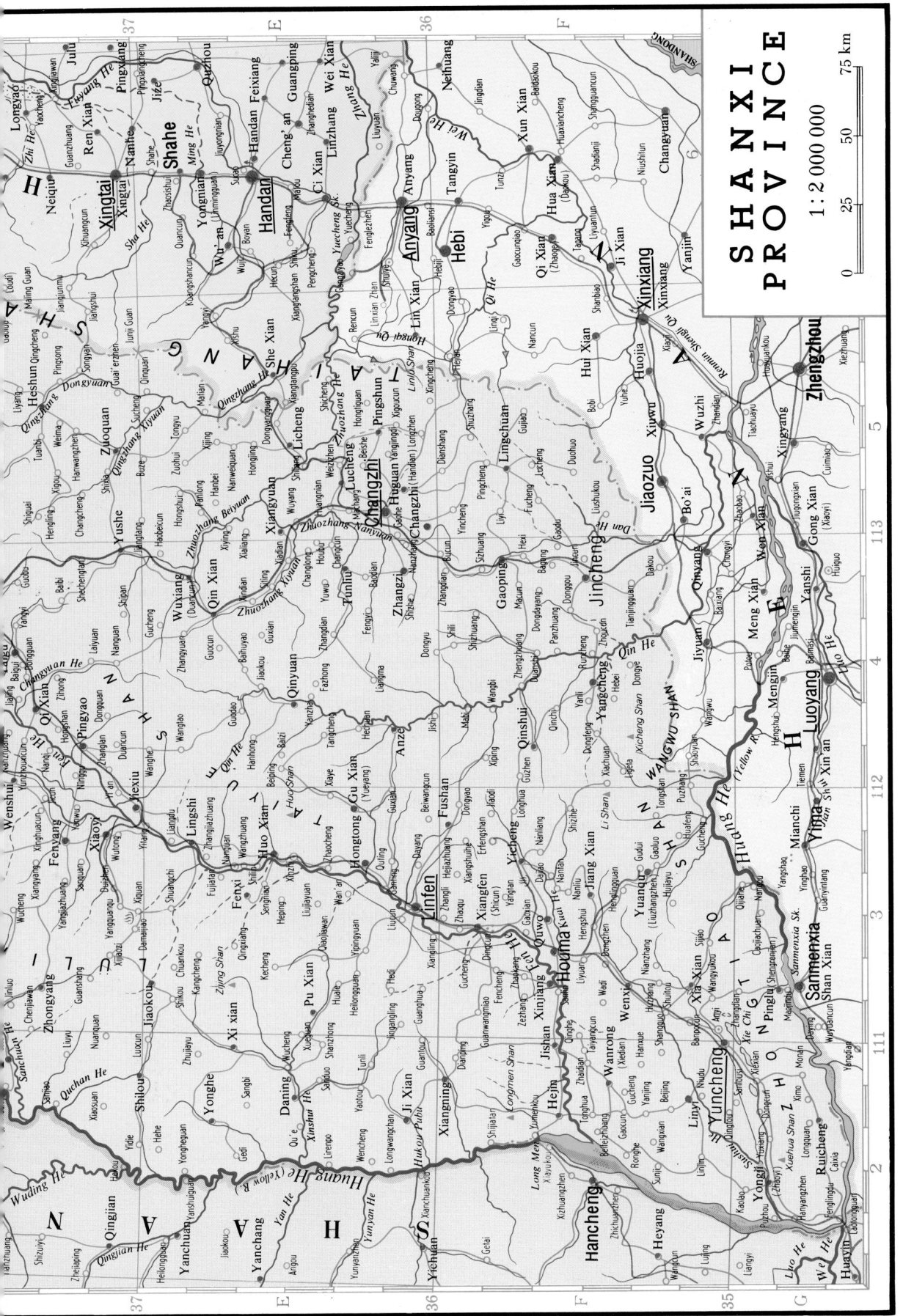

SHANXI
PROVINCE

1 : 2 000 000

0   25   50   75 km

Shanxi Province

Population: 26.6 million
Urban population: 15.1 million
Nationalities: Han, Hui, Mongolian, and Manchu

Area: 150,000 square kilometers
Climatic features: temperate, continental, monsoonal climate; long, cold winters and mild summers; warmer in the south than in the north
Average temperature: -16 — -2°C in January, 19 — 28°C in July
Annual average rainfall: 350 — 700 mm; high precipitation in the southeast and low in the northwest; 60 percent of the rain falls in summer
Physical features: located on the eastern part of the Loess Plateau; bounded by the Taihang Range in the east, the Yellow (Huanghe) River in the west and south, and the Great Wall in the north; valleys, basins, and lowlands in the central part are drained by the Fenhe River.
Mountains: the Taihang Range in eastern Shanxi includes Mount Wutai and Mount Hengshan; the Lüliang Mountains are the watershed of the Yellow and Fenhe Rivers.
Rivers: Fenhe River, a tributary of the Yellow River
Products: wheat, corn, sorghum, millet, potatoes, soybeans, sesame, peanuts, rape; cotton, ambary hemp, silk cocoons; tobacco; pears, dates, walnuts, persimmons; coal, iron
Specialties: Jishan dates, Yuanping pears, Qingxu grapes

Administrative divisions: 10 cities and 96 counties
Capital: Taiyuan
Neighboring areas: Hebei, Henan, and Shaanxi Provinces; Inner Mongolia Autonomous Region
Major cities: Taiyuan, Datong, Changzhi, Yuci, Yangquan, Linfen, Houma, Jiexiu

Tourist attractions: the ancient Yungang Grottoes near Datong; the Memorial Temple of Jin near Taiyuan

NEI MONGOL
(INNER MONGOLIA)
AUTONOMOUS REGION

1 : 7 330 000

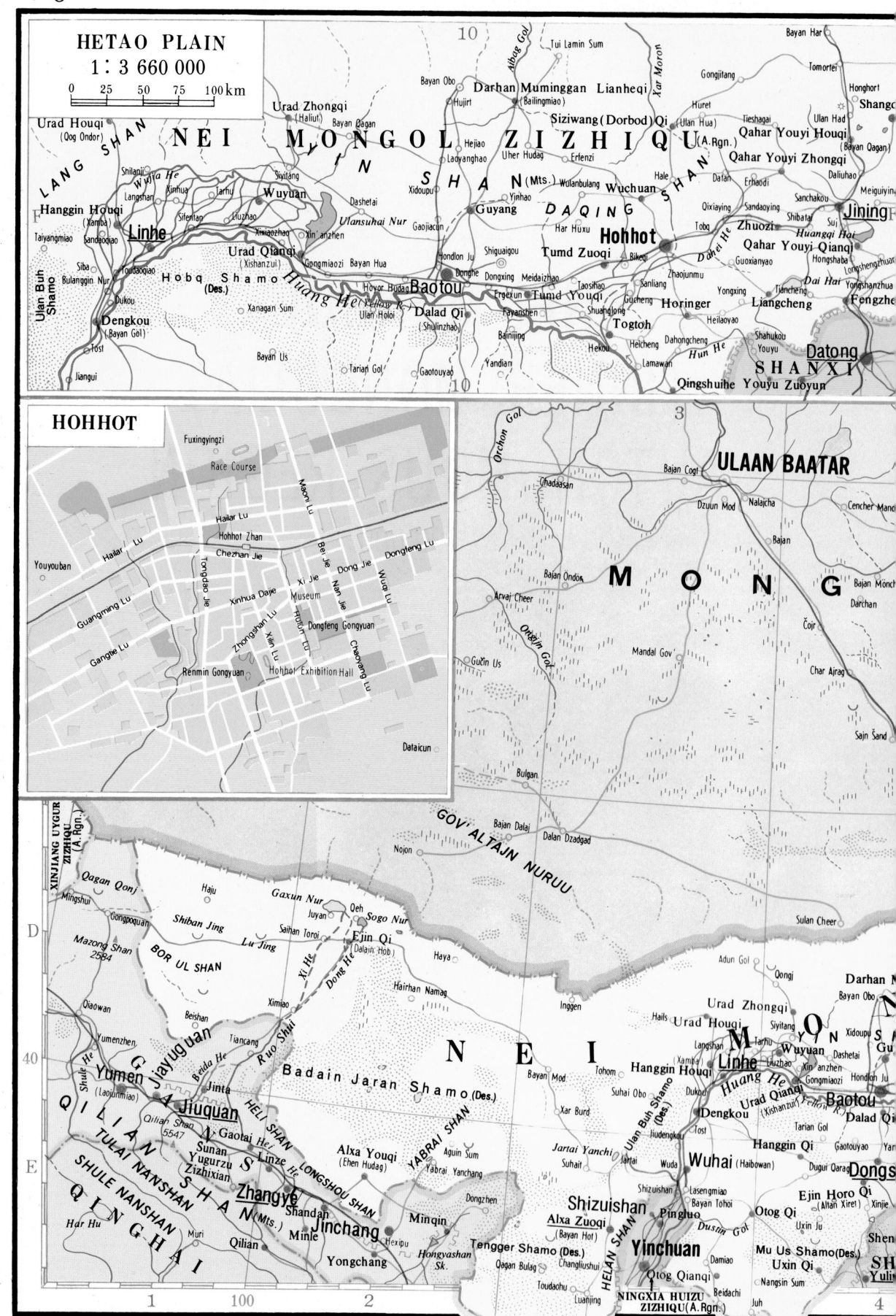

HETAO PLAIN
1 : 3 660 000
0 25 50 75 100 km

HOHHOT

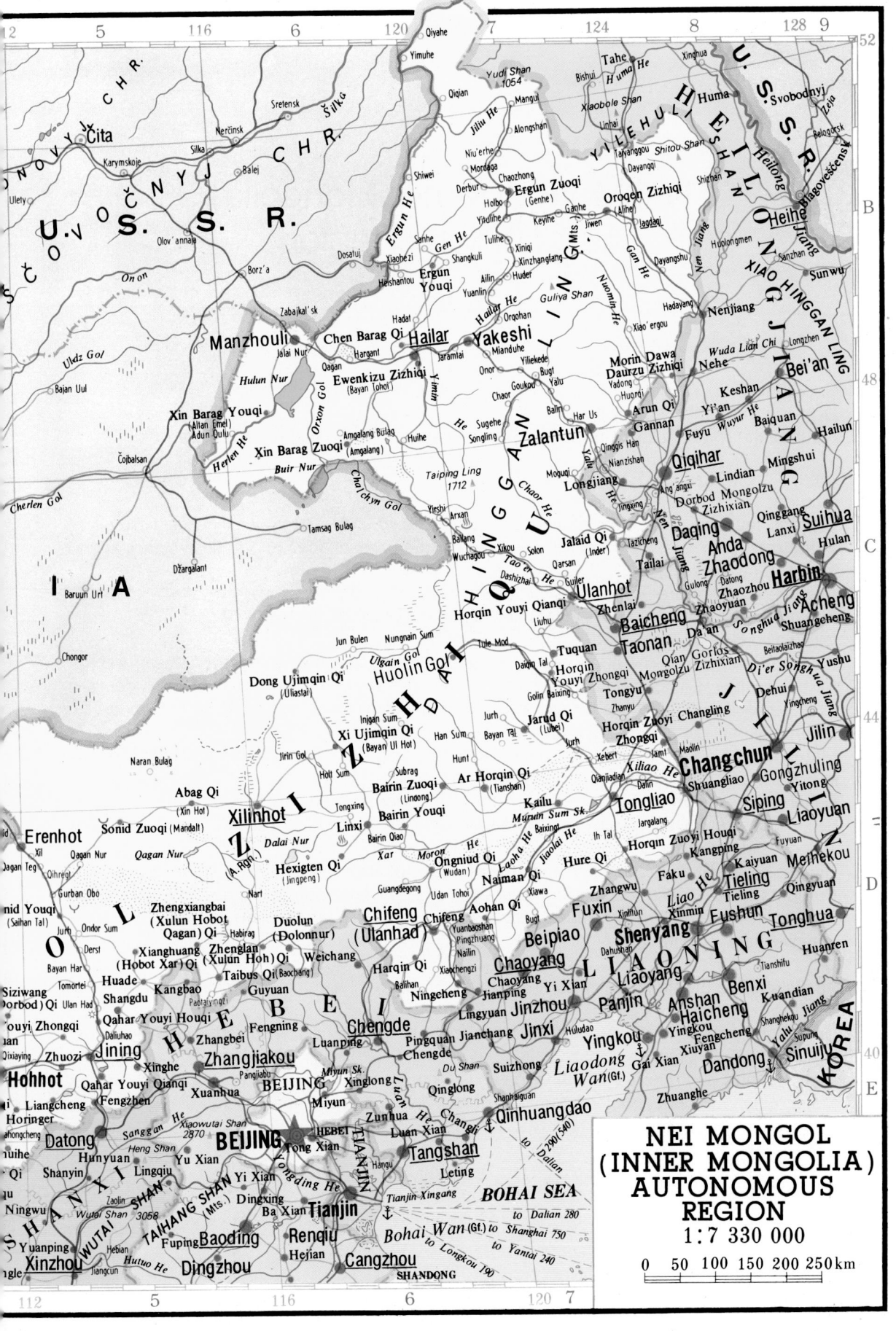

NEI MONGOL
(INNER MONGOLIA)
AUTONOMOUS
REGION
1:7 330 000

0   50   100 150 200 250km

Nei Mongol (Inner Mongolia) Autonomous Region

Population: 20.3 million
Urban population: 9.3 million
Nationalities: Mongolian, Han, Daur, Ewenki, Oroqen, Hui, Manchu, and Korean

Area: 1,100,000 square kilometers
Altitude: 1,000 meters in general
Climatic features: temperate, continental climate; cold, long winters with frequent blizzards; warm, short summers; from west to east, the climate changes from arid to semi-humid, and to humid in the northeast.
Average temperature: -23 — -10°C in January, 17 — 26°C in July
Annual average rainfall: 50 — 450 mm; high precipitation in the east; 70 percent of the rain falls during the summer
Physical features: in the northeast is the Greater Hinggan Range with dense forests; west of the range is the Hulunbuir Plateau, with vast grasslands for grazing; the rest of the Inner Mongolia Plateau consists of numerous deserts, sands, salt and alkali lakes, and scattered highlands.
Mountains: Greater Hinggan Range and Yinshan Mountains
Plateaus: Hulunbuir Plateau in the north; Xilingol and Ju Ud Plateaus in the east; Alxa Plateau in the west; Ordos Plateau south of the Yellow River
Deserts and sands: Hulunbuir Sands in the north; Horqin Sands in the east; Lesser Tengger Sands in the central east; Hobq Desert and Muus Sands south of the Yellow River; Ulanbuh and Tengger Deserts in the central west; Badainjaran Desert in the west
Rivers: Yellow River, Ergun River, and upper reaches of Liaohe River
Products: wheat, naked oats, millet, sorghum, corn, potatoes, rape, sugar beet, soybeans; flax, wool; shiny-leaved yellowhorn, musk, bezoar, licorice root, Chinese ephedra; iron, coal, alkali, salt, graphite, mica, sulphur

Administrative divisions: 16 cities, 18 counties, 51 banners, and 3 autonomous banners
Capital: Hohhot
Neighboring areas: Heilongjiang, Jilin, Liaoning, Hebei, Shanxi, Shaanxi, and Gansu Provinces; Ningxia Hui Autonomous Region
Neighboring countries: the Soviet Union and Mongolia
Major cities: Hohhot, Baotou, Wuhai, Hailar, Manzhouli, Tongliao, Chifeng, Jining, Erenhot, Ulanhot

LIAONING PROVINCE

1 : 2 330 000

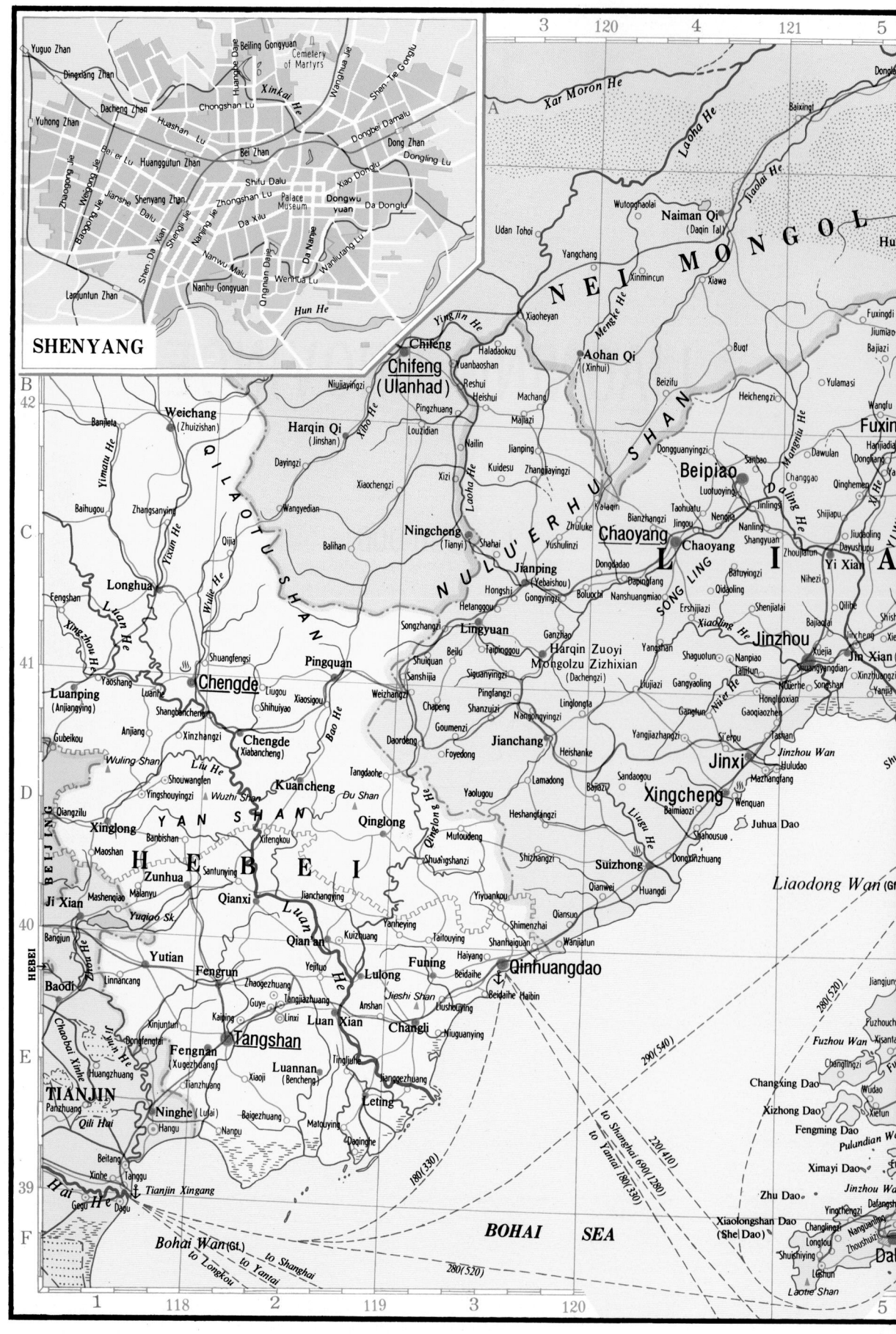

SHENYANG

Yuguo Zhan
Dingxiang Zhan
Dacheng Zhan
Yuhong Zhan
Huangwanggutun Zhan
Shenyang Zhan
Lanjuntun Zhan

Beiling Gongyuan
Cemetery of Martyrs
Xinkai He
Chongshan Lu
Huashan Lu
Bei er Lu
Zhongshan Lu
Shifu Dalu
Palace Museum
Nanwu Malu
Nanhu Gongyuan

Huanghe Dajie
Beiling Jie
Wanghua Jie
Shen-he Gonglu
Dongbei Damalu
Dong Zhan
Dongling Lu
Xiao Donglu
Da Donglu
Dongwu yuan

Hun He

3   120   4   121   5

Xar Moron He
Laoha He
Wutonghaolai

NEI MONGOL

Naiman Qi
(Daqin Tal)
Udan Tohoi
Yangchang
Xinmincun
Xiawa
Buqt

Baixingt
Fuxingdi
Jiumian
Bajiazi
Yulamasi
Wangfu
Fuxin
Hun

Yingjin He
Chifeng
Chifeng
(Ulanhad)
Haladaokou
Yuanbaoshan
Xiaoheyan

Aohan Qi
(Xinhui)
Beizifu
Heichengzi

Niujiayingzi
Reshui
Heishui
Pingzhuang
Machang
Majiazi

Weichang
(Zhuizishan)
Banjieta
Harqin Qi
(Jinshan)
Louzidian
Nailin
Jianping
Dongguanyingzi
Beipiao
Sanbao
Changgao
Dawulan
Qinghemen
Dongjiadiaz
Dongliang
Haidawanzi

QILAOTUSHAN
Dayingzi
Kuidesu
Zhangjiayingzi
Kalaqin
Bianzhangzi
Taohuatu
Jingou
Nengjia
Jinling
Shijiapu
Zhangsanying
Xizi
Xiaochengzi
Luotuoying
Nanling
Shangyuan
Jiudaoling
Dayushupu

NULU'ERHU SHAN

Longhua
Qijia
Ningcheng
(Tianyi)
Shahai
Dongdadao
Shangyan
Zhouliatun
Qilibe

Fengshan
Baihugou
Yaoshang
Wulie He
Balihan
Jianping
(Yebaishou)
Dapingfang
Batuying
Qidaoling
Shenjiatai
Shist

Shuangfengzi
Songzhangzi
Hongshi
Gongyingzi
Boluochi
Nanshuangmiao
Ershijiazi
Xiadling He
Bajiaolai
Yi Xian

CHENGDE
Liugou
Pingquan
Lingyuan
Hetanggou
Ganzhao
Taipingzhuang
Yangshan
Shaguotun
Nanpiao
Taimen
Nü'erhe
Songshan
Yanjia
Jinzhou
Jin Xian

Shuiquan
Sanshijia
Shuangyangdian
Xinzhzhuang

Xinzhangzi
Shihuiyao
Weizhangzi
Beijiu
Siguanyingzi
Chapeng
Shanzuizi
Pingfangzi
Linglongta
Nangongyingzi
Hongluoxian
Gaoqiaozhen
Xuejia
SONG LING

Chengde
(Xiabancheng)
Bao He
Daordeng
Goumenzi
Jianchang
Heishanke
Lamadong
Lüjiazi
Gangyaoling
Ganglun
Gaoqiaozhen
Si'erpu
Tashan

Liu He
Wuling Shan
Kuancheng
Du Shan
Foyedong
Bajiazi
Sandaogou
Jinxi

Shouwangfen
Yingshouyizi
Wuzhi Shan
Tangdaohe
Yaolugou
Heshangfangzi
Baimiaozi
Mazhifangfang
Huludao
Juhua Dao

Xinglong
Banbishan
Qinglong
Mutoudeng
Shizhangzi
Shahousue
Dongxinzhuang
Xingcheng
Wenquan

Maoshan
Xifengkou
Yiyuankou
Suizhong

Zunhua
Santunying
Jianchangying
Shuangshanzi
Qianwei
Qiansuo
Huangdi

YAN SHAN

Ji Xian
Mashenqiao
Malanyu
Qianxi
Yanheying
Taitouying
Shanhaiguan
Wanjiatun
Liaodong Wan
(Gl

Bangjun
Yuqiao Sk
Qian'an
Kuizhuang
Shimenzhai
Qinhuangdao

Baodi
Linnancang
Yutian
Fengrun
Yejiluo
Zhaogezhuang
Lulong
Funing
Haiyang
Beidaihe
Beidaihe Haibin

Luan He
Xinjuntun
Guye
Tangjiazhuang
Anshan
Liushoufing
Jieshi Shan

Panzhuang
Kaiping
Linxi
Luan Xian
Changli
Niuguanying

Fengnan
(Xugezhuang)
Tangshan
Xiaoji
Luannan
(Bencheng)
Tinghuhe
Haijianzhuang

TIANJIN
Huangzhuang
Tianzhuang
Nanpu
Leting
Matouying

Ninghe
(Lutai)
Baigezhuang
Hangu
Daqinghe

Qili Hai

HEBEI
Chaobai Xinhe
Beitang
Xinhe
Tanggu
Tianjin Xingang

Hai He
Gegu
Dagu

Bohai Wan (Gt.)
to Shanghai
to Longkou
to Shanghai
to Yantai

BOHAI   SEA

280(520)
290(540)
280(410)
280(330)
230(330)
180(330)
to Shanghai 600(280)
to Yantai 180(330)

Changxing Dao
Xizhong Dao
Fengming Dao
Ximayi Dao
Zhu Dao

Jiangjuns
Puzhou
Fuzhou Wan
Xisantun
Changlingzi
Wudao
Xietun
Pulandian Wa
Jinzhou Wa
Yingchengzi
Dafangshen

Xiaolongshan Dao
(Shel Dao)
Changling
Nanguantun
Zhoushulit
Da

Longtou
Shuishiying
Leshun
Laotie Shan

BEIJING
HEBEI
Qiangzixi
Gubeikou
Luanping
(Anjiangying)
Anjiang
Shangbancheng
Luanhe

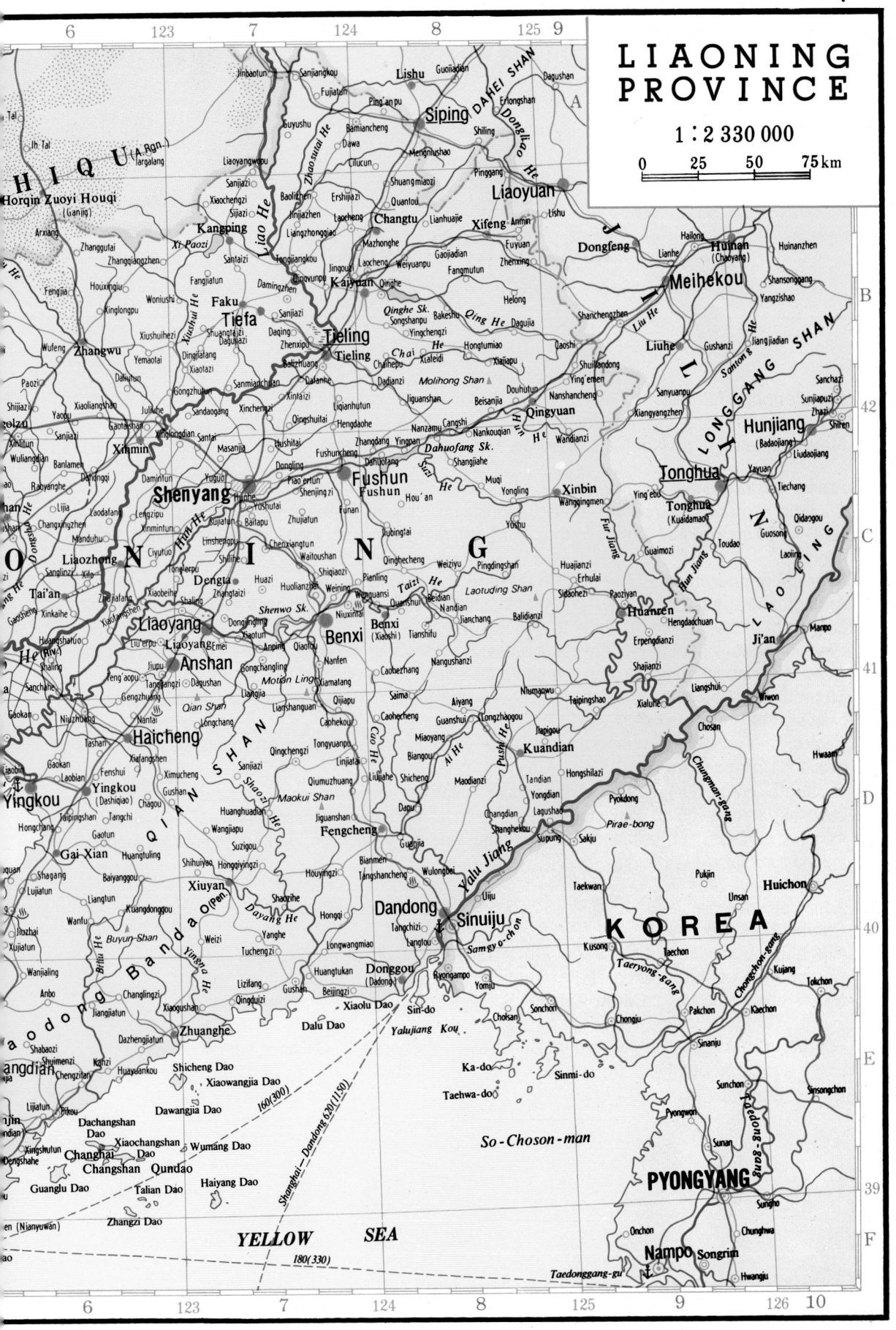

Liaoning Province

Population: 37.2 million
Urban population: 25.7 million
Nationalities: Han, Manchu, Mongolian, Hui, Korean, and Xibe

Area: 150,000 square kilometers
Climatic features: temperate, humid, monsoonal climate in the coastal region; subtropical, semi-humid, monsoonal climate in the north; hot, rainy summers; long, cold winters; short, windy springs
Average temperature: -17 — -5°C in January, 21 — 25°C in July
Annual average rainfall: 400 — 1,200 mm; high precipitation in the eastern mountain area; 60 percent of the rain falls from June to August
Physical features: high in the west and east; low plains in the central and the southern coastal areas; the Liaodong Peninsula in the south stretches out to enclose the Bohai Gulf
Mountains: Qianshan Mountains in the east, which are an extension of the Changbai Mountains; Nulu'erhu Mountains in the west
Rivers: Liaohe River, the principal waterway of the province; Yalu River, which forms the boundary between China and Korea
Products: corn, millet, sorghum, rice, wheat, potatoes, soybeans, peanuts, sesame; cotton, silk cocoons, ambary hemp, flax, tussah; apples, pears, grapes; ginseng, antlers; sea products including cutlass fish, yellow croaker, shrimp, and shellfish; iron, coal, oil shale, manganese, magnesium, talcum, petroleum, salt

Administrative divisions: 19 cities, 34 counties, and 5 autonomous counties
Capital: Shenyang
Neighboring areas: Jilin and Hebei Provinces; Inner Mongolia Autonomous Region
Neighboring country: Korea
Major cities: Shenyang, Dalian, Anshan, Fushun, Benxi, Dandong, Jinzhou, Yingkou

Tourist attractions: 350-year-old Imperial Palace in Shenyang; Dalian, a summer resort

JILIN PROVINCE

1 : 2 660 000

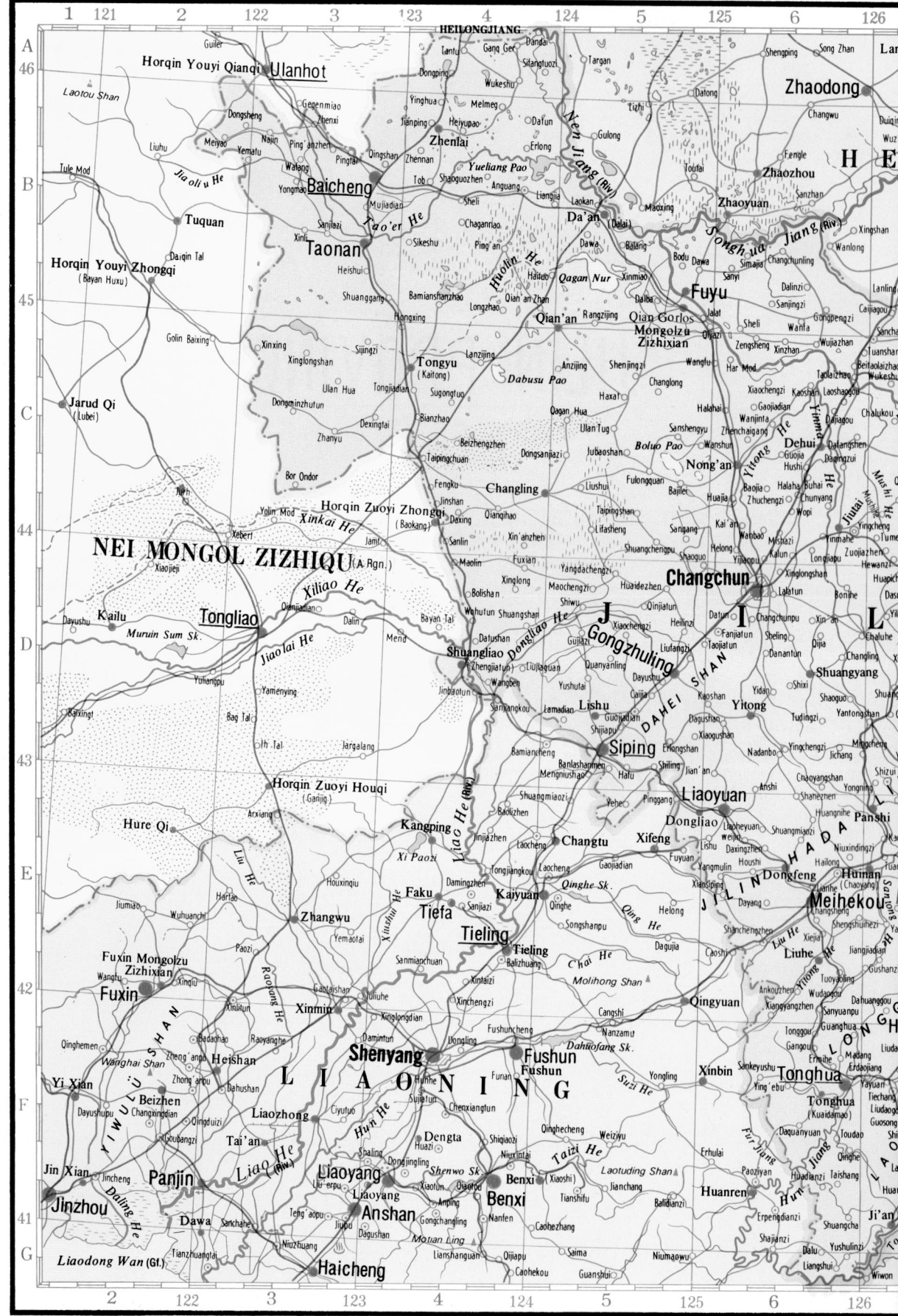

HEILONGJIANG

A
46

Horqin Youyi Qianqi   Ulanhot

Laotou Shan

Tule Mod

Tuquan

B
Baicheng

Taonan

Horqin Youyi Zhongqi
(Bayan Huxu)

45

Jarud Qi
(Lubei)

C

Zhenlai

Da'an (Dalai)

Qian'an

Tongyu
(Kaitong)

Changling

Fuyu

Qian Gorlos
Mongolzu
Zizhixian

Dehui

Nong'an

HE

Zhaodong

Zhaozhou

Zhaoyuan

44

NEI MONGOL ZIZHIQU (A. Rgn.)

Horqin Zuoyi Zhongqi
(Baokang)

Xinkai He

Changchun

Tongliao

Xiliao He

Jiaolai He

Shuangliao

Lishu

Siping

Gongzhuling

Yitong

Shuangyang

JILIN

D
Liaoyuan

43

Horqin Zuoyi Houqi
(Ganjig)

Hure Qi

Kangping

Changtu

Xifeng

Dongliao

Dongfeng

Meihekou

Huinan

Tonghua

E

Fuxin Mongolzu
Zizhixian

Fuxin

Zhangwu

Faku

Tiefa

Kaiyuan

Tieling
Tieling

Qingyuan

Xinmin

42

Yi Xian

Heishan

Shenyang

LIAONING

Fushun
Fushun

Xinbin

Tonghua

Jinzhou

Panjin

Liaozhong

Tai'an

Liaoyang
Liaoyang

Dengta

Benxi
Benxi

Huanren

F

YIWULÜ SHAN

Anshan

Liao He (Riv.)

Haicheng

Liaodong Wan (Gf.)

G
41

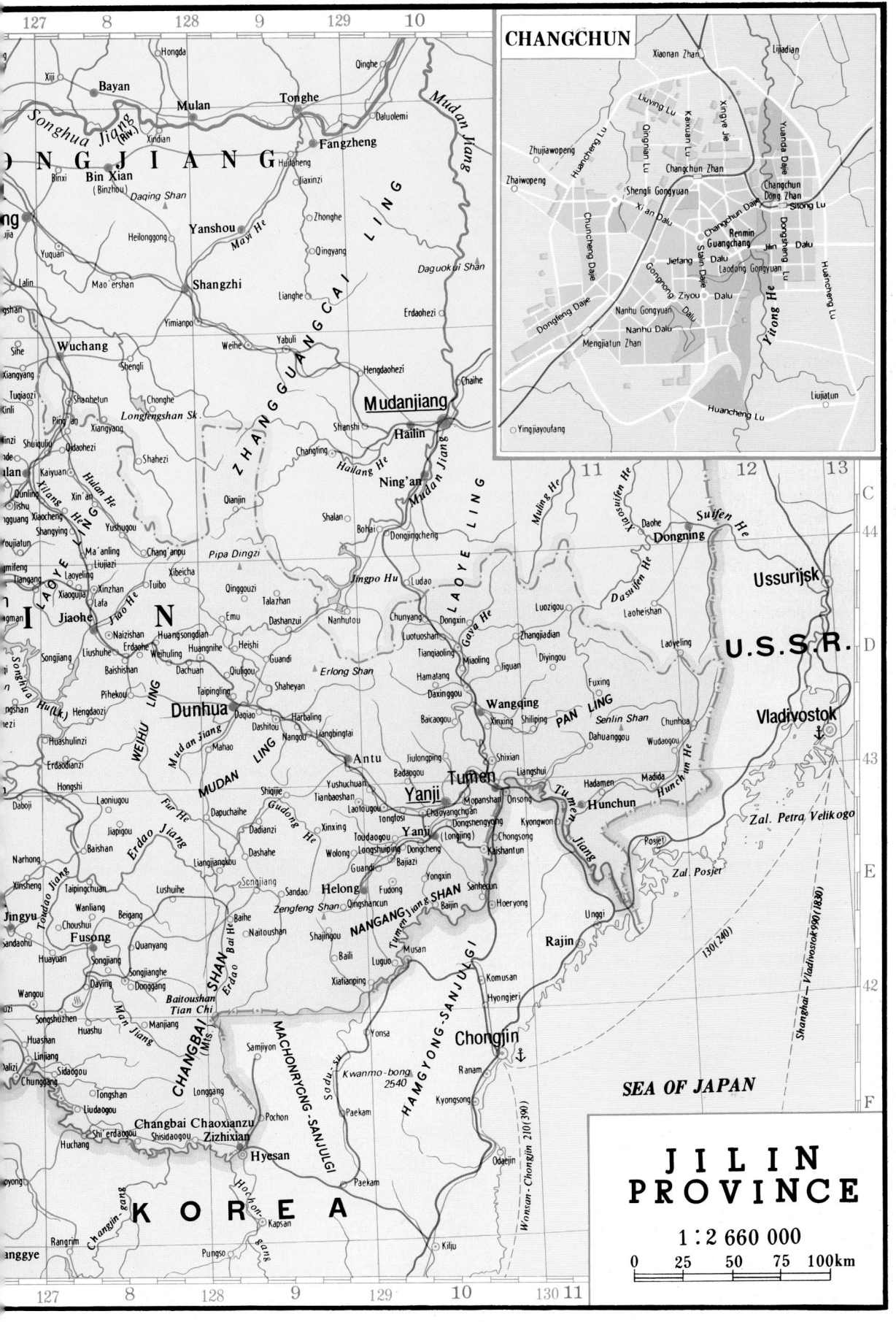

CHANGCHUN

Xiaonan Zhan · Lijiadian
Luying Lu · Xingye Jie · Yuanda Dajie
Zhujiawopeng · Qingnian Lu · Huancheng Lu · Kaixuan Lu · Changchun Zhan
Zhaiwopeng · Changchun Dong Zhan · Sitong Lu · Sitong Dajie
Shengli Gongyuan · Changchun Dan · Dongsheng Lu
Xi'an Dalu · Renmin Guangchang · Jilin Dalu
Chuncheng Lu · Stalin Dajie · Laodong Gongyuan
Jiefang Dalu · Gongnong Ziyou · Yitong He
Gongnong Dalu
Dongfeng Dajie · Nanhu Gongyuan
Changchun Dajie · Nanhu Dalu
Mengjiatun Zhan · Liujiatun
Huancheng Lu
Yingjiayoufang

D O N G J I A N G

Songhua Jiang (Riv.)
Hongda · Qinghe
Xiji · Bayan · Mulan · Tonghe
Daluolemi · Mudan Jiang
Bin Xian (Binzhou) · Xindian · Huifaheng · Fangzheng
Binxi · Jiaxinzi
Daqing Shan
Heilonggong · Yanshou · Zhonghe · Qingyang
Yuquan · Mayi He
Lalin · Mao'ershan · Shangzhi · Lianghe · Daguokui Shan
Erdaohezi
Xiangyang · Shanhetun · Chonghe
Tugiaozi · Ping'an · Xiangyang · Weihe · Yabuli
Kinli · Shuiqulu · Qidaohezi · Shahezi · Changting · Hengdaohezi · Chaihe
Sihe · Wuchang · Shengli · Longfengshan Sk. · Shanshi · Mudanjiang
Xiangyang · Kaiyuan · Qianjin · Hailin
Xiaochenq · Xinzhou · Ning'an
Shangying · Yushugou · Shalan · Bohai · Dongjingcheng
Z H A N G G U A N G C A I L I N G
youjiatun · Ma'anling · Chang'anpu · Pipa Dingzi
mifeng · Laoyeling · Liujiazi · Qinggouzi · Ludao · Jingpo Hu
Tiangang · Xiaoguija · Tuibo · Xinzhen · Talazhan · Chunyang
Jiaohe · Naizishan · Emu · Dashanzui · Nanhutou · Luotuoshan
Songjiang · Liushuhe · Erdaohe · Huangsongdian · Heishi · Tiangiaoling
Baishishan · Weihuling · Huangnihe · Guandi · Hamatang
Huashulinzi · Dachuan · Qiulgou · Erlong Shan · Daxinggou
Erdaodianzi · Pihekou · Shaheyan · Baicaogou
Hongshi · Dunhua · Daqiao · Dashitou · Harbaling
Laoniugou · Antu · Jiulongping · Shixian
Daboji · Dapuchaihe · Mahao · Nangou · Liangbingtai · Badagou
Jiapigou · Dadianzi · Shiqijie · Yushuchuan · Tianbaoshan · Tumen
Baishan · Dashahe · Xinxing · Laotougou · Yanji
Narhong · Lushuihe · Liangjiangkou · Toudaogou · Wolong · Longshuiping · Dongcheng
Xinsheng · Taipingchuan · Sandao · Songjiang · Guandi · Bajiazi
Wanliang · Beigang · Helong · Fudong · Yongxin
Jingyu · Choushui · Quanyang · Zengfeng Shan · Qingshancun · Baijin
Fusong · Songjiang · Baihe · Shajingou · Musan
Huayuan · Songjianghe · Naitoushan · Baili
Daying · Donggang · Baitoushan Tian Chi · Luguo · Xiatianping
Songshuzhen · Huashu · Manjiang · Yonsa · Komusan
Huashan · Sidaogou · Hyongjeri
Linjiang · Tongshan · Longgang · Samjiyon · Hoeryong
Chungyang · Liudaogou · Pochon · Chongjin
Changbai Chaoxianzu Zizhixian · Shi'erdaogou · Shisidaogou · Kwanmo-bong 2540 · Ranam
Huchang · Hyesan · Paekam · Kyongsong
Paekam · SEA OF JAPAN
KOREA · Odaejin
Rangrim · Kapsan · Pungso · Kiliu

L A O Y E L I N G
Mudan Jiang · LAOYE LING · PAN LING · Senlin Shan
WEIHU LING · MUDAN LING · Chunhua · Dahuanggou · Wudaogou
Fur He · Gudong He · Gaya He · Mopanshan · Onsong · Hunchun He
NANGANG SHAN · HAMGYONG-SANJULGI · Tumen Jiang · Hunchun
CHANGBAI (Mts) · Erdao Bai He · MACHONRYONG-SANJULGI · Sodu-su · Hochon-gang
Man Jiang · Changjin-gang · Hochon-gang

Suifen He · Dongning
Muling He · Xiaosuifen He · Daohe
Dasuifen He · Laoheishan · Laoyeling
Luozigou · Zhangjiadian
Miaoling · Diyingou · Jiguan · Fuxing
U.S.S.R.
Vladivostok
Zal. Petra Velikogo
Zal. Posjet
Posjet
Rajin · Unggi
Shanghai — Vladivostok 990 (1830)
130 (240)
Wonsan – Chongjin 210 (390)

C
44
D
43
E
42
F

**J I L I N
P R O V I N C E**

1 : 2 660 000

0 · 25 · 50 · 75 · 100km

Jilin Province

Population: 23.2 million
Urban population: 14.7 million
Nationalities: Han, Korean, Manchu, Hui, Mongolian, and Xibe

Area: 180,000 square kilometers
Climatic features: temperate, continental, monsoonal climate; cold, long winters; short, rainy summers; windy springs and autumns with unpredictable weather; low temperatures in the mountain area
Average temperature: -20 — -14°C in January, 16 — 24°C in July
Annual average rainfall: 350 — 1,000 mm; precipitation gradually decreases from the southeast to the northwest; 60 percent of the rain falls from June to August
Physical features: three topographical zones — Changbai Mountains in the southeast, Songliao Plain in the northwest, and hills, basins, and valleys in the center; volcanos scattered in the mountain areas
Rivers: Di'er Songhua River, the longest waterway in Jilin; Yalu and Tumen Rivers, which form the boundary between China and Korea
Lakes: Songhua Lake, also known as Fengman Reservoir, is a renowned artificial lake; other large lakes are the Yueliang Pao, Qagan Nur, and Dabusu Pao.
Products: corn, millet, sorghum, rice, wheat, potatoes, soybeans, sugar beet, sesame; sun-cured tobacco; flax, silk cocoons; mushrooms, edible fungus, ginseng; sable fur, antlers; timber; coal, oil shale

Administrative divistions: 1 autonomous prefecture, 14 cities, 31 counties, and 2 autonomous counties
Capital: Changchun
Neighboring areas: Heilongjiang and Liaoning Provinces; Inner Mongolia Autonomous Region
Neighboring countries: the Soviet Union and Korea
Major cities: Changchun, Jilin, Siping, Tonghua, Baicheng, Yanji, Hunjiang, Liaoyuan, Tumen

9

HEILONGJIANG PROVINCE

1 : 4 000 000

HARBIN

Songhua Jiang (Riv.)

Jiangxin Dao

Taiyangdao Gongyuan

Stalin Gongyuan

Youyi Lu

Jingwa Lu

Xinyang Lu

Kang'an Lu

Harbin Zhan

Museum

The Zoo

Hexing Lu

Ha-Ping Gonglu

Xuefu Lu

Daqing

Daqing Lu

Haping Lu

Cemetery of Martyrs

Zhongshan Lu

Fendou Lu

Majiagou He

Erlong Gongyuan

Wenchang Jie

Wangzhaotun Zhan

Gongbin Lu

Xiangfang Zhan

Sunjia Zhan

Buxexunuol

Dongzhan Zhan

Sankeshu Zhan

Taipingqiao Zhan

Dazhi Lu

Xianfeng Lu

Dazhan Zhan

Binjiang Zhan

Dazhi Lu

Binjiang Zhan

Dazhi jie

Taigu Jie

Hangi jie

Nanji Lu

Yiman Jie

Nangang Lu

Map area

CHABAROVSK

Fuyuan
Zhuali
Shuguang
Bacha
Qindeli
Smidovič
(Ürmi)

B U R E J N S K I J C H R.

B U R E J N S K I J C H R.

Bureja

U. S. S. R.

Zeja

Belogorsk

Svobodnyj

Simanovsk

Blagoveščensk

Heihe

Aihuixiang
Huormojin
Yaolun
Xun He
Xun ecun
Genchazi
Qihe
Qhelu
Xunke
Pojarkovo
Zavitinsk
Bureja
Changlutun
Furao
Xueshuiwei
Shuangshedagong
Daoländ
Wuyiling
Dongtang
Xinxiang
Tangwanghe
Hongxing
Weiguo
Wuying

K'urbin He

Jiayin (Chaoyang)
Baoxing
Beigou

Kusile

Chenqianqiao
Zhan He
Zhanhe
Longmen
Jusheng
Erfongshantun
Chaguanhe

H I N G G A N

H E I L O

Bei'an

Zhan He

Wudalianchi
Nemor
Longpe
Nenjiang
Nehe
Laolai
Jiujing
Xicheng
Nongkang
Tongnan
Keshan
Tailai

Keluo He

Dedu
(Qingshan)
Kedong Zhan

Sichun
Sanchun
Liaoming
Liming
Hailiang
Xibalin

Wuda Lian Chi

Oroqen Zizhiqi
(Alihe)

Nuomin He

Xiao'ergou

Wulubutie
Dayangshu
Olandabin
Nongyan
Hoduleng
Hadayang
Yilahe
Ding

Nen Jiang He

Nenjiang
Nehe
Longpe

Morin Dawa
Daurzu Zizhiqi (Nirji)

Zalantun

N E I M O N G O L

Arun Qi (Nai)
Arun He
Chaoyang
Yadong
Prinyang
Baoshan
Dahayang
Dongyang

Balin
Bel'in
Hat' Us
Huorqi
Charbaqi

Guliya Shan

Nuomin Dashan

Gan He
Ganhe
Jiwen
Keyihe
Yingchen
Duobukur He

Guyuan
Jagdaqi
Baihuasai

Tuozeminfulbke

Gulya Shan

H I N G G A N L I N G (MTS.)

Y I L E H U L I

Z I Z H I Q U

Narweng He

Shitou Shan

Shisanzhan
Shikanzhan
Shiyizhan
Zhongyaozhan
Xinlilun
Shizhan
Jiuzhan
Baihe
Bazhan
Qizhan
Yaozhan
Liuzhan
Wuzhan
Sizhan
Sanzhan

Taxi
Xinmin
Huolongmen
Handaqi
Wodagou

Hanmojin
Najinkovzi
Wdagou
Datoushan

Sunwu
Erzhan
Sanzhan

H E I

Xiaobole Shan

Dawusu
Xinlin
Jinhai
Tavan
Tajrenggou
Dayangqi
Xiaoyangqi (Songling)

Cangshan
Bishui
Huzhong
Huma
Neodahan
Xinglong
Xinlong
Hutongzhen
Laodadidian
Sandaoqie
Xinjilun
Zhangdiyingzi
Shangmachang
Baishilazi

Y I L E H U L I S H A N

Huma He

Ta He

Tahe

Fule
Cuigang
Bizhou

Tongbei He

Walagan
Erzhizhan
Shihezhan

Huma He

Qipan He

Ououi
Maodagezi
USumun
Iygda
Xinjiei
Jindian
Huma
Xinghua

Heilong Jiang

Kaikundang (Riv.)

Lianyin
Ershiyizhan
Tonghe
Dzalinda

Wusuli
Wusuli He
Eershiwuzhan

EMURSHAN

Ou He
Pangu
Zhangling
Fengshui Shan

Mohe
Xilinji
Laojinggou
Guilian

Mangui
Alongshan
Talangkong

Yidai Shan 1054

Fuleshan

Luoguhe

NEI MONGOL ZIZHIQU (A.Rgn.)

Scale markers: 122, 124, 126, 128

1 2 3 4 5

52 B 50 C 48

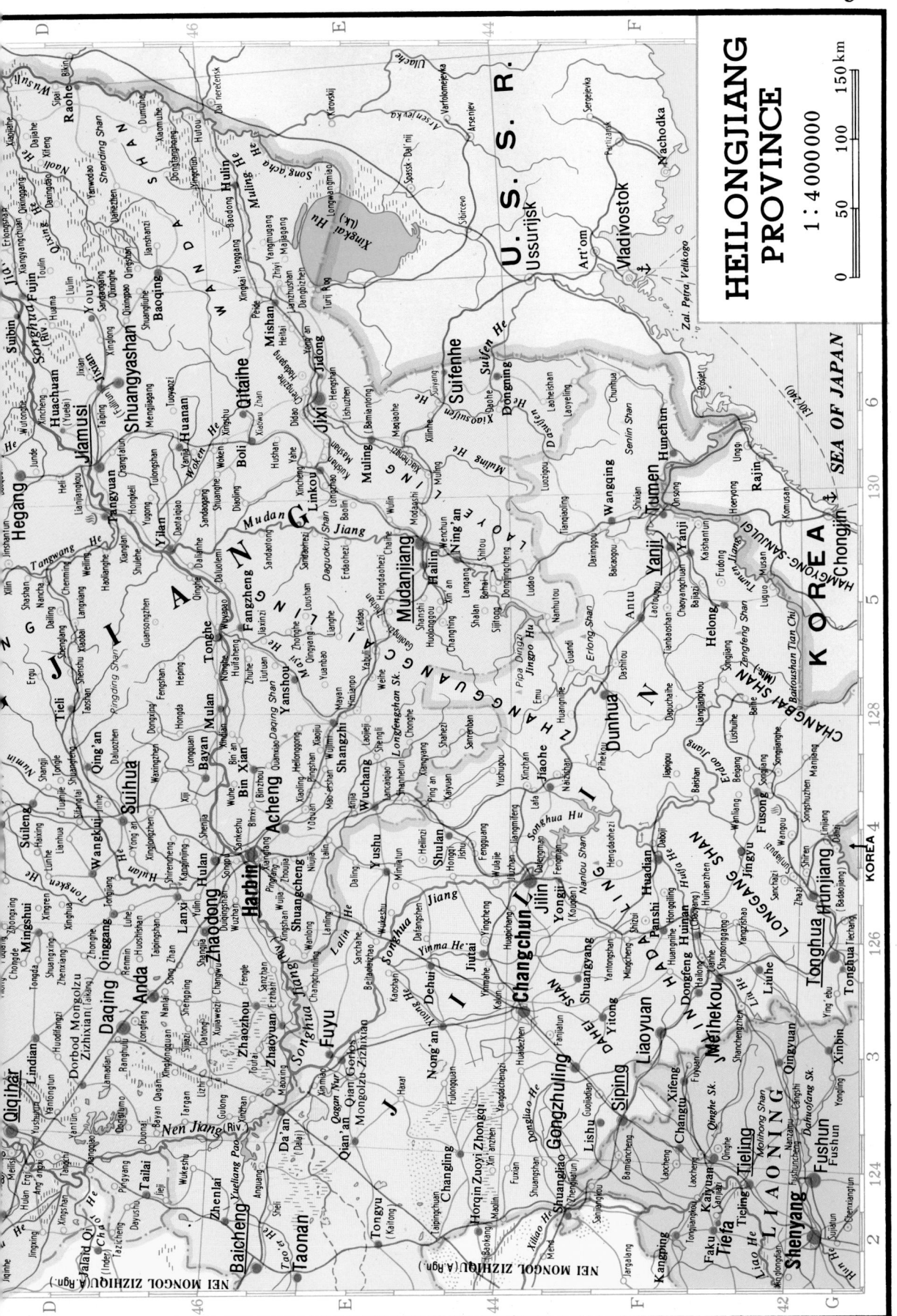

HEILONGJIANG PROVINCE

1 : 4 000 000

0   50   100   150 km

Heilongjiang Province

Population: 33.3 million
Urban population: 20.4 million
Nationalities: Han, Manchu, Korean, Mongolian, Hui, Daur, Oroqen, Hezhen, Kirgiz, and Ewenki

Area: 460,000 square kilometers
Climatic features: spans the cold-temperate/semi-humid and temperate/humid zones; short summers and long winters; no summer in the northwest; subject to spring droughts, summer flooding, and autumn frost
Average temperature: -32 — -17°C in January, 16 — 23°C in July; coldest in the northwest
Annual average rainfall: 250 — 700 mm; highest precipitation occurs on the southern side of the Lesser Hinggan Range and the Zhangguangcai Mountains; 60 percent of the rain falls from June to August
Physical features: mountainous in the north and south; plains in the east and west; intermittent volcanic eruptions in some sections
Mountains: Emur, Yilehuli, and Lesser Hinggan Mountains in the north; in the south, part of the Changbai Mountains
Plains: the Sanjiang Plain in the east consists of alluvial deposits from the Heilong, Songhua, and Wusuli Rivers; the Songnen Plain, named after the Nenjiang and Songhua Rivers, is connected to the Sanjiang Plain through the Songhua River Valley; a small plain lies north of Xingkai Lake in the east.
Rivers: Heilong River along the northern border; Nenjiang and Songhua Rivers in the middle; Wusuli River along the eastern border
Products: corn, sorghum, millet, wheat, rice, potatoes, soybeans, sugar beet, sesame, sunflower seeds; flax, tussah; timber; fur animals including squirrel, alpine weasel, sable, and otter; ginseng, antlers, tigerbone, musk, and other medicinal materials; edible fungus, mushrooms, pine nuts; chum salmon, sturgeon, huso sturgeon

Administrative divisions: 19 cities, 59 counties, and 1 autonomous county
Capital: Harbin
Neighboring areas: Jilin Province and Inner Mongolia Autonomous Region
Neighboring country: the Soviet Union
Major cities: Harbin, Qiqihar, Mudanjiang, Jiamusi, Jixi, Hegang, Shuangyashan, Daqing, Heihe

Tourist attractions: ice festival and Sun Island, Harbin; Jingpo Lake near Mudanjiang

SHANDONG PROVINCE

1 : 2'000 000

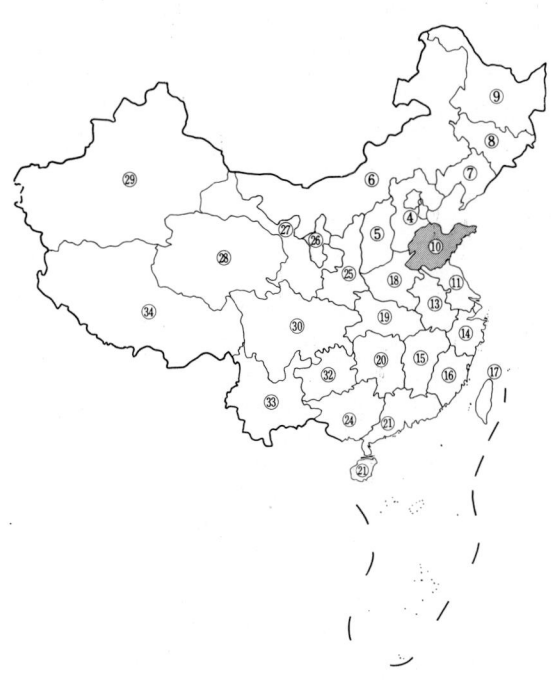

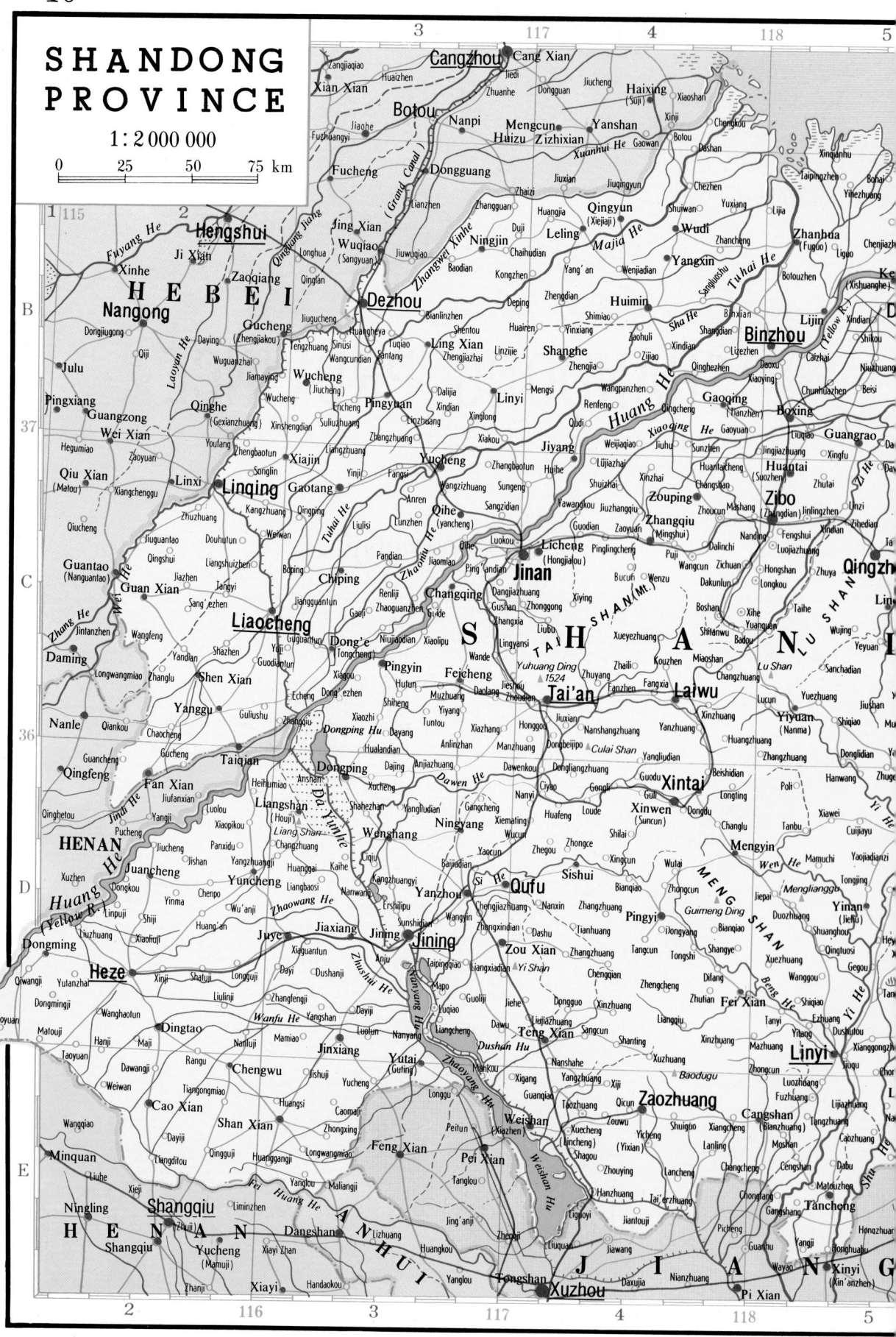

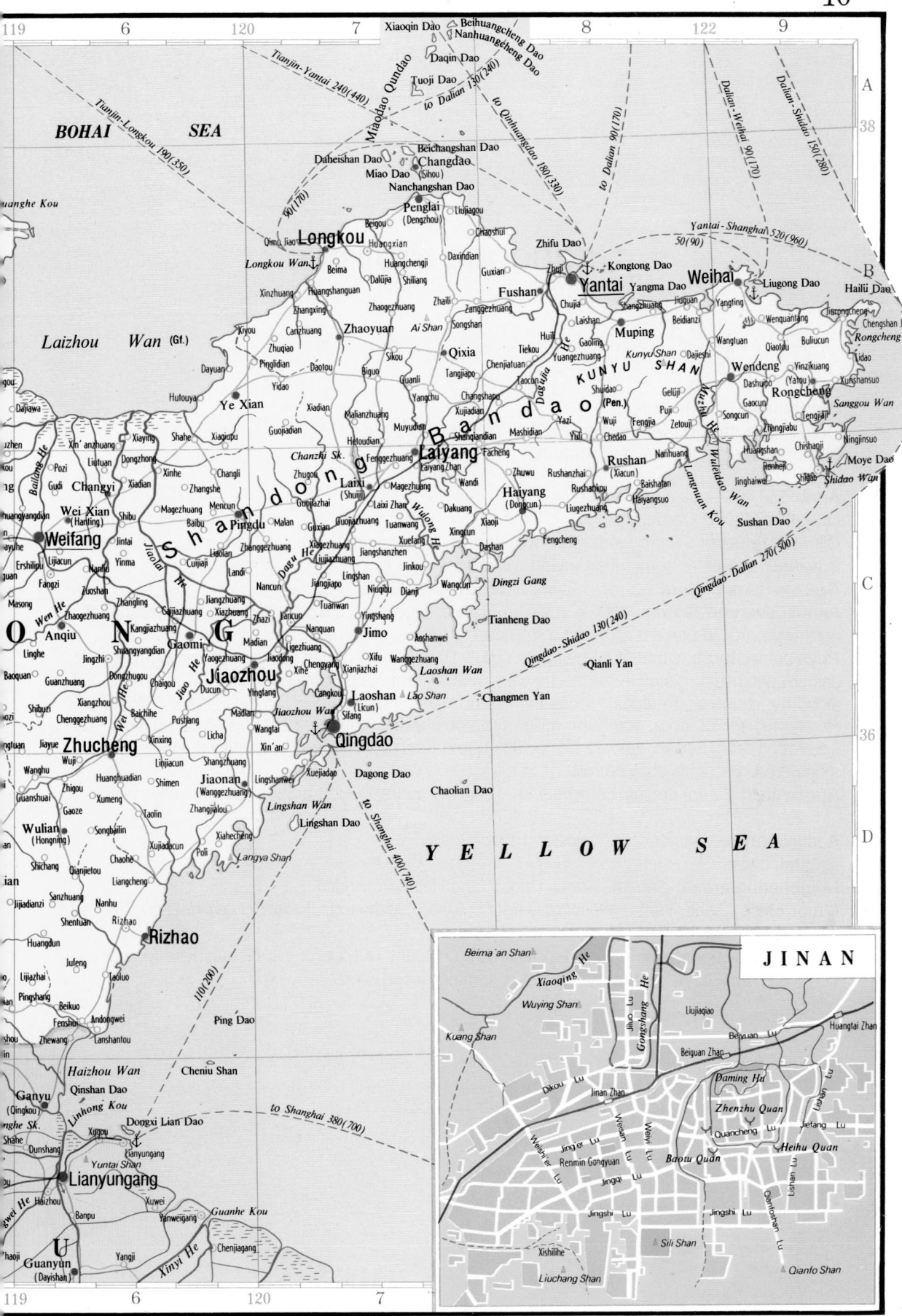

119   6   120   7   Xiaoqin Dao   Beihuangcheng Dao   8   122   9
                                      Nanhuangcheng Dao

Tianjin-Yantai 240(440)   Daqin Dao   A   38

Miaodao Qundao   Tuoji Dao   to Dalian 130(240)   to Dalian 90(170)   Dalian-Weihai 90(170)   Dalian-Shidao 150(280)

BOHAI   SEA
Tianjin-Longkou 190(350)   to Qinhuangdao 180(330)

90(170)

Daheishan Dao   Beichangshan Dao
Miao Dao   Changdao
(Sihou)   Nanchangshan Dao

Penglai   Yantai-Shanghai 520(960)
(Dengzhou)   Liujiagou   50(90)
Beigou   Chaoshui   Zhifu Dao

Longkou   Huangxian   Zhuji   Kongtong Dao
Qimu Dao   Beima   Huangchengji   Daxindian   Guxian   Yantai   Yangma Dao   Weihai   Liugong Dao   Hailü Dao
Longkou Wan   Dalüja   Shiliang   Fushan   Chujia   Shangzhuang   Huguan   Yangting   Jixrongcheng   B
Xinzhuang   Huangshanguan   Zhaogezhuang   Zhaili   Zanggezhuang   Laishan   Gaoling   Beidianzi   Wenquantang   Chengshan Jiao

Laizhou   Wan (Gf.)   Zhangxing   Zhaoyuan   Ai Shan   Songshan   Huili   Muping   Kunyu Shan   Dajieshi   Wangluan   Qiaotou   Buliucun   Rongcheng Wan
Xiyou   Canzhuang   Qixia   Tiekou   Yuangezhuang   KUNYU   SHAN   Wendeng   Yinzikuang   Idao
Dayuan   Zhuqiao   Pinglidian   Daotou   Biguo   Tangjiapo   Chenjiatuan   Taocun   Shuidao   Geliji   Dashujiao   Xunshansuo   Rongcheng
Hutouya   Yidao   Guanli   Changshapo   Mashidian   Yazi   (Pen.)   Puji   Gaocun   Songcun   Sanggou Wan
Ye Xian   Xiadian   Muyudian   Xujiadian   Yuli   Fengjia   Zetouji   Zhangjiabu
Shahe   Xinhe   Malianzhuang   Hetoudian   Shangqiandian   Chedao   Wuji   Chishanji
Xin'anzhuang   Guojiadian   Fengjia   Ningjinsuo
Pozi   Liutuan   Dongzhong   Chanzhi Sk.   Zhugou   Fengezhuang   Laiyang   Facheng   Rushan   Nanhuang   Huangshan   Moye Dao
Gudi   Changyi   Xiadian   Changli   Laiyang Zhan   Wandi   Zhuwu   Rushanzhai   (Xiacun)   Baishan   Shidao
Changyi   Zhangshe   Magezhuang   Haiyang   Rushankou   Baishatan   Renheji   Shidao Wan
Wei Xian   Shibu   Laixi   Guxian   Guojiazhuang   (Dongcun)   Liugezhuang   Haiyangsuo   Jinghaiwei
Weifang   Jintai   (Shuiji)   Malan   Tuanwang   Xiaoji   Sushan Dao
Lijiacun   Yinma   Landi   Jiangshanzhen   Jinkou   Dashan   Fengcheng
Fangzi   Zuoshan   Nancun   Lingshan   Jiangjiapo   Wangcun   Dingzi Gang
Masong   Kangjiazhuang   Jiangzhuang   Jimo   Niuqibu   Dianji
Anqiu   Gaomi   Shuangyangdian   Caijiazhuang   Xiazhuang   Yingshang   Qingdao-Dalian 270(500)   C
Linghe   Jingzhi   Jiao He   Kaikou   Nanquan   Koshanwei   Tianheng Dao
Baoquan   Jiaozhou   Dongzhougou   Chaigou   Yaogezhuang   Jiadong   Ligezhuang   Xifu   Wanggezhuang   Laoshan Wan   Qianli Yan
Shibuzi   Xiangzhou   Baichihe   Ducun   Xihe   Chengyang   Xianjiazhai   Qingdao-Shidao 130(240)
Jiayue   Pushiang   Yingtang   Cangkou   Changmen Yan
Zhucheng   Wuji   Licha   Madian   Jiaozhou Wan   Laoshan   Lao Shan   D   36
Wanghu   Zhigou   Huangluadian   Shimen   (Licun)   Silang
Zhucheng   Xumeng   Shangzhuang   Lingshanwei   Xin'an   Qingdao
Wulian   Xinxing   Lijiacun   Xuejiadan   Dagong Dao
(Hongning)   Gaoze   Taolin   Zhangjialou   Jiaonan   Chaolian Dao
Shichang   Songbailin   (Wanggezhuang)   Lingshan Wan   Y E L L O W   S E A
Qianjietou   Chaohe   Xiahecheng   Lingshan Dao
Xujiadacun   to Shanghai 400(740)

Langya Shan   Poli   Liangcheng   Nanhu

Shentuan
Huangdun   Rizhao

Jufeng

Lijiazhai   Taoluo

Pingshang   Beikou

Fenshou   Ping Dao
Andongwei
Zhewang   Lanshantou

Haizhou Wan   Cheniu Shan

Ganyu   Qinshan Dao
(Qingkou)   Linhong Kou
Dongxi Lian Dao   to Shanghai 380(700)
Xugou   Lianyungang

Yuntai Shan
Lianyungang

Xuwei
Banpu   Yanweigang   Guanhe Kou
Haizhou
Yangji   Chenjiagang

Guanyun
(Dayishan)   Xinyi He

119   6   120   7

JINAN

Beima'an Shan   Jihuo Lu   Gongshang He   Liujiaqiao   Huangtai Zhan
Xiaoqing He   Beiyuan Lu
Wuying Shan   Beiguan Zhan
Kuang Shan   Dikou Lu   Jinan Zhan   Daming Hu   Weiming Lu
Jinan Zhan   Zhenzhu Quan   Jietang Lu
Weiba Lu   Quancheng   Heihu Quan
Wenhua Lu   Baotu Quan
Weiqi Lu   Jingier Lu   Weiyi Lu   Jingqi   Qianfoshan Lu
Renmin Gongyuan   Jingqi
Jingshi Lu   Jingshi Lu
Xishilihe   Sili Shan   Qianfo Shan
Liuchang Shan

Shandong Province

Population: 77.8 million
Urban population: 44.5 million
Nationalities: Han, Hui, and Manchu

Area: 150,000 square kilometers
Coastline: 3,000 kilometers long
Climatic features: warm-temperate, semi-humid, monsoonal climate; influenced by the ocean, it is warmer and more humid than inland provinces; rainy summers; dry winters
Average temperature: -5 — -1°C in January, 24 — 28°C in July
Annual average rainfall: 560 — 1,170 mm; precipitation decreases from the southeast to the northwest; 60-70 percent of the rain falls during the summer
Physical features: situated in the lower Yellow River Valley; hills in the central region and on the eastern peninsula; plains in the north, west, and central east; narrow lowlands in the south and along the southeastern coast; faces the Bohai Gulf in the north and the Yellow Sea in the east.
Products: wheat, corn, sorghum, millet, potatoes, sweet potatos, rice, soybeans, peanuts, tea, sesame; cotton, tussah, ambary hemp; flue-cured tobacco; peaches, walnuts, chestnuts, persimmons; sea products; coal, petroleum, salt
Specialties: Yantai apples, Leling jujubes, Laiyang pears, Pingdu grapes, Dezhou watermelons

Administrative divisions: 25 cities and 86 counties
Capital: Jinan
Neighboring areas: Jiangsu, Anhui, Henan, and Hebei Provinces
Major cities: Jinan, Yantai, Weifang, Qingdao, Zibo, Zaozhuang, Jining, Dongying, Qufu

Tourist attractions: Confucius' Temple in Qufu; Mount Tai, one of the historic Five Mountains in the eastern China, in Tai'an; Qingdao, a summer resort city

SHANGHAI MUNICIPALITY
JIANGSU PROVINCE

1 : 2 000 000

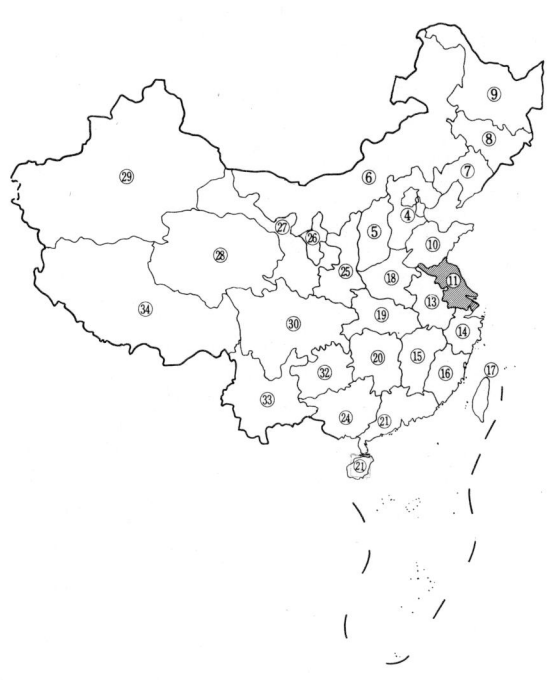

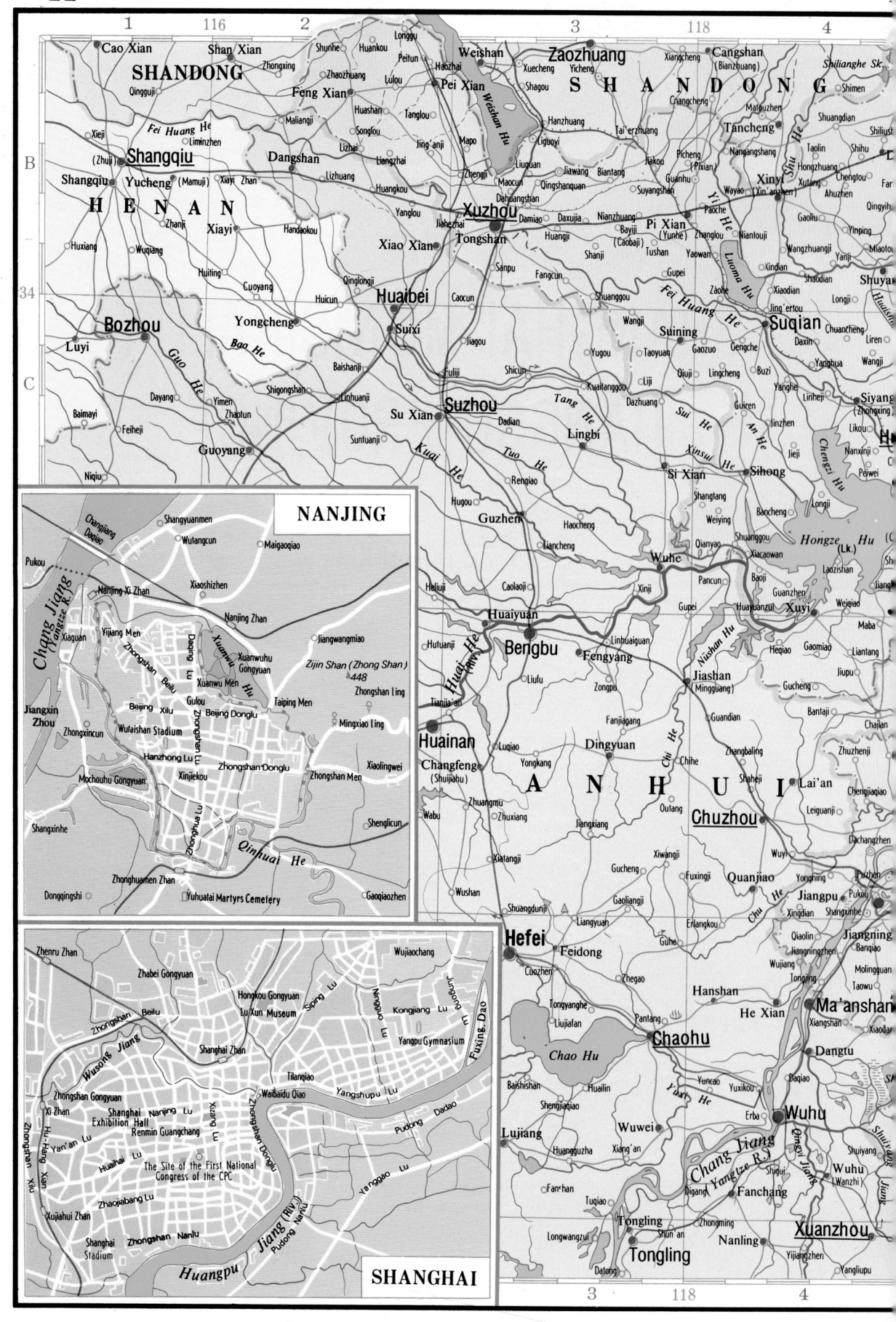

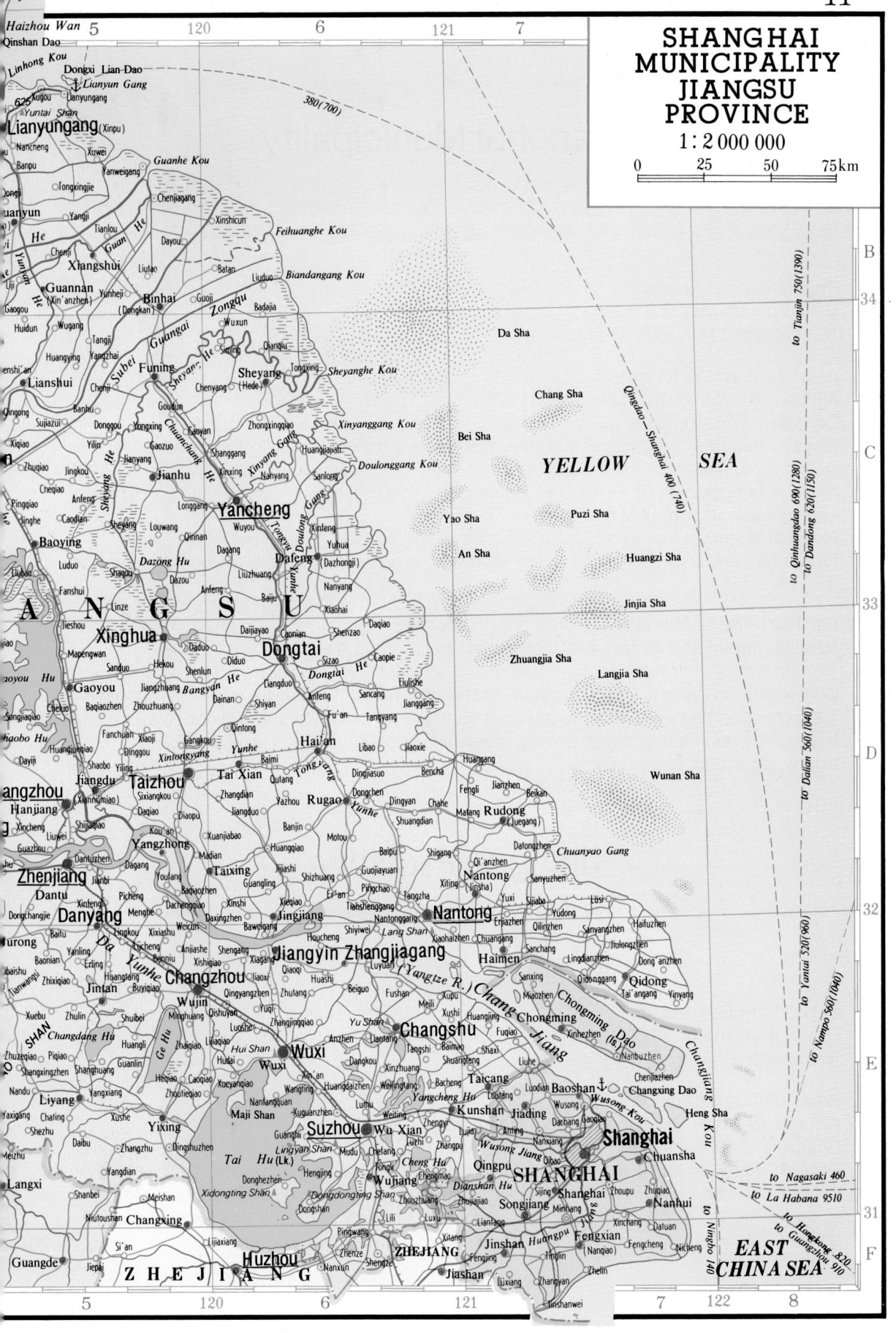

SHANGHAI
MUNICIPALITY
JIANGSU
PROVINCE
1 : 2 000 000

0   25   50   75km

Haizhou Wan
Qinshan Dao
Linhong Kou
Dongxi Lian-Dao
Lianyun Gang
Lianyungang
Yuntai Shan
Xugou
Lianyungang (Xinpu)
Nancheng
Banpu
Xuwei
Guanhe Kou
Xiangshui
Yanweigang
Guannan (Xin'anzhen) (Dongkan)
Binhai
Wugang
Yangzhai
Huangying
Funing
Sheyang
Lianshui
Chenji
Goudun
Yongxing
Gaoyan
Feihuanghe Kou
Biandangang Kou
Da Sha
YELLOW   SEA
Chang Sha
Bei Sha
Yao Sha
An Sha
Puzi Sha
Huangzi Sha
Jinjia Sha
Zhuangjia Sha
Langjia Sha
Wunan Sha

JIANGSU
Xinghua
Dongtai
Gaoyou
Taizhou
Tai Xian
Hai'an
Rugao
Rudong
Nantong
Haimen
Qidong
Chongming Dao
Changzhou
Jiangyin Zhangjiagang
Changshu
Wuxi
Suzhou
Kunshan
Shanghai
SHANGHAI
Songjiang
Nanhui
Zhenjiang
Danyang
Changzhou
Liyang
Yixing
Wujiang
Qingpu
Huzhou
ZHEJIANG
EAST
CHINA SEA

to Tianjin 750 (1390)
to Qinhuangdao 690 (1280)
to Dandong 620 (1150)
to Dalian 560 (1040)
to Yantai 520 (1040)
to Nampo 560 (1040)
to Nagasaki 460
to La Habana 9510
to Hongkong 820
to Guangzhou 910
Ningbo 140

Shanghai Municipality

Population: 12.3 million
Urban population: 7.8 million
Nationalities: Han, Hui, and Manchu

Area: 5,800 square kilometers
Altitude: 2 — 5 meters on the plains
Coastline: 200 kilometers long
Climatic features: subtropical, maritime, monsoonal climate; four distinct seasons; plum rains around June; typhoons in summer
Average temperature: 2 — 3.5°C in January, 27 — 28°C in July
Annual average rainfall: 1,000 mm
Physical features: low-lying and flat; situated on the Yangtze (Changjiang) River Delta
Products: rice, wheat, potatoes, rape, soybeans, peanuts; cotton, silk cocoons; pears; sea products

Administrative divisions: 12 districts and 10 counties
Neighboring areas: Jiangsu and Zhejiang Provinces

Comments: Shanghai is China's most comprehensive industrial and commercial city, ranking No. 1 in population and population density, and as a sea port, science and technology center, and business center. A tourist city, it attracts travelers from both home and abroad by its commercial activity rather than scenic beauty.

Jiangsu Province

Population: 62.7 million
Urban population: 20.6 million
Nationalities: Han, Hui, and Manchu

Area: 100,000 square kilometers
Altitude: less than 50 meters for most of the province
Coastline: 1,000 kilometers long
Climatic features: spans the warm-temperate/semi-humid and subtropical/humid zones; clear-cut seasonal changes; frequent "plum rains" between spring and summer; typhoons with rain-storms in late summer and early autumn; occasional frost, dry and hot winds, and hailstorms

—•— 12 —•—

SHANGHAI—
NANJING—HANGZHOU

1 : 1 330 000

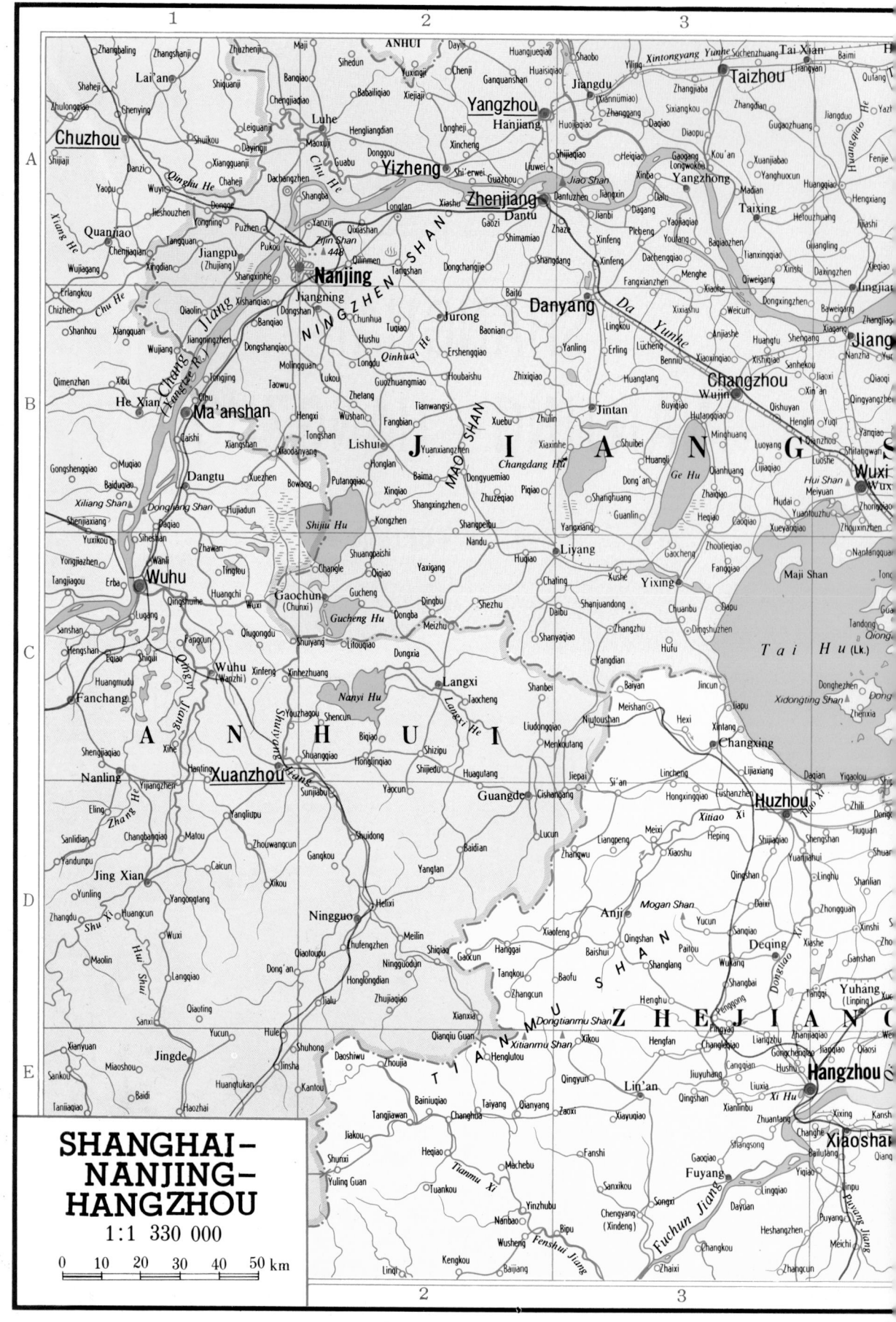

SHANGHAI-
NANJING-
HANGZHOU

1:1 330 000

0　10　20　30　40　50 km

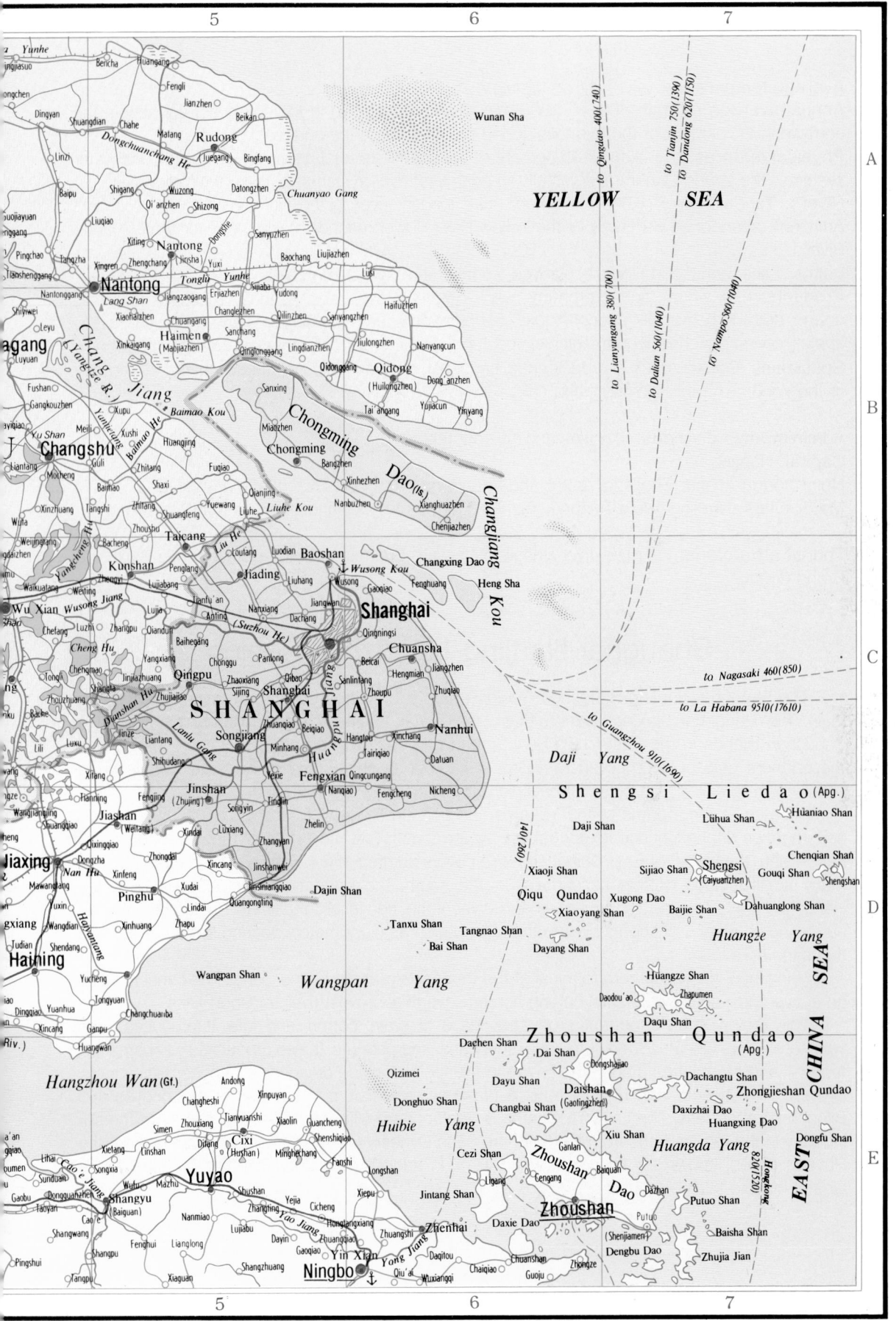

A

YELLOW SEA

to Qingdao 400(740)
to Tianjin 750(1390)
to Dandong 620(1150)
to Lianyungang 380(700)
to Dalian 560(1040)
to Nampo 560(1040)

Yunhe
ingjiasuo
ongchen
Dingyan
Shuangdian Chahe Malang Juegang Bingfang
Berita Huangang Fengli Jianzhen Beikan
Fengli
Linzi Dongchuanchang He Rudong
Baipu Shigang Wuzong Datongzhen Chuanyao Gang
Liuqiao Qi'anzhen Shizong
Guojiayuan Xiting Nantong Zhongzie Sanyuzhen Wunan Sha
inggang Zhengchang (Jinsha) Yuxi
Pingchao Xinren (Jinsha) Baochang Liujiazhen Haifuzhen Lusi
Tiansheng gang Nantong Tonglu Yunhe Jiaba Yudong Qidonggang
Nantonggang Lang Shan Jiangzaogang Enjiazhen Qilinzhen Sanyangzhen
Shiyiwei Xiaohaizhen Chuangang Changlezhen Sanchang Qingtonggang Lingdianzhen Jiulongzhen Nanyangcun
Leyu Haimen Qinglonggang Qidong
Luyuan Xinkaigang (Mabujiazhen) Sanxing (Huilongzhen) Dong'anzhen
Fushan Yu Shan Meili Xupu Huangjing Miaozhen Tai'angang Yujiacun Yinyang
Gangkouzhen Baimao Kou Xinzhen Nanbuzhen
Changshu Guli Zhitang Chongming Bangzhen Chongming Dao(Is.)
Xinzhuang Tangshi Baimao Fuqiao Xianghuazhen
Weijiangtang Zhoushu Shaxi Qianjing Chenjiazhen
gaizhen Bacheng Zhitang Shuangfeng Yuewang Liuhe Kou Nanbuzhen Changjiang Kou
Wu Xian Wusong Jiang Taicang Liu He Luodian Baoshan Changxing Dao
Shao Kunshan Penglang Liuhang Wusong Wusong Kou Heng Sha
Chefang Luzhi Zhangpu Lujiabang Jiading Jiangwan Gaoqiao Fenghuang
Waikualang Wenting Zhenyi Lujia Nanxiang Dachang Shanghai
Qiandun Anting Baihegang Qingningsi Chuansha
Cheng Hu Chengqiao Qingpu Zhaoxiang Chonggu Panlong Beicai Hengmian Jiangzhen
Tongli Jinjiazhuang Sijing Shanghai Sanlintang Zhoupu Zhuqiao
Zhouzhuang Lianta Linze Huangdu Beiqiao SHANGHAI Hangtou Xinchang Nanhui
Lili Baoche Dianshan Hu Lanlu Gang Songjiang Minhang Tairiqiao Datuan
Luxu Liantang Shibudang Xiejie Fengxian Qingcungang
Xifang Fengjing Songyin Tinggang Zhelin Fengcheng Nicheng
Hanning Jiashan Zhujing Nanqiao
Wangjianging Qixingqiao Xindai Lüxiang Zhangyan
gxiang Shuangqiao Dongzha Zhongdai Xincang Jinshanwei
Jiaxing Nan Hu Xinfeng Xudai Jinshanqiaqiao Dajin Shan
Mawangdui Yuxin Lindai Zhapu
Pinghu Xinhuang Zhapu
ngxiang Wangjiang Judian
Haining Yucheng Shendang Wangpan Shan
ao Dingxiao Yuanhua
Xincang Ganpu Changchuanba
Riv.) Huangwan

Chang *Yangtze R.)* *Jiang*
Baimao Kou
Chongming
Dao(Is.)
Changjiang
Kou
(Suzhou He)
Huangpu Jiang

to Nagasaki 460(850)
to La Habana 9510(17610)
to Guangzhou 910(1690)
140(260)

Daji Yang

Shengsi Liedao(Apg.)
Lühua Shan Hüaniao Shan
Daji Shan Chenqian Shan
Xiaoji Shan Sijiao Shan Shengsi Gouqi Shan
Qiqu Qundao Xugong Dao (Caiyuanzhen) Shengshan
Xiao yang Shan Baijie Shan Dahuanglong Shan
Tanxu Shan Tangnao Shan
Bai Shan Dayang Shan **Huangze Yang**
Huangze Shan
Daodou'ao Zhapumen
Wangpan Shan **Wangpan Yang** Daqu Shan
Dachen Shan **Zhoushan Qundao**
Qizimei Dai Shan (Apg.)
Dayu Shan Dongshajiao Dachangtu Shan
Donghuo Shan Daishan Zhongjieshan Qundao
Changbai Shan Daishan (Gaotingzhen) Daxizhai Dao
Huibie Yang Cezi Shan Ganlan Xiu Shan Huangxing Dao
Longshan **Zhoushan** **Huangda Yang**
Fanshi Baiquan Dongfu Shan
Xiepu Lingang Cengang Dazhan
Jintang Shan Baisha Shan
Daxie Dao Putuo Shan
Zhoushan Putuo
Zhenhai (Shenjiamen) Baisha Shan
Dengbu Dao Zhujia Jian

EAST CHINA SEA
Hongkong 820(1520)

Hangzhou *Wan* (Gt.)
Andong Xinpuyan
Changheshi Xiaolin Guancheng
Simen Zhouxiang Tianyuanshi Shenshiqiao
Xielang Linshan Cixi (Hushan) Minghezhen Changbai Shan
Dilang
Cixi
Yuyao
Shangyu Shushan Yejia Zhanting
(Baiguan) Nanmiao Hongtangxiang
Wuhu Mazhu Lianglong Zhuangshi Zhenhai
Fenghui Gaoqiao Yin Xian
Yong Jiang Ningbo
Cao E Jiang *Tao Jiang* *Yong Jiang*
Shangyu Nanmiao Dayin Daqitou
Fenghui Lujiabu Qiu'ai Wuxiangqi
Pingshui Tangqu Shangzhuang Xiaguan Chaijiao Chuanshan Zhongze Guoju

Average temperature: -2 — 4°C in January, 26 — 29°C in July
Annual average rainfall: 800 — 1,200 mm; high precipitation in the southeast and low in the northwest; 60 percent of the rain falls during the summer in the northeast
Physical features: plains cover 95 percent of the province's total area with well-developed water systems; the Grand Canal traverses all the east-west river systems; borders the Yellow Sea.
Rivers: Yangtze River (6,300 kilometers, third longest river in the world next to the Nile and Amazon); abandoned waterway of the Yellow River; lower reaches of Huaihe River; and Guanhe River
Lakes: Lake Taihu, and Hongze, Gaoyou, Luoma, and Yangcheng Lakes
Products: rice, wheat, corn, sorghum, millet, potatoes, soybeans, peanuts, rape, sesame, tea; cotton, ambary hemp, silk cocoons, jute; peppermint, spearmint, bamboo, and medicinal herbs; apples, pears, peaches, loquats, gingko; coal, phosphorus, salt, pottery clay; aquatic products
Specialties: Gaoyou duck and duck eggs, Langshan chicken, Taihu whitebait, shad and anchovy of the Yangtze, crabs of Yangcheng Lake

Administrative divisions: 21 cities and 54 counties
Capital: Nanjing
Neighboring areas: Zhejiang, Anhui, and Shandong Provinces; Shanghai Municipality
Major cities: Nanjing, Wuxi, Suzhou, Xuzhou, Lianyungang, Changzhou, Nantong, Zhenjiang

Tourist attractions: Yangtze River Bridge in Nanjing; Suzhou gardens; Lake Taihu in Wuxi; the Grand Canal

Shanghai-Nanjing-Hangzhou Region

The Shanghai-Nanjing-Hangzhou Region refers to the area covering the Ningbo-Shaoxing Plain, the Hangzhou-Jiaxing-Huzhou Plain, the Sunan Plain, Shanghai Municipality, and the Zhoushan Islands in the East China Sea. Spread over the southern tip of Jiangsu Province and the northern quarter of Zhejiang Province, the region is characterized by dense population, a prosperous economy, rich culture, convenient transportation, and natural beauty.

Situated at the mouths of the Yangtze and Fuchun Rivers, the land is crossed with canals and irrigation ditches, hence its epithet the "water country." At the center of the water network is Lake Taihu, the "pearl" of East China. The lake covers an area of 2,425 square kilometers and has many small islands dotting its surface. In the south, the Qiantang River connects with the Hangzhou Gulf, forming a trumpet shape. When the tide rises, the water is forced into the narrowing channel and shoots up into the sky as high as eight meters, roaring like a calvary of a thousand horses.

Hangzhou is the southern terminal of the thousand-year-old Grand Canal. The canal remains an active north-south waterway, cutting across several east-west river transport lines.

This region is an important production base of grain, cotton, and jute. It produces large volumes of rice, wheat, cotton, jute, rape, soybeans, and peanuts. It also produces *mao* bamboos, tung oil, and tea oil. Fruits and nuts grown in the region include oranges, red bayberries, loquats, Chinese torreya nuts, and hickory nuts. A tea-growing region, it is famous for its Longjing and Biluochun green teas. The Lake Taihu area is an important silkworm base. The history of the silk industry in the region dates from the Northern Song Dynasty (AD 960-1127). Also famous are the Huyang sheep, known for their soft, white wool. In addition, the Zhoushan Islands are China's largest inshore fishing ground.

—— 13 ——

ANHUI PROVINCE

1 : 2 000 000

13

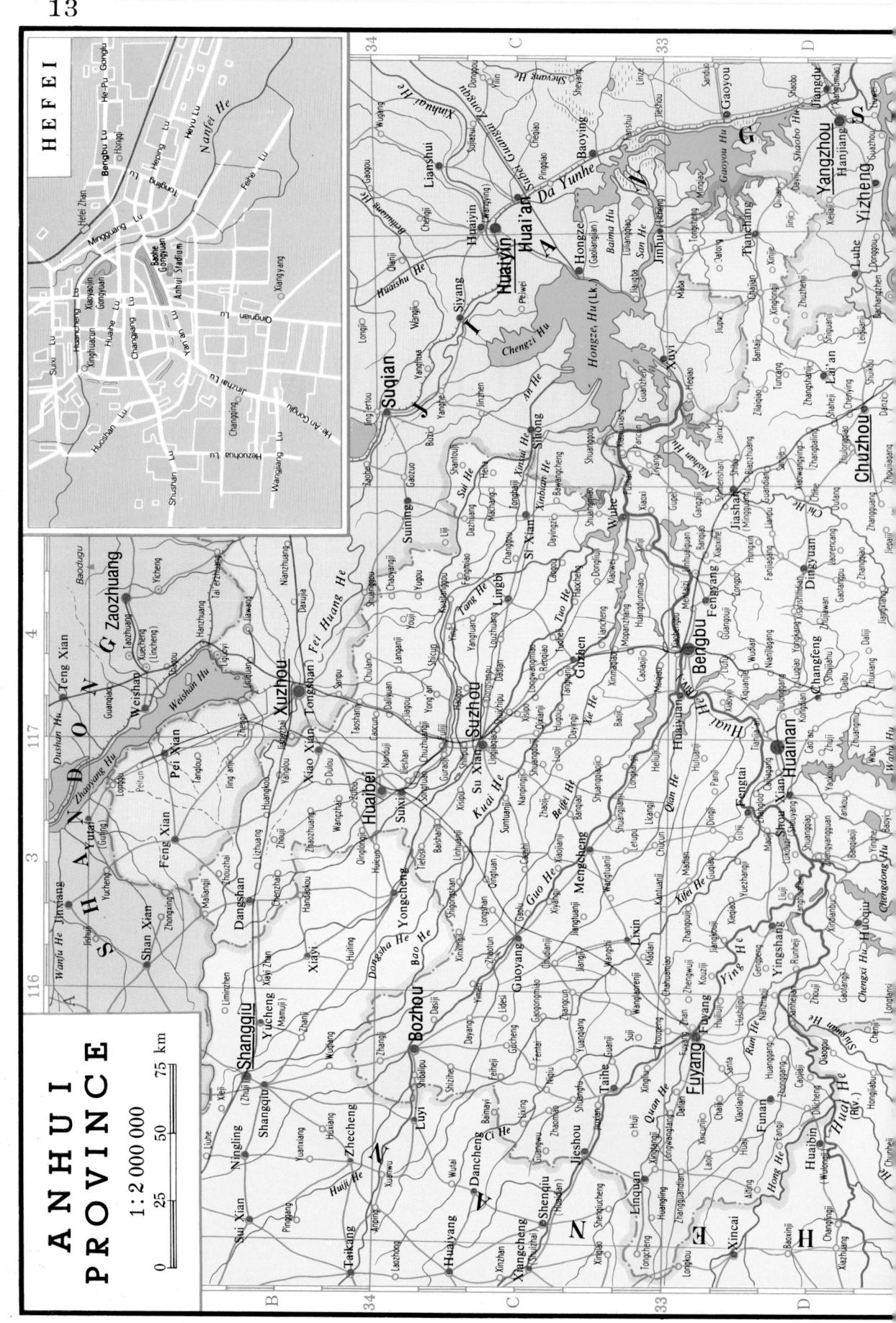

HEFEI

ANHUI
PROVINCE

1:2 000 000

0   25   50   75 km

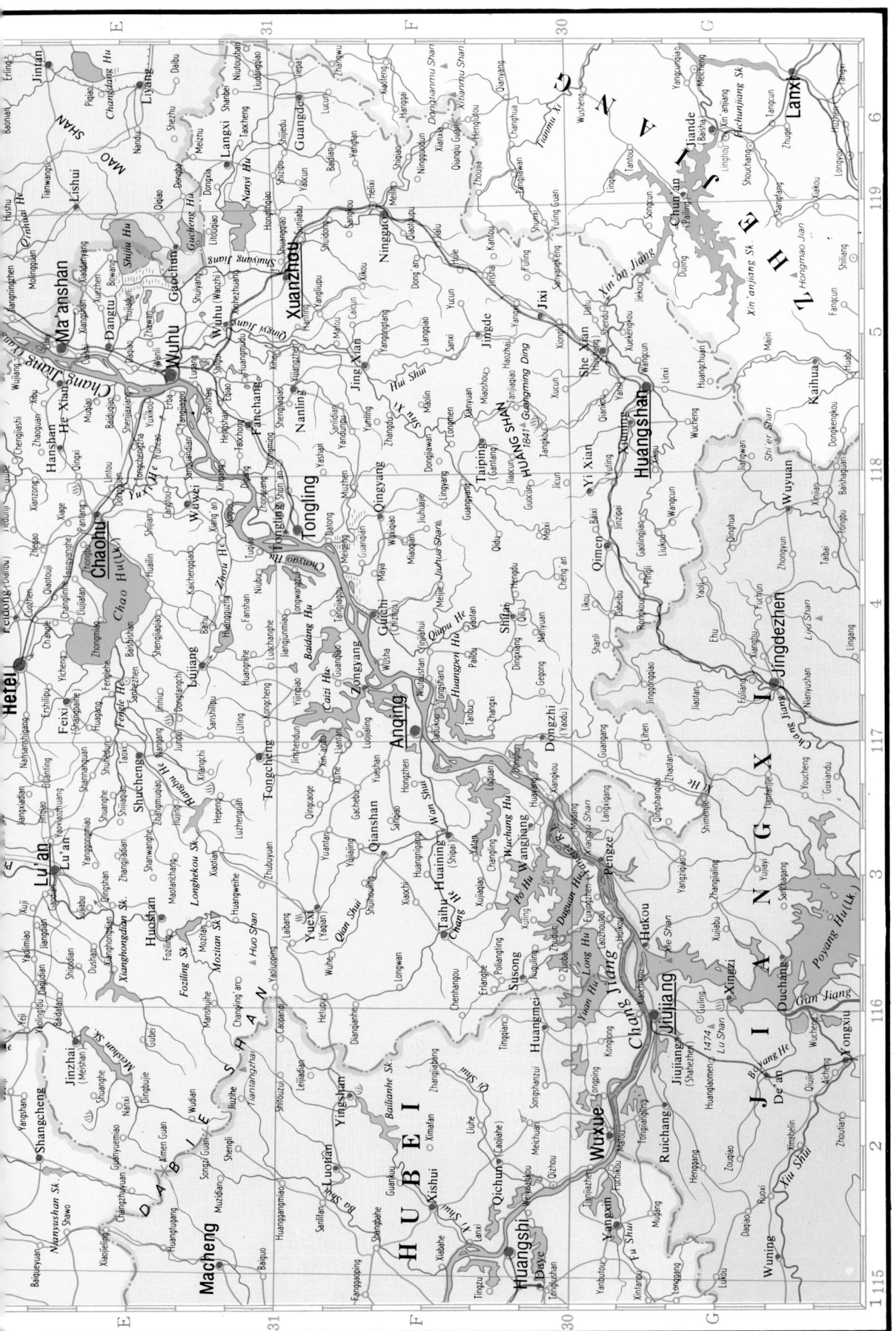

Anhui Province

Population: 52.2 million
Urban population: 15.3 million
Nationalities: Han, Hui, and She

Area: 130,000 square kilometers
Climatic features: warm-temperate, semi-humid, monsoonal climate north of the Huaihe River, with frequent spring droughts and summer floods; subtropical, humid, monsoonal climate in the south; clear-cut seasons; plum rains between spring and summer, sometimes followed by summer droughts
Average temperature: -1 — 4°C in January, 27 — 29°C in July
Annual average rainfall: 700 — 800 mm north of the Huaihe River, 800 — 1,700 mm south of the river; high precipitation in the mountain areas
Physical features: mainly plains and hills; the alluvial plain of the Huaihe River and its tributaries, 20 — 40 meters in altitude, makes up half of the province's farmland; hills line both sides of the Yangtze River.
Mountains: Dabie Mountains in the central west; in the south, the Huangshan and Jiuhua Mountains
Rivers: Yangtze and Huaihe Rivers
Lakes: Chaohu Lake in the center; Longgan and Pohu Lakes in the southwest; Nanyi Lake in the east
Products: rice, wheat, sorghum, corn, millet, potatoes, soybeans, peanuts, sesame, rape, peas; silk cocoons, cotton, ambary hemp, Chinese tallow tree, ramie; tobacco; apples, pears, *yangtao*, gingko; iron, coal copper
Specialties: Qimenhong, Tunxilu, Huangshan Maofeng, and Liu'an Guapian teas

Administrative divisions: 16 cities and 65 counties
Capital: Hefei
Neighboring areas: Jiangsu, Zhejiang, Jiangxi, Hubei, Henan, and Shandong Provinces
Major cities: Hefei, Huainan, Bengbu, Wuhu, Tongling, Anqing, Ma'anshan, Huaibei, Tunxi

Tourist attractions: Huangshan Mountain, famous for its sea of clouds, hot springs, precipitous rocks, and pines; Jiuhua Mountain, famous for its Buddhist temples; Mount Tianzhu in the Dabie Mountains, a well-known scenic spot

ZHEJIANG PROVINCE

1 : 2 000 000

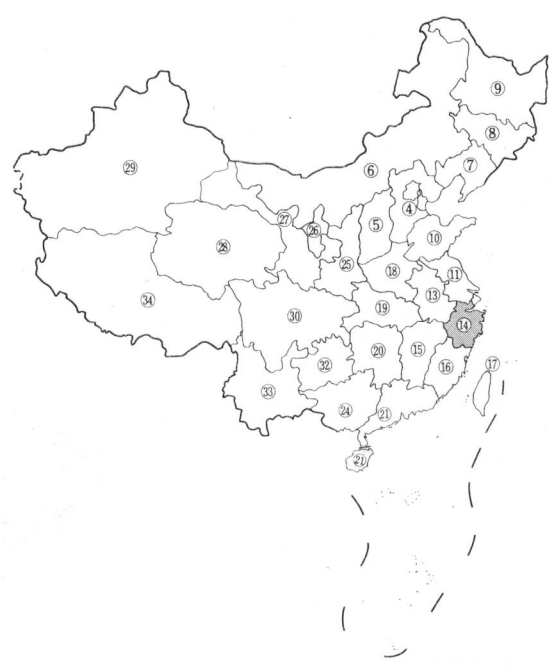

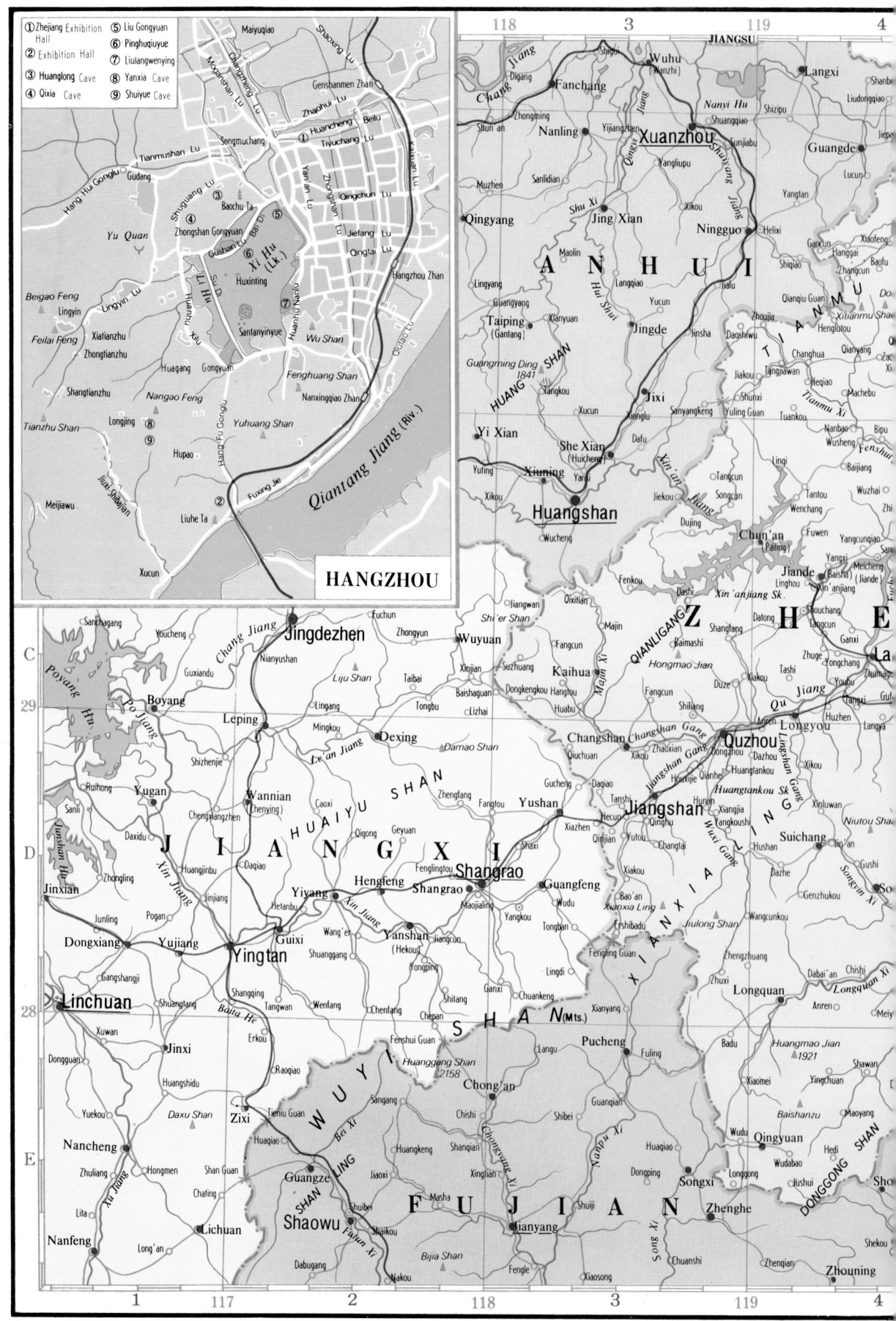

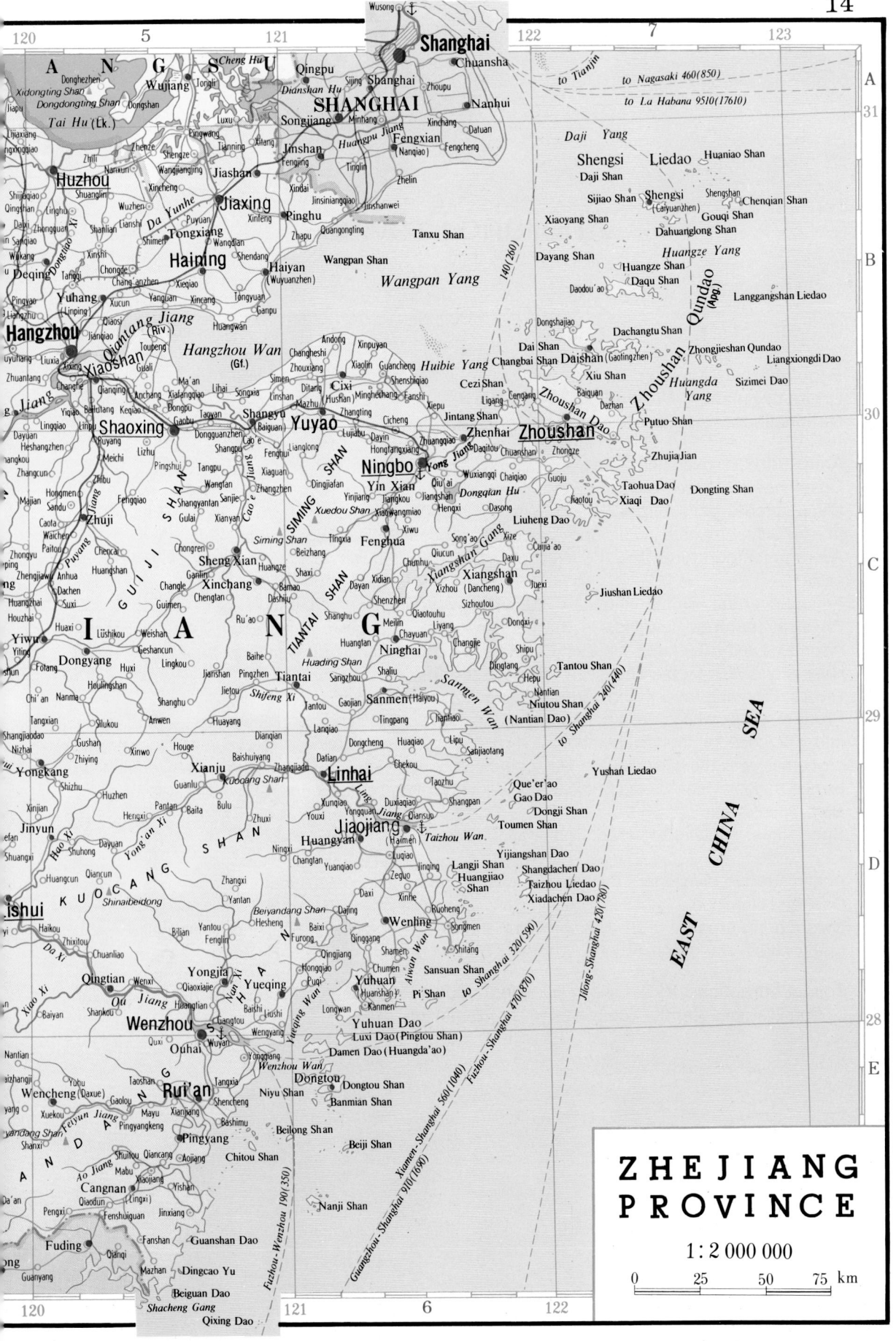

ZHEJIANG PROVINCE

1 : 2 000 000

0   25   50   75 km

Zhejiang Province

Population: 40.7 million
Urban population: 17.8 million
Nationalities: Han, She, Hui, Manchu, and Miao

Area: 100,000 square kilometers
Coastline: 2,200 kilometers long
Climatic features: subtropical, monsoonal climate; clear-cut seasons; plum rains from early June to early July; droughts in July and August; typhoons from late August to late September
Average temperature: 2 — 8°C in January, 27 — 30°C in July; high temperatures in the central basin
Annual average rainfall: 850 — 1,700 mm; low precipitation in the north
Physical features: lowlands in the northeast and mountains in the southwest; 70 percent mountains and hills; faces the East China Sea; the Hangzhou Gulf at the mouth of the Qiantang River is closed in by the Zhoushan Islands in the east.
Rivers: Qiantang River in the north; Oujiang River in the south
Products: rice, wheat, corn, potatoes, sugar cane, rape, sesame, peanuts, soybeans, tea; ramie, jute, silk cocoons, cotton, bamboo; tea-oil tree, tung tree, Chinese tallow tree; oranges, red bayberries, walnuts, Chinese torreya, loquats, peaches, persimmons, gingko, mushrooms, dried bamboo shoots; sea products including yellow croaker, hairtail, cuttlefish, shellfish, laver, kelp; alum, flourite, salt
Specialties: Fuchunjiang shad, Jinhua ham, Longjing tea, Huyang sheep

Administrative divisions: 18 cities, 57 counties, and 1 autonomous county
Capital: Hangzhou
Neighboring areas: Fujian, Jiangxi, Anhui, and Jiangsu Provinces: Shanghai Municipality
Major cities: Hangzhou, Ningbo, Wenzhou, Shaoxing, Jinhua, Jiaxing, Huzhou

Tourist attractions: West Lake in Hangzhou; Mount Putuo of the Zhoushan Islands, famous for its Buddhist temples; the tide waves of the Qiantang River

JIANGXI PROVINCE

1 : 2 000 000

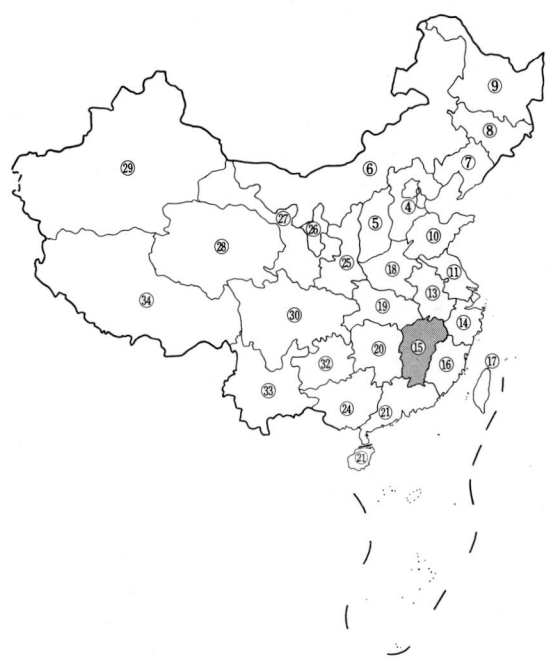

JIANGXI PROVINCE

1 : 2 000 000

0   25   50   75 km

HUI

ZHEJIANG

ANHUI

HUBEI

HUNAN

JIANGXI

Grid references: 30, B, 29, C, 28, A, H, S, N (Mts.)

114, 115, 116, 117 · 1, 2, 3, 4, 5

Major cities and places

Wuhan, Anqing, Huangshan, Xiuning, Yi Xian, Qimen, Wuyuan, Shangrao, Guangfeng, Chong'an, Yushan, Jingdezhen, Leping, Dexing, Yiyang, Hengfeng, Yanshan, Guixi, Yingtan, Jiujiang, Lu Shan, De'an, Yongxiu, Nanchang, Linchuan, Dongxiang, Jinxi, Xingzi, Duchang, Poyang Hu (Lk.), Boyang, Xinyu, Yichun, Pingxiang, Xianning, Huangshi, Ezhou, Wuxue, Huanggang, Daye, Ruichang, Wuning, Xiushui, Fengcheng, Gao'an, Shanggao, Zhangshu, Fengxin, Jing'an, Anyi, Xinjian, Qingjiang, Wan'zai

Rivers and features

Yangtze R., Chang Jiang, Gan Jiang, Xin Jiang, Fu He, Xiu Shui, Jin Jiang, Chang He, Po Hu, Huangpen Hu, Daguan Hu, Long Hu, Yuan Hu, Liangzi Hu, Huangou Hu, Xiaogu Shan, Lu Shan 1474, Jiugong Shan, Wumei Shan, Mufu Shan, Lianyun Shan, Fenghong Shan, Yuhua Shan, Huanggang Shan 2158

Scale bar and grid lines as shown.

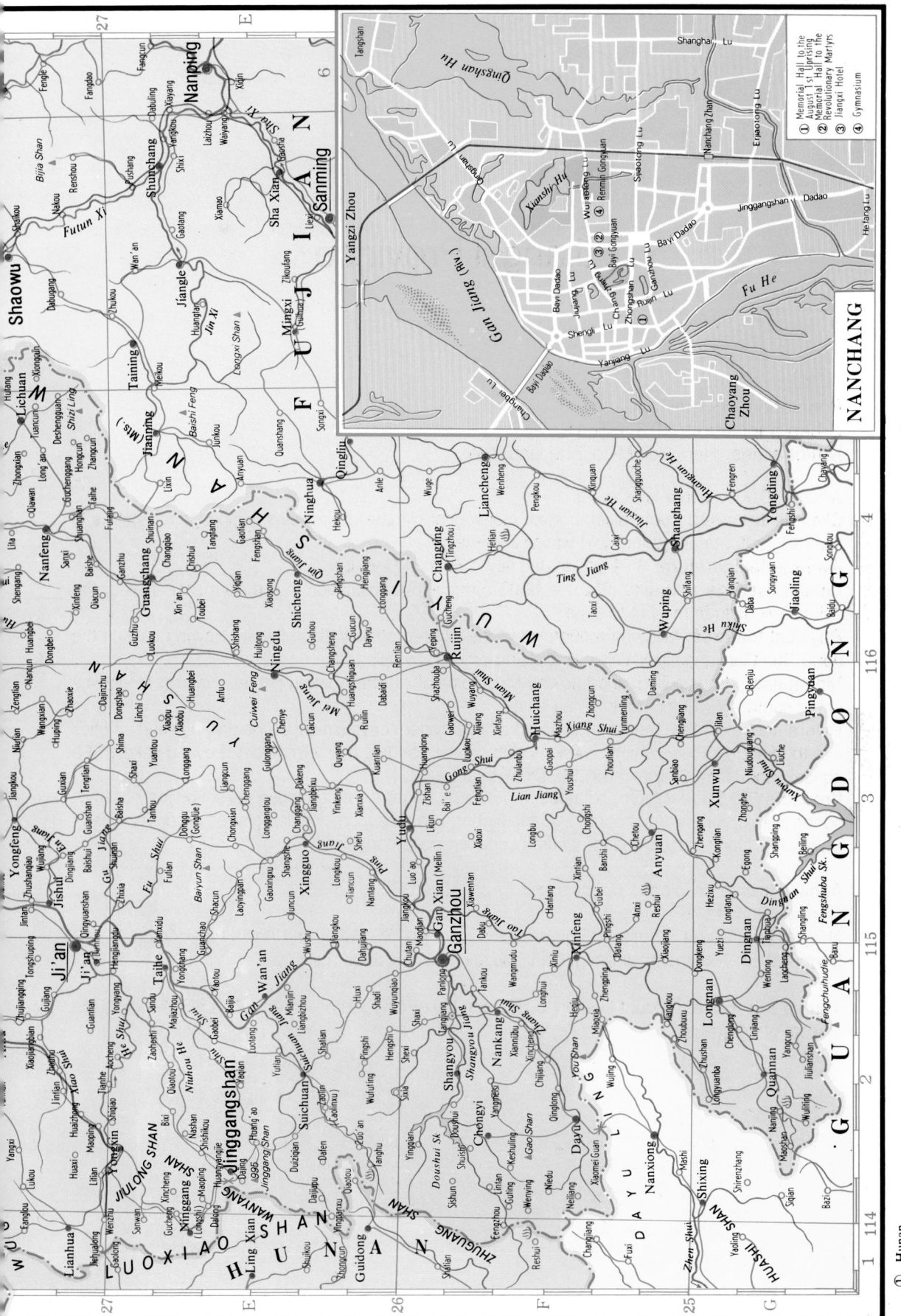

NANCHANG

① Memorial Hall to the August 1st Uprising
② Memorial Hall to the Revolutionary Martyrs
③ Jiangxi Hotel
④ Gymnasium

Qingshan Hu

Shanghai Lu

Tangshan

Nanchang Zhan

Erxiaoling Lu

Renmin Gongyuan

Wu'ai feng

Bayi Gongyuan

Spiaoting Lu

Jinggangshan Dadao

He'nang Lu

Xianshi Hu

Chanshan

Yangzi Zhou

Gan Jiang (Riv.)

Bayi Dadao

Fu He

Bayi Dadao

Ganzhou Lu

Bayi Jiang

Ruijin Lu

Zhongshan

Shengli Lu

Yanjiang Lu

Chaoyang Zhou

Changzheng Lu

Bayi Daqiao

Yanjiang

F U J I A N

Shaowu

Lichuan

Tuancun

Zhongxin

Qiawen

Long'an

Gucheng gang

Taihe

Fuhu

Shuangshan

Deshengguan

Hongcun

Zhanguan

Shizi Ling

Baishi Feng

Nanping

Fengle

Fengdo

Fandao

Fangkou

Wayang

Xijin

Gaosha

Sha Xi

Laizhou

Tangtou

Yongxin

Renshou

Ushang

Shunchang

Shixi

Shi Xian

Sha Xian

Gaolang

Xiamao

Wan'an

Sanming

Mingxi

Zhukoulang

Yangzi Zhou

Huangtan

Jin Xi

Jiangle

Quanshang

Junkou

Songxi

Anyuan

Lixin

Taining

Meikou

Longxi Shan

Jianning

Ninghua

Qingliu

Anle

Wuge

Hekou

Liancheng

Wenheng

Pengkou

Pengkou

Xinquan

Shangguoche

Huangguche He

Renfen

Fengren

Yongding

Chaying

Fenghu

Songbao

G U A N G D O N G

J I A N G X I

Shengang

Nanfeng

Xinfeng

Qiaozhu

Guangchang

Baishe

Ganzhu

Yijian

Changqiao

Gaolan

Fengshan

Hengjiang

Hengjiang

Qin Jiang

Shicheng

Xiaotong

Pingshan

Gucheng

Changting (Tingzhou)

Helan

Caixi

Ting Jiang

Taoxi

Shilang

Wuping

Shiku He

Yanqian

Songyuan

Baidu

Songlou

Qianzhu

Dongbei

Huangbei

Dajinzhu

Wangxan

Zenglian

Huping

Dongshao

Xinfeng

Shima

Xiaopu (Xiaolu)

Yuantou

Linchi

Anfu

Curwei Feng

Ningdu

Hulong

Zhangsheng

Gucun

Dayu

Huangshiguan

Dabaidi

Mian Shui

Wuyang

Gaowei

Xijiang

Xielang

Daming

Huichang

Zhongcun

Chengjiang

Jilan

Renjiu

Pingyuan

Guping

Heng tianqiao

Jinlian

Jintan

Shaxi

Longgang

Liangcun

Lixin

Laicun

Rujilin

Renlian

Leping

Ruijin

Shazhouba

Luokou

Zhulanbo

Yumenling

Zhoutian

Youshui

Zhongbao

Niuduoliang

Luche

Xunwu

Zhogghe

Shanglong

Beiling

H U N A N

① Hunan

Jiangxi Province

Population: 35.1 million
Urban population: 10.3 million
Nationalities: Han, Hui, Miao, She, and Yao

Area: 160,000 square kilometers
Climatic features: subtropical, humid, monsoonal climate; plum rains in spring; rainstorms in summer; autumn droughts; cold waves in winter
Average temperature: 3 — 9°C in January, 27 — 31°C in July
Annual average rainfall: 1,200 — 1,900 mm; high precipitation in the northeast; half of the annual rain falls from April to June
Physical features: hills and mountains in the south gradually slope toward Poyang Lake in the north; the Ganjiang River Valley is a plain bordered by hills to the east and west.
Mountains: Mufu, Jiuling, and Luoxiao Mountains along the western border; Nanling Mountains in the south; Wuyi Mountains in the east
Rivers and lake: the Ganjiang-Poyang drainage system covers most of the province and empties into the Yangtze River, which coincides with part of Jiangxi's northern border; Poyang Lake, 3,583 square kilometers, China's largest fresh water lake
Products: rice, wheat, corn, potatoes, millet, rape, sugar cane, tea, peanuts, soybeans, sesame; cotton, ramie, jute, silk cocoons; tea oil; timber; oranges, pomelos, lotus seeds; common carp, silver carp, black carp, bighead; wolfram, copper, coal; ceramics

Administrative divisions. 12 cities and 77 counties
Capital: Nanchang
Neighboring areas: Zhejiang, Fujian, Guangdong, Hunan, Hubei, and Anhui Provinces
Major cities: Nanchang, Jiujiang, Ganzhou, Jingdezhen, Ji'an, Ruijin

Tourist attractions: Mount Lushan, by Poyang Lake; Jingdezhen, an ancient town known as the "capital of ceramics"

FUJIAN PROVINCE

1 : 2 000 000

FUJIAN PROVINCE

1 : 2 000 000

0   25   50   75 km

FUZHOU

Min Jiang (Riv.)

Nantai Dao (Is.)

Nanchang
Linchuan
Yingtan
Shangrao
Jiangshan
Quzhou
Nanping
Shaowu
Jianyang
Ningde
Fu'an
Xiapu
Fuding
Shouning
Zhouning
Zhenghe
Songxi
Pucheng
Jianming
Taining
Guangchang
Nanfeng
Ningdu

ZHEJIANG
JIANGXI
FUJIAN

WUYILING

JIUFENG SHAN

DONGGONG SHAN

TAIMU SHAN

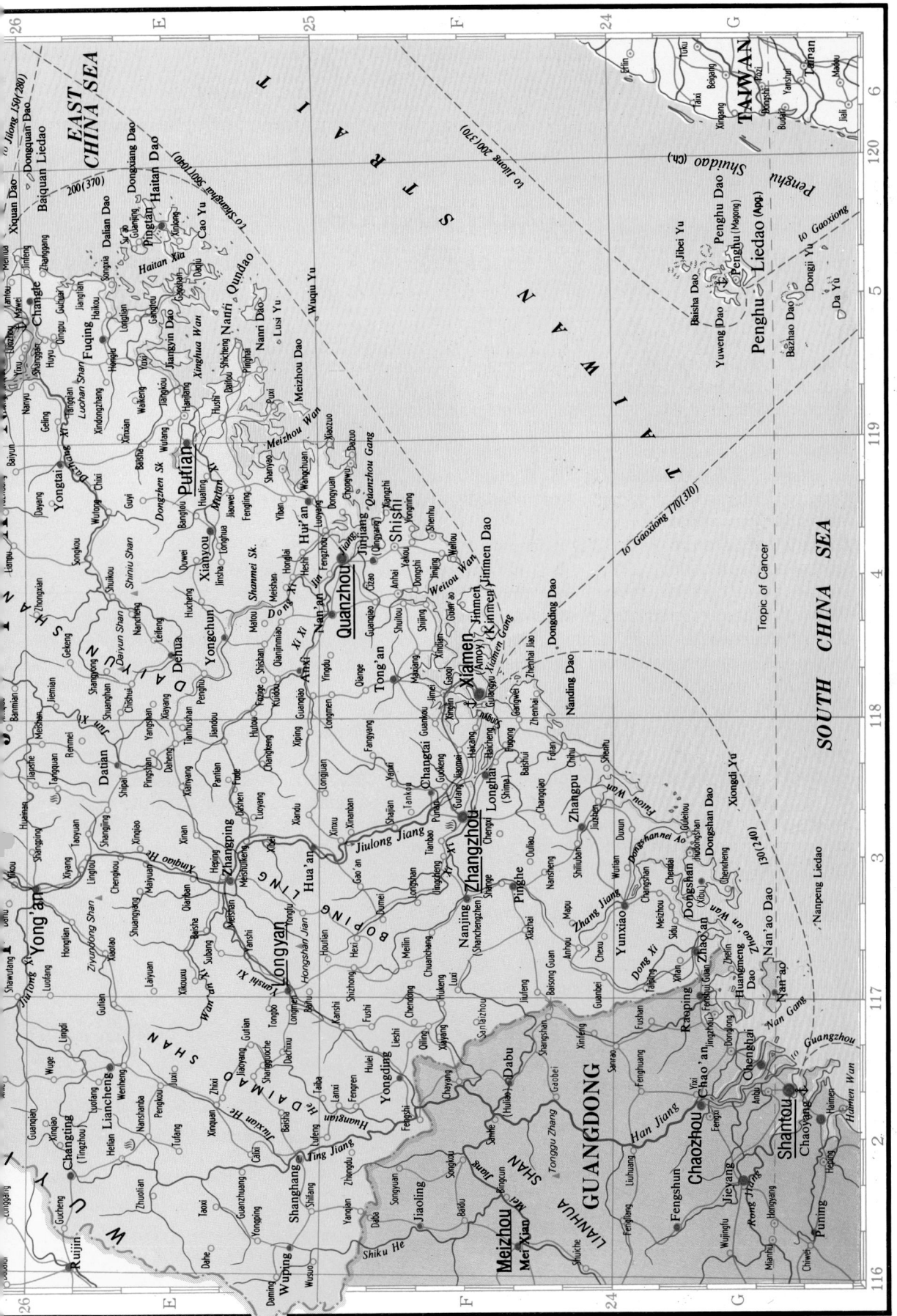

Fujian Province

Population: 27.5 million
Urban Population: 12 million
Nationalities: Han, She, Hui, Miao, Manchu, and Gaoshan

Area: 120,000 square kilometers
Coastline: 3,300 kilometers long
Climatic features: subtropical, humid, monsoonal climate; spring droughts; typhoons and rainstorms from summer to autumn
Average temperature: 5 — 13°C in January, 25 — 30°C in July
Annual average rainfall: 800 — 1,900 mm; low precipitation in the coastal lowlands, high in the northwestern mountains; the most rainfall occurs in May and June.
Physical features: graduated descent from the northwest to the southeastern seaboard; 90 percent mountains and hills; long and narrow plains along the coast; the East China Sea lies toward the northeast, the South China Sea toward the south, and Taiwan Province southeast across the Taiwan Strait.
Mountains: Wuyi, Jiufeng, Daiyun, Daimao, and Boping Mountains
River: the Minjiang River is the major waterway, with a drainage that covers about half of the province.
Products: rice, wheat, sweet potatoes, peanuts, sugar cane, rape, soybeans, sesame, tea; longans, oranges, lychees, pineapples, pomelos, loquats, bananas, lotus seeds; dried bamboo shoots, mushrooms, silver fungus; jute, tobacco, rosin, medicinal herbs; tea oil, tung oil, Chinese tallow tree; laver, lancelet, and other sea products; timber; iron, coal, molybdenum, manganese, salt, graphite

Administrative divisions: 11 cities and 59 counties
Capital: Fuzhou
Neighboring areas: Guangdong, Jiangxi, Zhejiang, and Taiwan Provinces
Major cities: Fuzhou, Xiamen, Nanping, Sanming, Zhangzhou, Quanzhou

Tourist attractions: Gulangyu Island, called the "garden on the sea," in Xiamen; Wuyishan, a scenic spot in Chong'an County

Comments: Xiamen Special Economic Zone is one of the four established in early 1980's, the other three being in Guangdong Province.

TAIWAN PROVINCE

1 : 2 000 000

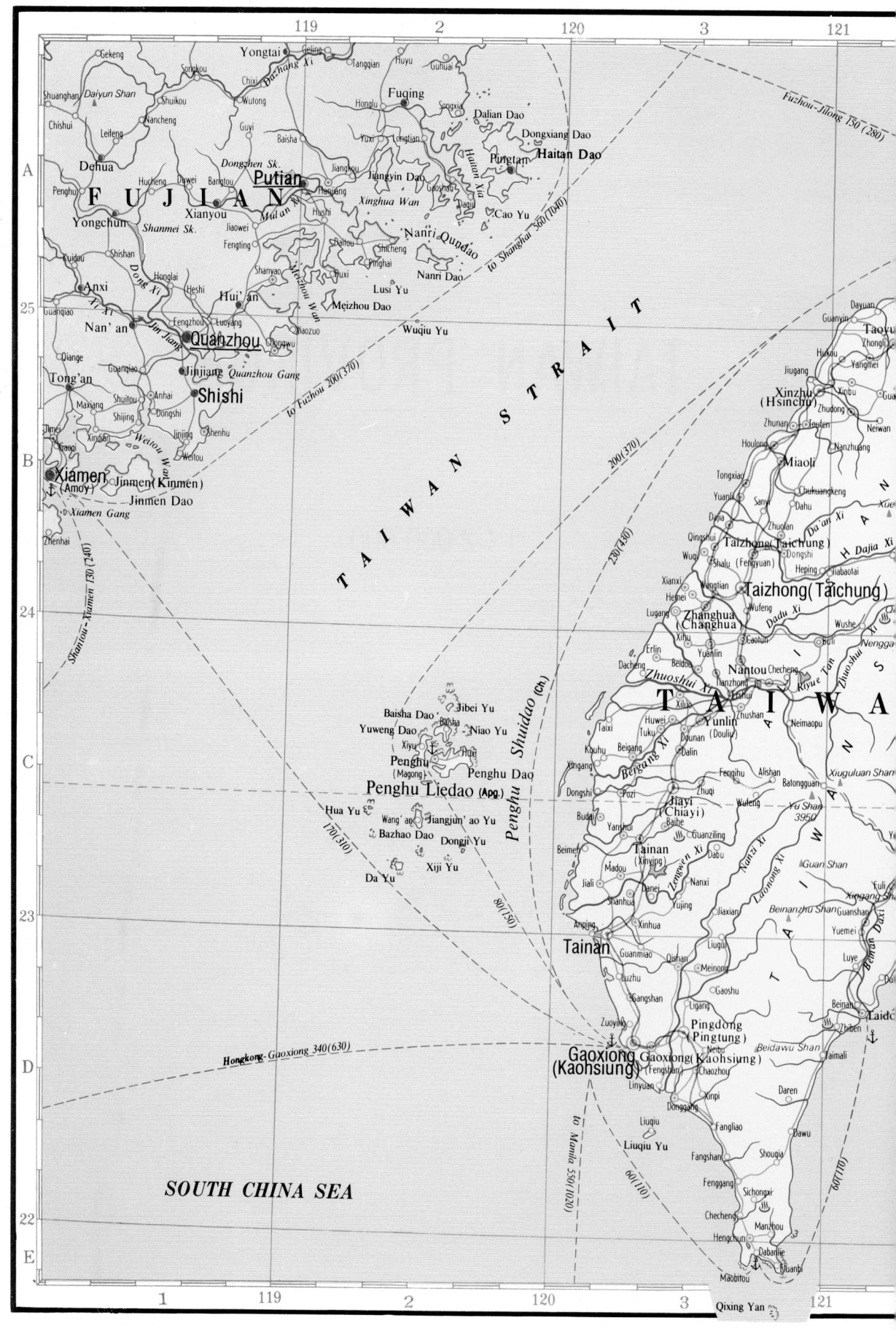

SOUTH CHINA SEA

EAST CHINA SEA

to Shanghai 420 (780)

to Nagasaki 560 (1170)

Pengjia Yu

Huangwei Yu

Chiwei Yu

Diaoyu Dao
Beixiao Dao · Nanxiao Dao

to Naha 340 (630)

Huaping Yu · Mianhua Yu

A

Jinshan

Jilong (Keelung)

Ruifang
Jinguashi

Nangang Shuanqi Aodi

ibei (Taipei)

Sandiao Jiao

25

ndian Huoshaoliao

Daxi

Pinglin

Toucheng

Yilan (Ilan)

Jiaoxi

Guishan Dao

Guiluan Dao

hui Xi

Luodong

xing

Su' ao

B

Nan' ao

Wushibi

Yonakuni-jima

Hatoma-jima

Ishigaki-jima

Tarama-jima

J A P A N

Dazhuoshui

Iriomote-jima

Komi

Ishigaki

Okinokami-shima

Kuro-shima

Y a e y a m a - r e t t ō

m (Hualien)

Hateruma-jima

R y ū k y ū – g u n t ō

24

C

Tropic of Cancer

P A C I F I C   O C E A N

23

D

oshao Dao

· Lan Yu

olan Yu

T A I W A N
P R O V I N C E

1 : 2 000 000

0   25   50   75 km

Taiwan Province

Situated in the Pacific Ocean, Taiwan lies southeast of the China mainland across the Taiwan Strait. The total coastline of Taiwan is 1,566 kilometers long. The province consists of Taiwan Island; the Penghu Islands in the Taiwan Strait; Pengjia, Diaoyu, Chiwei and other small islands northeast of Taiwan Island; Lan, Huoshao and islands in the southeast, most of which are volcanic cones. With a total area of 36,000 square kilometers, it is the second smallest province of China. It has a population of over 19 million, 97 percent of which are Han people. The Gaoshans are the province's main minority group, with a population of about 500,000.

The largest island of China, Taiwan Island is 380 kilometers long and 150 kilometers wide at maximum, with an area of 35,774.6 square kilometers. Mountains cover two-thirds of the island. The Taiwan Range consists of the parallel Hai'an, Zhongyang, Xueshan-Yushan, and Ali Mountains. Zhongyang Mountain, also known as Taiwan Mountain, is the largest on the island with most of its peaks above the 3,000-meter line. However, the highest peak in East China as well as in Taiwan is Yushan Peak, which tops 3,997 meters. Alluvial plains and hills spread along Taiwan Island's western coast. Rich soil and water resources make this an important agricultural area.

Located on the Pacific seismic belt, Taiwan is one of the most earthquake-prone regions in China. The resulting terrestrial heat is evidenced by its many volcanos and hot springs.

Situated on the Tropic of Cancer and influenced by the Kuroshio, a warm ocean current of the West Pacific, Taiwan has a subtropical-tropical monsoonal climate, which is characterized by long summers, much rainfall, and strong winds. The annual average temperature is 20 — 25°C: 13 — 20°C in January and 24 — 29°C in July. The annual average rainfall is 2,000 mm. Precipitation can reach 5,000 mm annually at the southern and northern tips of the island but diminishes to under 800 mm on the Penghu Islands. Jilong, the so-called rain port, has 214 rain days per year. Taiwan's typhoon season is from June to October, with August being the peak month.

The agricultural products of Taiwan are rice and sugar cane. Other crops include corn, tubers, peanuts, soybeans, jute, and sisal hemp. Taiwan produces fresh fruits all year round, earning the name "land of fruits." Taiwan has 55 percent forest coverage, making it one of China's major timber-producing bases.

Taiwan is famous for its camphor trees, as well as nutmeg, lemongrass, and cinchona. Fishing is a major industry. Aquatic products include porgy, yaito tuna, shark, oceanic bonito, sardine, agar, siliquose pelvetia, *zhegucai*, hawksbill turtle, coral, and pearl. Important terrestrial products are coal, petroleum, natural gas, gold, copper, salt, and sulphur.

The city of Taibei is the political, economic, and cultural center on the island. Other major cities are Jilong, Gaoxiong, Tainan, Taizhong, Xinzhu, Pingdong, and Taidong.

HENAN PROVINCE

1 : 2 330 000

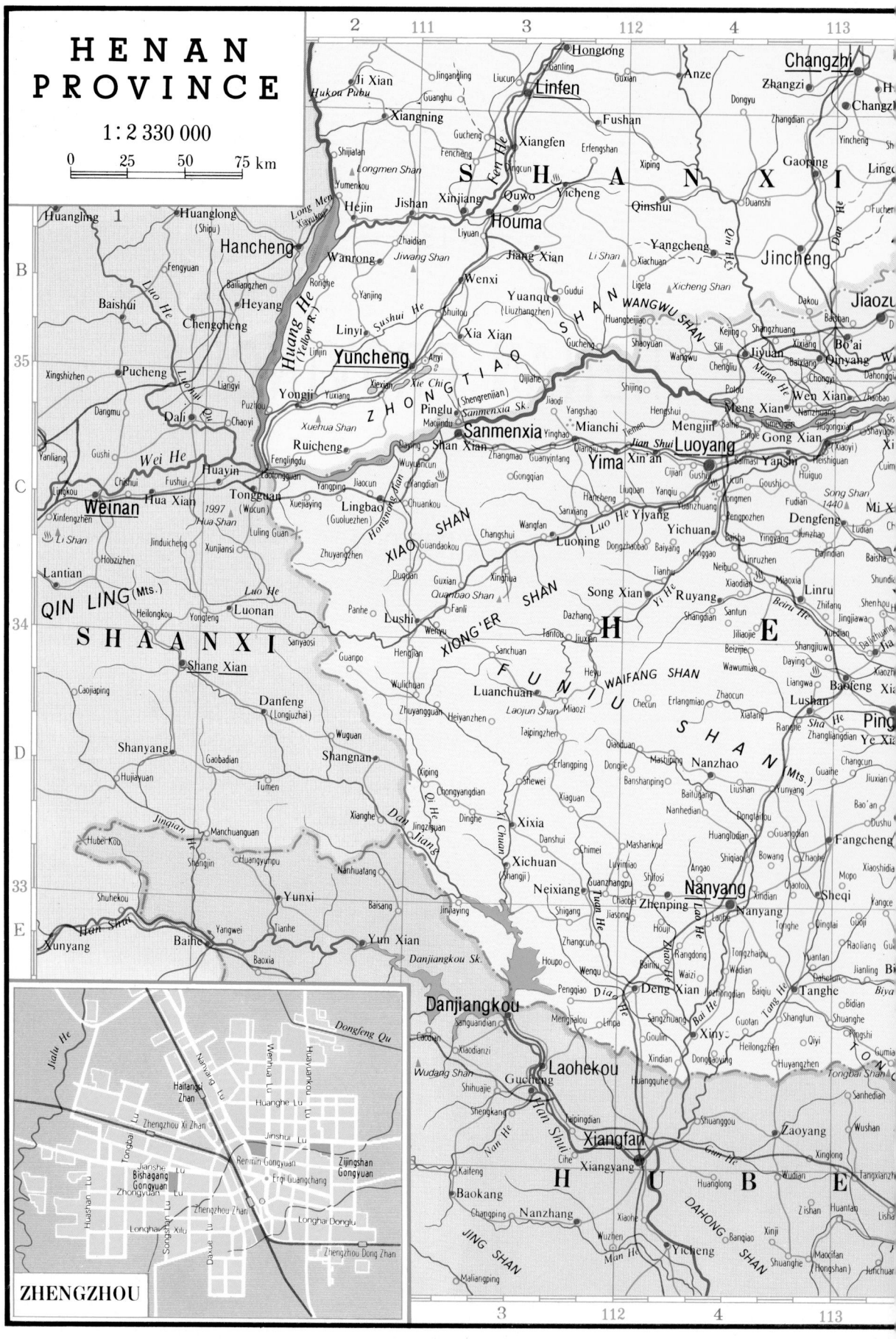

HENAN PROVINCE

1 : 2 330 000

0   25   50   75 km

SHANXI

SHAANXI

QIN LING (Mts.)

HENAN

HUBEI

ZHONGTIAO SHAN

WANGWU SHAN

XIAO SHAN

XIONG'ER SHAN

FUNIU SHAN

WAIFANG SHAN

DAHONG SHAN

JING SHAN

Ji Xian · Xiangning · Shijialan · Yumenkou · Hejin · Jishan · Xinjiang · Quwo · Yicheng · Houma · Jiang Xian · Wenxi · Yuanqu · Xia Xian · Yuncheng · Yongji · Pinglu · Sanmenxia · Shan Xian · Ruicheng · Mianchi · Yima · Luoyang · Yanshi · Gong Xian · Meng Xian · Jiyuan · Bo'ai · Jiaozuo · Qinyang · Wen Xian · Mengjin · Xin'an · Yichuan · Luoning · Dengfeng · Linru · Ruyang · Song Xian · Lushan · Baofeng · Nanzhao · Nanyang · Zhenping · Sheqi · Neixiang · Xichuan · Xixia · Deng Xian · Xinye · Tanghe · Zaoyang · Xiangfan · Xiangyang · Danjiangkou · Laohekou · Baokang · Nanzhang · Yicheng

Huangling · Huanglong · Hancheng · Baishui · Chengcheng · Heyang · Linyi · Pucheng · Dali · Huayin · Tongguan · Lingbao · Weinan · Hua Xian · Lantian · Shang Xian · Danfeng · Shanyang · Wuguan · Shangnan · Yunxi · Xunyang · Baihe · Yun Xian

ZHENGZHOU

Jialu He · Nanyang Lu · Wenhua Lu · Huayuankou Lu · Dongfeng Qu · Haitangsi Zhan · Huanghe Lu · Jinshui Lu · Zhengzhou Xi Zhan · Renmin Gongyuan · Zijingshan Gongyuan · Erqi Guangchang · Jianshe Lu · Bishagang Gongyuan · Zhongyuan Lu · Zhengzhou Zhan · Longhai Donglu · Zhengzhou Dong Zhan · Daxue Lu · Longhai Xilu

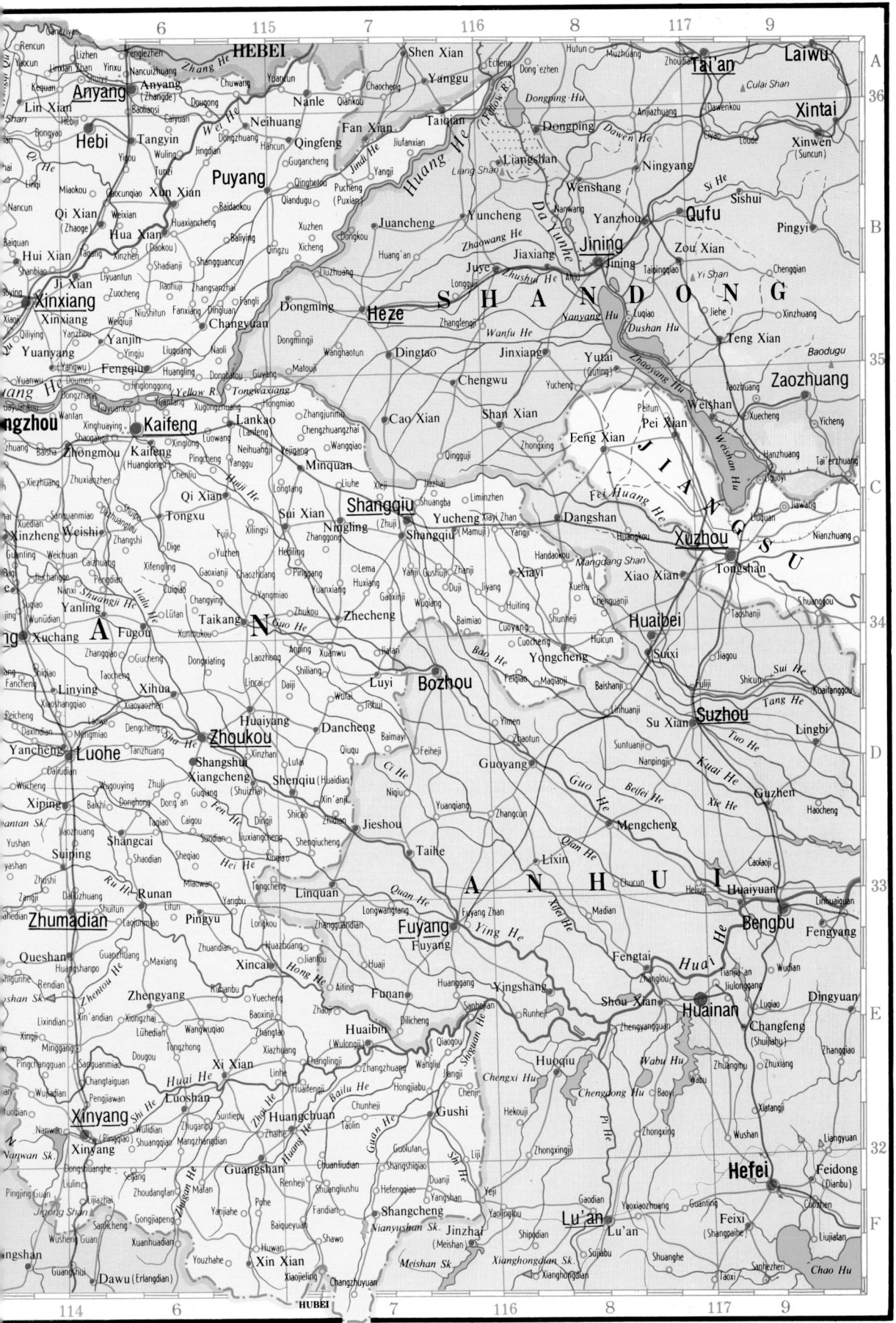

Henan Province

Population: 78.1 million
Urban population: 16.7 million
Nationalities: Han, Hui, Mongolian, and Manchu

Area: 160,000 square kilometers
Climatic features: spans the warm-temperate/semi-humid and subtropical/humid climates; dry, windy winters and springs; hot, rainy summers; strong sunlight in autumn
Average temperature: -3 — 3°C in January, 24 — 29°C in July
Annual average rainfall: 500 — 900 mm; high precipitation in the southern and northern mountains; 50 percent of the rain falls during the summer
Physical features: generally, plains cover the east and mountains, the west; part of the Yangtze River Basin lies in the southwest.
Mountains: Funiu, Waifang, Xiong'er, Xiaoshan Mountains in the west, which are extensions of the Qinling Range; southern foot of the Taihang Range in the north; Tongbai and Dabie Mountains in the south
Rivers: Yellow and Huaihe Rivers
Products: wheat, millet, sorghum, corn, rice, potatoes, sweet potatoes, peanuts, sesame, soybeans, sugar cane, rape, edible fungus; cotton, ambary hemp, tussah; flue-cured tobacco; oriental oak; apples, peaches, grapes, walnuts, gingko, persimmons; coal, bauxite, mica, nickel
Specialties: Lingbao dates, Huaiyang day lily, Huanghe common carp

Administrative divisions: 18 cities and 111 counties
Capital: Zhengzhou
Neighboring areas: Shandong, Anhui, Hubei, Shaanxi, Shanxi, and Hebei Provinces
Major cities: Zhengzhou, Luoyang, Kaifeng, Pingdingshan, Xinxiang, Anyang, Nanyang

Tourist attractions: Shaolin Temple, at the foot of Mount Songshan, one of the Five Mountains in eastern China; Longmen Grottoes in Luoyang

HUBEI PROVINCE

I : 2 330 000

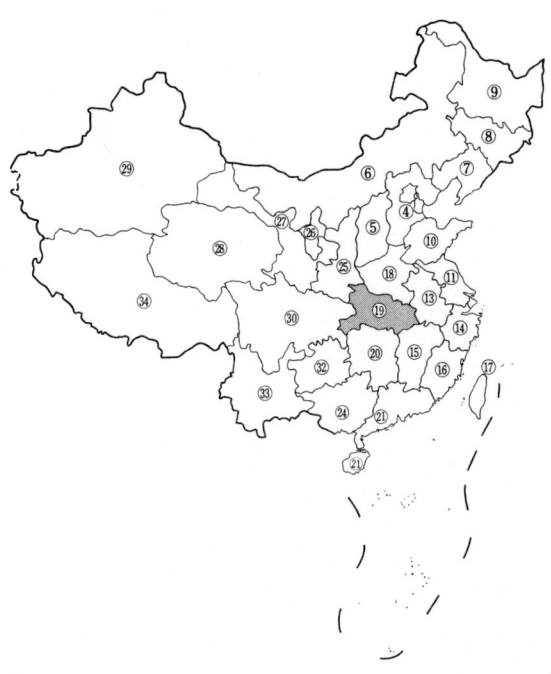

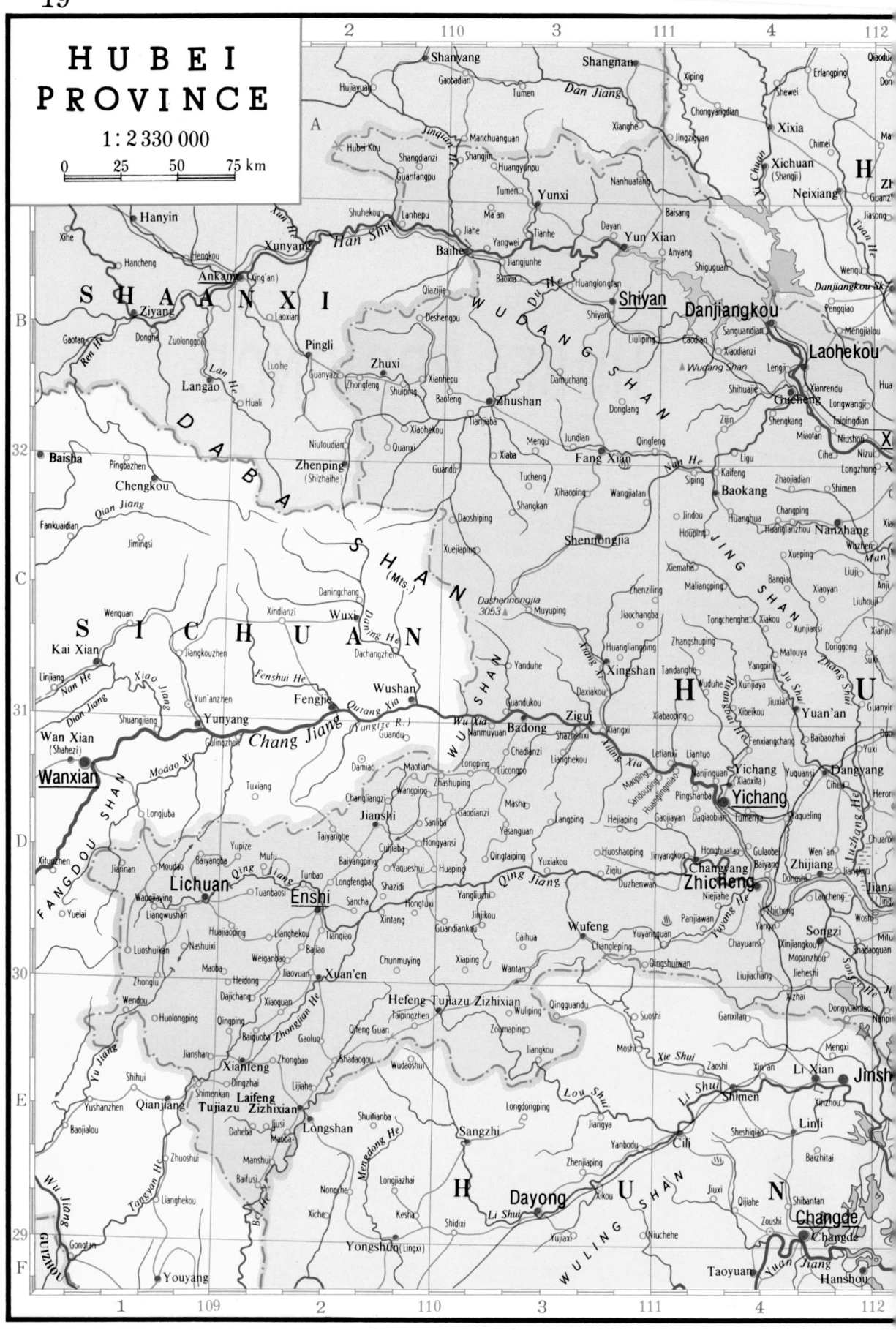

HUBEI PROVINCE

1 : 2 330 000

0   25   50   75 km

A

SHAANXI

Hanyin
Xihe
Hancheng
Hengkou
Xunyang
Han Shui
Ankang (Xing'an)
Ziyang
Gaotan
Donghe
Zuolonggou
Ren He
Langao
Huali
Laoxian
Pingli
Guanyazi
Zhongfeng
Shuiping
Zhuxi
Xianhepu
Baofeng
Damuchang

DABA SHAN

Baisha
Pingbazhen
Chengkou
Fankuaidian
Qian Jiang
Jimingsi
Zhenping (Shizhaihe)
Niutoudian
Quanxi
Xiaohekou
Daoshiping
Xiaba
Tucheng
Xihaoping
Wangjiatan

SICHUAN

Kai Xian
Linjiang
Nan He
Wenquan
Daningchang
Xindianzi
Wuxi
Xiao Jiang
Dian Jiang
Jiangkouzhen
Yun'anzhen
Fenshui He
Fengjie
Dang He
Wushan

Wan Xian (Shahezi)
Shuangjiang
Yunyang
Gulingzhen
Chang Jiang (Yangtze R.)
Qutang Xia
Guandu
Wanmuyuan
Wu Xia

Wanxian
Modao Xi

FANGDOU SHAN

Xituozhen
Jiannan
Moudao
Baiyangba
Yupize
Mufu
Tunbao
Changliangzi
Damiao
Maolian
Zhashuping

Lichuan
Wangjiaying
Longjiuba
Yuelai
Liangwushan
Qing Jiang
Tuanbaos
Tuanbao
Baiyangping
Yaqueshui
Sancha
Hongluxi
Yangliuchi
Jinjikou

Enshi
Huajiaoping
Chengkou
Bajiao
Shazidi
Huaping
Xintang
Guandiankou

Luoshuikan
Nashuixi
Maoba
Weiganbao
Jiaovuan
Tianqiao
Xiaping
Chunmuying
Wantar
Caihua

Zhonglu
Wendou
Heidong
Dajichang
Xiaoguan
Xuan'en
Hefeng
Tujiazu Zizhixian
Qifeng Guan
Wuliping
Qingguandu
Suoshi

Huolongping
Qingping
Baiguoba
Zhongbao
Gaolou
Taipingzhen
Jiangkou
Zoumaping
Moshi

Jianshan
Shadaogou
Wudaoshui
Xianfeng
Dingzhai
Lijiahe
Shimenkan
Jiusi
Maoba
Shuitianba
Longdongping
Jiangya
Xie Shui

Shihui
Yushanzhen
Qianjiang
Laifeng
Tujiazu Zizhixian
Daheba
Longshan
Mengdong He
Sangzhi
Yanbodu

Baojialou
Zhuoshui
Manshui
Baifusi
Nongche
Longjiazhai
Shidixi
Xikou
Jiuxi

Wu Jiang
Tangyan He
Be He
Xiche
Kesha
Li Shui
Xujiaxi
Niuchehe

GUIZHOU
Gongtan
Yongshun (Lingxi)

Youyang
Yongshun

F

B

SHANYANG
Hujiayuan
Gaobadian
Shangnan
Tumen
Dan Jiang
Xiping
Chongyangdian
Shewei
Xixia
Chimei
Qiaodu
Erlangping

Huber Kou
Shangdianzi
Shangjin
Manchuanguan
Xianghe
Jingziguan
Nanhualou
Neixiang
Guantangpu
Huangyunpu
Tumen
Yunxi
Baisang
Guanz

Shuhekou
Lanhepu
Jiahe
Ma'an
Dayan
Yun Xian
Anyang
Jiasong
Tuan Jir

Baihe
Yangwei
Tianhe
Jiangjunhe
Baoxia
Shiguguan
Wenqu

Qiazijie
Deshengpu
Du He
Huanglongfan
Danjiangkou Sk
Penggiao

WUDANG SHAN

Shiyan
Danjiangkou
Mengjialing

Zijin
Shengkang
Miaotan
Shihuajie
Sanguandian
Xiaodianzi
Caodian
Laohekou
Hua

Dongliang
Mengu
Jundian
Qingfeng
Fang Xian
Nan He
Ligu
Kaifeng
Zhaojiadian
Xianrendu
Longwangji
Taipingdian
Guicheng
Niushou
Nizui
Longzhong
X

Shenkang
Changping
Shimen
Nanzhang
Wuzhen
Man

Daoshiping
Xuejiaping
Houping
Huanglanzhou
Huanghua
Banjian
Xiaoyan
Anji
Liuhou

Dashennongjia 3053
Muyuping
Zhenziling
Jiaochangba
Tongchenghe
Xunjiansi
Donggong

Shennongjia
Xiemahe
Maliangping
C

SHAN (Mts.)

Yanduhe
Guandukou
Huangliangping
Zhangshuping
Yangping
Ju Shui
Yuxi

Xingshan
Tandanghe
Wudune
Xunjiaya
Jiuxian
Yuan'an

Wushan
WU SHAN
Wu Xia
Badong
Zigui
Xiangxi
Xiabaoping
Hejiaping
Xibeikou
Baibaozhai

Manmuyuan
Shazhenxi
Letianxi
Lianfuo
Sanyouping
Huanglingmiao
Nanjinguan
Yichang (Xiaoxita)
Dangyang
Heron

Chadianzi
Longping
Liucongpo
Lianghekou
Jling
Xia
Magang
Pingshanba
Yuquansi
Cihu

Longping
Masha
Yesangtan
Langping
Gaojiayan
Daqiaobian
Tumenya
Yaqueling

HUBU

Jianshi
Sanliba
Gaodianzi
Hongyansi
Qingtaiping
Yuxiakou
Huoshaoping
Jinyinkou
Gulaobei
Changyang
Baiyang
Zhijiang
Wen'an

Curiaba
Ziqiu
Qing Jiang
Duzhenwan
Zhicheng
Niejiahe
Yange
Dongshi
Jiangk

Yangliuchi
Ziqu
Panjiawan
Yuyanguan
Chayuansi
Xinjiangkou
Songzi
Mifu

Wufeng
Changleping
Qingshuiwan
Mopanzhou
Jieheshi
Shadaoguan

Xiaping
Guandiankou
Xizhai
Dongyuemiao

Hefeng
Tujiazu Zizhixian
Qingguandu
Ganxilan
Mengxi
Li Xian
Jinsh

Lou Shui
Zaoshi
Xin'an
Jinsh

Li Shui
Shimen
Xinzhou
Linli
Baizhitai

Cili
Sheshiqiao
Qijiahe

H
Dayong
Li Shui
U
WULING SHAN
N
Shibantan
Zoushi
Changde
Changde

Taoyuan
Nuan Jiang
Hanshou

1   109   2   110   3   111   4   112

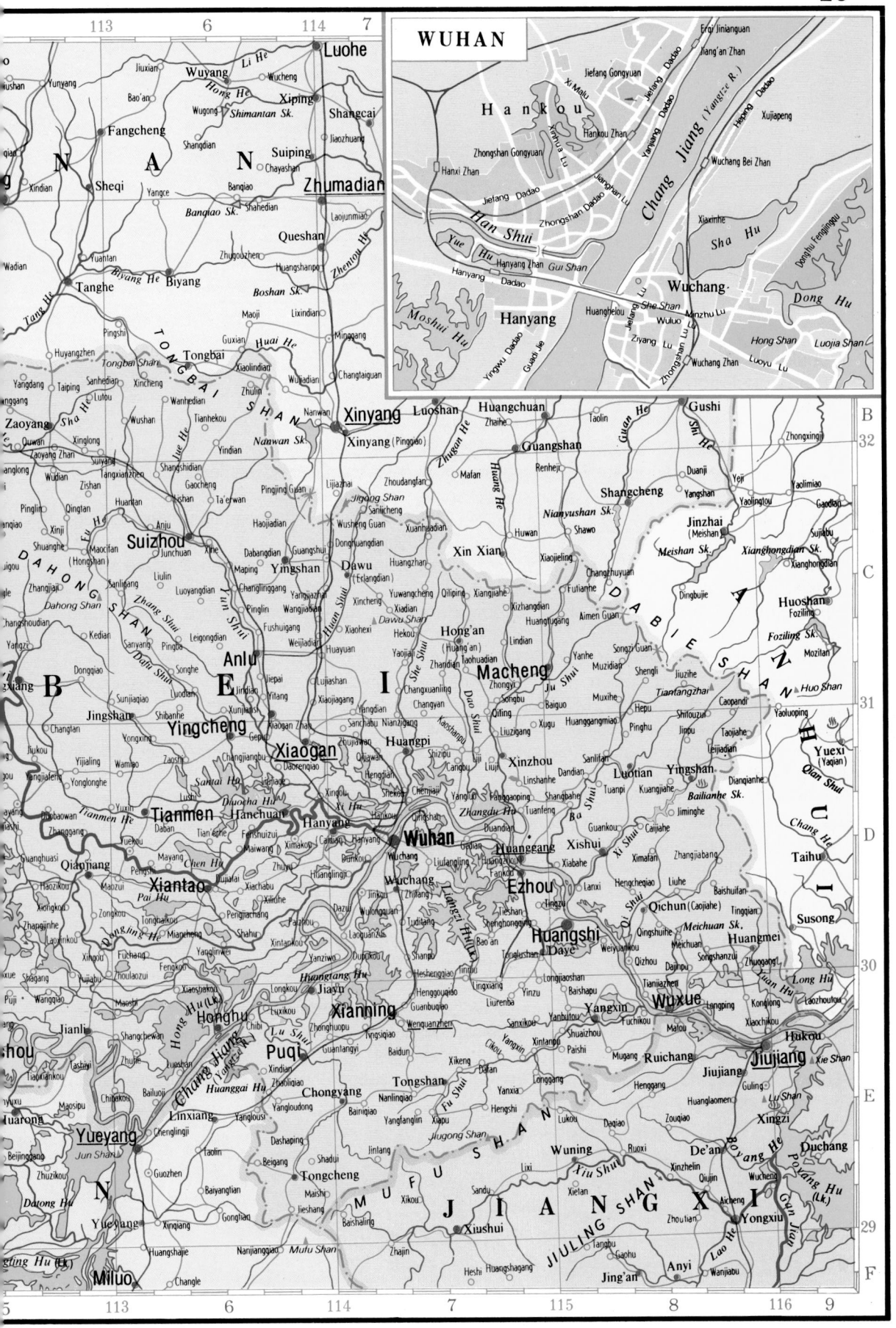

Hubei Province

Population: 49.9 million
Urban population: 23.6 million
Nationalities: Han, Tujia, Hui, Manchu, Miao, and Mongolian

Area: 180,000 square kilometers
Climatic features: subtropical, humid, monsoonal climate; changeable weather in spring; humid, hot summers; strong sunlight in autumn; dry winters; frequent droughts and floods
Average temperature: 1 — 6°C in January, 24 — 30°C in July; high temperatures on the northern side of the southeastern mountains and in the Three Gorges
Annual average rainfall: 750 — 1,500 mm; high precipitation in the southeastern and south-western mountains
Physical features: high in the west and low in the east; mountainous and hilly except in the south
Mountains: Wudang, Jingshan, and Wushan Mountains in the west; Dashennongjia Mountain in the Shennongjia Forest Region, among the western mountains; Tongbai and Dabie Mountains along the northeastern border; Mufu Mountains along the Hubei-Jiangxi border
Rivers: Yangtze River and its tributary the Hanshui River
Lakes: Honghu, Liangzi, Futou, Zhangdu, Longgan, Changhu, and Diaocha Lakes (Hubei is known as the land of a thousand lakes)
Products: rice, wheat, sorghum, millet, potatoes, corn, rape, sesame, tea, soybeans, peanuts, sugar cane; cotton, ramie, silk cocoons; sun-cured tobacco; freshwater products, such as blunt-snout bream, lotus seeds, water chestnuts, lotus roots, pearls, waterfowl; peaches, *yangtao*, oranges, chestnuts; tung oil, silver fungus, fir, Chinese tallow tree, metasequoia; iron, copper, rock salt, plaster stone

Administrative divisions: 1 autonomous prefecture, 25 cities, 51 counties, 2 autonomous counties, and 1 forest district
Capital: Wuhan
Neighboring areas: Anhui, Jiangxi, Hunan, Sichuan, Shaanxi, and Henan Provinces
Major cities: Wuhan, Huangshi, Yichang, Shashi, Xiangfan, Shiyan, Enshi, Jiangling

Tourist attractions: Gezhouba Dam project near Yichang; Shennongjia Natural Reserve in western Hubei

HUNAN PROVINCE

1 : 2 330 000

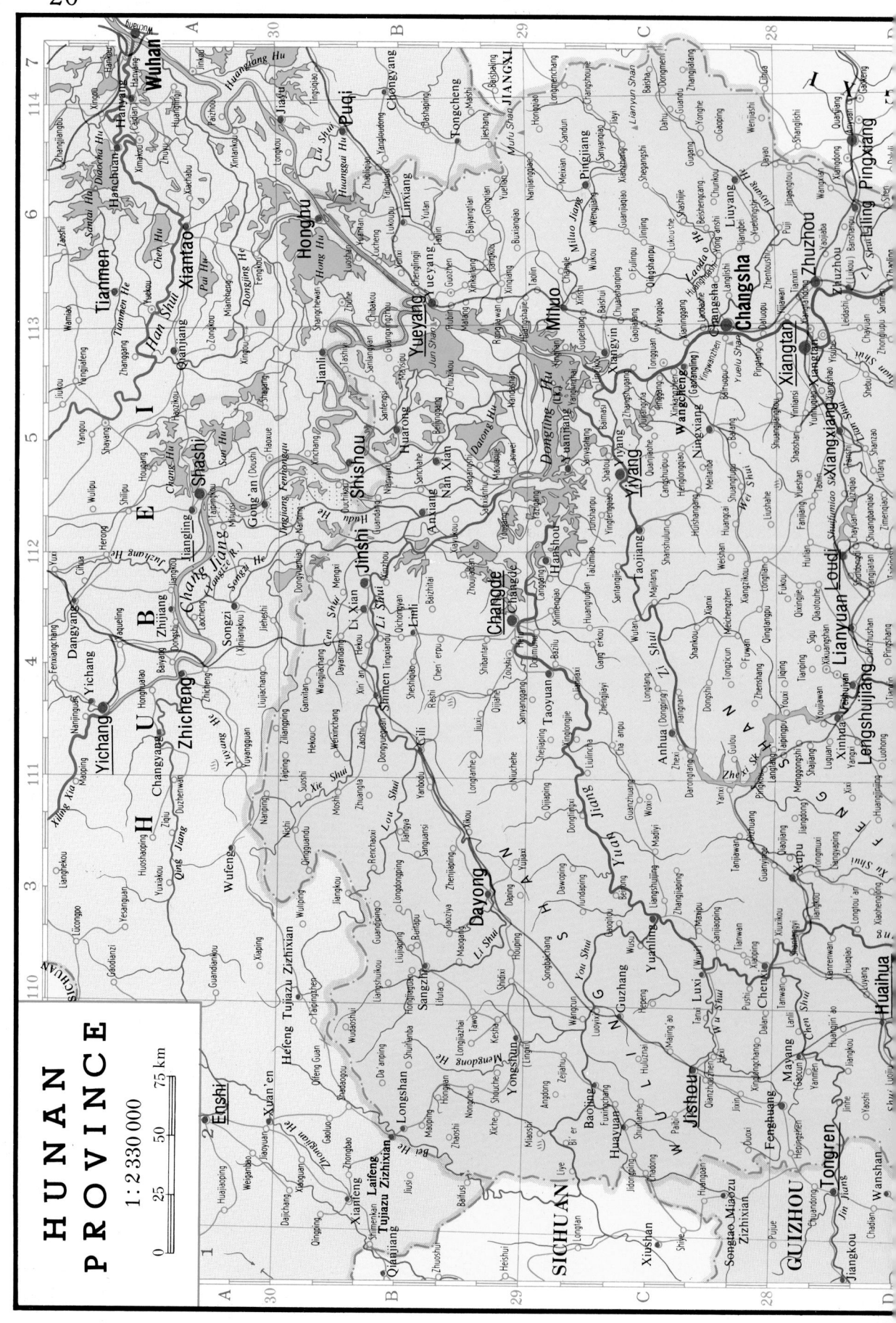

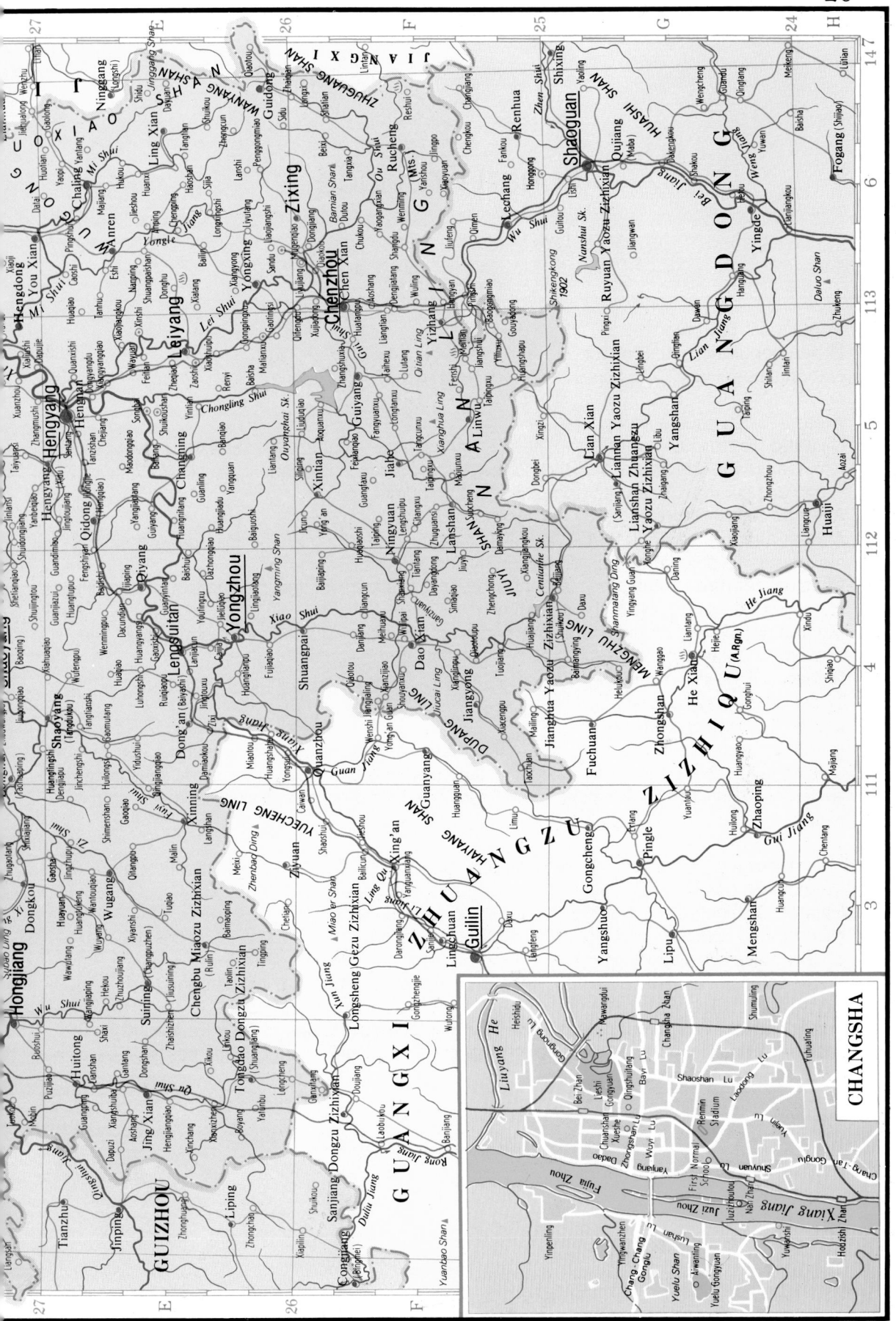

Hunan Province

Population: 57 million
Urban population: 18.8 million
Nationalities: Han, Tujia, Miao, Dong, Yao, Hui, Uygur, and Zhuang

Area: 210,000 square kilometers
Climatic features: subtropical, humid, monsoonal climate; short winters with low temperatures in the south and the northwestern mountains; frequent rainstorms between spring and summer; droughts from summer to autumn
Average temperature: 4 — 8°C in January, 26 — 30°C in July
Annual average rainfall: 1,250 — 1,750 mm; high precipitation on the seaward side of mountains; 40 percent of the rain falls from April to June
Physical features: mountains and hills cover 80 percent of the province; a small plain surrounds Dongting Lake in the central north.
Mountains: Wuling Mountains in the northwest; Xuefeng Mountains in the central west; Luoxiao Mountains in the east; Nanling Mountains in the south
Rivers: Xiangjiang, Yuanjiang, Zishui, and Lishui Rivers; the Yangtze River touches the border near Dongting Lake.
Lakes: Dongting and Datong Lakes
Products: rice, wheat, potatoes, corn, sorghum, millet, rape, soybeans, peanuts, sugar cane, sesame, tea; cotton, ramie, silk cocoons; flue-cured tobacco; tung oil, tea oil; lotus seeds, *yangtao*, oranges, lily; timber; pork, goose; antimony, lead, zinc, and other non-ferrous and rare metals

Administrative divisions: 1 autonomous prefecture, 24 cities, 74 counties, and 6 autonomous counties
Capital: Changsha
Neighboring areas: Jiangxi, Guangdong, Guizhou, Sichuan, and Hunan Provinces; Guangxi Zhuang Autonomous Region
Major cities: Changsha, Zhuzhou, Hengyang, Xiangtan, Shaoyang, Lengshuijiang

Tourist attractions: Mount Hengshan, 1,290 meters high, is one of the Five Mountains in eastern China; Dongting Lake, once the biggest fresh water lake in China, has an area of 2,820 square kilometers.

GUANGDONG PROVINCE
HAINAN PROVINCE

1 : 3 330 000

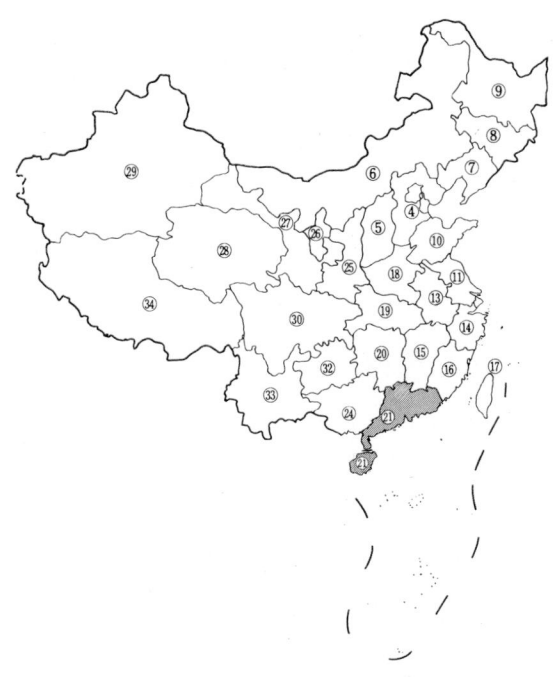

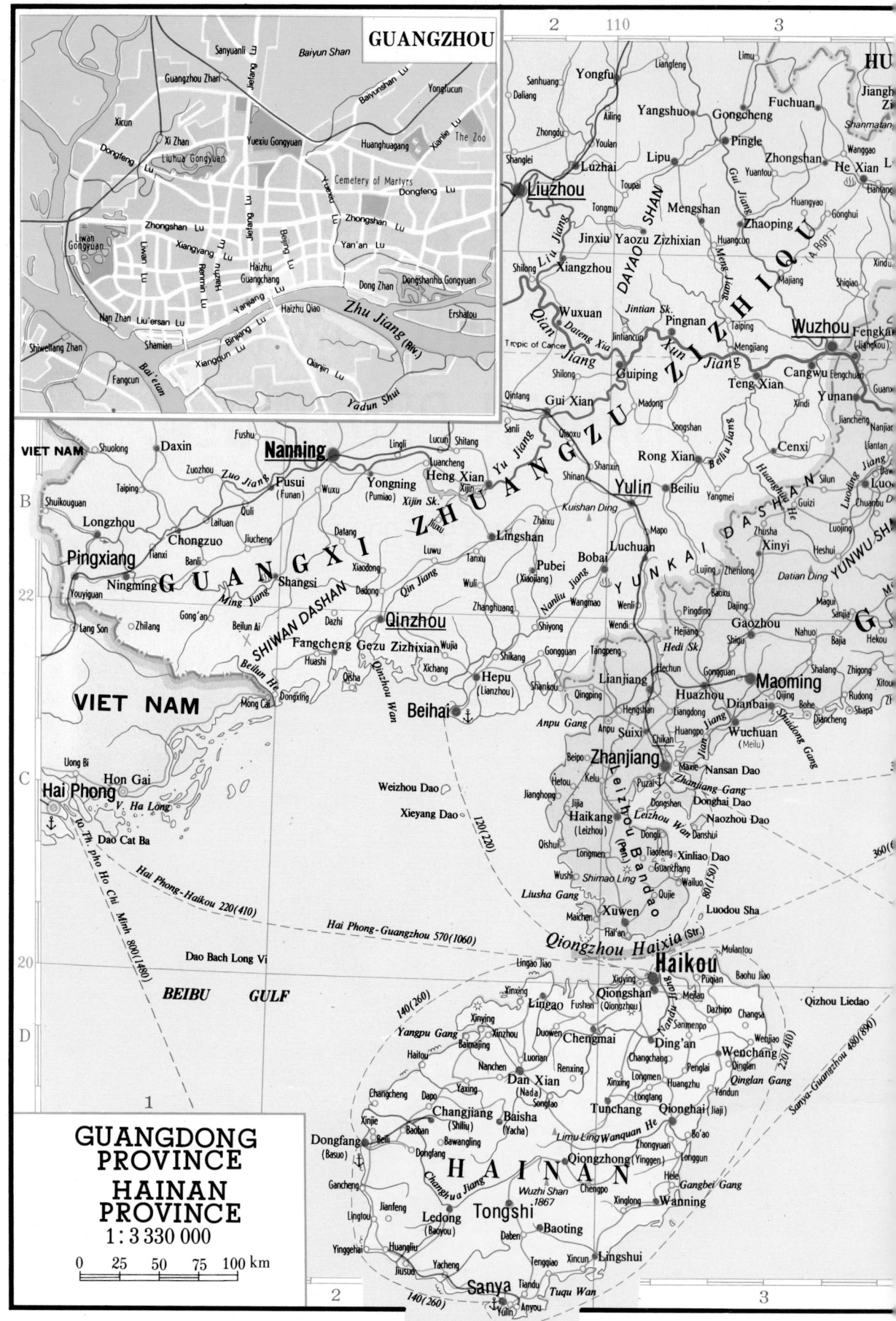

GUANGZHOU

Sanyuanli
Baiyun Shan
Guangzhou Zhan
Jiefang
Yongfucun
Baiyunshan Lu
Xicun
Xi Zhan
Yuexiu Gongyuan
Xianie Lu
The Zoo
Dongfeng
Liuhua Gongyuan
Huanghuagang
Cemetery of Martyrs
Dongfeng Lu
Zhongshan Lu
Jiefang
Zhongshan Lu
Yan'an Lu
Liwan
Gongyuan
Xiangyang Lu
Renmin Lu
Haizhu
Guangchang
Dong Zhan
Dongshanhu Gongyuan
Nan Zhan
Liu'ersan Lu
Yanjiang
Haizhu Qiao
Ershatou
Shiweitang Zhan
Shamian
Binjiang Lu
Xiangtun Lu
Qianjin Lu
Zhu Jiang (Riv.)
Fangcun
Bai'etan
Yadun Shui

2   110   3

Limu
HU
Sanhuang   Yongfu
Liangfeng
Jiangh
Daliang
Zi
Ailing
Yangshuo   Fuchuan
Shanmatan
Zhongdu
Youlan   Gongcheng
Wanggao
Shanglei
Lipu   Pingle   Zhongshan   He Xian
L
Luzhai   Yuantou   Huangyao   Jiantang
Liuzhou   Toupai   Zhaoping   Gonghui
Tongmu   Mengshan   Huangcun
DAYAO   Zhao   Majiang   Shiqiao
Jinxiu Yaozu Zizixian
Shilong   Liu   Meng Jiang   Wuzhou   Fengka
SHAN
Xiangzhou   Pingnan   (Jingkou)
Wuxuan   Jintian Sk.   Taiping   Mengjiang
Qian   Dateng Xia   Jintiancun   Cangwu   Fengchuan
Tropic of Cancer   Guiping   Teng Xian   Yunan
Shilong   Madong   Xindi   Jiancheng
Qintang   Gui Xian   Songshan   Beiliu Jiang   Cenxi
Sanli   Qiaoxu   Rong Xian   Silun   Luo
Lingli   Lucun Shitang   Shanxin   Guizi   Chuanbu
Nanning   Luancheng   Yu Jiang   Yulin   Luojing   SHA
Daxin   Fushu   Heng Xian   Beiliu   G
Shuolong   Xijin Sk.   Yangmei
Zuozhou   Zuo Jiang   Xijin   Kuishan Ding   Mapo   Datian D
Shuikouguan   Fusui   Yongning   Zhaixin   YUNWU
Taiping   (Funan)   Wuxu   (Pumiao)   Zhusha
Longzhou   Quli   Jiusu   Lingshan   Luchuan   Xinyi
Chongzuo   Laituan   Lujing Zhenlong   Heshui
Pingxiang   Tianxi   Datang   Luwu   Pubei   Bobai   Baoxu
Ningming   Banli   Xiaodong   Qin Jiang   (Xiaojiang)   Dajing   Magui
22   Youyiguan   Shangsi   Dadong   Tanxu   Wuli   Wangmao   Gaozhou   Sanjia
Lang Son   Zhilang   Gong'an   Ming Jiang   Zhanghuang   Wenli   Pingding   Nahuo   Bajia   Hekou
SHIWAN DASHAN   Dazhi   Nanliu Jiang   Wendi   Hejiang   Gongguan   Shalang   Zhigong
Beilun Ai   Qinzhou   Shiyong   Tangpeng   Hedi Sk.   Shigu   Maoming
Fangcheng Gezu Zizixian   Wujia   Shikang   Gongguan   Huazhou   Qijing   Shapa   Dianchen
VIET NAM   Huashi   Shankou   Qingping   Lianjiang   Dianbai   Bohe   Rudong
Qisha   Xichang   Hengshan   Liangdong   Wuchuan
Beilun He   Dongxing   Hepu   Anpu   Suixi   Huangpo   (Meilu)
Mong Cai   (Lianzhou)   Chikan
Anpu Gang   Beipo   Kelu   Maxie   Nansan Dao
Hai Phong   Hon Gai   Qinzhou Wan   Zhanjiang   Donghai Dao
Uong Bi   Beihai   Hetou   Puzai   Zhanjiang-Gang
V. Ha Long   Weizhou Dao   Jianghong   Jijia   Dongshan   Naozhou Dao
Dao Cat Ba   Xieyang Dao   Qishou   Haikang   Dongli   Danshui
120 (220)   Longmen   (Leizhou)   Xinliao Dao
Wushi   Guanchang
Shimao Ling   Wailuo
Liusha Gang   Qujie
Maichen   Xuwen   Luodou Sha
Hai Phong-Haikou 220(410)   360
Hai Phong-Guangzhou 570(1060)   Hai'an   Qiongzhou Haixia (Str.)   80 (150)
Dao Bach Long Vi   Lingao Jiao   Haikou   Mulantou
20   Xinxing   Qiongshan   Baohu Jiao
BEIBU   GULF   Lingao   Fushan   (Qiongzhan)   Qizhou Liedao
140 (260)   Xinying   Meilan
Yangpu Gang   Xinzhou   Duowen   Chengmai   Dazhipo   Changsa
Hailou   Baimajing   Luorian   Ding'an   Wehijiao   Wenchang
Nanchen   Renxing   Changchang   Penglai   Qinglan
Changcheng   Dapo   Yaxing   Xinxing   Longmen   Huangzhu   Qinglan Gang
Xinjie   Dan Xian   Songtao   Yandun   Sanya-Guangzhou 480(890)
Dongfang   Belli   (Nada)   Longlang
Changjiang   Baoban   Bawangling   Baisha   Qiongzhong   Longgun
Gancheng   (Shiliu)   (Yacha)   Tunchang   Qionghai (Jiaji)
Dongfang   Bawangling   Limu Ling   Wanquan He   Bo'ao
(Basuo)   HAINAN   Zhongyuan   Hele   Gangbei Gang
GUANGDONG   Changhua Jiang   Wuzhi Shan   Chengpo   Xinglong   Wanning
PROVINCE   Jianfeng   1867
HAINAN   Lingtou   Tongshi   Daben   Baoting
PROVINCE   Ledong   Lingshui
1 : 3 330 000   Yinggehai   (Baoyou)   Tenggiao   Xincun
Huangliu
0   25   50   75   100 km   Jiusuo   Yacheng   Sanya   Tiandu   Tuqu Wan
140 (260)   Yulin   Anyou

2   3

JIANGXI

FUJIAN

HUNAN

GUANGDONG

SOUTH CHINA SEA

Guangzhou

Shenzhen

Hongkong

Macao

Zhuhai

Foshan

Shantou

Chaozhou

Meizhou

Shaoguan

Zhaoqing

Jiangmen

Huizhou

Dongguan

Zhongshan

South China Sea routes (distances):

Jakarta-Guangzhou 1860(3440)
Conakry-Guangzhou 10380(19220)
Singapore-Hongkong 1440(2670)
Hongkong-Manila 630(1170)
Zhanjiang-Singapore 1340(2480)
Singapore-Guangzhou 1530(2830)
Durrësi-Guangzhou 7490(13870)
Hongkong-Shanghai 820(1520)
Guangzhou-Shanghai 910(1690)
Hongkong-Yokohama 1580(2930)
Guangzhou-Shantou 290(540)
Hongkong-Gaoxiong 340(630)

Dongsha Qundao (Apg.)
Dongsha Dao
Beiwei Tan
Nanwei Tan

Inset map:

HA NOI
Nanning
Guangzhou
TAIWAN
Gaoxiong
Hai Phong
Zhanjiang
Hongkong
Dongsha Qundao (Apg.)
Haikou
HAINAN
VIETNAM
LAOS
Xisha Qundao
Da Nang
Zhongsha Qundao (Apg.)
MANILA
PHILIPPINES
KAMPUCHEA
Th. pho Ho Chi Minh
SOUTH CHINA SEA
Nansha Qundao (Apg.)
Zengmu Ansha
BRUNEI MALAYSIA
MALAYSIA
INDONESIA

SOUTH CHINA SEA ISLANDS
1:33 300 000
0   250   500 km

① Guangdong ② Yunnan ③ Guangxi Zhuangzu Zizhiqu ④ Fujian ⑤ Thailand ⑥ Indonesia

Guangdong Province

Population: 56.5 million
Urban population: 17 million
Nationalities: Han, Yao, Zhuang, Hui, Manchu, and She

Area: 180,000 square kilometers
Coastline: 4,300 kilometers long
Climatic features: subtropical-tropical, humid monsoonal climate; rainy season from April to September; typhoons from May to November
Average temperature: 8 — 17°C in January, 27 — 29°C in July
Annual average rainfall: over 1,500 mm; high precipitation on the southern side of mountains; 40 percent of the rain falls during the summer
Physical features: situated on the Tropic of Cancer; hills in the north and lowlands in the south; hills scattered along the coastline; faces the South China Sea; includes the Pearl (Zhujiang) River Delta; the Leizhou Peninsula extends to the southwest.
Mountains: from west to east, arranged in an arc, are the Yunwu, Nanling, Jiulian, and Lianhua Mountains.
Rivers: Pearl River, which is the confluence of the Xijiang, Beijiang, and Dongjiang Rivers from the west, north, and east, respectively
Products: rice, potatoes, corn, sorghum, millet, wheat, sugar cane, peanuts, soybeans, sesame, tea; silk cocoons, ambary hemp, jute; sun-cured tobacco; bananas, oranges, lychees, pineapples, longans, and other tropical and subtropical fruits; rubber, oil palm, sisal hemp; coffee, cocoa, lemongrass, pepper; oyster, abalone, pearl, sea horse, and other sea products; timber; wolfram, tin, antimony, bismuth, molybdenum, copper, lead, zinc, oil shale, salt, sulphur

Administrative divisions: 15 cities, 73 counties, and 3 autonomous counties
Capital: Guangzhou (Canton)
Neighboring areas: Hunan, Jiangxi, Fujian, and Hainan Provinces; Guangxi Zhuang Autonomous Region; Hong Kong and Macao
Major cities: Guangzhou, Shantou, Foshan, Zhanjiang, Shenzhen, Zhuhai, Shaoguan

Tourist attraction: Seven Star Crags in Zhaoqing
Comments: Shenzhen, Zhuhai, and Shantou are three of China's four special economic zones established in early 1980's.

Hong Kong

Situated to the east of the mouth of the Pearl River, Hong Kong is a key outpost; it guards international navigation lines and is the gate to South China. It is composed of Kowloon Peninsula, its adjacent islands including Hong Kong and Dahao, and part of the Dapeng and Shenzhen Bays. Hong Kong has an area of 1,062 square kilometers with a population of 5.6 million (1988). Its urban core covers the northern part of Hong Kong Island and the southern part of Kowloon Peninsula. A deepwater port lies between the two areas.

In 1898, Britain obtained from China's Qing government a 99-year lease on Hong Kong. On December 19, 1984, the Chinese and British Governments signed a joint declaration concerning Hong Kong stating that Britain would restore Hong Kong to China on July 1, 1997.

Macao

Macao is located on the tip of Macao Peninsula in the southern part of the Pearl River Delta and includes Dangzai and Luhuan Islands in its domain. The territory's 16 square kilometers are inhabited by 426,400 (by the end of 1986) people, 96 percent of which are Chinese. It has been a Portuguese colony since the 16th century when some Portuguese businessmen made a landing on the pretext of sunning their water-soaked goods. The Chinese and Portuguese Governments signed a joint declaration on April 13, 1987 concerning Macao, stating that Portugal would restore

SOUTH CHINA SEA ISLANDS
ZHUJIANG DELTA

1 : 10 660 000   1 : 1 330 000

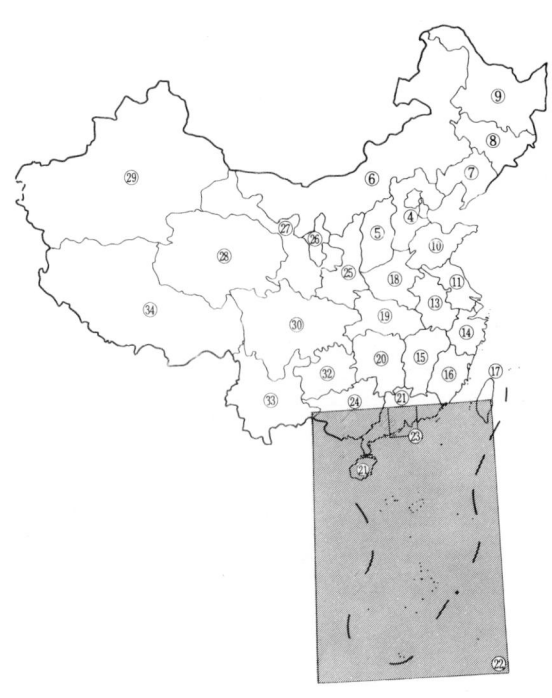

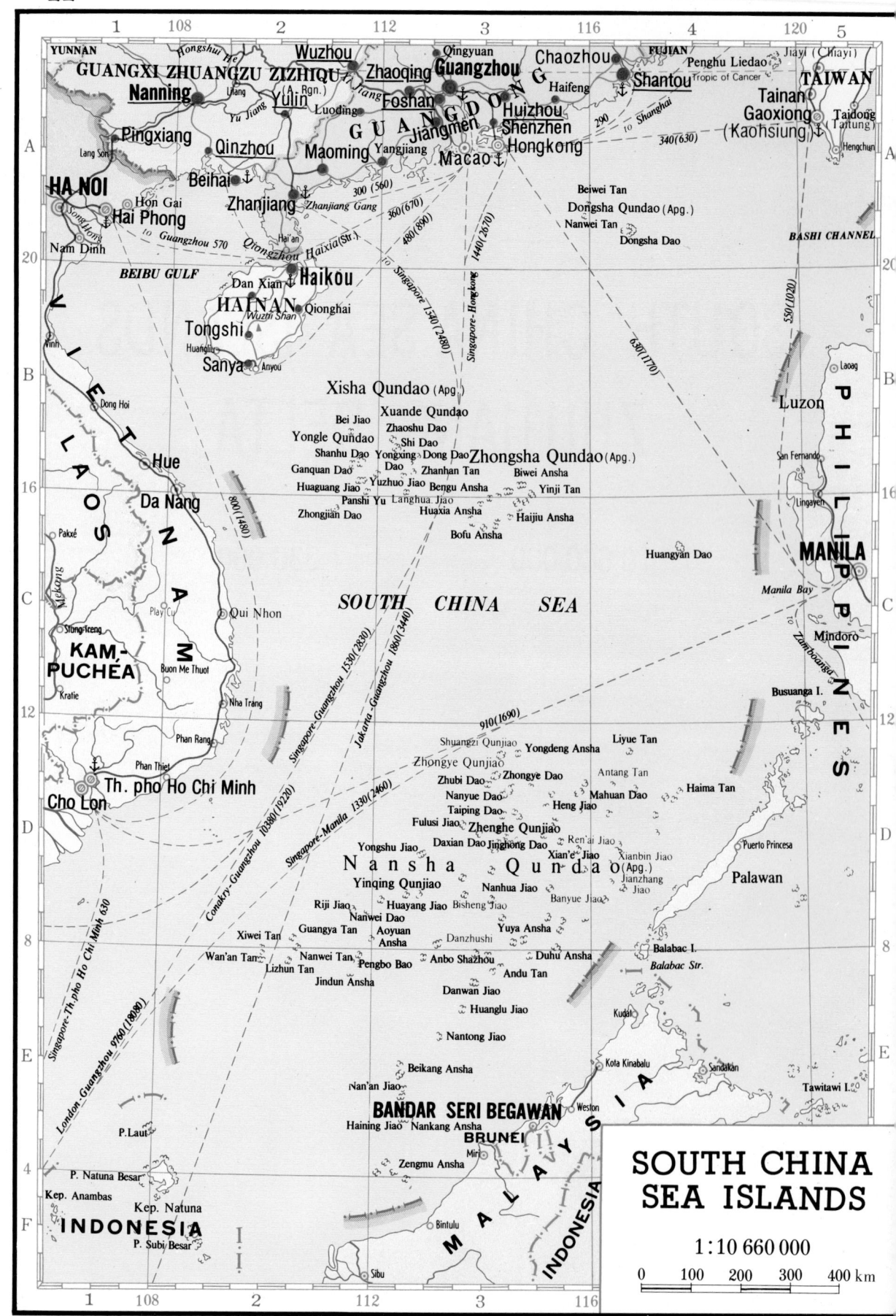

SOUTH CHINA
SEA ISLANDS

1 : 10 660 000

0   100   200   300   400 km

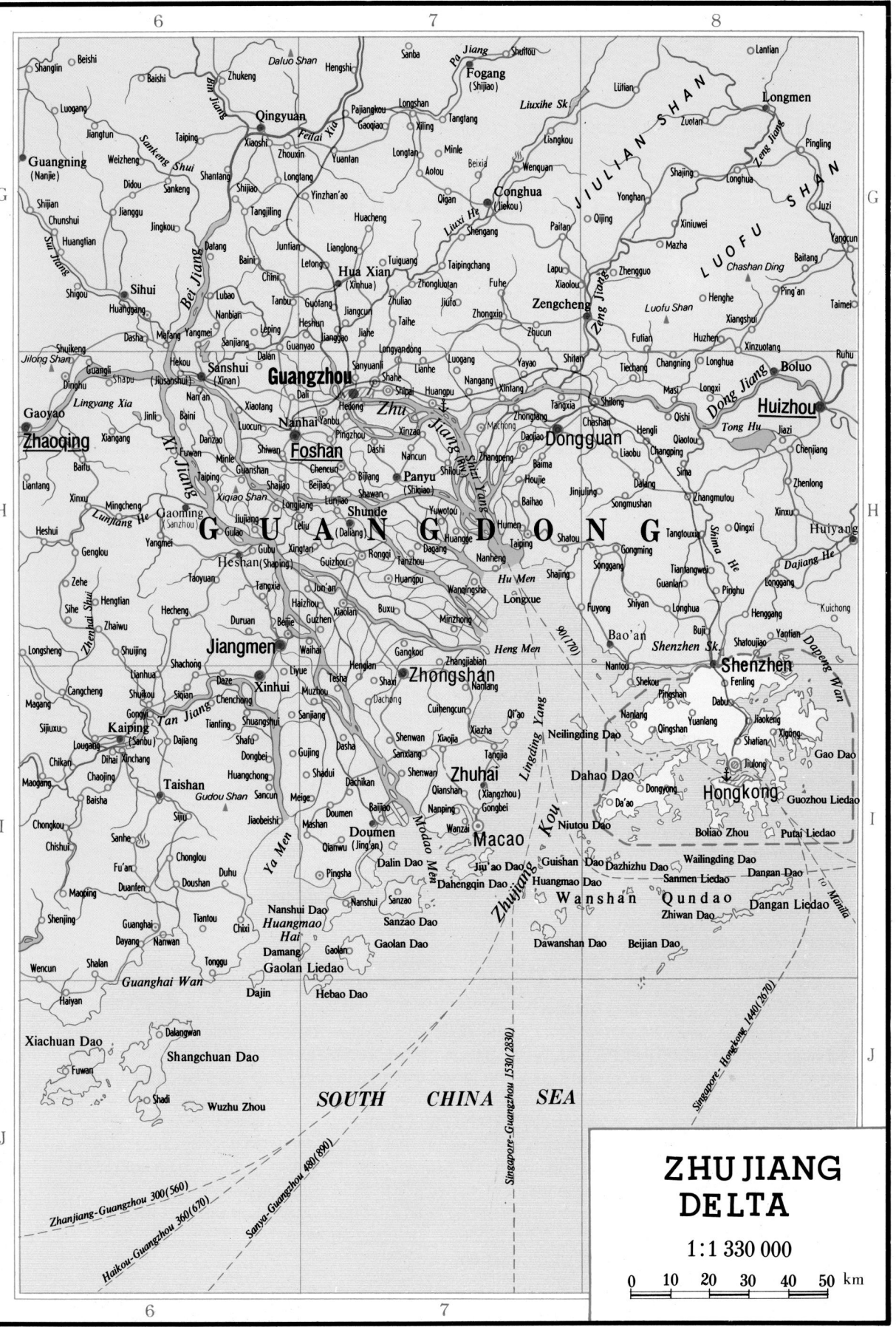

ZHU JIANG DELTA

1:1 330 000

0 10 20 30 40 50 km

Macao to China on December 20, 1999.

South China Sea Islands (See Hainan Province)

Hainan Province

Hainan Province is China's newest administrative division on the provincial level. It was formally established by the Seventh National People's Congress in April 1988. Consisting of Hainan Island and the South China Sea Islands, it is the smallest province, with an area of 34,000 square kilometers and a total coastline of 1,580 kilometers long. Besides Han people, people of the Li and Miao nationalities live there. The total population is 6.05 million, and urban population 1.8 million. The province administers 3 cities, 9 counties, and 7 autonomous counties. The provincial capital is Haikou.

Hainan Island, also known as Qiong'ai, is the second largest island in China with an area of 32,000 square kilometers. The parallel Wuzhi and Limu Mountains dominate the central area, taking up one third of the whole island. Their main peaks are 1,867 and 1,412 meters above sea level, respectively. Lowlands surround the mountains except on the southern coast, where precipices meet the South China Sea. The Qiongzhou Strait separates the Hainan Island from the mainland. Over 20 kilometers wide, the Qiongzhou Strait connects the Beibu Bay to the South China Sea.

The South China Sea Islands refer to all the islands, shoals, rocks, reefs, and shallows in the South China Sea. They are divided into four groups: Dongsha in the north; Xisha in the west; Zhongsha in the center, including Huangyan Island; and Nansha in the south, ending at the Zengmu Reef. The territory stretches 1,800 kilometers from north to south and over 900 kilometers from east to west. Neighboring countries are the Philippines in the east, Malaysia and Brunei in the south, Indonesia (Natuna Islands) in the southwest, and Vietnam in the west.

Situated between the 21st and 4th parallels north latitude, Hainan Province has a tropical maritime climate with high temperatures all year round. It is hard to distinguish the seasons. In the South China Sea Islands, the coldest month is February, with an average temperature of 22.9°C; the hottest month is August, with a 29.5°C average. Precipitation is heavy and evenly distributed throughout the year.

This province's natural resources include iron, salt, mined in Yinggehai on Hainan Island; petroleum from the South China Sea; minerals from the seabed; tropical plants; and all kinds of aquatic products. Xisha and its neighboring areas are a rich fishing ground. The islands are a haven for birds, whose abundant droppings are collected for natural fertilizer.

Pearl River Delta

The Pearl River Delta covers an area of 11,000 square kilometers and includes the cities of Xinhui, Gaoming, Sanshui, Zencheng, Dongguan, and Shenzhen. It is a densely populated, economically prosperous, and fertile region.

Originally a bay with many islands, the delta was formed by sand brought down by the tributaries of the Pearl River. Gradually an alluvial plain accumulated in the bay, and the original islands became hills on the delta. Today the land continues to grow into the sea, pushing back the water 10-15 meters every year. The plain is crossed in the west by the Xijiang and Beijiang Rivers and in the east by the Dongjiang and the Pearl Rivers.

The saying "four seasons of flowers and three winters without snow" accurately describes this region. The temperature seldom drops below 0°C, even when the region is struck by a cold wave from the north. However, flooding is frequent, especially from May to July.

In addition to being a fishing region, the delta is an important production base for sugar cane and a major silkworm base. Other delta products include rice, wheat, potatoes, peanuts, jute, lychees, longans, and ornamental plants and flowers.

GUANGXI ZHUANG AUTONOMOUS REGION

1 : 2 660 000

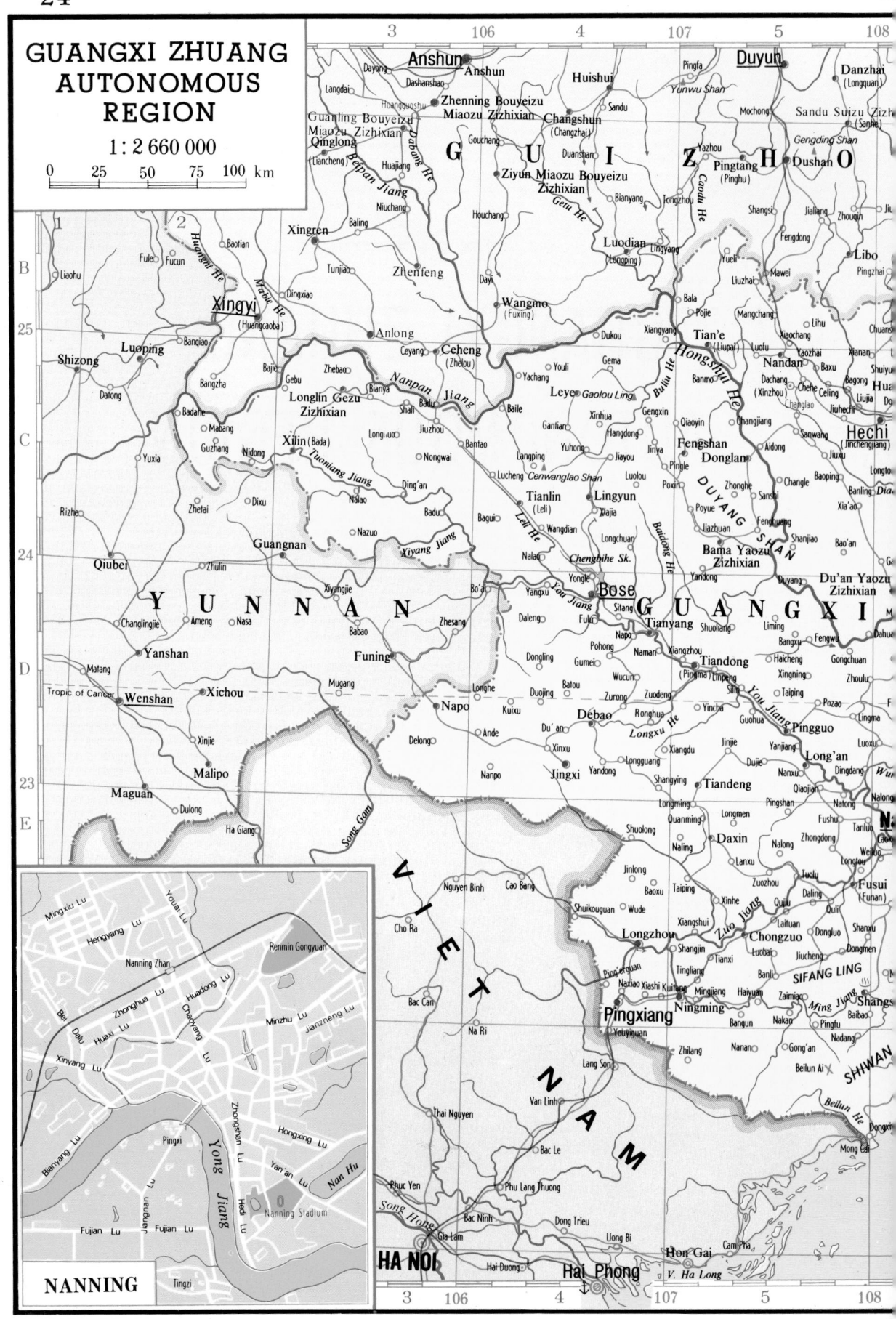

GUANGXI ZHUANG AUTONOMOUS REGION

1 : 2 660 000

NANNING

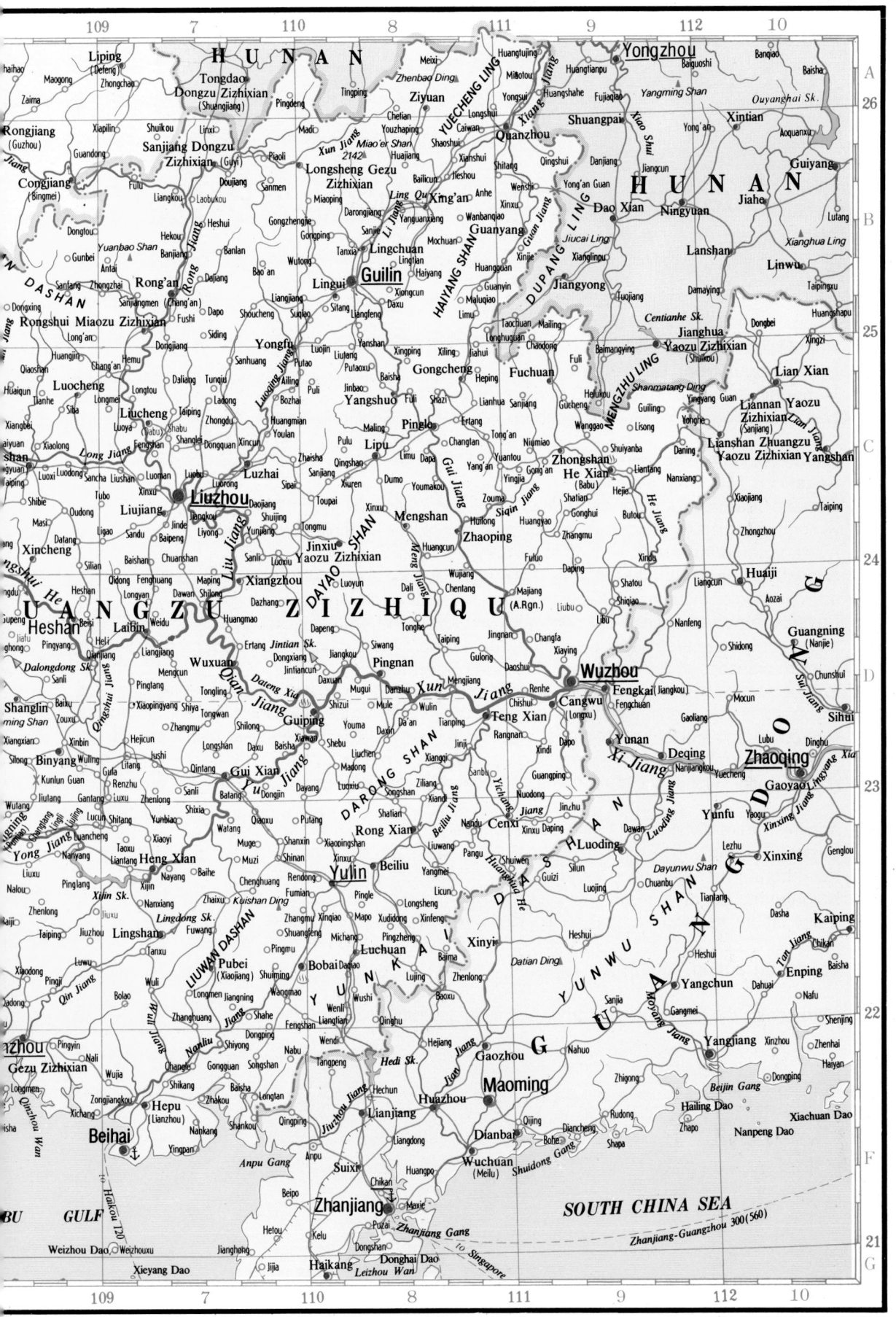

Guangxi Zhuang Autonomous Region

Population: 39.5 million
Urban population: 15.1 million
Nationalities: Zhuang (over 90 percent of the Chinese Zhuang people inhabit this region), Han, Yao, Miao, Tong, Mulam, Maonan, Hui, Jing, Yi, Shui, and Gelo

Area: 230,000 square kilometers
Coastline: 1,500 kilometers long
Climatic features: subtropical, humid, monsoonal climate; long, hot summers; warm, short winters; conspicuous dry and rainy seasons; one of China's most rainy areas
Average temperature: 6 — 16°C in January, 25 — 29°C in July
Annual average rainfall: 1,200 — 1,800 mm in most areas, with higher precipitation on the seaward side of mountains; 80 percent of the rain falls from April to September
Physical features: high in the northwest and low in the southeast; mountains on three sides; hills and plains in the middle and south; karst covers more than half of the region; drained by western branches of the Pearl River; faces the Beibu Bay.
Products: rice, wheat, corn, potatoes, millet, sorghum, rape, cassava, peanuts, sugar cane, tea, soybeans; ambary hemp, silk cocoons; tobacco; oranges, lychees, longans, bananas, pineapples; subtropical and tropical cash crops including rubber, coffee, pepper, sisal hemp, tea oil, and lemongrass; timber; aniseed, fennel oil, cassia bark; sea products; Manganese, bauxite, salt, coal, plaster stone, sulphur, tin, phosphorus, antimony, walfrom, iron, gold

Administrative divisions: 11 cities, 65 counties, and 12 autonomous counties
Capital: Nanning
Neighboring areas: Yunnan, Guizhou, Hunan, and Guangdong Provinces
Neighboring country: Vietnam
Major cities: Nanning, Liuzhou, Guilin, Wuzhou, Beihai, Pingxiang, Bose

Tourist attraction: karst hills in Guilin

Comments: the Beibu Gulf is a tropical fishing ground.

SHAANXI PROVINCE

1 : 2 660 000

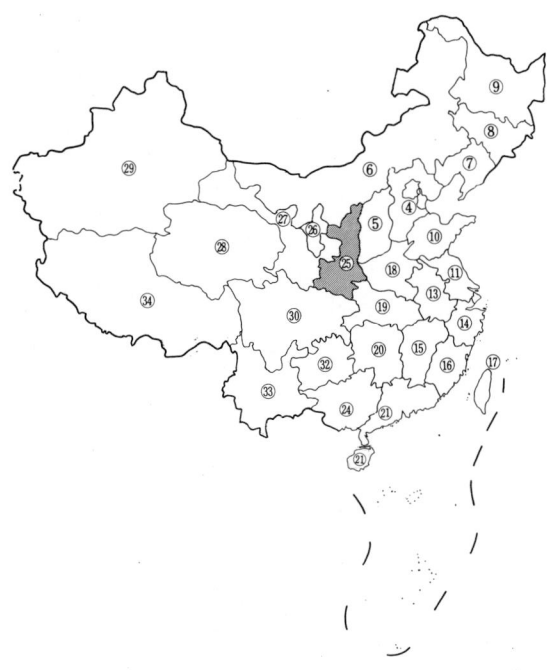

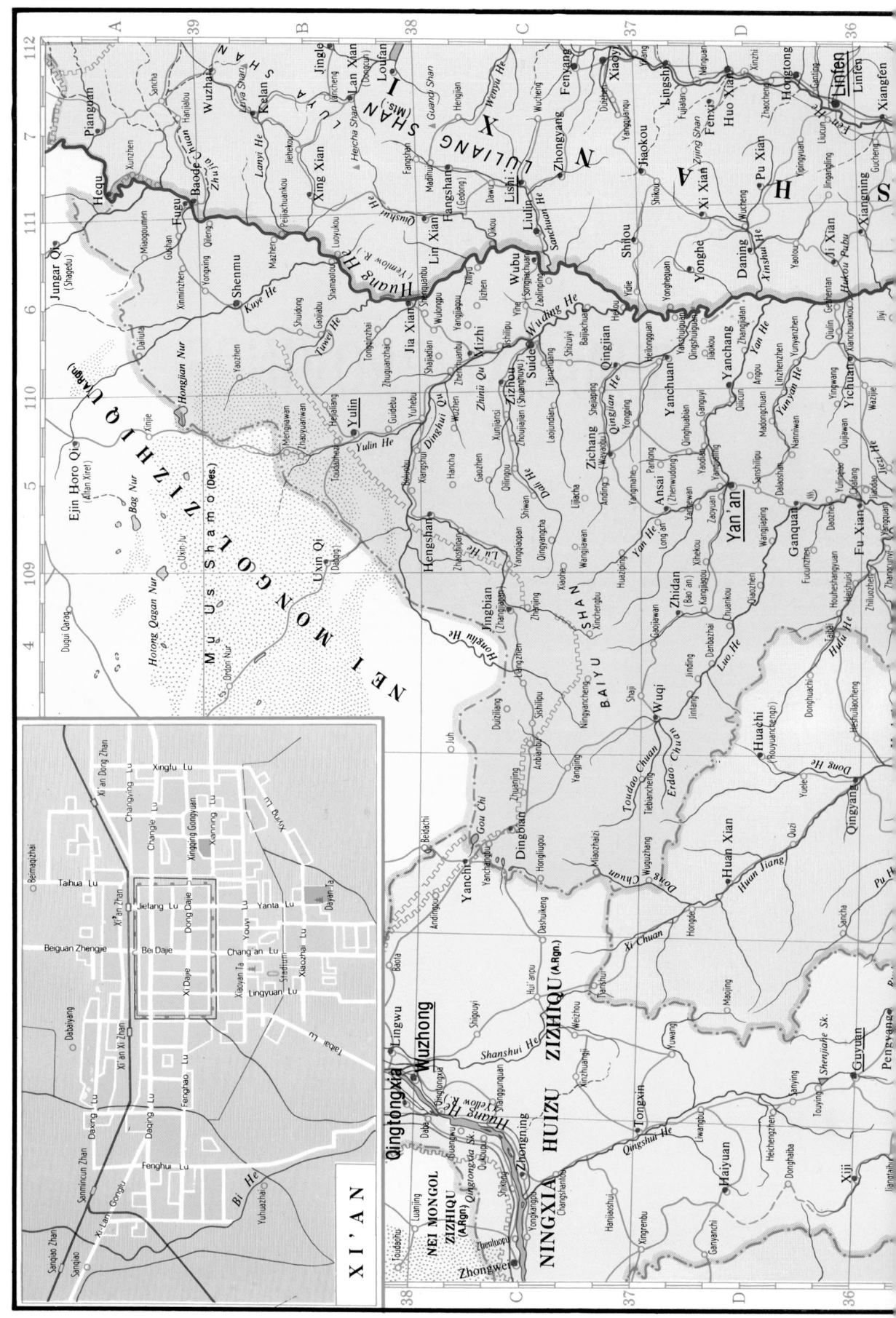

XI'AN

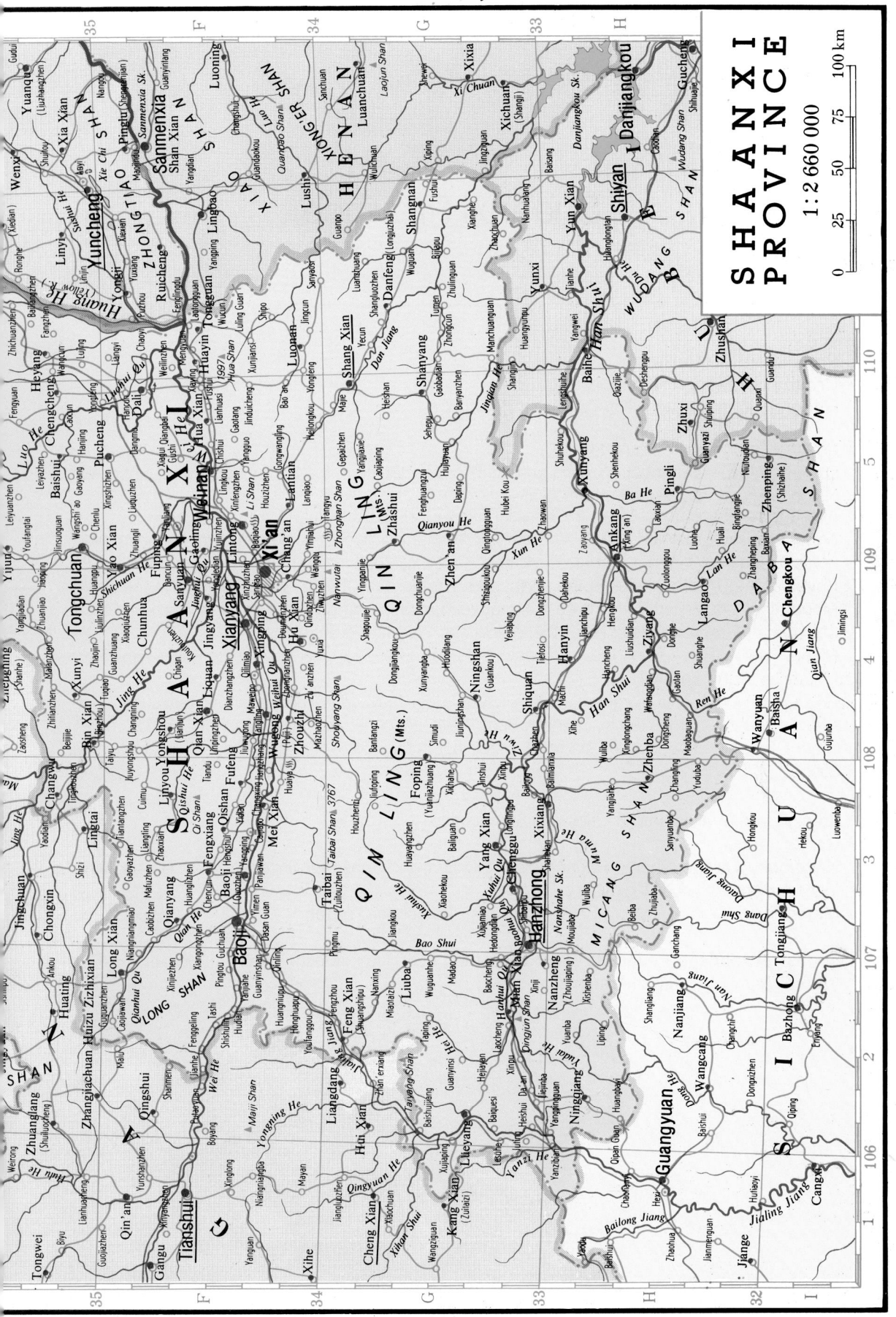

SHAANXI
PROVINCE

1 : 2 660 000

0   25   50   75   100 km

Shaanxi Province

Population: 30.4 million
Urban population: 12 million
Nationalities: Han, Hui, Mongolian, and Manchu

Area: 190,000 square kilometers
Climatic features: temperate, semi-arid, monsoonal climate in the north changes to subtropical, humid, monsoonal climate in the south
Average temperature: -11 — 3.5°C in January, 21 — 28°C in July
Annual average rainfall: 400 — 1,000 mm; precipitation highest in the southern mountain areas, lowest along the northern border; most of the rain falls occurs from July to September.
Physical features: plateaus in the north, plains in the central area, and mountains in the south
Mountains: the Qinling Range is an important geographical divide between northern and southern China and the major watershed of the Yellow and Yangtze Rivers
Rivers: Yellow River, along the northeastern border; Luohe, Jinghe, and Weihe Rivers, which are tributaries of the Yellow River
Products: wheat, corn, sorghum, rice, millet, potatoes, soybeans, rape, peanuts, tea, sugar cane, sesame, peas; cotton, ramie, ambary hemp, silk cocoons; walnuts, peaches, grapes, dates, chestnuts; palm, raw lacquer, bamboo, medicinal herbs; coal, iron, graphite, salt, molybdenum, copper

Administrative divisions: 8 cities and 89 counties
Capital: Xi'an
Neighboring areas: Shanxi, Henan, Hubei, Sichuan, and Gansu Provinces; Ningxia Hui and Inner Mongolia Autonomous Regions
Major cities: Xi'an, Xianyang, Baoji, Hanzhong, Tongchuan, Yan'an

Tourist attractions: terracotta army excavated near Xi'an; Mount Huashan, one of the Five Sacred Mountians, east of Xi'an

NINGXIA HUI
AUTONOMOUS REGION

1 : 1 330 000

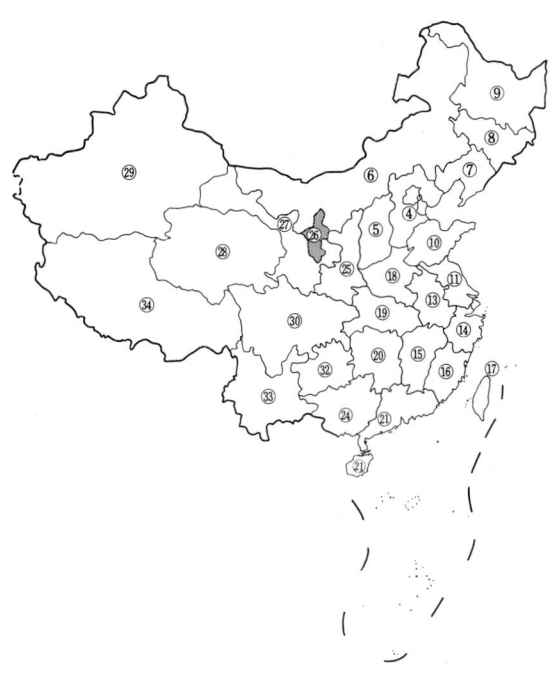

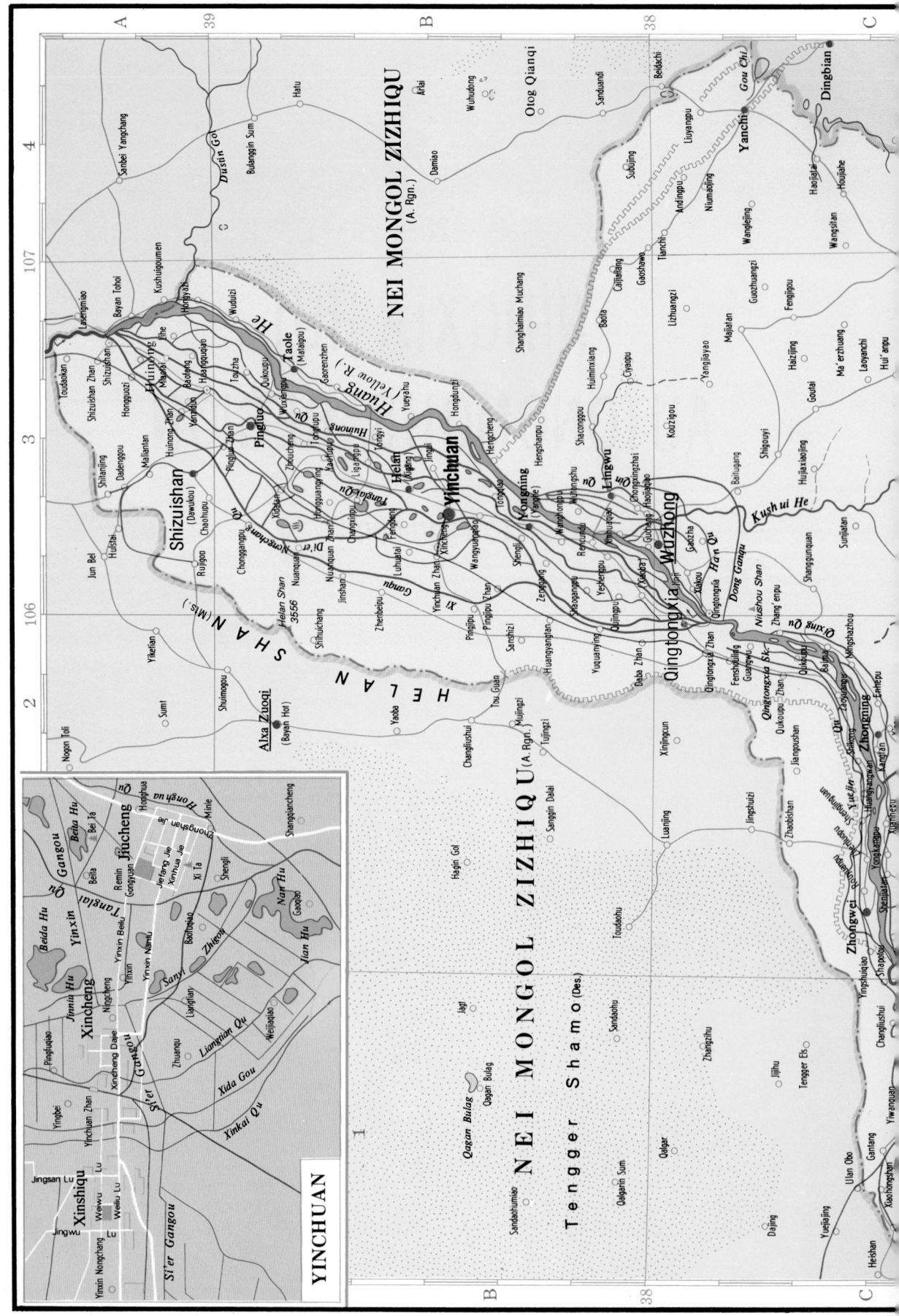

YINCHUAN

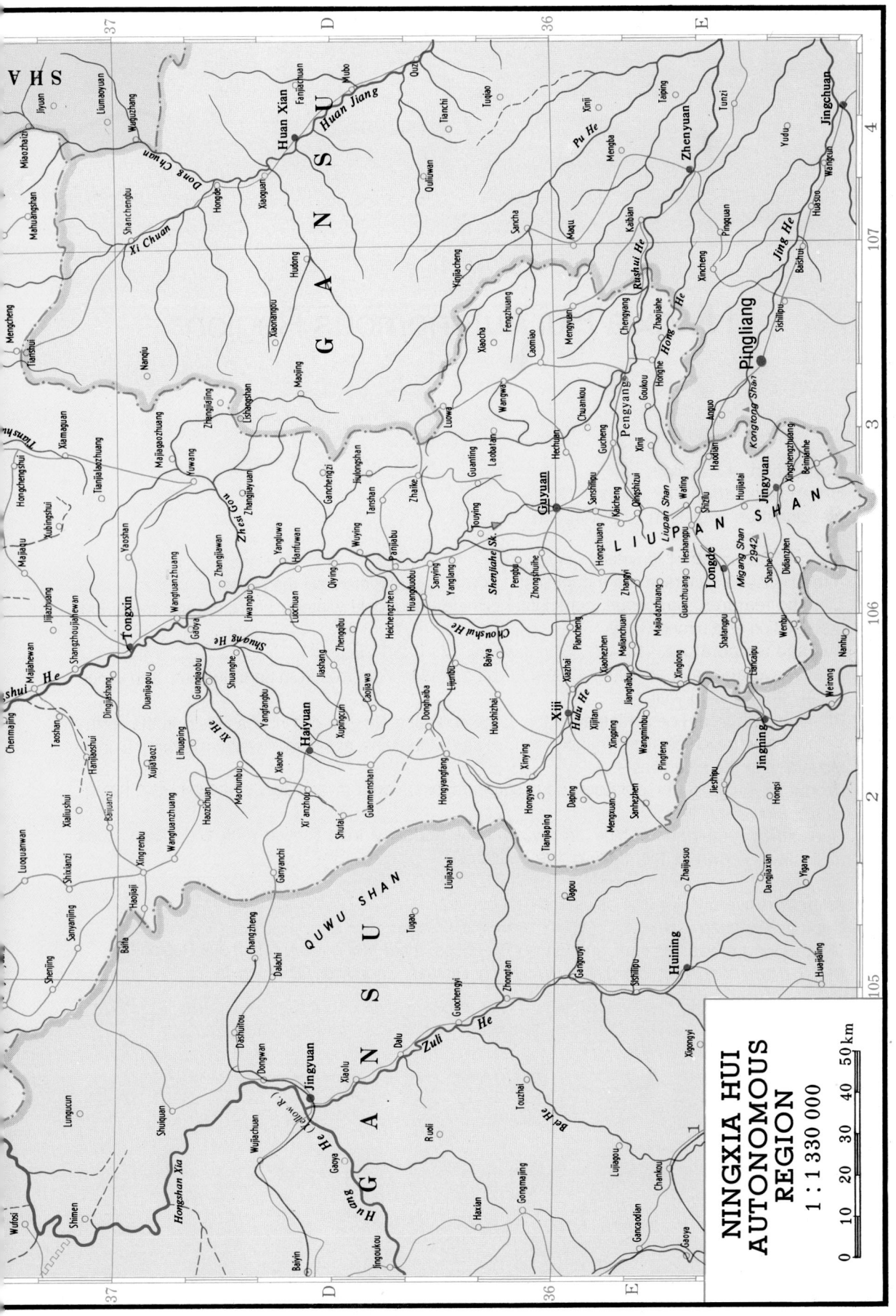

NINGXIA HUI
AUTONOMOUS
REGION
1 : 1 330 000

0 10 20 30 40 50 km

Ningxia Hui Autonomous Region

Population: 4.2 million
Urban population: 1.7 million
Nationalities: Hui, Han, and Manchu

Area: 66,000 square kilometers
Altitude: 2,000 meters in the mountains; 1,000 — 1,200 meters on the plains
Climatic features: temperate, continental climate; long, cold winters; short, hot summers; low precipitation and strong winds
Average temperature: -10 — -7°C in January, 17 — 24°C in July
Annual average rainfall: 190 — 700 mm; precipitation increases from north to south and varies greatly from year to year.
Physical features: Loess Plateau in the south and east; Ningxia or Yinchuan Plain, in the north; Yellow River traverses the Ningxia Plain; Helan Mountains along the western border; Liupan Mountains in the southwest
Products: wheat, millet, potatoes, corn, sorghum, broomcorn millet, rape, soybeans; flax, hemp; plaster stone, salt, iron
Specialties: argali sheep hide and wool, *facai*, wolfberry fruit, licorice root, and Helan stone (collectively known as the region's "five treasures")

Administrative divisions: 4 cities and 16 counties
Capital: Yinchuan
Neighboring areas: Shaanxi and Gansu Provinces; Inner Mongolia Autonomous Region
Major cities: Yinchuan, Shizuishan, Wuzhong, Guyuan, Zhongwei, Qingtongxia

GANSU PROVINCE

I : 4 660 000

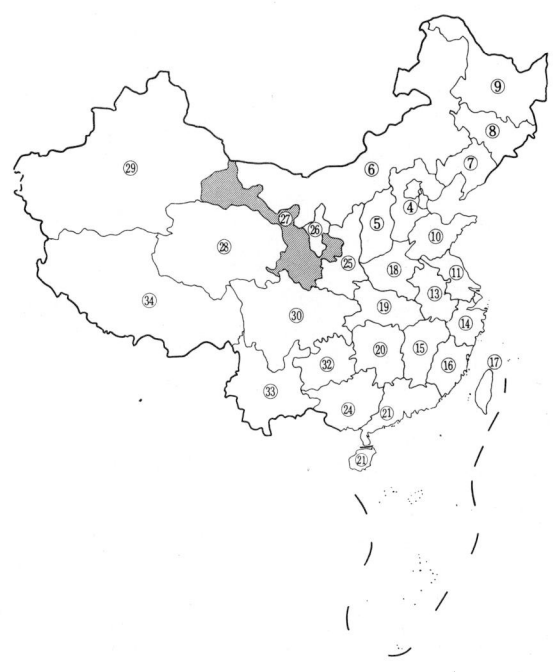

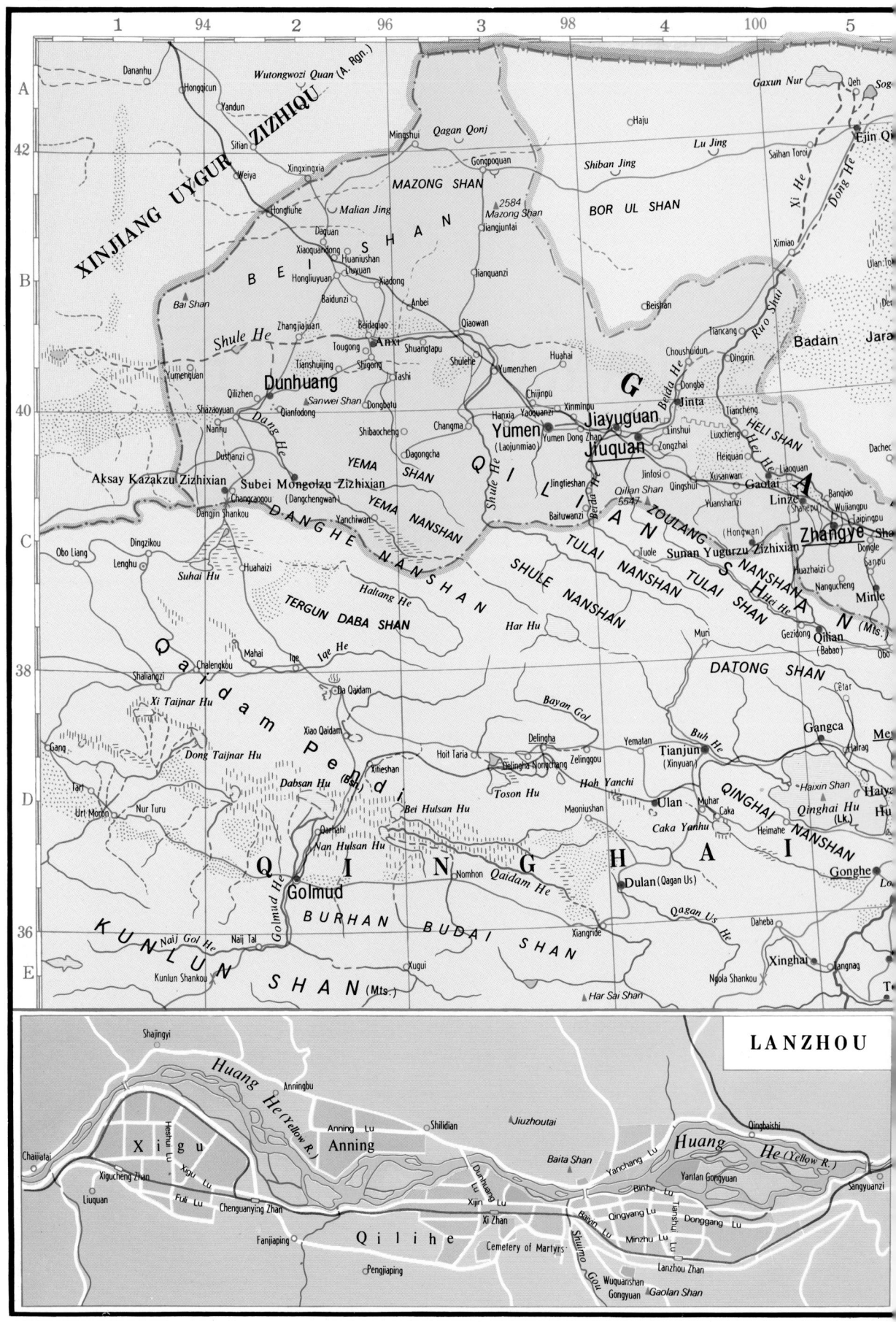

LANZHOU

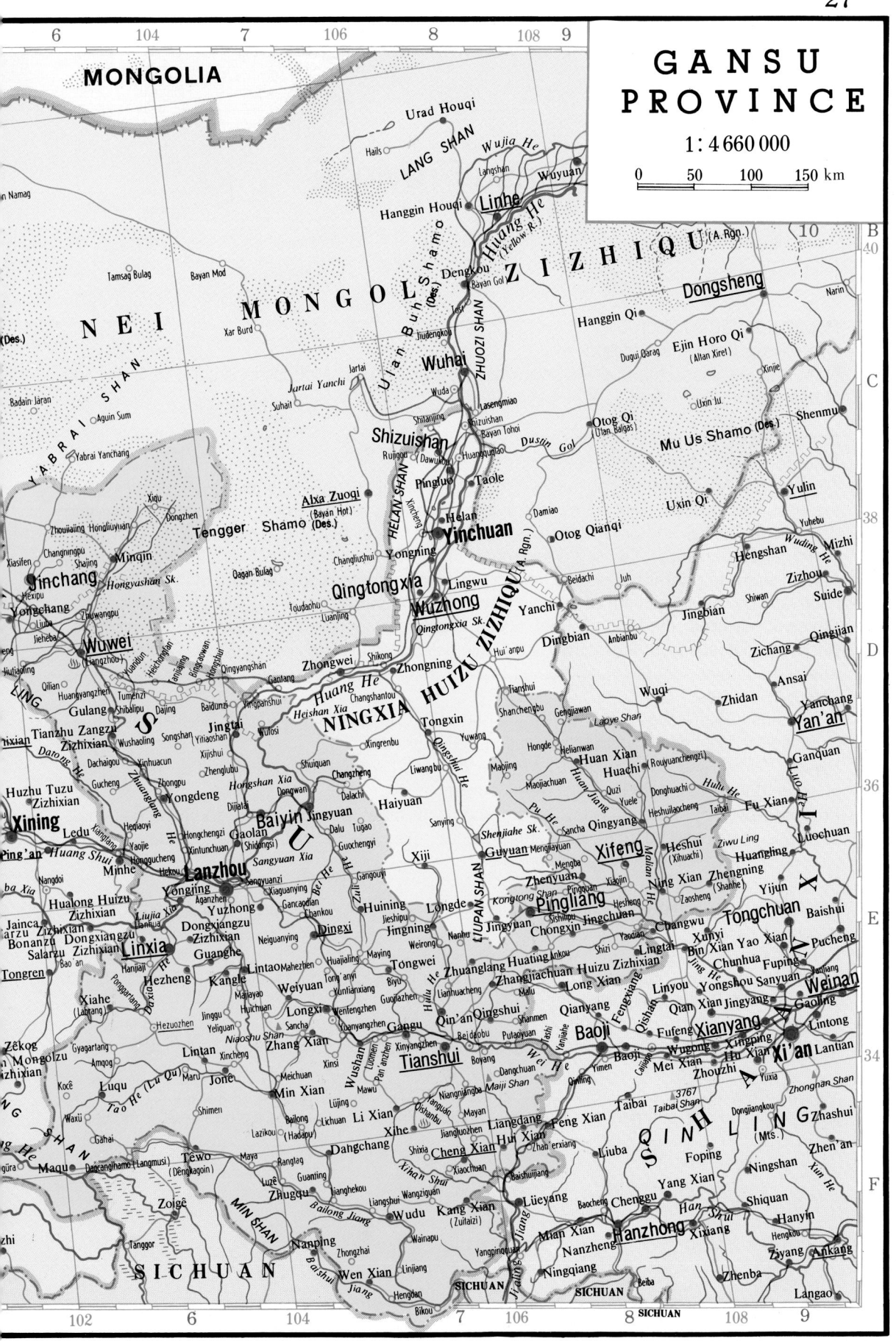

MONGOLIA

Urad Houqi

Hails

LANG SHAN

Wujia He

Langshan

Wuyuan

Hanggin Houqi

Linhe

HUANG HE (Yellow R.)

NEI MONGOL ZIZHIQU (A. Rgn.)

Dongsheng

Narin

Tamsag Bulag

Bayan Mod

Dengkou

Bayan Gol

Hanggin Qi

Ejin Horo Qi (Altan Xiret)

n Namag

Xar Burd

Jiudengkou

Dugui Qarag

Xinjie

Ulan Buh Shamo (Des.)

Wuhai

Jartai

Wuda

Lasengmiao

Otog Qi (Ulan Balgas)

Uxin Ju

Shenmu

Badain Jaran

Aguin Sum

Jartai Yanchi

Suhait

Shilanjing

Shizuishan

Bayan Tohoi

Dustin Gol

Mu Us Shamo (Des.)

Yulin

YABRAI SHAN

Yabrai Yancharg

Shizuishan

Ruigou

Dawukou

Huangquanliao

Otog Qianqi

Uxin Qi

Yuhebu

Wuding He

Mizhi

Zhouiialing Hongliuyuan

Xiqu

Dongzhen

Alxa Zuoqi (Bayan Hot)

Pingluo

Helan

Taole

Damiao

Beidachi

Hengshan

Zizhou

Xiasifen

Changningpu

HELAN SHAN

Xincheng

Yinchuan

Juh

Shiwan

Suide

Minqin

Changliushui

Yongning

Lingwu

Jinchang

Hongyashan Sk.

Qagan Bulag

Toudaohu

Qingtongxia

Yanchi

Jingbian

Zichang

Qingjian

Yongchang

Hexipu

Zhuwangpu

Luanjing

Wuzhong

Qingtongxia Sk.

Hui'anpu

Anbianbu

Ansai

Yanchang

Yan'an

epg

Jieheba

Wuwei (Liangzhou)

Liuba

Zhongwei

Shikong

Zhongning

Dingbian

Wuqi

Zhidan

Qilian

Huangyangzhen

Tumenzi

Baidunzi

Yingpanshui

Huang He

Changshantou

Tianshui

LING

Gulang

Shibalipu

Dajing

Qingyangzhen

Gantang

NINGXIA HUIZU ZIZHIQU (A. Rgn.)

Shanchengbu

Huan Xian

Donghuachi

Hulu He

Fu Xian

Luochuan

hixian

Tianzhu Zangzu Zizhixian

Dachaigou

Wushaoling

Songshan

Yitiaoshan

Zhenglubu

Shuiquan

Xingrenbu

Tongxin

Yuwang

Liwangbu

Helianwan

Mabjing

Laoye Shan

Quzi

Yuele

Heshuilaocheng

Taibai

Dato ng He

Gucheng

Hongshan Xia

Dongwan

Dalachi

Changzheng

Hongde

Maojiachuan

Huachi (Rouyuanchengzi)

Ziwu Ling

Huangling

Huzhu Tuzu Zizhixian

Yongdeng

Zhuanglang

Dijialu

Haiyuan

Pu He

Huan Jiang

Qingyang

Fu Xian

Xining

Ledu

Heqiaoyi

Baiyin

Jingyuan

Dalu

Tugao

Sanying

Shenjiahe Sk.

Sancha

Xifeng

Heshui (Xihuachi)

Ping'an

Huang Shui

Minhe

Hongchengzi

Xintunchuan

Gaolan

Guochengyi

Xiji

Guyuan

Mengjiayuan

Zhenyuan

Malian He

Ning Xian (Shanhe)

Zhengning

Tongchuan

Baishui

ba Xia

Nangdoi

Hekou

Sanyuan Xia

Gangouyi

Mengba

Kongtong Shan

Pingguan

Huangling

Pucheng

Jainca zu Zizhixian

Hualong Huizu Zizhixian

Liujia Xia

Lanzhou

Aganzhen

Xiaguanying

Longde

Zhenyuan

Pingliang

Hesheng

Zaosheng

Yijun

XI

Weinan

arzu Zizhixian

Yongjing

Yuzhong

Gancaodian

Chankou

Jingyuan

Chongxin

Jingchuan

Yaodian

Changwu

Xunyi

Bin Xian

Yao Xian

Gaoling

Bonanzu Dongxiangzu Salarzu Zizhixian

Dongxiang Zizhixian

Neiguanying

Huining

Jieshipu

Jingning

Nanhu

Weirong

Shizi

Lingtai

Jing He

Yongshou

Sanyuan

Tongren

Linxia

Guanghe

Lintao

Mahezhen

Huajialing

Maying

Zhuanglang He

Huating

Linkou

Zhangjiachuan Huizu Zizhixian

Malu

Long Xian

Linyou

Qian Xian

Jingyang

Lintong

Bao'an

Hezheng

Kangle

Majiayao

Tong'anyi

Yuntianxiang

Biyu

Guozhamen

Qianyang

Qishan

Fufeng

Wugong

Xingping

Xianyang

Xi'an

Lantian

Xiahe (Labrang)

Jinggu

Huichuan

Longxi

Wenfengzhen

Yuanyangzhen

Gangu

Qin'an

Qingshui

Shanmen

Fengxiang

Tianshui

Mei Xian

Zhouzhi

Hu Xian

Yuxia

Zêkog

Gyagarlang

Amqog

Lintan

Xincheng

Zhang Xian

Xinsi

Wushan

Tuomen

Pan Jiang

Boyang

Wei He

Yimen

Caijiapo

Baoji

Qinling

A

Mongolzu zhixian

Koçê

Luqu

Maru

Jonê

Meichuan

Mawu

Lüjing

Min Xian

Bailong

Lichuan

Li Xian

Dangchuan

Mayan

Maiji Shan

3767 Taibai Shan

Zhonghan Shan

NG SHAN

Waxü

Gahai

Lazikou (Hadapu)

Xihe

Jiangjuozhen

Shixia

Xihan Shui

Xiaochuan

Zhai'erxiang

Taibai

Liuba

Dongjiangkou

Zhashui

Maqu

Dagcanghamo (Langmusi)

Maya

Rangtag

Liangdang

Hui Xian

Baishuijiang

SICHUAN

Têwo (Dêngkagoin)

Zhugqu

Guanting

Jianghekou

Liangshui Wangziguan

Chena Xian

SICHUAN

QINLING (Mts.)

Zhen'an

Foping

Ningshan

Xun He

Zoigê

MIN SHAN

Bailong Jiang

Wudu

Kang Xian (Zuitaizi)

Lüeyang

Baocheng

Chenggu

Yang Xian

Shiquan

Hanyin

Tanggor

Nanping

Zhongzhai

Wen Xian

Yangpingguan

Jialing Jiang

Mian Xian

Nanzheng

Hanzhong

Han Shui

Xixiang

Hengkou

zhi

Zoigê

Bashui Jiang

Linjiang

Hengban

Ningqiang

Ziyang

Ankang

SICHUAN

Bikou

SICHUAN

Beiba

Zhenba

Langao

Gansu Province

Population: 20.7 million
Urban population: 8.1 million
Nationalities: Han, Hui, Tibetan, Dongxiang, Yugur, Baonan, Mongolian, Kazak, Tu, Salar, and Manchu

Area: 390,000 square kilometers
Altitude: mostly above 1,000 meters
Climatic features: subtropical, humid climate in the east changes to a temperate, dry climate in the west; cold, humid, highland climate in the Qilian Mountains; temperatures shift greatly from day to night as well as from season to season in the central and western parts of the province.
Average temperature: -14 — 3°C in January, 11 — 27°C in July
Annual average rainfall: 30 — 860 mm; precipitation decreases sharply north of the 37th parallel north latitude; 50-70 percent of the rain falls during the summer
Physical features: the Qinghai-Tibet, Loess, and Inner Mongolia Plateaus adjoin the province; where the plateaus meet is a narrow, 1,000-kilometer passage, the Hexi or Gansu Corridor, which was part of the ancient Silk Road leading to the Western Regions, present-day Xinjiang and areas further to the west.
Mountains: Qilian Range along the central part of the Gansu-Qinghai border; Beishan Mountains in the north; Dieshan-Minshan Mountains in the southwest
Rivers: Yellow River and tributaries, Weihe and Taohe Rivers; Bailong River in the south; Heihe, Shule and other inland rivers in the Hexi Corridor
Products: wheat, highland barley, millet, broomcorn millet, potatoes, corn, sorghum, rice, rape, soybeans, sugar beet; cotton; sun-cured tobacco; muskmelons, wool, leather; sausage casing; coal, petroleum, nickel, copper, sulphur, zinc

Administrative divisions: 2 autonomous prefectures, 13 cities, 60 counties, and 7 autonomous counties
Capital: Lanzhou
Neighboring areas: Shaanxi, Sichuan, and Qinghai Provinces; Inner Mongolia, Ningxia Hui, and Xinjiang Uygur Autonomous Regions
Neighboring country: Mongolia
Major cities: Lanzhou, Jiayuguan, Tianshui, Yumen, Dunhuang, Jinchang

Tourist attractions: Dunhuang, a post on the former Silk Road, famous for its Mogao Grottoes; the Jiayuguan Pass, an important outpost in ancient China and the western terminus of the Great Wall

—— 28 ——

QINGHAI PROVINCE

I : 4 000 000

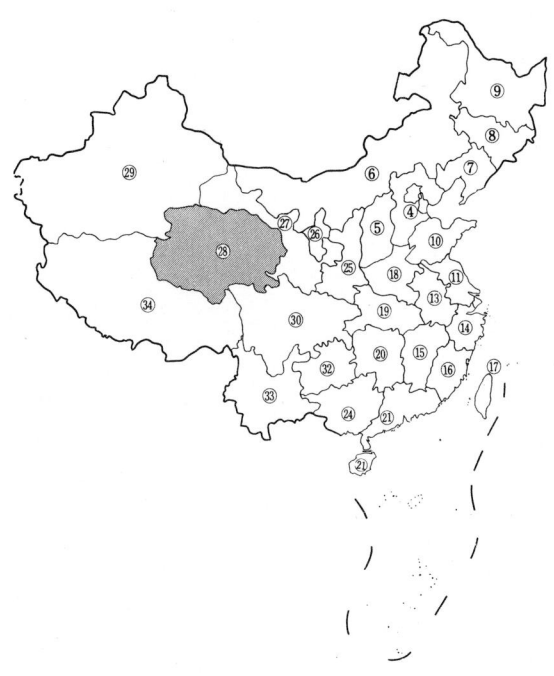

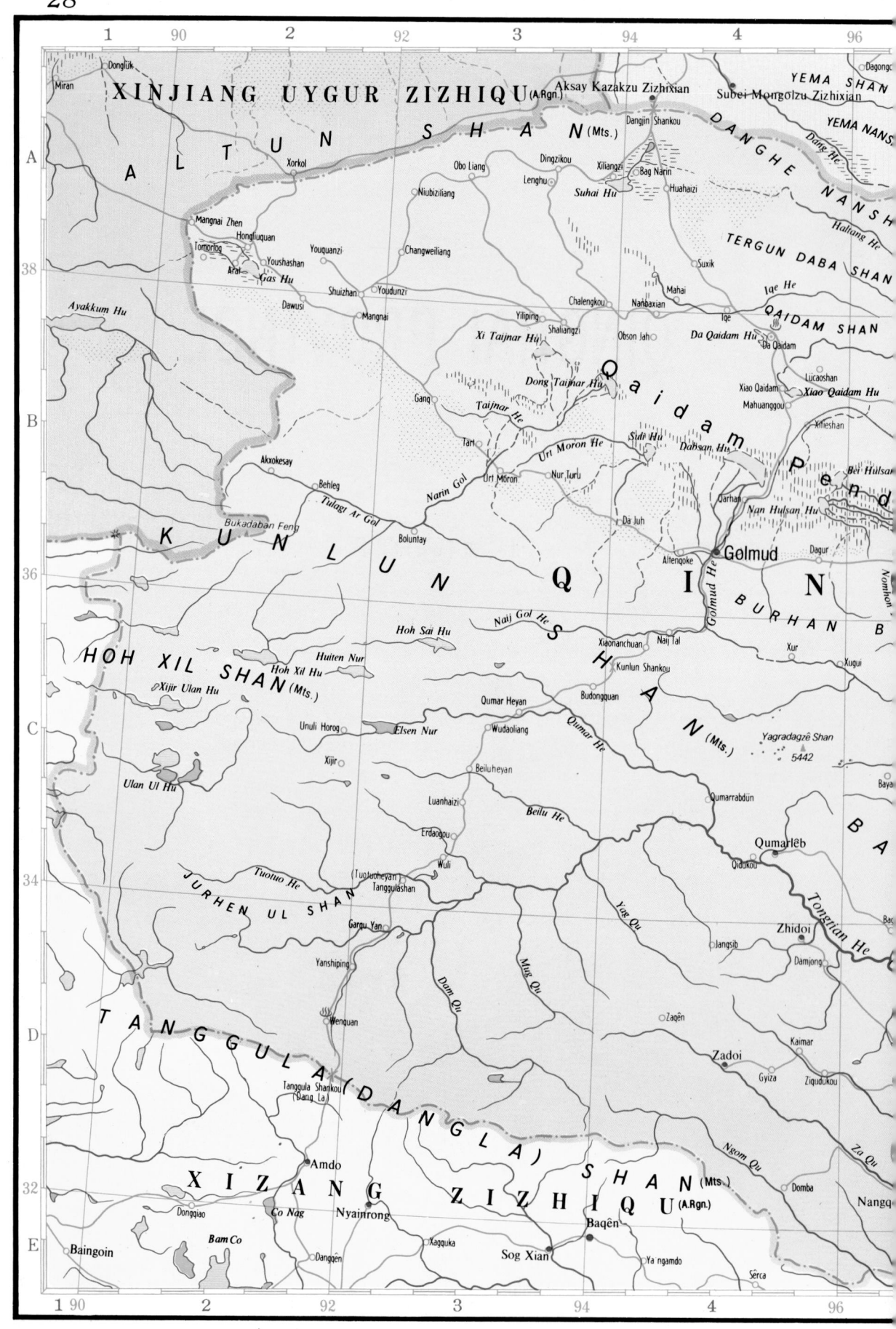

XINJIANG UYGUR ZIZHIQU (A.Rgn.)

A L T U N   S H A N (Mts.)

Miran   Dongluk

Aksay Kazakzu Zizhixian   YEMA SHAN

Subei Mongolzu Zizhixian   YEMA NANS

Dangjin Shankou   Dagongc

Xorkol

Obo Liang   Dingzikou   Xiliangzi   Bag Narin

Lenghu   Suhai Hu   Huahaizi

Niubiziliang

DANGHE NANSHAN

Dang He

Haitang He

TERGUN DABA SHAN

Mangnai Zhen   Hongliuquan   Youquanzi   Changweiliang

Tomorlog   Youshashan   Shuizhan   Youdunzi

Aral   Gas Hu   Dawusi   Mangnai

Suxik

Chalengkou   Nahbaxian   Mahai

QAIDAM SHAN

Iqe He   Iqe

Ayakkum Hu   Yiliping   Shaliangzi   Obsan Jah   Da Qaidam Hu   Da Qaidam

Xi Taijnar Hu   Lucaoshan

Dong Taijnar Hu   Xiao Qaidam   Xiao Qaidam Hu

Gang   Taijnar He   Mahuanggou

Qaidam Pend   Xileshan

Tari   Urt Moron He   Sidi Hu   Dabsan Hu   Bei Hulsan

Akxokesay   Urt Moron   Nur Turu   Qarhan   Nan Hulsan Hu

Behleg   Da Juh

Tulagi Ar Gol   Narin Gol   Golmud

Bukadaban Feng   Boluntay   Altenqoke   Dagur

K U N L U N   Q I   N   BURHAN   Nomhon

Hoh Sai Hu   Naij Gol He   Xiaonanchuan   Naij Tal   Xur

Huiten Nur   Kunlun Shankou   Xugui

HOH XIL SHAN (Mts.)   Budongquan   S H A N (Mts.)   Bayan

Xijir Ulan Hu   Qumar Heyan   Yagradagzê Shan

Unuli Horog   Elsen Nur   Wudaoliang   5442

Xijir   Beiluheyan   Qumar He   B A

Ulan Ul Hu   Luanhaizi   Beilu He   Qumarrabdûn

Erdaogou   Qidukou   Qumarlêb

Wuli   Yag Qu   Bac

Tuotuo He   Mug Qu   Zhidoi

JURHEN UL SHAN   Tugtuoheyan   Tanggulashan   Jangsib   Damjong

Gargu Yan   Zaqên   Kaimar

Yanshiping   Zadoi

Wenquan   Gyiza   Ziqudukou

T A N G G U L A (D A N G L A)   Zadoi

Tanggula Shankou   S H A N (Mts.)   Ngom Qu   Za Qu

(Dang La)   Domba

Amdo   Nangqc

X I Z A N G   Z I Z H I Q U (A.Rgn.)

Dongqiao   Co Nag   Nyainrong   Baqên

Baingoin   Bam Co   Xagguka   Sog Xian   Ya ngamdo

Dangqên   Sêrca

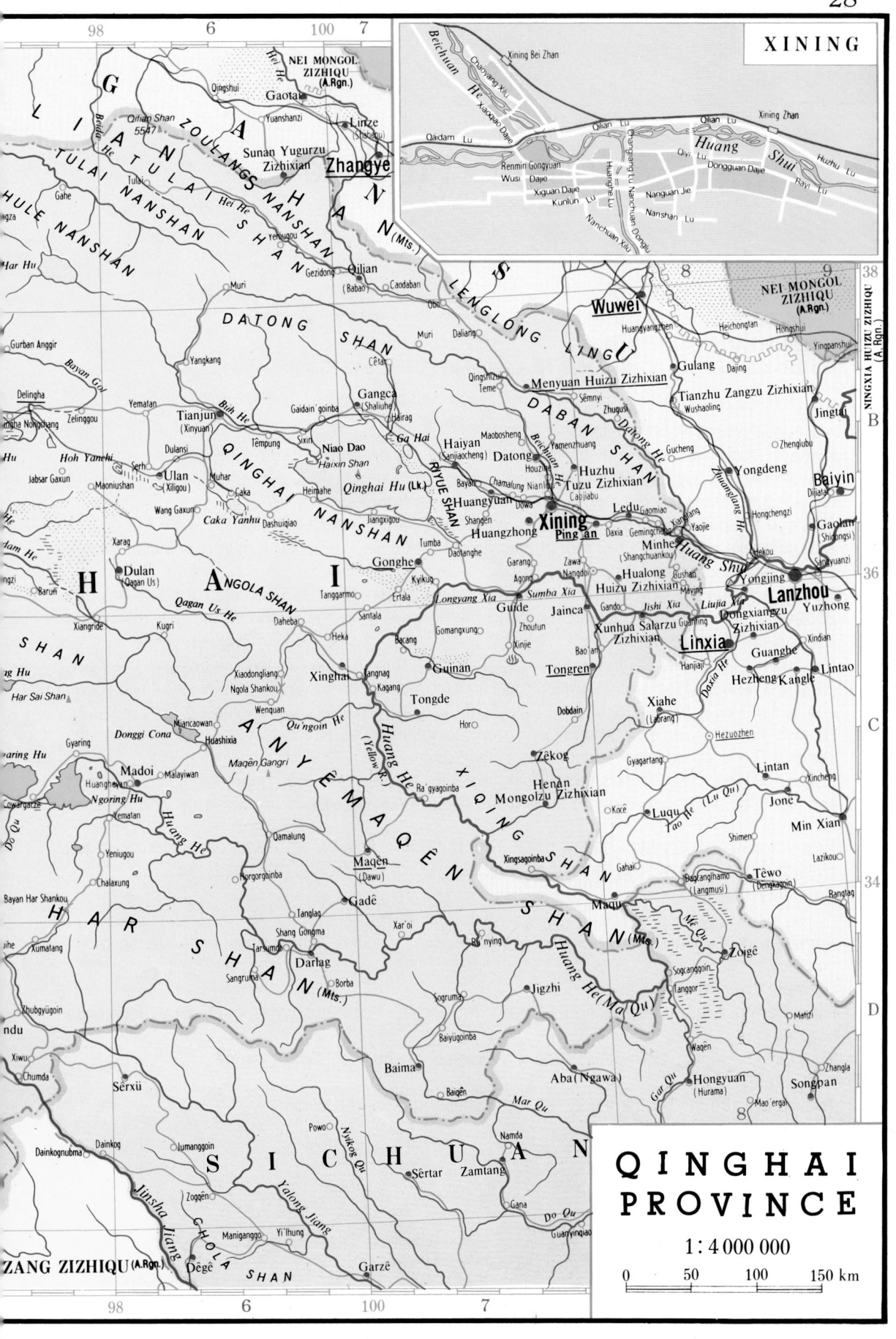

XINING

Beichuan He
Chaoyang Xilu
Xining Bei Zhan
Qilian Lu
Xining Zhan
Xiaoqiao Dajie
Qaidam Lu
Huangshui Lu
Huang Shui
Huzhu Lu
Xining Zhan
Qilian Lu
Renmin Gongyuan
Huang
Huzhu Lu
Wusi Dajie
Huanghe Lu
Qiyi Lu
Shui
Xiguan Dajie
Nanguan Jie
Rayi Lu
Kunlun Lu
Nanchuan Dajie
Nanshan Lu
Nanchuan Xilu

QINGHAI PROVINCE

1 : 4 000 000

0   50   100   150 km

Qinghai Province

Population: 4.1 million
Urban population: 1.4 million
Nationalities: Han, Tibetan, Hui, Tu, Salar, Mongolian, and Kazak

Area: 720,000 square kilometers
Altitude: 2,500 — 4,500 meters
Climatic features: continental highland climate; mostly dry and cold with frequent winds and little rainfall; long winters; short, cool summers; long hours of sunshine and strong sunlight; drastic temperature changes from day to night; sandstorms from February to April
Average temperature: -18.2 — -7°C in January, 5 — 21°C in July
Annual average rainfall: 700 mm in the eastern river valley, under 50 mm in the Qaidam Basin; precipitation decreases from east to west.
Physical features: covers the northeast portion of the Qinghai-Tibet Plateau; includes the 200,000-square-kilometer Qaidam Basin in the northwest; in the northeast are the Yellow and Huangshui River Valleys.
Mountains: Altun and Qilian Mountains in the north; Kunlun, Hoh Xil, and Qimantag in the west; Tanggula, where China's longest river, the Yangtze, has its source, in the southwest; A'nyêmaqen and Bayan Har in the southeast, with the 5,464-kilometer Yellow River originating from the latter
Rivers: Yellow River and tributaries; Tuotuo-Tongtian River, which is the upper reach of the Yangtze River; inland intermittent rivers in the basin
Lakes: Qinghai Lake, China's largest salt lake with an area of 4,583 square kilometers; Gyaring and Ngoring Lakes, two adjacent fresh water lakes; many smaller lakes, salt lakes, and marshes

Products: wheat, highland barley, millet, rice, potatoes, rape, broad beans, peas; leather, musk, antlers; rhubarb, Chinese caterpillar fungus; petroleum, salt, sylvite, coal, lead, zinc
Specialty: Xining Wool

Administrative divisions: 6 autonomous prefectures, 2 cities, 30 counties, and 7 autonomous counties
Capital: Xining
Neighboring areas: Gansu and Sichuan Provinces; Tibet and Xinjiang Uygur Autonomous Regions
Major cities: Xining, Golmud, Lenghu, Da Qaidam, Yushu, Gonghe, Delingha

Tourist attraction: Tar Lamasery, 20 kilometers southwest of Xining

XINJIANG UYGUR AUTONOMOUS REGION

1 : 6 660 000

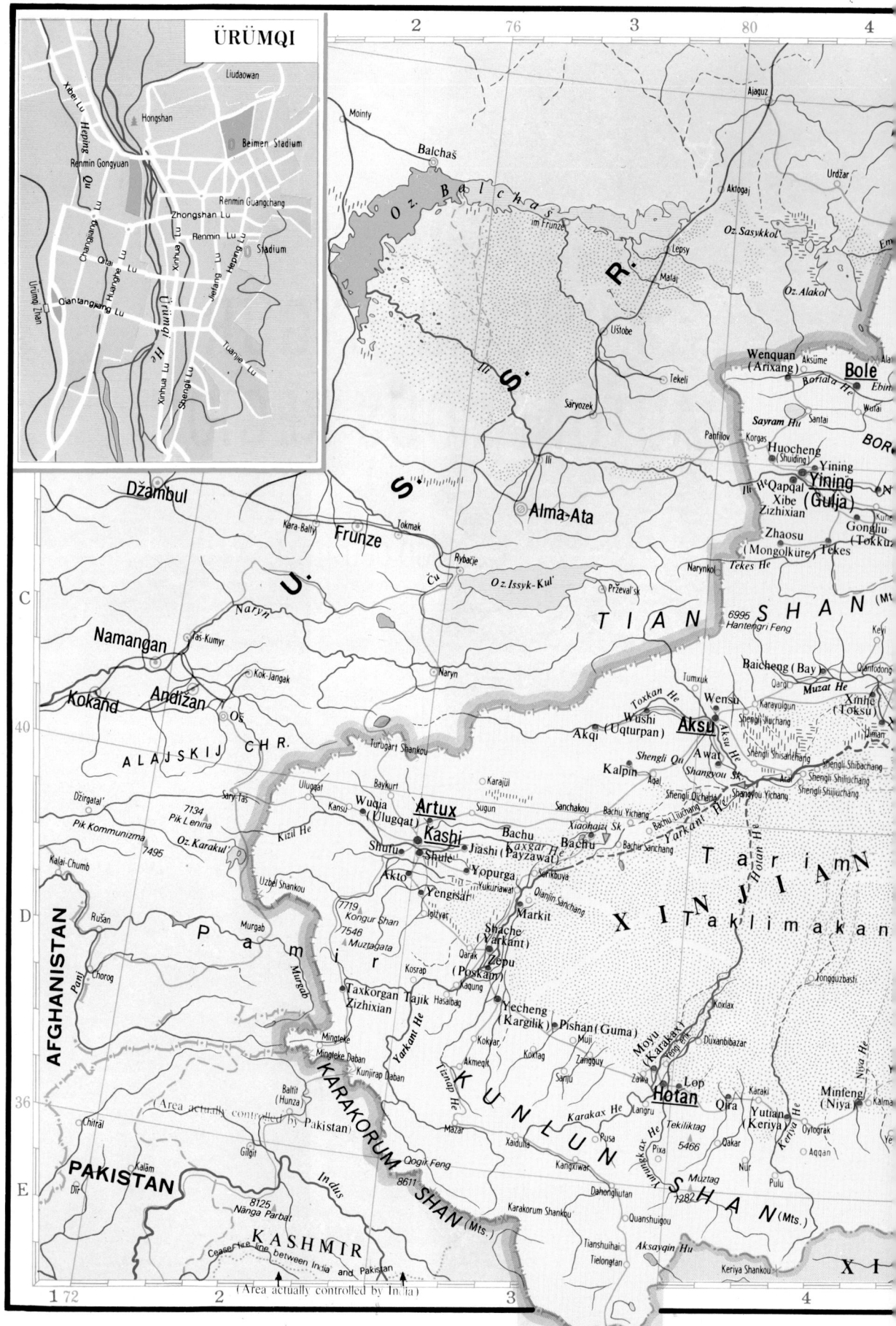

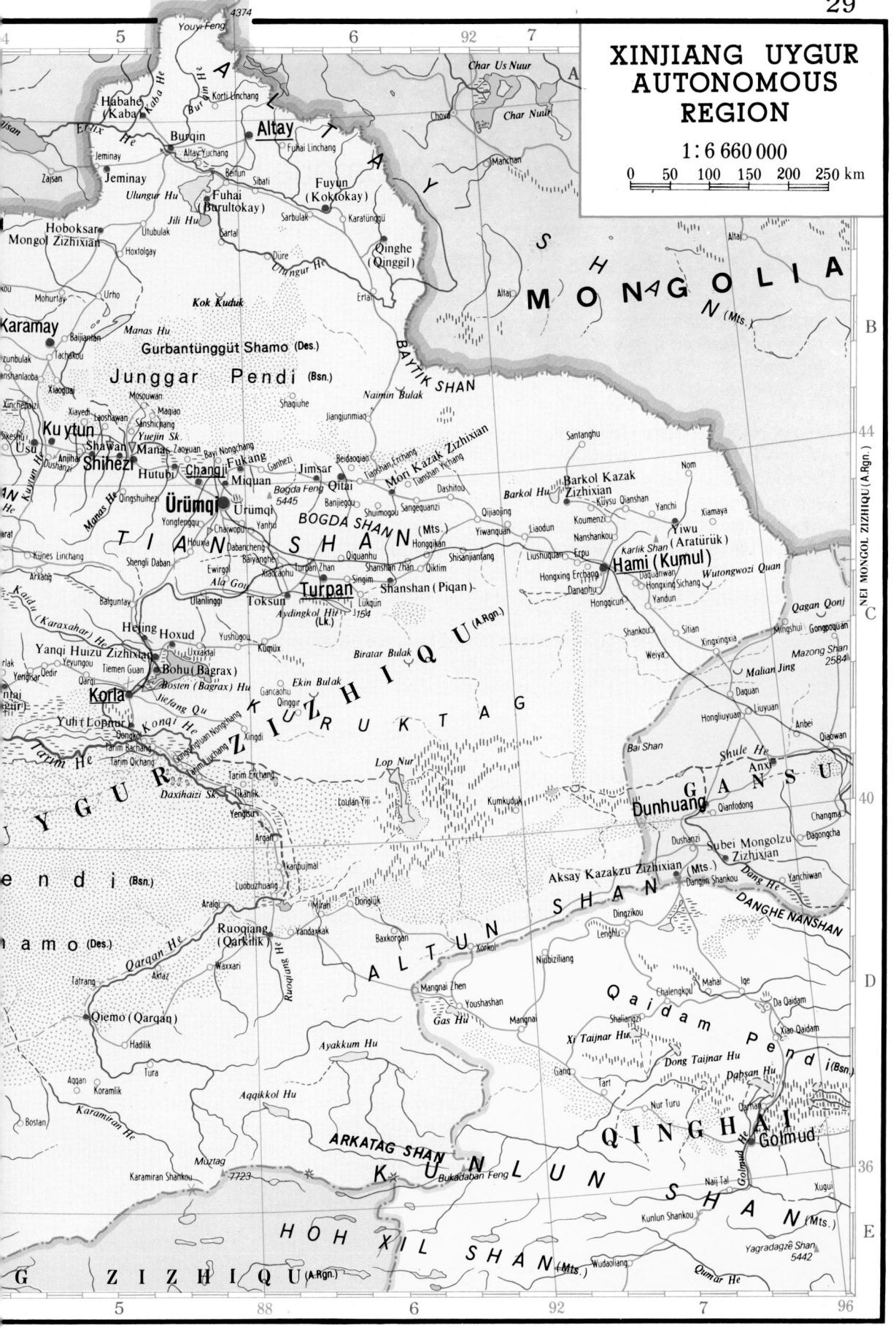

XINJIANG UYGUR AUTONOMOUS REGION

1 : 6 660 000

0 50 100 150 200 250 km

Xinjiang Uygur Autonomous Region

Population: 13.8 million
Urban population: 6 million
Nationalities: Uygur, Han, Kazak, Hui, Mongolian, Xibe, Kirgiz, Ozbek, Tajik, Russian, Manchu, Daur, and Tatar

Area: 1,600,000 square kilometers
Altitude: 8,611 meters at the Qogir Peak; 155 meters below sea level at the bottom of the Turpan Depression, the lowest point on the China continent
Climatic features: temperate, continental climate; warmer in the south; extreme temperature changes; little precipitation; frequent gales in spring and autumn
Average temperature: in January, -20 — -15°C in the north and -10 — -5°C in the south; in July, 22 — 26°C
Annual average rainfall: 150 mm; higher precipitation in the north; only 10 mm around Qarqan and Qarkilik
Physical features: three major mountain ranges separate the lowlands into various-sized basins and valleylands; conspicuous differences in land elevation
Mountains: Tianshan Range in the central area; Altay Range in the north; Karakorum, Kunlun, and Altun Mountains in the south
Deserts: Taklimakan Desert in the Tarim Basin; Gurbantunggut Desert in the Junggar Basin; Gumtay Desert in the east
Basins: Junggar Basin between the Tianshan and Altay Ranges; Tarim Basin between the Tianshan and Kunlun Ranges, over 500,000 square kilometers in area; Turpan Depression between the Bogda and Qoltag Mountains; east of the Turpan is the Hami Basin.
Rivers: the 2,137-kilometer Tarim River, China's longest inland river; Ili and Ertix Rivers
Lakes: Lop Nur, a famous salt lake; Bosten Lake, the largest fresh water lake of the region; Aydingkol Lake in the Turpan Depression, with the lowest altitude in China
Products: wheat, rice, corn, sorghum, millet, potatoes, rape, sesame, sugar beet, peanuts; peaches, grapes; cotton, silk cocoons; iron, coal, petroleum, gold, copper, salt, jade, sulphur
Specialties: Turpan grapes, Hami melons

Administrative divisions: 5 autonomous prefectures, 16 cities, 65 counties, and 6 autonomous counties
Capital: Ürümqi
Neighboring areas: Gansu and Qinghai Provinces; Tibet Autonomous Region
Neighboring countries: Mongolia, the Soviet Union, Afghanistan, Pakistan, and India
Major cities: Ürümqi, Kashi, Yining, Hami, Karamay, Aksu, Shihezi, Hotan, Korla

Tourist attraction: Tianchi Lake near Ürümqi, in the Tianshan Range

SICHUAN PROVINCE

I : 4 000 000

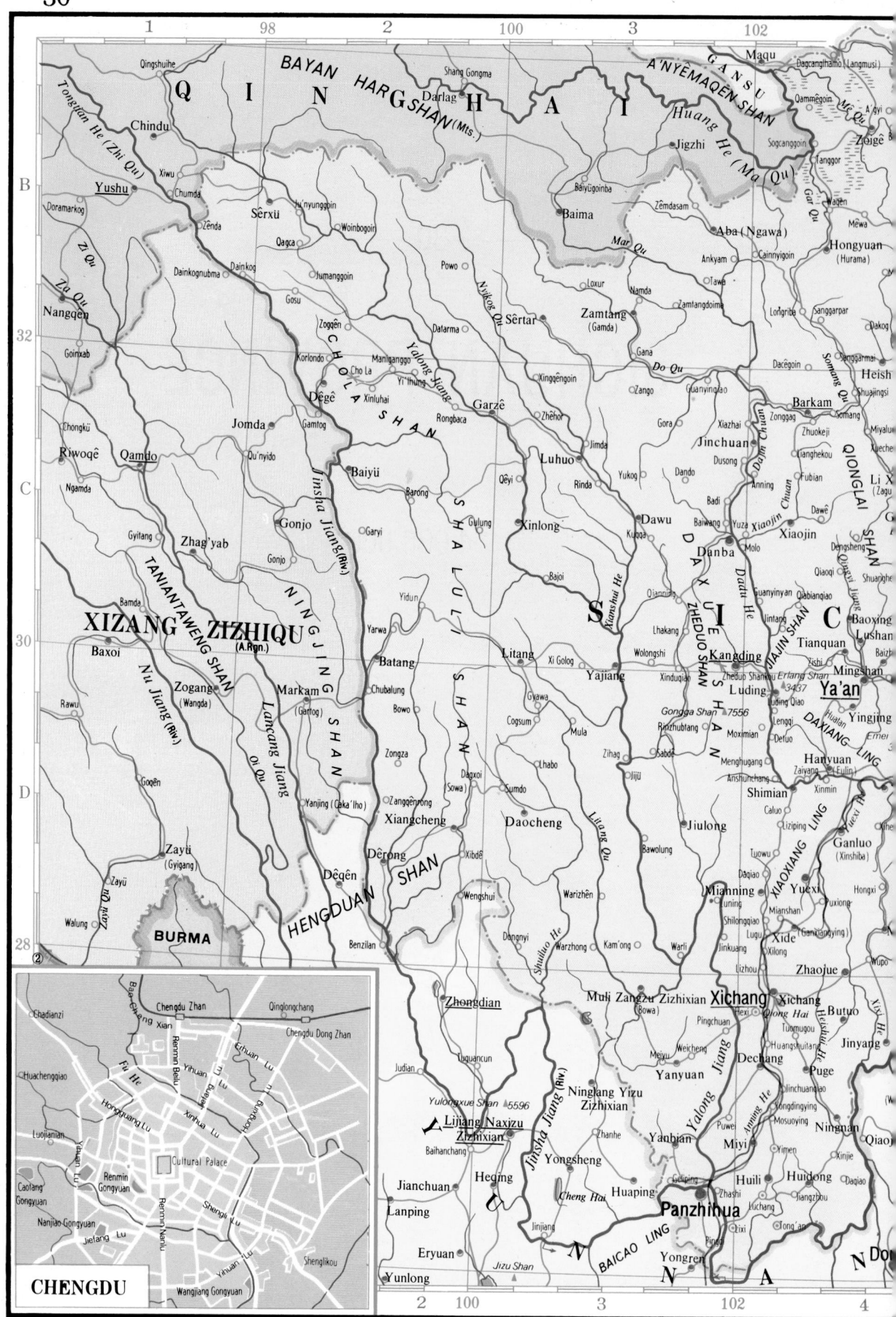

CHENGDU

① Guangxi Zhuangzu Zizhiqu ② India

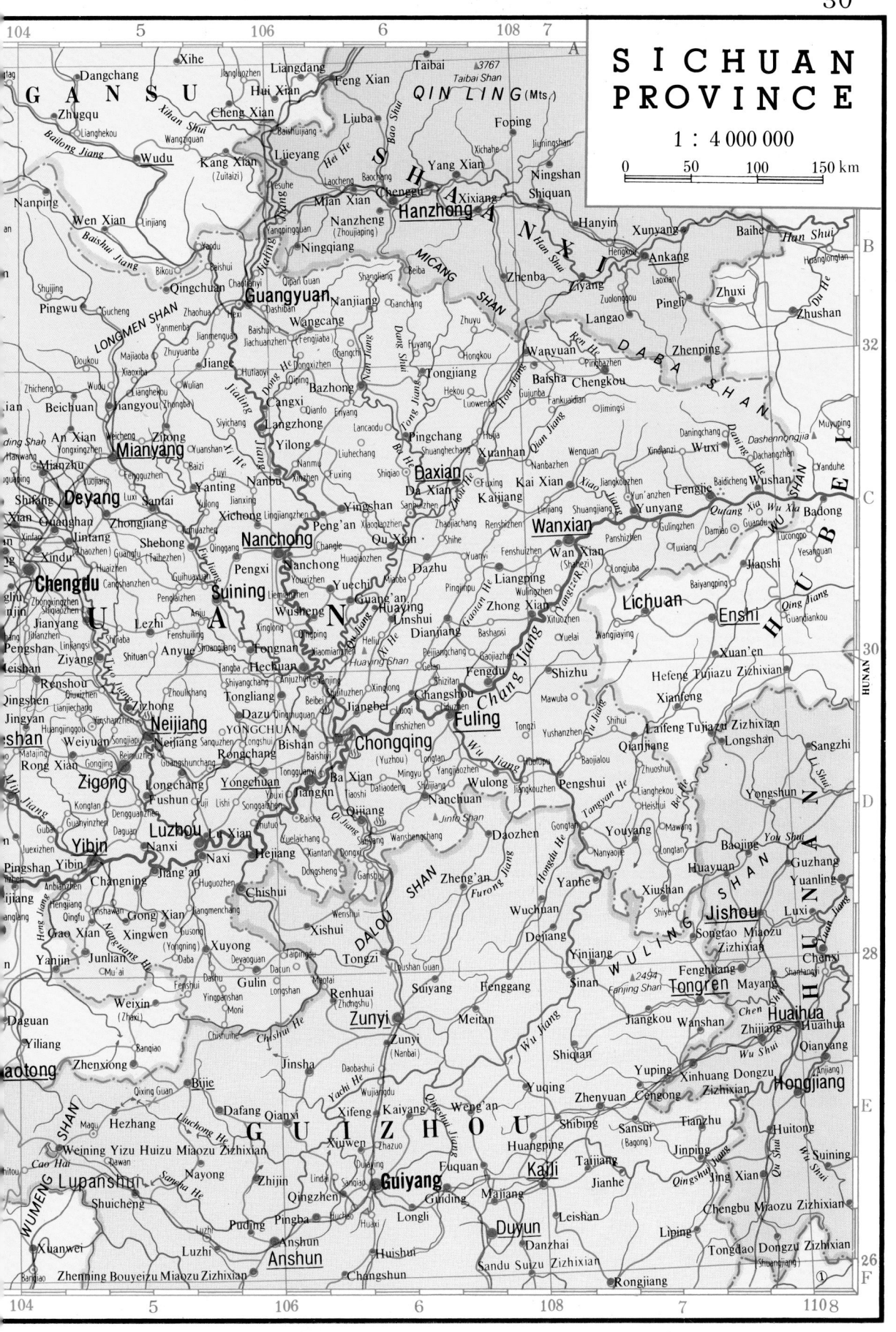

104   5   106   6   108   7

A

GANSU

Dangchang
Xihe
Jiangkouzhen   Liangdang
Hui Xian
Feng Xian
Taibai   3767
Taibai Shan   QIN LING (Mts.)

Zhugqu
Lianghekou
Cheng Xian
Liuba
Foping
Ningshan
Shiquan

Wangziquan
Lüeyang
Yang Xian
Xichahe
Jiuningshan

Wudu
Kang Xian
(Zuitaizi)
Laocheng   Baocheng   Chenggu   Xixiang
Hanyin   Xunyang   Baihe   Han Shui

Nanping
Yesuhe
Mian Xian
Hanzhong
Hanyin
Ankang   Huanglongtan

Wen Xian
Linjiang
Yangpingguan
Nanzheng
(Zhoujiaping)
Ziyang   Laoxian   Zhuxi

Shuijing
Bikou   Baishui
Ningqiang   Shangliang   Zhenba   Ziyang   Zuolongdou   Pingli   Zhushan

Pingwu
Gucheng
Qingchuan
Zhaohua
Dashihou   Nanjiang   Ganchang   Zhuyu   Langao   Zhenping

Beichuan
Jiangyou
Majiaoba
Zhuyuanba
Jiange
Wulian   Dongxizhen   Tongjiang   Hekou   Baisha   Chengkou   Jimingsi

An Xian
Weicheng   Zitong   Yuanshan   Bazhong   Qianfo   Enyang   Lancaodu   Pingchang   Wenquan   Nanbazhen   Wuxi   Dachanghe   Yanduhe

Mianyang
Fengguzhen   Baizi   Fuyi   Yilong   Nanmu   Fuxing   Shiqiao   Xuanhan   Yun'anzhen   Fengjie   Wushan

Mianzhu
Yanting
Jianxing   Peng'an   Yingshan   Kaijiang   Kai Xian   Yunyang   Qutang   Xia   Wu Xia   Badong

Deyang
Luxi   Santai
Xichong   Lingjiangzhen   Qu Xian   Zhaojiachang   Renshizhen   Linjiang   Shuangjiang   Yunyang   Gulingzhen   Damiao   Guandu

Guanghan
Jintang   Zhongjiang   Nanchong   Changle   Dazhu   Fenshuixi   Wan Xian   Panshizhen   Tuxiang   Lianshi

Chengdu   Shehong   Pengxi   Youxizhen   Yuechi   Miaoba   Yuanyi   (Shizi)   Longjiuba   Baiyangping

SICHUAN

Lezhi
Guihuaxiang
Anju   Huaying   Zhong Xian   Wulingzhen   Lichuan   Enshi   HUBEI

Suining
Linshui
Dianjiang
Fengdu
Shizhu

HUNAN

GUIZHOU

110 8

104   5   106   6   108   7

Sichuan Province

Population: 103.2 million
Urban population: 28.2 million
Nationalities: Han, Yi, Tibetan, Miao, Hui, and Qiang

Area: 560,000 square kilometers
Altitude: 300 — 700 meters in the lowlands; over 3,000 meters on the western plateau
Climatic features: subtropical, humid, monsoonal climate in the eastern lowlands with frequent fog; temperate-subtropical highland climate in the west, with intense sunlight but low temperatures
Average temperature: in January, 3 — 8°C in the lowlands, -9 — -3°C on the plateau, and 8 — 13°C in the south; in July, 25 — 29°C in the lowlands, 11 — 17°C on the plateau, and 22 — 26°C in the south
Annual average rainfall: 1,000 mm in the lowlands, 500 — 700 mm on the plateau, and 800 —1,200 mm in the south
Physical features: basin in the east, plateau in the west, mountain in the central south, highland swamps in the central north. Known as the Sichuan Basin, the eastern lowlands are closed off by mountains and plateaus on all sides. The drainage basin is crossed by the Yangtze River and is rich with red soil.
Mountains: Minshan, Longmen, Micang, and Daba Mountains in the north; Wushan Mountain in the east; Shaluli, Qionglai, and Daxue Mountains in the west
Plateau: the western Sichuan Plateau is an eastern extension of the Qinghai-Tibet Plateau.
Rivers: the Yangtze River flows along Sichuan's western and southern borders, with the southern segment called the Jinsha River. The Yangtze traverses the Sichuan Basin and is joined by several tributaries, the major ones being the Minjiang-Dadu, Tuojiang, and Jialing Rivers; on the plateau it meets another tributary, the Yalong River.
Products: rice, corn, sweet potatoes, wheat, sorghum, rape, sugar cane, peanuts, tea; ramie, silk cocoons, cotton, jute, ambary hemp; sun-cured tobacco; tung oil, camphor, Chinese tallow tree, raw lacquer, white wax; silver fungus, bulb of fritillary, bamboo; oranges, tangerines, pears, *yangtao*, lychees, longans, bananas; iron, coal, managnese, natural gas, petroleum, salt, alluvial gold, copper, nickel, phosphorus, sulphur, mica

Administrative divisions: 3 autonomous prefectures, 19 cities, 165 counties, 8 autonomous counties, and 1 industrial-agricultural district
Capital: Chengdu
Neighboring areas: Qinghai, Gansu, Shaanxi, Hubei, Hunan, Guizhou, and Yunnan Provinces; Tibet Autonomous Region
Major cities: Chengdu, Chongqing, Dukou, Zigong, Yibin, Neijiang, Wanxian, Nanchong, Leshan, Luzhou, Xichang

CHENGDU—CHONGQING

1 : 1 330 000

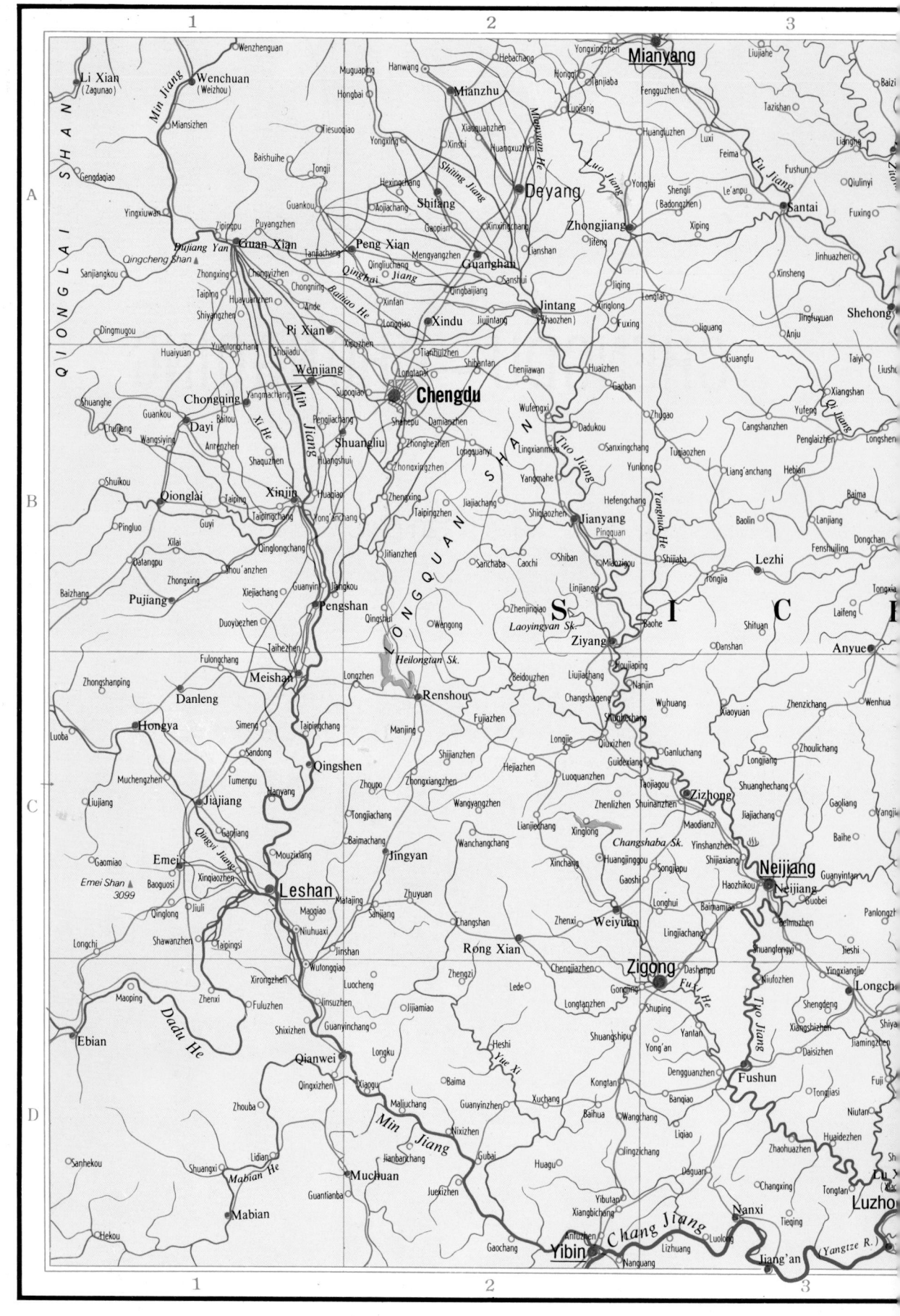

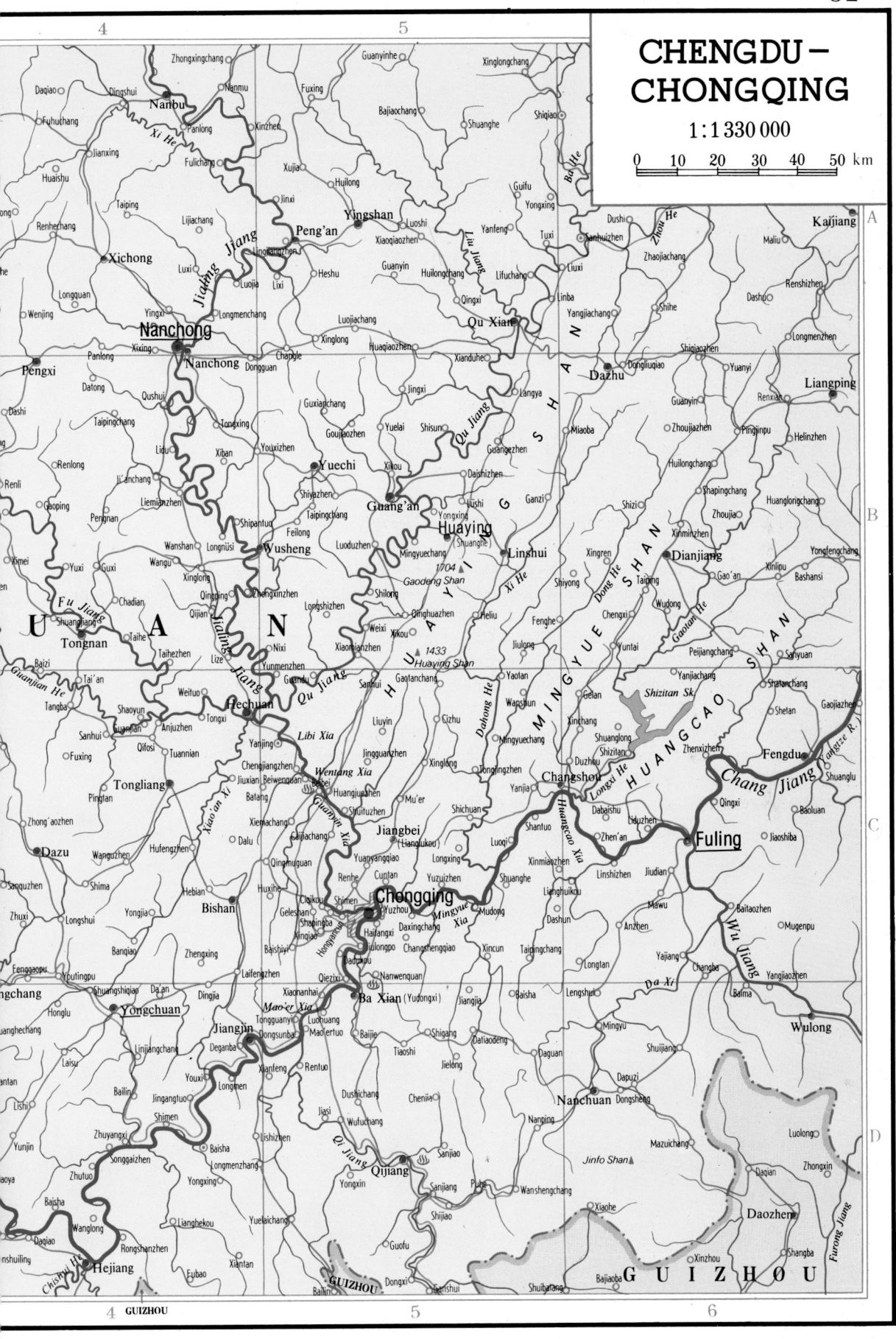

CHENGDU – CHONGQING

1 : 1 330 000

0 10 20 30 40 50 km

Tourist attractions: Mount Emei, 3,099 meters in elevation, one of the four mountains in China famous for their Buddhist temples; Mount Qingcheng, near Guanxian County, known historically as a center of the Taoist culture; Dujiangyan, on Minjiang River near Guanxian, built in 250 B.C., one of the earliest and most effective water conservancy projects; Baodingshan sculptures in Dazu County, about 100 kilometers west of Chongqing; Leshan Giant Buddha, the largest Buddha statue in the world, in Leshan; the Three Gorges on the Yangtze; Jiuzhaigou, a scene spot in Nanping County at the foot of the Minshan Mountain

Comments: Sichuan is the home of the giant panda and golden-haired monkey.

Chengdu-Chongqing Region

Because the abbreviated Chinese name for Chengdu is Cheng and for Chongqing, Yu, the Chengdu-Chongqing basin area is known as the Cheng-Yu Region. Encompassing the cities of Chengdu, Zigong, Neijiang, Chongqing, Nanchong, Suining, and Deyang, it is a region characterized by dense population, agricultural prosperity, and heavy industry.

The area is divided into three parts. To the east of the Qujiang River are parallel ridges and valleys with the hills having an average altitude of 700 — 800 meters. Between the Qujiang River and Longquan Mountain are fertile, flat-topped hills. The Chengdu Plain to the west of Longquan Mountain is the largest plain in Southwest China, with an area of 6,000 square kilometers. It is drained by the Minjiang and Tuojiang Rivers. Called the Heavenly Land, this region has an efficient irrigation network and is renowned for its farming products.

It is warm in winter and hot in summer with heavy precipitation and a frost-free period of over 300 days. Crops grow all the year round. A high percentage of the rice it produces is shipped out to meet consumption demands elsewhere. The region also produces cotton, rapeseed, corn, wheat, and sweet potatoes. Sugar cane is grown in Neijiang; silkworms are raised in Nanchong and Leshan; Biancha tea is produced in Ya'an, Qionglai, and Guanxian Counties; and oranges and tangerines are grown along the Yangtze and Jialing Rivers.

GUIZHOU PROVINCE

1 : 2 330 000

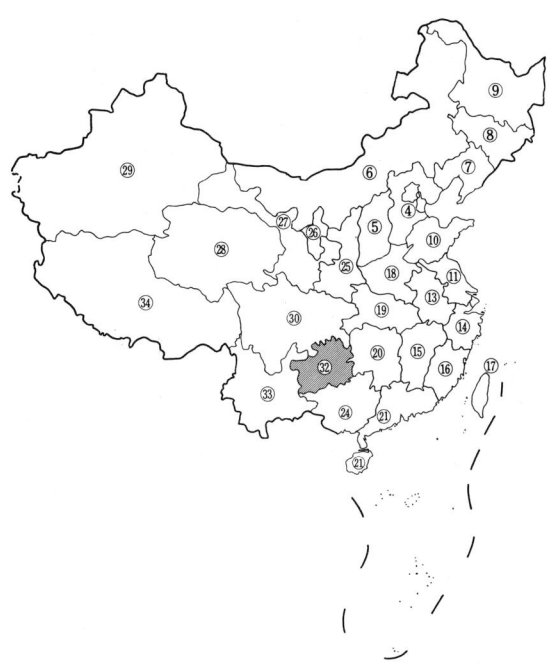

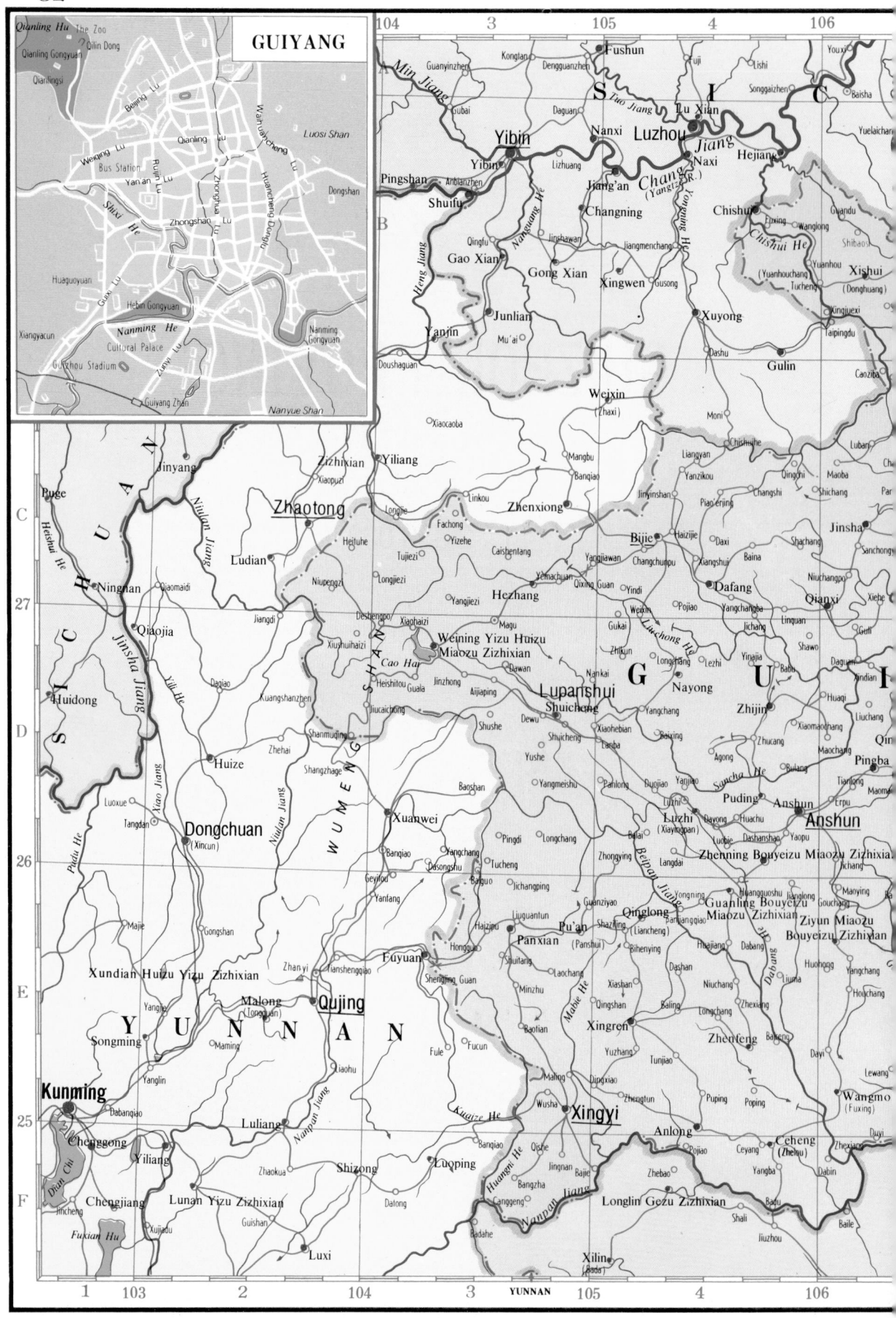

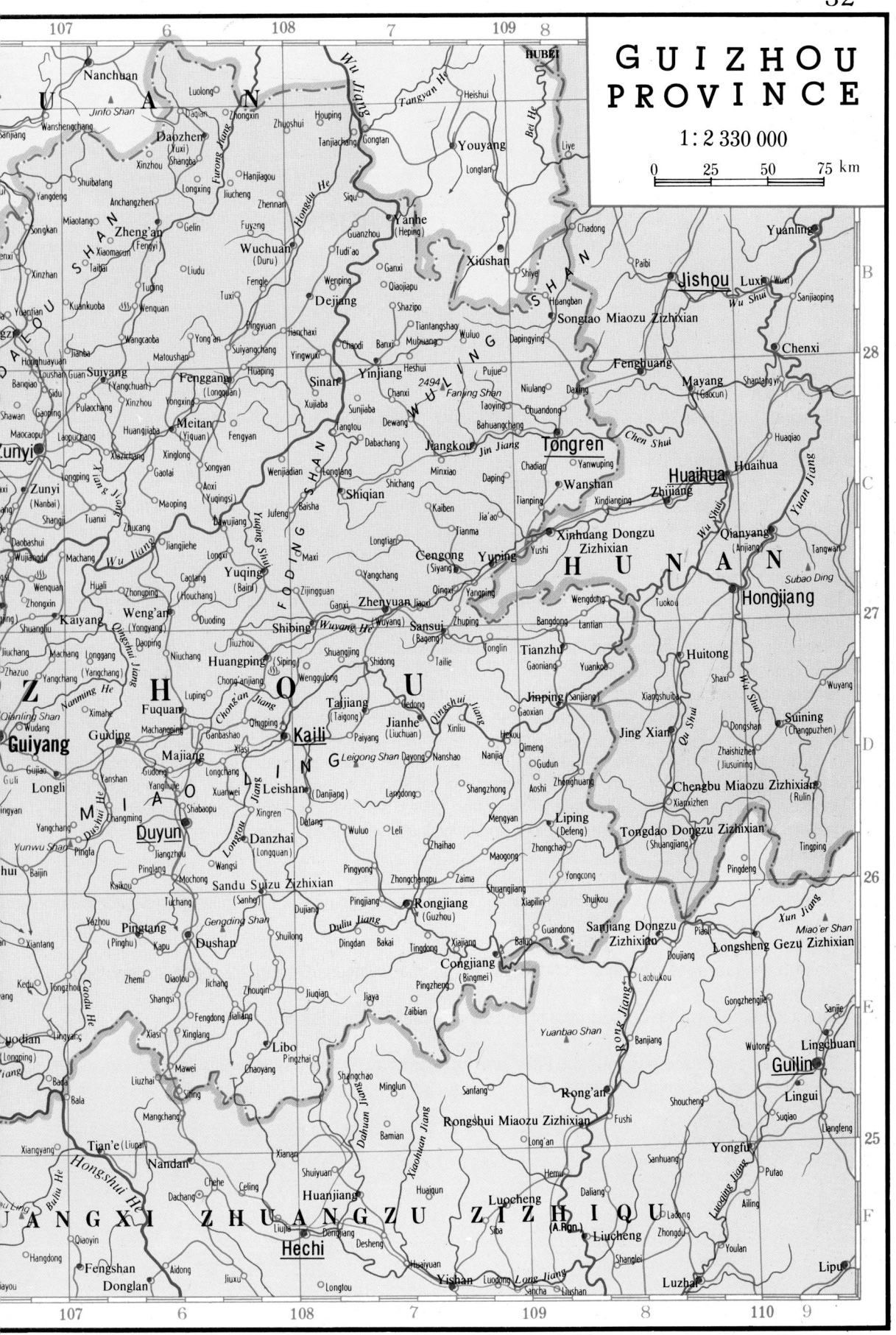

Guizhou Province

Population: 30.1 million
Urban population: 9 million
Nationalities: Han, Miao, Bouyei, Tong, Yi, Shui, Hui, Gelo, Zhuang, and Yao

Area: 170,000 square kilometers
Altitude: above 1,000 meters in most areas
Climatic features: subtropical, humid, monsoonal climate; few seasonal changes, with frequent cloudy and rainy weather; hailstorms in spring; occasional spring droughts in the west and summer droughts in the east
Average temperture: 1 — 10°C in January, 17 — 28°C in July
Annual average rainfall: 900 — 1,500 mm; high precipitation in the central and southwestern regions; half of the rain falls during the summer
Physical features: situated on the eastern Yunnan-Guizhou Plateau; mountains in the west slope down toward the north, east, and south
Mountains: Dalou, Miaoling, and Wumeng Mountains
Waterfall: the Huangguoshu is one of the leading falls in China in terms of height and volume. The major fall is over 20 meters wide and 60 meters high. The falls drain into the Pearl River.
Products: rice, wheat, corn, millet, potatoes, rape, sugar cane, soybeans, peanuts, sesame, tea; cotton, ramie, ambary hemp, tussah; flue-cured tobacco; timber; sisal hemp, lemongrass, raw lacquer, tung oil, Chinese tallow tree, cork, coffee, olives, bark of eucommia; gallnuts, silver fungus; pears, oranges, apples, bananas, pineapples, walnuts, chestnuts; mercury, coal, phosphorus, bauxite, natural gas

Administrative divisions: 3 autonomous   prefectures, 8 cities, 61 counties, 11 autonomous counties, and 3 special districts
Capital: Guiyang
Neighboring areas: Yunnan, Sichuan, and Hunan Provinces: Guangxi Zhuang Autonomous Region
Major cities: Guiyang, Zunyi, Lupanshui, Duyun, Anshun, Kaili, Bijie

Tourist attractions: Huangguoshu Falls, and its nearby caves and stone forests, located between Zhenning and Guanling Counties

YUNNAN PROVINCE

1 : 4 000 000

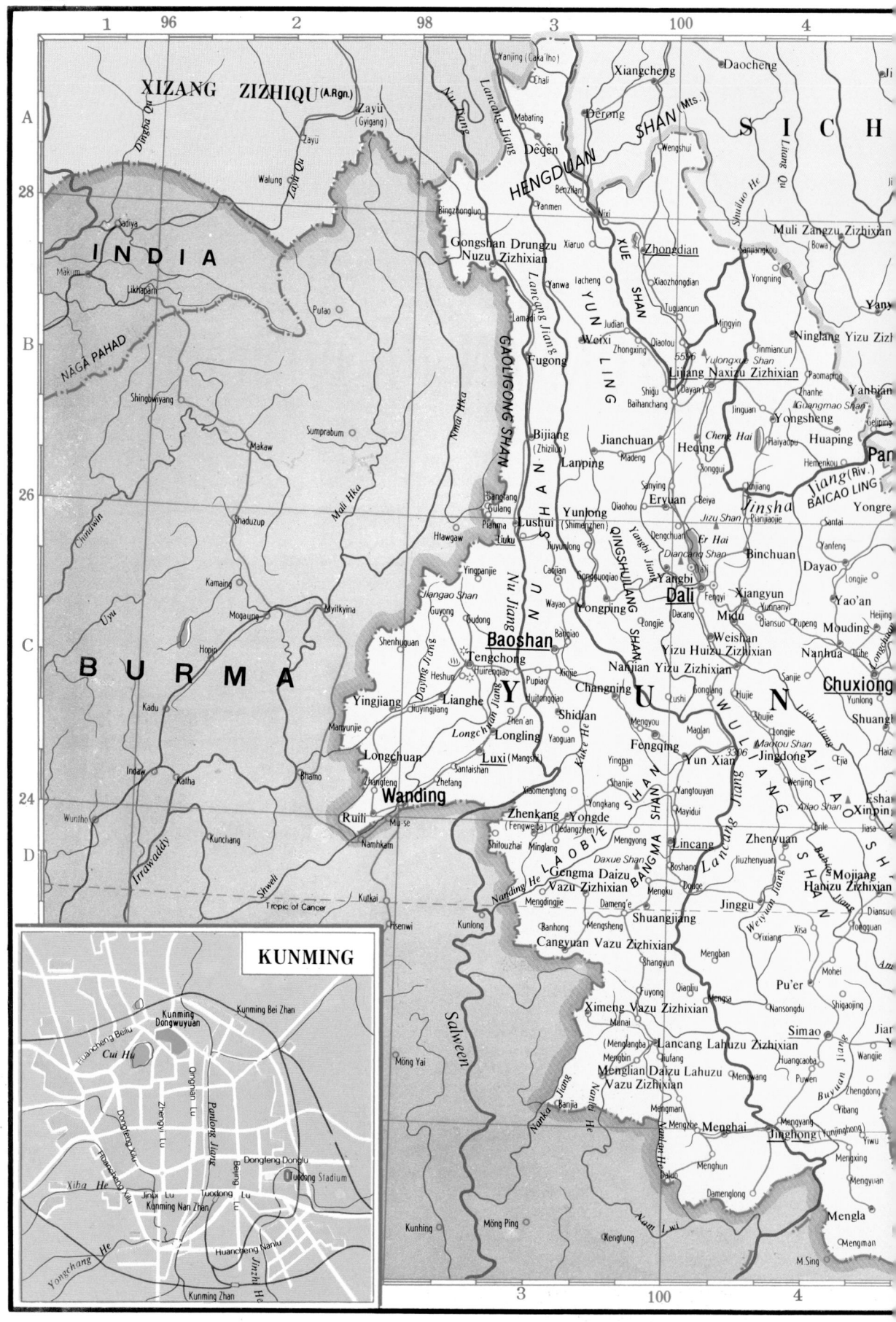

KUNMING

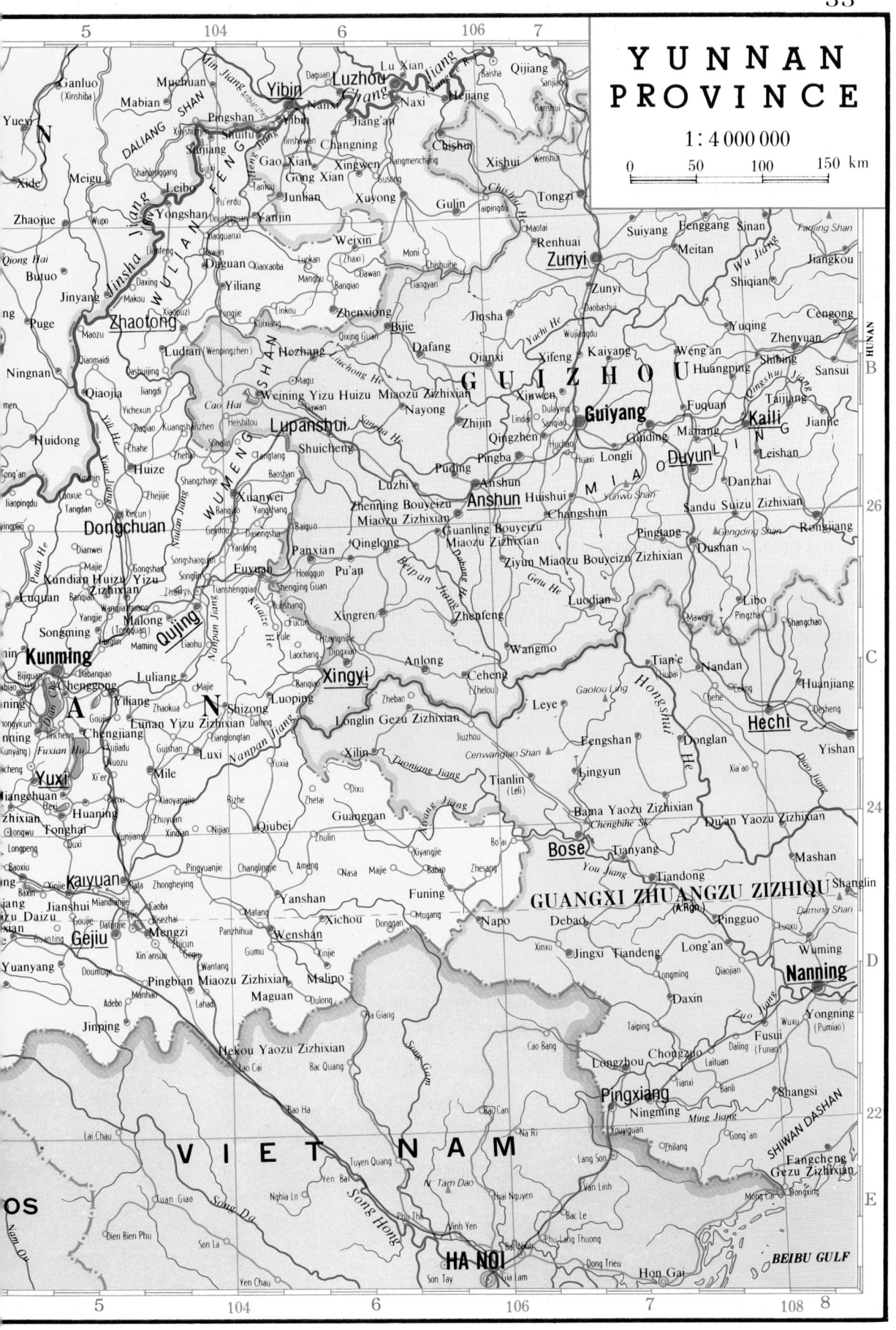

0   50   100   150 km

5   104   **6**   106   **7**

Ganluo
(Xinshiba)
Muchuan
Min Jiang
Daguan
Luzhou
Lu Xian
Baisha
Qijiang
Yibin
Mabian
Pingshan
Shuifu
Yibin
Nanxi
Naxi
Hejiang
Sanjiao
Gianshui
Yuexi
Gao Xian
Changning
Jiang'an
Xingwen
Chishui
Xide
Meigu
Leibo
Yongshan
Yanjin
Xuyong
Gulin
Tongzi
Zhaojue
Wupo
Daxing
Weixin
Renhuai
Maotai
Suiyang
Fenggang
Sinan
Faming Shan
Qiong Hai
Butuo
Jinyang
Daguan
Zhaxi
Dawan
Zunyi
Meitan
Shiqian
Jiangkou
Ningnan
Zhaotong
Ludian
Zhenxiong
Bijie
Dafang
Qianxi
Xifeng
Kaiyang
Weng'an
Huangping
Zhenyuan
Shibing
Cengong
Qiaojia
Jiangdi
GUIZHOU
Sansui
Nuidong
Huize
Lupanshui
Weining Yizu Huizu Miaozu Zizhixian
Nayong
Zhijin
Xinwen
Guiyang
Guiding
Majiang
Kaili
Jianhe
Leishan
Dongchuan
Xuanwei
Puding
Anshun
Huishui
Sandu Suizu Zizhixian
Rongjiang
Xundian Huizu Yizu Zizhixian
Fuyuan
Panxian
Qinglong
Pu'an
Guanling Bouyeizu Miaozu Zizhixian
Pingtang
Dushan
Libo
Qujing
Malong
Xingren
Zhenfeng
Ziyun Miaozu Bouyeizu Zizhixian
Luodian
Nandan
Huanjiang
Kunming
Chenggong
Luliang
Xingyi
Anlong
Ceheng
Wangmo
Tian'e
Hechi
Yishan
Yuxi
Yiliang
Shizong
Luoping
Longlin Gezu Zizhixian
Leye
Fengshan
Donglan
Kaiyuan
Jianshui
Gejiu
Mengzi
Wenshan
GUANGXI ZHUANGZU ZIZHIQU
Bose
Tiandong
Pingguo
Wuming
Nanning
Yongning
Fusui
Jinping
Hekou Yaozu Zizhixian
Longzhou
Chongzuo
Pingxiang
Ningming
Shangsi
Fangcheng Gezu Zizhixian

VIET NAM

HA NOI
Hon Gai
BEIBU GULF

5   104   **6**   106   **7**   108   **8**

Yunnan Province

Population: 34.6 million
Urban population: 10 million
Nationalities: Han, Yi, Bai, Hani, Zhuang, Dai, Miao, Lisu, Hui, Lahu, Va, Naxi, Yao, Tibetan, Jingpo, Blang, Pumi, Nu, Achang, Deang (Penglong), Mongolian, Drung and Jino

Area: 380,000 square kilometers
Altitude: 4,000 meters in the northern mountain region; 2,000 meters on the southern highland
Climatic features: from north to south the province spans three climatic zones — temperate, subtropical, and tropical; conspicuous changes in climate; two clear-cut seasons, dry and humid; rainy season from May to October
Average temperature: 8 — 17°C in January, 11 — 29°C in July
Annual average rainfall: 600 — 2,300 mm; low precipitation in the northwest, high in the southeast; 60 percent of the rain falls from June to August
Physical features: high in the northwest and low in the southeast; over 90 percent of the province is mountainous; the relative height of mountain peaks from river valleys can be as much as 3,000 meters.
Rivers: Nujiang, Lancang, Jinsha, Yuanjiang, and Nanpan Rivers
Products: rice, wheat, corn, sorghum, potatoes, sugar cane, peanuts, soybeans, peas, rape, tea; oranges, bananas, pineapples, cocoanuts, walnuts; cotton, silk cocoons; flue-cured tobacco; timber; tropical plants; tin, copper, zinc, marble, phosphorus

Administrative divisions: 8 autonomous prefectures, 11 cities, 86 counties, and 28 autonomous counties
Capital: Kunming
Neighboring areas: Sichuan and Guizhou Provinces; Tibet and Guangxi Zhuang Autonomous Regions
Neighboring countries: Burma, Laos, and Vietnam
Major cities: Kunming, Dongchuan, Gejiu, Dali, Luxi, Jinghong

Tourist attractions: Kunming, city of "eternal spring"; hot springs of Anning in Kunming; Dianchi Lake, south of Kunming; Stone Forest, a typical karst area, about 80 kilometers east of Kunming

Comments: Yunnan is the province with the largest number of nationalities in China.

XIZANG (TIBET)
AUTONOMOUS REGION

I : 6 660 000

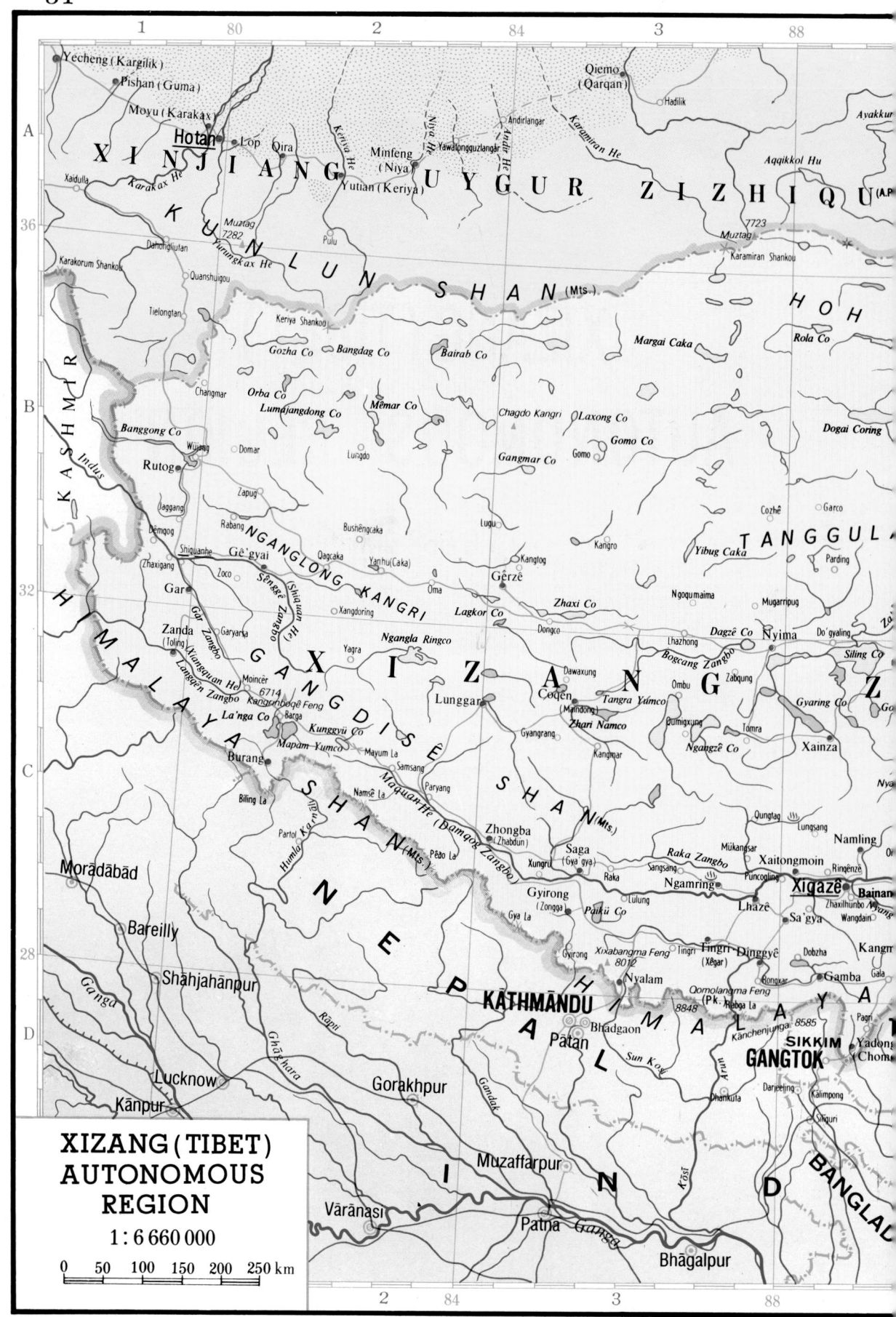

XINJIANG

Yecheng (Kargilik)
Pishan (Guma)
Moyu (Karakax)
Hotan
Lop
Qira
Xaidulla
Karakax He
Minfeng (Niya)
Yutian (Keriya)
Keriya He
Niya He
Andir He
Yawalongguzlangar
Andirlangar
Karamiran He
Qiemo (Qarqan)
Hadilik
Ayakkur

UYGUR ZIZHIQU (A.R.)

Aqqikkol Hu

KUN LUN SHAN (Mts.)

Muztag 7282
Dahongliutan
Quanshuigou
Karakorum Shankou
Tielongtan
Muoztagh
Yurungkax He
Pulu
Keriya Shankou
Muztag 7723
Karamiran Shankou

HOH

KASHMIR
Indus
Changmar
Gozha Co
Bangdag Co
Orba Co
Bairab Co
Margai Caka
Rola Co

Lumajangdong Co
Mêmar Co
Chagdo Kangri
Laxong Co

Banggong Co
Wujiang
Domar
Luingdo
Gangmar Co
Gomo
Gomo Co
Dogai Coring

Rutog
Zapug
Lugu
Kangro
Cozhê
Garco

Jaggang
Rabang
Bushêngcaka
Kangtog
Yibug Caka
Parding

Dêmqog
Shiquanhe
Gê'gyai
Qagcaka
Yanhu (Caka)
Gêrzê
Ngoqumaima
Mugarripug

Zhaxigang
Zoco
Oma
Zhaxi Co
Dagzê Co
Nyima
Do'gyaling

Gar
Garyarsa
Xangdoring
Lagkor Co
Dongco
Lhazhong
Bogcang Zangbo
Siling Co

Zanda (Toling)
Moincêr
Yagra
Ngangla Ringco
Dawaxung
Coqên
Tangra Yumco
Ombu
Zabung
Gyaring Co

Kangrinboqê Feng 6714
Barga
La'nga Co
Lunggar
Gyangrang
Zhari Namco
Qumigxung
Tomra
Ngangzê Co
Xainza

Burang
Mapam Yumco
Kunggyü Co
Mayum La
Samsang
Paryang
Kangmar

Biling La
Namsê La
Maquanhe (Damqog Zangbo)
Zhongba (Zhabdun)
Saga (Gya'gya)
Mükangsar
Qungtag
Lungsang
Namling

Partol
Pêdo La
Xungru
Raka Zangbo
Xaitongmoin
Ringênzê
Ori

Moradabad
Humla
Gyirong (Zongga)
Raka
Sangsang
Ngamring
Puncogling
Xigazê
Bainam

Bareilly
Gya La
Paiku Co
Lulung
Lhazê
Sa'gya
Zhaxilhünbo
Wangdain

Shahjahanpur
Gyirong
Xixabangma Feng 8012
Tingri (Xêgar)
Tingri
Dinggyê
Dobzha
Kangm

Nyalam
Rongxar
Gamba
Gala

Lucknow
Ghaghara
Rapti
Qomolangma Feng (Pk.) Rbaga La 8848
Bongxar
Pagri

Kanpur
KATHMANDU
Bhadgaon
Patan
Kanchenjunga 8585
SIKKIM
GANGTOK
Yadong
Chom

Ganga
Sun Kosi
Dhankuta
Darjeeling
Kalimpong
Siliguri

Gorakhpur
Gandak
Arun
Kosi

Muzaffarpur
BANGLAD

Varanasi
Patna
Ganga
Bhagalpur

XIZANG (TIBET)
AUTONOMOUS
REGION

1 : 6 660 000

0   50   100   150   200   250 km

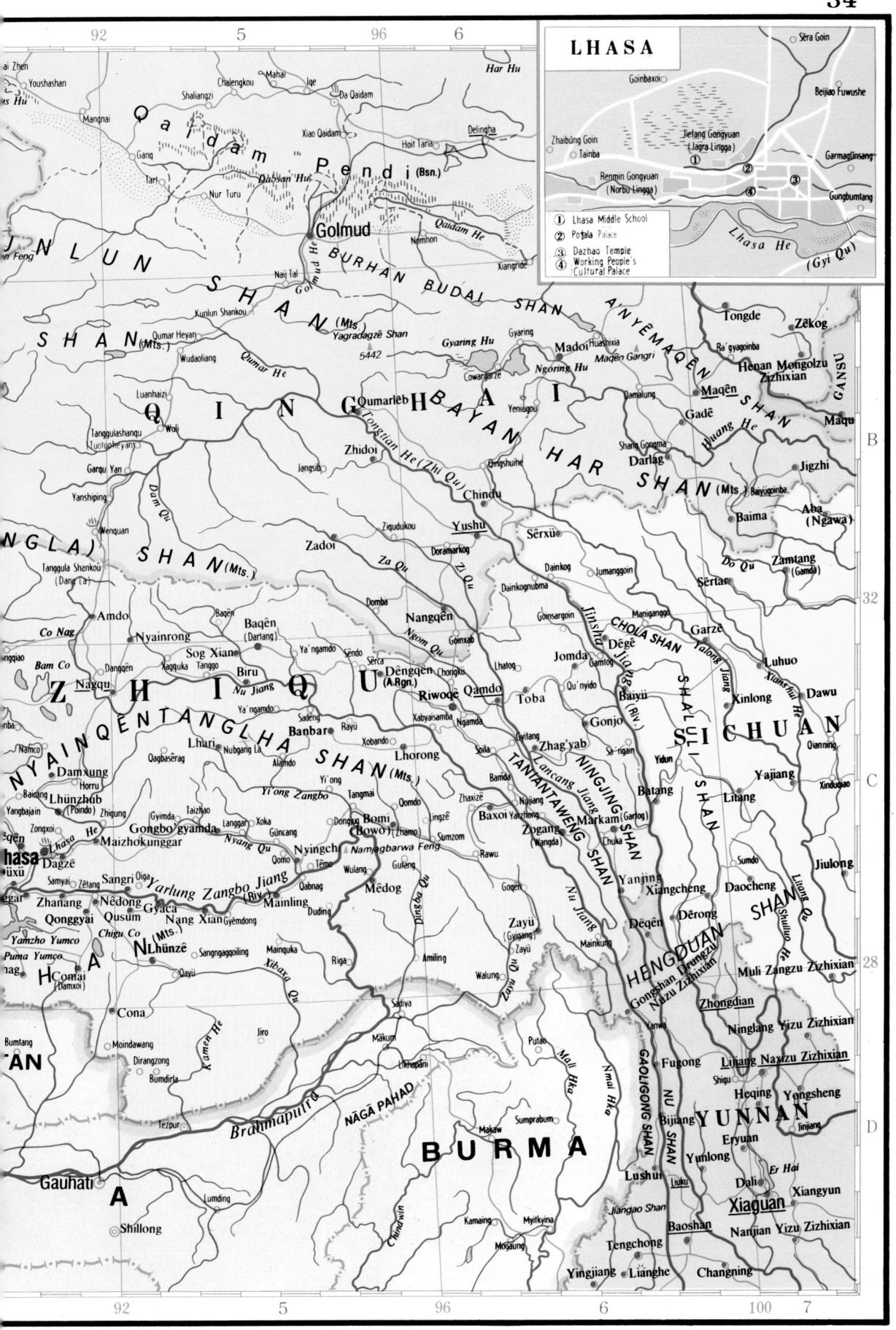

LHASA

Sëra Goin
Goinbaxoi
Beijiao Fuwushe
Zhaibúng Goin
Tainba
Jietang Gongyuan
(Jagra-Lingga)
① ② Garmagünsang
③
Renmin Gongyuan
(Norbu-Lingga) ④
Gungbumtang
Lhasa He
(Gyi Qu)

① Lhasa Middle School
② Potala Palace
③ Dazhao Temple
④ Working People's
　Cultural Palace

Youshashan
ai Zhen
s Hu
Mangnai
Chalengkou
Mahai
Har Hu
Shaliangzi
Iqe
Da Qaidam
Delingha
Xiao Qaidam
Hoit Taria

Qaidam Pendi (Bsn.)

Golmud
Qaidam He
Nemhon
Xiangride
Gang
Tarf
Dabsan Hu
Nur Turu

n Feng
Naij Tal
Golmud He
BURHAN BUDAI SHAN
A'NYEMAQEN
Tongde
Zêkog

KUNLUN SHAN
Kunlun Shankou
Yagradagzê Shan (Mts.)
Gyaring Hu
Gyaring
Madoi
Huashixia
Maqên Gangri
Ra'gyagoinba
Henan Mongolzu
Zizhixian

SHAN (Mts.)
Qumar Heyan
Wudaoliang
5442
Cowargarzê
Ngoring Hu
Damalung
Maqên
GANSU

QINGHBAYANHAR SHAN
Luanhaizi
Oumar He
Qumarleb
Zhidoi
Tongtian He (Zhi Qu)
Dingshuihe
Shang Gonma
Gadê
Darlag
Huang He
Maqu
Jigzhi
B

Tanggulashanqu
(Tuotuoheyan)
Woli
Jangsib
Chindu
SHAN (Mts.)
Baiyugoinba
Garqu Yan
Yanshiping
Zadoi
Za Qu
Yushu
Doramarkog
Sêrxü
Dainkog
Jumanggoin
Baima
Aba
(Ngawa)

DAM QU
Wenquan
Ziqudukou
Zl Qu
Dainkognubma
Do Qu
Zamtang
(Gamda)
Sêrtar

NGLA) SHAN (Mts.)
Tanggula Shankou
(Dang La)
Domba
Nangqên
Goinsargoin
Manigangqo
Garzê
32

Co Nag
Amdo
Baqên
Ngom Qu
Goinxab
Lhatog
Dêgê
Gamtog
CHOLA SHAN
Luhuo

Bam Co
nggiao
Nyainrong
Baqên
(Darlang)
Ya'ngamdo
Sêndo
Sêrca
Dênqên
(A.Rgn.)
Chongkü
Jomda
Qu'nyido
Yidun
Baiyü
Xinlong
Dawu
C

Namco
nba
Nagqu
ZHIQU
Xagquka
Tanggo
Sadeng
Ya'ngamdo
Riwoqê
Qamdo
Toba
Gonjo
Batang
Qianning

Damxung
Horru
NYAINQÊNTANGLHA SHAN
Lhari
Nubgang La
Xabya-samba
Ngamda
Soila
Gyitang
Zhag'yab
Sa-ngain
Litang
Yajiang
Xinduqiao

Baigoin
Lhünzhub
(Poindo)
Zhiguo
Qagbasêrag
Yi'ong
Alamdo
Bamda
TANTANTAWENG SHAN
NINGJING SHAN
SHALULI SHAN
SICHUAN

ên
Zongxoi
Lhasa He
Maizhokunggar
Gyimda
Taizhao
Yi'ong Zangbo
Tangmai
Oomdo
Zhaxize
Nujiang
Yanzhong
Baxoi
Rawu
Markam
(Gartog)
Chuka
Sumdo
Jiulong

hasa
Dagzê
üxü
Gongbo'gyamda
Langgar
Xoka
Güncang
Bomi
Bowo
Zhamo
lingzê
Sumzom
Zogang
(Wangda)
Yanjing
Xiangcheng
Daocheng

Samyai
Zêtang
Sangri
Oiga
Nyang Qu
Nyingchi
Têmo
Wulang
Gutang
Gogên
Dêqên
Dêrong
HENGDUAN SHAN

Zhanang
Nêdong
Gyaca
Gyêmdong
Mainling
Namjagbarwa Feng
Mêdog
Ding-bai Qu
Zayü
(Gyigang)
Gongshan Drungzu
Nüzu Zizhixian
Muli Zangzu Zizhixian
28

Qonggyai
Qusum
Nang Xian (Mts.)
Qabnag
Duding
Mainquka
Riga
Zayü
Zayü Qu
Mainkung
Zhongdian

Yamzho Yumco
Chigu Co
Nhünzê
Sangngagqoiling
Sadiya
Walung
Nu Jiang
Ninglang Yizu Zizhixian

Puma Yumço
Comai
(Damxoi)
Qayü
Xibaxa Qu
Amiling
Yanwo
Lijiang Naxizu Zizhixian

nag
Cona
Jiro
Makum
Mali Hka
Fugong
Shigu
Heqing
Yongsheng
YUNNAN

Bumtang
Moindawang
Dirangzong
Likhapani
Putao
N'mai Hka
Bijiang
Yunlong
Eryuan
Er Hai
Jinjiang
D

AN
Bumdirla
Tezpur
Brahmaputra
NĀGĀ PAHAD
Makaw
Sumprabum
GAOLIGONG SHAN
NU SHAN
Lushui
Liuku
Dali
Xiangyun

Gauhati
A
Lumding
Chindwin
BURMA
Jiangao Shan
Xiaguan
Nanjian Yizu Zizhixian

Shillong
Kamaing
Myitkyina
Mogaung
Baoshan
Tengchong
Changning

Yingjiang
Lianghe

Xizang (Tibet) Autonomous Region

Population: 2.03 million
Urban population: 250,000
Nationalities: Tibetan (1.97 million), Han, Moinba, Lhoba, and Hui

Area: 1,200,000 square kilometers
Altitude: over 4,000 meters on the whole; 8,848 meters at the peak of Qomolangma (Mount Everest)
Climatic features: highland climate, with lower temperatures and less precipitation than most of China; thin atmosphere; long hours of sunshine; intense solar radiation
Average temperature: -18 — 3.6°C in January, 7 — 19°C in July
Annual average rainfall: 60 — 1,000 mm; high precipitation in the east and south and low in the north; 90 percent of the rain falls from June to September
Physical features: almost the whole region is a plateau, known as the roof of the world; a small area in the southeast descends to the Brahmaputra River Valley; north of the Gangdisê Range and south of the Kunlun Range is the vast Northern Tibet Plateau with hills, basins, lakes, and snow-covered peaks; the southern valleys between the Gangdisê and the Himalayas are Tibet's principal farming and pastoral lands; in the east is a region of parallel mountains and valleys, which are the northern half of the Hengduan Mountains.
Mountains: the Himalayas in southern Tibet have an average elevation of 6,000 meters; in the north are the Kunlun and Tanggula Ranges; in the central southwest lies the Gangdisê Range; the Hengduan Mountains are to the immediate east of the Nyainqêntanglha Range.
Rivers: the Yarlung Zangbo River, which is the upper reach of the Brahmaputra River, winds its way through Tibet's southern valleys; the Nujiang, Lancang, and Jinsha Rivers, which are respectively the upper reaches of the Salween, Mekong, and Yangtze Rivers, cut through the Hengduan Mountains and enter Yunnan Province.
Lakes: Tibet has over 1,000 lakes, with the Nam Co (1,920 square kilometers) being the second largest salt lake in China; other major lakes are the Siling Co, Gyaring Co, Ngangzê Co, Tangra Yumco, and Yamzho Yumco
Products: wheat, highland barley, buckwheat; iron, coal, chromite, copper, borax, salt; medicinal herbs

Administrative divisions: 2 city and 76 counties
Capital: Lhasa
Neighboring areas: Qinghai, Sichuan, and Yunnan Provinces; Xinjiang Uygur Autonomous Region
Neighboring countries: India, Nepal, Sikkim, Bhutan, and Burma
Major towns: Lhasa, Xigazê, Gyangzê, Qamdo, Nyingchi, Gar, Nyalam

Tourist attraction: Potala Palace in Lhasa

TOPOGRAPHY OF CHINA

1 : 18 000 000

35

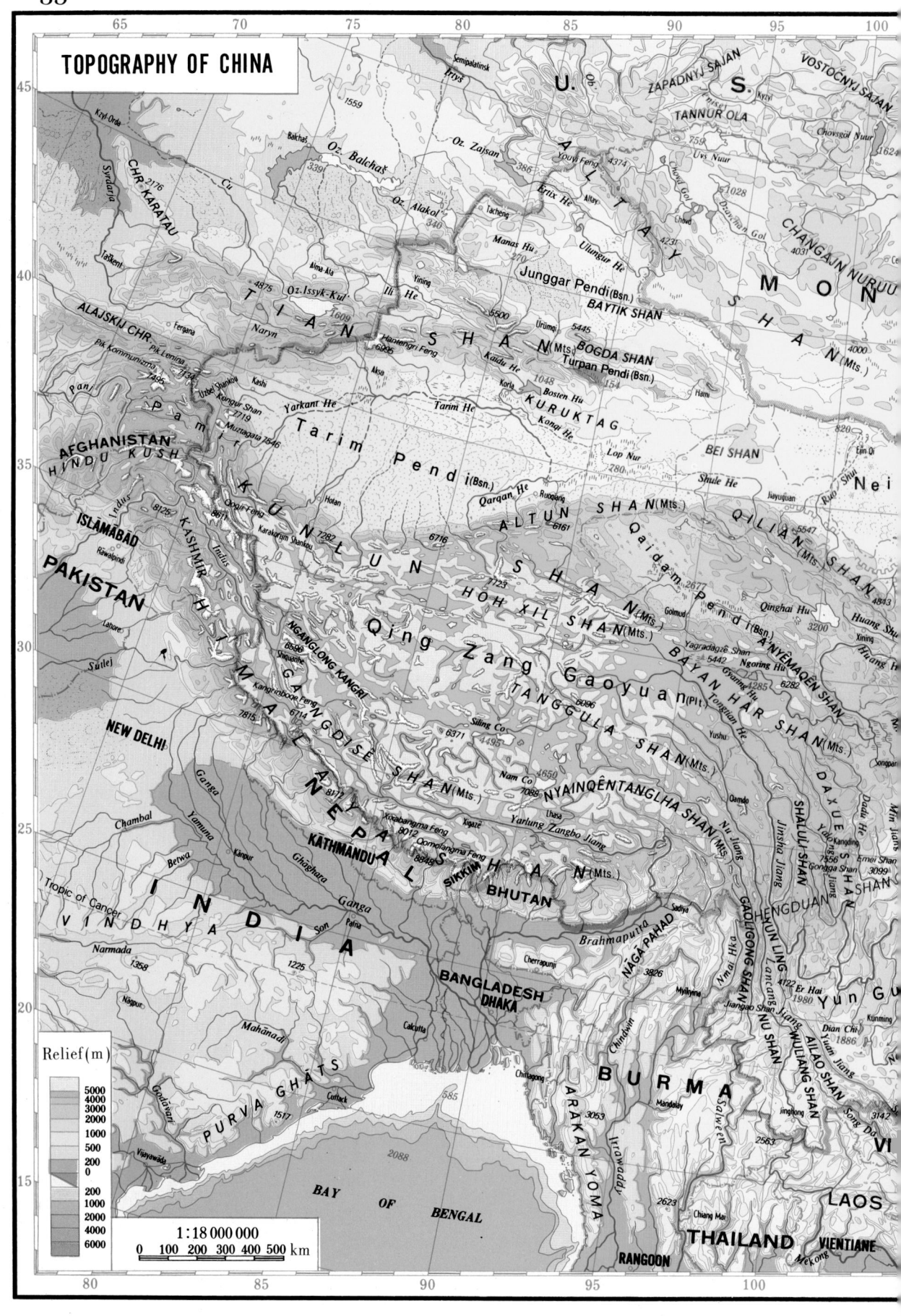

TOPOGRAPHY OF CHINA

Relief (m)

5000
4000
3000
2000
1000
500
200
0

200
1000
2000
3000
4000
6000

1:18 000 000

0 100 200 300 400 500 km

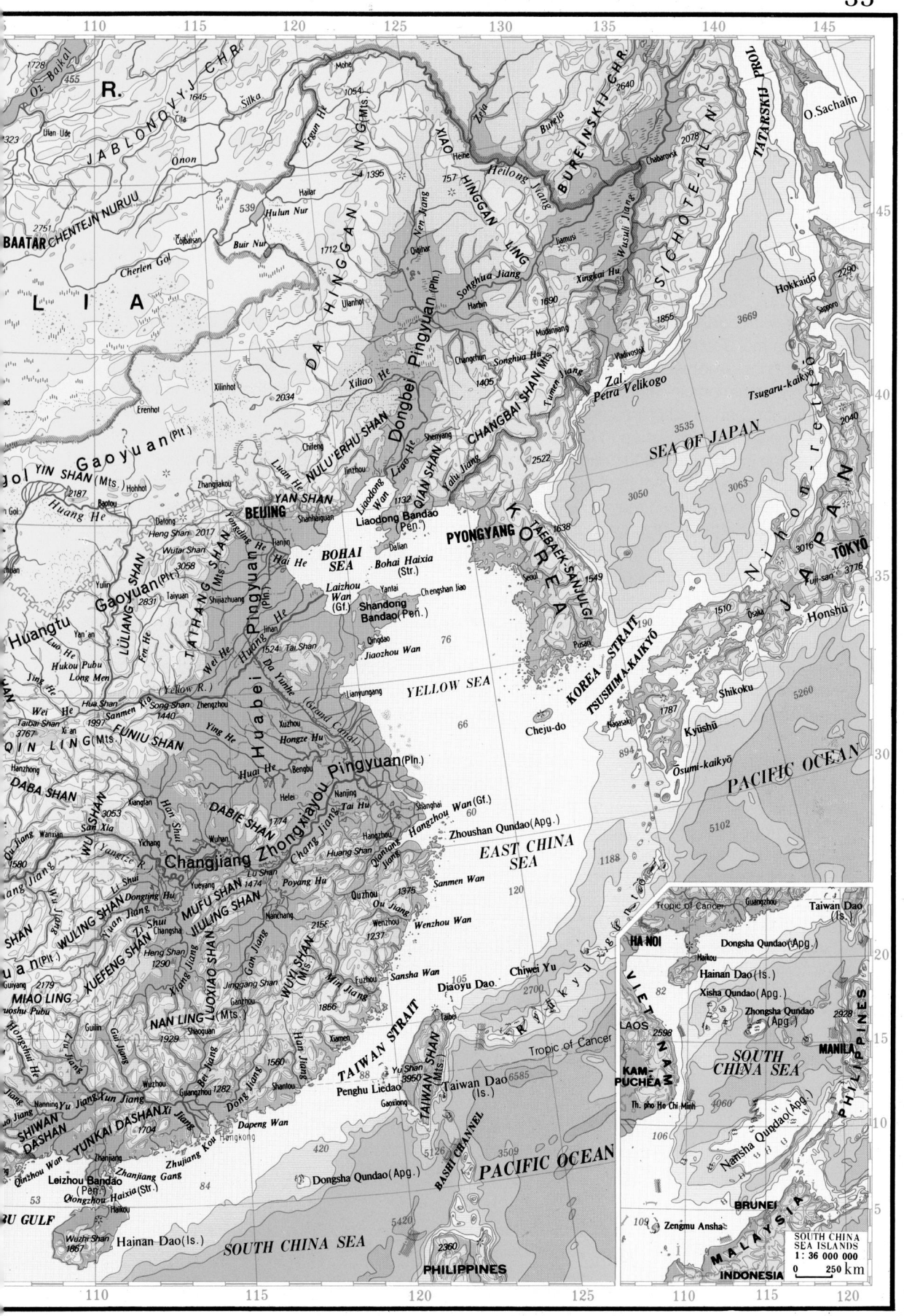

SOUTH CHINA
SEA ISLANDS
1 : 36 000 000
0 — 250 km

Climate and Topography

China's climate is characterized by monsoonal winds from the east and distinct seasonal changes, with northerly winds and little rainfall in the winter and southerly winds and plenty of rain in the summer. Common climatic phenomena include cold waves, cyclones, intermittent drizzles, and typhoons. Another characteristic is a distinct continental climate, with a wide temperature range and variations in rainfall. Temperatures in China are much lower in the winter and higher in the summer than in other countries of the same latitude.

The annual precipitation in China decreases progressively from the southeast coast (where the average is 1,000 to 2,000 millimeters) to the northwest interior (100 to 200 millimeters). Eastern Xinjiang, in the heartland of the Eurasian Continent, is China's most arid region. The average annual precipitation there is less than 50 millimeters; Toksun County in the Turpan Depression has the scantiest precipitation of any area in the country, with a mean annual precipitation of only 3.9 millimeters. China's record high annual precipitation of 8,408 millimeters was registered in Huoshaoliao, Taiwan Province.

One of the major features of China's physical geography is its mountains, plateaus, and hills which account for about 65 percent of the country's land mass. Of the world's nineteen mountains that exceed the 8,000-meter mark, seven are in China or on its borders, including the 8,848-meter Qomolangma (Mount Everest), which straddles the Sino-Nepalese border. In the southern foothills of the 5,445-meter, snow-covered Mount Bogda of the Tianshan Range is the Turpan Depression, where the dried-up surface of Lake Aydingkol lying 155 meters below sea level is the second lowest spot in the world.

Generally speaking, the land surface of China descends from west to east in a four-step staircase. At the top of the staircase is the Qinghai-Tibet Plateau, known as the "roof of the world," which towers in the southwest at an average elevation of 4,000 meters or more. The second step extends from east of the Qinghai-Tibet Plateau to the Greater Hinggan-Taihang-Wushan chain and consists mainly of plateaus and basins between 1,000 and 2,000 meters above sea level. These include the Yunnan-Guizhou, Inner Mongolia, and Loess Plateaus and the Tarim, Junggar, and Sichuan Basins. The third step extends further eastward and reaches the coast; it consists mainly of plains and low hills, 500 to 1,000 meters in elevation, such as the Northeast China, North China, and middle-lower Yangtze Plains. The bottom step of the staircase is the vast continental shelf formed by the shallows, plus the islands off the mainland.

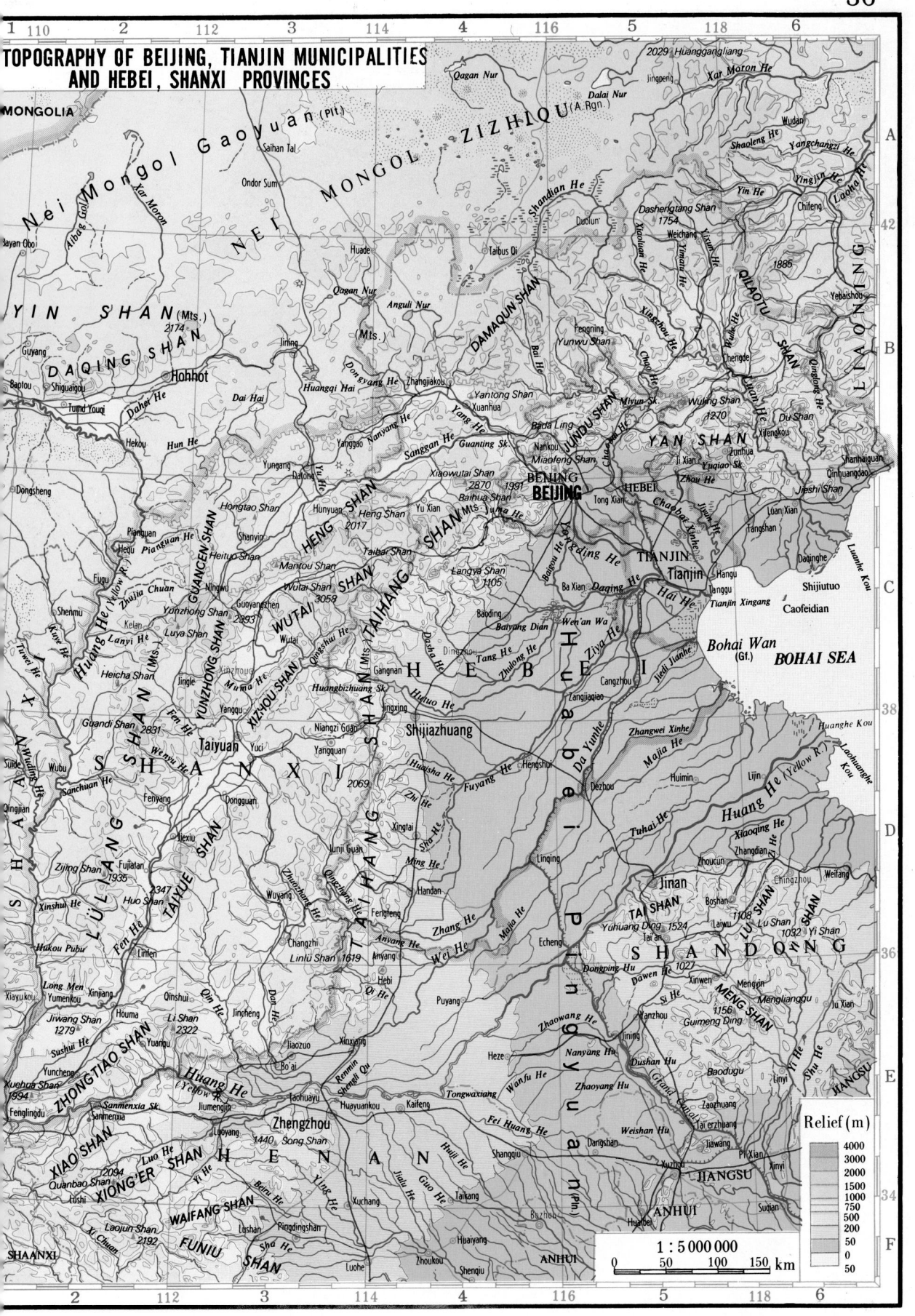

TOPOGRAPHY OF BEIJING, TIANJIN MUNICIPALITIES AND HEBEI, SHANXI PROVINCES

MONGOLIA

Nei Mongol Gaoyuan (Plt.)

NEI MONGOL ZIZHIQU (A. Rgn.)

2029 Huanggangliang

Qagan Nur

Dalai Nur

Jingpeng

Xar Moron He

Wudan

Shaoleng He

Yangchangzi He

YIN SHAN (Mts.)
2174

Guyang

Xar Moron

Aibao Gou

Baotou

Shiguaigou

DAQING SHAN

Hohhot

Dai Hai

Huade

Saihan Tal

Ondor Sum

Qagan Nur

Anguli Nur

(Mts.)

Jining

Dongyang He

DAMAQUN SHAN

Bai Hu

Shandian He

Duolun

Taibus Qi

Xiaoluan He

Yimai He

Yinai He

Dashengtang Shan
1754

Weichang

Yixun He

Chifeng

Yelaishou

Laoha He

QIAOTU SHAN

1885

LIAONING

Shaoleng He

Bayan Obo

Tuwei He

Huangqi Hai

Zhangjiakou

Yang He

Xuanhua

Yantong Shan

Fengning

Yunwu Shan

Xingzhou He

Chug He

Miyun Sk.

Chengde

Wuling Shan
1270

Du Shan

Xifengkou

Shanhaiguan

Qinhuangdao

Guyang

Hekou

Hun He

Yungang

Datong

Sanggan He

Guanting Sk.

Bada Ling

Nankou

Miaofeng Shan

BEIJING

BEINING

HEBEI

Tong Xian

Ji Xian

Zunhua

Yuqiao Sk.

Jieshi Shan

Luan Xian

Tangshan

YAN SHAN

Daqinghe

Luanhe Kou

Dongsheng

Dai Hai

Shanyin

Heng Shan
2017

HENG SHAN

Yu Xian

Juma He

Taibai Shan

TAIHANG SHAN (Mts.)

WUTAI SHAN

Langya Shan
1105

Chaobai Xinhe

TIANJIN

Tianjin

Hangu

Tanggu

Tianjin Xingang

Shijiutuo

Caofeidian

Fugu

Hequ

Piankuan He

Pianguan

Shenmu

Kelan

Lanyi He

Ningwu

Guoyangzhen

Wutai Shan
3058

WUTAI
2893

Qingshui He

Baoding

Dasha He

Baiyang Dian

Wen'an Wa

Ziya He

Jiedi Jianhe

Bohai Wan
(Gf.)

BOHAI SEA

Yunzhong Shan

Luya Shan

Guoyangzhen

Mutou Shan

XIZHOU SHAN

Xinzhou

Gangnan

Huangbizhuang Sk.

Niangzi Guan

Xingxing

Huhuo He

Zhulong He

Tang He

Dingzhou

Da Yunhe

Cangzhou

Zangjiaqiao

Heicha Shan

Yangqu

Jingle

Fen He

Mutou

Shijiazhuang

HEBEI

Zhangwei Xinhe

Majia He

Huimin

Huanghe Kou

Loohuanghe Kou

Guandi Shan
2891

Wenyu He

Taiyuan

Yuci

Huaisha He

Zhi He

Fuyang He

Hengshui

2069

Dezhou

Tuhai He

Huang He (Yellow R.)

Lijin

Xiaoqing He

Zhangdian

Weifang

Wubu

Sanchuan He

Fenyang

Dongguan

Sha He

Ming He

Xingtai

Linqing

Zhoucun

LÜLIANG SHAN

Zijing Shan
1935

Fujiatan

Huo Shan
2347

Zhuozhang He

Wuyang

Junji Guan

Handan

Fengfeng

Zhang He

Majia He

Echeng

Tuhai He

Linqing

Jinan

Boshan

Laiwu

TAI SHAN

Yuhuang Ding 1524

Tai'an

LU SHAN

1108

Lu Shan
1032

Yi Shan

Chingzhou

SHANDONG

Xinshui He

Jiexiu

Hukou Pubu

Linfen

TAIYUE SHAN

Anyang He

Anyang

Wei He

Dongping Hu

Dawen He

1027

Xinwen

Mengyin

MENG SHAN
1156

Menglianggu

Ju Xian

Xiayukou

Yumenkou

Long Men

Xinjiang

Houma

Qinshui

Jincheng

Dou He

Hebi

Qi He

Puyang

Si He

Yanzhou

Guimeng Ding

Linyi

JIANGSU

Jiwang Shan
1279

Li Shan
2322

Yuangu

Jiaozuo

Xinxiang

Jining

Baodugu

Shu He

Yi He

Sushui He

Yuncheng

Bo'ai

Renmin

Shengli Qu

Zhaowang He

Nanyang He

Dushan Hu

Zaozhuang

Tai'erzhuang

Xinyi

ZHONGTIAO SHAN

Huang He (Yellow R.)

Sanmenxia Sk.

Jiumengjin

Zhengzhou

Song Shan 1440

HENAN

Huayuankou

Kaifeng

Fei Huang He

Weishan Hu

Tiawang

Pi Xian

JIANGSU

Xuehua Shan
1994

Fenglingdu

Sanmenxia

Luoyang

Luoyang

Huili He

Jialu He

Guo He

Dangshan

Suqian

XIAO SHAN

XIONG'ER SHAN

Quanbao Shan
2094

Lushi

Yi He

Luo He

Befu He

Song He

Ying He

Xuchang

Taikang

Buzhou

Huaibei

ANHUI

SHAANXI

Laojun Shan
2192

WAIFANG SHAN

FUNIU SHAN

Lushan

Pingdingshan

Sha He

Zhoukou

Shenqiu

ANHUI

Huaiyang

Relief (m)

4000
3000
2000
1500
1000
750
500
200
50
0
50

1 : 5 000 000

0   50   100   150 km

37

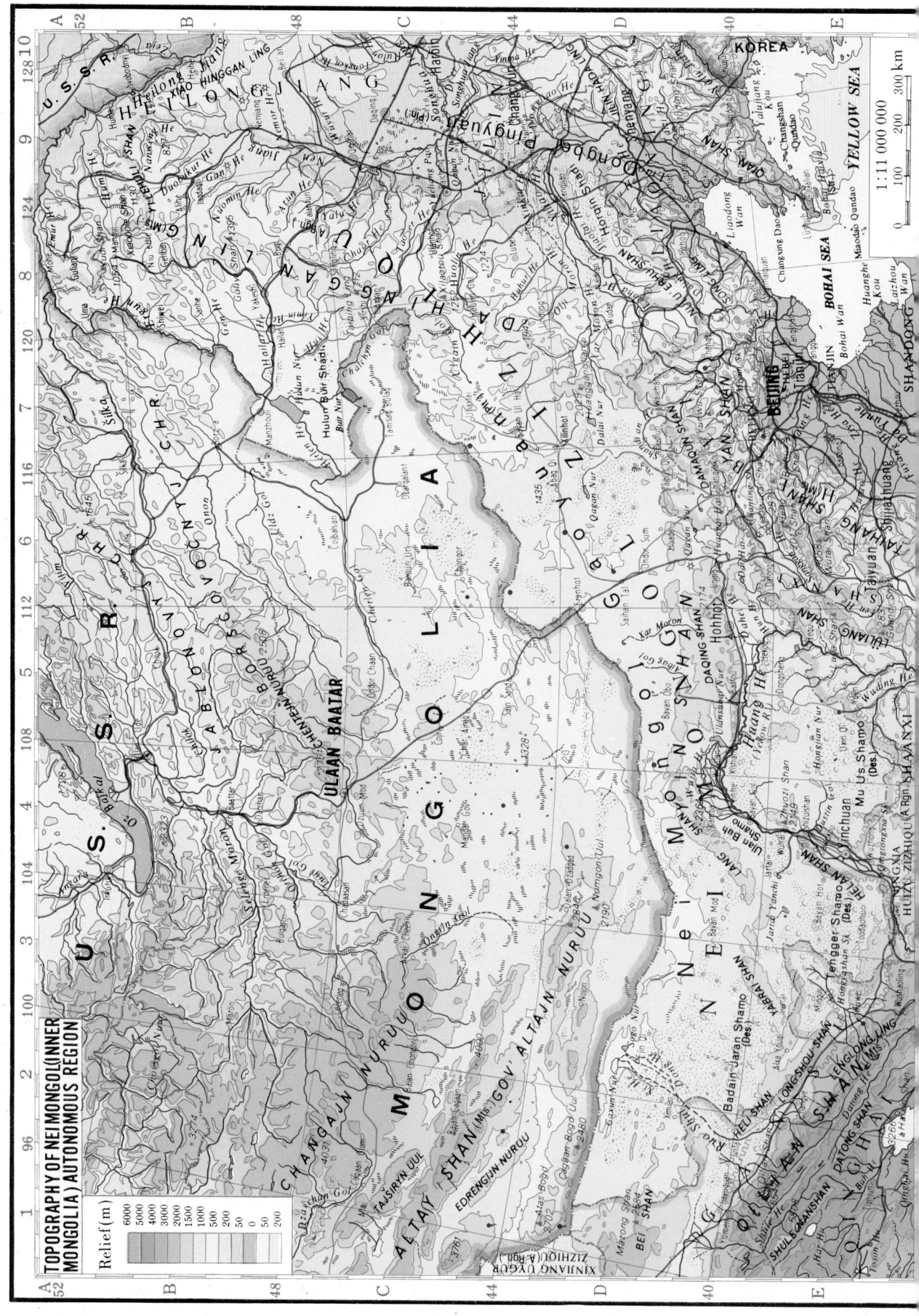

TOPOGRAPHY OF NEI MONGOL (INNER MONGOLIA) AUTONOMOUS REGION

Relief (m)

6000
5000
4000
3000
2000
1500
1000
500
200
50
0
50
200

1 : 11 000 000

0   100   200   300 km

KOREA

YELLOW SEA

BOHAI SEA

BEIJING

U. S. S. R.

HEILONGJIANG

DA HINGGAN LING

XIAO HINGGAN LING

ULAAN BAATAR

MONGOLIA

Nei MONGOL

ALTAY

SHAANXI

QI LIAN SHAN

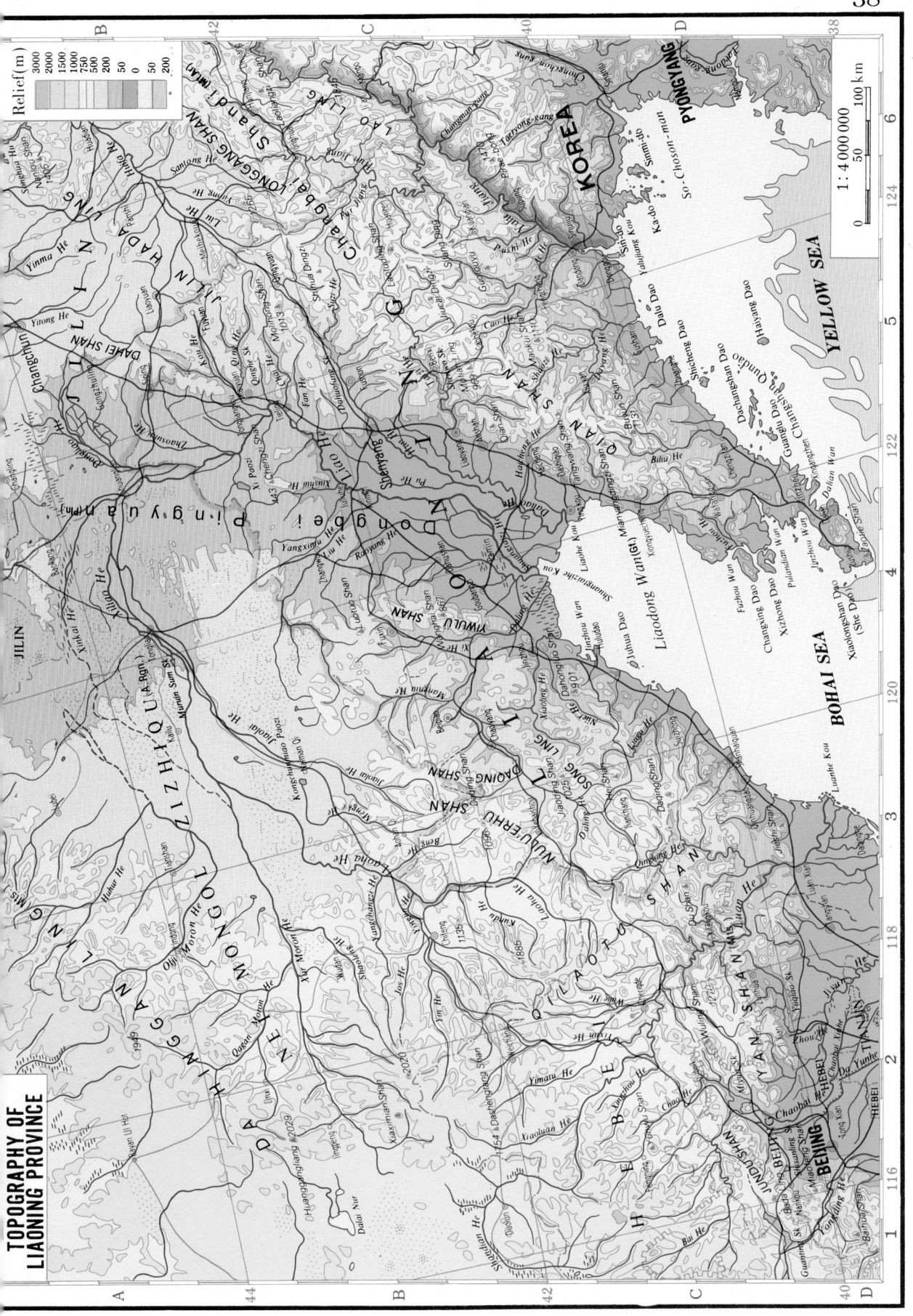

TOPOGRAPHY OF LIAONING PROVINCE

Relief (m)

3000
2000
1500
1000
750
500
200
50
0
50
200

1 : 4 000 000

0   50   100 km

YELLOW SEA

BOHAI SEA

KOREA

PYONGYANG

BEIJING

TIANJIN

HEBEI

JILIN

NEI MONGOL ZIZHIQU

DA HINGGAN LING

JILIN HADA LING

DAHEI SHAN

Changbai YONGGANG SHAN

LAO LING

Changchun

Liaodong Wan (Gulf)

Liaodong Wan

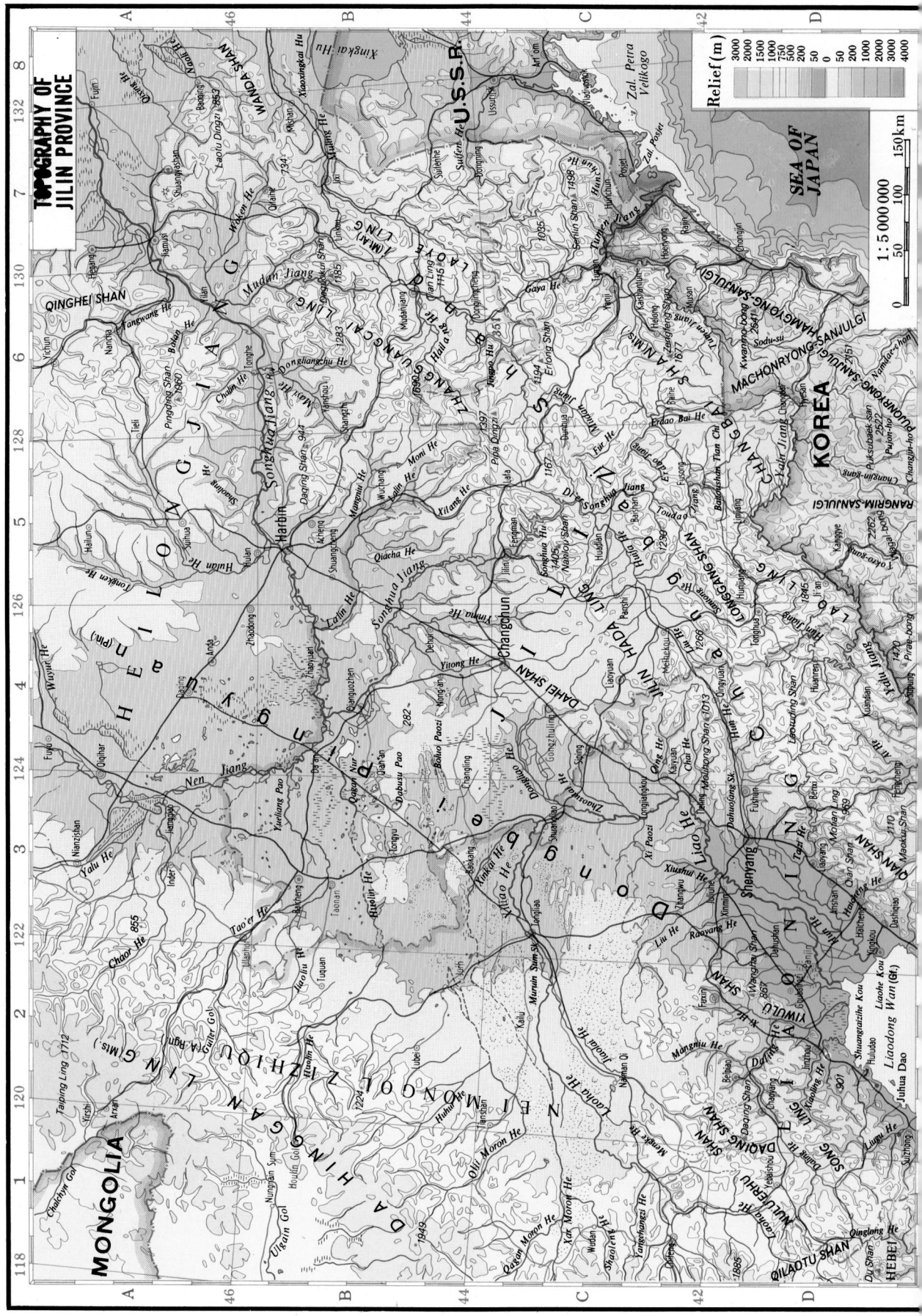

TOPOGRAPHY OF JILIN PROVINCE

Relief (m)

3000 2000 1500 1000 750 500 200 50 0 50 200 1000 2000 3000 4000

1 : 5 000 000

0 50 100 150 km

SEA OF JAPAN

MONGOLIA

HEILONGJIANG (Phn.)

QINGHEI SHAN

NEI MONGOL ZIZHIQU

DAXINGAN LING (Gr. Khingan Mts.)

ZHANGGUANGCAI LING

LAOYE LING (Maj.)

U.S.S.R.

JILIN

LIAONING

KOREA

DAHEI SHAN

JUN HADA LING

CHANGBAI SHAN

LONGGANG SHAN

LAOYE LING

QIAN SHAN

YIWULÜ SHAN

NULU'ERHU SHAN

SONG LING

DAQING SHAN

QILAODTU SHAN

HEBEI

MACHONRYONG-SANJULGI

HAMGYONG-SANJULGI

RANGRIM SANJULGI

PUORYONG-SANJULGI

Harbin

Changchun

Shenyang

Qiqihar

Fuyu

Anda

Daqing

Jilin

Tonghua

Vladivostok

Nongan

Ussurjsk

TOPOGRAPHY OF HEILONGJIANG PROVINCE

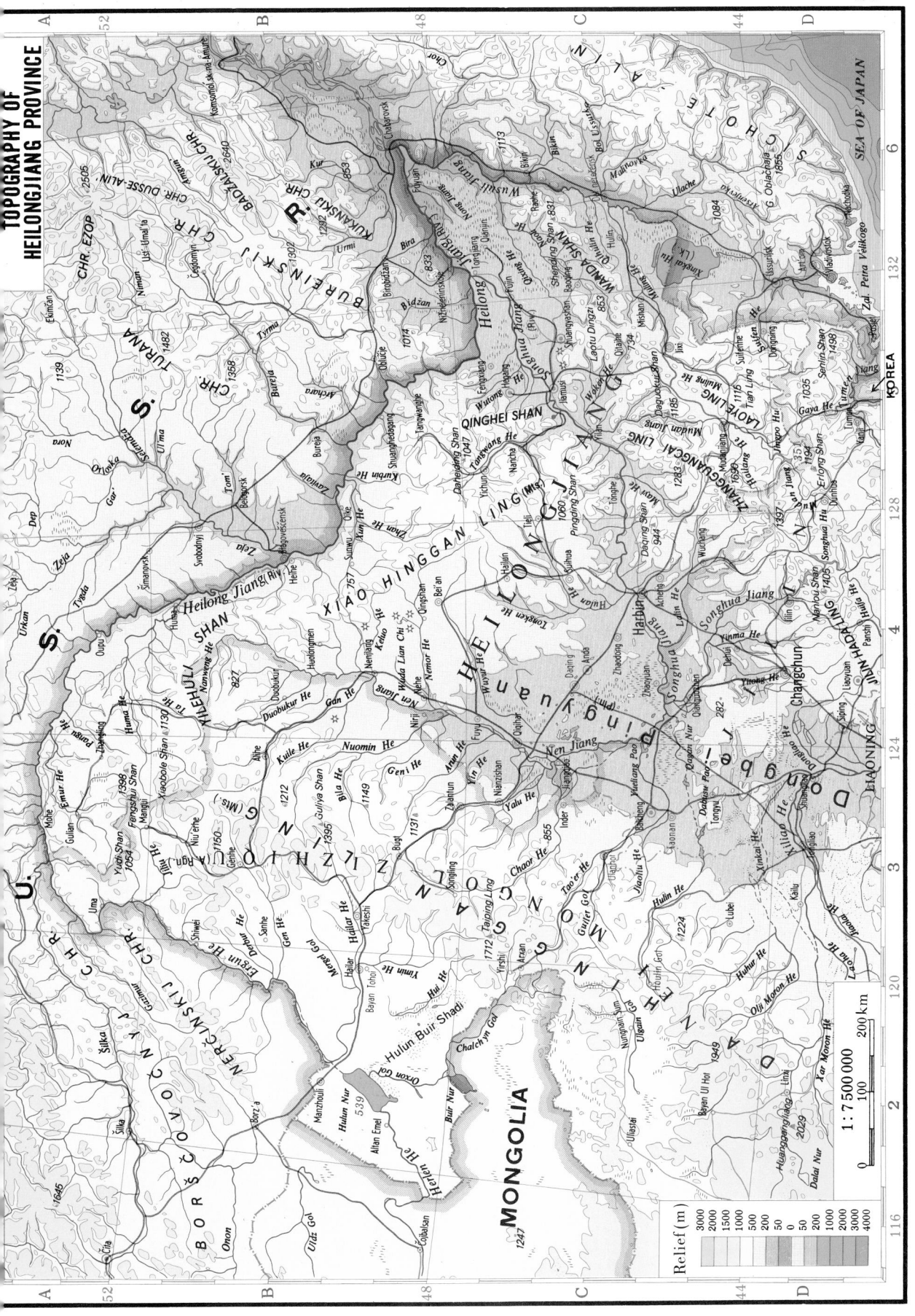

Relief (m)

3000
2000
1500
1000
500
200
50
0
50
200
1000
2000
3000
4000

1 : 7 500 000

0   100   200 km

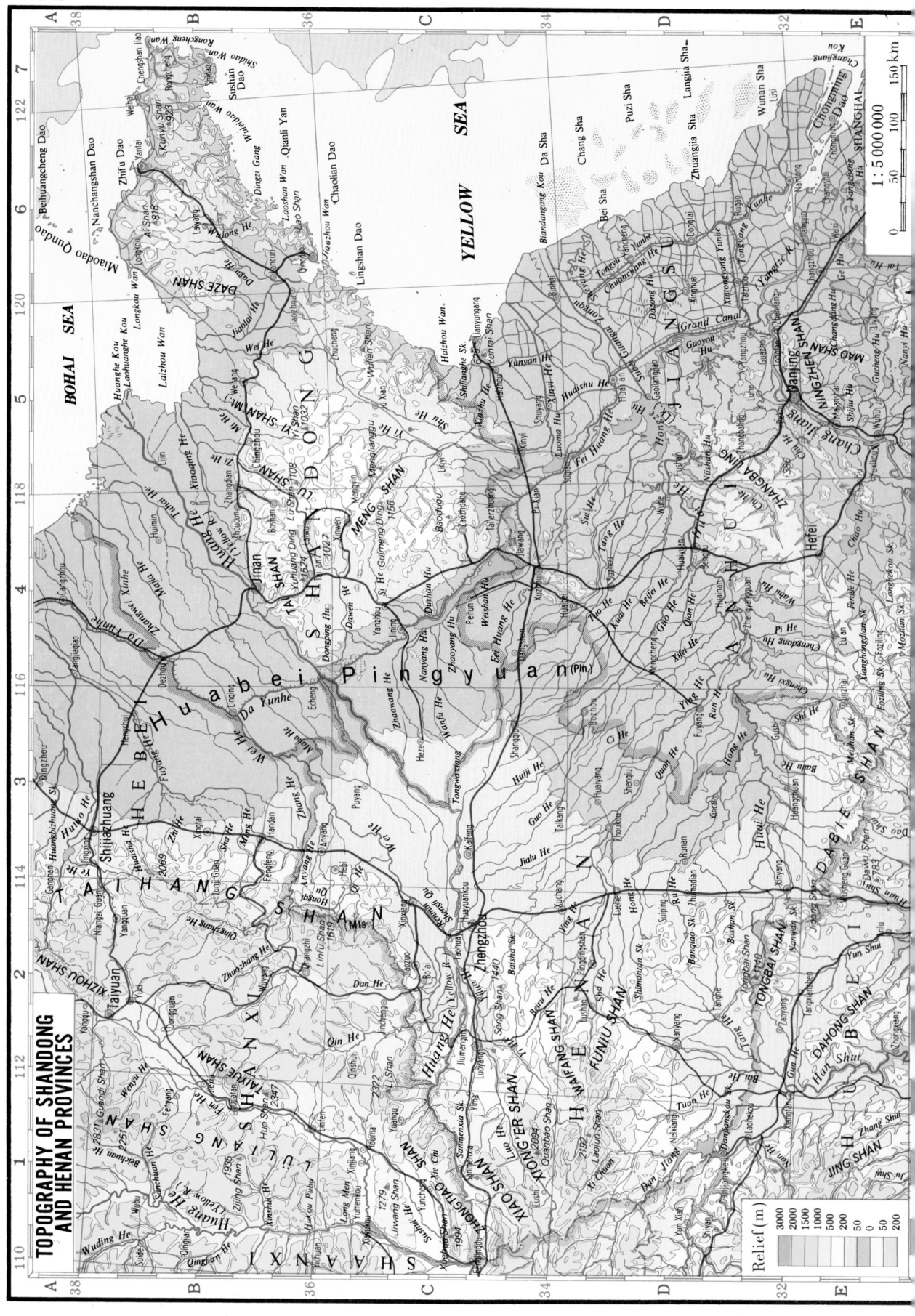

TOPOGRAPHY OF SHANDONG AND HENAN PROVINCES

41

1 : 5 000 000

Relief (m)

3000
2000
1500
1000
500
200
50
0
50
200

TOPOGRAPHY OF SHANGHAI MUNICIPALITY AND JIANGSU, ANHUI, ZHEJIANG PROVINCES

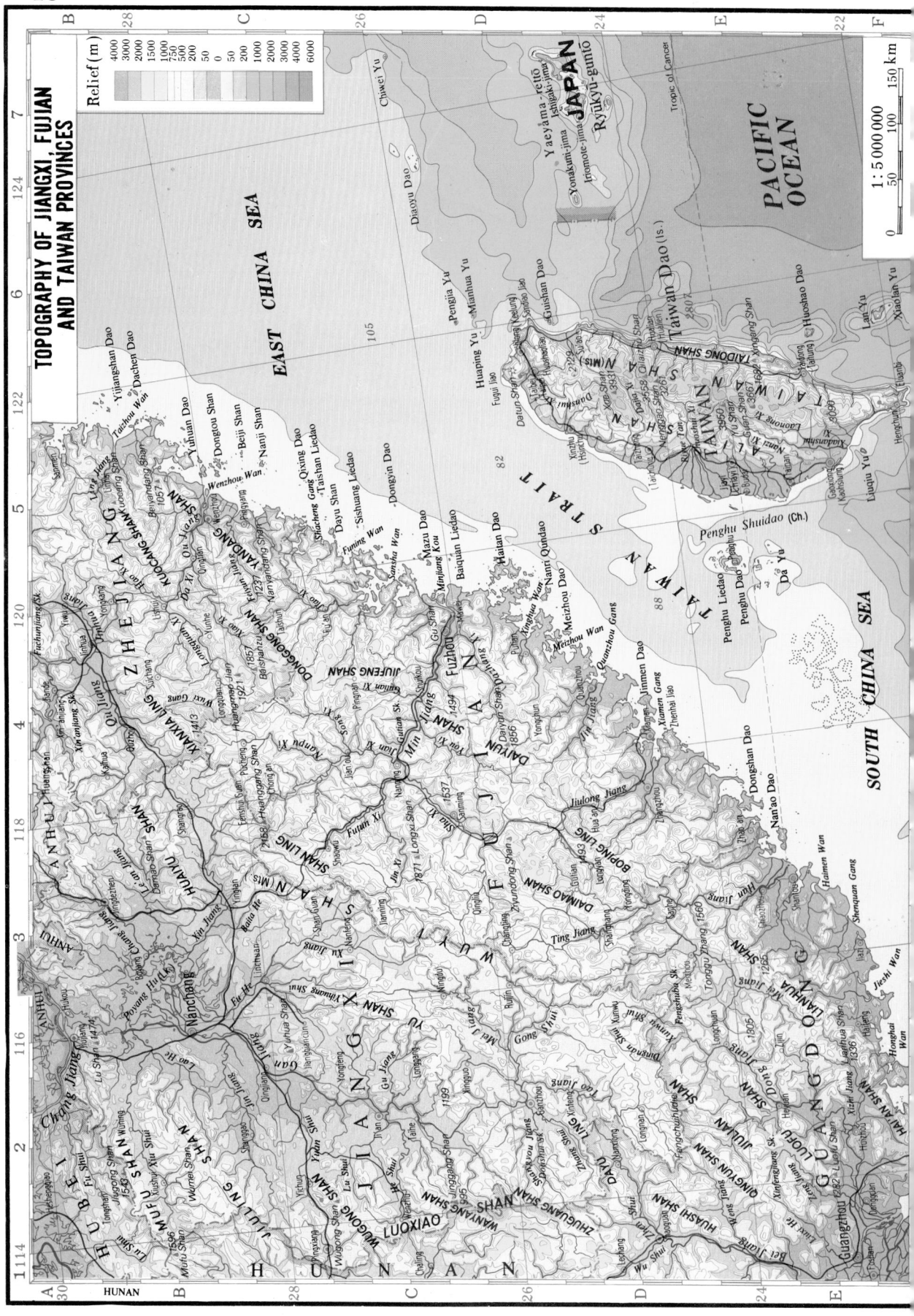

TOPOGRAPHY OF JIANGXI, FUJIAN AND TAIWAN PROVINCES

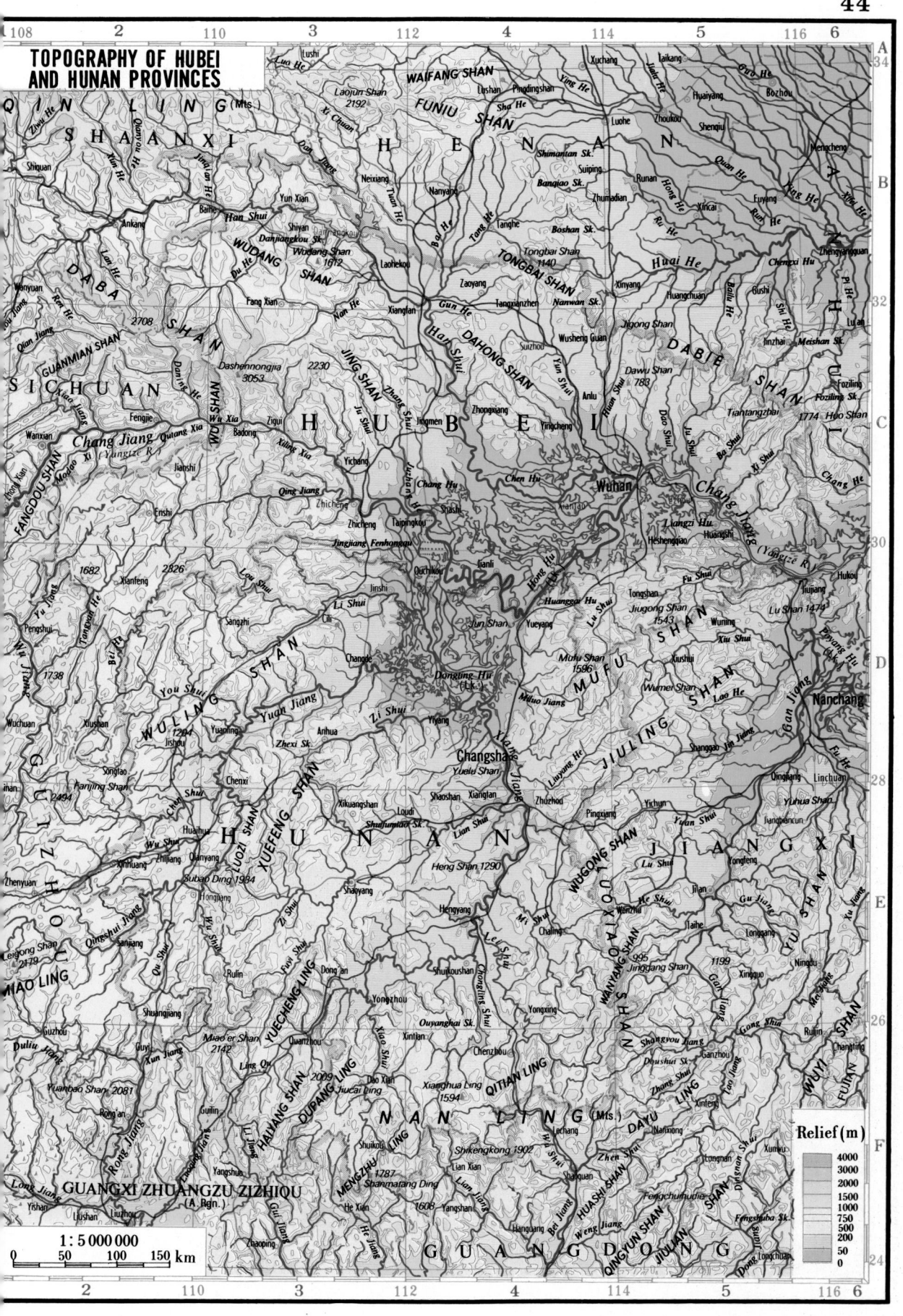

TOPOGRAPHY OF HUBEI AND HUNAN PROVINCES

1 : 5 000 000

0   50   100   150 km

Relief (m)

4000
3000
2000
1500
1000
750
500
200
50
0

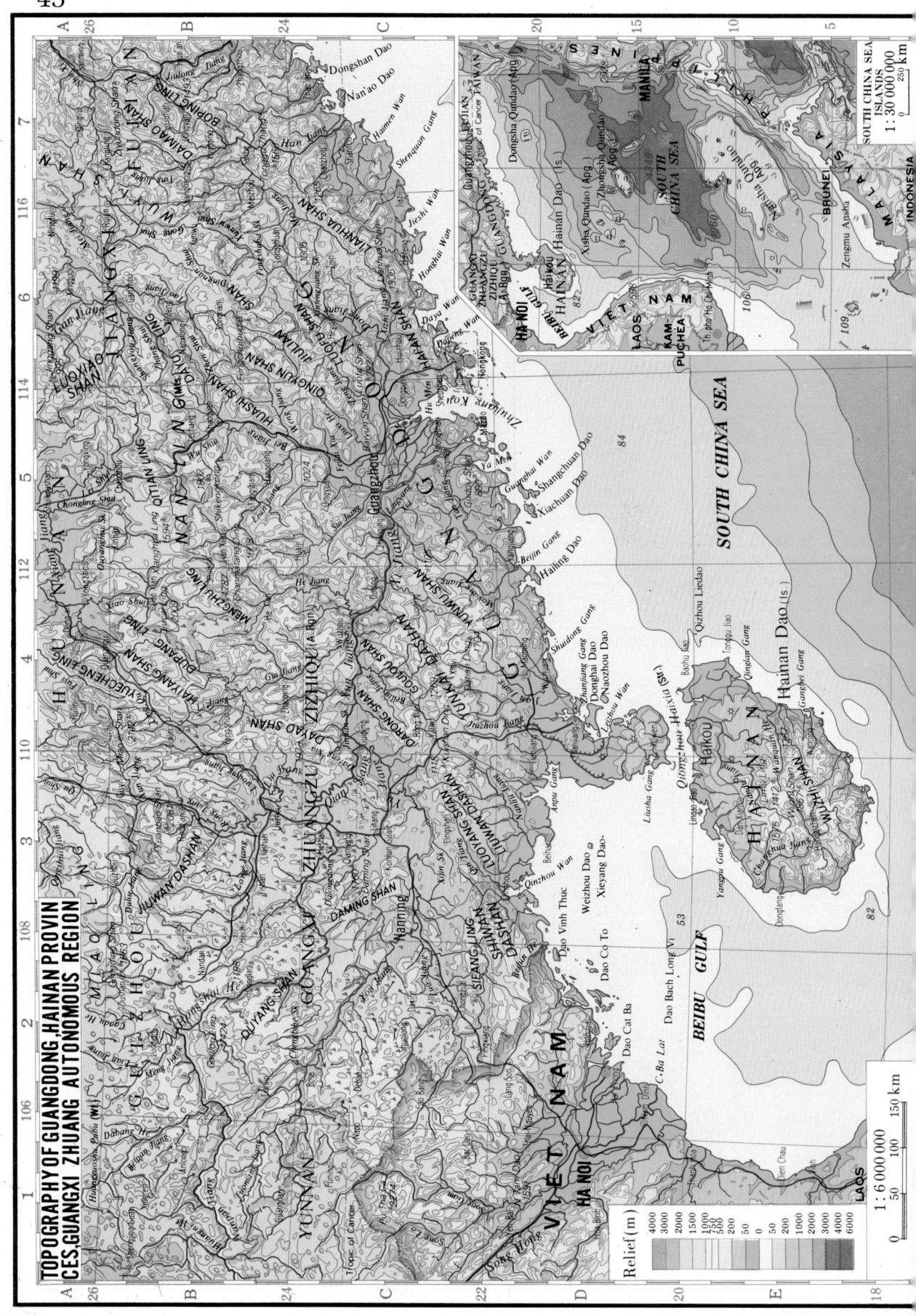

TOPOGRAPHY OF GUANGDONG, HAINAN PROVINCES, GUANGXI ZHUANG AUTONOMOUS REGION

1 : 6 000 000

SOUTH CHINA SEA ISLANDS
1 : 30 000 000

SOUTH CHINA SEA

BEIBU GULF

VIET NAM

HAINAN Dao (Is.)

Hainan Dao (Is.)

Relief (m)

4000 3000 2000 1500 1000 500 200 50 0 50 200 1000 2000 3000 4000 6000

TOPOGRAPHY OF SHAANXI PROVINCE

Relief(m)

6000
5000
4000
3000
2000
1500
1000
500
200
50

1 : 5 000 000

0   50   100   150 km

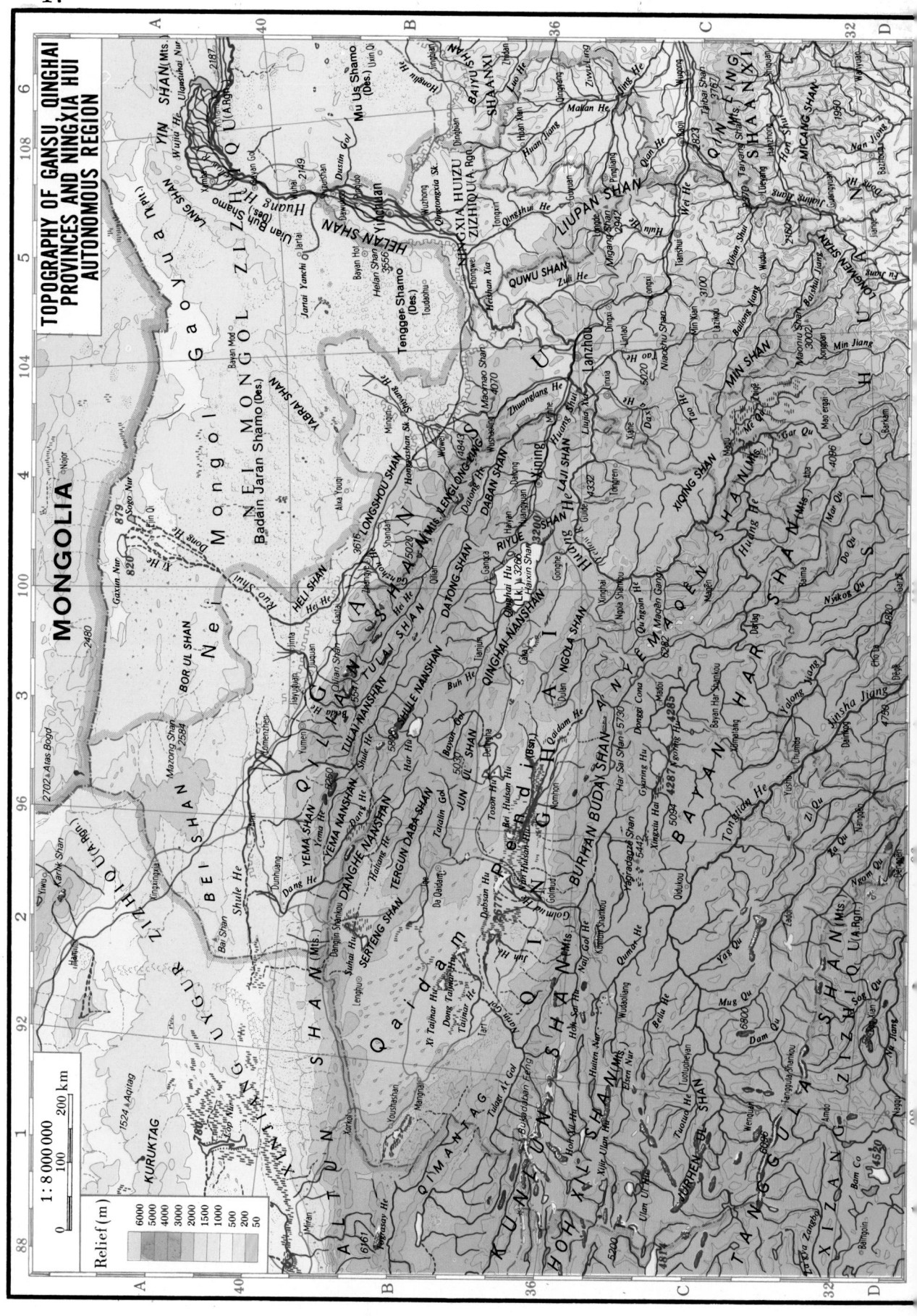

TOPOGRAPHY OF GANSU QINGHAI
PROVINCES AND NINGXIA HUI
AUTONOMOUS REGION

MONGOLIA

1 : 8 000 000

Relief (m)

0   100   200 km

6000
5000
4000
3000
2000
1500
1000
500
200
50

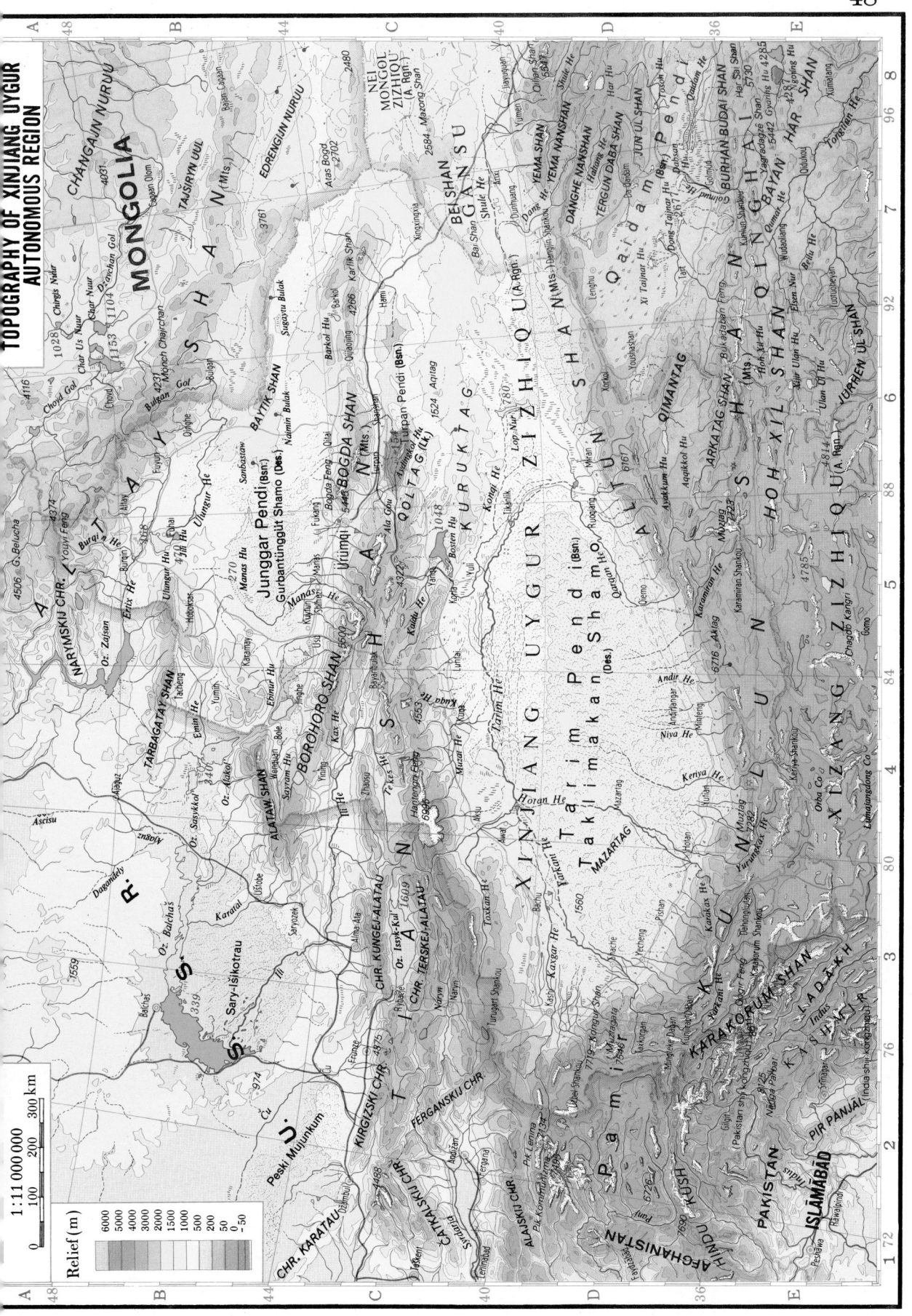

TOPOGRAPHY OF XINJIANG UYGUR AUTONOMOUS REGION

1:11 000 000

0   100   200   300 km

Relief (m)

6000
5000
4000
3000
2000
1500
1000
500
200
50
0
-50

MONGOLIA

CHANGAJN NURUU

TAJŠIRYN UUL

A L T A Y   S H A N (Mts.)

EDRENGIJN NURUU

NARYMSKIJ CHR.

TARBAGATAJ ŠAN

BAYTIK-SHAN

Junggar Pendi (Bsn.)

Gurbantünggüt Shamo (Des.)

BOGDA SHAN (Mts.)

BEISHAN

GANSU

NEI MONGOL ZIZHIQU (A. Rgn.)

BOROHORO SHAN

ALATAW SHAN

T I A N   S H A N

QOLTAG

KURUKTAG

A L T U N   S H A N

NEI MONGOL ZIZHIQU (A. Rgn.)

YEMA SHAN

YEMA NANSHAN

DANGHE NANSHAN

TERGÜN DABA SHAN

JUN UL SHAN

Qaidam Pendi

BURHAN-BUDAI SHAN

HAR SAI SHAN

BAYAN   HAR SHAN

Q I N G H A I

JÜRRÉN UL SHAN

XINJIANG UYGUR ZIZHIQU (A. Rgn.)

Tarim Pendi (Bsn.)

Taklimakan Shamo (Des.)

MAZARTAG

S'S'S'R'

TIAN   SHAN

KIRGIZSKIJ CHR.

CHR. KUNGEJ-ALATAU

CHR. TERSKEJ-ALATAU

FERGANSKIJ CHR.

ČATKALSKIJ CHR.

ALAJSKIJ CHR.

CHR. KARATAU

P a m i r

KARAKORUM SHAN

K U N L U N   S H A N

XIZANG ZIZHIQU (A. Rgn.)

HINDU KUSH

AFGHANISTAN

PAKISTAN

LADAKH

KASMIR

PIR PANJAL

ISLĀMĀBĀD

49

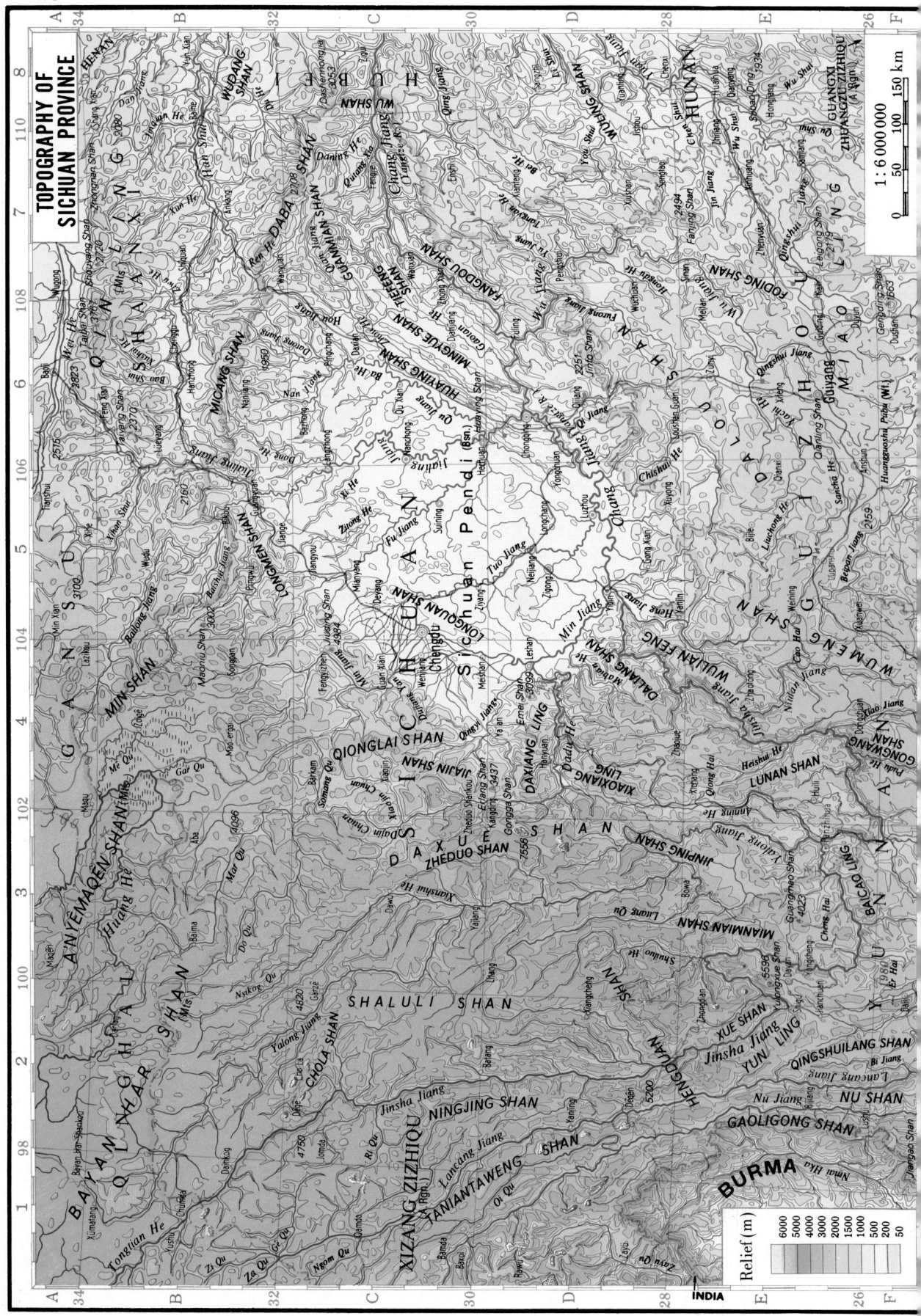

TOPOGRAPHY OF
SICHUAN PROVINCE

1 : 6 000 000

0   50   100   150 km

Relief (m)

6000
5000
4000
3000
2000
1500
1000
500
200
50

TOPOGRAPHY OF YUNNAN AND GUIZHOU PROVINCES

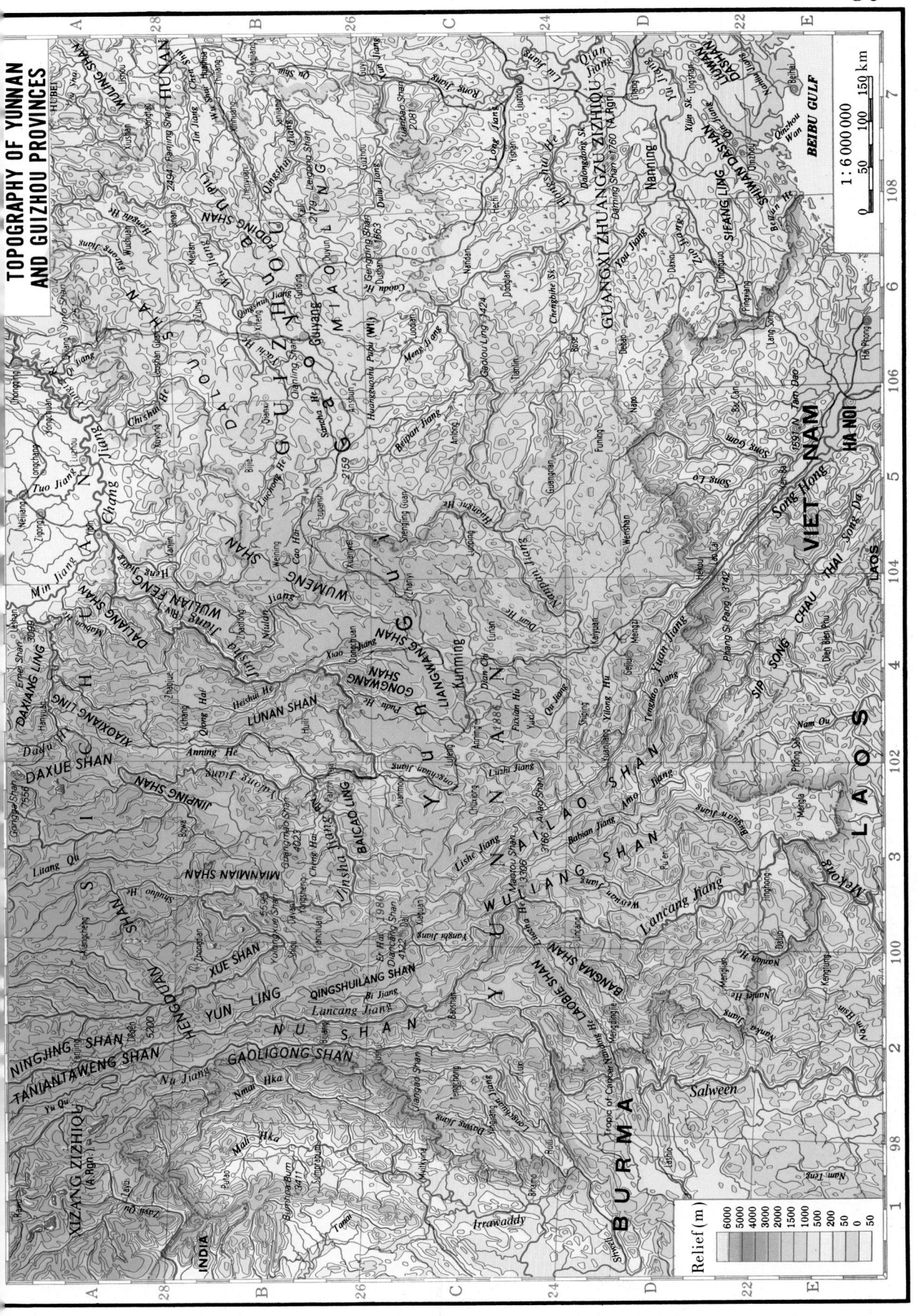

1 : 6 000 000

0 50 100 150 km

Relief (m)
6000
5000
4000
3000
2000
1500
1000
500
200
50
0
50

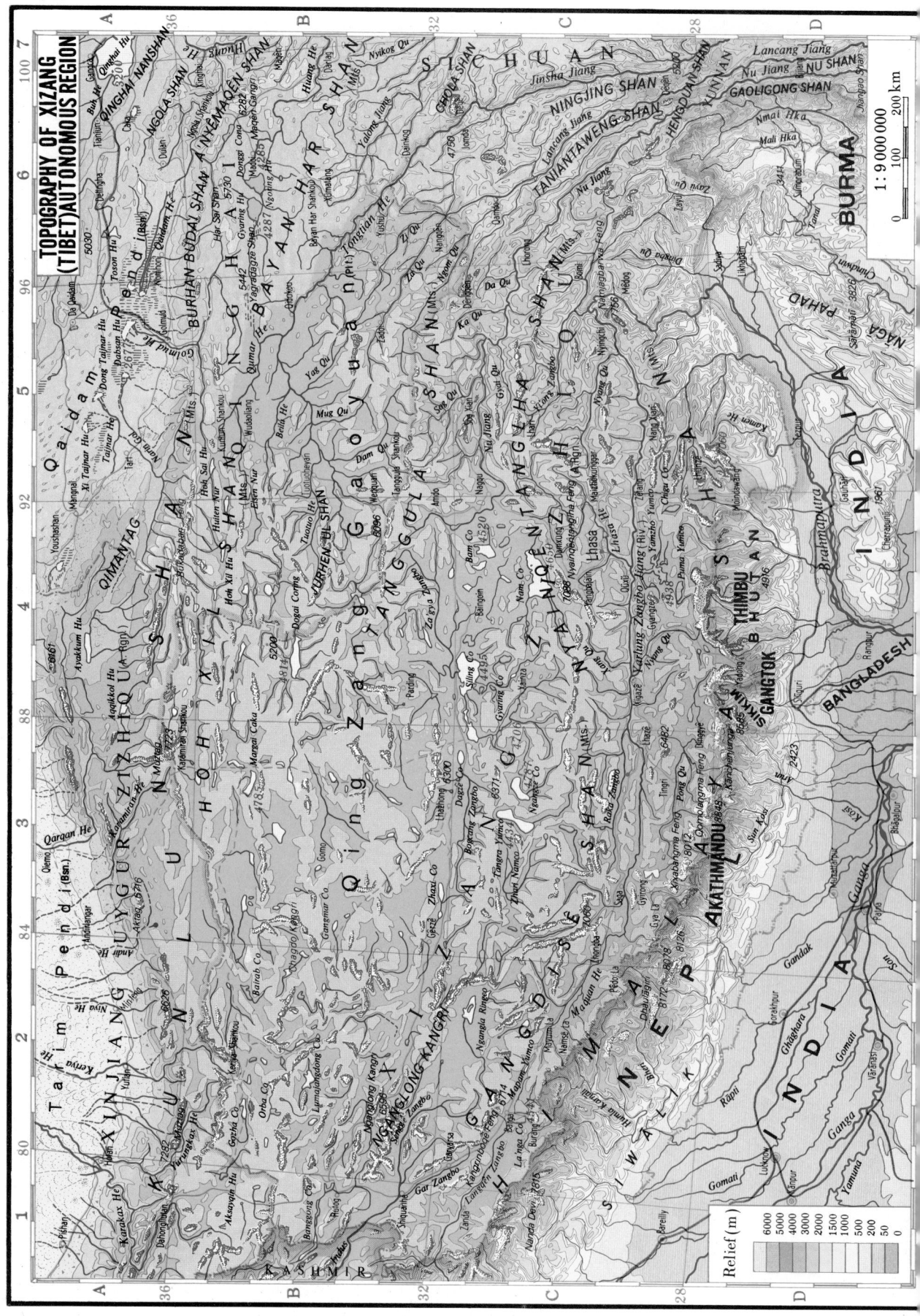

TOPOGRAPHY OF XIZANG (TIBET)AUTONOMOUS REGION

1 : 9 000 000

Relief (m)

6000
5000
4000
3000
2000
1500
1000
500
200
50
0

ATLAS OF
THE PEOPLE'S REPUBLIC
OF CHINA

INDEX TO
PLACE NAMES

ABBREVIATIONS OF PROVINCES, AUTONOMOUS REGIONS AND MUNICIPALITIES DIRECTLY UNDER THE CENTRAL GOVERNMENT

AH—Anhui ·········13

BJ—Beijing·············3

FJ—Fujian·············16

GD—Guangdong ·······21

GS—Gansu············· 27

GX—Guangxi ········· 24

GZ—Guizhou···········32

HB—Hubei·············19

HEB—Hebei············ 4

HEN—Henan···········18

HI—Hainan ·········21

HL—Heilongjiang ······ 9

HN—Hunan············20

JL—Jilin·············8

JS—Jiangsu············11

JX—Jiangxi ·········15

LN—Liaoning ··········· 7

NM—Nei Mongol······· 6

NX—Ningxia ···········26

QH—Qinghai·············28

SC—Sichuan ········· 30

SD—Shandong ········10

SH—Shanghai ·········11

SN—Shaanxi···········25

SX—Shanxi·············5

TJ—Tianjin ·············3

TW—Taiwan············17

XJ—Xinjiang············29

XZ—Xizang···········34

YN—Yunnan ·········33

ZJ—Zhejiang············14

The figure at the right indicates the page number for the map of administrative division of that province in the front section of this book.

A

Name	Region	Pg	Grid
Abag Qi (Xin Hot)	NM	6	C5
Aba (Ngawa)	SC	30	B3
Acheng	HL	9	E4
Adebo	YN	33	D5
Adun Gol	NM	6	D3
Adun Qulu	NM	6	B6
Aganzhen	GS	27	E6
Agong	GZ	32	D4
Agong	QH	28	B7
Aguin Sum	NM	6	E2
A'gyi	SC	30	B4
Ahuzhen	JS	11	B4
Aibag Gol	NM	6	F10
Aicheng	JX	15	B3
Aidong	GX	24	C5
Ai He	LN	7	D8
Aihui	HL	9	B4
Aihuixiang	HL	9	C4
Aijiaping	GZ	32	D3
Aikou	JX	15	B3
Ailao Shan	YN	33	C4
Ailao Shan	YN	33	C4-D4
Ailin	NM	6	B7
Ailing	GX	24	C7
Aimen Guan	AH	13	E2
	HB	19	C8
Ai Shan	SD	10	B7
Aiting	AH	13	D2
Aiwan Wan	ZJ	14	D6
Aiyang	LN	7	D8
Akmeqit	XJ	29	D3
Akqi	XJ	29	C3
Aksay Kazakzu Zizhixian	GS	27	C2
Aksayqin Hu	XJ	29	E3
Aksu He	XJ	29	C4
Aksüme	XJ	29	B4
Aksu	XJ	29	C4
Aktag	XJ	48	D5
Aktaz	XJ	29	D5
Akto	XJ	29	D2
Akxokesay	QH	28	B2
Alag Hu	QH	28	C5
Ala Gou	XJ	29	C5
Alamdo	XZ	34	C5
Alataw Shan	XJ	48	B3-4
Alataw Shankou	XJ	29	B4
(Ałihe) Oroqen Zizhiqi	NM	6	B7
Alishan	TW	17	C3
Ali Shan	TW	17	C3-B4
Alongshan	NM	6	B7
(Altan Emel) Xin Barag Youqi	NM	6	B6
(Altan Xiret) Ejin Horo Qi	NM	6	E4
Altay Shan (Mts.)	XJ	29	B6-7
Altay	XJ	29	B6
Altay Yuchang	XJ	29	B5
Altenqoke	QH	28	B4
Altun Shan (Mts.)	QH	28	A1-3
	XJ	29	D6-7
Alxa Youqi (Ehen Hudag)	NM	6	E2
Alxa Zuoqi (Bayan Hot)	NM	6	E3
Amdo	XZ	34	B4
Ameng	YN	33	D6
(Amgalang) Xin Barag Zuoqi	NM	6	B6
Amgalang Bulag	NM	6	B6
Amiling	XZ	34	C5
Amo Jiang	YN	33	D4
Amqog	GS	27	E6
Anbei	GS	27	B3
Anbianbu	SN	25	C4
Anbianzhen	SC	30	D5
Anbo	LN	7	E6
Anbo Shazhou	HI	22	E3
Anbu	GD	21	B6
Anchang	ZJ	14	B5
Anchangzhen	GZ	32	B6
Anchungoumen	HEB	3	A4
Anci	HEB	4	D4
Anda	HL	9	D3
Ande	GX	24	D4
Ande	SC	31	A1
Andi	GZ	32	C5
Anding	SN	25	C5
Andingpu	NX	26	C4
Anding Zhan	BJ	3	C3
Andir He	XJ	29	D4
Andirlangar	XJ	29	D4
Andong	ZJ	14	B6
Andongwei	SD	10	D6
Andun	GD	21	B5
Andu Tan	HI	22	E3
Anfeng	JS	11	C5
Anfeng	JS	11	C6
Anfeng	JS	11	D6
Anfengqiao	FJ	16	D4
Anfu	JX	15	E3
Anfu	JX	15	D2
Anfuzhen	SC	31	D2
Anfuzhen	SC	31	D3
Ang'angxi	HL	9	D2
Angao	HEN	18	D4
Angdong	HN	20	C2
Angou	SN	25	D6
Anguang	JL	8	B4
Anguli Nur	HEB	4	B2
Anguo	GS	26	E3
Anguo	HEB	4	E3
Anhai	FJ	16	F4
Anhe	GX	24	B8
An He	JS	11	C4
Anhou	FJ	16	F3
Anhua	ZJ	14	C5
Anhua (Dongping)	HN	20	C4
Anji	FJ	16	D4
Anji	HB	19	C5
Anjia	HL	9	E4
Anjiabu	HEB	4	C2
(Anjiang) Qianyang	HN	20	D3
Anjiang	HEB	4	C5
(Anjiangying) Luanping	HEB	4	C5
Anjiashe	JS	11	E5
Anjiazhuang	SD	10	D3
Anjihai	XJ	29	B5
Anji	ZJ	14	B4
Anju	SD	10	D3
Anju	HB	19	C6
Anju	SC	30	C5
Anju	SC	31	A3
Anjuzhen	SC	30	D6
Ankang (Xing'an)	SN	25	H5
Ankou	GS	27	E8
Ankouzhen	JL	8	E6
Ankyam	SC	30	B3
Anle	FJ	16	D2
Anling	HEB	4	F4
Anlinzhan	SD	10	C3
Anliu	GD	21	B5
Anlong	GZ	32	E4
Anlu	HB	19	C6
Anmin	LN	7	B8
Anning	SC	30	C4
Anning He	SC	30	E4
Anning	YN	33	C5
Anping	HEB	4	D4
Anping	LN	7	C7
Anping	TW	17	C3
Anping	HEN	18	D7
Anping	HN	20	E6
Anping	HEB	4	E3
Anpu	GD	21	C3
Anpu Gang	GD	21	C2
Anqing	AH	13	F4
Anqiu	SD	10	C6
Anren	SD	10	C3

Baidong He	GX	24	C4	Bailang	NM	6	C7	Bain'yai	SC	30	B4
Baidu	GD	21	A6	Bailang He	SD	10	C6-B6	Baipeng	GX	24	C7
Baidun	HB	19	E7	Baile	HEB	3	B1	Baipu	JS	11	D6
Baidunzi	GS	27	B2	Baile	GX	24	C4	Baiqên	QH	28	D7
Baidunzi	GS	27	D7	Baili	JL	8	E9	Baiqi	HEB	4	C5
Baiduqiao	AH	13	E5	Bailian	FJ	16	D3	Baiqiu	HEN	18	E4
Bai'e	JX	15	F3	Bailiangzhen	SN	25	E6	Baiquan	JL	8	E5
Baifang	HN	20	E5	Bailianhe Sk.	HB	19	D8	Baiquan	ZJ	14	B7
Baifusi	HB	19	E2	Bailicun	GX	24	B8	Baiquan	HEN	18	B5
Baigezhuang	HEB	4	D6	Bailin	FJ	16	C6	Baiquan Liedao	FJ	16	E5
Baigou	HEB	4	D4	Bailin	HN	20	E6	Baiquan	HL	9	D4
Baigou He	HEB	4	D4	Bailin	SC	31	D4	Baiquesi	SN	25	G2
(Baiguan) Shangyu	ZJ	14	B5	Bailin	SC	31	D5	Baiqueyuan	HEN	18	F7
				(Bailingmiao)	NM	6	D4	Bairab Co	XZ	34	B2
Baiguantun	HEB	3	B5	Darhan Muminggan				Bairin Qiao	NM	6	D6
Baigui	SX	5	D4	Lianheqi				Bairin Youqi	NM	6	D6
Baiguo	HB	19	C7	Bailong	SN	25	G3	Bairin Zuoqi	NM	6	D6
Baiguo	HN	20	D5	Bailong (Hadapu)	GS	27	E7	(Lindong)			
Baiguo	GZ	32	D3	Bailong Jiang	GS	27	F7	Bairuopu	HN	20	C5
Baiguoba	HB	19	E2	Bailu He	HEN	18	E7	Baisang	HB	19	B3
Baiguoshi	HN	20	E5	Bailuoji	HB	19	E6	(Baisha) Jiande	ZJ	14	C4
Baihanchang	YN	33	B3	Bailutang	ZJ	14	B5	Baisha	JX	15	E3
Baihao	GD	23	H7	Baima	JS	12	B2	Baisha	FJ	16	E3
Baihe	HEB	3	D1	Baima	GD	23	H7	Baisha	FJ	16	E4
Baihe	SC	31	C3	Baima	GX	24	E8	Baisha	TW	17	C2
Baihe	JL	8	E9	Baima	NX	26	C2	Baisha	HEN	18	C4
Baihe	TW	17	C3	Baima	SC	31	B3	Baisha	HEN	18	C5
Baihe	ZJ	14	C5	Baima	SC	31	D2	Baisha	HEN	18	C5
Baihe	HEN	18	C4	Baima	SC	31	D6	Baisha	HN	20	C7
Baihe	GX	24	E7	Baimachang	SC	31	C2	Baisha	HN	20	E5
Bai He	BJ	3	A3	Baimachuan	HEB	3	A5	Baisha	GD	21	A4
	HEB	4	C3	Baima Hu	JS	11	C5	Baisha	GD	21	B4
Bai He	HEN	18	E4	Baimajing	HI	21	D2	Baisha	GX	24	C8
Baihebu	BJ	3	A3	Baimamiao	SC	31	C3	Baisha	GX	24	D7
Baihegang	SH	12	C5	Baimangshen	SX	5	B5	Baisha	GX	24	F7
Baihe	SN	25	H6	Baimangying	HN	20	G4	Baisha	SC	30	D6
Baihou	GD	21	A6	Baimao	JS	11	E6	Baisha	SC	31	D4
Baihu	AH	13	E4	Baimao He	JS	12	B5	Baisha	SC	31	D5
Baihua	SC	31	D2	Baimao Kou	JS	12	B5	Baisha	GZ	32	C7
Baihuapai	NM	9	B3	Baimaoping	HN	20	E3	Baisha	FJ	16	E2
Baihua Shan	BJ	3	B2	Baimashi	ZJ	14	C3	Baisha Dao	TW	17	C2
Baihugou	HEB	4	B5	Baimasi	HEN	18	C4	Baisha Gongnongqu	SC	30	C7
Baihuyao	SX	5	E4	Baimasi	HN	20	C5	Baishaguan	JX	15	B6
Baiji	GX	24	E6	Baimatan	SN	25	E6	Baishaling	JX	15	B2
Baijia	JX	15	E2	Baima	QH	28	D7	Baishan	JL	8	E8
Baijiachuan	SN	25	C6	Baimayi	HEN	18	D7	Baishan	GX	24	C7
Baijiadian	SD	10	D3	Baimi	JS	11	D6	Baishan	HEN	18	B5
Baijian	HEB	4	D3	Baimianxia	SN	25	G3	Bai Shan	ZJ	12	D6
Baijiang	ZJ	14	C4	Baimiao	HEN	18	C7	Bai Shan	GS	27	B1
Baijiantan	XJ	29	B5	Baimiaozi	LN	7	D4	Baishanji	AH	13	C3
Baijiao	GD	23	I7	Baina	GZ	32	C4	Baishanzu	ZJ	14	E4
Baijiaping	HN	20	F4	Bainang	XZ	34	C4	Baishapu	HB	19	E8
Baijiazhuang	SX	5	D4	Baingoin	XZ	34	C4	Baisha Shan	ZJ	12	E7
Baijie	SC	31	D5	Baini	GD	23	G6	Baisha Sk.	HEN	18	C5
Baijie Shan	ZJ	12	D7	Baini	GD	23	H6	Baishatan	SD	10	C8
Baijin	JL	8	E10	(Baini) Yuqing	GZ	32	C6	Baisha (Yacha)	HI	21	D2
Baijin	GZ	32	D5	Bainijing	NM	6	F10	Baishe	JX	15	D4
Baiju	JS	11	C6	Bainiqiao	HB	19	E7	Baishi	ZJ	14	D5
Baijuanzi	NX	26	C2	Bainiu	HEN	18	E4	Baishi	GD	23	G6
Bailak	GZ	32	C5	Bainiuqiao	ZJ	12	E2	Baishi Feng	FJ	16	D2

Baishilazi	HL	9	B4
Baishishan	JL	8	D8
Baishishan	AH	13	E4
Baishiyi	SC	30	D6
Baishui	ZJ	14	B4
Baishui	JX	15	D3
Baishui	FJ	16	F3
Baishui	HN	20	C6
Baishui	HN	20	E4
Baishui	GS	26	E3
Baishui	SC	30	B5
Baishui	SC	30	B6
Baishuifan	HB	19	D8
Baishuihe	SC	31	A1
Baishuijiang	SN	25	G2
Baishui Jiang	GS	27	F7
Baishuijing	LN	7	E5
Baishui	SN	25	E5
Baishuiyang	ZJ	14	D5
Baisong Guan	FJ	16	F2
	GD	21	A6
Baisuo	GZ	32	E5
Baita	ZJ	14	D5
Baita	GS	26	D2
Baitabu	JS	11	B4
Baita He	JX	15	C5-D5
Baitang	QH	28	D5
Baitang	GD	23	G8
Baitaozhen	SC	31	C6
Baitapu	HEB	3	D2
Baitapu	LN	7	C7
Baitiao He	SC	31	A1-2
Baitou	SC	31	B1
Baitoushan Tian Chi	JL	8	E9
Baitu	FJ	16	E3
Baitu	GD	21	A4
Baitu	GD	23	H6
Baitu	GX	24	C6
Baitu	JS	11	E5
Baitugang	HEN	18	D4
Baitugang	NX	26	C3
Baituwanzi	GS	27	C3
Baiwang	SC	30	C3
Baiwang	GX	24	C6
Baiwen	SX	5	C3
Baixi	ZJ	14	D6
Baixi	AH	13	G4
Baixiang	HEN	18	B4
Baixiang	HEB	4	F2
Baixing	GZ	32	D4
Baixingt	NM	6	D7
Baixu	GX	24	D6
Baiya	NX	26	D2
Baiyan	ZJ	12	C3
Baiyan	ZJ	14	D5
Baiyang	HEN	18	C4
Baiyang	HB	19	D4
Baiyang	FJ	16	C5
Baiyangba	HB	19	D1
Baiyang Dian	HEB	4	E4
Baiyanggou	LN	7	D6
Baiyanghe	XJ	29	C6
Baiyangping	HB	19	D2
Baiyangtian	HN	20	B6
(Baiyashi) Dong'an	HN	20	E4
Baiyin	GS	27	D7
Baiyinna	HL	9	A3
Baiytigoinba	QH	28	D7
Baiyun	FJ	16	D4
Baiyun Shan	JX	15	E3
Baiyun Shan	GD	45	C5
Baiyu Shan	SN	25	C4
Baiyü	SC	30	C2
Baizao	JS	11	B5
Baizhang	SC	30	C4
Baizhangji	ZJ	14	E5
Baizhangkou	ZJ	14	E4
Baizhitai	HN	20	B4
Baizi	SX	5	E4
Baizi	SC	30	C5
Baizi	SC	31	B4
Bajia	GD	21	C3
Bajiao	SX	5	B3
Bajiao	HB	19	D2
Bajiaoba	GZ	31	D6
Bajiaochang	SC	31	A5
Bajiaotai	LN	7	C5
Bajiazi	LN	7	B5
Bajiazi	LN	7	D4
Bajiazi	JL	8	E10
Bajie	GZ	32	F4
Bajilei	JL	8	C5
Bajing	JX	15	C3
Bajoi	SC	30	C3
Bakai	GZ	32	E7
Bakeshiying	HEB	4	C5
Bakeshu	LN	7	B8
Bala	GX	24	B5
Balai	GZ	32	D4
Balang	JL	8	B5
Balan He	HL	39	A6
Balguntay	XJ	29	C5
Bali	TW	17	A4
Balidianzi	LN	7	C8
Baliguan	SN	25	G3
Balihan	NM	6	D6
Balin	NM	6	B7
Baling	GZ	32	E4
Balingshe	TW	17	B4
Baliying	HEN	18	B6
Balizhuang	LN	7	B7
Balougou	SX	5	C3
Baluo	GZ	32	E8
Bamao	ZJ	14	C5
Bama Yaozu Zizhixian	GX	24	C5
Bam Co	XZ	34	C4
Bamda	XZ	34	C6
Bamian	GX	24	B6
Bamiancheng	LN	7	A8
Bamian Shan	HN	20	F6
Bamianshanzhao	JL	8	B4
(Bamiantong) Muling	HL	9	E6
Banbar	XZ	34	C5
Banbishan	HEB	4	C5
Bancheng	JS	11	C4
Bandong	FJ	16	D4
Bandong	HEB	3	D3
Banfangzi	SN	25	G4
Bangdag Co	XZ	34	B2
Bangdong	GZ	32	D8
Bangong Co	XZ	34	B1
Bangjun	TJ	3	B4
Bangkog Co	XZ	34	C4
Bangma Shan	YN	33	D3-C3
Bangtou	FJ	16	E4
Bangun	GX	24	E5
Bangxu	GX	24	D5
Bangyan He	JS	11	D5-6
Bangzha	GZ	32	F3
Bangzhen	SH	12	B5
Banhong	YN	33	D3
Banhu	JS	11	C5
Banjia	YN	33	D3
Banjiang	GX	24	B7
Banjiegou	XJ	29	C6
Banjieta	HEB	4	B5
Banjin	JS	11	D6
Bankengting	FJ	16	D4
Banlamen	LN	7	C6
Banlan	GX	24	B7
Banlashanmen	JL	8	D5
Banli	GX	24	E5
Banling	GX	24	C5
Banmian	FJ	16	D4
Banmian Shan	ZJ	14	E6
Banmo	GX	24	C5
Banpocun	SX	5	F3
Banpu	JS	11	B5
Banqiao	BJ	3	B2
Banqiao	JS	11	E4
Banqiao	JS	12	A2
Banqiao	AH	13	C3
Banqiao	AH	13	D4
(Banqiao) Taibei (Taipei)	TW	17	A4
Banqiao	HEN	18	D5
Banqiao	HB	19	C4
Banqiao	HB	19	C5
Banqiao	HN	20	E5
Banqiao	GS	27	C5
Banqiao	SC	31	C4
Banqiao	SC	31	D3
Banqiao	GZ	32	C5
Banqiao	YN	33	B6
Banqiao	YN	33	B6
Banqiao	YN	33	C3
Banqiao	YN	33	C5

Banqiao	YN	33	C6	Baolin	HL	9	E5	Batongguan	TW	17	C3
Banqiaoji	AH	13	D3	Baolin	SC	31	B3	Batou	GX	24	D4
Banqiao Sk.	HEN	18	E5	Baolizhen	LN	7	B7	Batuyingzi	LN	7	C4
Banquan	SD	10	D5	Baoluan	SC	31	C6	Bawangcheng	AH	13	C4
Banshanping	HEN	18	D4	Baonian	JS	11	E5	Bawangling	HI	21	D2
Banshanpu	HN	20	D6	Baoping	GX	24	C5	Baweigang	JS	11	E6
Banshi	JX	15	F3	(Baoqing) Shaoyang	HN	20	D4	Bawolung	SC	30	D3
Bantaji	AH	13	D5					Baxi	SC	30	B4
Bantao	GX	24	C3	Baoqing	HL	9	D7	Baxian	SN	25	H5
Banxi	GZ	32	B7	Baoquan	HL	9	D3	Ba Xian	SC	30	D6
Banyanzhen	SN	25	G5	Baoquan	SD	10	C6	Ba Xian	HEB	4	D4
Banyue Jiao	HI	22	D3	Baoquanling	HL	9	D6	Baxin	YN	33	D5
Banzha	JS	11	C5	Baoshan	HL	9	C3	Bəxkorgan	XJ	29	D6
Bao'an	ZJ	14	D3	Baoshan	YN	33	B6	Baxoi	XZ	34	C6
Bao'an	HEN	18	D5					Baxu	GX	24	C5
Bao'an	HB	19	D7	Baoshansi	BJ	3	A3	Baxu	GD	15	G2
Bao'an	GX	24	B7	Baoshan	SH	11	E7	(Bay) Baicheng	XJ	29	C4
Bao'an	GX	24	C5	Baoshan	YN	33	C3	Bayan	QH	28	B7
(Bao'an) Zhidan	SN	25	D4	Baoshi	HEB	3	C1	Bayan	QH	28	C5
				Baoshou	JL	8	C7	Bayanbulak	XJ	29	C5
Bao'an	SN	25	F5	Bao Shui	SN	25	G3	(Bayan Gol) Dengkou	NM	6	F10
Bao'an	QH	28	C8	Baota	NX	26	B3				
Baoban	HI	21	D2	Baotian	GZ	32	E3	Bayan Gol	QH	28	B5
Baochang	JS	12	A5	Baoting	HI	21	D2	Bayan Har	NM	6	D5
(Baochang) Taibus Qi	NM	6	D5	Baotou	NM	6	D4	Bayan Har Shan(Mts.)	QH	28	C5-D6
				Baoxia	HB	19	B3	Bayan Har Shankou	QH	28	C5
Baocheng	SN	25	G2	Baoxing	HL	9	C6	(Bayan Hot) Alxa	NM	6	E3
Baode	SX	5	B3	Baoxing	SC	30	C4	Zuoqi			
Baodian	SD	10	B3	Baoxinji	HEN	18	E6	Bayan Hua	NM	6	F10
Baodian	SX	5	E4	Baoxiu	YN	33	D5	(Bayan Huxu) Horqin	NM	8	B2
				Baoxu	GD	21	B3	Youyi Zhongqi			
Baoding	HEB	4	E3	Baoxu	GX	24	E4	Bayan Mod	NM	6	D3
Baodi	TJ	3	C4	Baoyi	AH	13	D3	Bayannur Meng	NM	6	D3-4
Baodong	HL	9	E7	Baoying	JS	11	C5	Bayan Obo	NM	6	D4
Baodugu	SD	10	E4	(Baoyou) Ledong	GD	21	D2	Bayan Qagan	HL	9	D3
Baofeng	HB	19	B3					Bayan Qagan	NM	6	F10
Baofeng	NX	26	A3	Baqên	XZ	34	B5	(Bayan Qagan) Qahar	NM	6	F10
Baofeng	HEN	18	D5	Baqên	XZ	34	C5	Youyi Houqi			
Baofu	ZJ	14	B4	(Dartang)							
Baogongmiao	HN	20	F5	Baqi	HEN	18	C5	Bayan Tal	NM	8	D4
Baoguosi	SC	31	C1	Baqiao	SN	25	F5	Bayan Tal	NM	6	C7
Baohe	SC	31	B3	Baqiaozhen	JS	11	D5	(Bayan Tohoi)	NM	6	B6
Bao He	HEN	18	D7-8	Baqiaozhen	JS	11	D5	Ewenkizu Zizhiqi			
Bao He	HEB	3	D2	Barga	XZ	34	C2				
Bao He	HEB	4	C6	Barkam	SC	30	C4	Bayan Tohoi	NM	6	E3
Baohui Qu	SN	25	G3	Barkol Hu	XJ	29	C7	(Bayan Ul Hot) Xi	NM	6	C6
Baohu Jiao	HI	21	C3	Barkol Kazak	XJ	29	C7	Ujimqin Qi			
Baoji	AH	13	C4	Zizhixian							
Baoji	JS	11	C4	Barong	SC	30	C2	Bayan Us	NM	6	F10
Baojia	JL	8	C6	Barun	QH	28	B5	Bayan	HL	9	D4
Baojialou	SC	30	D7	Bashansi	SC	30	C6	Bayiji (Caobaji)	JS	11	B3
Baojing	HN	20	C2	Bashimu	ZJ	14	E5				
				Ba Shui	HB	19	D8				
Baoji	SN	25	F3	(Basuo) Dongfang	GD	21	D2				
Baoji	SN	25	F3								
(Guozhen)				Batan	JS	11	B6	Bayi Nongchang	XJ	29	B5
(Baokang) Horqin	NM	8	C4	Batang	GX	24	D7	Baykurt	XJ	29	D2
Zuoyi Zhongqi				Batang	SC	31	C5	Baytik Shan	XJ	29	B6
Baokang	HB	19	C4	Batang	HN	20	C5	Bayuquan	LN	7	D6
Baoliansi	HEN	18	A6	Batang	SC	30	C2	Bazhan	HL	9	B3

Biguo	SD	10	B7
Bihenying	GZ	32	E4
Bihu	ZJ	14	D4
Bijiang	GD	23	H7
Bi Jiang	YN	50	C2
Bijiang	YN	33	B3
(Zhiziluo)			
Bijiapu	SN	25	G6
Bijiaquan	HEB	4	D6
Bijia Shan	FJ	16	C3
Bijie	GZ	32	C4
Bijiguan	YN	33	C5
Bikeqi	NM	6	D4
Bikou	GS	27	F7
Bila He	NM	40	B3
Bilian	ZJ	14	D5
Biling La	XZ	34	C2
Biliu He	LN	7	E6-D6
Bin'an	HL	9	E4
Binchuan	YN	33	C4
Bingcaowan	GS	27	D6
Bingcun	GD	21	A6
Bingfang	JS	12	A5
Bingfangjie	SN	25	H5
(Bingmei) Congjiang	GZ	32	E7
Bingzhongluo	YN	33	B3
Binhai	JS	11	B5
(Dongkan)			
Binjiang	JX	15	D2
Bin Jiang	GD	21	B4
Binxi	HL	9	E4
Bin Xian (Binzhou)	HL	9	E4
Bin Xian (Binzhou)	SN	25	E4
Bin Xian	SD	10	B4
Binyang	GX	24	D6
(Binzhou) Bin Xian	SN	25	E4
(Binzhou) Bin Xian	HL	9	E4
Bipu	ZJ	14	C4
Biqiao	AH	12	C2
Biratar Bulak	XJ	29	C6
Biru	XZ	34	C5
Bisezhai	YN	33	D5
Bishan	SC	30	D6
Bisheng Jiao	HI	22	D3
Bishui	HL	9	A2
Biwei Ansha	HI	22	B3
Bixi	JX	15	E2
Biyang He	HEN	18	E5
Biyang	HEN	18	E5
Biyong	HN	20	D2
Biyu	GS	27	E7
Bizhou	HL	9	B3
Bo'ai	YN	33	D7
Bo'ai	HEN	18	B5
Bo'ao	HI	21	D3
Bobai	GX	24	E7
Bobi	HEN	18	B5

Bobso	SC	30	B4
Bodu	JL	8	B5
Bofu Ansha	HI	22	C3
Bogcang Zangbo	XZ	34	C3
Bogda Feng	XJ	29	C6
Bogda Shan	XJ	29	C6
Bogenli	HL	9	C3
Bohai	HL	9	E5
Bohai	SD	10	B5
Bohai Sea	HEB	4	E6-7
	LN	7	F3-4
	SD	10	A6-7
Bohai Wan (Gf.)	TJ	3	D5
	HEB	4	E5-6
Bohe	GD	21	C3
Bohu (Bagrax)	XJ	29	C5
Bolao	GX	24	E7
Bole (Bortala)	XJ	29	B4
Boliao Zhou	GD	23	I8
Bolishan	JL	8	D4
Boli	HL	9	E6
Boluntay	QH	28	B3
Boluobu	SN	25	B5
Boluochi	LN	7	C3
Boluokeng	GD	21	A4
Boluonuo	HEB	4	B5
Boluo Pao	JL	8	C5
Boluo Paozi	JL	39	B4
Boluo	GD	21	B5
Bomei	GD	21	B5
Boming	SX	5	C4
Bomi (Bowo)	XZ	34	C5
(Zhamo)			
Bonihe	JL	8	D6
Boping	SD	10	C3
Boping Ling	FJ	16	F3-E3
Borba	QH	28	D6
Borohoro Shan	XJ	29	B4-C5
Bor Ondor	JL	8	C3
(Bortala) Bole	XJ	29	B4
Bortala He	XJ	29	B4
Bor Ul Shan	NM	6	D1
Bose	GX	24	D4
Boshan	SD	10	C4
Boshang	YN	33	D4
Boshan Sk.	HEN	18	E5
Bostan	XJ	29	C4
Bostan	XJ	29	D5
Bosten (Bagrax) Hu	XJ	29	C5
Botou	SD	10	A4
Botouzhen	SD	10	B5
(Bowa) Muli Zangzu	SC	30	E3
Zizhixian			
Bowang	AH	13	E5
Bowang	HEN	18	D4
Bowo	SC	30	D2
(Bowo) Bomi	XZ	34	C5

(Zhamo)			
(Bo Xian) Bozhou	AH	13	C2
Boxing	SD	10	B5
Boyan	HEB	5	E6
Boyang	GS	27	E8
Boyang	HN	20	E2
Boyang He	JX	15	B3
Boyang	JX	15	B4
Boye	HEB	4	E3
Bozhai	GX	24	C7
(Bozhen) Botou	HEB	4	E4
Bozhou	HN	20	D2
Bucun	SX	5	F4
Bucun	SD	10	C4
Budai	TW	17	C3
Budongquan	QH	28	C3
Bugt	NM	6	D7
Bugt	NM	6	B7
(Bügür) Luntai	XJ	29	C5
Buhai	JL	8	C6
Buhe	HB	19	D5
Buh He	QH	28	B6
Buir Nur	NM	6	C6
Buji	GD	23	H8
Bukadaban Feng	QH	28	B2
	XJ	29	D6
Bukou	HB	19	B5
Bulang	GZ	32	D4
Bulanggin Nur	NM	6	F10
Bulanggin Sum	NM	26	B4
Bulaotun	BJ	3	A4
Buli	TW	17	C3
Buliucun	SD	10	B9
Buliu He	GX	24	C4
Bulu	ZJ	14	D5
Bumdirla	XZ	34	D5
Buqian	GD	21	B5
Burang	XZ	34	C2
Burhan Budai Shan	QH	28	B4
Burqin He	XJ	29	A5
Burqin	XJ	29	B5
(Burultokay) Fuhai	XJ	29	B5
Bushêngcaka	XZ	34	B2
(Butha) Zalantun	NM	6	B7
Butou	GX	24	C9
Butuo	SC	30	E4
Buxianqiao	HN	20	B6
Buxu	GD	23	H7
Buyiqiao	JS	11	E5
Buyuan Jiang	YN	33	D4
Buyun Shan	LN	7	D6
Buze	SX	5	E5
Buzi	JS	11	C4
Buzidian	HEB	3	B5

C

Caicun	AH	13	F5	Cangzhou	HEB	4	E4	Cao Xian	SD	10	E2
(Caidian) Hanyang	HB	19	D7					Caoyan	JS	11	C5
				Canzhuang	SD	10	B7	Cao Yu	FJ	16	E5
Caigongzhuang	TJ	3	D4	Cao'an	AH	13	D4	(Caozhou) Heze	SD	10	D2
Caigou	HEN	18	D6	Caoba	SC	30	D4	Caozhuang	SD	10	E5
Caihua	HB	19	D3	Caoba	YN	33	D5	Caoziba	GZ	32	C5
Caijia	JL	8	D5	(Caobaji) Bayiji	JS	11	B3	Ceheng (Zhelou)	GZ	32	F4
Caijia	HN	20	E4					Celing	GX	24	C5
Caijiachang	SC	31	C5	Caobizhen	SN	25	F3	Cengang	ZJ	14	B6
Caijiagang	AH	13	D3	Caobo	HN	20	D6	Cengong	GZ	32	C7
Caijiagou	JL	8	B7	Caochi	SC	31	B2	(Siyang)			
Caijiahe	HB	19	D8	Caocun	AH	13	B4	Cengshan	SD	10	E5
Caijialiang	NX	26	B3	Caocun	SN	25	E5	Cenhe	HB	19	D5
Caijiapo	SN	25	F3	Caodaban	QH	28	A7	Cen Shui	HN	20	B4
Caijiaya	SX	5	C3	Caodian	HB	19	B4	Centianhe Sk.	HN	20	F4
Caijiaying	HEB	4	B3	Caodian	JS	11	C5	Cenwanglao Shan	GX	24	C4
Caijiazhuang	SD	10	C6	Caodongzhuang	HEB	4	D7	Cenxi	GX	24	E9
Cainnyigoin	SC	30	B4	Caodu He	GZ	32	E6	Ceshi	SX	5	D5
Caishentang	GZ	32	C3	Cao'e	ZJ	14	C5	Cetar	QH	28	B7
Caishi	AH	13	E5	Cao'e Jiang	ZJ	14	C5	Ceyang	GZ	32	F4
Caitingqiao	HEB	4	D5	Caofeidian	HEB	36	C6	Ceyu	HEB	4	F2
Caiwan	GX	24	B8	Caogou	AH	13	C4	Cezi Shan	ZJ	14	B6
Caixi	FJ	16	E2	Caogoubu	HEB	4	D2	Cha'anpu	HN	20	C4
Caixia	SX	5	G2	Cao Hai	GZ	32	D3	Chabu	FJ	16	C3
Caiyu	BJ	3	C3	Caohe	HEB	4	E3	Chadao	HEB	4	C3
Caiyuan	HEN	18	B6	Cao He	LN	7	D8	Chadian	SC	31	B4
(Caiyuanzhen)	ZJ	14	B7	Cao He	HEB	3	D1	Chadian	GZ	32	C8
Shengsi				Caohecheng	LN	7	D8	Chadian	TJ	3	C5
Caizhai	SD	10	B5	Caohekou	LN	7	D7	Chadianzi	HB	19	D3
Caizhuang	HEN	18	C6	Caohezhang	LN	7	C8	Chadong	HN	20	C2
Caizi Hu	AH	13	F4	Caojiabu	QH	28	B7	Chadong	GD	21	B3
Caka	QH	28	B6	Caojiachuan	SX	5	G3	Cha'ensi	HN	20	D5
(Caka) Yanhu	XZ	34	B2	(Caojiahe) Qichun	HB	19	D8	Chafang	SN	25	D5
(Caka'lho) Yanjing	XZ	34	C6					Chagannao	JL	8	B4
Caka Yanhu	QH	28	B6	Caojiaji	AH	13	D2	Chagdo Kangri	XZ	34	B3
Caluo	SC	30	D4	Caojialu	BJ	3	A4	Chagou	LN	7	D6
Cangbu	HB	19	D7	Caojian	YN	33	C3	Cha'gyüngoinba	XZ	34	C4
Cangcheng	GD	23	I6	Caojiaping	SN	25	G5	Chahayang	HL	9	C3
Cang'erhui	SX	5	D3	Caojiawa	NX	26	D2	Chahe	JS	11	C5
Canggang	HN	20	C4	Caojiawan	SN	25	F2	Chahe	JS	11	D6
Canggeng	GZ	32	F3	Caojiawu	HEB	3	C3	Chahe	YN	33	B5
Cangkou	SD	10	C7	Caolaoji	AH	13	C4	Chaheji	AH	12	A1
Cangnan	ZJ	14	E5	(Caolinxu) Zaolin	JX	15	E2	Chahuamiao	AH	13	D2
(Lingxi)				Caomaji	SD	10	E3	Chaichangtun	BJ	3	C3
Cangqian	ZJ	12	E3	Caomiao	NX	26	D3	Chaigou	SD	10	C6
Cangqian	FJ	16	D4	Caonian	JS	11	D6	(Chaigoubu) Huai'an	HEB	4	C2
Cangshan	HL	9	B2	Caopandi	HB	19	D8				
Cangshan	SD	10	E5	Caopie	JS	11	D6	Chaihe	HL	9	E5
(Bianzhuang)				Caopu	JS	11	B4	Chai He	LN	7	B8
Cangshanzhen	SC	30	C5	Caoqiao	JS	11	E5	Chaihepu	LN	7	B8
Cangshi	LN	7	C8	Caoshi	LN	7	B9	Chaihudian	SD	10	B3
Cangshuipu	HN	20	C5	Caoshi	HB	19	D5	Chaiji	AH	13	D2
Cangtou	AH	13	E4	Caoshi	HN	20	E6	Chaiqiao	ZJ	14	C6
Cangtou He	SX	5	A4	Caoshi	AH	13	C3	Chaiwopu	XJ	29	C5
Cangwu	GX	24	D9	Caosi	HEB	3	D3	Chajian	AH	13	D5
(Longxu)				Caota	ZJ	14	C5	Chajianling	HEB	4	D2
Cang Xian	HEB	4	E4	Caotang (Houchang)	GZ	32	C6	Chakou	SX	5	C5
Cangxi	SC	30	C5	Caotun	TW	17	C3	Chakou	SX	5	D3
Cangyuan Vazu	YN	33	D3	Caowei	HN	20	B5	Chalaxung	QH	28	C5
Zizhixian				Caoxi	JX	15	C5	Chalengkou	QH	28	A3

Chengyang	NX	26	E3	Chi'an	ZJ	14	C5	Chongkou	GD	23	I6
Chengyuan	FJ	16	C5	(Chiayi) Jiayi	TW	17	C3	Chongkü	XZ	34	C6
Chengzhuang	SX	5	C3	Chibakou	HB	19	E6	Chongling Shui	HN	20	E5
Chengzhuangzhai	HEN	18	C7	Chibi	HB	19	E6	Chongli	HEB	4	C3
Chengzi	BJ	3	B2	Chicheng	HEB	4	C3	(Xiwanzi)			
Chengzi	HEB	4	B5	Chifeng (Ulanhad)	NM	6	D6	Chonglou	GD	21	B4
Chengzihe	HL	9	E6					Chongming Dao(ls.)	SH	11	E7
Chengzi Hu	JS	11	C4	Chifeng	NM	6	D6	Chongming	SH	11	E7
Chengzi Shan	LN	38	B5	Chigan	SN	25	F4	Chongning	SC	31	A1
Chengzitan	LN	7	E6	Chigang	JX	15	C4	Chongqing	SC	30	D6
Chenhangou	AH	13	F2	Chigu Co	XZ	34	C4	(Yuzhou)			
Chen Hu	HB	19	D6	Chihe	AH	13	D4				
Cheniu Shan		10	E6	Chi He	AH	13	D4	Chongqing	SC	30	C4
Chenji	JS	11	B5	Chihu	FJ	16	F3	Chongren	ZJ	14	C5
Chenji	JS	11	C4	Chijiang	JX	15	F2	Chongren He	JX	15	D4
Chenji	JS	11	C5	Chijinpu	GS	27	B3	Chongren	JX	15	D4
Chenji	JS	11	D5	Chikan	GD	21	B4	Chongru	FJ	16	D5
Chenji	HEN	18	E7	Chikan	GD	21	C3	Chongshi	JX	15	F3
Chenjia	SC	31	D5	Chimei	HEN	18	D3	Chongwu	FJ	16	F4
Chenjiagang	JS	11	B5	Chindu	QH	28	D5	Chongxian	JX	15	E3
Chenjiaji	HB	19	D7	Chini	GD	23	G6	Chongxingzhai	NX	26	B3
Chenjiang	GD	23	H8	Chini'ao	SX	5	C4	Chongxin	GS	27	E8
Chenjiaqian	AH	12	A1	Chiping	SD	10	C3	Chongyangdian	HEN	18	D3
Chenjiatuan	SD	10	B8	Chishanji	SD	10	C9	Chongyang Xi	FJ	16	C4
Chenjiawan	SX	5	D3	Chishi	ZJ	14	D4	Chongyang	HB	19	E7
Chenjiawan	SC	31	B2	Chishi	FJ	16	C3	Chongyi	HEN	18	B4
Chenjiazhen	SH	11	E7	Chishui	JX	15	E4	Chongyi	JX	15	F2
Chenjiazhuang	SX	5	C5	Chishui	FJ	16	E4	Chongyizhen	SC	31	A1
Chenjiazhuang	SD	10	B5	Chishui	GD	21	B4	Chongzuo	GX	24	E5
Chenliu	HEN	18	C6	Chishui	GX	24	D9	Choushui	JL	8	E8
Chenlu	SN	25	E5	Chishui	SN	25	F5	Choushuidun	GS	27	B4
Chenmajing	NX	26	C2	Chishuihe	SC	30	E5	Choushui He	NX	26	D2
Chenming	HL	9	D5	Chishui He	SC	30	E5-6	Chuaigutuan	HEB	4	C2
Chenpo	SD	10	D2		GZ	32	B4	Chuanbu	JS	12	C3
Chenqian Shan	ZJ	14	B7	Chishui	GZ	32	B4	Chuanbu	GD	21	B3
Chenqingqiao	HL	9	C4	Chitou Shan	ZJ	14	E5	Chuanchang	FJ	16	F3
Chenshi	HEB	4	E3	Chiwei	GD	21	B6	Chuanchang He	JS	11	C5-6
Chenshi'an	JS	11	C5	Chiwei Yu	TW	17	A7	Chuancheng	JS	11	C4
Chenshu	JS	12	B4	Chixi	JX	15	C4	Chuandong	GZ	32	C8
Chen Shui	HN	20	D2-3	Chixi	FJ	16	E4	Chuangang	JS	11	E7
Chentang	GX	24	D8	Chixi	GD	21	C4	Chuankeng	JX	15	C6
Chen Xian	HN	20	F6	Chiyan	FJ	16	C5	Chuankou	SX	5	E3
Chenxiangtun	LN	7	C7	Chiyuan	FJ	16	D4	Chuankou	HEN	18	C2
Chenxi Xian	HN	20	C3	Chizhen	AH	13	E5	Chuankou	SN	25	D4
Chenyang	JS	11	C6	(Chizhou) Guichi	AH	13	F4	Chuankou	NX	26	E3
Chenyao Hu	AH	13	F4					Chuanliao	ZJ	14	D5
Chenye	JX	15	E3	Cho La	SC	30	C2	Chuanliudian	HN	18	E7
Chenying	AH	13	D5	Chola Shan	SC	30	B2-C2	Chuanshan	GX	24	B6
(Chenying) Wannian	JX	15	C5	(Chomo) Yadong	XZ	34	D4	Chuanshan	ZJ	14	C6
				Chong'anjiang	GZ	32	D6	Chuanshan	GX	24	C7
Chenzhai	AH	13	B3	Chong'an Jiang	GZ	32	D6	Chuanshanping	HN	20	C6
				Chong'an	FJ	16	C4	Chuansha	SH	11	E7
Chenzhou	HN	20	F6	Chongde	HL	9	D3	Chuanshi	FJ	16	C4
Chenzhuang	HEB	4	E2	Chongde	ZJ	14	B5	Chuantan	JX	15	B2
Chepan	JX	15	D5	Chongfang	SD	10	E5	Chuantang	GD	21	A5
Cheqiao	JS	11	C5	(Chongfu) Chongde	ZJ	12	D4	Chuanxindian	HB	19	D5
Chetian	GX	24	A8	Chonggangpu	NX	26	B3	Chuanyao Gang	JS	11	D7
Chetou	JX	15	F3	Chonggou	SD	10	D5	Chubalung	SC	30	D2
Chexu	FJ	16	F3	Chonggu	SH	12	C5	Chucha	JX	15	C4
Chezhen	SD	10	B4	Chonghe	HL	9	E4	Chucun	AH	13	C3

Chudianji	AH	13	C3	Cixi (Hushan)	ZJ	14	B6	Dabai'an	ZJ	14	D4

Chudianji	AH	13	C3
Chu He	JS	12	A2
Chuiyang	HEB	4	F3
Chujia	SD	10	B8
Chujiang	SC	31	B1
Chuka	XZ	34	C6
Chukou	HN	20	F6
Chukuangkeng	TW	17	B3
Chulan	AH	13	B4
Chumda	QH	28	D5
Chumen	ZJ	14	D6
Chun'an	ZJ	14	C4
(Pailing)			
Chunchi	FJ	16	C5
Chunheji	HEN	18	E7
Chunhu	ZJ	14	C6
Chunhua	JL	8	D12
Chunhua	JS	11	E4
Chunhua	SN	25	F4
Chunhuazhen	SD	10	B5
Chunkou	HN	20	C6
Chunmuying	HB	19	D2
Chunshui	HEN	18	D5
Chunshui	GD	21	B4
Chunwan	GD	21	B3
(Chunxi) Gaochun	IS	12	C2
Chunyang	JL	8	C6
Chunyang	JL	8	D10
Chutan	JX	15	F2
Chutoulang	NM	4	A6
Chuwang	HEN	18	A6
Chuzhou	AH	13	D5
Chuxiong	YN	33	C4
Chuzhuangji	AH	13	C4
Cicheng	ZJ	14	C6
Cigou	HEN	18	D5
Cihe	HB	19	B4
Ci He	AH	13	C2
	HEN	18	D7
Ci He	HEB	4	E2
Cihu	AH	13	E5
Cihua	JX	15	C2
Cihua	HB	19	D4
Cijian	HEN	18	C4
Cijiawu	BJ	3	B2
Cikou	HB	19	E7
Cili	HN	20	B4
Cilucun	LN	7	A8
(Ciping)	JX	15	E2
Jinggangshan			
Ciqikou	SC	31	C5
Ciqiu	SD	10	D3
Cishan	HEB	4	G2
Cishangang	AH	12	D3
Citangxu	HN	20	F5
Ci Xian	HEB	4	G2

Cixi (Hushan)	ZJ	14	B6
Ciyao	SD	10	D4
Ciyaopu	NX	26	B3
Ciyingzi	HEB	3	A3
Ciyu	HEB	4	E2
Ciyutuo	LN	7	C6
Cizao	FJ	16	F4
Cizhu	SC	31	C5
Cogsum	SC	30	D3
Comai (Damxoi)	XZ	34	C4
Co Nag	XZ	34	B4
Cona	XZ	34	D4
Conghua	GD	21	B4
Congjiang	GZ	32	E7
(Bingmei)			
Congluoyu	SX	5	D2
Coqên	XZ	34	C3
(Maindong)			
Cowargarzê	QH	28	C5
Cozhê	XZ	34	B3
Cuigang	HL	9	A3
Cuihengcun	GD	23	I7
Cuihuangkou	TJ	3	C4
Cuijia'ao	ZJ	14	C6
Cuijiaba	HB	19	D2
Cuijiaji	SD	10	C6
Cuijiayu	SD	10	D5
Cuiluan	HL	9	D5
Cuimiao	HEN	18	C5
Cuimu	SN	25	F3
Cuiqiao	HEN	18	C6
Cuiwei Feng	JX	15	E3
Culai Shan	SD	10	C4
Cunqian	JX	15	C3
Cuntan	SC	31	C5
Cuocheng	HEN	18	D8
Cuoyang	HEN	18	C8
Cuozhen	AH	13	E4

D

Da'an	ZJ	14	E4
Da'an	FJ	16	C3
Da'an	GD	21	B5
Da'an	GX	24	C6
Da'an	GX	24	D8
Da'an	SN	25	G2
Da'an	SC	31	D4
Da'anping	HN	20	B2
Da'anshan	BJ	3	B2
Da'an Xi	TW	17	B3-4
Da'an (Dalai)	JL	8	B5
Da'ao	GD	23	I8
Daba	LN	7	B6
Daba	GD	21	A6
Daba	NX	26	C2
Daba	SC	30	D5
Daba	GZ	32	B5
Dabachang	GZ	32	C7

Dabai'an	ZJ	14	D4
Dabaichi	HEB	3	D2
Dabaidi	JX	15	E3
Dabailou	BJ	3	C3
Dabaishu	SC	31	C6
Dabaizhuang	TJ	3	C4
Daban	HB	19	D6
Dabancheng	XJ	29	C6
Dabang	GZ	32	E4
Dabangdian	HB	19	C6
Dabang He	GZ	32	E4
Dabanlie	TW	17	E3
Dabanqiao	YN	33	C5
Daban Shan (Mts.)	QH	28	B7-8
Dabao	SC	30	D4
Daba Shan	SN	25	H4-I5
	SC	30	B7-C7
Daba Zhan	NX	26	B2
Dabeibu	AH	13	G4
Daben	HI	21	D2
Dabie Shan	AH	13	E2-3
	HB	19	C8-9
Dabin	GZ	32	F5
Dabizhuang	TJ	3	C4
Daboji	JL	8	E7
(Dabqig) Uxin Qi	NM	25	B5
Dabsan Hu	QH	28	B4
Dabu	FJ	16	C4
Dabu	TW	17	C3
Dabu	GD	23	I8
(Dabu) Liucheng	GX	24	C7
Dabu	SD	10	E5
Dabu	JX	15	F3
Dabu	HEB	3	B1
Dabugang	FJ	16	C3
Dabuling	FJ	16	D3
Dabusu Pao	JL	8	C4
Dabu (Huliao)	GD	21	A6
Dabuzi	HEB	3	A1
Dacang	YN	33	C4
Dacêgoin	SC	30	B4
Dachaigou	GS	27	D6
Dachang (Xinzhou)	GX	24	C5
Dachang	SH	11	E7
Dachang Huizu	HEB	4	D4
Zizhixian			
Dachangshan Dao	LN	7	E6
Dachangtu Shan	ZJ	14	B7
Dachangzhen	JS	11	D4
Dachangzhen	SC	30	C7
Dachechang	NM	27	C5
Dachen	ZJ	14	C5
Dachen Dao	ZJ	42	D5
Dacheng	JX	15	C3
Dacheng	TW	17	C3
Dachengqiao	JS	11	D5
Dachengwei	HEB	4	E3
Dachengzi	BJ	3	B4
(Dachengzi) Harqin	LN	7	C3

Name	Prov	Map	Grid
Zhoyi Mongolzu Zizhixian			
Dachen Shan	ZJ	12	E6
Dachenzhuang	HEB	4	F2
Dachikan	GD	23	I7
Dachixu	FJ	16	E2
Dachong	GD	23	I7
Dachuan	JL	8	D8
Daciyao	SX	5	B5
Dacun	BJ	3	B2
Dacun	SC	30	D6
Dacundian	HN	20	E4
Dadenggou	NX	26	A3
Dadian	SD	10	D5
Dadian	AH	13	C4
Dadianzi	LN	7	B8
Dadianzi	JL	8	E9
(Dadong) Donggou	LN	7	E8
Dadong	GX	24	E6
Daduan	JX	15	C2
Dadu He	SC	30	C3-4
Dadukou	AH	13	F4
Dadukou	SC	31	B2
Dadukou	SC	31	C5
Daduo	JS	11	D6
Dadu Xi	TW	17	B3
Daduzhuang	HEB	3	D4
Da'erhao	HEB	4	B4
Dafan	HB	19	E7
Dafangshen	LN	7	E5
Dafangshen	JL	8	C6
Dafang	GZ	32	C4
Dafanhe	LN	7	B7
Dafen	JX	15	E2
Dafengman	JL	8	D7
Dafeng (Dazhongji)	JS	11	C6
Dafu	AH	13	G5
Dafu Shui	HB	19	C6
Dagan	FJ	16	D3
Dagang	JS	11	C6
Dagang	JX	15	C4
Dagang	GD	23	H7
Dagang	TJ	3	D4
Dagang	JS	11	D5
Dagangkou	TW	17	C4
Dagangtou	ZJ	14	D4
Dagcanglhamo (Langmusi)	GS	27	E6
(Dagezhen) Fengning	HEB	4	B4
Daglung	XZ	34	C4
Dagongcha	GS	27	C3
Dagong Dao	SD	10	D7
Dagou	GS	26	E2
Dagu	TJ	3	D5
Daguan	SC	30	D5
Daguan	SC	31	D5
Daguan	GZ	32	D5
Daguan Hu	AH	13	F3-G3
Daguantou	BJ	3	A3
Daguan	YN	33	B5
Dagudian	AH	13	E3
Dagu He	SD	10	C7
Dagujia	LN	7	B8
Dagujia He	SD	10	B8
Dagujiazi	LN	7	B7
Daguokui Shan	HL	9	E5
Dagur	QH	28	B4
Dagushan	LN	7	C7
Dagushan	JL	8	D6
Dagxoi (Sowa)	SC	30	D2
Dagzê Co	XZ	34	B3
Dagzê	XZ	34	C4
Dagzhuka	XZ	34	C4
Dahaibei	TJ	3	C5
Dahaituo Shan	BJ	3	A2
	HEB	4	C3
Dahao Dao	GD	21	B4
Dahe	FJ	16	E2
Daheba	HB	19	E2
Daheba	QH	28	C6
Daheiding Shan	HL	9	D5
Dahei He	NM	6	F10
Dahei Shan	JL	8	D5-6
Daheishan Dao	SD	10	B7
Dahekou	NM	4	A4
Dahekou	SN	25	H4
Dahenan	HEB	4	D3
Daheng	FJ	16	E3
Dahengqin Dao	GD	23	I7
Dahetun	HEN	18	E5
Dahezhen	HL	9	D7
Da Hinggan Ling (Mts.)	NM	6	C6-B7
Dahongcheng	NM	6	D4
Dahong He	SC	31	C5
Dahongliutan	XJ	29	E3
Dahongluo Shan	LN	38	C4
Dahongmen	BJ	3	B3
Dahongqi	LN	7	C6
Dahongqiao	HEN	18	B5
Dahong Shan	HB	19	C5
Dahong Shan	HB	19	C5-6
Dahu	FJ	16	D3
Dahu	TW	17	B3
Dahu	HN	20	C6
Dahua	GX	24	D5
Dahuai	GD	21	B4
Dahuanggou	JL	8	D11
Dahuanggou	JL	8	E7
Dahuanglong Shan	ZJ	14	B7
Dahuangshan	JS	11	B3
Dahuan Jiang	GX	24	B6
Dahuashan	BJ	3	B4
Dahuichang	BJ	3	B2
Dahujiang	JX	15	E2
Dahulun	HEB	4	B3
Dahuofang	LN	7	C8
Dahuofang Sk.	LN	7	C8
Dahushan	LN	7	C6
Dahutu	NM	4	B1
Daibu	JS	11	E5
Daibu	AH	13	D4
Daicheng	HEB	4	E4
Daifang	JX	15	D3
Dai Hai	NM	6	F10
Daihua	GZ	32	E5
Daiji	HEN	18	D7
Daiji	FJ	16	D5
Dai Jiang	FJ	16	D5
Daijiapu	JX	15	E2
Daijiayao	JS	11	D6
Dailing	HL	9	D5
Daimao Shan	FJ	16	E2
Dainan	JS	11	D6
Dainkog	SC	30	B1
Dainkognubma	XZ	34	B6
Daiqin Tal	NM	6	C7
Dai Shan	ZJ	14	B7
Daishan (Gaotingzhen)	ZJ	14	B7
Daishizhen	SC	31	B5
Daisizhen	SC	31	D3
Daitou	FJ	16	E5
Daiwang	HEN	18	B5
Daiwangcheng	HEB	4	D2
Daixi	ZJ	14	B5
Daixi	FJ	16	D5
Dai Xian	SX	5	B4
(Daiyue) Shanyin	SX	5	B4
Daiyun Shan	FJ	16	E4
Daiyun Shan	FJ	16	E4-D4
Daji	ZJ	14	E4
Dajia	TW	17	B3
Dajiagou	JL	8	C6
Dajiahe	HL	9	D7
Dajiang	GD	23	I6
Dajiang	GX	24	B7
Dajiang He	GD	23	H8
Dajiao	SX	5	F3
Dajiawa	SD	10	B5
Dajia Xi	TW	17	B4
Dajichang	HB	19	E2
Dajieshi	SD	10	B8
Dajin	GD	23	J6
Dajin Chuan	SC	30	C4
Dajindian	HEN	18	C4
Dajing	SD	10	D3
Dajing	JX	15	E2
Dajing	GD	21	B3
Dajing	NM	26	C1
Dajing	ZJ	14	D6
Dajing	GS	27	D6
Dajinpu	HB	19	D8
Dajin Shan	SH	12	D5
Dajinzhu	JX	15	D3
Daji Shan	ZJ	14	B7

Name	Region	No.	Grid
Daji Yang	ZJ	14	B7
Da Juh	QH	28	B4
Dakeng	JX	15	E3
Dakengkou	GD	21	A4
Dakog	SC	30	B4
Dakou	SX	5	F4
Dakoutun	TJ	3	C4
Dakuang	SD	10	C7
Dakunlun	SD	10	C4
Dalàchi	GS	27	D7
Dalad Qi	NM	6	D4
(Dalai) Da'an	JL	8	B5
(Dalain Hob) Ejin Qi	NM	6	D2
Dalai Nur	NM	6	D6
Dalan	GD	21	B5
Dalan	GD	23	H6
Dalan	HN	20	C2
Dalang	GD	23	H8
Dalangwan	GD	21	C4
Dalaoba	XJ	29	C4
Dalaoshan	SN	25	D5
Dalaozi	SD	10	C5
Dalba	JL	8	B5
Daleng	GX	24	D4
Dali	GD	23	H6
Dali	GX	24	D8
(Dalian) Shahe	HEB	4	G2
Dalian Dao	FJ	16	E5
(Daliang) Shunde	GD	23	H7
Daliang	GX	24	C7
Daliang	QH	28	B7
Dalianggang	HEB	3	C1
Daliang Shan	SC	30	D4
Dalianhe	HL	9	D5
Dalian	LN	7	F5
Dalianwan	LN	7	E5
Dalian Wan	LN	7	F5
Daliao He	LN	38	C5
Dali He	SN	25	C5
Daliji	AH	13	D4
Dalijia	SD	10	B3
Dalikou	FJ	16	D3
Dalin	NM	6	D7
Dalin	TW	17	C3
Dalinchi	SD	10	C4
Dalin Dao	GD	23	I7
Daling	JL	8	B7
Daling	GX	24	E5
(Dalinghe) Jin Xian	LN	7	C5
Daling He	LN	7	C4-5
Dalinhe	SX	5	B5
Dalinzi	JL	8	B6
Daliudian	HEN	18	D5
Daliuhao	NM	6	D5
Daliuhe	HEB	3	D3
Daliuta	SN	25	A6
Daliutun	LN	7	B6
Daliuzhen	HEB	3	D3
Daliuzhuang	HEN	18	D6
Dali	SN	25	F5
Dali	YN	33	C4
Daliyuan	AH	13	C4
Dalizhuang	HEN	18	D5
Dalizi	JL	8	F7
Dalong	JX	15	E2
Dalongdong Sk.	GX	24	D6
Dalonghua	HEB	3	C1
Dalongwan	TJ	3	C4
Dalou Shan	GZ	32	B5-6
Dalu	GS	27	D7
Dalu	JL	8	G6
Dalu	JS	12	A3
Dalu	SC	31	C4
Dalü	GX	24	F6
Dalu Dao	LN	7	E7
Dalüjia	SD	10	B7
Daluli	JX	15	D1
Daluo	YN	33	E4
Daluolemi	HL	9	E5
Daluo Shan	GD	21	B4
Daluozhen	HL	9	D4
Damachang	AH	13	D5
Damafang	HEB	3	D1
Damaijiao	SX	5	D3
Damang	GD	23	I6
Damanzhuang	HEB	4	E4
Damao Shan	JX	15	C5
Damaqun Shan	HEB	4	B2-3
Damaying	HN	20	F5
Damen Dao (Huangda'ao)	ZJ	14	E6
Dameng'e	YN	33	D3
Damenglong	YN	33	E4
Damianzhen	SC	31	B2
Damiao	NM	4	A6
Damiao	HEB	4	B5
Damiao	NM	6	E3
Damiao	JS	11	B3
Damiao	JX	15	C2
Damiao	SC	30	C7
Damiaokou	HN	20	E4
Daming	FJ	16	E1
Daming Shan	GX	24	D6
Daming Shan	GX	45	C3
Daming	HEB	4	G3
Damingzhen	LN	7	B7
Damintun	LN	7	C6
Damjong	QH	28	D4
(Damqog Zangbo) Maquan He	XZ	34	C2-3
Dam Qu	QH	28	D3
Damuchang	HB	19	B3
Damuzhi Shan	FJ	16	D4
(Damxoi) Comai	XZ	34	C4
Damxung	XZ	34	C4
Dananhu	XJ	29	C7
Dananqiao	JX	15	C6
Danantun	JL	8	D6
Danba	SC	30	C3
Danbazhai	SN	25	D4
(Dancheng) Xiangshan	ZJ	14	C6
Dancheng	HEN	18	D7
Dancun	SN	25	F5
Dandai	JL	8	A4
Dandian	HB	19	D8
Dando	SC	30	C3
Dandong	LN	7	D8
Danei	TW	17	C3
Danfeng (Longjuzhai)	SN	25	G6
Dangan Dao	GD	23	I8
Dangan Liedao	GD	21	C5
Dangba	HEB	4	C6
Dangbizhen	HL	9	E7
Dangchang	GS	27	F7
Dangcheng	HEB	4	E2
(Dangchengwan) Subei Mongolzu Zizhixian	GS	27	C2
Dangchuan	GS	27	E8
Dang He	GS	27	C2
Danghe Nanshan	GS	27	C2-3
	QH	28	A4-5
Dangjiaxian	GS	26	E2
Dangjiazhuang	SD	10	C3
Dangjin Shankou	GS	27	C2
	QH	28	A4
Dangkou	JS	11	E6
(Dangla) Tanggula Shan	QH	28	D2-4
	XZ	34	B3-5
(Dang La) Tanggula Shankou	QH	28	D2
	XZ	34	B4
Dangmu	SN	25	F5
Dangqên	XZ	34	C4
Dangshan	AH	13	B3
Dang Shui	SC	30	B6-C6
Dangtu	AH	13	E5
Dangyang	HB	19	D4
Dangyu	HEB	3	B5
Dan He	SX	5	F5
Daning	GX	24	C9
Daningchang	SC	30	C7
Daning He	SC	30	C7
Daning	SX	5	E2
Daniudian	SX	5	C4
Danjiangkou	HB	19	B4
(Danjiang) Leishan	GZ	32	D7
Danjiang	HN	20	F4
Dan Jiang	HEN	18	D2-3
	SN	25	G6

Name	Prov	No	Grid
Data	YN	33	D5
Datai	BJ	3	B2
Datai	HN	20	E6
Datan	HEB	4	B4
Datan	NM	6	F10
Datang	JX	15	F2
Datang	GD	23	G6
Datang	GX	24	C6
Datang	GX	24	E6
Datang	GZ	32	D7
Datangpu	SC	31	B1
Datarma	SC	30	B2
Dateng Xia	GX	24	D7
Datian	AH	13	D2
Datian	ZJ	14	D6
Datian	GD	21	B4
Datian Ding	GD	21	B3
Datian	FJ	16	E3
Datiaodeng	SC	30	D6
Datong	HL	9	D3
Datong	ZJ	14	C4
Datong	YN	33	C6
Datong	AH	13	D5
Datong	AH	13	F4
Datong	SC	31	B4
Datong He	GS	27	D6
	QH	28	B8
Datong Hu	HN	20	B5
Datong Jiang	SC	25	H3
Datong Shan	QH	28	B6-7
Datong	SX	5	A5
Datong (Xiping)	SX	5	A5
Datong	QH	28	B7
Datongzhen	JS	11	D7
Datoushan	HL	9	B4
Datuan	SH	11	F7
Datun	JL	8	B4
Datun	JL	8	D6
Datunjie	YN	33	D5
Datun Shan	TW	17	A4
Datuopu	HN	20	C5
Datushan	JL	8	D4
Dawa	LN	7	A7
Dawa	JL	8	B5
Dawa	JL	8	B5
Dawan	GD	21	A4
Dawan	GD	21	B3
Dawan	GX	24	D7
Dawan	GZ	32	D3
Dawan	YN	33	B5
Dawan	YN	33	B6
Dawang	SD	10	C5
Dawangdian	HEB	4	D3
Dawangji	SD	10	E2
Dawangjia Dao	LN	7	E7
Dawang Shan	JX	15	D4
Dawangzhuang	HEB	3	D2
Dawanshan Dao	GD	23	I7
Dawa	LN	7	D6
Dawaxung	XZ	34	C3

Name	Prov	No	Grid
Dawê	SC	30	C4
Dawei	HEB	3	D1
Daweizhen	HEN	18	C5
Dawen He	SD	10	D3
Dawenkou	SD	10	D4
Dawoping	HN	20	C3
Dawu	SD	10	D3
Dawu	SX	5	D3
Dawu	TW	17	D3
(Dawu) Maqên	QH	28	C7
Dawujiang	GZ	32	C6
Dawujiazi	HL	9	C4
(Dawukou) Shizuishan	NX	26	A3
Dawulan	LN	7	C5
Dawulan	HEB	4	C7
Dawu Shan	HB	19	C7
Dawusi	QH	28	B2
Dawusu	HL	9	B3
Dawu (Erlangdian)	HB	19	C7
Dawu	SC	30	C3
Daxi	ZJ	14	D6
Daxi	TW	17	B4
Daxi	TW	17	B4
Daxi	GZ	32	C4
Da Xi	ZJ	14	D5
Da Xi	SC	31	D6
Daxia	QH	28	B8
Daxia He	GS	27	E6
Daxiakou	HB	19	C3
Da Xian	SC	30	C6
Daxiang Ling	SC	30	D4
Daxian Jiao	HI	22	D3
Daxian	SC	30	C6
Daxidu	JX	15	C4
Daxie Dao	ZJ	12	E6
Daxihaizi Sk.	XJ	29	C5
Daxin	JS	11	C4
Daxin	GX	24	D8
Daxindian	SD	10	B7
Daxindian	HEN	18	D5
Daxing	JL	8	C4
Daxing	GZ	32	C8
Daxing	YN	33	B5
Daxingchang	SC	31	C5
Daxingdao	HL	9	D7
Daxinggou	JL	8	D10
Daxing (Huangcun)	BJ	3	C3
Daxingzhen	JL	8	E6
Daxingzhe	SD	10	E5
Daxingzhen	JS	11	D6
Daxin	GX	24	E5
Daxizhai Dao	ZJ	12	E7
Daxu	HN	20	G4
Daxu	GX	24	B8
Daxu	GX	24	D7
Daxu	ZJ	14	C6

Name	Prov	No	Grid
Daxuan	GX	24	D8
Daxucun	JX	15	C6
(Daxue) Wencheng	ZJ	14	E5
Daxue Shan	SC	30	C3-D3
Daxue Shan	YN	33	D3
Daxujia	JS	11	B3
Daxu Shan	JX	15	D4
(Dayan) Lijiang Naxizu Zizhixian	YN	33	B4
Dayan	ZJ	14	C6
Dayan	HB	19	B3
Dayandang	HN	20	B4
Dayang	SD	10	C3
Dayang	SX	5	E3
Dayang	JL	8	E6
Dayang	AH	13	C2
Dayang	FJ	16	E4
Dayang	GD	23	I6
Dayang	GX	24	D7
Dayangdong	HN	20	F4
Dayang He	LN	7	D7
Dayangqi	NM	6	B8
Dayang Shan	ZJ	14	B7
Dayangshu	NM	6	B8
Dayangzhuang	HEB	3	D2
Dayao	HN	20	D6
Dayao Shan	GX	24	D8-C8
Dayao	YN	33	C4
Daya Wan	GD	21	B5
Daye	HB	19	D7
Dayi	SD	10	D3
Dayi	GZ	32	E5
Dayiji	SD	10	D3
Dayiji	SD	10	E2
Dayiji	JS	11	D5
Dayin	HEB	3	D2
Dayin	ZJ	14	C6
Daying	HEB	3	D2
Daying	HEB	4	F3
Daying	SX	5	B5
Daying	SX	5	C4
Daying	JL	8	E8
Daying	HEN	18	C3
Daying	HEN	18	D4
Dayingji	AH	12	A1
Dayingji	AH	13	C3
Daying Jiang	YN	33	C3
Dayingpan	HEB	3	B5
Dayingpan	HEB	4	B2
Dayingzi	NM	4	B6
Dayingzi	AH	13	C4
Dayiqiao	IS	12	B4
(Dayishan) Guanyun	JS	11	B5
Dayi	SC	30	C4
Dayong	GZ	32	D4
Dayong	GZ	32	D7
Dayong	HN	20	B3
Dayou	JS	11	B5

Name	Prov.	Map	Grid
Dongjiugong	HEB	4	F3
Dongji Yu	TW	17	C2
Dongjug	XZ	34	C5
(Dongkan) Binhai	JS	11	B5
Dongkeng	ZJ	14	E4
Dongkeng	JX	15	D2
Dongkeng	JX	15	G2
Dongkengkou	ZJ	14	C3
Dongkou	SD	10	D2
Dongkou	HN	20	D3
Donglai	NM	7	A5
Donglang	HB	19	B3
Donglan	GX	24	C5
Dongle	GS	27	C5
Dongli	GD	21	C3
Dongliang	SX	5	C5
Dongliang	LN	7	C5
Dongliang Shan	AH	12	B1
Dongliangzhuang	SD	10	D4
Dongliangzhu He	HL	39	B6
Dongliao He	JL	8	D4-5
Donglidian	SD	10	C5
Dongling	LN	7	C7
Dongling	GX	24	D4
Donglingjing	SX	5	C4
Dongling Shan	BJ	3	B2
	HEB	4	C3
Dongliu	AH	13	F3
Dongliu	JX	15	B5
Dongliuji	AH	13	C4
Dongliuqiao	SC	31	B6
Donglong	GD	21	B6
Donglou	SX	5	C4
Donglü	HEB	3	D2
Donglük	XJ	29	D6
Dongluo	GX	24	E5
Dongluo Dao	FJ	16	D6
Dongmajuan	TJ	3	C3
Dongmao	HEB	4	C4
Dongmen	HN	20	C7
Dongmen	GX	24	E5
Dongmiaohe	HEB	3	A5
Dongmingji	SD	10	D2
Dongming	SD	10	D2
Dongminzhutun	JL	8	C3
Dongning	HL	9	E6
Dongnyi	SC	30	D3
Dongping	FJ	16	C4
Dongping	GD	21	C4
Dongping	GX	24	E7
(Dongping) Anhua	HN	20	C4
Dongping	JL	8	A4
Dongping Hu	SD	10	C3
Dongping	SD	10	D3
Dongpo	YN	33	C5
Dongpu	ZJ	14	B5
Dongqian	ZJ	12	D4
Dongqian Hu	ZJ	14	C6
Dongqiao	XZ	34	C4
Dongqiao	JX	15	D1
Dongqiao	HB	19	C5
Dongquan	SX	5	D4
Dongquan	GX	24	C7
Dongquan Dao	FJ	16	E6
Dongsanjiazi	JL	8	C5
Dongsanpu	AH	13	C4
Dongsha Dao	FJ	16	D6
Dongsha Dao	GD	21	C6
Dongsha He	LN	7	C6
Dongsha He	HEN	13	B3-C3
Dongshajiao	ZJ	14	B7
Dongshan	JS	11	E6
(Dongshan) Jiangning	JS	12	B2
Dongshan	HN	20	E2
Dongshan	GD	21	C3
Dongshan Dao	FJ	16	G3
Dongshanmiao	HEB	3	A2
Dongshannei Ao	FJ	16	G3
Dongshanqiao	JS	12	B1
Dongshan (Xibu)	FJ	16	G3
Dongshao	JX	15	E3
Dongsha Qundao (Apg.)	GD	21	C6
Dongshe	SX	5	C4
Dongshe	SX	5	D3
Dongshe	SX	5	D4
Dongshe	JS	12	A5
Dongsheng	JL	8	B2
Dongsheng	SN	25	H4
Dongsheng	SC	30	D6
Dongsheng	SC	31	D6
Dongsheng	NM	6	E4
Dongshengyong	JL	8	E10
Dongshi	FJ	16	F4
Dongshi	TW	17	C3
Dongshi	TW	17	B3
Dongshi	HN	20	C4
Dongshi	HB	19	D4
Dongshiqiao	HEB	3	D2
Dongshuanghe	HEN	18	E6
Dongshui	GD	21	A5
Dongsunba	SC	31	D5
Dongtai He	JS	11	D6
Dong Taijnar Hu	QH	28	B3
Dongtaitou	HEN	18	D4
Dongtai	JS	11	D6
Dongtang	HL	9	C5
Dongtangchi	AH	13	E4
Dongtiangezhuang	BJ	3	A4
Dongtianmu Shan	ZJ	14	B4
Dongtiao Xi	ZJ	14	B5
Dongting	HEB	4	E3
Dongting Hu (Lk.)	HN	20	C5
Dongting Shan	ZJ	14	C7
Dongtingxi	HN	20	C3
Dongtou	GX	24	B6
Dongtou Shan	ZJ	14	E6
Dongtou	ZJ	14	E6
Dongtuanbu	HEB	3	C1
Dongtumo	HL	9	D3
Dong Ujimqin Qi (Uliastai)	NM	6	C6
Dongwan	GS	27	D7
Dongwang	HEB	4	F3
Dongwangzhuang	HEB	4	E2
Dongwankou	HEB	4	B4
Dongwu Yang	FJ	16	D5
Dongxi	ZJ	14	C6
Dongxi	SC	30	D6
Dong Xi	FJ	16	E4
Dong Xi	FJ	16	G3
Dongxia	AH	13	E6
Dongxiang	GX	24	D7
Dongxiang Dao	FJ	16	E5
Dongxiang	JX	15	C4
Dongxiangzu Zizhixian	GS	27	E6
Dongxiating	HEN	18	D6
Dongxi Lian Dao	JS	11	B5
Dongxin	JL	8	D10
Dongxing	NM	6	F10
Dongxing	HL	9	D4
Dongxing	GX	24	B6
Dongxing	GX	24	F6
Dongxingzhen	JS	12	B3
Dongxinzhuang	LN	7	D4
Dongxinzhuang	HEB	3	B5
Dongxiuzhuang	SX	5	C3
Dongxizhen	SC	30	B6
Dongyang	SX	5	D4
Dongyang	HL	9	C3
Dongyang	SD	10	D4
Dongyangdu	HN	20	E5
Dongyangguan	SX	5	E5
Dongyang He	HEB	4	C1-2
Dongyang	ZJ	14	C5
Dongyao	SX	5	F3
Dongyao	HEN	18	B5
Dongye	SX	5	C5
Dongye	SX	5	F4
Dongyetou	SX	5	D5
Dongyin Dao	FJ	16	D6
Dongying	SD	10	B5
Dongyingzi	HEB	3	A4
Dongyong	GD	23	I8
Dongyou	FJ	16	C4
Dongyu	SX	5	E4
Dongyuan	FJ	16	F4
Dongyuan	GD	21	B6
Dongyueguan	HN	20	B4
Dongyuemiao	JS	12	B2
Dongyuemiao	HB	19	E4
Dongyulin	SX	5	B4
Dongzha	ZJ	12	D4
Dongzhai	SX	5	C4
Dongzhang	HEN	18	C6
Dongzhaobao	HEN	18	C4

Dongzhen	HEB	4	F2	Duanjiagou	NX	26	D2	Duobukur He	NM	9	B3
Dongzhen	SX	5	F3	Duanjialing	HEB	3	B4	Duodao	HB	19	D5
Dongzhen	GS	27	C6	Duanshan	GZ	32	E5	Duoding	GZ	32	C6
Dongzhenjie	SN	25	G4	Duanshi	SX	5	F4	Duohuo	SX	5	F5
Dongzhen Sk.	FJ	16	E4	Duanting	SX	5	D4	Duojiao	GZ	32	D4
Dongzhi (Yaodu)	AH	13	F4	Duanxin	JX	15	B5	Duojing	GX	24	D4
Dongzhong	SD	10	C6	Du'an Yaozu Zizhixian	GX	24	D6	Duolun(Dolonnur)	NM	6	D6
Dongzhou	ZJ	14	D3								
Dongzhuang	HEN	18	B6	Duchang	JX	15	B4	Duonai	HL	9	D2
Dongzhugou	SD	10	C6	Ducun	SD	10	C6	Duowen	HI	21	D2
Dongziya	TJ	3	D3	Dudang	HEB	4	G2	Duoxi	HN	20	C2
Do Qu	QH	28	C5	Duding	XZ	34	C5	Duoyuezhen	SC	31	B1
Do Qu	SC	30	B3-C3	Duguan	HEN	18	C2	Duozhu	GD	21	B5
Doramarkog	QH	28	D5	Dugui	YN	33	D4	Duozhuang	SD	10	D5
(Dorbiljin) Emin	XJ	29	B4	Dugui Qarag	NM	6	E4	Dupang Ling	HN	20	F4
				Du He	HB	19	B3		GX	24	B9
(Dorbod) Siziwang Qi	NM	6	D4	Duhu	GD	21	B4	Dupukou	HB	19	D7
Dorbod Mongolzu Zizhixian(Taikang)	HL	9	D3	Duhu Ansha	HI	22	E3	Düre	XJ	29	B6
				Duiqingshan	HL	9	E4	(Duru) Wuchuan	GZ	32	B7
				Duiyingzi	BJ	3	A3	Duruan	GD	23	H6
Doucun	SX	5	C5	Duizhen	SX	5	D3	Dushan	AH	13	E3
Doudian	BJ	3	C2	Duiziliang	SN	25	C4	Du Shan	HEB	4	C6
Douge	YN	33	D4	Duiziqian	JX	15	E2	Dushan Hu	SD	10	D3
Dougong	HEN	18	A6	Duji	SD	10	B3	Dushanji	SD	10	D3
Dougou	HEN	18	E6	Duji	HEN	18	C7	Dushan	GZ	32	E6
Dou He	HEB	3	C5	Dujiang	GZ	32	E7	Dushanzi	GS	27	C2
Douhutun	LN	7	B8	Dujiang Yan	SC	30	C4	Dushanzi	XJ	29	B5
Douhutun	SD	10	C2	Dujiatai	HB	19	D6	Dusheng	HEB	4	E4
Doujiang	GX	24	B7	Dujie	GX	24	D5	Dushi	SC	31	A6
Doukou	SC	30	B5	Dujie	GX	24	C6	Dushichang	SC	31	D5
(Douliu) Yunlin	TW	17	C3	Dujing	ZJ	14	C3	Dushikou	HEB	4	B3
Doulong Gang	JS	11	C6	Dukou	JX	15	C6	Dushu	HEN	18	D5
Doulonggang Kou	JS	11	C6	Dukou	HEB	4	G2	Dushui He	GZ	32	D6
Douluo	SX	5	C4	Dukou	NM	6	D3	Dushutou	SD	10	D5
Doumen	ZJ	12	E4	Dukou	GX	24	B4	Dusong	SC	30	C3
Doumen	GD	23	I7	(Dukou)Panzhihua	SC	30	E3	Dustin Gol	NM	6	E3
Doumen	HEN	18	C6					Dutou	HN	20	F6
Doumen	GD	21	B4	Dulan	TW	17	D4	Duwei	FJ	16	E4
Doumenzhen	SN	25	F4	Dulansi	QH	28	B6	Duwu	FJ	16	D5
Doumuge	YN	33	D5	Dulan (Qagan Us)	QH	28	B6	Düxanbibazar	XJ	29	D4
Doumuhu	HN	20	C4					Duxiaqiao	ZJ	14	D6
Dounan	TW	17	C3	Dulaying	GZ	32	D5	Duxun	FJ	16	G3
Doushaguan	YN	33	A6	Dule	HEB	3	D1	Duya	HEB	3	C1
Doushan	GD	23	I6	Dulin	HEB	4	E4	Duyang	GX	24	D5
(Doushi) Gong'an	HB	19	D5	Duliu	TJ	3	D4	Duyang Shan	GX	24	C5
				Duliu Jiang	GZ	32	E7	Duyi	GZ	32	E5
Doushui	JX	15	F2	Duliu Jianhe	TJ	3	D4	Duyun	GZ	32	D6
Doushui Sk.	JX	15	F2	Dulong	YN	33	D6	Duyun	GZ	32	D6
Douyu	HEB	4	F2	Dulou	AH	13	B3	Duze	ZJ	14	C3
Douzhangzhuang	TJ	3	C4	Duluhe	HL	9	D6	Duzhenwan	HB	19	D3
Douzhuang	HEB	3	C2	Dumei	FJ	16	F3	Duzhou	SC	31	C6
Dowa	QH	28	B7	Dumo	GX	24	C8	Duzhuang	SX	5	B5
Du'an	GX	24	D4	Dumuhe	HL	9	D7	Duzhuang	SX	5	D5
Duancun	SX	5	D4	(Dunhou) Ji'an	JX	15	D2				
(Duancun) Wuxiang	SX	5	E4	Dunhuang	GS	27	B2				
				Dunhua	JL	8	D9	**E**			
Duancun	HEB	3	D2	Dunkou	HB	19	D7				
Duandian	HB	19	D7	Dunshang	JS	11	B5	Ebian	SC	30	D4
Duanfen	GD	23	I6	Duobaowan	HB	19	D5	Ebinur Hu	XJ	29	B4
Duanji	HEN	18	F7	Duobukur	NM	40	B4	Echeng	SD	10	C3

Name	Prov	No	Grid
Fanshi	ZJ	14	B6
Fanshi	SX	5	B5
Fanshui	JS	11	C5
Fan Xian	HEN	18	B7
Fanxiang	HEN	18	B6
Fanzhen	SD	10	C4
Fanzipai	BJ	3	A4
Fate	JL	8	C7
Fayanshen	NM	6	F10
Fazhong	SX	5	E4
Feicheng	SD	10	C3
Feidong (Dianbu)	AH	13	E4
Feiheji	AH	13	C2
Fei Huang He	SD	10	E3
	JS	11	B3-C4
Feihuanghe Kou	JS	11	B6
Feilai Xia	GD	21	B4
Feilong	SC	31	B5
Feiluan	FJ	16	D5
Feima	SC	31	A3
Feiqiao	HEN	18	D8
Feishuiyan	HN	20	D4
Feitian	HN	20	E5
Fei Xian	SD	10	D4
Feixiang	HEB	4	G2
Feixianqiao	HN	20	F5
Feixi (Shangpaihe)	AH	13	E4
Feiyun Jiang	ZJ	14	E5
Fencheng	SX	5	F3
Fengbin	TW	17	C4
Fengcheng	SD	10	C5
Fengcheng	GS	27	C5
Fengcheng	SD	10	C8
Fengcheng	SH	11	F7
Fengcheng	LN	7	D8
Fengcheng	JX	15	C3
Fengchuan	GD	21	B3
Fengchuihudie	GD	21	A5
Fengdeng	NX	26	B3
Fengdengwu	HEB	3	C5
Fengding Shan	JX	15	C2
Fengdong	GZ	32	E6
Fengdu	FJ	16	D4
Fengdu	SC	30	D6
Fengfeng	HEB	4	G2
Fenggang	JX	15	D4
Fenggang	TW	17	D3
Fenggang (Longquan)	GZ	32	C6
Fenggaopu	SC	31	C4
Fenggeling	SN	25	F2
Fenggezhuang	SD	10	C7
Fengguang	JL	8	C7
Fengguzhen	SC	30	C5
Fenghe	SC	31	B5
Feng He	BJ	3	C3
Fengheying	BJ	3	C3
Fenghuang	SH	12	C6
Fenghuang	GD	21	B6
Fenghuang	GX	24	C5
Fenghuang	GX	24	D7
Fenghuang	HN	20	D2
Fenghuangzui	SN	25	G5
Fenghua	ZJ	14	C6
Fenghui	ZJ	14	C5
Fengjia	LN	7	B6
Fengjia	SD	10	B8
(Fengjiaba) Wangcang	SC	30	B6
Fengjiakou	HEB	4	E4
Fengjiang	JX	15	D2
Fengjiapu	HEB	4	E5
Fengjiayu	BJ	3	A4
Fengjie	SC	30	C7
Fengjigou	NX	26	C3
Fengjing	SH	11	F7
Fengkai (Jiangkou)	GD	21	B3
Fengkou	HB	19	D6
Fengku	JL	8	C4
Fengle	HL	9	E3
Fengle	FJ	16	C4
Fengle	HB	19	C5
Fengle	GZ	32	B6
Fenglehe	AH	13	E4
Fengle He	AH	13	E4
Fenglezhen	HEN	18	A6
Fengli	JS	11	D7
Fengliang	GD	21	B6
Fenglin	TW	17	C4
Fenglin	ZJ	14	D5
Fenglingdu	SX	5	G2
Fengling Guan	ZJ	14	D3
	FJ	16	B4
Fenglingtou	JX	15	C5
Fengman	JL	8	D7
Fengmiao	AH	13	C4
Fengming Dao	LN	7	E5
Fengnan (Xugezhuang)	HEB	4	D6
Fengning (Dagezhen)	HEB	4	B4
Fengqiao	ZJ	14	C5
Fengqing	YN	33	C3
Fengqiu	HEN	18	B6
Fengren	FJ	16	F2
Fengrun	SX	5	C3
Fengrun	HEB	4	D6
Fengshan	JX	15	E4
Fengshan	HEB	4	B5
Fengshan	HL	9	D5
(Fengshan) Gaoxiong (Kaohsiung)	TW	17	D3
Fengshan	GX	24	C7
Fengshan	GX	24	E7
Fengshan	GX	24	C5
Fengshi	FJ	16	F2
Fengshiyan	HN	20	E4
Fengshuba Sk.	GD	21	A5
Fengshui	SD	10	C5
Fengshui Shan	HL	9	A2
Fengshun	GD	21	B6
Fengtai	BJ	3	B3
Fengtai	AH	13	D3
Fengtian	JX	15	C2
Fengtian	JX	15	F3
Fengtian	TW	17	C4
Fengtian	JX	15	D2
Fengting	FJ	16	E4
(Fengweiba) Zhenkang	YN	33	D3
Fengwu	GX	24	D5
Fengxi	FJ	16	D2
Fengxi	GD	21	B6
Feng Xian	JS	11	B2
Feng Xian (Shuangshipu)	SN	25	G2
(Fengxiang) Luobei	HL	9	D6
Fengxiangba	GZ	32	C5
Fengxiang	SN	25	F3
Fengxian (Nanqiao)	SH	11	F7
Fengxin	JX	15	C3
Fengyan	GZ	32	C6
Fengyang	AH	13	D4
(Fengyi) Zheng'an	GZ	32	B6
Fengyi	YN	33	C4
Fengyi	SX	5	E4
(Fengyizhen) Maowen Qiangzu Zizhixian	SC	30	C4
(Fengyuan) Taizhong (Taichung)	TW	17	B3
Fengyuan	SN	25	E5
Fengzhen	NM	6	D5
Fengzhou	FJ	16	F4
Fengzhou	SN	25	G2
Fengzhou	JX	15	F1
Fengzhuang	NX	26	D3
Fen He	SX	5	F3
Fen He	HEN	18	D6
Fenhe Sk.	SX	5	C3
Fenjie	JS	12	A4
Fenkou	ZJ	14	C3
Fenling	GD	23	I8
Fenqihu	TW	17	C3
Fenshi	HN	20	F5
Fenshouling	NX	26	C2
Fenshui	LN	7	D6
Fenshui	JX	15	C5
Fenshui	SC	30	E5
Fenshui	SD	10	D6
Fenshuiguan	ZJ	14	E5
Fenshui Guan	JX	15	D5
	FJ	16	C3
Fenshui Guan	FJ	16	G3
	GD	16	G3

Gaocheng	JS	12	C3	Gaolingzi	HL	9	E5	Gaotangpu	AH	13	D4
Gaocheng	HEB	4	E2	Gaoliu	JS	11	B4	Gaotang	SD	10	C3
Gaochun	JS	11	E4	Gaoliying	BJ	3	B3	Gaotan He	SC	30	C6
Gaocun	SX	5	C4	Gaolong	HN	20	E6	Gaotian	JX	15	E4
Gaocun	SX	5	F2	Gaolou	HEB	3	B4	Gaotingsi	HN	20	E5
Gaocun	SD	10	B9	Gaolou	ZJ	14	E5	(Gaotingzhen)	ZJ	14	B7
Gaocun	ZJ	14	B4	Gaolou Ling	GX	24	C4	Daishan			
Gaocun	JX	15	C2	Gaolu	AH	13	C3	Gaotouyao	NM	6	D4
(Gaocun) Mayang	HN	20	D2	Gaoluo	SX	5	D5	Gaotun	LN	7	D6
				Gaoluo	SX	5	F3	Gaowan	HEB	4	E5
Gaocunqiao	HEN	18	B6	Gaoluo	HB	19	E2	Gaowei	JX	15	F3
Gao Dao	ZJ	14	D6	Gaomiao	JS	11	D4	Gaoxian	SX	5	F3
Gao Dao	GD	23	I8	Gaomiao	QH	28	B8	Gaoxian	GZ	32	D7
Gaodeng Shan	SC	31	B5	Gaomiao	SC	31	C1	Gao Xian	SC	30	D5
Gaodian	AH	13	E3	Gaomingxian	GD	21	B4	Gaoxianji	HEN	18	C6
Gaodianzi	HB	19	D3	Gaomi	SD	10	C6	Gaoxingxu	JX	15	E3
Gaodu	SX	5	F4	Gaomutang	HN	20	E4	Gaoxinji	HEN	18	C7
Gaofu	JX	15	D5	Gaoniang	GZ	32	D8	Gaoxiong (Kaohsiung)	TW	17	D3
Gaogang	JS	12	A3	Gaopai	JX	15	F3				
Gaogongmiao	AH	13	C2	Gaopian	SC	31	A2	Gaoxiong (Kaohsiung)	TW	17	D3
Gaogou	JS	11	B5	Gaoping	HN	20	C6	(Fengshan)			
Gaohe	SX	5	E5	Gaoping	SC	31	B4	Gaoxishi	HN	20	E4
Gaohebu	AH	13	F3	Gaoping	GZ	32	C5	Gaoya	SD	10	C5
Gaohu	JX	15	C3	Gaoping	SX	5	F4	Gaoya	GS	26	D1
Gaoji	SD	10	C3	Gaoqi	FJ	16	F4	Gaoya	NX	26	D2
Gaojiabu	SX	5	B4	Gaoqian	HEB	4	F2	Gaoya	GS	26	E1
Gaojiabu	SN	25	B6	Gaoqiao	SD	10	D5	Gaoyakou	BJ	3	B2
Gaojiacun	NM	6	F10	Gaoqiao	SH	11	E7	Gaoyan	JS	11	C4
Gaojiadi	HEB	4	B2	Gaoqiao	ZJ	12	E3	Gaoyang	SN	25	E5
Gaojiadian	LN	7	B8	Gaoqiao	ZJ	12	E5	Gaoyang	HEB	4	E3
Gaojiadian	JL	8	C6	Gaoqiao	FJ	16	D3	Gaoyao	GD	21	B4
Gaojiafang	HN	20	C6	Gaoqiao	HN	20	E3	Gaoyazhen	SN	25	F3
Gaojian	ZJ	14	C6	Gaoqiao	GD	23	G7	Gaoyi	HEN	18	E5
Gaojiawan	SN	25	D4	Gaoqiao	GZ	32	B5	Gaoyi	HEB	4	F2
Gaojiayan	HB	19	D4	Gaoqiaozhen	LN	7	D4	Gaoyou	JX	15	C3
Gaojiazhen	SC	30	C6	Gaoqing (Tianzhen)	SD	10	B4	Gaoyou Hu	JS	11	D5
Gaojingzhuang	TJ	3	C5	Gaoqitou	HN	20	C3	Gaoyou	JS	11	D5
Gaokan	LN	7	D6	Gaorenzhen	NX	26	B3	Gaoyu	HEB	4	G2
Gaokan	LN	7	D6	Gaosha	HN	20	E3	Gaoyuan	SD	10	B4
Gaokeng	JX	15	D1	Gaosha	FJ	16	D3	Gaoze	SD	10	D6
Gaolan	JX	15	C2	Gaoshan	SX	5	A4	Gaozha	NX	26	C3
Gaolan	GD	23	I7	Gaoshan	FJ	16	E5	Gaozhen	SN	25	C5
Gaolan Dao	GD	21	C4	Gao Shan	JX	15	F2	Gaozhou	GD	21	C3
Gaolan Liedao	GD	23	I6-7	Gaoshanzi	LN	7	C6	Gaozi	JS	12	A2
Gaolan	GS	27	D6	Gaoshawo	NX	26	B4	Gaozuc	JS	11	C4
(Shidongsi)				Gaosheng	LN	7	C6	Gaozuo	JS	11	C5
Gaoli	HEB	3	C2	Gaoshi	SC	31	C3	Garang	QH	28	B7
Gaoliang	GD	21	B3	Gaoshu	TW	17	D3	Garco	XZ	34	B4
Gaoliang	SC	31	C3	Gaositai	HEB	4	B5	Gar Qu	SC	30	B4
Gaoliangji	AH	13	D4	Gaotai	GZ	32	C6	Garqu Yan	QH	28	D3
(Gaoliangjian)	JS	11	C4	Gaotaishan	LN	7	B6	(Gartog) Markam	XZ	34	C6
Hongze				Gaotai	GS	27	C4				
Gaoligong Shan	YN	33	B3	Gaotan	AH	13	F4	Gar	XZ	34	B1
Gaolincun	HEB	3	D2	Gaotan	SN	25	H4	Garyarsa	XZ	34	C2
Gaoling	BJ	3	A4	Gaotanchang	SC	31	C5	Garyi	SC	30	C2
Gaoling	GX	24	C6	Gaotang	FJ	16	D3	Gar Zangbo	XZ	34	C2
Gaoling	SD	10	B8	Gaotang	SN	25	F5	Garzê	SC	30	C2
Gaolingjiao	AH	13	G4	Gaotangji	AH	13	D3				
Gaolingkou	HEB	3	B1	(Gaotangling)	HN	20	C5				
Gaoling	SN	25	F5	Wangcheng				Gas Hu	QH	28	A2

Gaxun Nur	NM	6	D2
Gaya He	JL	8	D10
Gebu	GX	24	C3
Gedi	SX	5	E2
Gedian	HB	19	D7
(Gedong) Fangshan	SX	5	D3
Gedong	GZ	32	D7
Gefan	ZJ	14	D4
Gegenmiao	NM	8	B3
Gegong	AH	13	F4
Gegou	SD	10	D5
Gegu	YN	33	D5
Gegu	TJ	3	D4
Gê'gyai	XZ	34	B2
Ge Hu	JS	11	E5
Gejiu	YN	33	D5
Gekeng	FJ	16	E4
Gelan	SC	30	C6
Geleshan	SC	31	C5
Gelin	GZ	32	B6
Geling	FJ	16	E5
Geliping	SC	30	E3
Gelüji	SD	10	B8
Gema	GX	24	C4
Gemingcheng	QH	28	B8
Gengche	JS	11	C4
Gengdaqiao	SC	31	A1
Gengding Shan	GZ	32	E6
Gengjiawan	GS	27	D8
Gengle	HEB	4	G1
Genglou	GD	21	B4
Gengma Daizu Vazu Zizhixian	YN	33	D3
Gengpeng	AH	13	D3
Gengxin	GX	24	C4
Gengzhen	SX	5	C5
Gengzhuang	LN	7	D6
(Genhe) Ergun Zuoqi	NM	6	B7
Gen He	NM	6	B7
Geni He	NM	40	B3
Genzhukou	ZJ	14	D4
Gepaizhen	SN	25	G5
Gepu	HB	19	D6
Gê Qu	XZ	49	C1
Gêrzê	XZ	34	B3
Geshancun	ZJ	14	C5
Getai	SN	25	E6
Getu He	GZ	32	E5
(Gexianzhuang) Qinghe	HEB	4	F3
Geyitou	YN	33	C6
Geyuan	JX	15	C5
Geyucheng	HEB	3	C3
Gezhentan	SN	25	D6
Gezidong	QH	28	A7
Gobi	QH	28	B5
Goinsargoin	XZ	34	C6
Goinxab	QH	28	E5
Golin Baixing	NM	6	C7
Golmud He	QH	28	C4-B4
Golmud	QH	28	B4
Gomang Co	XZ	34	C4
Gomangxung	QH	28	C7
Gomo	XZ	34	B3
Gomo Co	XZ	34	B3
Gong'an	GX	24	C9
Gong'an	GX	24	F5
Gong'an (Doushi)	HB	19	D5
Gongbei	GD	23	I7
Gongbo'gyamda	XZ	34	C5
Gongchangling	LN	7	C7
Gongche	GX	24	F6
Gongcheng	GX	24	C8
Gongchenqiao	ZJ	12	E3
Gongchuan	FJ	16	D3
Gongchuan	GX	24	D5
Gongcun	HEB	4	D4
Gongfang	JX	15	D3
Gonggar	XZ	34	C4
Gongga Shan	SC	30	D3
Gongguan	GD	21	C3
Gongguan	GX	24	E7
Gongguoqiao	YN	33	C3
Gonghe	QH	28	B7
Gonghui	HEB	4	B2
Gonghui	GX	24	C9
Gongjiapeng	HEN	18	F6
Gongjiatai	HEB	4	F3
Gongjing	SC	30	D5
Gongjitang	NM	6	F10
Gonglang	YN	33	C4
Gongli	SD	10	D4
Gongliu (Tokkuztara)	XJ	29	C4
(Gonglüe) Donggu	JX	15	E3
Gongmajing	GS	26	D1
Gongmiaozi	NM	6	D4
Gongming	GD	23	H8
Gongpengzi	JL	8	B6
Gongpengzi	JL	8	C7
Gongping	GD	21	B5
Gongping	GX	24	B8
Gongpingxu	HN	20	E5
Gongpoquan	GS	27	B3
Gongqian	HEN	18	C3
Gongqingtuan Nongchang	XJ	29	C5
Gongshan	YN	33	C5
Gongshan Drungzu Nuzu Zizhixian	YN	33	B3
Gongshengqiao	AH	12	B1
Gong Shui	JX	15	F3
Gongtan	SC	30	D7
Gongtian	HN	20	B6
Gongwangling	SN	25	F5
Gongwang Shan	YN	50	C4-B4
Gongxi	JX	15	D3
Gong Xian (Xiaoyi)	HEN	18	C4
Gong Xian	SC	30	D5
Gongyi	GD	23	I6
Gongyingzi	LN	7	C3
Gongzheng	GX	24	E6
Gongzhengjie	GX	24	B8
Gongzhutun	LN	7	B7
Gonjo	XZ	30	C2
Gonjo	XZ	34	C6
Goqên	XZ	34	C6
Gora	SC	30	C3
Gosu	SC	30	B2
Goubangzi	LN	7	C5
Gouchang	GZ	32	E5
Gou Chi	SN	25	C3
Goudun	JS	11	C5
Gougezhuang	HEB	3	D3
Goujiaozhen	SC	31	B5
Goujie	YN	33	C5
Goujie	YN	33	D5
Goukou	NM	6	B7
Goukou	NX	26	E3
Goulin	HEN	18	E4
Goulou Shan	GX	45	C4
Goumen	HEB	3	A5
Goumenzi	LN	7	D3
Gouqi Shan	ZJ	14	B7
Goushi	HEN	18	C4
Goutai	NX	26	C3
Gouyadong	HN	20	F5
Gozha Co	XZ	34	B2
Guabu	JS	11	D4
Guai'erzhen	SX	5	D5
Guaihe	HEN	18	D4
Guaimozi	LN	7	C9
Guala	GZ	32	D3
Gualanyu	HEB	4	C5
Guali	ZJ	14	B5
Guan'ao	FJ	16	F4
Guanbei	JX	15	D1
Guanbei	FJ	16	F3
Guanbuqiao	HB	19	E7
Guancen Shan	SX	5	B4
Guancen Shan	SX	5	C4
Guanchang	GD	21	C3
Guanchao	JX	15	E2
Guancheng	HEB	3	D2
Guancheng	SX	5	C4
Guancheng	SD	10	D2
Guancheng	ZJ	14	B6
Guandang	HN	20	B5
Guandaokou	HEN	18	C3
Guandi	HEB	4	B4
Guandi	JL	8	D9
Guandi	JL	8	E10
Guandian	GZ	32	B5
Guandian	AH	13	D5
Guandiankou	HB	19	D3

Guandimiao	HN	20	E5	Guangyang	AH	13	F4	Guantao	HEB	4	G3
Guandiping	HN	20	B3	Guangya Tan	HI	22	D2	(Nanguantao)			
Guandi Shan	SX	5	D3	Guangyuan	SC	30	B5	Guantian	JX	15	D2
Guandong	GZ	32	E8	Guangze	FJ	16	C3	Guantianba	SC	31	D2
Guandu	HB	19	C3	Guangzhou	GD	21	B4	Guantianjie	JS	11	B4
Guandu	HN	20	C6					Guanting	HEB	4	C3
Guandu	GD	21	A4	Guangzong	HEB	4	F3	Guanting	NX	26	D3
Guandu	SC	30	C7	Guan He	JS	11	B5	Guanting	YN	33	D5
Guandu	SC	31	C5	Guan He	HEN	18	E7	Guanting	AH	13	E3
Guandu	GZ	32	B5	Guanhekou	SX	5	B3	Guanting	HEN	18	C5
Guandukou	HB	19	C3	Guanhe Kou	JS	11	B5	Guanting	GS	27	F7
Guan'er	SX	5	B5	Guanhu	JS	11	B3	Guanting	QH	28	C8
Guanfangpu	HB	19	A2	Guanji	AH	13	C2	Guanting Sk.	HEB	4	C3
Guangang	AH	13	G3	Guanjia	LN	7	D8	Guanting Zhan	HEB	3	B2
Guang'an	SC	30	C6	Guanjian	SC	31	C4	Guantou	FJ	16	D5
Guangchang	JX	15	E4	Guan Jiang	GX	24	B9	Guantou	SX	5	E2
Guangdegong	NM	6	D6	Guanjian He	SC	31	C4	Guantunbu	NM	5	A5
Guangde	AH	13	F6	Guanjiaqiao	HN	20	C6	Guanwangmiao	SX	5	F3
Guangdian	HEN	18	D4	Guanjiawu	HEB	3	D3	Guanxi	TW	17	B4
Guangezhen	SC	31	B5	Guanjiazui	HN	20	E4	Guan Xian	SD	10	C2
Guangfaxu	HN	20	F5	Guanjing	FJ	16	E5	Guan Xian	SC	30	C4
Guangfeng	JX	15	C6	Guankou	HB	19	D8	Gu'an	HEB	4	D4
Guangfu	SC	30	C5	(Guankou) Ningshan	SN	25	G4	Guanxu	GD	21	B3
Guangfu	JS	11	E6					Guanyang	FJ	16	C6
Guanghai	GD	21	C4	Guankou	SC	31	A1	Guanyang	GX	24	B9
Guanghai Wan	GD	23	J6	Guankou	FJ	16	F3	Guanyao	GD	23	G6
Guanghan	SC	30	C5	Guankou	SC	31	B1	Guanyazi	HB	19	B2
Guanghe	GS	27	E6	Guanlan	GD	23	H8	Guanyin	TW	17	A4
Guanghua	SX	5	E3	Guanli	SD	10	B7	Guanyin	GX	24	B8
Guanghua	JL	8	F6	Guanlin	JS	11	E5	Guanyin	SC	31	A5
Guanghuasi	HB	19	D5	Guanling	HN	20	E5	Guanyin	SC	31	B1
Guanghua	HB	19	B4	Guanling Bouyeizu	GZ	32	E4	Guanyin	SC	31	B6
(Guangji)	HB	19	E8	Miaozu Zizhixian				Guanyinchang	SC	31	D2
Wuxue				Guanlu	ZJ	14	D5	Guanyinge	HN	20	C3
Guangli	GD	21	B4	Guanmenshan	NX	26	D2	Guanyinhe	SC	31	A5
Guangling	JS	11	D6	Guanmian Shan	SC	49	C7	Guanyinqiao	SC	30	C3
Guangling	SX	5	B6	Guanmiao	TW	17	D3	Guanyinshan	SN	25	F2
Guanglu	HEB	4	G2	Guannan	JS	11	B5	Guanyinsi	HB	19	C4
Guanglu Dao	LN	7	E6	(Xin'anzhen)				Guanyinsi	SN	25	G2
Guangmao Shan	YN	33	B4	Guanpo	HEN	18	D2	Guanyintan	HN	20	E4
Guangming Ding	AH	13	F5	Guanputou	TJ	3	D4	Guanyintan	SC	31	C3
Guangnan	YN	33	C6	Guanqian	AH	13	F4	Guanyintang	HEN	18	C3
Guangningsi	LN	7	E5	Guanqian	FJ	16	C4	Guanyintang	HEN	18	C5
Guangning	GD	21	B4	Guanqian	FJ	16	E2	Guanyin Xia	SC	31	C5
(Nanjie)				Guanqian	FJ	16	D3	Guanyinyan	SC	30	C4
Guan Gou	BJ	3	B2	Guanqiao	SD	10	E4	Guanyinzhen	SC	30	D5
Guangouji	AH	13	D4	Guanqiao	AH	13	F4	Guanyuemiao	AH	13	E2
Guangping	FJ	16	D3	Guanqiao	FJ	16	E4	Guanyun	JS	11	B5
Guangping	GX	24	D9	Guanqiao	FJ	16	F4	(Dayishan)			
Guangping	HN	20	E2	Guanqiaobu	NX	26	D2	Guanzhangpu	HEN	18	D3
Guangping	HEB	4	G2	Guanshan	TW	17	C4	Guanzhen	JS	11	C4
Guangrao	SD	10	B5	Guanshan	GD	23	H6	Guanzhou	GZ	32	B7
Guangshan	HEN	18	E6	Guanshan	JX	15	D3	Guanzhuang	NX	26	E3
Guangshui	HB	19	C7	Guan Shan	TW	17	C3	Guanzhuang	HEB	4	F2
Guangshun	GZ	32	D5	Guanshan Dao	ZJ	14	E5	Guanzhuang	SD	10	C6
Guangshunchang	SC	30	D5	Guanshang	SX	5	D3	Guanzhuang	FJ	16	E2
Guangwu	HEN	18	C5	Guanshuai	SD	10	D6	Guanzhuang	HEN	18	E5
Guangwu	NX	26	C2	Guanshui	LN	7	D8	Guanzhuang	HEN	18	E6
Guangwu	AH	13	C2	Guansongzhen	HL	9	D5	Guanzhuang	HB	19	C5
Guangxingzhou	HN	20	B5	Guantangyi	HB	19	E7	Guanzhuang	HN	20	C3

Guanzhuang	SN	25	F4	Guhou	JX	15	E4	Guli	JS	12	B5
Guanziling	TW	17	C3	Guhuai	FJ	16	E5	Guli	GZ	32	D5
Guanziyao	GZ	32	E3	Guichi	AH	13	F4	Guli	SD	10	D4
Guazhou	JS	11	D5	(Chizhou)				Guli	GZ	32	D5
Gubai	SC	30	D5	Guide	SD	10	C3	Gulian	HL	9	A2
Gubei	JX	15	F3	Guidebu	SN	25	B5	Guling	GX	24	D6
Gubei	AH	13	E2	Guide	QH	28	B7	Guling	JX	15	B3
Gubeikou	BJ	3	A4	Guidexiang	SC	31	C3	Gulingzhen	SC	30	C7
Gubu	JX	15	C4	Guiding	GZ	32	D6	Gulin	SC	30	D5
Gubu	GD	23	H6	Guidong	HN	20	E6	Guliushu	SD	10	C2
Gucheng	HEB	4	F4	Guifu	SC	31	A5	Guliya Shan	NM	6	B7
Gucheng	SX	5	A5	(Guihua) Mingxi	FJ	16	D3	(Gulja) Yining	XJ	29	C4
Gucheng	SX	5	F2	Guihuayuan	SC	30	C5	Gulong	HL	9	E3
Gucheng	SX	5	F3	Guiji	AH	13	D3	Gulong	GX	24	D8
Gucheng	SX	5	F3	Gui Jiang	GX	24	C8	Gulonggang	JX	15	E3
Gucheng	NM	6	F10	Guiji Shan	ZJ	14	C5	Gulou	HN	20	C4
Gucheng	HL	9	D3	Guiler	NM	6	C7	Gulougang	AH	13	D4
Gucheng	SD	10	D2	Guiler Gol	NM	39	A2	Gulung	SC	30	C2
Gucheng	JS	11	D4					(Guma) Pishan	XJ	29	D3
Gucheng	AH	13	C2	Guiling	GX	24	C9	Gumei	GX	24	D4
Gucheng	AH	13	D4	Guilin	GX	24	B8	Gumiao	HEN	18	E5
Gucheng	JX	15	C6					Gumu	YN	33	D6
Gucheng	JX	15	E1	Guiluan Dao	TW	17	B4	Gunbei	GX	24	B6
Gucheng	FJ	16	E2	Guimen	ZJ	14	C5	Güncang	XZ	34	C5
Gucheng	GX	24	C9	Guimeng Ding	SD	10	D4	Gun He	HB	19	B5
Gucheng	NX	26	B3	Guinan	QH	23	C7	Guobei	SC	31	C3
Gucheng	NX	26	E3	Guiping	GX	24	D8	Guobu	SX	5	D4
Gucheng	GS	27	D6	Guiren	JS	11	C4	Guochengyi	GS	27	D7
Gucheng	SC	30	B5	Guishan	YN	33	C5	Guocun	SX	5	E4
Gucheng	HEB	3	C3	Guishan Dao	TW	17	B4	Guocun	AH	13	F4
Gucheng	HEB	4	D3	Guishan Dao	GD	23	I7	Guocun	HEB	4	C3
Gucheng	JS	12	C2	Gui Shui	HN	20	F5	Guodao	SX	5	E4
Gucheng	HEN	18	D6	Guitai	GX	24	E6	Guodian	SD	10	C4
Gucheng	SX	5	E4	Guitou	GD	21	A4	Guodian	HEN	18	C5
Guchenggang	JX	15	D4	Guixi	YN	33	A5	Guodiantun	SD	10	C2
Gucheng Hu	JS	11	E4	Gui Xian	GX	24	D7	Guodu	SD	10	D4
Gucheng	HB	19	B4	Guixi	JX	15	C5	Guofu	HL	9	D4
Gucheng	HEB	4	F3	Guiyang	HN	20	E5	Guofu	SC	31	D5
(Zhengjiakou)				Guiyang	GZ	32	D5	Guo He	AH	13	C3
Guchuan	SN	25	F2	Guiyang	HN	20	F5		HEN	18	C7
Gucun	JX	15	D3	Guizhou	GD	23	H7	Guohua	GX	24	D5
Gucun	JX	15	E4	Guizi	GD	21	B3	Guoji	JS	11	B5
Gudatun	SX	5	A6	Gujiang	JX	15	D2	Guoji	HEN	18	E5
Gudi	SD	10	C6	Gu Jiang	JX	15	D3	Guojia	JL	8	C6
Gudian	SX	5	A5	Gujiao	SX	5	D4	Guojiadian	JL	8	D5
Gudianzi	JL	8	D7	Gujiao	SX	5	F5	Guojiadian	SD	10	B7
Gudingqiao	SX	5	B5	Gujiao	GZ	32	D5	Guojiatun	HEB	4	B5
Gudong	GZ	32	D6	Gujiazi	JL	8	D5	Guojiayao	SX	5	A5
Gudong	YN	33	C3	Gujing	GD	23	I6	Guojiayuan	JS	11	D6
Gudong He	JL	8	E9	Gujunba	SC	30	C7	Guojiazhai	SD	10	C7
Gudou Shan	GD	21	B4	Gukai	GZ	32	C4	Guojiazhen	GS	27	E7
Gudui	SX	5	F3	Gukou	FJ	16	D4	Guojiazhuang	SD	10	C7
Gudun	GZ	32	D8	Gula	GX	24	D6	Guoju	ZJ	14	C7
Gufang	ZJ	14	C4	Gulai	ZJ	14	C5	Guokeng	FJ	16	F3
Gugancheng	HEN	18	B7	Gulang	YN	33	B3	Guoleizhuang	HEB	4	C2
Gugang	HN	20	C6	Gulang	GS	27	D6	Guoliji	SD	10	D3
Gugaozhuang	JS	12	A4	Gulangyu	FJ	16	F4	(Guolüezhen)	HEN	18	C2
Guguantun	SD	10	C3	Gulao	GD	23	H6	Lingbao			
Guguanzhen	SN	25	F2	Gulaobei	HB	19	D4	Guolutan	HEN	18	E7
Guhe	AH	13	E4	Guleitou	FJ	16	G3	Guoqiao	JX	15	B4

Guosong	JL	8	F7	Gu Xian (Yueyang)	SX	5	E3	Hagin Gol	NM	26	B2
Guotan	HEN	18	E4	Guxianchang	SC	31	B5	Hai'an	GD	21	C3
Guotang	GD	23	G7	Guxiandu	JX	15	B4	Hai'an Shan	GD	21	B5
Guotouyu	LN	38	C6	Guxiang	GD	21	B6	Hai'an	JS	11	D6
Guoxianyao	NM	6	F10	Guxiansi	AH	13	D3	Haibei	HL	9	D4
Guoyang	AH	13	C3	Guyang	HEN	18	C6				
Guoyangzhen	SX	5	C4	Guyang	NM	6	D4				
Guozhen	HN	20	B6	Guye	HEB	4	D6	(Haibowan) Wuhai	NM	6	E3
(Guozhen) Baoji	SN	25	F3	Guyi	FJ	16	E4				
Guozhou Liedao	GD	23	I8	(Guyi) Sanjiang	GX	24	B7	Haicang	FJ	16	F3
Guozhuang	HEB	4	E2	Dongzu Zizhixian				Haicheng	GX	24	D5
Guozhuangmiao	JS	11	E5	Guyi	SC	31	B1	Haicheng	FJ	16	F3
Guozhuangzi	NX	26	C3	Guyong	YN	33	C3	Haicheng He	LN	38	C5
Gupei	JS	11	B3	Guyuan	NM	9	B3	Haicheng	LN	7	D6
Gupei	AH	13	D4					Haidian	BJ	3	B3
Gupeitang	HN	20	C6	Guyuan	NX	26	D3				
Gupeng	GX	24	D6	Guyuan	HEB	4	B3	Haifeng	HI	21	B5
Guqiang	HEN	18	D6	(Pingdingbu)				Haifuzhen	JS	11	E7
Gŭqiao	AH	13	D3	Guyushu	LN	7	A7	Hai He	TJ	3	D4
Guraoji	AH	13	C3	Guzhang	GX	24	C2	Haihui	JX	15	B4
Gurban Anggir	QH	28	B5	Guzhang	HN	20	C2	Haijiang	HL	9	C3
Gurban Obo	NM	6	D5	Guzhen	GD	23	H7	Haijiu Ansha	HI	22	C3
Gurbantünggüt Shamo	XJ	29	B5-6	Guzhen	SX	5	F4	Haikang	GD	21	C3
				Guzhen	AH	13	C4	(Leizhou)			
Gushan	ZJ	14	D5	(Guzhou) Rongjiang	GZ	32	E7	Haikou	ZJ	14	D5
Gushan	QH	28	B8					Haikou	JX	15	B5
Gushan	SX	5	A5	Guzhu	JX	15	E4	Haikou	FJ	16	E5
Gushan	LN	7	D6	Guzhu	GD	21	B5	Haikou	HI	21	C3
Gushan	LN	7	E7	Gyaca	XZ	34	C5	Hailang He	HL	8	C9-10
Gushan	SN	25	A6	Gyagartang	GS	27	E6	Hailar He (Riv)	NM	6	B7
Gushan	SD	10	C3	(Gya'gya) Saga	XZ	34	C3	Hailar	NM	6	B6
Gu Shan	FJ	16	D5	Gyai Qu	XZ	51	C5	Hailing Dao	GD	21	C3
Gushanzi	JL	8	E7	Gya La	XZ	34	C3	Hailin	HL	9	E5
Gushi	ZJ	14	D4	Gyangrang	XZ	34	C3	Hailong	JL	8	E6
Gushi	JX	15	B2	Gyangzê	XZ	34	C4	Hailong	JL	8	E6
Gushi	SN	25	F5	Gyaring	QH	28	C5	(Meihekou)			
Gushi	HEN	18	E7	Gyaring Co	XZ	34	C4	Hails	NM	6	D3
Gushu	HEB	3	B5	Gyaring Hu	QH	28	C5	Hailü Dao	SD	10	B9
Gushui	GD	21	B4	Gyawa	SC	30	D3	Hailun	HL	9	D4
Gushui	HEN	18	C4	Gyêmdong	XZ	34	C5	Haima Tan	HI	22	D4
Gushuji	HEN	18	C7	(Gyigang) Zayü	XZ	34	C6	(Haimen) Jiaojiang	ZJ	14	D6
Gusong	SC	30	D5	Gyimda	XZ	34	C5				
Gutang	FJ	16	F3	Gyirong	XZ	34	C3	Haimen	GD	21	B6
Gutang	XZ	34	C5	Gyirong	XZ	34	C3	Haimen Wan	GD	21	B6
Gutian [nan]	FJ	16	E2	(Zongga)				Haimen	JS	11	E7
Gutian [bei]	FJ	16	E2	Gyitang	XZ	34	C6	Hainan Dao(Is.)	GD	21	D3
Gutian Sk.	FJ	16	D4	Gyiza	QH	28	D4				
Gutian Xi	FJ	16	D4								
Gutian	FJ	16	D4	**H**							
Guting	JX	15	F2								
(Guting) Yutai	SD	10	E3								
Guxi	SC	31	B4	Habahe (Kaba)	XJ	29	A5	Haining Jiao	HI	22	E3
Guxian	SX	5	E3	Habirag	NM	6	D5	Haining	ZJ	14	B5
Guxian	JX	15	D3	Hadagang	HL	9	E6	(Xiashi)			
Guxian	SD	10	C7	Hadamen	JL	8	E11	Haiqing	HL	9	D8
Guxian	SD	10	B8	(Hadapu) Bailong	GS	27	E7	Hairag	QH	28	B7
Guxian	HEN	18	E5	Hadat	NM	6	B6	Hairhan Namag	NM	6	D2
Guxian	SX	5	E4	Hadayang	NM	6	B8	Haitan Dao	FJ	16	E5
Guxian	JX	15	C3	Hadilik	XJ	29	D5	Haitangxi	SC	31	C5
Guxian	HEN	18	C3	Hafu	JL	8	D5	Haitan Xia	FJ	16	E5

Haitou	JS	11	B5	Handaqi	HL	9	B4	Hanyuan (Fulin)	SC	30	D4
Haitou	HI	21	D2	(Handian) Changzhi	SX	5	E5				
Haituo	JL	8	B4					Hanzhong	SN	25	G3
				Hanfang	JX	15	F3	Hanzhuang	BJ	3	B4
				Hanfuwan	NX	26	D3	Hanzhuang	SD	10	E4
				Hangbu He	AH	13	E3	Haobeicun	SX	5	E4
Haixing	HL	9	D4	Hangdong	GX	24	C4	Haocheng	AH	13	C4
Haixing (Suji)	HEB	4	E5	Hanggai	ZJ	14	B4	Haocun	HEB	4	E4
Haixin Shan	QH	28	B7	Hanggin Houqi	NM	6	D3	Haodian	NX	26	E3
Haiyan	GD	21	C4	(Xamba)				Haogou	AH	13	C4
Haiyang	HEB	4	D7	Hanggin Qi	NM	6	E4	Haojiadian	HB	19	C6
Haiyang	GX	24	B8	Hangkou	JX	15	B2	Haojiaji	NX	26	D2
Haiyang Dao	LN	7	E7	Hangkouping	ZJ	14	C4	Haojiapo	SX	5	C3
Haiyang Shan	GX	24	B8	Hangou	TJ	3	C4	Haojiaqiao	NX	26	B3
Haiyangsuo	SD	10	C8	Hangtou	SH	12	C6	Haojiatai	NX	26	C4
Haiyang	SD	10	C8	Hangtou	ZJ	14	C3	Haokou	HEB	3	D1
(Dongcun)				Hangu	TJ	3	C5	Haolianghe	HL	9	D5
Haiyantang	ZJ	12	D4-5	Hanguang	GD	21	A4	Haoqiao	HEB	4	F2
Haiyan	ZJ	14	B5	Hangzhou	ZJ	14	B5	Haoshan	HN	20	E6
(Wuyuanzhen)				Hangzhou Wan (Gf.)	ZJ	14	B5	Hao Xi	ZJ	14	D5
Haiyan	QH	28	B7	Hanhong	SX	5	E4	Haoxue	HB	19	D5
(Sanjiaocheng)				Hanhui Qu	SN	25	G2	Haozhai	JS	11	B2
Haiyaopu	YN	33	B4	Hanji	SD	10	E2	Haozhai	AH	13	F5
(Haiyou) Sanmen	ZJ	14	C6	Hanjiadian	LN	7	C5	Haozhikou	SC	31	C3
				Hanjiagou	GZ	32	B6	Haozhuang	HEN	18	D5
Haiyuan	GX	24	E5	Hanjiaji	GS	27	E6	Haozichuan	NX	26	D2
Haiyuan	NX	26	D2	Hanjialou	SX	5	B3	Haozikou	HB	19	D5
Haizhou	JS	11	B5	Hanjiang	FJ	16	E5	Harbaling	JL	8	D9
Haizhou	GD	23	H7	Han Jiang	GD	21	B6-A6	Harbin	HL	9	E4
Haizhou Wan	JS	11	B5	Hanjiang	JS	11	D5	Hargant	NM	6	B6
Haizidi	YN	33	C4	Hanjiang	JS	11	D5	Har Hu	QH	28	A5
Haizijie	GZ	32	C4	Hanjiaoshui	NX	26	C2	Har Huxu	NM	6	F10
Haizijing	NX	26	C3	Hanjiawa	HEB	4	E2	Har Mod	JL	8	C6
Haizipu	GZ	32	E3	Hanjiaying	HEB	4	B2	Harqin Qi	NM	6	D6
Haju	NM	6	D1	Hanjing	SN	25	E5	Harqin Zuoyi	LN	7	C3
Haladaokou	LN	7	B3	Hankou	HB	19	D7	Mongolzu Zizhixian			
Halagang	HEB	4	D4	Hanmaying	HEB	4	B5	(Dachengzi)			
Halaha	JL	8	C6	Han Qu	NX	26	C3	Har Sai Shan	QH	28	C5
Halahai	JL	8	C6	Hanshan	AH	13	E5	Hartao	LN	7	B6
(Haliut) Urad	NM	6	F10	Hanshou	HN	20	C4	Har Us	NM	6	B7
Zhongqi				Han Shui (Riv.)	HB	19	C5	Hasalbag	XJ	29	D3
Haltang He	QH	28	A4-5		SN	25	H4	Hatu	NM	26	B4
Hamatang	JL	8	D10	Han Sum	NM	6	C6	Haxat	JL	8	C5
				Hantai	HEB	4	E2	Haxian	GS	26	D1
Hami (Kumul)	XJ	29	C7	Hantan	JX	15	C5	Haya	NM	6	D2
Hami	XJ	29	C7	Hantang	JX	15	C2	Hebachang	SC	31	A2
Hanbei	SX	5	E5	Hantengri Feng	XJ	29	C4	Hebao Dao	GD	23	J7
Hancha	SN	25	C5	(Hanting) Wei Xian	SD	10	C6	Hebei	BJ	3	B2
Hancheng	SN	25	H4	Hanting	AH	13	F5	Hebei	SX	5	F4
Hancheng	HEB	4	D6	Hanwang	SC	30	C5	Hebeitun	TJ	3	C4
Hancheng	HEN	18	C3	Hanwang	SD	10	D5	Hebian	SX	5	C5
Hancheng	SN	25	E6	Hanwangzhen	SX	5	D5	Hebian	SC	31	B3
Hanchuan	HB	19	D6	Hanxia	GS	27	C3	Hebian	SC	31	C4
Hancun	SN	25	F5	Hanxue	SX	5	F2	Hebiji	HEN	18	B6
Hancun	HEB	4	D4	Hanyang	HB	19	D7	Hebi	HEN	18	B6
Hancun	HEN	18	B7	Hanyang	SC	31	C1	Hebu	JX	15	D3
				Hanyang	HB	19	D7	Hecheng	GD	21	B4
Handan	HEB	4	G2	(Caidian)							
Handan	HEB	4	G2	Hanyangzhen	SX	5	G2	Hechi	GX	24	C6
Handaokou	HEN	18	C8	Hanyin	SN	25	H4	(Jinchengjiang)			

Name	Region	Sheet	Grid
Hechuan	SX	5	E4
Hechuan	NX	26	E3
Hechuan	SC	30	C6
Hechun	GD	21	C3
Hecun	HEB	5	E6
Hecun	ZJ	14	D3
(Hede) Sheyang	JS	11	C6
Hedi	SX	5	C5
Hedi	SX	5	E3
Hedi	ZJ	14	E4
Hedi He	YN	33	D5-C5
Hediling	HEN	18	C7
Hedi Sk.	GD	21	C3
Hedong	GD	23	H7
Hedongdian	SN	25	G2
Hefei	AH	13	E4
Hefengchang	SC	31	B2
Hefengqiao	HEN	18	F7
Hefeng Tujiazu Zizhixian	HB	19	E3
Hefu	HN	20	B4
Hegang	HL	9	D6
Hegumiao	HEB	4	G3
Hehe	SX	5	E2
Hehuanyakou	TW	17	B4
Heicha Shan	SX	5	C3
Heicheng	NM	6	F10
Heichengzhen	NX	26	D3
Heichengzi	LN	7	B4
Heichongtan	GS	27	D6
Heidong	HB	19	E2
Hei He	HEB	4	C4
Hei He	HEN	18	D6
Hei He	SN	25	G2
Hei He	GS	27	C4
	QH	28	A6
Hei He	GS	46	D3
Heihe Shi	HL	9	B4
Heihumiao	SD	10	D2
Heijing	YN	33	C4
Heilangkou	TJ	3	C4
Heilaoyao	NM	6	F10
Heilin	JS	11	A4
Heilinzi	JL	8	C7
Heilinzi	JL	8	D5
Heilonggong	HL	9	E4
Heilongguan	SX	5	E3
Heilongguan	SN	25	D6
Heilong Jiang (Riv.)	HL	9	D6-7
Heilongkou	SN	25	F5
Heilongtan Sk.	SC	31	C2
Heilongzhen	HEN	18	E4
Heimahe	QH	28	B6
Heiqiao	JS	12	A3
Heiquan	GS	27	C4
Heishan	SN	25	G5
Heishan	NM	26	C1
Hei Shan	LN	38	C3
Heishanke	LN	7	D3
Heishansi	HEB	3	B1
Heishantou	NM	6	B6
Heishan Xia	NX	26	C1
	GS	27	D7
Heishan	LN	7	C6
Heishenmiao	GZ	32	C5
Heishi	JL	8	D9
Heishi	JL	8	E7
Heishiguan	HEN	18	C4
Heishitou	GZ	32	D3
Heishui	LN	7	B3
Heishui	JL	8	B3
Heishui	SN	25	G2
Heishui	SC	30	D7
Heishui He	SC	30	E4
Heishuisi	SN	25	D4
Heishui	SC	30	B4
Heita	AH	13	C5
Heitai	HL	9	E6
Heituhe	GZ	32	C2
Heituo Shan	SX	5	B4
Heiyanzhen	HEN	18	D3
Heiyanzi	HEB	4	D6
Heiyukou	SX	5	C2
Heiyupao	JL	8	B4
Hejia	JX	15	C4
Hejialiang	SN	25	B5
Hejian	HEN	18	B5
Hejiang	GD	21	C3
He Jiang	GX	24	C9
Hejiang	SC	30	D5
Hejian	HEB	4	E4
Hejiao	NM	6	F10
Hejiaping	HB	19	D3
Hejiayan	SN	25	G2
Hejiazhen	SC	31	C2
Hejiazhuang	SX	5	F3
Hejicun	GX	24	D7
Hejie	GX	24	C9
Hejing	XJ	29	C5
Hejin	SX	5	F2
Heka	QH	28	C6
Hekou	FJ	16	D2
Hekou[dong]	HN	20	B4
Hekou	SX	5	C3
Hekou	SX	5	D4
Hekou	NM	6	F10
Hekou	JS	11	D5
(Hekou) Yanshan	JX	15	C5
Hekou	HB	19	C7
Hekou[xi]	HN	20	B4
Hekou	HN	20	E3
Hekou	GD	21	B4
Hekou	GD	21	C3
Hekou	GX	24	B7
Hekou	SN	25	C6
Hekou	GS	27	D6
Hekou	SC	30	C6
Hekou	SC	31	D1
Hekou	GZ	32	D7
Hekouji	AH	13	D3
Hekou Yaozu Zizhixian	YN	33	D5
Helan Shan	NM	6	E3
	NX	26	B2
Helan Shan	NX	26	B2
Helan (Xigang)	NX	26	B3
Hele	HI	21	D3
Heli	GX	24	D6
Heli	HL	9	D6
Helianwan	GS	27	D8
Helinzhen	SC	31	B6
Heli Shan	GS	27	C4-5
Heliu	SC	30	C6
Heliuji	AH	13	C3
Helixi	AH	13	F6
Helong	JL	8	C6
Helong	LN	7	B8
Helong	JL	8	E9
Helukou	HN	20	G4
Hemei	TW	17	B3
Hemenkou	YN	33	B4
Hemu	GX	24	C7
Henan Mongolzu Zizhixian	QH	28	C7
Hengcheng	NX	26	B3
Hengcheqiao	HB	19	D8
Hengchun	TW	17	D3
Hengdan	GS	27	F7
Hengdaochuan	LN	7	C9
Hengdaohe	LN	7	B7
Hengdaohezi	JL	8	D7
Hengdaohezi	HL	9	E5
Hengdaozi	JL	8	D8
Hengdian	HB	19	D7
Hengdong	HN	20	D5
Hengdu	AH	13	F4
Hengduan Shan(Mts.)	YN	33	A2-B3
	XZ	34	C6-D6
Hengfan	ZJ	14	B4
Hengfeng	JX	15	C5
Henggang	GD	23	H8
Henggang	JX	15	B3
Henggouqiao	HB	19	E7
Henghe	GD	23	G8
Heng He	SC	31	D3
Henghu	ZJ	14	B4
Hengjian	SX	5	D3
Hengjian	HEN	18	D3
Hengjiang	JX	15	E4
Hengjiang	SC	30	D5
Heng Jiang	SC	30	D5
	YN	33	A6
Hengjiangdu	JX	15	E2
Hengjiangqiao	HN	20	E2
Heng Jiao	HI	22	D3
Hengjing	JS	11	E6

Hengkou	SN	25	H4	Hepu	HB	19	C8	Hexia	JX	15	D2
Henglan	GD	23	I7	Hepu	ZJ	14	C6	He Xian	AH	13	E5
Hengli	GD	21	B5	Hepu	GX	24	F7	He Xian (Babu)	GX	24	C9
Hengli	GD	23	H8	(Lianzhou)				Hexiangqiao	HN	20	D3
Hengliangdian	JS	12	A2	Heqiao	JS	11	E5	Hexigten Qi	NM	6	D6
Henglin	JS	12	B3	Heqiao	JS	11	D4	(Jingpeng)			
Hengling	HEB	3	B2	Heqiao	ZJ	14	B4	Hexijie	HEB	4	G3
Hengling	SX	5	D5	Heqiaoyi	GS	27	D6	Hexingchang	SC	31	A2
Henglingguan	SX	5	F3	Heqing	YN	33	B4	Hexipu	GS	27	C6
Henglongqiao	HN	20	C5	Heqiu	JX	15	F2	Hexiwu	TJ	3	C4
Henglu	JX	15	B3	Hequ	SX	5	B3	Heyang	SD	10	D5
Henglu	JX	15	B5	Herlen He	NM	6	B6	Heyang	SN	25	E6
Henglutou	ZJ	14	B4	Herong	HB	19	D4	Heyu	HEN	18	D3
Heng Men	GD	21	B4	Heshan	GD	21	C4	Heyuan	GD	21	B5
Hengmian	SH	12	C6	Heshan	GX	24	D6				
Hengnan	HN	20	E5	Heshan	HL	9	C3	Heze (Caozhou)	SD	10	D2
Heng Sha	SH	11	E7	Heshangfangzi	LN	7	D3	Hezhang	GZ	32	C3
Hengshan	HL	9	E6	Heshangpu	NX	26	E3	Hezheng	GS	27	E6
Hengshan	AH	13	E5	Heshangzhen	ZJ	14	C5	Hezhi	SX	5	B3
Hengshan	GD	21	C3	Heshan	GX	24	D6	Hezixu	JX	15	G3
Hengshan	JS	12	C4	Heshan	GD	21	B4	Hezuozhen	GS	27	E6
Heng Shan	SX	5	B5	Hesheng	GS	27	E8	Himalaya Shan (Mts.)	XZ	34	C3-5
Heng Shan	SX	5	B5	Hesheng	ZJ	14	D5				
Heng Shan	HN	20	D5	Heshengqiao	HB	19	D7	Hoboksar Mongol	XJ	29	B5
Hengshanpu	NX	26	B3	Heshi	SC	31	D2	Zizhixian			
Hengshan	SN	25	C5	Heshi	JX	15	C2	(Hobot Xar)	NM	6	D5
Hengshan	HN	20	D5	Heshi	FJ	16	E4	Xianghuang Qi			
Hengshi	JX	15	E2	Heshu	SC	31	A5	Hobq Shamo	NM	6	F10
Hengshi	HB	19	E7	Heshui	GD	21	B3	Hohhot	NM	6	D4
Hengshi	GD	23	G7	Heshui	GD	21	B3	Hoh Sai Hu	QH	28	C3
Hengshui	SX	5	F3	Heshui	GD	23	H6	Hoh Xil Hu	QH	28	C2
Hengshui	HEN	18	C4	Heshui	GX	24	B7	Hoh Xil Shan (Mts.)	QH	28	C1-2
Hengshui	SN	25	F3	Heshui	GZ	32	B7		XZ	34	B4-5
				He Shui	JX	15	E2	Hoh Yanchi	QH	28	B5
Hengshui	HEB	4	F3	Heshuilaocheng	GS	27	D9	Hoit Taria	QH	28	B5
Hengtian	GD	23	H6	Heshui	GS	27	E9	Holbo	NM	6	B7
Hengxi	JS	12	B1	(Xihuachi)				Holt Sum	NM	6	C6
Hengxi	ZJ	14	C4	Heshun	FJ	16	C3	Hondlon Ju	NM	6	D4
Hengxi	ZJ	14	C6	Heshun	GD	23	G7	Hong'an	HB	19	C7
Hengxi	ZJ	14	D5	Heshun	YN	33	C3	(Huang'an)			
Heng Xian	GX	24	E7	Heshun	SX	5	D5	Hongbai	SC	31	A2
Hengxiang	JS	12	A4	Hetanbu	JX	15	C5	Hongchang	LN	7	D6
	HN	20	E4-5	Hetang	FJ	16	D5	Hongchang	HEN	18	C5
Hengyang	HN	20	E5	Hetanggou	LN	7	C3	Hongchengshui	NX	26	C3
Hengyang	HN	20	E5	Hetian	FJ	16	E2	Hongchengzi	GS	27	D6
(Xidu)				Hetian	GD	21	B5	Hongcibu	SX	5	A5
Hepeng	AH	13	E3	Hetou	GD	21	A4	Hongcun	JX	15	D4
Hepeng	HN	20	C3	Hetou	GD	21	C2	Hongda	HL	9	D4
Heping	FJ	16	C3	Hetoudian	SD	10	B7	Hongdao	SX	5	C4
Heping	SX	5	E3	Hetouzhuang	JS	12	A3	Hongde	GS	27	D8
Heping	HL	9	D5	Hetupu	AH	13	F3	Hongdu	GX	24	D6
Heping	ZJ	14	B4	Hewanzi	JL	8	C7	Hongdu He	GZ	32	B7
Heping	FJ	16	E3	Hexi	ZJ	14	A4	Hongdunzi	NX	26	B3
Heping	TW	17	B3	Hexi	SX	5	F4	Honggong	GD	21	A4
Heping	GD	21	B6	Hexi	SC	30	B5	Honggou	SD	10	C4
Heping	GX	24	C8	Hexi	SC	30	E4	Hongguangying	NX	26	B3
(Heping) Yanhe	GZ	32	B7	Hexi	YN	33	C5	Honggucheng	GS	27	D6
Heping	GD	21	A5	Hexi	HN	20	C2	Hongguo	GZ	32	E3
Hepingzhen	HN	20	D2	Hexi	FJ	16	F3	Hongguozi	NX	26	A3
(Hepo) Jiexi	GD	21	B5	Hexi	ZJ	14	E4	Honghai Wan	GD	21	B5

Honghe	NX	26	E3	(Hongqizhen)Tongshi	HI	21	D2	Horqin Shadi	NM	37	D8
Hong He	AH	13	D2	Hongquan	NX	26	C2	Horqin Youyi	NM	6 ·	C7
	HEN	18	D5	Hongshaba	NM	6	F10	Qianqi			
Hong He	NX	26	E3	Hongshan	SD	10	C5	Horqin Youyi	NM	6	C7
				(Hongshan) Maocifan	HB	19	C5	Zhongqi			
Honghe	YN	33	D5	Hongshan	SX	5	D4	Horqin Zuoyi Houqi	NM	6	D7
Honghort	NM	6	F10	Hongshan Jian	FJ	16	E3				
Hong Hu	HB	19	E6	Hongshanqiao	FJ	16	D5	Horqin Zuoyi	NM	6	C7
Honghuabu	SD	10	E5	Hongshan Xia	GS	27	D7	Zhongqi			
Honghuapu	SN	25	F2	Hongshi	LN	7	C3	Horru	XZ	34	C4
Honghuatao	HB	19	D4	Hongshi	JL	8	E8				
Honghuayuan	GZ	32	B5	Hongshila	HEB	4	B4	Hotan He	XJ	29	D4
Honghu (Xindi)	HB	19	E6	Hongshilazi	LN	7	D9	Hotan	XJ	29	D3
Hongjiabu	HEN	18	E7	Hongshiyan	HEN	18	D5	Hotong Qagan Nur	NM	25	A4
Hongjiaguan	HN	20	B3	Hongshui	GS	27	D6	Hou'an	LN	7	C8
(Hongjialou)	SD	10	C4	Hongshui	SX	5	E5	Houbachang	GZ	32	C5
Licheng				Hongshui He (Riv.)	GX	24	C6-D6	Houbaishu	JS	11	E5
Hongjiang	HN	20	D2	Hongshuizhuang	TJ	3	B4	Houbu	SX	5	E4
Hongjian Nur	SN	25	A5	Hongsi	GS	26	E2	(Houchang) Caotang	GZ	32	C6
	NM	37	E5	Hongsipu	NX	26	C3	Houchang	GZ	32	E5
Hongjing	SX	5	E5	Hongtangsi	HEB	4	B4	Houcheng	HEB	4	C4
Hongkeli	HL	9	D5	Hongtangxiang	ZJ	14	C6	Houcheng	JS	11	E6
Hongkong	GD	21	B5	Hongtao Shan	SX	5	B4	Hougang	HB	19	D5
				Hongtian	FJ	16	E3	Houge	ZJ	14	D5
Hongkou	SC	30	B6	Hongtiguan	SX	5	E5	Houheshangyuan	SN	25	D4
Honglai	FJ	16	E4	Hongtong	SX	5	E3	(Houji) Liangshan	SD	10	D3
Honglan	JS	11	E4	Hongtumiao	LN	7	B8				
Honglinqiao	AH	13	F5	Hongtuxi	HB	19	D2	Houji	HEN	18	E4
Hongliugou	SN	25	C3	(Hongwan) Sunan	GS	27	C4	Houjiagang	JX	15	B4
Hongliuhe	GS	27	B2	Yugurzu Zizhixian				Houjiahe	NX	26	C4
Hongliu He	NM	25	C4	Hongxi	SC	30	D4	Hou Jiang	SC	30	C6-7
Hongliuquan	QH	28	A2	Hongxin	AH	13	D4	Houjiaping	SC	31	C2
Hongliuyuan	GS	27	B2	Hongxing	BJ	3	B3	Houjiaying	TJ	3	B4
Hongliuyuan	GS	27	C6	Hongxing	HL	9	C5	Houjie	GD	21	B4
Honglongdian	AH	12.	D2	Hongxing	JL	8	C4	Houlingshan	ZJ	14	C5
Honglu	SC	31	D4	Hongxing Erchang	XJ	29	C7	Houliugusi	HEB	3	D3
Honglu	FJ	16	E5	Hongxingqiao	ZJ	14	B4	Houlong	TW	17	B3
Hongluoxian	LN	7	C4	Hongxing Sichang	XJ	29	C7	Houma	SX	5	F3
Hongmao Jian	ZJ	14	C3	Hongyan	HN	20	B2	Houmen	GD	21	B5
Hongmen	ZJ	14	C5	Hongyan	HN	20	F6	Houping	HB	19	C4
Hongmen	JX	15	D4	Hongyan	NM	9	C3	Houping	HN	20	B3
Hongmiao	HEN	18	C6	Hongyancun	SC	31	C5	Houping	GZ	32	B7
(Hongning) Wulian	SD	10	D6	Hongyang	GD	21	B6	Houpo	HEN	18	E3
				Hongyangfang	NX	26	D2	Houshayu	BJ	3	B3
Hongnong Jian	HEN	18	C2	Hongyansi	HB	19	D2	Houshi	JL	8	E6
Hongqi	LN	7	D7	Hongyao	NX	26	D2	Housuo	SX	5	B4
Hongqi	JL	8	C7	Hongyashan Sk.	GS	27	C6	Houtanba	GZ	32	B5
Hongqi	SC	31	A2	Hongya	SC	30	D4	Houtengzhuang	HEB	4	E5
Hongqiao	HEB	4	D5	Hongyazi	NX	26	A3	Houtian	FJ	16	F3
Hongqiao	ZJ	14	D6	Hongyuan	SC	30	B4	Houxia	XJ	29	C5
Hongqiao	HN	20	C6	(Hurama)				Houxijie	ZJ	14	D3
(Hongqiao) Qidong	HN	20	E5	Hongze Hu (Lk.)	JS	11	C4	Houxinqiu	LN	7	B6
				Hongze	JS	11	C4	Houyi	HEB	3	C3
Hongqicun	XJ	29	C7	(Gaoliangjian)				Houyingzi	LN	7	D7
Hongqikan	XJ	29	C6	Hongzhen	AH	13	F3	Houzhai	ZJ	14	C5
Hongqiling	JL	8	E7	Hongzhuang	NX	26	E3	Houzhen	SD	10	C5
Hongqi Qu	HEN	18	A5	Hongzhuang	JS	11	B4	Houzhenzi	SN	25	G3
Hongqiyingzi	LN	7	D7	Hor	QH	28	C7	Houzihe	QH	28	B7
				Horgorgoinba	QH	28	C6	Houzizhen	SN	25	F5
				Horinger	NM	6	D4	Hoxtolgay	XJ	29	B5

Name	Prov	Map	Grid
Hoxud	XJ	29	C5
Hoyor Hudag	NM	6	F10
(Hsinchu) Xinzhu	TW	17	B3
Hua'an	FJ	16	E3
Huabei Pingyuan (Pln.)		36	C5-E5
		41	B3-C4
Huabu	ZJ	14	C3
Huacheng	GD	21	A5
Huacheng	GD	23	G7
Huachi (Rouyuanchengzi)	GS	27	D8
Huachong	JS	11	B4
Huachu	GZ	32	D4
Huachuan (Yuelai)	HL	9	D6
Huade	NM	6	D5
Huadian	JL	8	E7
Huadianzi	JL	8	F6
Huading Shan	ZJ	14	C6
Huafeng	SD	10	D4
Huafeng	SX	5	F3
Huagang	AH	13	E4
Huagu	SC	31	D2
Huaguang Jiao	HI	22	B2
Huagutang	AH	12	D2
Huahai	GS	27	B3
Huahaizi	QH	28	A4
Huai'an (Chaigoubu)	HEB	4	C2
Huai'an	JS	11	C5
Huaibai	SN	25	E5
Huaibei	AH	13	C3
	AH	13	C3
Huaibin (Wulongji)	HEN	18	E7
(Huaide) Gongzhuling	JL	8	D5
Huaidezhen	JL	8	D5
Huaidezhen	SC	31	D3
(Huaidian) Shenqiu	HEN	18	D7
Huaifengji	HEN	18	E7
Huai He (Riv.)	AH	13	D4
	HEN	18	E6
Huaihua	HN	20	D2
Huaihua	HN	20	D2
Huaiji	GD	21	B4
Huailai (Shacheng)	HEB	4	C3
Huailin	AH	13	E4
Huainan	FJ	16	E3
Huainan	AH	13	D3
Huaining (Shipai)	AH	13	F3
Huaiqun	GX	24	C6
Huairen	SD	10	B4
Huairen	SX	5	B5
Huairou Sk.	BJ	3	B3

Name	Prov	Map	Grid
Huairou	BJ	3	B3
Huaisha He	HEB	4	F2
Huaishu	SC	31	A4
Huaishu He	JS	11	B4-C4
Huaishuzhuang	SN	25	E4
Huaisiqiao	JS	12	A2
Huaiya	SN	25	F3
Huaiyang	HEN	18	D6
Huaiyin (Wangying)	JS	11	C5
Huaiyuan	GX	24	C6
Huaiyuan	SC	30	C4
Huaiyuan	AH	13	D4
Huaiyushan	JX	15	C5
Huaiyu Shan	JX	15	C5
Huaizhen	HEB	4	E4
Huaizhen	SC	30	C5
Huaizhong	JX	15	D2
Huaji	AH	13	D2
Huajia	JL	8	C6
Huajialing	GS	27	E7
Huajiang	GX	24	B8
Huajiang	HN	20	F4
Huajiang	GZ	32	E4
Huajianzi	LN	7	C9
Huajiaoping	HB	19	D2
Hualandian	SD	10	C3
Huale	SX	5	E3
Huali	SN	25	H5
Huali	GZ	32	C6
Hualian Xi	TW	17	C4
Hualian (Hualien)	TW	17	C4
(Hualien) Hualian	TW	17	C4
Hualin	JX	15	C3
Hualong Huizu Zizhixian	QH	28	B8
Huama	HL	9	D6
Huamenlou	HN	20	D5
Huanan	HL	9	D6
Huandun	JS	11	B4
Huang'an	SD	10	D2
(Huang'an) Hong'an	HB	19	C7
Huangang	JS	11	D7
Huang'ao	JX	15	E2
Huangbai	JL	8	F7
Huangbai	JX	15	C5
Huangbai He	HB	19	C4-D4
Huangban	GZ	32	B8
Huangbayi	SN	25	H2
Huangbei	JX	15	D4
Huangbei	JX	15	E3
Huangbeijiao	HEN	18	B4
Huangbizhuang Sk.	HEB	4	E1-2
Huangcai	HN	20	C5
(Huangcaoba) Xingyi	GZ	32	E3

Name	Prov	Map	Grid
Huangcaoba	YN	33	D4
Huangcao Shan	SC	31	C6-B6
Huangcao Xia	SC	31	C6
Huangcheng	GS	27	D5
Huangchengji	SD	10	B7
Huangchi	AH	12	C1
Huangchong	GD	23	I6
Huangchuan	AH	13	G5
Huangchuan	HEN	18	E7
(Huangcun) Daxing	BJ	3	C3
Huangcun	AH	12	D1
Huangcun	ZJ	14	D5
Huangcun	GD	21	B5
Huangcun	GX	24	C8
(Huangda'ao) Damen Dao	ZJ	14	E6
Huangdaizhen	JS	11	E6
Huangda Yang	ZJ	14	B7
Huangdi	LN	7	D4
Huangdun	SD	10	D6
Huangdun	FJ	16	D4
Huangdunmiao	AH	13	C4
Huangduobu	NX	26	D3
Huangfengqiao	HN	20	D6
Huanggai	SD	10	D3
Huanggai Hu	HB	19	E6
	HN	20	B6
Huanggang	GD	21	B4
Huanggang	AH	13	D2
Huanggang	JX	15	B4
Huanggangji	SD	10	E3
Huanggangkou	JX	15	C2
Huanggangliang	NM	37	D7
Huanggangmiao	HB	19	D8
Huanggang Shan	JX	15	D5
	FJ	16	C3
Huanggang (Huangzhou)	HB	19	D7
Huangge	GD	23	H7
Huangguan	GX	24	B9
Huangguoshu	GZ	32	E4
Huangguoshu Pubu (Wf.)	GZ	50	C5
Huangguzha	AH	13	E4
Huang He (Yellow R.)	SX	5	E2
	NM	6	D3-4
	SD	10	B4
	HEN	18	C5
	SN	25	F6-E6
	NX	26	B3
	GS	27	E5
	QH	28	C7
	SC	30	B3
Huang He	HEN	18	E7
Huanghe Kou	SD	10	B5
Huangheya	SD	10	B3

Huize	YN	33	B5	Hunyuanyao	NM	5	A5	Hutuanji	AH	13	D3
				Huocheng	XJ	29	B4	Hutubi	XJ	29	B5
Huizhou	GD	21	B5	(Shuiding)				Hutun	SD	10	C3
Huji	JS	11	C4	Huodifangzi	HL	9	D3	Hutuo He	HEB	4	E3
Huji	AH	13	C2	Huoditang	SN	25	G4		SX	5	C5
Huji	HB	19	C5	Huodoushan	HEB	3	A4	Huwan	HEN	18	F6
Hujia	LN	7	C5	Huohong	GZ	32	E5	Huwei	TW	17	C3
Hujia	SC	30	C6	Huojiaqiao	JS	12	A3	Huxi	TW	17	C2
Hujiadun	AH	13	E5	Huojia	HEN	18	B5	Huxi	ZJ	14	C5
Hujiatuo	HEB	4	D7	Huokou	FJ	16	D5	Huxi	JX	15	E2
Hujiaxiaojing	NX	26	C3	Huolianzhai	LN	7	C7	Hu Xian	SN	25	F4
Hujiayu	SX	5	F3	Huolin He	JL	8	B4	Huxiang	HEN	18	C7
Hujiayuan	SN	25	G5		NM	37	C8	Huxihe	SC	31	C5
Hujie	YN	33	C4	Huolonggou	HL	9	E5	Huyangzhen	HEN	18	E4
Hujirt	NM	6	F10	Huolongmen	HL	9	C3	Huyu	FJ	16	E5
Hukeng	FJ	16	F2	Huolongping	HB	19	E1	Huzhang	SX	5	F3
Hukou	TW	17	B4	Huolupu	SC	30	D6	Huzhen	ZJ	14	D5
Hukou	HN	20	E6	Huolu	HEB	4	E2	Huzhen	ZJ	14	C4
Hukou Pubu	SX	5	E2	Huoqiu	AH	13	D3	Huzhen	GD	23	G8
	SN	25	D6	Huormojin	HL	9	C4	Huzhong	HL	9	A2
Hukou	JX	15	B4	Huorqi	NM	6	B7	Huzhou	ZJ	14	B5
Hulan	JL	8	D7	Huo Shan	SX	5	E3	Huzhu Tuzu	QH	28	B7
Hulan Ergi	HL	9	D2	Huo Shan	AH	13	E3	Zizhixian			
Hulan He	JL	8	C8	Huo Shan	AH	42	C2				
Hulan He	HL	9	D4	Huoshan	AH	13	E3				
Hulan	HL	9	D4	Huoshao Dao	TW	17	D4	**I**			
Hule	AH	13	F5	Huoshaoliao	TW	17	B4				
Hulei	FJ	16	F2	Huoshaoping	HB	19	D3	Igizyar	XJ	29	D3
(Huliao) Dabu	GD	21	A6	Huoshishan	HL	9	D3				
Hulin	HL	9	E7	Huoshiying	HEB	3	B5	Ih Tal	NM	6	D7
Huliu He	HEB	4	D2	Huoshizhai	NX	26	D2	Ikanbujmal	XJ	29	D6
Hulstai	NM	26	A3	Huotian	HN	20	E6	(Ilan) Yilan	TW	17	B4
Huludao	LN	7	D4	Huotong	FJ	16	D5	Ili He	XJ	29	C4
Hulu He	SN	25	D4	Huotong Xi	FJ	16	C5-D5				
	GS	27	D9	Huoxian	BJ	3	C3				
Hulu He	NX	26	E2	Huo Xian	SX	5	E3	(Inder) Jalaid Qi	NM	6	C7
	GS	27	E7	Huping	JX	15	D3	Inggen	NM	6	D3
				Huqiao	JS	12	C2	Injgan Sum	NM	6	C6
Hulun Buir Shadi	NM	37	B7	(Hurama) Hongyuan	SC	30	B4	Iqe	QH	28	A4
Hulun Nur	NM	6	B6					Iqe He	QH	28	A4
Hulushan	FJ	16	D4	Hure Qi	NM	6	D7				
Huluzhai	HN	20	C2	Huret	NM	6	F10				
Huma He	HL	9	A3	Hurleg Hu	QH	28	B5	**J**			
Huma	HL	9	B4	Hushan	HL	9	E6				
Humen	GD	23	H7	(Hushan) Cixi	ZJ	14	B6				
Hu Men	GD	21	B4	Hushan	ZJ	14	D4	Jabsar Gaxun	QH	28	B5
Humu	HEB	3	D2	Hushan	JX	15	C2	Jagdaqi	NM	6	B8
Hunan	ZJ	14	D3	Hushan	JL	8	C6	Jaggang	XZ	34	B1
Hunchun He	JL	8	E11-D12	Hushi	FJ	16	E5	Jagt	NM	26	B1
Hunchun	JL	8	E11	Hushiha	HEB	4	C4	Jainca	QH	28	C7
Hunhe	LN	7	C7	Hushitai	LN	7	C7	Jalaid Qi(Inder)	NM	6	C7
Hun He	SX	5	B5	Hushu	ZJ	12	E3				
Hun He	NM	6	F10	Hushu	JS	11	E4	Jalai Nur	NM	6	B6
Hun He	LN	7	C7	Hutangqiao	JS	12	B3	Jalat	JL	8	B5
Hun Jiang	LN	7	C9	Hutian	HN	20	D5	Jamati	XJ	29	B4
	JL	8	F6	Hutiaoyi	SC	30	C5	Jamt	NM	6	C7
Hunjiang	JL	8	F7	Hutongzhen	HL	9	B4	Jangsib	QH	28	D4
(Badaojiang)				Hutou	HL	9	D7	Jaramtai	NM	6	B7
Hunt	NM	6	C6	Hutou	FJ	16	E4	Jargalang	NM	6	D7
Hunyuan	SX	5	B5	Hutouya	SD	10	B6	Jartai	NM	6	E3

Jartai Yanchi	NM	6	E3	Jiangao Shan	YN	33	C3	Jiangkou	HN	20	D3
Jarud Qi(Lubei)	NM	6	C7	Jiangba	JS	11	C4	(Jiangkou) Fengkai	GD	21	B3
				Jiangbei	JL	8	D7				
Jeminay	XJ	29	B5	Jiangbei	HN	20	C6	Jiangkou	GX	24	C7
Jeminay	XJ	29	B5	Jiangbei	SC	30	D6	Jiangkou	GX	24	D8
Jia'ao	GZ	32	C7	Jiangbeixu	JX	15	E3	Jiangkou	SN	25	G3
Jiabaotai	TW	17	B4	Jiangbiancun	JX	15	D3	Jiangkou	SC	31	B1
Jiachuanzhen	SC	30	B6	Jiangcheng	HEB	4	E3	Jiangkou	FJ	16	C4
Jiading	SH	11	E7	Jiangcheng Hanizu	YN	33	D4	Jiangkouji	AH	13	D3
Jiadou	SX	5	B6	Yizu Zizhixian				Jiangkou	GZ	32	C7
Jiafang	GX	24	D6	Jiangchuan	YN	33	C5	Jiangkouzhen	SC	30	C7
Jiafu	GX	24	D6	Jiangcun	JX	15	B5	Jiangkouzhen	SC	30	D6
Jiagou	AH	13	C4	Jiangcun	JX	15	C5	Jiangle	FJ	16	D3
Jiagui	GX	24	C6	Jiangcun	HN	20	F4	Jiangling	HB	19	D5
Jiahe	HB	19	B3	Jiangcun	GD	21	B4	(Jingzhou)			
Jiahe	GD	23	G7	Jiangcun	SX	5	C5	Jianglong	GZ	32	E4
Jiahe	HN	20	F5	Jiangdi	YN	33	B5	Jiangluozhen	GS	27	F7
Jiahezhai	JS	11	B3	Jiangdian	AH	13	E3	Jiangmenchang	SC	30	D5
Jiahui	GX	24	C8	Jiangdong	HN	20	D3	Jiangmen	GD	21	B4
(Jiaji) Qionghai	GD	21	D3	Jiangduo	JS	11	D6	Jiangmifeng	JL	8	D7
				Jiangdu	JS	11	D5	Jiangnan	JL	8	E7
Jiajiachang	SC	31	B2	(Xiannümiao)				Jiangnan	HN	20	C4
Jiajiachang	SC	31	C3	Jiange	SC	30	B5	Jiangning	GX	24	E7
Jiajiang	SC	30	D4	Jianggang	JS	11	D6	Jiangning	JS	11	E4
Jiajiatun	SX	5	A6	Jianggao	GD	23	G7	Jiangningzhen	JS	11	E4
Jiajin Shan	SC	30	C4	Jianggezhuang	HEB	4	D7	Jiangoushan	NX	26	C2
Jiakou	JS	11	B3	Jianggu	GD	23	G6	Jiangpu	JS	11	D4
Jiakou	ZJ	14	B4	Jiangguantun	SD	10	C3	Jiangqiao	HL	9	D2
Jiakou Wa	TJ	3	D3-4	Jianghong	GD	21	C2	Jiangshan	ZJ	14	C6
Jialequan	SX	5	D4	Jianghua Yaozu	HN	20	G4	Jiangshan Gang	ZJ	14	D3
Jiali	TW	17	C3	Zizhixian(Shuikou)				Jiangshan	ZJ	14	D3
Jialiang	GZ	32	E6	Jiangji	AH	13	C3	Jiangshanzhen	SD	10	C7
Jialing	SX	5	D4	Jiangji	HEN	18	E7	Jiangshijie	HN	20	D5
Jialing Jiang (Riv.)	SN	25	G2	Jiangjia	SC	31	D5	Jiangshui	HEB	4	F1
	SC	30	C5	Jiangjiabu	JX	15	C4	Jiangshui	HN	20	F5
Jialou	HEN	18	E5	Jiangjiadian	HEB	4	A5	Jiangtaibu	NX	26	E2
Jialu	AH	13	F5	Jiangjiadian	JL	8	E7	Jiangtang	SX	5	D5
Jialu He	HEN	18	C6	Jiangjialing	HN	20	F4	Jiangtian	FJ	16	E5
Jiamaying	SD	10	B2	Jiangjiapo	SD	10	C7	Jiangtuanji	AH	13	C3
Jiamingzhen	SC	31	D3	Jiangjiatun	LN	7	E6	Jiangtun	GD	23	G6
Jiamusi	HL	9	D6	Jiangjiehe	GZ	32	C6	Jiangui	NM	6	F10
Jian'an	JL	8	D6	Jiangjin	SC	30	D6	Jiangwan	SH	12	C5
Jianba	GZ	32	B6	Jiangjun'ao Yu	TW	17	C2	Jiangwan	JX	15	B6
Jianbanchang	SC	31	D2	Jiangjunguan	BJ	3	B4	Jiangwan	GD	21	A4
Jianbi	JS	11	D5	Jiangjunhe	HB	19	B3	Jiangxi	YN	33	D4
Jianchang	LN	7	C8	Jiangjunmiao	AH	13	F4	Jiangxiadian	AH	13	E3
Ji'anchang	SC	31	B4	Jiangjunmiao	XJ	29	B6	Jiang Xian	SX	5	F3
Jianchang	LN	7	D3	Jiangjunmu	HEB	4	F2	Jiangxiang	AH	13	D4
Jianchangying	HEB	4	C6	Jiangjunshi	LN	7	E5	Jiangxiang	JX	15	C4
Jianchapu	HEB	3	D3	Jiangjuntai	GS	27	B3	Jiangxigou	QH	28	B7
Jianchaxi	GZ	32	B6	Jiangkou	ZJ	14	C6	Jiangxikou	FJ	16	C4
Jiancheng	GD	21	B3	Jiangkou	JX	15	D2	Jiangxin	JS	12	A3
Jianchipu	SN	25	H4	Jiangkou	JX	15	D3	Jiangya	HN	20	B3
Jianchuan	YN	33	B3	Jiangkou	JX	15	F2	(Jiangyan) Tai Xian	JS	12	A3
(Jiande) Meicheng	ZJ	14	C4	Jiangkou	JX	15	F3	Jiangyi	JX	15	B3
Jiande (Baisha)	ZJ	14	C4	Jiangkou	FJ	16	E5	Jiangyi	YN	33	B4
				Jiangkou	HB	19	D4	Jiangyin Dao	FJ	16	E5
Jiandou	FJ	16	E3	Jiangkou	HB	19	E3	Jiangyin	JS	11	E6
Jianfeng	HI	21	D2	Jiangkou	HN	20	D2	Jiangyong	HN	20	F4
Jian'an	SC	30	D5	Jiangkou	HN	20	D3	Jiangyou (Zhongba)	SC	30	C5

Jiangyu	SD	10	C5	Jiaocheng	SX	5	D4	Jiashan	ZJ	14	B5
Jiangzaogang	JS	12	B5	Jiaocun	AH	13	F5	Jiashi(Payzawat)	XJ	29	D3
Jiangzhang	SN	25	F3	Jiaocun	HEN	18	C2				
Jiangzhen	SH	12	C6	Jiaodao	BJ	3	C2	Jiashizhuang	HEB	4	F2
Jiangzhou	SC	30	E4	Jiaodao	SN	25	E5	Jiasi	SC	31	D5
Jiangzhou	GZ	32	D6	Jiaodi	SX	5	F3	Jiasong	HEN	18	E4
Jiangzhuang	SD	10	C6	Jiaodi	HEN	18	C3	Jiatan	HEN	18	D7
Jiangzhuang	JS	11	D5	Jiaoding Shan	LN	38	C4	Jiawang	JS	11	B3
Jianhe	SN	25	F2	Jiaodong	SD	10	C7	Jiaxian	TW	17	C3
Jianhe	HEB	3	C5	Jiao He	SD	10	C6	Jia Xian	HEN	18	D5
Jianhe	GZ	32	D7	Jiao He	JL	8	D8	Jia Xian	SN	25	B6
(Liuchuan)				Jiaohekou	SN	25	E5	Jiaxiang	SD	10	D3
Jianhu	JS	11	C5	Jiaohe	HEB	4	E4				
Jianjiang	FJ	16	D5	Jiaohe	JL	8	D8	Jiaxing	ZJ	14	B5
Jian Jiang	GD	21	C3	Jiaohuji	HEN	18	B6	Jiaxinzi	HL	9	E5
Jianjiaxi	HN	20	C4	Jiaojiang	ZJ	14	D6	Jiaya	GZ	32	E7
(Jianjun) Yongshou	SN	25	F4	(Haimen)				Jiayi	HN	20	C6
				Jiaokeng	GD	23	I8	Jiayin	HL	9	C6
Jianling	HEN	18	E5	Jiaokou	SX	5	E4	(Chaoyang)			
Jianli	HB	19	E5	Jiaokou	SN	25	D6	Jiayi(Chiayi)	TW	17	C3
Jianmenguan	SC	30	B5	Jiaokou	SX	5	E3	Jiayou	GX	24	C4
Jiannan	HB	19	D1	Jiaolai He	SD	10	C6	Jiayue	SD	10	C6
Jianning	FJ	16	D2	Jiaolai He	NM	6	D7	Jiayuguan	GS	27	C4
Jian'ou	FJ	16	C4	Jiaoling	GD	21	A6	Jiayu	HB	19	E6
Jianping	LN	7	C3	Jiaoliu He	NM	8	B2	Jiazhai	HEN	18	C7
Jianping	JL	8	B4		JL	39	B2	Jiazhen	SD	10	C2
Jianping	LN	7	C3	Jiaomei	FJ	16	F3	Jiazhuan	GX	24	C5
(Yebaishou)				Jiaomiao	SD	10	C3	Jiazi	GD	21	B6
Jianqiao	HEB	4	F4	Jiaonan	SD	10	D6	Jiazi	GD	23	H8
Jianqiao	ZJ	14	B5	(Wanggezhuang)				Jiazi Gang	GD	21	B6
Jianquanzi	GS	27	B3	Jiaoping	SN	25	E4	Jibei Yu	TW	17	C2
Jianshan	ZJ	14	C5	Jiaopingdu	YN	33	B5	Jichang	JL	8	D6
Jianshan	HB	19	E1	Jiao Shan	JS	12	A3	Jichang	GZ	32	C4
Jianshan	JX	15	C3	Jiaoshiba	SC	31	C6	Jichang	GZ	32	D5
Jianshanzi	HL	9	D7	Jiaotan	JX	15	B5	Jichang	GZ	32	E6
Jianshe	FJ	16	E3	Jiaotang	JX	15	B3	Jichangping	GZ	32	E3
Ji'an	JX	15	D2	Jiaotou	ZJ	14	C7	Jichangzhuang	HEB	4	F3
Jianshi	HB	19	D2	Jiaowei	FJ	16	E4	Jicun	AH	13	F4
Jian Shui	HEN	18	C4	Jiaoxi	JS	11	E6	Jicun	SX	5	D3
Jianshui	YN	33	D5	Jiaoxi	FJ	16	C3	Jicun	HN	20	F5
Jiantian	JX	15	B4	Jiaoxi	GZ	32	C7	Jidongping	HN	20	C2
Jiantiao	ZJ	14	C6	Jiaoxi	TW	17	B4	Jidong	HL	9	E6
Jiantou	HEN	18	E7	Jiao Xi	FJ	16	C5	Jiebu	JX	15	C3
Jiantouji	SD	10	E4	Jiaozhou	SD	10	C7	Jiebu	JX	15	D3
Jianxi	AH	13	D5	Jiaoxie	JS	11	D6	Jiedi	HEB	4	E4
Jian Xi	FJ	16	D4	Jiaoyang	FJ	16	E2	Jiedi Jianhe	HEB	4	E5
Ji'an (Dunhou)	JX	15	D2	Jiaoyuan	SD	10	D1	Jiedu	SX	5	D5
Ji'an	JL	8	F7	Jiaoyuan	HB	19	D2	Jiedunji	AH	13	E4
Jianxing	SC	30	C5	Jiaozhou Wan	SD	10	C7	Jiefang Qu	XJ	29	C5
Jianyang	JS	11	C5	Jiaozhuang	HEN	18	D6	Jiehe	SD	10	D4
				Jiaozhuanghu	BJ	3	B4	Jieheba	GS	27	C6
Jianyang	FJ	16	C4	Jiaoziya	HN	20	B3	Jiehedian	HEB	4	G2
Jianyang	SC	30	C5	Jiaozuo	HEN	18	B5	Jiehekou	SX	5	C3
Jianyangyi	HB	19	D5	Jiapigou	LN	7	D8	Jieheshi	HB	19	D4
Jianzhang Jiao		22	D4	Jiapigou	JL	8	E8	(Jiehu) Yinan	SD	10	D5
Jianzhen	JS	11	D7	Jiapu	ZJ	14	A4	Jiehualong	JX	15	D1
Jianzhong	HEB	4	G3	Jiasa	YN	33	C4	Jieji	JS	11	C4
Jiaobeishi	GD	23	I6	Jiashang	NX	26	D2	Jieji	HL	9	D2
Jiaochangba	SC	30	B4	Jiashan	AH	13	D4	Jiejinkou	HL	9	D7
Jiaochangba	HB	19	C3	(Mingguang)				Jiekou	AH	13	G5

(Jiekou) Conghua	GD	23	G7	Jilong(Keelung)	TW	17	A4	(Ciping)			
				Jimda	SC	30	C3	Jinggang Shan	JX	15	E2
Jielong	SC	31	D5	Jimei	FJ	16	F4	Jinggongqiao	JX	15	B5
Jieluqiao	HN	20	E4	Jiminghe	HB	19	D8	Jinggu	GS	27	E6
Jiemian	FJ	16	E4	Jimingsi	SC	30	C7	Jingguanzhen	SC	31	C5
Jiepai	SD	10	D5	Jimo	SD	10	C7	Jinggu	YN	33	D4
Jiepai	AH	13	F6	Jimsaɪ	XJ	29	B6	Jinghai	GD	21	B6
Jiepai	HB	19	C6	Jin'an	ZJ	14	D4	Jinghaiwei	SD	10	C9
Jiepaiji	AH	13	D4	Jinancheng	HB	19	D5	Jinghai	TJ	3	D4
Jieshang	HB	19	E6	Jinan	SD	10	C4	Jinghe	JS	11	C5
Jiesheng	GD	21	B5					Jinghe	HEB	4	E4
Jieshi	SC	31	C3	Jinbao	GX	24	C8	Jing He	SN	25	F4
Jieshi	GD	21	B5	Jinbaotun	NM	7	A7		GS	26	E3-4
Jieshipu	GS	27	E7	Jinchai	GX	24	C6	Jinghe(Jing)	XJ	29	B4
Jieshi Shan	HEB	4	D7					Jinghong Dao	HI	22	D3
Jieshi Wan	GD	21	B5	Jinchang	GS	27	C6	Jinghong	YN	33	E4
Jieshou	SD	10	C3	Jincheng	LN	7	C5	(Yunjinghong)			
Jieshou	JS	11	C5	Jincheng	YN	33	C5	Jinghui Qu	SN	25	F4
Jieshou	JX	15	D2	(Jinchengjiang)	GX	24	C6	Jingjiangdian	ZJ	12	E4
Jieshou	FJ	16	C3	Hechi				Jingjiang Fenhongqu	HB	19	E5
Jieshou	HN	20	E6	Jinchengshi	HN	20	E4	Jingjiang	JS	11	D6
Jieshou	GX	24	B8	Jincheng	SX	5	F4	Jingjiawa	HEN	18	C5
Jieshou	AH	13	C2	Jinchuan	JL	8	E7	Jingjiazhuang	BJ	3	A2
Jieshouzhen	AH	13	D5	Jinchuanqiao	SC	30	E4	Jingjiazhuang	SD	10	B4
Jietou	ZJ	14	C5	Jinchuan	SC	30	C4	Jingjukou	ZJ	14	D4
Jiexiu	SX	5	D3	Jinci	SX	5	D4	Jingkou	JS	11	C5
Jiexi (Hepo)	GD	21	B5	Jincun	SX	5	F4	Jingkou	GD	23	G6
Jieyang	GD	21	B6	Jincun	ZJ	14	A4	Jingle	SX	5	C3
Jiezhenxi	GZ	32	B5	Jinde	GX	24	C7	Jinglonggong	HEN	18	C6
Jiezhongdian	HEN	18	E4	Jindian	HB	19	C6	Jingmen	HB	19	C5
Jiezhudu	JX	15	C5	Jindi He	HEN	18	B7	Jingmen	HB	19	C5
Jiezi He	SN	25	E5	Jinding	SN	25	D4	Jingnan	GX	24	D9
Jifeng	SC	31	A2					Jingnan	GZ	32	F3
Jigong Shan	HEN	18	F6	Jindou	HB	19	C4	Jingning	GS	27	E7
	HB	19	C7	Jinduicheng	SN	25	F5	Jingou	LN	7	C4
Jiguan	JL	8	D10	Jindun Ansha	HI	22	E2	Jingoukou	GS	26	D1
Jiguang	SC	31	A3	Jinfeng	FJ	16	E5	Jingoutun	HEB	4	B5
Jiguanshan	LN	7	B8	Jinfo Shan	SC	30	D6	Jingouzi	LN	7	B7
Jiguanshan	LN	7	D7	Jinfosi	GS	27	C4	(Jingpeng) Hexigten	NM	6	D6
Jigzhi	QH	28	D7	(Jing) Jinghe	XJ	29	B4	Qi			
Jiji	TW	17	C3	(Jing'an) Doumen	GD	23	I7	(Jingping) Pinglu	SX	5	B4
Jijia	GD	21	C2								
Jijiadianzi	SD	10	D5	Jingangling	SX	5	E3	Jingpo	HN	20	F6
Jijiamiao	SC	31	D2	Jingangtou	HN	20	D6	Jingpo Hu	HL	9	F5
Jijiashi	JS	11	D6	Jingangtuo	SC	31	D4	Jingpu	TW	17	C4
Jijiazhuang	HEB	4	C2	Jing'anji	JS	11	B2	Jing Shan	HB	19	C4
Jijiazhuang	NX	26	C2	Jing'an	JX	15	C3	Jingshan	HB	19	C6
Jijie	YN	33	D5	Jingbian	SN	25	C4	Jingshuizi	NM	26	C2
Jijihu	NM	26	C1	(Zhangjiapan)				Jingtai	GS	27	D7
Jijü	SC	30	D3	Jingcheng	FJ	16	F3	(Yitiaoshan)			
Jiliaojie	HEN	18	C4	Jingchuan	GS	27	E8	Jingtieshan	GS	27	C3
Jili Hu	XJ	29	B5	Jingcun	SN	25	F6	Jingtoujiang	HN	20	E5
Jiling	GS	27	C5	Jingde	AH	13	F5	Jingtouxu	HN	20	E4
Jilin Hada Ling	JL	8	E6-D7	Jingdezhen	JX	15	B5	Jinguan	YN	33	B4
Jilin	JL	8	D7	Jingdian	HEN	18	B6	Jinguashi	TW	17	A4
				Jingdong	YN	33	C4	Jingui	NX	26	B3
Jiliu He	NM	6	B7	Jing'ertou	JS	11	B4	Jingxi	SC	31	B5
Jilong	GD	21	B5	Jingfuyuan	SC	31	A3	Jingxi	FJ	16	D3
Jilongjie	HN	20	E5	Jinggang	HN	20	C5	Jing Xian	AH	13	F5
Jilong Shan	GD	23	H6	Jinggangshan	JX	15	E2	Jing Xian	HEB	4	F4

Jiucai Dingzi	LN	38	C6	Jiulong	JX	15	C4	Jiuxu	GX	24	E6
Jiucai Ling	HN	20	F4	Jiulong	GD	21	B5	Jiuyi	HN	20	F4
	GX	24	B9	Jiulong	SC	31	B5	Jiuyingjiang	YN	33	C3
Jiucaizhuang	NM	5	B3	Jiulonggang	AH	13	D4	Jiuyi Shan	HN	20	F4-5
Jiuchang	GZ	32	D5	Jiulong Jiang	FJ	16	F3	Jiuyongnian	HEB	4	G2
Jiuchangge	HEN	18	C5	Jiulongping	JL	8	D10	Jiuyongshou	SN	25	F4
Jiucheng	HEB	4	E3	Jiulongpo	SC	31	C5	Jiuyuhang	ZJ	14	B4
Jiucheng	HEB	4	E3	Jiulongshan	NX	26	D3	Jiuyunlong	YN	33	C3
Jiucheng	HEB	4	E5	Jiulong Shan	ZJ	14	D3	Jiuzhai	LN	7	D6
(Jiucheng) Wucheng	SD	10	B3	Jiulong Shan	JX	15	E2	Jiuzhan	JL	8	D7
				Jiulong Xi	FJ	16	D2-E3	Jiuzhan	HL	9	B3
Jiucheng	SD	10	D2	Jiulong	SC	30	D3	Jiuzhanbu	HEB	3	A2
Jiucheng	GX	24	E5	Jiulongzhen	JS	11	E7	Jiuzhangqiu	SD	10	C4
Jiucheng	GZ	32	B6	Jiumengjin	HEN	18	C4	Jiuzhen	FJ	16	F3
Jiudaoling	LN	7	C5	Jiumiao	LN	7	B5	Jiuzhenyuan	YN	33	D4
Jiudengkou	NM	6	E3	Jiumu	FJ	16	B4	Jiuzhou	HEB	3	C3
Jiudian	HEB	4	G2	Jiuninghe	TJ	3	C5	Jiuzhou	GX	24	C3
Jiudian	SC	31	C6	Jiuningshan	SN	25	G4	Jiuzhou	GX	24	E6
Jiuding Shan	SC	30	C4	Jiupu	LN	7	C6	Jiuzhou	GZ	32	D6
Jiudongshan	FJ	16	G3	Jiupu	JS	11	D4	Jiuzhou Jiang	GD	24	F8
Jiuduhe	BJ	3	B3	Jiuqian	GZ	32	E7	Jiuzhuang	GZ	32	C5
Jiufang	YN	33	D3	Jiuqingyun	HEB	4	F5	Jiuzhuangwo	HEB	3	B2
Jiufanxian	HEN	18	B7	Jiuqu	SD	10	D5	Jiuzihe	HB	19	C8
Jiufeng	FJ	16	F3					Jiwang Shan	SX	36	E2
Jiufeng	GD	21	A4	Jiuquan	GS	27	C4	Jiwen	NM	6	B7
Jiufeng Shan	FJ	16	C5-D5	(Suzhou)				Jixian	HL	9	D6
Jiufo	GD	23	G7	Jiurongcheng	SD	10	B9	Jixian	HL	9	D6
Jiufoping	SN	25	G3	(Jiusanshui) Hekou	GD	23	H6	Ji Xian	SX	5	E2
Jiugang	TW	17	B3	Jiushan	SD	10	C5	Ji Xian	HEN	18	B6
Jiugongkou	HEB	3	B1	Jiushan Liedao	ZJ	14	C7	Ji Xian	TJ	3	B4
Jiugongqiao	HN	20	D4	Jiusi	HB	19	E2	Ji Xian	HEB	4	F3
Jiugong Shan	JX	15	B2	(Jiusuining)	HN	20	E3	Jixian	HL	9	D6
	HB	19	E7	Zhaishizhen				(Fulitun)			
Jiugongxian	HEN	18	C5	Jiusuo	HI	21	D2	Jixin	HN	20	C2
Jiuguan	ZJ	12	D4	Jiutai	JL	8	C6	Jixi	HL	9	E6
Jiuguan	SD	10	B8	Jiutang	GX	24	D6	Jixi	AH	13	F5
Jiuguantao	SD	10	C2	Jiutiaoling	GS	27	D6	Jiyang	FJ	16	C4
Jiugucheng	HEB	4	F4	Jiuwan Dashan	GX	24	B6	Jiyang	HEN	18	C7
Jiuguling	AH	13	F3	Jiuwugong	SN	25	F4	Jiyang	SD	10	C4
Jiuhe	GD	21	B5	Jiuwuqiang	HEB	4	E3	Jiyi	SN	25	E6
Jiuhechi	GX	24	C5	Jiuwuqiao	HEB	4	F4	Jiyuan	SN	26	C4
Jiuhu	SD	10	B4	Jiuwuqing	TJ	3	C4	Jiyuan	HEN	18	B4
Jiuhuai'an	HEB	4	C2	Jiuxi	HN	20	B4	Jiyun He	TJ	3	C5
Jiuhuajie	AH	13	F4	Jiuxian	BJ	3	A2	Jize	HEB	4	G2
Jiuhua Shan	AH	13	F4	Jiuxian	HEB	4	F5	Jizhen	SN	25	C6
Jiujiang	GD	21	B4	Jiuxian	SX	5	B3	Jizhong Yunhe	HEB	4	E4
				Jiuxian	SD	10	C4	Jizu Shan	YN	33	C4
Jiujiang	JX	15	B3	Jiuxian	AH	13	C2	Jogdor	NM	4	A4
Jiujiang	JX	15	B3	Jiuxian	ZJ	14	C4	Jomda	XZ	34	C6
(Shahezhen)				Jiuxian	HEN	18	C3	Jonê	GS	27	E6
Jiujing	HL	9	C3	Jiuxian	HEN	18	D5	Jos He	NM	38	B3
Jiujing	AH	13	E3	Jiuxian	HB	19	C4	Juancheng	SD	10	D2
Jiujingxing	HEB	4	E2	Jiuxian	SN	25	E5	Juan Shui	HN	20	D5
Jiujintang	SC	31	A2	Jiuxian	SC	31	C4	Jubaoshan	JL	8	C5
Jiukou	HB	19	D5	Jiuxiangcheng	HEN	18	D6	Jucun	ZJ	14	D4
Jiuli	SC	31	C1	Jiuxian He	FJ	16	E2	Judian	YN	33	B3
Jiulianshan	JX	15	G2	Jiuxiantang	JX	15	C2	(Juegang) Rudong	JS	11	D7
Jiulian Shan	GD	21	A5	Jiuxincheng	HEB	4	D3				
Jiuling Shan	JX	15	C2-B3	Jiuxinle	HEB	5	C6	Jue He	HB	19	B6
Jiulong	ZJ	14	D4	Jiuxu	GX	24	C5	Juexi	ZJ	14	C6

Kecheng	SX	5	E3
Kedian	HB	19	C5
Kedong	HL	9	C4
Kedong Zhan	HL	9	C4
Kedu	GZ	32	E5
(Keelung) Jilong	TW	17	A4
Kejing	HEN	18	B4
Kelan	SX	5	C3
Kelegou	HEB	4	B6
Kelu	GD	21	C2
Keluo He	HL	9	C3-4
Keluotun	HL	9	C3
Kengkou	ZJ	12	E2
Kengkou	JX	15	C5
Kengkou	FJ	16	C4
Kengxi	JX	15	D1
Kenli	SD	10	B5
(Xishuanghe)			
Keqiao	ZJ	14	B5
Kequan	HEN	18	A6
(Keriya) Yutian	XJ	29	D4
Keriya He	XJ	29	D4
Keriya Shankou	XJ	29	E4
	XZ	34	B2
Kesha	HN	20	B2
Keshan	HL	9	C3
Keshuling	JX	15	F2
Keyi	XJ	29	C4
Keyihe	NM	6	B7
(Kinmen) Jinmen	FJ	16	F4
Kizil He	XJ	29	D2
Kocê	GS	27	E6
Kok Kuduk	XJ	29	B5
(Koktokay) Fuyun	XJ	29	B6
Kokyar	XJ	29	D3
Kongcheng	AH	13	E4
Kongchunmiao Paozi	NM	38	B4
Kongdian	AH	13	D4
Kongfang	JX	15	D4
Kongjiawan	HB	19	C5
Kongjiazhuang	HEB	4	C2
Konglong	HB	19	E8
Kongtan	SC	30	D5
Kongtian	JX	15	G3
Kongtong Dao	SD	10	B8
Kongtong Shan	GS	27	E8
Kongur Shan	XJ	29	D2
Kongzhen	SD	10	B4
Kongzhen	JS	11	E5
Konqi He	XJ	29	C5
Koramlik	XJ	29	D5
Korgas	XJ	29	B4
Korla	XJ	29	C5
Korla	XJ	29	C5
Korlondo	SC	30	C2
Korti Linchang	XJ	29	A5
Kosrap	XJ	29	D3
Kou'an	JS	11	D5
Koubu	SD	10	C5
Kou He	LN	38	B6
Kouhu	TW	17	C3
Koumenzi	XJ	29	C7
(Kouqian) Yongji	JL	8	D7
Kouquan	SX	5	A5
Koutou	HEB	4	E2
Koutouzhen	SN	25	F4
Kouzhen	SD	10	C4
Kouzhuang	HEB	4	C6
Kouzigou	NX	26	C3
Kouziji	AH	13	D3
Koxlax	XJ	29	D4
Koxtag	XJ	29	D3
(Kuaidamao) Tonghua	JL	8	F6
Kuai He	SX	5	F3
Kuai He	AH	13	C3
Kuaitanggou	AH	13	C4
Kuaize He	YN	33	C6
Kuancheng	HEB	4	C6
Kuandian	LN	7	D8
Kuangdonggou	LN	7	D6
Kuangjiahe	HB	19	D8
Kuangshancun	HEB	4	G2
Kuangshanzhen	YN	33	B5
Kuankuoba	GZ	32	B6
Kuantian	JX	15	E3
Kugqa	SC	30	C3
Kugri	QH	28	C6
Kuichong	GD	21	B5
Kuidesu	LN	7	C3
Kuidou	FJ	16	E4
Kuile He	NM	40	B3
Kuishan	HL	9	E6
Kuishan Ding	GX	24	E7
Kuitan	GD	21	B5
Kuitang	GX	24	E4
Kuixiang	YN	33	B6
Kuixu	GX	24	D4
Kuizhuang	HEB	4	D6
Kuke He	YN	33	C3
Kumkuduk	XJ	29	C6
(Kumul) Hami	XJ	29	C7
Kümüx	XJ	29	C6
Kundu He	NM	38	C3
(Künes) Xinyuan	XJ	29	C4
Künes Chang	XJ	29	C4
Künes He	XJ	29	C4
Künes Linchang	XJ	29	C5
Kunggyü Co	XZ	34	C2
Kunjirap Daban	XJ	29	D2
Kunlun Guan	GX	24	D6
Kunlun Shan (Mts.)	QH	28	B2-C4
	XJ	29	D3-E4
Kunlun Shankou	QH	28	C4
Kunming	YN	33	C5
Kunshan	JS	11	E6
(Kunyang) Jinning	YN	33	C5
Kunyu Shan	SD	10	B8
Kunyu Shan	SD	10	B8
Kuocang Shan	ZJ	14	D5
Kuocang Shan	ZJ	14	D5
Kuqa Chang	XJ	29	C4
Kuqa	XJ	29	C4
Kuqiao	JX	15	C5
Kurbin He	HL	9	C5
Kuruktag	XJ	29	C6
Kushuigoumen	NM	26	A3
Kushui He	NX	26	C3
Kusite	HL	9	C5
Kuye He	SN	25	B6
Küysu	XJ	29	C7
Kuytun He	XJ	29	C5-B5
Kuytun	XJ	29	B5
Kyikug	QH	28	B7

L

Labagoumen	BJ	3	A3
(Labrang) Xiahe	GS	27	E6
Ladong	GX	24	C7
Lafa	JL	8	D8
Lagkor Co	XZ	34	B2
Lagushao	LN	7	D8
Laha	HL	9	C3
Lahadi	YN	33	D5
Lai'an	AH	13	D5
Laibang	AH	13	F3
Laibin	GX	24	D7
Laicun	JX	15	E3
Laifeng	SC	31	B3
Laifeng Tujiazu Zizhixian	HB	19	E2
Laifengzhen	SC	31	C4
Laishan	SD	10	B8
Laishui	HEB	4	D3
Laisu	SC	31	D4
Laituan	GX	24	E5
Laiwu	SD	10	C4
Laixi (Shuiji)	SD	10	C7
Laixi Zhan	SD	10	C7
Laiyang	SD	10	C7
Laiyang Zhan	SD	10	C7
Laiyuan	SX	5	D4
Laiyuan	FJ	16	E3
Laiyuan	HEB	4	D2
Laizhou	FJ	16	D4
Laizhou Wan (Gt.)	SD	10	B6
Lalang	GX	24	C6
Lalatun	JL	8	D6
Lalie	GX	24	C6

Name	Prov	Sheet	Grid
Lalin	HL	9	E4
Lalin He	JL	8	B7
	HL	9	E3-4
Lamadi	YN	33	B3
Lamadian	JL	8	D5
Lamadian	HL	9	D3
Lamadong	LN	7	D3
Lamawan	NM	6	D4
Lanba	GZ	32	D4
Lancaiqiao	HL	9	E4
Lancang Jiang (Riv.)	YN	33	D4-C4
	XZ	34	C6
Lancang Lahuzu	YN	33	D3
Zizhixian			
(Menglangba)			
Lancaodu	SC	30	C6
Lancheng	SD	10	E4
Lancheng	SX	5	C3
Lancun	SD	10	C7
Landi	SD	10	C6
(Lanfeng) Lankao	HEN	18	C6
La'nga Co	XZ	34	C2
Langang	HL	9	E5
Langanji	AH	13	C4
Langao	SN	25	H4
Langdai	GZ	32	D4
Langdong	GZ	32	D7
Langfang	HEB	4	D4
Langgangshan Liedao	ZJ	14	B7
Langgar	XZ	34	C5
Langhua Jiao	GD	22	C3
Langjia Sha	JS	11	D7
Langji Shan	ZJ	14	D6
Langju	JX	15	D4
Langlishi	HN	20	C6
(Langmusi)	GS	27	E6
Dagcanglhamo			
Langnuan Kou	SD	10	C8
Langping	GX	24	C4
Langping	HB	19	D3
Langqên Zangbo	XZ	34	C1-2
(Xiangquan He)			
Langqi	FJ	16	D5
Langqiao	AH	13	F5
Langru	XJ	29	D3
Langshan	HN	20	E3
Langshan	HEB	4	C3
Langshan	NM	6	D3
Lang Shan	NM	6	F10
Lang Shan	JS	11	E6
Langtang	HN	20	C4
Langtou	LN	7	D8
Langu	FJ	16	C4
Langwogou	HEB	4	B2
Langxiang	HL	9	D5
Langxigang	JX	15	B4
Langxi He	AH	12	C2
Langxi	AH	13	E6
Langya	ZJ	14	C4
Langya	SC	31	B5
Langya Shan	HEB	4	D3
Langya Shan	SD	10	D6
Langzhong	SC	30	C5
Lan He	SN	25	H4-5
Lanheba	HEB	3	B2
Lanhepu	HB	19	B2
Lanjiacun	HN	20	E4
Lanjiang	SC	31	B3
Lankao	HEN	18	C6
(Lanfeng)			
Lankou	GD	21	B5
Lanli	HN	20	D2
Lanling	SD	10	E4
Lanling	HL	9	E4
Lanlu Gang	SH	12	C5
Lanping	YN	33	B3
Lanqiao	ZJ	14	C6
Lanqiao	SN	25	F5
Lanqiying	HEB	3	B5
Lanshantou	SD	10	D6
Lanshan	HN	20	F5
Lanshi	HN	20	E6
Lantang	GD	21	B5
Lantian	JX	15	C4
(Lantian) Lianyuan	HN	20	D4
Lantian	GD	23	G8
Lantian	GZ	32	C8
Lantianba	SC	31	D3
Lantian	SN	25	F5
Lanxi	FJ	16	F2
Lanxi	HB	19	D8
Lanxia	FJ	16	D3
Lan Xian (Dongcun)	SX	5	C3
Lanxi	HL	9	D4
Lanxi	ZJ	14	C4
Lanxu	GX	24	E5
Lanyi He	SX	5	C3
Lan Yu	TW	17	D4
Lanzhou	GS	27	D6
Lanzijing	JL	8	C4
Laobatan	NX	26	D3
Laobian	LN	7	D6
Laobie Shan	YN	33	D3-C3
Laobukou	GX	24	B7
Laochang	GZ	32	E3
Laochang	YN	33	C6
Laocheng	LN	7	B7
Laocheng	LN	7	B8
Laocheng	JX	15	G2
Laocheng	HB	19	D4
Laocheng	SN	25	G2
Laodafang	LN	7	C6
Laodaodian	HL	9	B4
Laodaohe	HN	20	C5
Laodao He	HN	20	C6
Laofengkou	XJ	29	B4
Laofu	NM	4	A6
Laoguan	JX	15	D1
Laoguanzui	HB	19	D7
Laoguo	HEB	4	C6
Laoha He	NM	6	D7
	LN	7	C3
Laohe	HEN	18	E4
Lao He	JX	15	C3
Lao He	HEN	18	E4
Laoheishan	HL	9	F6
Laohekou	HB	19	B4
Laohetou	HEB	3	D2
Laohuanghe Kou	SD	41	B5
Laohutun	LN	7	E5
Laoji	AH	13	D2
Laojieji	HL	9	E4
Laojingou	HL	9	A2
Laojundian	SN	25	C5
Laojunmiao	HEN	18	E6
(Laojunmiao) Yumen	GS	27	C3
Laojun Shan	HEN	18	D3
Laokan	JL	8	B5
Laokou	GX	24	E6
Laolai	HL	9	C3
Laoliangzi Shan	JL	38	C7
Laoling	JL	8	F7
Lao Ling	JL	8	F7
(Laolong) Longchuan	GD	21	A5
Laoniugou	JL	8	E8
Laoniuwan	SX	5	B3
Laonong Xi	TW	17	C3
Laopo	SD	10	D5
Laopu	HEB	3	C5
Laopuchang	GZ	32	C6
Laorencang	AH	13	D4
Lao Shan	SD	10	C7
Laoshan Wan	SD	10	C7
Laoshan	SD	10	C7
(Licun)			
Laoshaogou	JL	8	C6
Laoshawan	XJ	29	B5
Laotie Shan	LN	7	F5
Laotongguan	SN	25	F6
Laotougou	JL	8	E10
Laotou Shan	NM	8	B1
Laotuding Shar	LN	7	C8
Laotu Dingzi	HL	40	C5
Laowo	HEN	18	D6
Laowuchang	GD	21	B6
Laoxian	SN	25	H5
Laoxinkou	HB	19	D5
Laoyanchi	NX	26	C3
Laoyanghao	NM	6	F10
Laoyan He	HEB	4	F3
Laoyeling	JL	8	D8
Laoyeling	HL	9	F6

Laoye Ling	JL	8	D8-C8	Lengshuijiang	HN	20	D4	Lianggezhuang	HEB	4	D3
Laoye Ling	JL	8	D10	Lengshuipu	HB	19	C5	Lianghe	SC	31	A3
	HL	9	F5-E6	Lengshuipu	HN	20	F5	Lianghe	HL	9	E5
Laoye Shan	GS	27	D8	Lengshuitan	HN	20	E4	Lianghekou	HB	19	D2
Laoying	SX	5	B3	Lengzipu	LN	7	C6	Lianghekou	HB	19	D3
Laoyingpan	JX	15	E3	Leping	GD	23	G6	Lianghekou	GS	27	F7
Laoyingyan Sk.	SC	31	B2	Leping	JX	15	C5	Lianghekou	SC	30	C4
Laozhong	HEN	18	D6					Lianghekou	SC	30	C5
Laozhoutou	AH	13	G3	Leshan	SC	30	D4	Lianghekou	SC	30	D7
Laozhu	ZJ	14	D4	Lesuhe	SN	25	G2	Lianghekou	SC	31	D4
Laozhuangzi	HEB	3	C5	Letianxi	HB	19	D4	Lianghe	YN	33	C3
Laozishan	JS	11	C4	Leting	HEB	4	D6	Lianghuikou	SC	31	C6
Lapu	GD	23	G7	Letong	GD	23	G7	Liangjia	JL	8	B4
Laren	GX	24	C6	Letupu	AH	13	C3	Liangjia	LN	7	C7
Lasengmiao	NM	6	E3	Lewang	GZ	32	E5	Liangjia	LN	7	E6
Laxong Co	XZ	34	B3	Leye	GX	24	C4	Liangjiadian	HEB	3	B5
Lazikou	GS	27	E7	Leyu	JS	12	B4	Liangjiadian	LN	7	E5
Le'an Jiang	JX	15	C5	Lezhengwu	BJ	3	B4	Liangjiadu	JX	15	C4
Le'anpu	SC	31	A3	Lezhi	GZ	32	D4	Liangjiang	GX	24	B8
Le'an	JX	15	D3	Lezhi	SC	30	C5	Liangjiang	GX	24	D6
Lechang	GD	21	A4	Lezhu	GD	21	B4	Liangjiang	GX	24	D7
Lecheng	GD	21	B4	Lhabo	SC	30	D3	Liangjiangkou	JL	8	E9
Lede	SC	31	D2	Lhakang	SC	30	C3	(Liangjiayoufang)	SX	5	B4
Ledong	HI	21	D2	Lhari	XZ	34	C5	Youyu			
(Baoyou)				Lhasa He	XZ	34	C4	Liangkou	JX	15	E2
Ledu	QH	28	B8	Lhasa	XZ	34	C4	Liangkou	GD	21	B4
Lehua	JX	15	C3					Liangkou	GX	24	B7
Leibo	SC	30	D4	Lhatog	XZ	34	C6	Lianglong	GD	23	G7
Leidashi	HN	20	D6	Lhazê	XZ	34	C3	Lianglong	ZJ	14	C6
Leifeng	FJ	16	E4	Lhazhong	XZ	34	B3	Lianglongtan	YN	33	C5
Leigongdian	HB	19	C6	Lhorong	XZ	34	C5	(Lianglukou)	SC	31	C5
Leigong Shan	GZ	32	D7	Lhozhag	XZ	34	C4	Jiangbei			
Leiguanji	AH	13	D5	Lhünzê	XZ	34	C5	Liangma	SX	5	E4
Leihe	HB	19	C5	Lhünzhub	XZ	34	C4	Liangmianjing	HEB	4	B2
Leijiadian	HB	19	D8	(Poindo)				Liangpeng	ZJ	12	D3
Leishan	GZ	32	D7	Liancaipu	NX	26	E2	Liangping	SC	30	C6
(Danjiang)				Liancheng	AH	13	C4	Liangqing	GX	24	E6
Lei Shui	HN	20	E5-6	(Liancheng)	GZ	32	E4	Liangqiu	SD	10	D4
Leiyang	HN	20	E5	Qinglong				Liangsan	HN	20	D1
Leiyazhen	SN	25	E5	Liancheng	FJ	16	E2	Liangshan	JX	15	D2
Leiyuanzhen	SN	25	E5	Lianfeng	YN	33	B5	Liang Shan	SD	10	D3
(Leizhou) Haikang	GD	21	C3	Liang'anchang	SC	31	B3	Liangshan	SD	10	D3
				Liangbaosi	SD	10	D3	(Houji)			
Leizhou Bandao(Pen.)	GD	21	C3	Liangbingtai	JL	8	D9	Liangshan Yizu	SC	30	E3-4
Leizhou Wan(Gt.)	GD	21	C3	Liangbizhou	JX	15	E2	Zizhizhou			
Leizhuang	HEB	4	D6	Liangcheng	SD	10	D3	(Liangshizhen)	HN	20	D4
(Leli) Tianlin	GX	24	C4	Liangcheng	SD	10	D6	Shaodong			
Leli	GZ	32	D7	Liangcheng	NM	6	D5	Liangshui	GS	27	F7
Leli He	GX	24	C4	Liangcun	HEB	4	E2	Liangshui	JL	8	E11
Leling	SD	10	B4	Liangcun	JX	15	E3	Liangshui	JL	8	G6
Leliu	GD	23	H7	Liangcun	GZ	32	B5	Liangshuihezi	JL	8	E7
Lema	HEN	18	C7	Liangcun	HEB	4	E3	Liangshuijing	HN	20	C3
Lenghu	QH	28	A3	Liangcun	GD	21	B4	Liangshuikou	HN	20	B3
Lengji	HB	19	B4	Liangdang	GS	27	F8	Liangshuiyuanzi	NX	26	C1
Lengkou	HEB	4	C6	Liangdawa	HEB	3	A5	Liangshuizhen	SD	10	C2
Lenglong Ling	GS	27	C5-D6	Liangditou	SD	10	E2	Liangtian	HN	20	F5
	QH	28	A7-B8	Liangdong	GD	21	C3	Liangtian	GX	24	E8
Lengqi	SC	30	D4	Liangdu	SX	5	E3	Liangting	SN	25	F3
Lengshui	SC	31	D6	Liangduo	JS	11	D6	Liangtun	LN	7	D6
Lengshuihe	SN	25	H5	Liangfeng	GX	24	B8	Liangwa	HEN	18	D4

Name	Prov.	Map	Grid	Name	Prov.	Map	Grid	Name	Prov.	Map	Grid
Liangwang Shan	YN	50	C4	(Liantang) Nanchang	JX	15	C3	(Licun) Laoshan	SD	10	C7
Liangwangzhuang	TJ	3	D4								
Liangwushan	HB	19	D1	Liantang	FJ	16	C3	Licun	HEN	18	C4
Liangxiadian	SD	10	D3	Liantang	HN	20	E5	Licun	JX	15	F3
Liangxiangzhen	BJ	3	C2	Liantang	GD	23	H6	Licun	GX	24	E8
Liangxiongdi Dao	ZJ	14	B7	Liantang	GX	24	C9	Lidang	FJ	16	C5
Liangyan	GZ	32	C4	Liantang	GX	24	E7	Lidao	SD	10	B9
Liangyaping	HN	20	D3	Liantuo	HB	19	D4	Lidesi	AH	13	C2
Liangyi	SN	25	F6	Lian Xian	GD	21	A4	Lidian	SC	30	D4
Liangyuan	AH	13	E4	Lianxing	HL	9	C3	Lidong	GD	21	B4
Liangzhai	JS	11	B2	Lianyin	HL	9	A2	Lidu	SC	31	B4
Liangzhao	HEB	3	D3					Liduzhen	SC	30	D6
Liangzhen	SN	25	C4	Lianyuan	HN	20	D4	Liebu	SX	5	B3
Liangzhongqiao	LN	7	B7	(Lantian)				Liejinba	SN	25	G2
(Liangzhou) Wuwei	GS	27	D6	Lianyungang	JS	11	B5	Liemianzhen	SC	30	C6
				Lianyun Gang	JS	11	B5	Lieqiao	JX	15	C5
Liangzhu	ZJ	14	B5	Lianyungang	JS	11	B5	Lieshan	AH	13	C3
Liangzhuang	SD	10	C3	(Xinpu)				Lieshi	FJ	16	F2
Liangzi Hu	HB	19	D7	Lianyun Shan	HN	20	C6	Liexi	FJ	16	D3
Liangzizhong	SN	25	E6	Lianzhen	HEB	4	F4	Lifasheng	JL	8	C5
Lianhe	JL	8	E6	(Lianzhou) Hepu	GX	24	F7	Lifuchang	SC	31	A5
Lianhe	JX	15	C5					Lifuta	HN	20	B3
Lianhe	GD	23	H7	Lianzhushan	HL	9	E6	Ligang	JX	15	C3
Lianhua	HL	9	D4	Liaobin	LN	7	D6	Ligang	ZJ	14	B6
Lianhua	GD	23	I6	Liaobu	GD	23	H8	Ligang	TW	17	D3
Lianhua	GX	24	C8					Ligangpu	NX	26	B3
Lianhua	GS	27	E6	Liaocheng	SD	10	C2	Ligao	GX	24	C7
Lianhuacheng	GS	27	E7	Liaodong Bandao (Pen.)	LN	7	E5-D7	Ligeta	SX	5	F4
Lianhuajie	LN	7	B8	Liaodong Wan (Gt.)	LN	7	D5	Ligezhuang	SD	10	C7
Lianhua Shan	GD	21	B5	Liaodun	XJ	29	C7	Ligou	HEB	4	C2
Lianhua Shan	GD	21	B5	Liao He (Riv.)	LN	7	C5-6	Ligu	HB	19	B4
Lianhuasi	SN	25	F5	Liaohe Kou	LN	7	D6	Liguo	SD	10	B5
Lianhua	JX	15	D1	Liaoheyuan	JL	8	E6	Liguoyi	JS	11	B3
Lian Jiang	GD	21	A4	Liaohu	YN	33	C5	Lihai	ZJ	14	B5
Lian Jiang	GZ	32	E5	Liaojiangshi	HN	20	E6	Lihe	NX	26	A3
Lian Jiang	JX	15	F3	Liaolan	SD	10	C6	Li He	HEN	18	D5
Lianjiangkou	GD	21	A4	Liaoquan	GS	27	C5	Lihen	AH	13	G3
Lianjiangkou	HL	9	D6	Liaoyang	LN	7	C7	Lihu	GX	24	B5
Lianjiang	FJ	16	D5					Lihu	GD	21	B6
Lianjiang	GD	21	C3	Liaoyangwopu	LN	7	A7	Lihuaping	NX	26	D2
Lianjiechang	SC	30	D5	Liaoyang	LN	7	C7	Liji	JS	11	B5
Liannan Yaozu	GD	21	A4	Liaoyuan	JL	8	E6	Liji	JS	11	C3
Zizhixian (Sanjiang)				Liaozhong	LN	7	C6	Liji	HB	19	D7
Lianping	GD	21	A5	Libao	JS	11	D6	Liji	HEN	18	E7
Lianpu	AH	13	D4	Libazhuang	SX	5	B5	Lijia	LN	7	C6
Lianpu	FJ	16	D4	Libei	JX	15	D4	Lijia	SD	10	B5
Lianqiao	HN	20	D4	Libi Xia	SC	31	C5	Lijiacha	SN	25	C5
Lianshan	HN	20	E2	Libo	GZ	32	E6	Lijiachang	SC	31	A4
Lianshan	SC	31	A2	Libu	GD	21	A4	Lijiacun	SD	10	C6
Lianshanguan	LN	7	D7	Libu	GX	24	D9	Lijiadu	JX	15	C4
Lianshan Zhuangzu	GD	21	A4	Licangji	AH	13	C3	Lijiahe	HB	19	E2
Yaozu Zizhixian				Licha	SD	10	C6	Lijiajie	SC	31	C3
Lianshi	ZJ	14	B5	(Licheng) Jinhu	JS	11	C5	Lijiakou	HEB	3	C3
Lian Shui	HN	20	D5	Licheng	SD	10	C4	Lijian	GX	24	D6
Lianshui	JS	11	C5	(Hongjialou)				Lijiang	JX	15	D3
Liantan	GD	21	B3	Licheng	SX	5	E5	Li Jiang	GX	24	B8
Liantan	AH	13	F3	Licheng	GS	27	E7				
Liantang	JS	11	E6	Lichuan	HB	19	D1	Lijiang Naxizu	YN	33	B4
Liantang	SH	11	E7	Lichuan	JX	15	D4	Zizhixian (Dayan)			
Liantang	JS	11	D4	Licun	HEB	3	D4	Lijiaping	HN	20	E4

Name	Prov.	Sheet	Grid
Lijiaqiao	JS	11	E6
Lijiaqiao	BJ	3	B3
Lijiashi	HB	19	D5
Lijiatun	LN	7	E6
Lijiaxiang	ZJ	14	B4
Lijiaying	HEB	4	B6
Lijiazhai	SD	10	D6
Lijiazhai	HEN	18	F6
Lijiazhuang	SD	10	E5
Lijin	SD	10	B5
Lijunbu	NX	26	D2
Liju Shan	JX	15	B5
Likou	AH	13	G4
Likou	JS	11	C4
Lili	JS	11	F6
Liling	HN	20	D6
Limin	SX	5	B4
Liming	GX	24	D5
Liminzhen	HEN	18	C7
Limu	GX	24	B8
Limu	GX	24	C8
Limu Ling	HI	21	D2
Lin'an	ZJ	14	B4
Linba	SC	31	A5
Lincai	HEN	18	D6
Lincang	YN	33	D4
Lincheng	ZJ	14	B4
(Lincheng) Xuecheng	SD	10	E4
Lincheng	HEB	4	F2
Linchi	JX	15	E3
Linchuan (Shangdundu)	JX	15	D4
Lindai	ZJ	12	D5
Lindai	GZ	32	D5
Lindian	HB	19	C7
Lindian	HL	9	D3
(Lindong) Bairin Zuoqi	NM	6	D6
Linfen	SX	5	E3
Linfen	SX	5	E3
Ling'an	ZJ	12	D4
Lingang	JX	15	B5
Lingao Jiao	HI	21	C2
Lingao	HI	21	D2
Lingbao (Guolüezhen)	HEN	18	C2
Lingbei	GD	21	A4
Lingbi	AH	13	C4
Lingcheng	JS	11	C4
Lingchuan	GX	24	B8
Lingchuan	SX	5	F5
Lingdi	FJ	16	E2
Lingdi	JX	15	C6
Lingdianzhen	JS	11	E7
Lingding Yang	GD	23	I7
Lingdong Sk.	GX	24	E7
Linghe	SD	10	C6
Linghou	ZJ	14	C4
Linghu	ZJ	14	B5
Lingjiachang	SC	31	C3
Ling Jiang	ZJ	14	D6
Lingjiangkou	JX	15	C2
Lingjiangzhen	SC	30	C6
Lingjiaotang	HN	20	E4
Lingjiaqiao	AH	13	C4
Lingjing	HEN	18	C5
Lingjing	SX	5	C5
Lingkou	ZJ	14	C5
Lingkou	JS	11	E5
Lingkou	SN	25	F5
Lingli	GX	24	E6
(Lingling) Yongzhou	HN	20	E4
Linglongta	LN	7	D3
Lingma	GX	24	D5
Lingqiao	ZJ	14	B5
Lingqiu	SX	5	B6
Ling Qu	GX	24	B8
Lingshan	HEB	4	E2
Lingshan	SD	10	C7
Ling Shan	HEB	3	B1
Lingshan Dao	SD	10	D7
Lingshan Gang	ZJ	14	D4
Lingshan Wan	SD	10	D7
Lingshanwei	SD	10	D7
Lingshan	GX	24	E7
Lingshi	SX	5	E3
Lingshou	HEB	4	E2
Lingshui	HI	21	D3
Lingtai	GS	27	E8
Lingtian	GX	24	B8
Lingtou	FJ	16	E3
Lingtou	HI	21	D2
Lingui	GX	24	B8
Lingwu	NX	26	B3
(Lingxi) Cangnan	ZJ	14	E5
Lingxi	JX	15	C6
(Lingxi) Yongshun	HN	20	B2
Lingxi	HEB	4	D3
Ling Xian	SD	10	B3
Ling Xian	HN	20	E6
Lingxiang	HB	19	E7
Lingxianmiao	SC	31	B2
Lingyang	AH	13	F4
Lingyang	GZ	32	E5
Lingyang Xia	GD	21	B4
Lingyan Shan	JS	11	E6
Lingyansi	SD	10	C3
Lingyuan	LN	7	C3
Lingyun	GX	24	C4
Lingzê	XZ	34	C6
Linhai	HL	9	B3
Linhai (Taizhou)	ZJ	14	D6
Linhe	HEN	18	E6
Linheji	JS	11	C4
Linhe	NM	6	D3
Linhong Kou	JS	11	B5
Linhuaiguan	AH	13	D4
Linhuanji	AH	13	C3
Linjiacun	SD	10	D6
Linjiang	JL	8	F7
Linjiang	JX	15	C3
Linjiang	JX	15	G2
Linjiang	FJ	16	C4
Linjiang	GS	27	F7
Linjiang	SC	30	C7
Linjiangchang	SC	31	D4
Linjianghu	JX	15	C5
Linjiangsi	SC	30	C5
Linjiaping	SX	5	D2
Linjiatai	LN	7	D7
Linjin	SX	5	F2
Linkou	YN	33	B6
Linkou	HN	20	E2
Linkou	HL	9	E6
Linli	HN	20	B4
Linlü Shan	SX	5	E5
	HEN	18	A5
(Linmingguan) Yongnian	HEB	4	G2
Linnancang	HEB	4	D5
Linpa	HEN	18	E3
Linpeng	GX	24	D5
(Linping) Yuhang	ZJ	14	B5
Linpingzhen	SN	25	F4
Linpu	ZJ	14	B5
Linpuji	SD	10	D2
Linqi	ZJ	14	C4
Linqi	HEN	18	B5
Linqing	SD	10	C2
Linquan	GZ	32	C4
Linquan	AH	13	C2
Linqu	SD	10	C5
Linru	HEN	18	C4
Linruzhen	HEN	18	C4
Linshan	ZJ	14	B5
Linshanhe	HB	19	D7
Linshengpu	LN	7	C7
Linshizhen	SC	30	D6
Linshui	GS	27	C4
Linshui	SC	30	C6
Linshu (Xiazhuang)	SD	10	E5
Lintan	JX	15	E2
Lintan	GS	27	E6
Lintao	GS	27	E6
Lintingkou	TJ	3	C4
Lintong	SN	25	F5
Lintou	AH	13	E4
Linwu	HN	20	F5
Linxi	HEB	4	D6
Linxi	GX	24	B7
Linxi	AH	13	G5

Name	Prov	No	Grid
Lin Xian	HEN	18	A5
Lin Xian	SX	5	D2
Linxiang	HN	20	B6
Linxian Zhan	HEN	18	A5
Linxia	GS	27	E6
Linxi	NM	6	D6
Linxi (Tongcun)	HEB	4	G3
Linying	HEN	18	D5
Linyi	SX	5	F2
Linyi	SD	10	B3
Linyi	SD	10	D5
Linyou	SN	25	F3
Linyuan	TW	17	D3
Linze	JS	11	C5
Linze (Shahepu)	GS	27	C5
Linzhang	HEB	4	G2
Linzhenzhen	SN	25	D5
Linzheyu	SX	5	C2
Linzhuang	SD	10	B3
Linzi	JS	12	A4
Linzi	SD	10	C5
Linzijie	SD	10	B3
Linzikou	HN	20	C5
Liping	SN	25	H2
Liping (Defeng)	GZ	32	D8
Lipu	ZJ	14	D6
Lipu	ZJ	14	C4
Lipu	GX	24	C8
Liqianhutun	LN	7	B7
Liqiao	SC	31	D3
Liqizhuang	HEB	3	B4
Liqizhuang	TJ	3	D4
Liquan	SN	25	F4
Liren	JS	11	C4
Lirenpo	SX	5	E2
Lishan	HB	19	C6
Lishan	TW	17	B4
Li Shan	SX	5	F3
Li Shan	SN	25	F5
Lishangshan	GS	26	D3
Lishe Jiang	YN	33	C4
Lishi	SC	30	D5
Lishi	GD	21	A4
Lishi	SX	5	D3
Lishizhen	SC	31	D3
Lishizhen	SC	31	D4
Lishu	JL	8	E6
Li Shui	HN	20	B4
Lishui	ZJ	14	D4
Lishui	JS	11	E5
Lishu	JL	8	D5
Lishuzhen	HL	9	E6
Lisong	GX	24	C9
Lisui	BJ	3	B3
Lita	JX	15	D4
Litan	HEB	4	E4
Litang	GX	24	D7
Litang Qu	SC	30	D3
Litang	SC	30	C3
Litan He	JX	15	D4
Litian	JX	15	D2
Litouqiao	AH	13	E5
Litun	HEN	18	E6
Liuba	GS	27	C6
Liubao	JS	11	C5
Liuba	SN	25	G2
Liubinbu	BJ	3	A3
Liubu	GX	24	D9
Liubu	SD	10	C4
Liuchang	GZ	32	D5
Liuchang	HEB	4	F3
Liuche	JX	15	G3
Liuchen	GX	24	D8
Liucheng	ZJ	14	D4
Liucheng (Dabu)	GX	24	C7
Liuchong He	GZ	32	D4
(Liuchuan) Jianhe	GZ	32	D7
Liucun	HEB	3	D3
Liucun	SX	5	E3
Liucun	HEB	4	E3
Liudaogou	JL	8	F7
Liudaogou	JL	8	F8
Liudaohezi	HEB	4	C5
Liudaojiang	JL	8	F7
Liudaokou	TJ	3	C4
Liudongqiao	AH	13	E6
Liudu	GD	21	B3
Liudu	GZ	32	B6
Liuduo	JS	11	B6
Liuduqiao	HN	20	F5
Liuduzhai	HN	20	D3
Liu'erpu	LN	7	C6
Liufang	JX	15	B4
Liufangling	HB	19	D7
Liufangzi	JL	8	D5
Liufu	AH	13	D4
Liugezhuang	HEB	4	E4
Liugezhuang	SD	10	C8
Liugong Dao	SD	10	B9
Liugou	HEB	4	C6
Liuguang	GZ	32	C5
Liuguang	HEN	18	B6
Liuguantun	GZ	32	E3
Liugu He	LN	7	D4
Liugui	TW	17	D3
Liuhang	SH	12	C5
Liuhe	HB	19	D8
Liuhe	JS	11	E7
Liuhe	HEN	18	C7
Liuhe	HEB	3	D3
Liu He	HEB	4	C5-6
Liu He	LN	7	B6
Liu He	JL	8	E6
Liu He	SH	12	B5
Liuhechang	SC	30	C6
Liuhekou	HEB	3	A5
Liuhe Kou	JS	12	B5
Liuheng Dao	ZJ	14	C7
Liuhe	JL	8	E6
Liuheying	HEB	3	C2
Liuhouji	HB	19	C5
Liuhu	NM	6	C7
Liuhu	SD	10	B5
Liuhuang	GD	21	B6
Liuji	AH	13	D3
Liuji	HB	19	C4
Liuji	HB	19	D7
Liujia	GX	24	C5
Liujia	JX	15	C4
Liujiachang	HB	19	D4
Liujiachang	SC	31	C2
Liujiafan	AH	13	E4
Liujiage	HB	19	D6
Liujiagou	SD	10	B7
Liujiaguan	JL	8	D4
Liujiahe	LN	7	D7
Liujiahe	SC	31	A3
Liujiang	SC	31	C1
Liu Jiang	GX	24	D7-C7
Liu Jiang	SC	31	A5
Liujiang	GX	24	C7
Liujiaping	HN	20	B3
Liujiata	SX	5	B3
Liujia Xia	GS	27	E6
Liujiayuan	SX	5	E3
Liujiazhai	GS	26	D2
Liujiazhen	JS	12	A5
Liujiazhuang	SD	10	C7
Liujiazhuang	SD	10	D4
Liujiazi	LN	7	C4
Liujiazi	JL	8	D8
Liujing	GX	24	E6
Liukesong	HL	9	D4
Liukou	AH	13	G4
Liuku	YN	33	C3
Liulihezhen	BJ	3	C2
Liulimiao	BJ	3	A3
Liulin	HL	9	D6
Liulin	HEN	18	F6
Liulin	HB	19	C6
Liulincha	HN	20	C4
Liulinji	SD	10	D2
Liulinshui	BJ	3	B2
Liulin	SX	5	D2
Liulinzhen	SN	25	E4
Liuliping	HB	19	B3
Liulishe	JS	11	D6
Liulisi	SD	10	C3
Liuma	GZ	32	E4
Liumaoyuan	SN	26	C4
(Liupai) Tian'e	GX	24	B5
Liupan Shan	NX	26	E3
Liupan Shan	NX	26	E3
Liuqiao	JS	12	A5
Liuqiao	SD	10	B5

Liuqiu	TW	17	D3
Liuqiu Yu	TW	17	D3
Liuquan	HEB	3	C3
Liuquan	JS	11	B3
Liuquan	HEN	18	C4
Liuquzhen	SN	25	F5
Liurenba	HB	19	E7
Liusha Gang	GD	21	C2
Liushahe	HN	20	C5
Liushan	GX	24	C7
Liushan	HEN	18	D4
Liushanzhai	SD	10	C5
Liushi	JX	15	D1
Liushi	ZJ	14	D5
Liushi	HEB	4	E3
Liushilipu	AH	13	D2
Liushouying	HEB	4	D7
Liushu	SC	31	B3
Liushuhe	JL	8	D8
Liushui	JL	8	C5
Liushuidian	SN	25	H4
Liushuigou	HB	19	C5
Liushukou	SX	5	F5
Liushuquan	XJ	29	C7
Liushuquan	HEB	3	C5
Liusiqiao	JX	15	B4
Liusong	HEB	3	C4
Liutaizhuang	HEB	4	D7
Liutang	GX	24	C8
Liutao	JS	11	B5
Liutuan	HL	9	E5
Liutuan	SD	10	C6
Liutun	HEB	3	D4
Liuwan Dashan	GX	24	E7
Liuwang	GX	24	E8
Liuwei	JS	11	D5
Liuxi	SC	31	A6
Liuxia	ZJ	14	B5
Liuxi He	GD	21	B4
Liuxihe Sk.	GD	23	G7
Liuxu	GX	24	E6
Liuyang He	HN	20	C6
Liuyangpu	NX	26	C4
Liuyang	HN	20	C6
Liuyin	SC	31	C5
Liuyu	SX	5	D2
Liuyuan	HEB	4	G2
Liuyuan	GS	27	B2
Liuyuankou	HEN	18	C6
Liuzan	HEB	4	D6
Liuzhai	GX	24	B5
Liuzhan	HL	9	B3
(Liuzhangzhen) Yuanqu	SX	5	F3
Liuzhao	NM	6	D4
Liuzhou	GX	24	C7
Liuzhuang	SD	10	D2
Liuzhuang	JS	11	C6
Liuzigang	HB	19	D7
Liwangbu	NX	26	D3
Lixi	SC	31	A5
Lixi	JX	15	B2
Lixi	JX	15	D4
Lixi	SC	30	E3
Lixian	BJ	3	C3
Li Xian	GS	27	E7
Li Xian (Zagunao)	SC	30	C4
Li Xian	HN	20	B4
Li Xian	HEB	4	E3
Lixin	FJ	16	D2
Lixindian	HEN	18	E6
Lixing	AH	13	C2
Lixin	AH	13	C3
Lixu	JX	15	C4
Liyang	ZJ	14	C6
Liyang	SX	5	D5
Liyang	JS	11	E5
Liye	HN	20	C2
Liyi	SX	5	F5
Liyong	GX	24	C7
Liyuan	SX	5	F3
Liyuantun	HEN	18	B6
Liyue	GD	23	I6
Liyue Tan	HI	22	D4
Liyujiang	HN	20	F6
Liyutang	HN	20	E6
Lize	SC	31	B4
Lizezhen	SD	10	B4
Lizhai	JX	15	B5
Lizhai	JS	11	B2
Lizhen	HEN	18	A6
Lizhi	HL	9	E3
Lizhou	SC	30	D4
Lizhu	ZJ	14	C5
Lizhuang	AH	13	B3
Lizhuang	SC	31	D3
Lizhuang	SC	32	B3
Lizhuangzi	NX	26	C3
Lizhun Tan	HI	22	E2
Liziba	GZ	32	B5
Lizifang	LN	7	E7
Liziping	SC	30	D4
Lizui	GD	21	A5
Long'an	JX	15	D4
Long'an	SN	25	D5
Long'an	GX	24	B6
Long'anqiao	HL	9	D3
Long'an	GX	24	D5
Longbu	JX	15	F3
Longchang	GZ	32	D3
Longchang	GZ	32	D4
Longchang	GZ	32	E4
Longchang	LN	7	D7
Longchang	GZ	32	D6
Longchang	SC	30	D5
Longcheng	HN	20	E2
Longchi	SC	30	D4
Longchuan	GX	24	C4
Longchuan Jiang	YN	33	C3
Longchuan Jiang	YN	33	C4
Longchuan (Laolong)	GD	21	A5
Longchuan	YN	33	C2
Longcun	GD	21	B5
Longde	NX	26	E3
Longdongping	HN	20	B3
Longdu	JS	11	E4
Longfang	SN	25	E5
Longfeng	HL	9	D3
Longfengba	HB	19	D2
Longfengchang	SC	31	B4
Longfengshan Sk.	HL	9	E4
Longgang	JL	8	F9
Longgang	SD	10	C5
Longgang	JS	11	C6
Longgang	JX	15	E3
Longgang	JX	15	E4
Longgang	GD	21	B5
Longgang	GZ	32	D6
Longgang (Yangchang)			
Longgang	HB	19	E7
Longgang Shan	JL	8	F6-E7
Longgangtou	JX	15	E3
Longgong	ZJ	14	E3
Longgu	JS	11	B2
Longguan	HEB	4	C3
Longguang	GX	24	D4
Longgudu	JX	15	D4
Longguji	SD	10	D2
Longgun	HI	21	D3
Longhai (Shima)	FJ	16	F3
Longhe	GX	24	D4
Longhe	HL	9	A2
Longhe	HL	9	C3
Longheji	JS	12	A2
Longhekou Sk.	AH	13	E3
Longhu	JX	15	D4
Long Hu	AH	13	C3
Longhua	HEB	4	F4
Longhua	FJ	16	E4
Longhua	GD	21	B5
Longhua	GD	23	H8
Longhua	GD	23	H8
Longhua	SX	5	F3
Longhua	HEB	4	B5
Longhuguan	GX	24	B8
Longhui	JX	15	F2
Longhui	SC	31	C3
Longhui (Taohuaping)	HN	20	D4
Longhuo	GX	24	C3
Longji	JS	11	C4
Longji	JS	11	B4
Longjiang	FJ	16	D3
Longjiang	GD	23	H6
Longjiang	SC	31	C3
Longjiang	GD	21	B6

Name	Prov	No.	Grid
Long Jiang	GX	24	C6-7
Longjiang	HL	9	D2
Longjiaoshan	HB	19	E7
Longjiapu	JL	8	C6
Longjiazhai	HN	20	B2
Longjie	SC	31	C2
Longjie	YN	33	B6
Longjie	YN	33	C3
Longjie	YN	33	C4
Longjie	YN	33	C4
Longjie	GD	21	A5
Longjiezi	GZ	32	C3
(Longjing) Yanji	JL	8	E10
Longjingguan	HEB	3	B5
Longju	JS	11	B5
Longjuan	FJ	16	F3
Longjuba	SC	30	C7
(Longjuzhai) Danfeng	SN	25	G6
Longkangji	AH	13	C3
Longkou	SD	10	B7
Longkou	SD	10	C4
Longkou	JX	15	E3
Longkou	HEN	18	E6
Longkou	HB	19	E6
Longkou Wan	SD	10	B7
Longku	SC	31	D2
Longlin Gezu Zizhixian	GX	24	C3
Longling	YN	33	C3
Longli	GZ	32	D5
Longmei	GX	24	C7
Longmen	HL	9	C4
Longmen	AH	13	F5
Longmen	FJ	16	E2
Longmen	FJ	16	F4
Longmen	HEN	18	C4
Longmen	GD	21	C3
Longmen	HI	21	D3
Longmen	GX	24	E5
Longmen	GX	24	E7
Longmen	GX	24	F6
Longmen	SC	31	D4
Long Men	SX	5	F2
	SN	25	E6
Longmenchang	HN	20	C7
Longmenchang	SC	31	A4
Longmen Shan	SX	5	F2
Longmen Shan	ZJ	14	C4
Longmen Shan	SC	30	B5
Longmensuo	HEB	4	C3
Longmen	GD	21	B5
Longmenzhang	SC	31	D4
Longmenzhen	SC	31	A6
Longming	GX	24	E5
Longnan	JX	15	G2
Longnüsi	SC	31	B4
Longpeng	YN	33	D5
Longping	HB	19	D3
Longping	HB	19	E8
Longping	GZ	32	C6
(Longping) Luodian	GZ	32	E5
Longqiao	SC	31	A2
Longquan	SX	5	G2
Longquan	JL	8	E7
Longquan	HL	9	D4
Longquan	SC	31	A4
(Longquan) Fenggang	GZ	32	C6
(Longquan) Danzhai	GZ	32	D6
Longquanguan	HEB	4	E1
Longquan Shan	SC	31	B2
Longquan Xi	ZJ	14	D4
Longquan	ZJ	14	D4
Longquanyi	SC	31	B2
Longriba	SC	30	B4
Longshan	ZJ	12	E6
Longshan	AH	13	C3
Longshan	FJ	16	F3
Longshan	GD	21	B4
Longshan	GX	24	D7
Longshan	SC	30	E5
Long Shan	SN	25	F2
Longshan	HN	20	B2
Longsheng	GD	21	B4
Longsheng	GX	24	E8
Longsheng	SC	31	B3
Longsheng Gezu Zizhixian	GX	24	B8
Longshengzhuang	NM	6	F10
(Longshi) Ninggang	JX	15	E1
Longshizhen	SC	31	B5
Longshou Shan	NM	6	E2
Longshou Shan	GS	27	C5
Longshui	GX	24	A8
Longshui	SC	30	D5
Longshuiping	JL	8	E10
Longtai	SC	31	A3
Longtaichang	SC	31	C4
Longtan	JS	11	D5
Longtan	HN	20	D3
Longtan	HI	23	G7
Longtan	GX	24	F7
Longtan	SC	30	D6
Longtan	SC	30	D7
Longtang	JX	15	G3
Longtang	HEN	18	C7
Longtang	HN	20	C4
Longtang	GD	21	D3
Longtang	GD	23	G6
Longtang	GZ	32	C7
Longtanhe	HN	20	B4
Longtansi	AH	13	D2
Longtansi	SC	31	B2
Longtanxu	HN	20	F5
Longtanzhen	SC	31	D2
Longtian	FJ	16	E5
Longtian	HN	20	C4
Longtian	GD	21	A5
Longtian	GZ	32	C7
Longting	SD	10	D4
Longtingpu	SN	25	G3
Longtou	LN	7	F5
Longtou	GX	24	C6
Longtou	GX	24	C7
Longtou	GX	24	E5
Longtou'an	HN	20	D3
Longtou Jiang	GZ	32	D6
Longwan	AH	13	F3
Longwan	ZJ	14	D6
Longwangchan	SX	5	E2
Longwangji	HB	19	B4
Longwangmiao	HEB	4	G3
Longwangmiao	LN	7	D7
Longwangmiao	HL	9	E7
Longwangmiao	SD	10	E3
Longwangmiao	AH	13	C4
Longwangtang	AH	13	D2
Longwangzui	AH	13	F4
Longwo	GD	21	B5
Longwokou	JS	12	A3
Longwu	YN	33	C5
Longxi	HN	20	F6
Longxi	GD	23	H8
Longxi	GZ	32	C6
(Longxian) Wengyuan	GD	21	A5
Long Xian	SN	25	F2
Longxi He	SC	31	C6
Longxing	SX	5	B5
Longxing	SC	31	C5
Longxing	GZ	32	B6
Longxingshi	HN	20	E6
Longxi Shan	FJ	16	D3
Longxi	GS	27	E7
(Longxu) Cangwu	GX	24	D9
Longxue	GD	23	H7
Longxu He	GX	24	D4-5
Longyan	GX	24	D7
Longyandong	GD	23	H7
Longyang Xia	QH	28	B7
Longyan	FJ	16	E3
Longyao	HEB	4	F2
Longyou	ZJ	14	C4
Longyuanba	JX	15	G2
Longzhao	HL	9	E6
Longzhao	JL	8	B4
Longzhaogou	LN	7	D8
Longzhen	SX	5	E5
Longzhen	HL	9	C4
Longzhen	SC	31	C2
Longzhong	HB	19	B5
Longzhou	GX	24	E4

Name	Prov	Pg	Grid	Name	Prov	Pg	Grid	Name	Prov	Pg	Grid
(Lopnur) Yuli	XJ	29	C5	Luding	SC	30	D4	Lunan Shan	SC	49	E4
Lop Nur	XJ	29	C6	Luduo	JS	11	C5	Lunan Yizu	YN	33	C5
Lop	XJ	29	D4	Lüeyang	SN	25	G2	Zizhixian			
Loubanzhai	SX	5	C4	Lufeng	FJ	16	F2	Lungdo	XZ	34	B2
Loude	SD	10	D4	Lufeng	GD	21	B5	Lunggar	XZ	34	C2
Loudi	HEB	4	F2	Lufeng	YN	33	C5	Lungsang	XZ	34	C4
Loudi	HN	20	D4	Lugang	TW	17	B3	Lungucun	GS	26	C1
Loufan	SX	5	C3	Lugang	AH	13	E5	Lunhe	HL	9	D4
Lougang	GD	23	I6	Lügongbao	HEB	4	E4	Luning	SC	30	D3
Lougou	SX	5	B3	Lugouqiao (Wanping)	BJ	3	B3	Lunjiang He	GD	23	H6
Loulan Yiji	XJ	29	C6	Lugu	SC	30	D4	Lunjiao	GD	23	H7
Loushan	HL	9	E5	Lugu	XZ	34	B3	Luntai (Bügür)	XJ	29	C5
Loushan Guan	GZ	32	B5	Luguan	HN	20	D4	Lunzhen	SD	10	C3
Lou Shui	HN	20	B3	Luguan	AH	13	F3	Luo'ao	JX	15	F3
Loutang	SH	11	E7	Luguo	JL	8	E10	Luoba	SC	31	C1
Louwang	JS	11	C5	Luhe	HL	9	D4	Luobai	GX	24	E5
Louzhuang	AH	13	C4	Lühe	YN	33	C4	Luobei	HL	9	D6
Louzidian	NM	4	A7	Lu He	SN	25	C5	(Fengxiang)			
Loxur	SC	30	B3	Lühedian	HEN	18	E6	Luobie	GZ	32	D4
Luancheng	GX	24	E6	Luhe	JS	11	D4	Luobo Ding	FJ	16	D3
Luancheng	HEB	4	F2	Luhongshi	HN	20	E4	Luobu	GX	24	C7
Luanchuan	HEN	18	D3	Lühua Shan	ZJ	12	D7	Luobuzhuang	XJ	29	D6
				Luhuatai	NX	26	B3	Luochanghe	AH	13	E4
Luanhaizi	QH	28	C3	Luhuo	SC	30	C3	Luocheng	GS	27	C4
Luanhe	HEB	4	C5	Lujia	JL	8	C7	Luocheng	SC	31	D2
Luan He	HEB	4	C6	Lujia	JS	11	E7	Luocheng	GX	24	C6
Luanhe Kou	HEB	4	D7	Lujiabang	JS	12	C5	Luochuan	NX	26	D3
Luanjing	NM	6	E3	Lujiabu	ZJ	14	C6	Luochuan	SN	25	E5
Luannan	HEB	4	D6	Lujiagou	GS	26	E1	Luoci	YN	33	C5
(Bencheng)				Lujiang	AH	13	E4	Luocun	SX	5	E2
Luanping	HEB	4	C5	Lüjiaqiao	HEB	4	E5	Luocun	GD	23	H6
(Anjiangying)				Lujiashan	HB	19	C6	Luodian	SH	11	E7
Lu'an	AH	13	E3	Lujiatun	LN	7	D6	Luodian	HB	19	C6
Luan Xian	HEB	4	D6	Lüjiazhai	SD	10	C4	Luodian	GZ	32	E5
Lu'an	AH	13	E3	Lujiazhuang	SX	5	D5	(Longping)			
Luanzhuang	SN	25	G6	Lujing	GX	24	E8	Luoding Jiang	GD	21	B3
Luban	GZ	32	C5	Lujing	SN	25	E6	Luoding	GD	21	B3
Lubao	GD	21	B4	Lüjing	GS	27	E7	Luodong	TW	17	B4
(Lubei) Jarud Qi	NM	6	C7	Lu Jing	NM	6	D1	Luodong	GX	24	C6
				(Lukou) Zhuzhou	HN	20	D6	Luodou Sha	GD	21	C3
Lubiao	YN	33	C5					Luoduzhen	SC	31	B5
Lubu	GD	21	B4	Lukou	JS	12	B2	Luofa	HEB	3	C3
Lücaoshan	QH	28	B4	Lukou	JX	15	B3	Luofang	JX	15	C3
Luchang	SC	30	E4	Lukou	JX	15	D2	Luofang	JX	15	D3
Lucheng	HN	20	B6	Lukoupu	HN	20	B6	Luofang	FJ	16	E2
Lucheng	SX	5	F5	Lukoushe	HN	20	C6	Luofang	FJ	16	E3
Lucheng	GX	24	C4	Lukouzi	AH	13	D3	Luofu	GD	21	A5
Lücheng	JS	11	E5	Lükqün	XJ	29	C6	Luofu	GX	24	C5
Lucheng	SX	5	E5					Luofu Shan	GD	21	B5
Luchuan	GX	24	E8	Lüliangqiao	JS	11	C5	Luofu Shan	GD	21	B5
Lüchun	YN	33	D5	Lüliang Shan (Mts.)	SX	5	D3-C3	Luogang	GD	23	H7
Lücongpo	HB	19	D3	Luliang	YN	33	C5	Luogang	GD	23	G6
Lucun	AH	13	F6	Luling Guan	HEN	18	C2	Luoguhe	HL	9	A1
Lucun	GX	24	E6		SN	25	F6	Luohan	SC	31	D3
Lucun	SD	10	C5	Lulong	HEB	4	D6	Luohan Shan	FJ	16	E5
Ludao	HL	9	F5	Lulou	JS	11	B2	Luohe	SN	25	H5
Ludian	HEN	18	C5	Lülung	XZ	34	C3	Luo He	HEN	18	C3
Ludian	YN	33	B5	Luluo	HEB	4	F1	Luo He	SN	25	E5
(Wenpingzhen)				Lumajangdong Co	XZ	34	B2	Luohe	HEN	18	D6
Luding Qiao	SC	30	D4	Lumu	JS	11	E6	Luoheya	SD	10	D5

Luohong	HN	20	D4		HN	20	D6	Lüting	AH	13	E4
Luohuang	SC	31	D5	Luoxiu	GX	24	C7	Lutou	HB	19	B5
Luohui Qu	SN	25	F5-6	Luoxiu	GX	24	D8	Luwo	GX	24	D6
Lu ji	AH	13	C3	Luoxu	GX	24	D6	Luwu	GX	24	E6
Lu ji	AH	13	D4	Luoxue	YN	33	B5	Luxi	JX	15	D2
Lu jia	SC	31	A4	Luoya	GX	24	C7	Luxi	FJ	16	F3
Lu jiachang	SC	31	A5	Luoyang	JS	12	B3	Luxi	SC	30	C5
Lu jialing	AH	13	F4	Luoyang	FJ	16	E3	Luxi	SC	31	A4
Luojiang	SC	30	C5	Luoyang	FJ	16	F4	Lüxia	FJ	16	D6
Luo Jiang	SC	31	A2	Luoyang	GX	24	C6	Lu Xian	SC	30	D5
Luojiaqu	SX	5	C3	Luoyangdian	HB	19	C6	Lüxiang	SH	11	F7
Luojiazhuang	SD	10	C5					Luxi Dao (Pingtou	ZJ	14	E6
Luojin	GX	24	B8	Luoyang Shan	GX	45	C3	Shan)			
Luojing	GD	21	B3	Luoyang	HEN	18	C4	Luxikou	HB	19	E6
Luojiu	HN	20	D2	Luoyixi	HN	20	C2	Luxi	YN	33	C5
Luokan	YN	33	B6	Luoyuan Wan	FJ	16	D5	Luxi (Wuxi)	HN	20	C3
Luokeng	GD	21	A4	Luoyuan	FJ	16	D5	Luxi (Mangshi)	YN	33	C3
Luokou	SD	10	C3	Luoyukou	SX	5	C2	Luxu	JS	11	E6
Luokou	JX	15	E4	Luoyun	GX	24	D8	Luxu	GX	24	D7
Luokou	JX	15	F3	Luozha He	YN	50	C3	Luyang	HN	20	D3
Luokun	GZ	32	E5	Luozhen	SD	10	B5	Lüyang	LN	7	C5
Luolong	SC	31	D3	Luozhou	FJ	16	E5	Lüyanyi	HB	19	B5
Luolong	GZ	32	A6	Luozhuang	SD	10	E5	Luya Shan	SX	5	C3
Luolou	SD	10	D2	Luozigou	JL	8	D11	Luya Shan	SX	5	C3
Luolou	GX	24	C4	Luozi Shan	HN	44	E3	Luye	TW	17	D4
Luoma Hu	JS	11	B4	Lupanshui	GZ	32	D3	Luyimiao	HEN	18	D4
Luoman	GX	24	C7					Luyi	HEN	18	D7
Luomen	GS	27	E7	Luping	GZ	32	D6	Luyuan	JS	11	E6
Luonan	HI	21	D2	Luqiao	AH	13	D4	Luzê	GS	27	F7
Luonan	SN	25	F6	Luqiao	SD	10	D3	Luzhai	GX	24	C7
Luoning	HEN	18	C3	Luqiao	ZJ	14	D6	Luzhenguan	AH	13	E3
Luoping	YN	33	C6	(Lu Qu) Tao He	GS	27	E6	Luzhi	GZ	32	D4
Luoqi	SC	30	D6	Luquan	YN	33	C5	Luzhi	JS	11	E6
Luoqiao	JX	15	C5	Luqu	GS	27	E6	Lüzhi Jiang	YN	33	C4
Luoqiao	FJ	16	D4	Lu Shan	JX	15	B3	Luzhi Tequ	GZ	32	D4
Luoqing Jiang	GX	24	C7	Lu Shan	SD	10	C5	(Xiayingpan)			
Luoquanwan	NX	26	C2	Lu Shan	SD	10	C5	Luzhou	SC	30	D5
Luoquanzhen	SC	31	C2	Lushan	SC	30	C4	Luzhu	TW	17	D3
Luorong	GX	24	C7	Lushan	HEN	18	D4				
Luoshan	HB	19	E6	Lüshanzhen	ZJ	12	D3				
Luoshan	HEN	18	E6	Lushi	HB	19	D6		**M**		
Luoshe	JS	11	E6	Lushi	YN	33	C3				
Luoshi	SC	31	A5	Lüshi	SC	31	B5	Ma'an	ZJ	14	B5
Luoshuihe	SX	5	B6	Lüshikou	ZJ	14	C5	Ma'an	HB	19	B3
Luoshuikan	HB	19	D1	Lushi	HEN	18	C3	Ma'anling	JL	8	C8
Luotang	JX	15	E2	Lu Shui	HB	19	E6	Ma'anshan	AH	13	E5
Luotian	HB	19	D8	Lu Shui	JX	15	D2	Ma'ao	JX	15	B2
Luotun	SD	10	D3	Lu Shui	HN	20	D6	Maba	JS	11	D4
Luotuodian	HEN	18	E5	Lushuihe	JL	8	E8	(Maba) Qujiang	GD	21	A4
Luotuoshan	JL	8	D10	Lushui	YN	33	C3	Mabang	GX	24	C2
Luotuo Shan	LN	38	B4	Lüshun	LN	7	F5	Mabating	YN	33	A3
Luotuoying	LN	7	C4	Lüsi	JS	11	D7	Mabi	FJ	16	D5
Luowa	NX	26	D3	Lusikou	JX	15	C4	Mabi	SX	5	F4
Luowang	HEN	18	C6	Lusi Yu	FJ	16	E5	Mabian He	SC	30	D4
Luowenba	SC	30	C6	(Lutai) Ninghe	TJ	3	C5	Mabian	SC	30	D4
Luowenyu	HEB	3	B5	Lutai	HEN	18	D7	Mabie He	GZ	32	E3
Luowenzao	SX	5	A5	Lütan	HEN	18	C6	Mabu	JX	15	D3
Luoxi	JX	15	B2	Lutang	HN	20	F5	Mabu	ZJ	14	E5
Luoxi	GX	24	C6	Lutian	JX	15	C4	Macao	GD	21	B4
Luoxiao Shan	JX	15	E1	Lütian	GD	21	B4				

Machang	HEB	4	E4	Mahuiling	JX	15	B3	Malin	HN	20	E3
Machang	SX	5	E5	Maichen	GD	21	C2	Maling	GX	24	C8
Machang	LN	7	B3	Maiji Shan	GS	27	E8	Maling	GZ	32	E3
Machang	JS	11	B5	Mailing	GX	24	B9	Maling Guan	HEB	4	F1
Machang	AH	13	C4	(Maindong) Coqên	XZ	34	C3	Malipo	YN	33	D6
Machang	GZ	32	C5					Maliu	SC	31	A6
Machang	GZ	32	D5	Mainkung	XZ	34	C6	Maliuchang	SC	31	D2
Machang	GZ	32	D5	Mainling	XZ	34	C5	Malong	YN	33	C5
Machang Jianhe	TJ	3	D4	Mainquka	XZ	34	C5	(Tongquan)			
Machangping	GZ	32	D6	Maishi	HB	19	E6	Malu	GS	27	E8
Machangying	BJ	3	B4	Maiwang	HB	19	D6	Maluqiao	GX	24	B8
Machebu	ZJ	14	B4	Maixie	JX	15	D3	Mamiao	SD	10	D3
Macheng	HB	19	C8	Maiyuan	FJ	16	E3	Maming	YN	33	C5
Machi	SN	25	H4	Maizhokunggar	XZ	34	C4	Mamuchi	SD	10	D5
Machikou	BJ	3	B3	Maji	SD	10	D2	(Mamuji) Yucheng	HEN	18	C7
Machong	GD	23	H7	Maji	JS	11	D4				
Machunbu	NX	26	D2	Majiadazhuang	NX	26	E3	Manas He	XJ	29	C5
Macun	SX	5	F4	Majiadian	TJ	3	C4	Manas Hu	XJ	29	B5
Madang	JL	8	F6	Majiagang	HL	9	E7	Manas	XJ	29	B5
Madang	JX	15	B4	Majiagaozhuang	NX	26	D3	Mancheng	HEB	4	E3
Madao	SN	25	G2	Majia He	SD	10	B4	Manchuanguan	SN	25	G6
Madeng	YN	33	B3	Majiahewan	NX	26	C2	(Mandalt) Sonid	NM	6	D5
Madi	GX	24	B8	Majian [bei]	ZJ	14	C4	Zuoqi			
Madian	JS	11	D5	Majian [nan]	ZJ	14	C4	Manduhu	LN	7	C6
Madian	HEB	4	E3	Majiang	HN	20	E6	Mangbu	YN	33	B6
Madian	SD	10	C7	Majiang	GX	24	D9	Mangchang	GX	24	B5
Madian	SD	10	C7	Majiang	GZ	32	D6	Mangdang Shan	HEN	18	C8
Madian	AH	13	C3	Majiaoba	SC	30	B5	Mang He	HEN	18	B4-C4
Madian	AH	13	D3	Majiaqu	NX	26	C3	Mangla He	QH	47	C4
Madida	JL	8	E11	Majiatan	NX	26	C3	Mangnai	QH	28	B2
Madihui	SX	5	D3	Majiayao	GS	27	E6	Mangnai Zhen	QH	28	A2
Madiyi	HN	20	C3	Majiazao	SX	5	A6	Mangniu He	HEB	3	C3-D3
Madoi	QH	28	C6	Majiazhou	JX	15	E2	Mangniu He	LN	7	C5-B5
Madong	GX	24	D8	Majiazi	LN	7	B3	Mangniu He	HL	39	B5
Madongchuan	SN	25	D5	Majie	YN	33	C5	(Mangshi) Luxi	YN	33	C3
Madou	TW	17	C3	Majie	YN	33	C5	Mangui	NM	6	A7
Ma'erzhuang	NX	26	C3	Majie	YN	33	D6	Mangzhangdian	HEN	18	E6
Mafan	HEN	18	F6	Majie	SN	25	G5	Manhao	YN	33	D5
Mafang	BJ	3	B4	Majin	ZJ	14	C3	Man He	HB	19	C4-5
Mafang	SX	5	C3	Majing'ao	HN	20	C2	Maniganggo	SC	30	C2
Mafang	SX	5	D5	Majin Xi	ZJ	14	C3	Manjiang	JL	8	F8
Mafang	GD	23	G6	Maji Shan	JS	11	E6	Man Jiang	JL	8	E8-F8
Mafuzhen	SN	25	F3	Majitang	HN	20	C4	Manjing	SC	31	C2
Magang	GD	23	I6	Majuqiao	BJ	3	C3	Mankou	SD	10	E3
Magezhuang	SD	10	C6	Makou	JX	15	C3	Manshui	HB	19	E2
Magezhuang	SD	10	C7	Makou	YN	33	B5	Manshuihe	AH	13	E3
(Magong) Penghu	TW	17	C2	Malan	SD	10	C7	Mantou Shan	SX	5	B4
				Malanguan	HEB	3	B5	Manyunjie	YN	33	C2
Magong	GD	21	B5	Malanyu	HEB	4	C5	Manzhou	TW	17	D3
Magu	GZ	32	D3	Malanzhen	SN	25	E4	Manzhouli	NM	6	B6
Maguan	YN	33	D6	Malayiwan	QH	28	C6	Manzhuang	SD	10	C4
Magui	GD	21	B3	Malianchuan	NX	26	E2	Maoba	HB	19	D2
Magushan	JX	15	D4	Maliang	HB	19	D5	Maoba	HB	19	E2
Magutian	HEN	18	E5	Maliangji	AH	13	B3	Maoba	GZ	32	C5
Mahai	QH	28	A4	Maliangping	HB	19	C4	Maobaguan	SN	25	H4
Mahao	JL	8	D9	Malian He	GS	27	E8	Maobitou	TW	17	E3
Mahezhen	GS	27	E7	Malianjing	GS	27	C5	Maobosheng	QH	28	B7
Mahuan Dao	HI	22	D4	Malian Jing	GS	27	B2	Maocaojie	HN	20	B5
Mahuanggou	QH	28	B4	Maliantan	NX	26	A3	Maocaopu	GZ	32	C5
Mahuangshan	NX	26	C4	Malianzhuang	SD	10	B7	Maochang	GZ	32	D5

Name	Prov	Map	Grid
Maochengzi	JL	8	D5
Maocifan (Hongshan)	HB	19	C5
Maocun	JS	11	B3
Maodian	JX	15	F3
Maodianzi	LN	7	D8
Maodianzi	SC	31	C3
Maodongqiao	HN	20	E5
Mao'ergai	SC	30	B4
Mao'ershan	HL	9	E4
Mao'ertuo	SC	31	D5
Mao'er Xia	SC	31	D5
Maogang	GD	23	I6
Maogang	HN	20	B3
Maogong	GZ	32	D7
Maoji	AH	13	D3
Maoji	HEN	18	E5
Maojiachuan	GS	27	D8
Maojialing	JX	15	C5
Maojiazao	SX	5	B5
(Maojiazhen) Haimen	JS	12	B5
Maojindu	SX	5	G3
Maojing	GS	27	D8
Maojunxu	HN	20	F5
Maokui Shan	LN	7	D7
Maolan	YN	33	C4
Maolin	JL	8	D4
Maolin	AH	13	F5
Maoling	GX	24	F6
Maoling	GZ	32	D5
Maomaodong	GD	21	C3
Maoming	QH	28	B5
Maoniushan	SC	49	B5
Maoniu Shan	SC	31	D1
Maoping	JX	15	D2
Maoping	JX	15	E2
Maoping	HB	19	D3
Maoping	HN	20	B2
Maoping	GD	23	I6
Maoping	GZ	32	C6
Maoping	SC	31	C1
Maoqiao	HEB	4	C5
Maoshan	JX	15	G2
Mao Shan	JS	11	E5
Maoshi	HB	19	E6
Maosipu	HN	20	B5
Maotai	GZ	32	C5
Maotanchang	AH	13	E3
Maotian	HB	19	D2
Maotiao He	GZ	32	D5
Maotou Shan	YN	33	C4
Mao Xian	SC	30	C4
(Fengyizhen)			
Maoxing	HL	9	E3
Maoxuji	JS	12	A2
Maoyang	ZJ	14	E4
Maoyanma	HEB	3	D3
Maoying	GZ	32	E5
Maozhou	HEB	4	E4
Maozu	YN	33	B5
Maozui	HB	19	D6
Mapam Yumco	XZ	34	C2
Mapengwan	JS	11	D5
Maping	HB	19	C6
Maping	GX	24	C7
Mapo	SD	10	D3
Mapo	JS	11	B3
Mapo	GX	24	E8
Mapu	FJ	16	F3
Maqên Gangri	QH	28	C6
Maqên (Dawu)	QH	28	C7
Maqiao	XJ	29	B5
Maqiaohe	HL	9	E6
Maqiaoji	HEN	18	D8
Maqu	GS	26	E3
(Ma Qu) Huang He	QH	28	D7-8
Maquan He (Riv.)	XZ	34	C2-3
(Damqog Zangbo)			
Maqu	GS	27	E6
Margai Caka	XZ	34	B3
Margyang	XZ	34	C4
Markam	XZ	34	C6
(Gartog)			
Markit	XJ	29	D3
Mar Qu	SC	30	B3
Maru	GS	27	E6
Masanjia	LN	7	C7
Masha	FJ	16	C3
Masha	HB	19	D3
Mashan	GD	23	I7
Mashan	HL	9	E6
Mashang	SD	10	C4
Mashankou	HEN	18	D4
Mashan	GX	24	D6
Mashenqiao	TJ	3	B5
Mashi	GD	21	A5
Mashidian	SD	10	B8
Mashikou	HEB	4	C2
Mashiping	HEN	18	D4
Mashou	SX	5	D5
Masi	GX	24	C6
Masi	GD	23	H8
Masong	SD	10	C5
(Mataigou) Taole	NX	26	B3
Matajing	SC	30	D4
Matang	JS	11	D7
Matang	YN	33	D6
Matang	HN	20	B6
Matian	SX	5	E5
Matianxu	HN	20	E5
Matizi	SC	30	B4
Matou	BJ	3	C3
Matou	HEB	4	G2
(Matou) Qiu Xian	HEB	4	G3
Matou	AH	13	F5
Matou	HEB	3	C2
Matou	HEB	4	D4
Matou	HEB	4	F4
Matou	JX	15	B3
Matou	FJ	16	E4
Matoucun	HEB	3	C2
Matouji	AH	13	D3
Matouji	SD	10	D2
Matouli	HEB	4	F3
Matoushan	GZ	32	B6
Matouya	HB	19	C4
Matouying	HEB	4	D6
Matouzhen	SD	10	E5
(Matsu) Mazu Dao	FJ	16	D5
Mawang	SC	30	D7
Mawangtang	ZJ	12	D4
Mawei	FJ	16	E5
Mawei	GZ	32	E6
Maweipo	SN	25	F4
Mawu	GS	27	E7
Mawu	SC	31	C6
Mawuba	SC	30	D7
Maxi	GZ	32	C7
Maxiang	HEN	18	E6
Maxiang	FJ	16	F4
Maxie	GD	21	C3
Maxipu	HN	20	C3
Maya	AH	13	F4
Maya	GS	27	F6
Mayan	HL	9	E5
Mayan	GS	27	E7
Mayang	HB	19	D6
Mayang (Gaocun)	HN	20	D2
Mayidui	YN	33	C4
Mayi He	HL	9	E5
Maying	GS	27	E7
Maying	QH	28	B8
Mayu	HEB	4	F3
Mayu	ZJ	14	E5
Mayum La	XZ	34	C2
Mazar	XJ	29	D3
Mazartag	XJ	48	D3-4
Mazartag	XJ	48	D4
Mazha	GD	23	G8
Mazhan	SD	10	C5
Mazhan	ZJ	14	E5
Mazhangfang	LN	7	D4
Mazhaozhen	SN	25	F4
Mazhen	SN	25	B6
Mazhonghe	LN	7	B8
Mazhou	JX	15	F3
Mazhu	ZJ	14	B6
Mazhuang	HEB	3	C3
Mazhuang	SD	10	D5
Mazong Shan	GS	27	B3
Mazong Shan	GS	27	B3
Mazu (Matsu) Dao	FJ	16	D5
Mazuichang	SC	31	D6
Mêdog	XZ	34	C5
Meichang	TJ	3	C4
Meicheng (Jiande)	ZJ	14	C4
Meichengzhen	HN	20	C4
Meichi	ZJ	14	C5

Name			
Meichuan	HB	19	D8
Meichuan	GS	27	E7
Meichuan Sk.	HB	19	D8
Meicun	JS	12	B4
Meidaizhao	NM	6	F10
Meige	GD	23	I7
Meigeng	AH	13	F4
Meiguiying	NM	6	F10
Meigu	SC	30	D4
(Meihekou) Hailong	JL	8	E6
Meihua	FJ	16	D5
Meihuaxu	HN	20	F4
Mei Jiang	JX	15	E3
Mei Jiang	GD	21	A6
Meijie	AH	13	F4
Meikeng	GD	21	A5
Meikou	FJ	16	D3
Meilan	HI	21	D3
Meili	JS	11	E6
Meilin	AH	13	F6
Meilin	ZJ	14	C6
Meilin	JX	15	C3
(Meilin) Gan Xian	JX	15	F3
Meilin	FJ	16	F3
Mei Ling	JX	15	C3
Meilisi	HL	9	D2
Meilong	GD	21	B5
(Meilu) Wuchuan	GD	21	C3
Meinong	TW	17	D3
Meiqiao	AH	13	C4
Meishan [nan]	FJ	16	E3
(Meishan) Jinzhai	AH	13	E2
Meishan [bei]	FJ	16	E3
Meishan	FJ	16	E4
Meishan	ZJ	14	A4
Meishan Sk.	AH	13	E2
Meishan	SC	30	C4
Meishuikeng	FJ	16	E3
Meitanba	HN	20	C5
Meitan (Yiquan)	GZ	32	C6
Meitian	HN	20	F5
Meixi	HL	9	D5
Meixi	AH	13	F4
Meixi	ZJ	14	B4
Meixi	GX	24	A8
Meixian	FJ	16	D4
Meixian	HN	20	C6
Mei Xian	SN	25	F3
Mei Xian	GD	21	A6
Meiyao	JL	8	B2
Meiyu	SC	30	E3
Meiyuan	JS	12	B4
Meiyuan	ZJ	14	D4
Meiyukou	SX	5	A5
Meizhou	FJ	16	G3
Meizhou Dao	FJ	16	E5
Meizhou	GD	21	A6
Meizhou Wan	FJ	16	E5-F5
Meizhu	AH	13	E6
Meizhuang	JX	15	C4
Melmeg	JL	8	B4
Mêmar Co	XZ	34	B2
Mencun	SD	10	C6
Mend	NM	8	D4
Mengba	GS	27	E8
Mengban	YN	33	D4
Mengbin	YN	33	D3
Mengcheng	NX	26	C3
Mengcheng	AH	13	C3
Mengcun	GX	24	D7
Mengcun Huizu Zizhixian	HEB	4	E5
Mengdingjie	YN	33	D3
Mengdong He	HN	20	B2
Mengfeng	SX	5	D4
Menggongshi	HN	20	D4
Mengguying	HEB	4	B2
Menghai	YN	33	E4
Menghe	JS	11	D5
Menghugang	SC	30	D4
Menghun	YN	33	E4
Mengji	AH	13	D3
Mengjiagang	HL	9	D6
Mengjialou	HEN	18	E3
Mengjiang	GX	24	D8
Meng Jiang	GX	24	C8-D8
Meng Jiang	GZ	32	E5
Mengjiawan	SN	25	B5
Mengjiawan	NX	26	C1
Mengjiayuan	GS	27	E8
Mengjin	HEN	18	C4
Mengke He	NM	7	B4
Mengku	YN	33	D3
(Menglangba) Lancang Lahuzu Zizhixian	YN	33	D4
Mengla	YN	33	E4
Menglian Daizu Lahuzu Vazu Zizhixian	YN	33	D3
Menglianggu	SD	10	D5
Mengman	YN	33	D4
Mengman	YN	33	E4
Mengmiao	HEN	18	D6
Mengniushao	LN	7	A8
Mengquan	TJ	3	B4
Mengsa	YN	33	D4
Meng Shan	SD	10	D4-5
Mengshan	GX	24	C8
Mengsheng	YN	33	D3
Mengsi	SD	10	B4
Mengtuan	SD	10	C6
Mengu	HB	19	B3
Mengwang	YN	33	D4
Mengxi	HN	20	B4
Meng Xian	HEN	18	C4
Mengxing	YN	33	E4
Mengxuan	NX	26	E2
Mengyan	GZ	32	D7
Mengyang	YN	33	D4
Mengyangzhen	SC	31	A2
Mengying	HEB	3	A3
Mengyin	SD	10	D4
Mengyong	YN	33	D3
Mengyou	YN	33	C3
Mengyuan	SN	25	F6
Mengyuan	NX	26	E3
Mengyuan	YN	33	E4
Mengzhe	YN	33	E4
Mengzhu Ling	HN	20	G4
	GX	24	C9
Mengzi	YN	33	D5
Menkoutang	AH	12	C2
Mentaizi	AH	13	D4
Mentougou	BJ	3	B2
Menyuan Huizu Zizhixian	QH	28	B7
Mê Qu	SC	30	B4
Mergel Gol	NM	40	B2-3
Mêwa	SC	30	B4
Miancaowan	QH	28	C6
Miancheng	HB	19	D6
Mianchi	HEN	18	C3
Miandianjie	YN	33	D5
Mianduhe	NM	6	B7
Mianhu	GD	21	B6
Mianhua Yu	TW	17	A5
Mianjin	JX	15	E2
Mianmian Shan	SC	49	E3
	YN	50	B3
Mianning	SC	30	D4
Mianshan	SC	30	D4
Mian Shui	JX	15	F3
Miansizhen	SC	30	C4
Mian Xian	SN	25	G2
Mianxu	GX	24	D6
Mianyangdingzi Shan	LN	38	C5
Mianyang	SC	30	C5
(Mianyang) Xiantao	HB	19	D6
Mianyuan He	SC	31	A2
Mianzhu	SC	30	C5
Miaoba	SC	30	C6
Miaocheng	BJ	3	B3
Miao Dao	SD	10	B7
Miaodao Qundao	SD	10	A7
Miao'ergou	XJ	29	B4
Miao'er Shan	GX	24	B8
Miaofeng Shan	BJ	3	B2
Miaogoumen	SN	25	A6
Miaokou	HEN	18	B6
Miaoling	JL	8	D10
Miao Ling	GZ	32	D6-7
Miaoli	TW	17	B3
Miaoping	GX	24	B8

Miaoqian	AH	13	F4	Mingyuechang	SC	31	C5	Molihong Shan	LN	7	B8
Miaoqian	JX	15	B3	Mingyuegou	JL	8	D9	Molingguan	JS	11	E4
Miaoshan	SD	10	C4	Mingyue Shan	SC	31	C5-B6	Molo	SC	30	C3
Miaoshi	HN	20	C2	Mingyue Xia	SC	31	C5	Monan	SX	5	G2
Miaoshou	AH	13	F5	Minhang	SH	11	E7	(Mongolküre) Zhaosu	XJ	29	C4
Miaotai	NX	26	A3	Minhe	QH	28	B8				
Miaotaizi	SN	25	G2	(Shangchuankou)				Moni	SC	30	E5
Miaotan	HB	19	B4	Minhou	FJ	16	D5	Moni He	HL	39	B5
Miaotang	GZ	32	B6	(Ganzhe)				Mopanshan	JL	8	E10
Miaotou	JS	11	B4	Min Jiang (Riv)	SC	30	D4-5	Mopanzhang	AH	13	C4
Miaotou	GX	24	A9	Min Jiang	FJ	16	D4	Mopanzhou	HB	19	D4
Miaowan	HEN	18	D6	Minjiang Kou	FJ	16	D5	Mopo	HEN	18	D5
Miaoxia	JX	15	F2	Minjiatun	JL	8	C7	Mordaga	NM	6	B7
Miaoxia	HEN	18	C4	Minle	GD	23	G7	Mori Kazak	XJ	29	C6
Miaoyang	LN	7	D8	Minle	GD	23	H6	Zizhixian			
Miaozhaizi	SN	25	C3	Minle	GS	27	C5	Morin Dawa Daurzu	NM	6	B8
Miaozhen	SH	11	E7	Minqiao	JS	11	D5	Zizhiqi			
Miaozi	HEN	18	D3	Minqing	FJ	16	D4	Moshan	SD	10	E5
Miaozigou	SC	31	B2	Minqin	GS	27	C6	Moshi	HN	20	B3
Micang Shan	SN	25	H3	Minquan	HEN	18	C7	Mosouwan	XJ	29	B5
Michang	GX	24	E8	Min Shan	GS	27	F6	Mosuoying	SC	30	E4
Midu	YN	33	C4		SC	30	B4	Motian Ling	LN	7	C7
Migang Shan	NX	26	E3	Min Xian	GS	27	E7	Motou	JS	11	D6
Mi He	SD	10	C5	Minxiao	GZ	32	C7	Moudao	HB	19	D1
Mile	YN	33	C5	Minzhong	GD	23	H7	Mouding	YN	33	C4
Miliangpu	JX	15	B3	Minzhu	HL	9	D7	Moujiaba	SN	25	H3
Miluo Jiang	HN	20	C6	Minzhu	GZ	32	E3	Mouzixiang	SC	31	C1
Miluo	HN	20	C6	Miquan	XJ	29	B5	Mowu	FJ	16	D3
Minfeng	SD	10	B5	Miran	XJ	29	D6	Moximian	SC	30	D4
Minfeng (Niya)	XJ	29	D4	Mishan	HL	9	E6	Moxitou	JX	15	B3
Mingcheng	JL	8	D6	Mishazi	JL	8	C6	Moyang Jiang	GD	21	B3
Mingcheng	GD	21	B4	Mi Shui	HN	20	D6-E6	Moye Dao	SD	10	C9
Minggang	HEN	18	E6	Mituo	SC	31	D4	Moyu (Karakax)	XJ	29	D3
Minggao	HEN	18	C4	Mituosi	HB	19	D5	Mozitan	AH	13	E3
(Mingguang) Jiashan	AH	13	D4	Mi Xian	HEN	18	C5	Mozitan Sk.	AH	13	E3
				Mixinguan	SX	5	A6	Mu'ai	SC	30	D5
Ming He	HEB	4	G2	Miyaluo	SC	30	C4	Mubo	GS	26	D4
Minghechang	ZJ	14	B6	Miyi	SC	30	E4	Muchangpu	AH	13	E3
Minghua	HEB	4	F3	Miyun Sk.	BJ	3	A3	Muchengzhen	SC	31	C1
Minghuang	JS	11	E5	Miyun	BJ	3	B4	Muchuan	SC	30	D4
Mingjiang	GX	24	E5	Miyuzhen	SX	5	D3	Mudan Jiang	JL	8	D8-9
Ming Jiang	GX	24	E5	Mizhi	SN	25	C6		HL	9	E5
Mingkou	JX	15	C5	Mobin	HN	20	D2				
Minglang	YN	33	D3	Mocheng	JS	12	B4	Mudanjiang	HL	9	E5
Mingli	SX	5	D4	Mochong	GZ	32	D6	Mudan Ling	JL	8	E9
Minglun (Yibei)	GX	24	B6	Mochuan	GX	24	B8	Mudong	SC	31	C5
Mingshan	HL	9	D6	Mocun	GD	21	B4	Mudu	JS	11	E6
Mingshan	SC	30	C4	Modao Men	GD	23	I7	Mu'er	SC	31	C5
Mingshazhou	NX	26	C2	Modaoshi	HL	9	E5	Mufu	HB	19	D2
(Mingshui) Zhangqiu	SD	10	C4	Mogan Shan	ZJ	14	B4	Mufu Shan	JX	15	B1-2
				Moguqi	NM	6	C7		HB	19	E7
Mingshui	GS	27	A3	Mohe	HL	9	A2	Mufu Shan	HN	20	B6
Mingshui	HL	9	D3	Mohei	YN	33	D4	Mugang	YN	33	D6
Mingteke	XJ	29	D2	Mohe (Xilinji)	HL	9	A2	Mugang	HB	19	E8
Mingteke Daban	XJ	29	D2					Mugarripug	XZ	34	B3
Mingxi (Guihua)	FJ	16	D3	Mohurtay	XJ	29	B5	Muge	GX	24	E7
Mingyin	YN	33	B4	Moincêr	XZ	34	C2	Mugenpu	SC	31	C6
Mingyu	SC	30	D6	Moindawang	XZ	34	D4	Mugenqiao	HN	20	F6
Mingyue	SC	31	B4	Mojiang Hanizu	YN	33	D4	Mug Qu	QH	28	D3
Mingyuechang	SC	31	B5	Zizhixian				Muguaping	SC	30	C4

Name	Prov	#	Grid	Name	Prov	#	Grid	Name	Prov	#	Grid
Mugui	GX	24	D8	Nagarzê	XZ	34	C4	Nanchong	SC	30	C6
Muhar	QH	28	B6					Nanchong	SC	30	C6
Muhuang	GZ	32	B7	Nagqu	XZ	34	C5	Nanchuan	SC	30	D6
Muji	XJ	29	D3	Nagza	QH	28	A5	Nancuizhuang	HEN	18	A6
Mujiadian	JL	8	B3	Nahuo	GD	21	C3	Nancun	SX	5	B6
Mujingzi	NM	26	B2	Naij Gol He	QH	28	C3	Nancun	SD	10	C7
Mukangsar	XZ	34	C3	Naij Tal	QH	28	C4	Nancun	JX	15	D3
Mula	SC	30	D3	Nailin	NM	6	D6	Nancun	HEN	18	B5
Mulantou	HI	21	C3	Naiman Qi	NM	6	D7	Nancun	GD	23	H7
Mulan Xi	FJ	16	E4	Naimin Bulak	XJ	29	B6	Nandagang	HEB	3	D4
Mulan	HL	9	E5	Naitoushan	JL	8	E9	Nandan	GX	24	C5
Mule	GX	24	D8	Naizishan	JL	8	D8	(Nandaran) Qingyuan	HEB	4	E3
Mulin	BJ	3	B3	(Naji) Arun Qi	NM	9	C2				
Muling	HL	9	E6	Najin	JL	8	B3	Nandashan	HN	20	B5
Muling Guan	SD	10	C5	Najinkouzi	HL	9	B4	Nandian	LN	7	C8
Muling He	HL	9	E7	Nakan	GX	24	E5	Nanding	SD	10	C5
Muling	HL	9	E6	Nakou	FJ	16	C3	Nanding Dao	FJ	16	F4
(Bamiantong)				Nalao	GX	24	C4	Nanding He	YN	33	D3
Muli Zangzu	SC	30	E3	Nalao	GX	24	C3	Nandu	JS	11	E5
Zizhixian (Bowa)				Nali	GX	24	F6	Nandu	GX	24	E8
Muma He	SX	5	C4	Naling	GX	24	E5	Nanduji	AH	13	C3
Muma He	SN	25	H3	Nalong	GX	24	E6	Nandu Jiang	HI	21	D3-C3
Munai	YN	33	D3	Nalong	GX	24	E5	Nandulehe	BJ	3	B4
Muping	SD	10	B8	Nalou	GX	24	E6	Nanfan	SX	5	F3
Muqi	LN	7	C8	Naman	GX	24	D4	Nanfangquan	JS	11	E6
Muqiao	AH	13	E5	Namco	XZ	34	C4	Nanfen	LN	7	C7
Muri	QH	28	A6	Nam Co	XZ	34	C4	Nanfeng	GD	21	B3
Muri	QH	28	B7	Namda	SC	30	B3	Nanfeng	JX	15	B4
Muruin Sum Sk.	NM	6	D7	Namjagbarwa Feng	XZ	34	C5	Nanfeng	JX	15	D4
Mushihe	JL	8	C7	Namling	XZ	34	C4	Nangang	GD	23	H7
Mushi He	JL	8	C7	Namse La	XZ	34	C2	Nangang	AH	13	E3
Mutoudeng	HEB	4	C7	Nanan	GX	24	F5	Nangang	TW	17	A4
Mutougou	NM	4	A6	Nan'an	GD	23	H6	Nan Gang	GD	21	B6
Mu Us Shamo	NM	6	E4	Nan'an Jiao	HI	22	E3	Nangang Shan	JL	8	E9-10
Muxihe	HB	19	C8	Nan'an	FJ	16	F4	Nangangshang	JS	11	B4
Muyang	FJ	16	C5	Nan'ao	TW	17	B4	Nangaocun	HEB	3	C2
Muyang Xi	FJ	16	C5-D5	Nan'ao Dao	GD	21	B6	Nangdoi	QH	28	B8
Muyudian	SD	10	B7	Nan'ao	GD	21	B6	Nangezhuang	BJ	3	C3
Muyuping	HB	19	C3	(Nanbai) Zunyi	GZ	32	C5	Nangong	HEB	4	F3
Muzat He	XJ	29	C4	Nanbao	ZJ	14	C4	Nangongyingzi	LN	7	D3
Muzhen	AH	13	F4	Nanbaxian	QH	28	B4	Nangou	SX	5	G3
Muzhou	GD	23	I7	Nanbazhen	SC	30	C7	Nangou	JL	8	D9
Muzhuang	SD	10	C3	Nanbian	GD	23	G6	Nangqên	QH	28	D5
Muzhu He	SD	10	B8	Nanbozi	HEB	3	A2	Nangsin Sum	NM	6	E4
Muzi	GX	24	E7	Nanbu	SC	30	C6	Nanguan	HEB	3	C3
Muzidian	HB	19	C8	Nanbuzhen	JS	11	E7	Nanguan	SX	5	D4
Muztag	XJ	29	D5	Nancaicun	TJ	3	C4	Nanguan	SX	5	E3
	XZ	34	A3	Nancha	HL	9	D5	Nanguang	SC	31	D2
Muztag	XJ	29	D4	Nanchangshan Dao	SD	10	B7	Nanguang He	SC	30	D5
Muztagata	XJ	29	D2	Nanchang	JX	15	C3	Nanguanling	LN	7	E5
								(Nanguantao)	HEB	4	G3
N				Nanchangtan	NX	26	C1	Guantao			
				Nanchang	JX	15	C3	Nanguantou	HEB	3	D1
				(Liantang)				Nangucheng	GS	27	C5
Nabu	GX	24	F7	Nanchen	HI	21	D2	Nangunlonggou	HEB	4	E1
Nachen	GX	24	E6	Nancheng	JS	11	B5	Nangushanzi	LN	7	C8
(Nada) Dan Xian	GD	21	D2	Nancheng	FJ	16	E4	Nanguzhuang	SD	10	E5
Nadanbo	JL	8	D6	Nanchengsi	HEB	3	C1	Nang Xian	XZ	34	C5
Nadang	GX	24	F5	Nancheng	JX	15	D4				
Nafu	GD	21	B4								

Name	Prov	No.	Grid
Nanhai	GD	21	B4
(Nanhaoqian) Shangyi	HEB	4	B1
Nanhe	SD	10	B5
Nan He	HB	19	C4-B4
Nanhedian	HEN	18	D4
Nanheng	GD	23	H7
Nanhe	HEB	4	F2
Nanhu	SD	10	D6
Nanhu	GS	27	C2
Nanhu	GS	27	E7
Nan Hu	ZJ	12	D4
Nanhua Jiao	HI	22	D3
Nanhuang	SD	10	C8
Nanhuangcheng Dao	SD	10	A7
Nanhuatang	HB	19	A3
Nanhua	YN	33	C4
Nanhu Dashan	TW	17	B4
Nanhui	SH	11	E7
Nan Hulsan Hu	QH	28	B4
Nanhutou	HL	9	F5
Nanjia	GZ	32	D7
Nan Jiang	SC	30	C6-B6
Nanjiangkou	GD	21	B3
Nanjiangqiao	HN	20	C6
Nanjiang	SC	30	B6
Nanjian Yizu Zizhixian	YN	33	C4
(Nanjie) Guangning	GD	21	B4
Nanjin	SC	31	C2
Nanjing	JX	15	G2
Nanjing	JS	11	D4
Nanjinguan	HB	19	D4
Nanjing (Shanchengzhen)	FJ	16	F3
Nanji Shan	ZJ	14	E6
Nanjuma He	HEB	3	C2-D2
Nankai	GZ	32	D3
Nanka Jiang	YN	33	D3
Nankang	GX	24	F7
Nankang Ansha	HI	22	E3
Nankang	JX	15	F2
Nankeng	JX	15	D1
Nankou	FJ	16	D3
Nankouqian	LN	7	C8
Nankouzhen	BJ	3	B2
Nanku	JS	12	C4
Nanlai	HL	9	D3
Nanlang	GD	23	I8
Nanlang	GD	21	B4
Nanlan He	YN	33	D4-E4
Nanlei He	YN	33	D3-E3
Nanle	HEN	18	A7
Nanliang	SX	5	F3
Nanliao	TW	17	D4
Nanling	LN	7	C4
Nanling	GD	21	B5
Nan Ling (Mts.)	HN	20	F5-6
	GD	21	A4
Nanlingcheng	HEB	3	D3
Nanling	AH	13	F5
Nanlinqiao	HB	19	E7
Nanliu	SX	5	F3
Nanliu	SD	10	C6
Nanliu Jiang	GX	24	F7-E7
Nanlou Shan	JL	8	D7
Nanluji	SD	10	D2
Nanma	ZJ	14	C5
(Nanma) Yiyuan	SD	10	C5
Nanmeng	HEB	3	C3
Nanmiao	ZJ	12	E5
Nanmiao	JX	15	D2
Nanming He	GZ	32	D6
Nanmu	SC	30	C6
Nanmuping	HN	20	D2
Nanmuyuan	HB	19	D3
Nanning	GX	24	E6
Nanniwan	SN	25	D5
Nanpan Jiang	GX	24	C3
	GZ	32	F3
	YN	33	C6
Nanpeng Dao	GD	21	C4
Nanpeng Liedao	GD	21	B6
Nanpiao	LN	7	C4
Nanping	HB	19	E5
Nanping	HN	20	A3
Nanping	HN	20	E6
Nanping	SC	31	D5
Nanping	GD	23	I7
Nanpingji	AH	13	C3
Nanping	FJ	16	D4
Nanping	SC	30	B5
Nanpi	HEB	4	E4
Nanpo	GX	24	D4
Nanpu	HEB	4	D6
Nanpu	HEB	4	D6
Nanpu Xi	FJ	16	C4
Nanqi	SX	5	D4
Nanqi	HEB	3	D1
(Nanqiao) Fengxian	SH	11	F7
Nanqiao	HB	19	C5
Nanqiu	GS	26	D3
Nanquan	SX	5	B5
Nanquan	SD	10	C7
Nanri Dao	FJ	16	E5
Nanri Qundao	FJ	16	E5
Nansan Dao	GD	21	C3
Nansanshigang	AH	13	E4
Nanshahe	SD	10	D4
Nanshahe Sk.	SN	25	H3
Nanshanba	FJ	16	E2
Nanshanbu	HEB	3	A2
Nanshancheng	LN	7	B9
Nanshangtun	HEB	4	D2
Nanshangzhuang	SD	10	C4
Nanshankou	XJ	29	C7
Nanshao	GZ	32	D7
Nansha Qundao (Apg.)	HI	22	D2-4
Nansheng	FJ	16	F3
Nanshuang Dao	FJ	16	D6
Nanshuangmiao	LN	7	C4
Nanshui	GD	23	I7
Nanshui Dao	GD	23	I6
Nansongdu	YN	33	D4
Nantai	LN	7	D6
Nantang	JX	15	E3
Nantian	ZJ	14	C6
Nantian	ZJ	14	E4
(Nantian Dao) Niutou Shan	ZJ	14	C6
Nantonggang	JS	11	D6
Nantong Jiao	HI	22	E3
Nantong	JS	11	D6
Nantong (Jinsha)	JS	11	D7
Nantou	GD	21	B4
Nantou	TW	17	C3
Nanwan	HEN	18	E5
Nanwan	GD	23	I6
Nanwang	SD	10	D3
Nanwangzhuang	HEB	4	E3
Nanwan Sk.	HEN	18	E5
Nanwei Dao	HI	22	D2
Nanweiquan	SX	5	E5
Nanwei Tan	GD	21	C5
Nanwei Tan	GD	22	E2
Nanweng He	NM	9	B3
Nanwenquan	SC	31	C5
Nanwutai	SN	25	G4
Nanxi	HEN	18	C6
Nanxi	AH	13	E2
Nanxi	TW	17	C3
Nan Xi	ZJ	14	D5
Nanxiakou	HEB	4	F4
Nan Xian	HN	20	B5
Nanxiang	GX	24	C9
Nanxiang	GX	24	E7
Nanxiang	SH	11	E7
Nanxiao	GX	24	E6
Nanxiao Dao	TW	17	A6
Nanxin	SD	10	D4
Nanxing	SN	25	G2
Nanxinji	JS	11	C4
Nanxinzhuang	HEB	3	C3
Nanxiong	GD	21	A5
Nanxi	SC	30	D5
Nanxu	GX	24	D5
Nanxun	ZJ	14	B5
Nanya	FJ	16	D4
Nanyandang Shan	ZJ	14	E5
Nanyang	SD	10	D3
Nanyang [nan]	JS	11	C6

Panlong [nan]	SC	31	A4	Penglai	SD	10	B7	Pingdingshan	LN	7	C8
Panlong	GZ	32	D4	(Dengzhou)				Pingding Shan	HL	9	D5
Panlongzhen	SC	31	C3	Penglaizhen	SC	30	C5	Pingdingshan	HEN	18	D5
Panqiao	JX	15	D3	Penglang	JS	12	C5	Pingding	SX	5	D5
Pan Shan	TJ	3	B4	Pengnan	SC	31	B4	Pingdiquan	SX	5	C4
Panjin	LN	7	C6	Pengpozhen	HEN	18	C4	Pingdong (Pingtung)	TW	17	D3
Panshi	JL	8	E7	Pengqiao	HEN	18	E3				
Panshi Yu	HI	22	C2	Pengshan	SC	30	C4	Pingdu	SD	10	C6
Panshizhen	SC	30	C7	Pengshi	HB	19	D6	Ping'erguan	GX	24	E4
Panshui	GZ	32	C5	Pengshui	SC	30	D7	Pingfa	GZ	32	D6
(Panshui) Pu'an	GZ	32	E3	Pengting	GZ	32	E5	Pingfang	E4	9	E4
				Pengtoucun	HEB	3	C1	Pingfangzi	LN	7	D3
Pantan	ZJ	14	D5	Pengxi	ZJ	14	E5	Pingfeng	NX	26	E2
Pantang	AH	13	E4	Peng Xian	SC	30	C4	Pingfu	GX	24	E5
Pantian	FJ	16	E3	Pengxi	SC	30	C5	Pinggang	GD	21	C3
Panxi	YN	33	C5	Pengyang	NX	26	E3	Pinggang	LN	7	B8
Panxian Tequ	GZ	32	E3	Pengze	JX	15	B4	Pinggang	HEN	18	C7
Panxidu	SD	10	D2	Piancheng	NX	26	E2	Pingguo	GX	24	D5
Panyu (Shiqiao)	GD	21	B4	Pianguan He	SX	5	B3	Pinggu	BJ	3	B4
Panzhihua	YN	33	D6	Pianguan	SX	5	B3	Pinghai	FJ	16	E5
Panzhuang	TJ	3	C4	Pianjiaojie	YN	33	B4	Pinghai	GD	21	B5
Panzhuang	SX	5	F4	Pianling	LN	7	C7	Pinghe	FJ	16	F3
Paoche	JS	11	B4	Pianma	YN	33	B3	Pinghu	FJ	16	D4
Paomaping	YN	33	B4	Pianqiao	SN	25	E5	Pinghu	HB	19	D8
Paotai	LN	7	E5	Piao'erjing	GZ	32	C4	Pinghu	GD	21	B5
Paotaiyingzi	NM	6	D5	Piao'ertun	LN	7	C7	(Pinghu) Pingtang	GZ	32	E6
Paozi	LN	7	B6	Piaoli	GX	24	B7				
Paoziyan	LN	7	C9	Picheng (Pixian)	JS	11	B3	Pinghu	ZJ	14	B6
Parding	XZ	34	B4	Picheng	JS	11	D5	Pingji	GX	24	E6
Paryang	XZ	34	C2	Pi He	AH	13	E3	Pingjiang	GZ	32	E7
(Payzawat) Jiashi	XJ	29	D3	Pihekou	JL	8	D8	Ping Jiang	JX	15	E3
				Pikou	LN	7	E6	Pingjiang	HN	20	C6
Pêdo La	XZ	34	C2	Ping'an	JL	8	B4	Pingjing Guan	HEN	18	F5
Peicheng	HEN	18	D5	Ping'an	JL	8	C8		HB	19	C6
Peide	HL	9	E6	Ping'an	GD	23	G8	Pingjinpu	SC	30	C6
Peijiachuankou	SX	5	C2	Ping'anbu	HEB	4	B4	Pingjipu	NX	26	B3
Peijiangchang	SC	30	C6	Ping'ancheng	HEB	4	C5	Pingjipu Zhan	NX	26	B3
Peishan	HEB	3	C2	Ping'andian	SD	10	C3	Pingkou	HN	20	C4
Peitun	JS	11	B2	Ping'anpu	HEB	3	A5	Pinglang	GX	24	E6
Peiwei	JS	11	C4	Ping'anpu	LN	7	A8	Pinglang	GZ	32	D6
Pei Xian	JS	11	B2	Ping'an	QH	28	B8	Pingle	HEN	18	C4
Peng'an	SC	30	C6	Ping'anzhen	JL	8	B3	Pingle	GX	24	C4
Pengbo Bao	HI	22	E3	Pingba	HB	19	C6	Pingle	GX	24	E8
Pengbu	NX	26	D3	Pingba	GZ	32	D5	Pingle	GX	24	C8
Pengcheng	HEB	4	G2	Pingbazhen	SC	30	C7	Pingli	AH	13	G4
Pengdian	HEN	18	C6	Pingbian Miaozu	YN	33	D5				
Penggong	ZJ	14	B4	Zizhixian				Pingliang	GS	27	E8
Penggongmiao	HN	20	E6	Pingchangguan	HEN	18	E5	Pinglidian	SD	10	B7
Penghu	FJ	16	E4	Pingchang	SC	30	C6	Pinglin	HB	19	C5
Penghu Dao	TW	17	C2	Pingchao	JS	11	D6	Pinglin	HB	19	C6
Penghu Liedao (Apg.)	TW	17	C2	Pingcheng	SX	5	F5	Pinglin	TW	17	B4
Penghu Shuidao(Ch.)	TW	17	C2	Pingcheng	HEN	18	C6	Pingling	GD	21	B5
Penghu	TW	17	C2	Pingchuan	SC	30	E3	Pinglingcheng	SD	10	C4
(Magong)				Ping Dao		10	D6	Pingli	SN	25	H5
Pengjiachang	HB	19	D6	Pingdeng	GX	24	A7	Pinglucheng	SX	5	B4
Pengjiachang	SC	31	B1	Pingdi	SC	30	E3	Pingluo	SC	31	B1
Pengjiawan	HEN	18	E6	Pingdi	GZ	32	D3	Pingluo	NX	26	B3
Pengjia Yu	TW	17	A5	Pingding	GD	21	B3	Pingluo Zhan	NX	26	B3
Pengkou	FJ	16	E2	(Pingdingbu) Guyuan	HEB	4	B3	Pinglu	SX	5	G3
Penglai	HI	21	D3					(Shengrenjian)			

Pinglu	SX	5	B4	Pingyang	HL	9	C3	Pu'an (Panshui)	GZ	32	E3
(Jingping)				Pingyang	GX	24	D6	Pubei	GX	24	E7
(Pingma) Tiandong	GX	24	D5	Pingyang	HL	9	D2	(Xiaojiang)			
				Pingyangkeng	ZJ	14	E5	Pucheng (Puxian)	HEN	18	B7
Pingmu	SN	25	G3	Pingyang	ZJ	14	E5	Pucheng	FJ	16	C4
Pingmu	GX	24	E7	Pingyao	ZJ	14	B4	Pucheng	SN	25	F5
Pingnan	GX	24	D8	Pingyao	SX	5	D4	Puding	GZ	32	D4
Pingnan	FJ	16	D4	Pingyin	GX	24	F6	Pudu He	YN	33	C5
Pingqiao	JS	11	C5	Pingyin	SD	10	C3	Pu'erdu	YN	33	A6
(Pingqiao) Xinyang	HEN	18	E6	Pingyi	SD	10	D4	Pu'er	YN	33	D4
				Pingyong	GZ	32	D7	Puge	SC	30	E4
Pingquan	GS	27	E8	Pingyuan	GZ	32	B6	Puhe	SC	31	D5
Pingquan	SC	31	B2	Pingyuanjie	YN	33	D5	Pu He	GS	27	D8
Pingquan	HEB	4	B6	Pingyuan	GD	21	A5	Pu He	LN	38	C5
Pingsha	GD	21	B4	Pingyuan	SD	10	B3	Puji	HB	19	E5
Pingshan	HL	9	E4	Pingyu	HEN	18	E6	Puji	HN	20	D6
(Pingshan) Huidong	GD	21	B5	Pingzhai	GZ	32	E7	Puji	SD	10	C4
				Pingzhen	ZJ	14	C5	(Puji) Wugong Xi	SN	25	F4
Pingshan	GD	23	I8	Pingzheng	GZ	32	E7	Puji	SD	10	B8
Pingshan	JX	15	E4	Pingzheng	GX	24	E8	Pujiang	ZJ	14	C4
Pingshan	FJ	16	E3	Pingzhou	GD	23	H7	Pujiang	SC	30	C4
Pingshan	GX	24	E5	Pingzhuang	NM	6	D6	Pujue	GZ	32	C7
Pingshanba	HB	19	D4	Pipa Dingzi	JL	8	D9	Pukou	JS	11	D4
Pingshang	SD	10	D6	(Piqan) Shanshan	XJ	29	C6	Pukou	FJ	16	D5
Pingshang	HN	20	D4					(Pulandian) Xinjin	LN	7	E5
Pingshan	HEB	4	E2	Piqiao	JS	11	E5				
Pingshan	SC	30	D5	Pi Shan	ZJ	14	D6	Pulandian Wan	LN	7	E5
Pingshe	SX	5	C4	Pishan (Guma)	XJ	29	D3	Pulaochang	GZ	32	C6
Pingshi	HEN	18	E5	Pixa	XJ	29	D3	Puli	GX	24	C8
Pingshi	JX	15	E2	(Pixian) Picheng	JS	11	B3	Pulu	XJ	29	D4
Pingshi	JX	15	F3	Pi Xian (Yunhe)	JS	11	B3	Pulu	GX	24	C8
Pingshi	GD	21	A4	Pi Xian	SC	30	C4	Puma Yumco	XZ	34	C4
Pingshui	ZJ	14	C5	Pogan	JX	15	C4	(Pumiao) Yongning	GX	24	E6
Pingshui	HN	20	E6	Pogan	JX	15	D4				
Pingshun	SX	5	E5	Pohe	HEN	18	F6	Puming	SX	5	C3
Pingsong	SX	5	D5	Pohong	GX	24	D4	Punan	FJ	16	F3
Pingtai	JL	8	B3	Po Hu	AH	13	F3	Püncogling	XZ	34	C4
Pingtan	SC	31	C4	(Poindo) Lhünzhub	XZ	34	C4	Puning	GD	21	B6
Pingtan	GD	21	B5					Pupeng	YN	33	C4
Pingtang	GX	24	D7	Po Jiang	JX	15	B4-C4	Pupiao	YN	33	C3
Pingtang	HN	20	C5	Pojiao	GZ	32	C4	Puping	GZ	32	E4
Pingtang	GZ	32	E6	Pojiao	GZ	32	F4	Puqi	ZJ	14	D6
(Pinghu)				Pojie	GX	24	B5	Puqian	HI	21	C3
Pingtan	FJ	16	E5	Poli	SD	10	D5	Puqi	HB	19	E6
Pingtou	SX	5	D4	Poli	SD	10	D6	Pusa	XJ	29	D3
Pingtou	SN	25	F2	Poliangting	AH	13	F3	Pushang	FJ	16	D3
(Pingtou Shan) Luxi	ZJ	14	E6	Polu	SX	5	A4	Pushang	SD	10	C6
Dao				Ponggartang	GS	27	E6	Pushi	HN	20	C3
(Pingtung) Pingdong	TW	17	D3	Pong Qu	XZ	51	C3	Pushi He	LN	7	D8
				Poping	GZ	32	E4	Putai Liedao	GD	23	I8
Pingwang	SX	5	A5	(Poskam) Zepu	XJ	29	D3	Putang	GX	24	E7
Pingwang	JS	11	F6	Potou	HEN	18	C4	Putangqiao	JS	12	B2
Pingwu	SC	30	B5	Powo	SC	30	B2	Putao	GX	24	C8
Pingxi	GD	21	A4	Poxi	FJ	16	D5	Putaoxu	GX	24	C8
Ping Xi	HN	20	D3	Poxin	GX	24	C5	Putaoyuan	GS	27	E8
Pingxiangcheng	HEB	4	G2	Poyang Hu (Lk.)	JX	15	B4	Putian	JX	15	B2
Pingxiang	GX	24	E4	Poyue	GX	24	C5				
Pingxiang	JX	15	D1	Pozao	GX	24	D5	Putian	FJ	16	E4
Pingxiang	HEB	4	F3	Pozi	TW	17	C3	Putuo Shan	ZJ	14	B7
Pingxing Guan	SX	5	B5	Pozi	SD	10	C6	Putuo	ZJ	14	C7

(Shenjiamen)			
Puwa	BJ	3	C2
Puwang	SD	10	D5
Puwei	SC	30	E3
Puwen	YN	33	D4
Puxi	FJ	16	E5
(Puxian) Pucheng	HEN	18	B7
Pu Xian	SX	5	E3
Puxiong	SC	30	D4
Puyang	ZJ	14	C5
Puyang Jiang	ZJ	14	C5
Puyang	HEN	18	B7
Puyangzhen	SC	31	A1
Puyuan	ZJ	14	B5
Puzai	GD	21	C3
Puzhang	SX	5	F4
Puzhen	JS	11	D4
Puzhou	SX	5	G2
Puzijiao	HN	20	E2
Puzi Sha	JS	11	C7

Q

Qabnag	XZ	34	C5
Qagan	NM	6	B6
Qagan Bulag	NM	6	E3
Qagan Bulag	NM	26	B1
Qagan Hua	JL	8	C5
Qagan Moron He	NM	38	B3
Qagan Nur	JL	8	B5
Qagan Nur	NM	4	B1
Qagan Nur	NM	6	D5
Qagan Nur	NM	6	D5
Qagan Qonj	GS	27	A3
Qagan Teg	NM	6	D5
(Qagan Us) Dulan Xian	QH	28	B6
Qagan Us He	QH	28	B6-C6
Qagbasêrag	XZ	34	C5
Qagca	SC	30	B2
Qagcaka	XZ	34	B2
Qahar Youyi Houqi	NM	6	D5
Qahar Youyi Qianqi	NM	6	D5
Qahar Youyi Zhongqi	NM	6	D5
Qaidam He	QH	28	B5
Qaidam Pendi (Bsn.)	QH	28	B3-5
Qaidam Shan	QH	28	A4-B5
Qakar	XJ	29	D4
Qalgar	NM	26	C1
Qalgarin Sum	NM	26	B1
Qamalung	QH	28	C6
Qamdo	XZ	34	C6
Qammêgoin	SC	30	B4
Qapqal Xibe Zizhixian	XJ	29	C4

Qarak	XJ	29	D3
Qarhan	QH	28	B4
(Qarkilik) Ruoqiang	XJ	29	D6
(Qarqan) Qiemo	XJ	29	D5
Qarqan He	XJ	29	D5
Qarqi	XJ	29	C5
Qarqi	XJ	29	C4
Qarsan	NM	6	C7
Qayü	XZ	34	C5
Qedir	XJ	29	C5
Qeh	NM	6	D2
Qêyi	SC	30	C3
Qiabianqiao	SC	30	C4
Qiacha Hê	JL	8	C7-B7
Qiacun	JX	15	D4
Qian'an	HEB	4	C6
Qian'an	JL	8	B5
Qian'an Zhan	JL	8	B4
Qianban	FJ	16	E3
Qiancang	ZJ	14	E5
Qiancheng	HN	20	D2
Qiancun	ZJ	14	D5
Qiandalabin	NM	9	C3
Qiandugu	HEN	18	B7
Qiandun	JS	12	C5
Qianfang	JX	15	C4
Qianfeng	HL	9	D4
Qianfo	SC	30	C6
Qianfodong	GS	27	B2
Qianfodong	XJ	29	C4
Qiangbai	SN	25	F5
Qiange	FJ	16	F4
Qian Gorlos Mongolzu Zizhixian	JL	8	B5
Qiangu'ao	HN	20	D3
Qiangwei He	JS	11	B4-5
Qiangzilu	BJ	3	A4
Qianhe	ZJ	14	D3
Qian He	SN	25	F3
Qian He	AH	13	D3
Qianhuang	JS	12	B3
Qianhui Qu	SN	25	F2
Qianji	JS	11	C4
Qianjiadian	BJ	3	A3
Qianjiadian	NM	6	D7
Qianjiang	GX	24	D6
Qian Jiang	SC	30	C7
Qian Jiang (Riv.)	GX	24	D7
Qianjiang	HB	19	D5
Qianjiang	SC	30	D7
Qianjietou	SD	10	D6
Qianjin	JL	8	C9
Qianjin (Weidongmen)	HL	9	D7
Qianjing	JS	12	B5
Qianjinmiao	FJ	16	F4
Qianjin Sanchang	XJ	29	D3
Qiankou	HEN	18	A7

Qiankou	AH	13	G5
Qianligang	ZJ	14	C3
Qianling Shan	GZ	32	D5
Qianliu	YN	33	D4
Qianli Yan	SD	10	C8
Qianmotou	HEB	4	F3
Qianning	SC	30	C3
Qianqi	FJ	16	C6
Qianqihao	JL	8	C4
Qianqing	ZJ	14	B5
Qianqiu	JS	11	C6
Qianqiu	HEN	18	C3
Qianqiu Guan	AH	13	F6
	ZJ	14	B4
Qianshan	GD	23	I7
Qianshan	XJ	29	C7
Qian Shan	LN	7	D6-7
Qian Shan	LN	7	D7
Qianshanlaoba	XJ	29	B5
Qianshan	AH	13	F3
Qian Shui	AH	13	F3
Qiansuo	LN	7	D3
Qiansuo	ZJ	14	D6
Qiansuo	YN	33	C4
Qiantang Jiang	ZJ	14	B5
Qianwei	LN	7	D4
Qianweitang	HEB	3	B4
Qianwei	SC	30	D4
Qianwu	GD	21	B4
Qian Xian	SN	25	F4
Qianxi	HEB	4	C6
Qianxi	GZ	32	C5
Qianyang	FJ	16	C5
Qianyang	ZJ	14	B4
Qianyang	SN	25	F3
Qianyang (Anjiang)	HN	20	D3
Qianyao	JS	11	C4
Qianyou He	SN	25	G5
Qianzhai	SX	5	B4
Qi'anzhen	JS	11	D7
Qianzhou	JS	12	B4
Qianzhouzhen	HN	20	C2
Qı'ao	GD	23	I7
Qiaocun	SX	5	B4
Qiaodong	JX	15	C3
Qiaoduan	HEN	18	D4
Qiaodun	ZJ	14	E5
Qiaogou	HEN	18	E7
Qiaoguan	SD	10	C5
Qiaohou	YN	33	B3
Qiaojian	GX	24	D5
Qiaojiang	HN	20	D3
Qiaojiapu	GZ	32	B7
Qiaojiawan	SX	5	E3
Qiaojia	YN	33	B5

Qiaokou	HN	20	F6
Qiaoli	GX	24	D6
Qiaolin	JS	11	E4
Qiaomaidi	YN	33	B5
Qiaoqi	JS	11	E6
Qiaoqi	SC	30	C4
Qiaoshan	GX	24	C6
Qiaoshe	JX	15	C3
Qiaosi	ZJ	14	B5
Qiaoting	AH	12	D1
Qiaotou	NM	4	A6
Qiaotou	SX	5	C3
Qiaotou	LN	7	C7
Qiaotou	SD	10	B9
Qiaotou	JX	15	E2
Qiaotou	HEN	18	D4
Qiaotou	HN	20	E7
Qiaotou	HN	20	F4
Qiaotou	GD	23	H8
Qiaotou	GZ	32	E6
Qiaotou	YN	33	B4
Qiaotouhe	HN	20	D4
Qiaotouhu	ZJ	14	C6
Qiaotouji	AH	13	E4
Qiaotoupu	AH	13	F5
Qiaotoupu	HN	20	F4
Qiaowan	GS	27	B3
Qiaoxiajie	ZJ	14	D5
Qiaoxu	GX	24	E7
Qiaoyin	GX	24	C5
Qiaozhen	SN	25	D4
Qiawan	JX	15	D4
Qiazijie	SN	25	H5
Qibao	SH	11	E7
Qibu	FJ	16	C5
Qibu	FJ	16	D5
Qichongyan	HN	20	B4
Qichun	HB	19	D8
(Caojiahe)			
Qicun	SD	10	E4
Qicun	SX	5	C4
Qidao	SX	5	D2
Qidaogou	JL	8	F7
Qidaohe	BJ	3	A3
Qidaohezi	JL	8	C8
Qidaoling	LN	7	C4
Qidong	GX	24	C7
Qidonggang	JS	11	E7
Qidong	HN	20	E5
(Hongqiao)			
Qidong	JS	11	E7
Qidu	AH	13	F4
Qidukou	QH	28	C4
Qidun	SX	5	B4
Qiemo(Qarqan)	XJ	29	D5
Qiezixi	SC	31	C5
Qifanggang	HB	19	B5
Qifengcha	BJ	3	A3
Qifengdu	HN	20	F6
Qifeng Guan	HB	19	E2
Qifosi	SC	31	C4
Qigan	GD	23	G7
Qigong	GD	21	A4
Qigong	JX	15	C5
Qigou	HEB	4	C6
Qihe	SD	10	C3
Qi He	HEN	18	B5
Qi He	HEN	18	D3
Qihe	SD	10	C3
(Yancheng)			
Qihregt	NM	6	D5
Qihulin He	HL	40	C6
Qiji	HEB	4	F3
Qijia	HEB	4	B6
Qijia	JL	8	D6
Qijiahe	SX	5	G3
Qijiahe	HN	20	B4
Qijian	SC	31	B4
Qi Jiang	SC	31	B3
Qi Jiang	SC	30	D6
Qijiang	SC	30	D6
Qijiaojing	XJ	29	C6
Qijiaping	HN	20	C3
Qijiapu	LN	7	D7
Qijiawan	HB	19	D7
Qijiawu	HEB	4	E5
Qijiazhuang	BJ	3	B2
Qijiazi	JL	8	B5
Qijing	GD	21	C3
Qijing	GD	23	G8
(Qike) Xunke	HL	9	C5
Qikeshu	HL	9	D2
Qikou	HEB	4	E5
Qikou	SX	5	D2
Qiktim	XJ	29	C6
Qilaizhu Shan	TW	17	B4
Qilaotu Shan	HEB	4	B5-6
Qileng	SN	25	B6
(Qili) Shitai	AH	13	F4
Qilian	GS	27	D6
Qilian Shan(Mts.)	GS	27	C3-5
	QH	28	A5-7
Qilian Shan	GS	27	C4
	QH	28	A6
Qilian (Babao)	QH	28	A7
Qilicun	SN	25	D5
Qili Hai	TJ	3	C4-5
Qilihe	LN	7	C5
Qililong	ZJ	14	C4
Qilimiao	SN	25	F4
Qiling	FJ	16	F2
Qiling	GD	21	A5
Qilingou	SN	25	C5
Qilinmen	JS	12	A2
Qilinzhen	JS	11	E7
Qiliping	HB	19	C7
Qiliying	HEN	18	B5
Qilizhen	SN	25	E5
Qilizhen	GS	27	B2
Qiman	XJ	29	C4
Qimantag	XJ	48	D6
Qimen	GD	21	A4
Qimeng	GZ	32	D8
Qimen	AH	13	G4
Qimenzhan	AH	12	B1
Qimu Jiao	SD	10	B7
Qin'an	GS	27	E7
Qincheng	BJ	3	B3
Qinchi	SX	5	F4
Qincun	HEB	4	F4
Qindeli	HL	9	C7
Qinduzhen	SN	25	F4
Qing'an	HL	9	D4
Qingbaijiang	SC	31	A2
Qingbai Jiang	SC	31	A2
Qingbaikou	BJ	3	B2
Qingcaoge	AH	13	F3
Qingcheng	SX	5	D5
Qingcheng	SD	10	B4
Qingcheng	SX	5	C5
Qingcheng Shan	SC	31	A1
Qingchengzi	LN	7	D7
Qingchi	GZ	32	C4
Qingchuan	SC	30	B5
Qingcungang	SH	12	C6
	SD	10	C6-7
Qingdao	SD	10	C7
Qingduizi	LN	7	C5
Qingduizi	LN	7	E7
Qingfeng	HB	19	B3
Qingfengdian	HEB	4	E3
Qingfeng	HEN	18	B7
Qingfu	SC	30	D5
Qinggang	SC	30	C5
Qinggang	ZJ	14	D6
Qinggang	HL	9	D4
(Qinggil) Qinghe	XJ	29	B6
Qinggir	XJ	29	C6
Qinggis Han	NM	6	C7
Qinggouzi	JL	8	D9
Qingguandu	HN	20	B3
Qingguji	SD	10	E2
Qinghai Hu(Lk.)	QH	28	B7
Qinghai Nanshan	QH	28	B6-7
Qinghe	HL	9	C3
Qinghe	BJ	3	B3
Qinghe	SX	5	F3
Qinghe	LN	7	B8
Qinghe	JL	8	F6
Qinghe	HL	9	D5
Qing He	LN	7	B8
Qinghecheng	LN	7	C8
Qinghei Shan	HL	40	C5
Qinghemen	LN	7	C5
Qinghe Sk.	LN	7	B8
Qinghetou	HEN	18	B7
Qinghe(Qinggil)	XJ	29	B6
Qinghe	HEB	4	F3

(Gexianzhuang)			
Qinghezhen	SD	10	B4
Qinghu	ZJ	14	D3
Qinghu	GX	24	E8
Qinghua	JX	15	B5
Qinghuabian	SN	25	D5
Qinghuazhen	SC	31	B5
Qingjiang	ZJ	14	D6
Qing Jiang	HB	19	D3
Qingjiangqiao	HN	20	E3
(Qingjiang)Huaiyin	JS	11	C5
Qingjiang	JX	15	C3
(Zhangshuzhen)			
Qingjian He	SN	25	C5-6
Qingjian	SN	25	C6
(Qingkou)Ganyu	JS	11	B5
Qinglan	HEB	4	F4
Qinglan	HI	21	D3
Qinglan Gang	HI	21	D3
Qinglian	GD	21	A4
Qingliangdian	HEB	4	F3
Qingliang Jiang	HEB	4	F3
Qingliangsi	SX	5	C2
Qingliuchang	SC	31	A2
Qingliu He	AH	12	A1
Qingliu	FJ	16	D2
Qinglong	JX	15	F2
Qinglong	SC	31	C1
Qinglong	YN	33	D5
Qinglongchang	SC	30	C4
Qinglonggang	JS	12	B5
Qinglong He	HEB	4	C6-7
Qinglongji	AH	13	B3
Qinglongqiao	BJ	3	B2
Qinglongshan	NX	26	C3
Qinglongwan He	TJ	3	C4
Qinglong	HEB	4	C6
Qinglong	GZ	32	E4
(Liancheng)			
Qingmuguan	SC	30	D6
Qingningsi	SH	12	C6
Qingong	JS	11	C5
Qingping	GD	21	C2
Qingping	SD	10	C3
Qingping	SC	30	C6
Qingping	GZ	32	D6
Qingping	HB	19	E2
Qingpu	FJ	16	E5
Qingpu	SH	11	E7
Qingshan	JL	8	B3
Qingshan	JL	8	B7
(Qingshan)Dedu	HL	9	C4
Qingshan	HL	9	D7
Qingshan	ZJ	12	D3
Qingshan	AH	13	E3
Qingshan	ZJ	14	B4
Qingshan	ZJ	14	B5
Qingshan	HB	19	D7
Qingshan	GD	23	I8
Qingshan	GX	24	C8
Qingshan	GZ	32	E4
Qingshancun	JL	8	E9
Qingshanpu	HN	20	C6
Qingshanqiao	AH	13	G3
Qingshanquan	JS	11	B3
Qingshen	SC	30	D4
Qingshi	JL	8	F7
Qingshila	HEB	4	B4
Qingshizui	NX	26	E3
Qingshizui	QH	28	B7
Qingshui	BJ	3	B2
Qingshui	SD	10	C2
Qingshui	TW	17	B3
Qingshui	GX	24	B9
Qingshui	GS	27	C4
Qingshui	SC	31	B2
Qingshuiguan	SN	25	D6
Qingshuihe	SX	5	B5
Qingshuihe	AH	12	C1
Qingshuihe	HB	19	D8
Qingshuihe	QH	28	D5
Qingshui He	SX	5	C5
Qingshui He	NX	26	C2
Qingshuihe	NM	6	E4
Qingshuihezi	XJ	29	C5
Qingshui Jiang	GX	24	D6-7
Qingshui Jiang	GZ	32	C6-D6
Qingshui Jiang	GZ	32	D7
Qingshuilang Shan	YN	33	C3
Qingshuitai	LN	7	B7
Qingshuiwan	HB	19	D3
Qingshui	GS	27	E8
Qingshuping	HN	20	D5
Qingtai	HEN	18	E4
Qingtaiping	HB	19	D3
Qingtan	HB	19	C5
Qingtang	GD	21	A4
Qingtangpu	HN	20	C4
Qingtazhen	HEB	3	D2
Qingtian	ZJ	14	D5
Qingtongguan	SN	25	G5
Qingtongxia	NX	26	C3
Qingtongxia Sk.	NX	26	C2
Qingtongxia	NX	26	B3
(Xiaoba)			
Qingtongxia Zhan	NX	26	C2
Qingtou	SX	5	F2
Qingtuan	AH	13	C3
Qingtuosi	SD	10	D5
Qinguanzhen	SN	25	E5
Qingxi	GZ	32	C7
Qingxi	HL	9	C4
Qingxi	AH	13	E5
Qingxi	GD	23	H8
Qingxi	SC	31	A5
Qingxi	SC	31	C6
Qing Xian	HEB	4	E4
Qingxiang	SX	5	E3
Qingxizhen	SC	31	D1
Qingxu	SX	5	D4
Qingyan	GZ	32	D5
Qingyang	HL	9	E5
(Qingyang)Jinjiang	FJ	16	F4
Qingyangcha	SN	25	C5
Qingyangshan	NM	27	D7
Qingyang	GS	27	D8
Qingyang	AH	13	F4
Qingyangzhen	JS	11	E6
Qingyihu	JS	11	B4
Qingyi Jiang	AH	13	F5-E5
Qingyi Jiang	SC	30	C4
(Qingyuan)Yishan	GX	24	C6
Qingyuan He	GS	25	G1
Qingyuanshan	JX	15	D3
Qingyuan	ZJ	14	E4
Qingyuan	GD	21	B4
Qingyuan	HEB	4	E3
(Nandaran)			
Qingyuan	LN	7	B8
Qingyun	ZJ	14	B4
Qingyundian	BJ	3	C3
Qingyunpu	LN	7	B7
Qingyun Shan	GD	21	B4-A5
Qingyun	SD	10	B4
(Xiejiaji)			
Qingzhang Dongyuan	SX	5	D5
Qingzhang He	HEB	4	G1
Qingzhang Xiyuan	SX	5	D5-E5
Qingzhen	GZ	32	D5
Qingzhou	FJ	16	D3
Qingzu	HEN	18	B7
Qin He	SX	5	F4
Qinhuai He	JS	11	E5
Qinhuangdao	HEB	4	D7
Qinjian	ZJ	14	D3
Qin Jiang	GX	24	E6
Qin Jiang	JX	15	E4
Qinjiatun	JL	8	D5
Qinlan	AH	13	D6
Qinling	SN	25	F2
Qin Ling (Mts.)	SN	25	G3
Qinling Shandi	SN	46	E3-5
Qinnan	JS	11	C5
Qin Qu	NX	26	B3
Qinquan	SX	5	D5
Qinquan	SX	5	E5
Qinshan Dao	JS	11	B5
Qinshui	SX	5	F4
Qintang	GX	24	D7
Qintong	JS	11	D6
Qin Xian	SX	5	E4
Qinyang	FJ	16	C5
Qinyang	HEN	18	B4
Qinyu	FJ	16	C6
Qinyuan	SX	5	E4

Qu Xian	SC	30	C6
Qüxü	XZ	34	C4
Quyang	JX	15	E3
Quyang	HEB	4	E2
Quzhou	ZJ	14	D3
Quzhou	HEB	4	G2
Quzi	GS	27	D8

R

Rabang	XZ	34	B2
Rabga La	XZ	34	D3
Ra'gyagoinba	QH	28	C7
Raka	XZ	34	C3
Raka Zangbo	XZ	34	C3
Rangdong	HEN	18	E4
Ranghe	HEN	18	D4
Ranghulu	HL	9	D3
Rangnan	GX	24	D9
Rangtag	GS	27	F6
Rangu	SD	10	E2
Rangzijing	JL	8	B5
Ranzhuang	HEB	4	E3
Ranzhuang	SX	5	B6
Rao'er	JX	15	C5
Raohe	HL	9	D7
Raoliang	HEN	18	E5
Raoping	GD	21	B6
Raoqiao	JX	15	D5
Raoshi	JX	15	D2
Raoyanghe	LN	7	C6
Raoyang He	LN	7	C6
Raoyang	HEB	4	E3
Rawu	XZ	34	C6
Rayü	XZ	34	C5
Ren'ai Jiao	HI	22	D3
Renchaoxi	HN	20	B3
Rencun	HEN	18	A5
Rencundu	NX	26	B3
Rendian	HEN	18	E5
Rendong	GX	24	E8
Renfeng	SD	10	B4
Renfengzhuang	TJ	3	C5
Rengezhuang	HEB	3	C5
Renhe	GX	24	D9
Renhe	SC	31	C5
Renhe	JX	15	D3
Renhe	SC	31	A4
Ren He	SN	25	H4
	SC	30	B7
Renhechang	SC	31	A4
Renheji	SD	10	C9
Renheji	HEN	18	F7
Renhuai (Zhongshu)	GZ	32	C5
Renhua	GD	21	A4
Renju	GD	21	A5
Renli	SC	31	B4
Renliji	SD	10	C3

Renlong	SC	31	B4
Renmei	FJ	16	E3
Renmin	HL	9	D3
Renmin Shengli Qu	HEN	18	B5
Renqiao	AH	13	C4
Renqiu	HEB	4	E4
Renshan	GD	21	B5
Renshizhen	SC	30	C6
Renshou	FJ	16	C3
Renshou	SC	30	D5
Rentian	JX	15	F4
Rentuo	SC	31	D5
Renxian	SC	31	B6
Ren Xian	HEB	4	F2
Renxing	HI	21	D2
Renyi	HN	20	E5
Renyichang	SC	31	C3
Renzhu	GX	24	D7
Reshi	HN	20	B4
Reshui	NM	4	A7
Reshui	JX	15	F3
Reshui	HN	20	F6
Riga	XZ	34	C5
Riji Jiao	HI	22	D2
Rinbung	XZ	34	C4
Rinda	SC	30	C3
Rinqênzê	XZ	34	C4
Rinzhubtang	SC	30	D3
Ri Qu	XZ	49	C2
Riwoqê	XZ	34	C6
Riyue Shan	QH	28	B7
Riyue Tan	TW	17	C3
Rizhao	SD	10	D6
Rizhe	YN	33	C6
Rola Co	XZ	34	B4
Rong'an (Chang'an)	GX	24	B7
Rongbaca	SC	30	C2
Rongchang	SC	30	D5
Rongcheng Wan	SD	10	B9
Rongcheng (Yatou)	SD	10	B9
Rongcheng	HEB	4	D3
Ronghe	SX	5	F2
Ronghua	GX	24	D4
Rong Jiang	GD	16	G2
Rong Jiang	GX	24	B7
Rongjiang (Guzhou)	GZ	32	E7
Rongjiawan	HN	20	B6
Rongkou	AH	13	G4
Ronglongchang	SC	31	C3
Rongqi	GD	21	B4
Rongshanzhen	SC	31	D4
Rongshui Miaozu Zizhixian	GX	24	B7
Rongxar	XZ	34	C3
Rong Xian	SC	30	D5
Rong Xian	GX	24	E8
(Rouyuanchengzi)	GS	27	D8

Huachi			
Rouyuanpu	NX	26	C2
Ru'ao	ZJ	14	C5
Rucheng	HN	20	F6
Rucun	SX	5	C5
Rudong	GD	21	C3
Rudong (Juegang)	JS	11	D7
Rugao	JS	11	D6
Ru He	HEN	18	D6
Ruhu	GD	23	H8
Rui'an	ZJ	14	E5
Ruichang	JX	15	B3
Ruicheng	SX	5	G2
Ruifang	TW	17	A4
Ruihong	JX	15	C4
Ruijin	JX	15	F4
Ruilin	JX	15	E3
Ruili	YN	33	C2
Ruiqiaopu	HN	20	E4
Ruisui	TW	17	C4
Ruitapu	HN	20	B3
Rujigou	NX	26	A3
(Rulin) Chengbu Miaozu Zizhixian	HN	20	E3
Runanbu	HEN	18	E6
Runan	HEN	18	E6
Runcheng	SX	5	F4
Run He	AH	13	D2
Runheji	AH	13	D3
Ru'nying	QH	28	D7
Ruoheng	ZJ	14	D6
Ruoli	GS	26	D1
Ruoqiang He	XJ	29	D6
Ruoqiang (Qarkilik)	XJ	29	D6
Ruoshui	HN	20	D2
Ruo Shui	NM	6	D1-2
	GS	27	B4-5
Ruoxi	JX	15	B3
Rushankou	SD	10	C8
Rushan (Xiacun)	SD	10	C8
Rushanzhai	SD	10	C8
Rushui He	NX	26	E3
Rutog	XZ	34	B1
Ruyang	HEN	18	C4
Ruyuan Yaozu Zizhixian	GD	21	A4

S

Sabdê	SC	30	D3
Sadêng	XZ	34	C5
Saga (Gya'gya)	XZ	34	C3
Sa'gya	XZ	34	C4
Saheqiao	HEB	4	C6
(Saihan Tal) Sonid Youqi	NM	6	D5

Name	Prov	Map	Grid	Name	Prov	Map	Grid	Name	Prov	Map	Grid
Saihan Toroi	NM	6	D2	Sandu	FJ	16	D5	Sanhekou	JS	12	B3
Saima	LN	7	D8	Sandu	HN	20	E6	Sanhekou	SC	31	D1
Saiqi	FJ	16	D5	Sandu	GX	24	C7	Sanhe	HEB	4	D5
Saiyu	SX	5	D5	Sandu	GZ	32	D5	Sanhezhan	HL	9	A3
Samsang	XZ	34	C2	Sanduandi	NM	26	B4	Sanhezhen	NX	26	E2
Samyai	XZ	34	C4	Sandu Ao	FJ	16	D5	Sanhezhen	AH	13	E4
Sanba	GD	23	G7	Sandun	HN	20	C6	Sanhu	JX	15	D3
Sanbao	LN	7	C4	Sanduo	SX	5	E2	San Hu	HB	19	D5
Sanbastaw	XJ	48	B6	Sanduo	JS	11	D5	Sanhuang	GX	24	C7
Sanbei Yangchang	NM	26	A4	Sandu Suizu	GZ	32	D6	Sanhui	SC	31	C4
Sanbiao	JX	15	F3	Zizhixian (Sanhe)				Sanhui	SC	31	C5
(Sanbu) Kaiping	GD	23	I6	Sanfang	GX	24	B6	Sanhuizhen	SC	30	C6
Sanbu	GX	24	D8	Sanfengsi	HN	20	B5	Sanjia	GD	21	B3
Sancang	JS	11	D6	Sa'ngain	XZ	34	C6	Sanjia	HEB	4	B6
Sancha	SX	5	B3	Sangang	JL	8	C5	Sanjiachang	YN	33	C4
Sancha	HB	19	D2	Sangang	FJ	16	C3	Sanjiadian	BJ	3	B2
Sancha	GX	24	C6	Sangbi	SX	5	E2	(Sanjiang) Liannan	GD	21	A4
Sancha	GS	27	D8	Sangcun	SD	10	D4	Yaozu Zizhixian			
Sancha	GS	27	E7	Sangequanzi	XJ	29	C6	Sanjiang	GD	21	B4
Sanchaba	SC	31	B2	Sang'ezhen	SD	10	C2	Sanjiang	GD	23	G6
Sanchabu	HB	19	D7	Sanggan He	HEB	4	D1-C2	Sanjiang	GX	24	C8
Sanchadian	SD	10	C5		SX	5	B5-6	Sanjiang	GX	24	C9
Sanchagang	JX	15	B4	Sanggarmai	SC	30	B4	Sanjiang	SC	30	D6
Sanchahe	LN	7	C6	Sanggarpar	SC	30	B4	Sanjiang	SC	31	C2
Sanchahe	JL	8	C7	Sanggin Dalai	NM	26	B2	(Sanjiang) Jinping	GZ	32	D8
Sanchahe	HN	20	B5	Sanggin Dalai	NM	4	A3				
Sancha He	GZ	32	D4	Sanggou Wan	SD	10	B9	Sanjiang Dongzu	GX	24	B7
Sanchakou	HEB	3	A2	Sanglinzi	LN	7	C6	Zizhixian (Guyi)			
Sanchakou	NM	6	F10	Sangluoshu	SD	10	B4	Sanjiangkou	LN	7	A7
Sanchakou	XJ	29	D3	Sangmu	GZ	32	B5	Sanjiangkou	JX	15	C3
Sanchang	JS	11	E7	Sangngagqoiling	XZ	34	C5	Sanjiangkou	SC	31	A1
Sanchazi	JL	8	E7	Sangou	HEB	4	B6	Sanjiangkou	YN	33	B4
Sanchong	TW	17	A4	Sangri	XZ	34	C5	Sanjiangmen	GX	24	B7
Sanchongyan	GZ	32	C5	Sangruma	QH	28	D6	Sanjiao	SX	5	C4
Sanchuan	HEN	18	D3	Sangsang	XZ	34	C3	Sanjiao	SX	5	D2
Sanchuan He	SX	5	D2-3	Sanguandian	AH	13	E5	Sanjiao	SX	5	D2
Sancun	GD	23	I6	Sanguandian	HB	19	B4	Sanjiao	SC	31	D5
Sandao	JL	8	E9	Sanguanmiao	HEN	18	C5	(Sanjiaocheng)	QH	28	B7
Sandaogang	LN	7	B7	Sanguanmiao	HEN	18	E6	Haiyan			
Sandaogang	HL	9	D6	Sanguansi	HN	20	B3	Sanjiaoping	HN	20	C3
Sandaogang	HL	9	D6	(Sangyuan) Wuqiao	HEB	4	F4	Sanjiaotang	ZJ	14	D6
Sandaogou	LN	7	D4					Sanjiazhen	SC	31	B4
Sandaogoumen	HEB	4	A5	Sangyuan	FJ	16	C6	Sanjiazi	LN	7	B6
Sandaohezi	HL	9	E5	Sangyuan Xia	GS	27	D7	Sanjiazi	LN	7	B7
Sandaohu	JL	8	E7	Sangyuanzi	GS	27	D6	Sanjiazi	LN	7	B7
Sandaohu	NM	26	B1	Sangzhi	HN	20	B3	Sanjiazi	LN	7	D7
Sandaohumiao	NM	26	B1	Sangzhou	ZJ	14	C6	Sanjiazi	JL	8	B3
Sandaoqia	HL	9	B4	Sangzhuang	HEN	18	E4	Sanjie	AH	13	D5
Sandaoqiao	NM	6	F10	Sangzidian	SD	10	C3	Sanjie	ZJ	14	C5
Sandaotong	HL	9	E5	Sanhe	GD	23	I6	Sanjie	GX	24	B8
Sandaoying	NM	6	F10	Sanhe	GZ	32	B5	Sanjie	YN	33	C4
Sandaozhen	HL	9	D4	Sanhe	GZ	32	C5	Sanjieshou	SD	10	D5
Sandiao Jiao	TW	17	A5	(Sanhe) Sandu Suizu	GZ	32	D6	Sanjing	SX	5	C3
Sandong	SC	31	C1	Zizhixian				Sanjingzi	JL	8	B6
Sandouping	HB	19	D4	Sanhe	NM	6	B7	Sanju	XJ	29	D3
Sandu	ZJ	14	C4	Sanhe	GD	21	A6	Sankeng	GD	21	B4
Sandu	ZJ	14	C5	San He	JS	11	C4-5	Sankeng Shui	GD	23	G6
Sandu	JX	15	B2	Sanhecun	JL	8	E10	Sankeshu	HL	9	E4
Sandu	JX	15	C2	Sanhedian	HB	19	B6	Sankeyushu	JL	8	F6
Sandu	JX	15	E2	Sanhejian	HEN	18	E7	Sankou	AH	12	E1

Shangtang	JX	15	C3	Shanmatang Ding	HN	20	G4	Shaoleng He	NM	38	B3
Shangtang	JX	15	D4		GX	24	C9	Shaoling He	HL	39	A5
Shangtun	HEN	18	E4	Shanmei Sk.	FJ	16	E4	Shaoshan	HN	20	D5
Shan Guan	JX	15	D5	Shanmen	HN	20	D3	Shaoshui	GX	24	B8
	FJ	16	C3	Shanmen	GS	27	E8	Shaowen	HL	9	D3
Shangwang	ZJ	12	E4	Shanmuqing	GZ	32	D2	Shaowu	FJ	16	C3
Shangxi	ZJ	14	C4								
Shang Xian	SN	25	G5	Shannanguan	AH	13	E3	Shaoxing	ZJ	14	B5
Shangxingzhen	JS	11	E5	Shanpen	GZ	32	C5				
Shangxinhe	JS	11	D4	Shanpo	HB	19	D7	Shaoyang	HN	20	D4
Shangxizhuang	SX	5	B4	Shanqian	FJ	16	C3	(Baoqing)			
Shangyangwu	SX	5	C4	Shanqiandian	SD	10	B7	Shaoyang	HN	20	E4
Shangyantan	ZJ	14	C5	Shanshan (Piqan)	XJ	29	C6	(Tangdukou)			
Shangye	SD	10	D4	Shanshan Zhan	XJ	29	C6	Shaoyuan	HEN	18	B4
Shangying	GX	24	D4	Shanshi	HL	9	E5	Shaoyun	SC	31	C4
Shangying	JL	8	C8	Shanshulun	HN	20	C5	Shaozihe	LN	7	D7
Shangyi	HEB	4	B1	Shansonggang	JL	8	E7	Shaozi He	LN	7	D7
(Nanhaoqian)				Shantang	GD	23	G6	Shapa	GD	21	C3
Shangyong	FJ	16	E4	Shantangyi	HN	20	D3	(Shaping) Heshan	GD	23	H6
Shangyou Jiang	JX	15	F2	Shanting	SD	10	D4				
Shangyou Sk.	XJ	29	C4	Shantou	JX	15	D3	Shapingba	SC	31	C5
Shangyou	JX	15	F2					Shapingchang	SC	31	B6
Shangyou Yichang	XJ	29	C4	Shantouji	AH	13	C5	Shapotou	NX	26	C1
Shangyuan	LN	7	C4	Shantou	GD	21	B6	Shapu	GD	23	H6
Shangyun	YN	33	D3	Shantuo	SC	31	C5	Shaqiuhe	XJ	29	B6
Shangyu	ZJ	14	B5	Shanwanghe	AH	13	E3	Shaquan	SX	5	B3
(Baiguan)				Shanwanzi	HEB	4	A5	Shaquanzi	XJ	29	B4
Shangzhage	YN	33	B5	Shanwei	GD	21	B5	Shaquzhen	SC	31	B1
Shangzhai	SX	5	B6	Shanxi	ZJ	14	E5	Shashan	HL	9	D5
Shangzhenzi	SN	25	E4	Shan Xian	SD	10	E3	Shashijie	HN	20	C6
Shangzhi	HL	9	E4	Shan Xian	HEN	18	C3	Shashi	HB	19	D5
Shangzhong	GZ	32	D7	Shanxiang	HN	20	F4	Shashiyu	HEB	4	C6
Shangzhoujiahewan	NX	26	C2	Shanxin	GX	24	E7	Shatanchang	SC	31	C6
Shangzhuang	HEB	4	D2	Shanxu	GX	24	E5	Shatangpu	NX	26	E2
Shangzhuang	SX	5	C4	Shanyang	FJ	16	D5	Shatian	JX	15	E2
Shangzhuang	SD	10	B8	Shanyang	SN	25	G5	Shatian	HN	20	F6
Shangzhuang	ZJ	12	E5	Shanyao	FJ	16	E4	Shatian	GD	23	I8
Shangzhuang	SD	10	D6	Shanyaqiao	JS	12	C2	Shatian	GX	24	C9
Shangzhuang	HEN	18	B4	Shanyincheng	SX	5	B4	Shatian	GX	24	E8
Shanhaiguan	HEB	4	C7	Shanyin	SX	5	B4	Shatou	HN	20	C5
Shanhe	NX	26	E3	(Daiyue)				Shatou	GD	23	H7
(Shanhe) Zhengning	GS	27	E9	Shanzao	HN	20	D5	Shatou	GX	24	D9
				Shanzhai	SX	5	B3	Shatoujiao	GD	23	I8
Shanhetun	HL	9	E4	Shanzhong	SX	5	E2	Shatu	GZ	32	C5
Shanhou	AH	12	B1	Shanzhuang	JX	15	D2	Shatuji	SD	10	D2
Shanhua	TW	17	C3	Shanzuizi	LN	7	D3	Shawan	ZJ	14	E4
Shanhu Dao	HI	22	B2	Shaobo	JS	11	D5	Shawan	HN	20	D3
Shanji	JS	11	B3	Shaobo Hu	JS	11	D5	Shawan	GD	23	H7
Shanjiao	GX	24	C5	Shaodian	JS	11	B4	Shawan	GZ	32	C5
Shanjie	YN	33	C3	Shaodian	HEN	18	D6	Shawan	XJ	29	B5
Shanjuandong	JS	12	C3	Shaodong	HN	20	D4	Shawanzhen	SC	30	D4
Shankou	ZJ	14	D5	(Liangshizhen)				Shawo	HEN	18	F7
Shankou	JX	15	C2	Shaogangji	HEN	18	C6	Shawo	GZ	32	D4
Shankou	HN	20	C4	Shaogangpu	NX	26	B3	Shawutang	FJ	16	D3
Shankou	GX	24	F7					Shaxi	JS	11	E7
Shankou	XJ	29	C7	Shaoguan	GD	21	A4	Shaxi	ZJ	14	C6
Shanlenggang	SC	30	D4					Shaxi	JX	15	C6
Shanli	AH	13	G4	Shaoguo	JL	8	D5	Shaxi	JX	15	E3
Shanlian	ZJ	14	B5	Shaoguo	JL	8	D6	Shaxi	JX	15	F2
Shan Ling	FJ	16	C3	Shaoguozhen	JL	8	B4	Shaxi	HN	20	E2

Shaxi	GD	23	I7
Sha Xi	FJ	16	D3
Sha Xian	FJ	16	D3
Shayang	HB	19	D5
Shayu	BJ	3	B3
Shayugou	HEN	18	C5
Shazaoyuan	GS	27	C2
Shazhen	SD	10	C2
Shazhenxi	HB	19	D3
Shazhouba	JX	15	F3
(Shazhou)Zhangjiagang	JS	11	E6
Shazi	GX	24	C8
Shazidi	HB	19	D2
Shaziling	GZ	32	E4
Shazipo	GZ	32	B7
Shebiya	NM	5	A3
Shebu	GX	24	D8
Shebu	HN	20	D5
Shechengtan	SX	5	D4
(She Dao) Xiaolongshan Dao	LN	7	F4
Shefu	JX	15	E3
Shegangshi	HN	20	C6
Shegeng	JX	15	C4
Shehong (Taihezhen)	SC	30	C5
Shejiang	GD	21	A5
Shejiaping	HN	20	C4
Shejiaping	SN	25	C5
Shekou	FJ	16	C5
Shekou	GD	23	I8
Shekou	HB	19	D7
Sheli	JL	8	B6
Sheli	JL	8	B4
Sheling	JL	8	D6
Shencheng	ZJ	14	E5
Shenchi	SX	5	B4
Shencun	AH	12	C2
Shendang	ZJ	14	B5
Shending Shan	HL	9	D7
Shendu	AH	13	G5
Shengang	JS	11	E6
Shengang	GD	23	G7
Shengang	JX	15	D4
Shengdeng	SC	31	D3
Shengfang	HEB	4	D4
Shenghang	GD	21	B4
Shenghongqing	HB	19	D7
Shengjiaqiao	AH	13	E4
Shengjiaqiao	AH	13	F5
Shengjing Guan	GZ	32	E3
	YN	33	C6
Shengjinguan	NX	26	C2
Shengkang	HB	19	B4
Shenglang	HL	9	D5
Shengli	HL	9	E4
Shengli	HB	19	C8
Shengli	NX	26	B3
Shengli(Badongzhen)	SC	31	A3
Shengli Daban	XJ	29	C5
Shengli Jiuchang	XJ	29	C4
Shengli Qichang	XJ	29	C4
Shengli Qu	XJ	29	C3
Shengli Shibachang	XJ	29	C4
Shengli Shijiuchang	XJ	29	C4
Shengli Shiliuchang	XJ	29	C4
Shengli Shisanchang	XJ	29	C4
Shengmijie	JX	15	C3
Shengping	HL	9	D3
(Shengrenjian) Pinglu	SX	5	G3
Shengshan	ZJ	12	D4
Shengshan	ZJ	14	B7
Shengshuihezi	JL	8	E6
Shengsi Liedao	ZJ	14	B7
Shengsi (Caiyuanzhen)	ZJ	14	B7
Sheng Xian	ZJ	14	C5
Shengze	JS	11	F6
Shenhekou	SN	25	H5
Shenhou	HEN	18	C5
Shenhu	FJ	16	F4
Shenhuguan	YN	33	C2
Shenjia	HL	9	D4
Shenjiahe Sk.	NX	26	D3
Shenjiaji	HB	19	D5
(Shenjiamen) Putuo	ZJ	14	C7
Shenjiatai	LN	7	C4
Shenjiatan	NX	26	C2
Shenjiaxiang	AH	13	E5
Shenjing	HEB	4	C2
Shenjing	GD	21	C4
Shenjing	NX	26	C1
Shenjingzi	LN	7	C7
Shenjingzi	JL	8	C5
Shenlou	HEN	18	D5
Shenlun	JS	11	D5
Shenmu	SN	25	B6
Shennan	HEB	4	E2
Shennongjia Linqu	HB	19	C3
Shenqiucheng	HEN	18	D7
Shenqiu (Huaidian)	HEN	18	D7
Shenquan	GD	21	B6
Shenquanbu	SN	25	C6
Shenquan Gang	GD	21	B6
Shenshiqiao	ZJ	14	B6
Shenshizhuang	HEB	3	C1
Shenshu	HL	9	D5
Shentou	SX	5	B4
Shentou	SD	10	B3
Shentu	FJ	16	F3
Shentuan	SD	10	D6
Shenwan[nan]	GD	23	I7
Shenwan[bei]	GD	23	I7
Shenwo Sk.	LN	7	C7
Shen Xian	SD	10	C2
Shen Xian	HEB	4	E3
Shenxing	HEB	4	D3
Shenyang	LN	7	C7
Shenzao	JS	11	D6
Shenze	HEB	4	E3
Shenzhen	ZJ	14	C6
Shenzhen	GD	21	B5
Shenzhen Sk.	GD	23	H8
Sheqiao	HEN	18	D6
Sheqi	HEN	18	D4
Sheshiqiao	HN	20	B4
She Shui	HB	19	C7
Shetan	SC	31	C6
Shetianqiao	HN	20	D4
Shewei	HEN	18	D3
Shexi	JX	15	F2
She Xian	HEB	4	G1
She Xian(Huicheng)	AH	13	G5
Sheyang	JS	11	C5
Sheyang He	JS	11	C5
Sheyanghe Kou	JS	11	C6
Sheyang (Hede)	JS	11	C6
Shezhu	JS	11	E5
Shiba	AH	13	D5
Shibalipu	AH	13	C2
Shibalipu	SN	25	G3
Shibalipu	GS	27	D6
Shiban	SC	31	B2
Shibanhe	HB	19	C6
Shiban Jing	NM	6	D1
Shibantan	HN	20	B4
Shibantan	SC	31	B2
Shibanyan	HEN	18	A5
Shibaocheng	GS	27	C3
Shibaosi	GZ	32	B5
Shibaqing	NM	4	B1
Shibatai	NM	6	F10
Shibazhan	HL	9	A3
Shibei	FJ	16	C4
Shibi	JX	15	C3
Shibie	GX	24	C6
Shibing	GZ	32	C7
Shibishan	JX	15	B4
Shibu	SD	10	C6
Shibuzi	SD	10	C6
Shicao	HEN	18	D7
Shichang	SD	10	D6
Shichang	GZ	32	C4
Shichang	GZ	32	C7
Shicheng	SX	5	E5
Shicheng	LN	7	D8
Shicheng	FJ	16	E5
Shicheng Dao	LN	7	E6
Shicheng	JX	15	E4
Shichuan	SC	31	C5
Shichuan He	SN	25	F4
(Shicun) Xiangfen	SX	5	F3
Shicun	AH	13	C4
Shidao	SD	10	C9

(Shipu) Huanglong	SN	25	E5	Shitougang	JX	15	C3	Shizilu	NX	26	E3

Name	Prov	Col1	Col2
(Shipu) Huanglong	SN	25	E5
Shipuqiao	ZJ	12	C4
Shiqian	GZ	32	C7
Shiqiao	SD	10	C5
Shiqiao	SD	10	D5
Shiqiao	JX	15	D4
Shiqiao	JX	15	E2
Shiqiao	HEN	18	D4
Shiqiao	HEN	18	D5
Shiqiao	HB	19	C5
Shiqiao	GX	24	D9
Shiqiao	SC	30	C6
(Shiqiao) Panyu	GD	21	B4
Shiqiao	AH	13	F6
Shiqiaozhen	SC	30	C5
Shiqiaozhen	SC	31	B6
Shiqiaozi	LN	7	C7
Shiqijie	JL	8	E9
(Shiqizhen) Zhongshan	GD	23	I7
Shiquanhe	XZ	34	B1
(Shiquan He) Sênggê Zangbo (Riv.)	XZ	34	B2-C2
Shiquan	SN	25	G4
Shiren	JL	8	F7
Shirencheng	HL	9	D4
Shirengou	HEB	4	B5
Shirenzhang	GD	21	A5
Shisanjianfang	XJ	29	C6
Shisanjingzi	HL	9	D4
Shisanling	BJ	3	B3
Shisanling Sk.	BJ	3	B3
Shisanzhan	HL	9	B3
Shishan	LN	7	C5
Shishan	FJ	16	E4
Shishang	JX	15	E4
Shishi	FJ	16	F4
Shishikou	JX	15	E2
Shishou	HB	19	E5
Shishulin	SN	25	F2
Shisidaogou	JL	8	F8
Shisizhan	HL	9	B3
Shisun	SC	31	B5
Shitai (Qili)	AH	13	F4
Shitan	JX	15	C3
Shitan	GD	21	B4
Shitan	GD	21	A4
Shitang	ZJ	14	D6
Shitang	JX	15	C5
Shitang	JX	15	D3
Shitang	GX	24	B9
Shitang	GX	24	E7
Shitangwan	JS	12	B4
Shitanjing	NX	26	A3
Shitanwu	SD	10	C4
Shitie	SX	5	D4
Shiting	HEB	3	C2
Shiting Jiang	SC	31	A2
Shitou	HL	9	E5

Name	Prov	Col1	Col2
Shitougang	JX	15	C3
Shitou Shan	NM	6	B8
Shitouzhai	YN	33	D3
Shitouzui	HB	19	D8
Shituan	SC	30	C5
Shiwan	HN	20	D5
Shiwan	GD	23	H6
Shiwan	SN	25	C5
Shiwan Dashan	GX	24	F5-E6
Shiwei	NM	6	B6
Shiwu	JL	8	D5
Shixi	JL	8	D6
Shixi	JX	15	C5
Shixi	FJ	16	D3
Shixia	HEB	3	B1
Shixia	SX	5	D5
Shixia	GX	24	E7
Shixia	GS	27	F7
Shixiajiang	HN	20	D3
Shixian	JL	8	D10
Shixianzi	NX	26	C2
Shixing	GD	21	A5
Shixizhen	SC	31	D1
Shiya	GX	24	D7
Shiyan	HB	19	B3
Shiyan	GD	23	H8
Shiyan	JS	11	D6
Shiyangchang	SC	30	D5
Shiyang He	GS	47	B4
Shiyangzhen	SC	31	A1
Shiyanqiao	SC	31	D3
Shiyan	HB	19	B3
Shiyazhen	SC	31	B5
Shiye	SC	30	D7
Shiyidu	JX	15	C6
Shiyiwei	JS	11	E6
Shiyizhan	HL	9	B3
Shiyong	SC	31	B6
Shiyong	GX	24	F7
(Shizhaihe) Zhenping	SN	25	I5
Shizhan	HL	9	B4
Shizhangzi	LN	7	D3
Shizhe	SX	5	E4
Shizheng	GD	21	A5
Shizhenjie	JX	15	C4
Shizhong	FJ	16	F3
Shizhu	ZJ	14	D5
Shizhuang	JS	11	D6
Shizhuang	SX	5	F4
Shizhu	SC	30	D7
Shizi	GS	27	E8
Shizi	SC	31	B6
Shizigou	HEB	4	B3
Shizigoukou	SN	25	G4
Shizihe	SX	5	F3
Shizihe	AH	13	C2
Shizi Ling	JX	15	D4
(Shizilu) Junan	SD	10	D5

Name	Prov	Col1	Col2
Shizilu	NX	26	E3
Shizipu	AH	13	F6
Shizipu	HB	19	D7
Shizitan	SC	30	D6
Shizitan Sk.	SC	31	C6
Shizi Yang	GD	23	H7
Shizong	JS	12	A5
Shizong	YN	33	C5
Shizui	SX	5	C5
Shizui	JL	8	D7
Shizui	GX	24	D8
Shizuishan	NX	26	A3
Shizuishan (Dawukou)	NX	26	A3
Shizuishan	NX	26	B3
Shizuishan Zhan	NX	26	A3
Shizuiyi	SN	25	C6
Shou'anzhen	SC	31	B1
Shouchang	ZJ	14	C4
Shouche	HN	20	B2
Shoucheng	GX	24	B7
Shoufeng	TW	17	C4
Shouguang	SD	10	C5
Shouning	FJ	16	C5
Shouqia	TW	17	D3
Shouwangfen	HEB	4	C5
Shou Xian (Shouyang)	AH	13	D3
(Shouyang) Shou Xian	AH	13	D3
Shouyang Shan	SN	25	G4
Shouyang	SX	5	D5
Shouyanxu	HN	20	F4
Shuaizhou	HB	19	E8
Shuajingsi	SC	30	C4
Shuangba	HEN	18	C7
Shuangbai	YN	33	C4
Shuangbanqiao	HN	20	D5
Shuangcha	JL	8	F6
Shuangchengpu	JL	8	C5
Shuangcheng	HL	9	E4
Shuangchi	SX	5	E3
Shuangdian	JS	11	D6
Shuangdian	JS	11	B4
Shuangduiji	AH	13	C3
Shuangdunji	AH	13	D4
Shuangfeng	HL	9	D4
Shuangfeng	JS	11	E7
Shuangfeng	GX	24	E7
Shuangfengsi	HEB	4	B5
Shuangfeng (Yongfeng)	HN	20	D5
Shuangfengyi	SC	31	C3
Shuangfeng Zhan	HN	20	D4
Shuangfu	AH	13	C2
Shuangfupu	HN	20	C5
Shuanggang	JL	8	B3
Shuanggang	JX	15	C5
Shuanggou	JS	11	B3
Shuanggou	JS	11	C4
Shuanggou	JS	11	C4
Shuanggou	HB	19	B5

Name	Prov	Map	Grid
Shuanghan	FJ	16	E4
Shuanghe	HL	9	E6
Shuanghe	AH	13	E2
Shuanghe	AH	13	E3
Shuanghe	HEN	18	E4
Shuanghe	HB	19	C5
Shuanghe	HB	19	C5
Shuanghe	SN	25	H4
Shuanghe	NX	26	D2
Shuanghe	SC	30	C4
Shuanghe	SC	31	A5
(Shuanghe) Huayun Gongnongqu	SC	31	B5
Shuanghe	SC	31	C5
Shuang He	NX	26	D2
Shuanghechang	SC	30	C6
Shuanghechang	SC	31	C3
Shuanghechang	SC	31	D4
Shuanghedagang	HL	9	C5
Shuanghezhen	JL	8	D7
Shuanghou	SD	10	D5
(Shuanghuyu) Zizhou	SN	25	C6
(Shuangjiang) Tongdao Dongzu Zizhixian	HN	20	E2
Shuangjiang	SC	30	C5
Shuangjiang	SC	30	C7
Shuangjiang	GZ	32	E7
Shuangjiangkou	HN	20	D5
Shuangjiang	YN	33	D3
Shuangjianji	AH	13	C3
Shuangjie	GD	21	C3
Shuangji He	HEN	18	C6
Shuangjing	GZ	32	D7
Shuangjingji	HEB	4	G2
Shuangkou	TJ	3	C4
Shuangliao (Zhengjiatun)	JL	8	D4
Shuanglin	ZJ	14	B5
Shuanglin	JX	15	D2
Shuangliu	GZ	32	C5
Shuangliuhe	HL	9	D7
Shuangliushu	HEN	18	F7
Shuangliu	SC	30	C4
Shuanglong	NM	6	F10
Shuanglong	SC	31	C6
Shuanglongzhen	SN	25	E4
Shuanglu	HL	9	D4
Shuanglu	SC	31	C6
Shuangmiao	AH	13	C4
Shuangmiao	AH	13	D3
Shuangmiaozi	LN	7	B8
Shuangmiaozi	JL	8	E6
Shuangpaishan	HN	20	E6
Shuangpaishi	JS	12	C2
Shuangpai	HN	20	F4
Shuangqiao	BJ	3	B3
Shuangqiao	ZJ	12	D4
Shuangqiao	AH	13	D3
Shuangqiao	AH	13	F5
Shuangqiao	HEN	18	E6
Shuangqiao	GX	24	D6
Shuangqiaoji	AH	13	C3
Shuangshan	JL	8	D4
Shuangshanzi	HEB	4	C7
(Shuangshipu) Feng	SN	25	G2
Shuangshipu	SC	31	D2
Shuangshiqiao	SC	31	D4
Shuangshui	GD	23	I6
Shuangtaizi	LN	7	B7
Shuangtaizi He	LN	38	C4-5
Shuangtaizihe Kou	LN	7	D5
Shuangtang	HEB	3	D3
Shuangtang	TJ	3	D4
Shuangtang	JX	15	C4
Shuangtapu	GS	27	B3
Shuangtian	JX	15	D4
Shuangxi	ZJ	14	D4
Shuangxi	FJ	16	C5
Shuangxi	FJ	16	D5
Shuangxi	TW	17	A4
Shuangxi	SC	31	D1
Shuangxing	HL	9	D3
Shuangyang	HL	9	D3
Shuangyang	FJ	16	E3
Shuangyangdian	LN	7	C5
Shuangyangdian [nan]	SD	10	C6
Shuangyangdian [bei]	SD	10	C6
Shuangyang	JL	8	D6
Shuangyashan	HL	9	D6
Shuangzihe	HL	9	D5
Shuangzi Qunjiao	HI	22	D3
Shucheng	HEB	4	E4
Shucheng	AH	13	E3
Shufu	XJ	29	D2
Shuguang	HL	9	C8
Shu He	SD	10	E5
	JS	11	B4
Shuhedun	AH	13	E4
Shuhekou	SN	25	H5
Shuhong	ZJ	14	D5
Shuhong	AH	12	E1
Shuibatang	GZ	32	B6
Shuibei	JS	11	E5
Shuibei	JX	15	C3
Shuibei	FJ	16	C3
Shuibei	FJ	16	C4
Shuibian	JX	15	D3
Shuiche	GD	21	A6
Shuicheng	GZ	32	D3
Shuicheng Tequ	GZ	32	D3
Shuichipu	AH	13	C4
Shuidao	SD	10	B8
(Shuiding) Huocheng	XJ	29	B4
Shuidong	AH	13	F5
Shuidong	SN	25	B6
Shuidongdi	HN	20	D4
Shuidong Gang	GD	21	C3
Shuidongjiang	HN	20	D5
Shuifumiao Sk.	HN	20	D5
Shuifu	YN	33	A6
Shuiguo	SD	10	E4
Shuihouling	AH	13	F3
Shuiji	FJ	16	C4
(Shuiji) Laixi	SD	10	C7
(Shuijiahu) Changfeng	AH	13	D4
Shuijiang	SC	30	D6
Shuijing	GD	23	H6
Shuijing	GX	24	C7
Shuijing	SC	30	B5
Shuijingtou	HN	20	D4
Shuikeng	GD	23	H6
Shuikou	AH	13	D5
Shuikou	FJ	16	D4
Shuikou	FJ	16	E4
Shuikou	HN	20	E6
(Shuikou) Jianghua Yaozu Zizhixian	HN	20	G4
Shuikou	GD	21	B4
Shuikou	GD	21	B5
Shuikou	SC	31	B1
Shuikou	GZ	32	E8
Shuikouguan	GX	24	E4
Shuikoushan	HN	20	E5
Shuikousi	GZ	32	C5
Shuikouxu	GD	21	A5
Shuiliandong	LN	7	B9
Shuilong	GZ	32	E6
Shuiluo He	SC	30	D3
Shuimenzi	LN	7	E6
Shuiming	GX	24	E7
Shuimogou	NM	26	B2
Shuimogou	XJ	29	C6
Shuinan	JX	15	E3
Shuinan	JX	15	E4
Shuinan	FJ	16	C4
Shuinanzhen	SC	31	C3
Shuiping	HB	19	B2
Shuipo	HEN	18	C6
Shuiqian	FJ	16	D2
Shuiquan	HEB	3	A1
Shuiquan	HEB	4	B4
Shuiquan	LN	7	C3
Shuiquan	GS	27	D7
Shuiquanzi	GS	27	C5
Shuiquliu	JL	8	C8
Shuishi	JX	15	F2
Shuishiying	LN	7	F5
Shuitang	GZ	32	E3
Shuitianba	HN	20	B2
Shuitianhe	HN	20	C2
Shuitou	SX	5	F3
Shuitou	ZJ	14	E5
Shuitou	FJ	16	F4
Shuitou	GD	23	G7
Shuitun	HEN	18	E6

Shuituzhen	SC	30	D6	Sidu	HN	20	E6	Siming Shan	ZJ	14	C6
Shuiwan	SD	10	B4	Sidu	GZ	32	C5	Simudi	SN	25	G4
Shuiwen	GX	24	E9	Si'erpu	LN	7	D4	Sinan	GZ	32	C7
Shuixi	JX	15	D3	Sifang	SD	10	C7	Singim	XJ	29	C6
Shuiyanba	GX	24	C9	Sifang Ding	LN	38	C6	Sinüsi	SD	10	B3
Shuiyang	AH	13	E5	Sifang Ling	GX	24	E5	Sipai	HL	9	D8
Shuiyang Jiang	JS	11	E4	Sifangtai	HL	9	D4	Sipai	GX	24	C7
	AH	13	F5-E5	Sifangtuozi	JL	8	A4	(Siping) Huangping	GZ	32	D6
Shuiye	HEN	18	A6	Sifen	HN	20	D6				
Shuiyuan	GX	24	C6	Sifentan	NM	6	F10	Siping	HB	19	C4
Shuizhai	SD	10	C4	Sigezhuang	HEB	3	C1				
(Shuizhai)	HEN	18	D6	Sigu	HN	20	D4	Siping	JL	8	D5
Xiangcheng				Siguanyingzi	LN	7	C3	Sipu	JX	15	C5
(Shuizhai) Wuhua	GD	21	B5	Sihai	BJ	3	A3	Siqian	FJ	16	C3
				Sihaidian	HL	9	D4	Siqian	GD	21	A5
Shuizhan	QH	28	A2	Sihe	GD	23	H6	Siqian	GD	23	I6
Shujiadu	SC	31	B1	Sihe	JL	8	C7	Siqian	JX	15	C4
Shujie	YN	33	C4	Si He	SD	10	D3	Siqin Jiang	GX	24	C8-9
Shulan	JL	8	C7	Sihedun	JS	12	A2	Siqu	GZ	32	B7
Shulehe	HL	9	D5	Siheshan	AH	12	C1	Sishibadu	JX	15	C6
Shulehe	GS	27	B3	Siheyong	HEB	4	B5	Sishilijie	JX	15	B4
Shule He	GS	27	B2	Sihong	JS	11	C4	Sishilipu	SD	10	D5
Shule Nanshan	QH	28	A5-6	(Sihou) Changdao	SD	10	B7	Sishilipu	SN	25	C4
Shule	XJ	29	D3					Sishilipu	SN	25	C6
(Shulinzhao) Dalad	NM	6	F10	Sihui	GD	21	B4	Sishilipu	GS	26	E1
Qi				Sijia	HN	20	E6	Sishilipu	GS	27	E8
(Shulu) Xinji	HEB	4	F3	Sijiaba	JS	11	D7	Sishuang Liedao	FJ	16	D6
Shun'an	AH	13	F4	Sijiao	SX	5	F3	Sishui	HEN	18	C5
Shunchang	FJ	16	D3	Sijiao Shan	ZJ	14	B7	Sishui	SD	10	D4
Shunde	GD	21	B4	Sijiazi	LN	7	B7	Sishun	JX	15	F2
Shundian	HEN	18	C5	Sijiazi	HL	9	D3	Sitang	GX	24	B8
Shunhe	JS	11	B2	Sijing	SH	11	E7	Sitang	GX	24	D4
Shunhechang	SC	31	C2	Sijingzi	JL	8	C3	Sitang	GX	24	E6
Shunheji	HEN	18	C8	Sijitong	HL	9	E5	Sitian	XJ	29	C7
Shunxi	ZJ	14	B3	Sijiu	GD	23	I6	Siting	GZ	32	E6
Shunyi	BJ	3	B3	Sijiuxu	GD	23	I6	Siting	SX	5	E4
Shuoliang	GX	24	D5	Sikeshu	JL	8	B4	Siwang	GX	24	D8
Shuolong	GX	24	E4	Sikeshu	XJ	29	B5	Sixi	JX	15	C3
Shuo Xian	SX	5	B4	Sikou	SD	10	B7	Sixia	JX	15	E2
Shuping	SC	31	D3	Sikou	JX	15	B5	Si Xian	AH	13	C4
Shushan	ZJ	12	E5	Silaogou	SX	5	B5	Sixiangkou	JS	11	D5
Shushe	GZ	32	D3	Sili	JX	15	C5	Sixin	QH	28	B6
Shu Shui	JX	15	E2	Sili	HEN	18	B4	(Siyang) Cengong	GZ	32	C7
Shutai	NX	26	D2	Silian	GX	24	C6				
Shu Xi	AH	13	F5	Silin	GX	24	D5	Siyang	JS	11	C4
Shuyang	JS	11	B4	Siling Co	XZ	34	C4	(Zhongxing)			
Shuzhang	SX	5	F5	Siliping	HN	20	F5	Siyichang	SC	30	C5
Si'an	ZJ	14	B4	Silong	GX	24	D6	Siyitang	NM	6	D4
Siba	NM	6	F10	Silukou	ZJ	14	C5	Sizao	JS	11	D6
Siba	GX	24	C6	Silun	GD	21	B3	Sizhan	HL	9	C3
Sibati	XJ	29	B6	Sima	GD	23	H8	Sizhoutou	ZJ	14	C6
Sichakou	HEB	4	B4	Simajia	JL	8	B6	Sizhuang	SX	5	F4
Sichongxi	TW	17	D3					Sizhuang	HEB	3	C2
Sichuan Pendi (Bsn.)	SC	49	C4-6	Simao	YN	33	D4	Sizimei Dao	ZJ	14	B7
Sidangkou	TJ	3	D4	Simaqiao	HN	20	F4	Siziwang (Dorbod) Qi	NM	6	D4
Sidaogou	JL	8	F8	Simen	ZJ	14	B6	Sogcanggoin	SC	30	B4
Sidaohezi	LN	7	C9	Simeng	SC	31	C1	Sogo Nur	NM	6	D2
Siding	GX	24	B7	Simenqian	HN	20	D3	Sog Qu	XZ	51	B5-C5
Sidu	JX	15	B2	Siming	JS	11	C6	Sogruma	QH	28	D7
Sidu	FJ	16	G3	Siming Shan	ZJ	14	C5	Sog Xian	XZ	34	C5

Name	Prov	Map	Grid	Name	Prov	Map	Grid	Name	Prov	Map	Grid
Soila	XZ	34	C6	Songshanpu	LN	7	B8	Sugun	XJ	29	D3
Solon	NM	6	C7	Songshanzui	HB	19	D8	Suhai Hu	QH	28	A3
Somang	SC	30	C4	Songshaoguan	YN	33	C5	Suhai Obo	NM	6	D3
Somang Qu	SC	30	B4-C4	Songshi	JX	15	D4	Suhait	NM	6	E3
Song'acha He	HL	9	E7	Songshu	LN	7	E6	Suibin	HL	9	D6
Song ao	ZJ	14	C6	Songshuzhen	JL	8	E8	Suichang	ZJ	14	D4
Songbai	HN	20	E5	Songta	SX	5	D5	Suicheng	HEB	4	D3
Songbaichang	HN	20	C3	Songtang	GD	21	A5	Suichuan Jiang	JX	15	E2
Songbailin	SD	10	D6	Songtao	HI	21	D2	Suichuan	JX	15	E2
Songbu	HB	19	C7	Songtao Miaozu	GZ	32	B8	Suide	SN	25	C6
Songcun	SD	10	B9	Zizhixian				Suidong	HL	9	D7
Songcun	ZJ	14	C3	Songtuan	AH	13	C3	Suifen He	HL	9	E6
Songgaizhen	SC	30	D5	Songxi	ZJ	14	B4	Suifenhe	HL	9	E6
Songgang	GD	21	B4	Songxi	FJ	16	D2	Sui He	AH	13	C4-5
Songgui	YN	33	B4	Song Xi	FJ	16	C4				
Songhe	HB	19	C6	Songxia	FJ	16	E5	Suihua	HL	9	D4
Songhu	JX	15	C3	Songxia	ZJ	14	B5	Sui Jiang	GD	21	B4
Songhua Hu	JL	8	D7-8	Song Xian	HEN	18	C4	Suijiang	YN	33	A5
Songhua Jiang (Riv.)	JL	8	B6	Songxi He	SX	5	D5-6	Suileng	HL	9	D4
	HL	9	D6-7	Songxi	FJ	16	C4	Suining	HN	20	E3
				Songyan	SX	5	D5	(Changpuzhen)			
(Songjiachuan) Wubu	SN	25	C6	Songyan	GZ	32	C6	Suining	SC	30	C5
				Songyankou	SX	5	C5	Suining	JS	11	C3
Songjiagou	SX	5	C3	Songyin	SH	12	D5	Suiping	HEN	18	D5
Songjiang	JL	8	D8	Songyin Xi	ZJ	14	D4	Sui Xian	HB	19	C6
Songjiang	JL	8	E8	Songyu	FJ	16	F4	Sui Xian	HEN	18	C7
(Songjiang) Antu	JL	8	E9	Songyuan	GD	21	A6	Suixi	GD	21	C3
				Songzhai	HEN	18	C5	Suixi	AH	13	C3
Songjianghe	JL	8	E8	Song Zhan	HL	9	D3	Suiyang	HL	9	E6
Songjiang	SH	11	E7	Songzhangzi	LN	7	C3	Suiyang	HB	19	B5
Songjiapu	SC	30	D5	Songzhuang	BJ	3	B3	Suiyangchang	GZ	32	B6
Songjiaqiao	JS	11	D5	Songzi Guan	AH	13	E2	Suiyang	GZ	32	C6
Songjiaying	HEB	3	A1		HB	19	C8	(Yangchuan)			
Songjiaying	HEB	4	D6	Songzi He	HB	19	D4-E4	Suizhong	LN	7	D4
Songjiazhuang	SX	5	B5	Songzi	HB	19	D4	Suizhou	HB	19	C6
Songkan	GZ	32	B5	(Xinjiangkou)				Suj	NM	6	F10
Songkou	GD	21	A6	Sonid Youqi (Saihan	NM	6	D5	(Suji) Haixing	HEB	4	E5
Songkou	FJ	16	D2	Tal)				Suji	AH	13	C2
Songkou	FJ	16	E4	Sonid Zuoqi	NM	6	D5	Sujiabu	AH	13	E3
Songlin	SD	10	C2	South China Sea	TW	17	D1-2	Sujiaqiao	HEB	3	C3
Songlin	YN	33	B6	(Sowa) Dagxoi	SC	30	D2	Sujiatun	LN	7	C7
Songlin	YN	33	C5	Su'ao	FJ	16	E5	Sujiazui	JS	11	C5
Songlindian	HEB	4	D3	Su'ao	TW	17	B4	Suli Hu	QH	28	B4
Songling	NM	6	B7	Subang	FJ	16	E3	Sulin Gol He	QH	28	B5
(Songling)	NM	9	B3	Subao Ding	HN	20	D3	Suliuzhuang	SD	10	B3
Xiaoyangqi				Subei Guangai	JS	11	C5-B6	Sumba Xia	QH	28	B7
Song Ling	LN	7	C4	Zongqu				Sumdo	SC	30	D3
Songlou	JS	11	B2	Subei Mongolzu	GS	27	C2	Sumt	NM	26	A2
Songmen	ZJ	14	D6	Zizhixian				Sumzom	XZ	34	C6
Songming	YN	33	C5	(Dangchengwan)				Sunan Yugurzu	GS	27	C4
Songmushan	GD	23	H8	Subrag	NM	6	C6	Zizhixian (Hongwan)			
Songpan	SC	30	B4	Subujing	NX	26	B4	(Suncun) Xinwen	SD	10	D4
Songpu	HL	9	E4	Sucao	HEB	4	G2	Sundian	HEN	18	D6
Songshan	LN	7	C5	Sucheng	SX	5	E5	Sunduan	ZJ	12	E4
Songshan	SD	10	B7	Suchenzhuang	JS	12	A3	Sunfang	JX	15	D4
Songshan	JX	15	D2	Sucun	HEB	4	F3	Sungeng	SD	10	C4
Songshan	GX	24	E8	Sucun	SD	10	D5	Suning	HEB	4	E3
Songshan	GX	24	F7	Sugaytu Bulak	XJ	48	B7	Sunji	SX	5	F2
Songshan	GS	27	D6	Sugehe	NM	6	B7	Sunjiaba	GZ	32	C7
Song Shan	HEN	18	C5	Sugongtuo	JL	8	C4	Sunjiabu	AH	13	F5

Sunjiapuzi	JL	8	E7	Tai'an	LN	7	C6	Tainan	TW	17	D3
Sunjiaqiao	HB	19	C6	Tai'an	SD	10	C4	Tainan	TW	17	C3
Sunjiatan	NX	26	C3	Taiba	FJ	16	F2	(Xinying)			
Sunshi	HEB	3	D3	Taibai	JX	15	B5	Taining	FJ	16	D3
Sunshidian	SD	10	D3	Taibai	GS	27	D9	(Taipei) Taibei	TW	17	A4
Suntiepu	HEN	18	E6	Taibai	GZ	32	B6	(Taipei) Taibei	TW	17	A4
Suntuanji	AH	13	C3	Taibai Shan	SX	5	B6	(Banqiao)			
Sunwu	HL	9	C4	Taibai Shan	SN	25	G3	Taiping	HL	9	D6
Sunzhen	SD	10	B4	Taibai	SN	25	F3	Taiping	FJ	16	D4
Sunzhuang	HEB	3	C2	(Zuitouzhen)				Taiping	FJ	16	G3
Suocheng	HN	20	F5	Taibei	JS	11	B5	Taiping	HB	19	B5
Suohuang	SX	5	D5	Taibei(Taipei)	TW	17	A4	Taiping	HN	20	B4
Suoshi	HN	20	B3	Taibei(Taipei)	TW	17	A4	Taiping	HN	20	F5
(Suozhen) Huantai	SD	10	C5	(Banqiao)				Taiping	GD	21	A4
				Taibus Qi(Baochang)	NM	6	D5	Taiping	GD	21	B4
Supoqiao	SC	31	B2					Taiping	GD	23	G6
Suqian	JS	11	C4	Taicang	JS	11	E7	Taiping	GD	23	H6
Suqiao	JX	15	C4	(Taichung) Taizhong	TW	17	B3	Taiping	GX	24	C6
Suqiao	HEN	18	C5					Taiping	GX	24	C7
Suqiao	GX	24	B8	(Taichung) Taizhong	TW	17	B3	Taiping	GX	24	D5
Sushan Dao	SD	10	C9	(Fengyuan)				Taiping	GX	24	D8
Sushui He	SX	5	G2-F2	Taidong	HL	9	D3	Taiping	GX	24	E5
Susong	AH	13	F3	Taidong Shan	TW	17	C4	Taiping	GX	24	E6
Sutuo	BJ	3	B3	Taidong(Taitung)	TW	17	D4	Taiping	GS	26	E4
Suxi	ZJ	14	C5					Taiping	SC	31	A1
Suxi	HB	19	C4	Tai'erzhuang	SD	10	E4	Taiping	SC	31	A4
Su Xian	AH	13	C3	(Taigong) Taijiang	GZ	32	D7	Taiping	SC	31	B1
								Taiping	SC	31	B6
Suxik	QH	28	A4	Taigu	SX	5	D4	Taipingbu	HEB	3	B1
Suxu	GX	24	E6	Taihang Shan (Mts.)	HEB	4	E2-D3	Taipingchang	GD	21	B4
Suyangshan	JS	11	B3		SX	5	E5-D5	Taipingchang	SC	31	B1
(Suzhou) Jiuquan	GS	27	C4		HEN	18	B5-A5	Taipingchang	SC	31	B4
				Taihe	SD	10	C5	Taipingchang	SC	31	B5
				Taihe	JX	15	D4	Taipingchang	SC	31	C1
(Suzhou He) Wusong	SH	12	C5	Taihe	GD	21	B4	Taipingchang	SC	31	C5
Jiang				Taihe	SC	31	B4	Taipingchuan	JL	8	C4
Suzhou	JS	11	E6	Taihe	AH	13	C2	Taipingchuan	JL	8	E8
Suzhou	AH	13	C3	Taihe	JX	15	E2	Taipingcun	TJ	3	D4
Suzhuang	ZJ	14	C3	Taihexu	HN	20	F5	Taiping Dao	HI	22	D3
Suzigou	LN	7	D7	(Taihezhen) Shehong	SC	30	C5	Taipingdian	HB	19	B4
Suzi He	LN	7	C8					Taipingdu	SC	30	D6
				Taihezhen	SC	31	B1	Taipinggou	LN	7	C3
T				Taihezhen	SC	31	B4	Taipinggou	HL	9	C6
				Tai Hu (Lk.)	JS	11	E6	Taipingguan	JX	15	B4
				Taihu	AH	13	F3	Taipingkou	HB	19	D5
Tachakou	XJ	29	B5	Taijiang	GZ	32	D7	Taipingling	JL	8	D9
Tacheng	YN	33	B3	(Taigong)				Taiping Ling	NM	6	C7
				Taijitun	LN	7	C4	Taipingpu	HN	20	D4
Tacheng(Qoqek)	XJ	29	B4	Taijnar He	QH	28	B3	Taipingpu	GS	27	C5
				(Taikang) Dorbod	HL	9	D3	Taipingqiao	SD	10	D3
Tadou	FJ	16	D4	Mongolzu Zizhixian				Taipingshan	LN	7	D6
Ta'ercun	HEB	3	A1					Taipingshan	JL	8	C5
Ta'erwan	HB	19	C6	Taikang	HEN	18	C6	Taipingshan	HL	9	D4
Tagang	HEN	18	B6	Tailai	HL	9	D2	Taipingshao	LN	7	D9
Taha	HL	9	D3	Tailie	GZ	32	D7	Taipingsi	HN	20	D5
Ta He	HL	9	B3	Tailing	BJ	3	B3	Taipingsi	SC	31	C1
Tahe	HL	9	A3	Tailuge	TW	17	B4	Taiping	AH	13	F5
Tai'an	SC	31	C4	Taimali	TW	17	D4	(Gantang)			
				Taimei	GD	21	B5	Taipingxu	HN	20	F5
Tai'angang	JS	11	E7	Taimu Shan	FJ	16	D5-C5	Taipingxu	HN	20	F5

Taiping Yang	TW	17	C5-6	Tamsag Bulag	NM	27	B6	Tangjiapo	SD	10	B7
Taipingzhai	HEB	4	C6	Tanbo	HN	20	D5	Tangjiawan	ZJ	14	B4
Taipingzhen	SD	10	B5	Tanbu	SD	10	D5	Tangjiazhuang	HEB	4	D6
Taipingzhen	HEN	18	D3	Tanbu	AH	13	F4	Tangjiling	GD	23	G6
Taipingzhen	HB	19	E2	Tanbu	GD	23	G6	Tangkou	ZJ	12	D2
Taipingzhen	SC	31	B2	Tanbu	JX	15	C2	Tangkou	AH	13	F5
Taipingzhuang	HEB	4	B5	Tancheng	SD	10	E5	Tangkou	FJ	16	D5
Taiqian	HEN	18	B7	Tandanghe	HB	19	C4	Tanglag	QH	28	C6
Tairiqiao	SH	12	C6	Tandian	LN	7	D8	Tanglai Qu	NX	26	B3
Taishan	SX	5	B5	Tandong	JS	12	C4	Tanglou	JS	11	B2
Tai Shan (Mt.)	SD	10	C4	Tanfang	JX	15	D4	Tangmai	XZ	34	C5
Taishang	JL	8	F6	Tangang	JX	15	C3	Tangmiao	HEB	3	A2
Taishan Liedao	FJ	16	D6	Tangba	SC	30	C5	Tangnag	QH	28	C7
Taishan	GD	21	B4	Tangbu	JX	15	C3	Tangnanji	AH	13	C4
Taishitun	BJ	3	A4	Tangcheng	SX	5	E4	Tangnao Shan	ZJ	12	D6
Taishun	ZJ	14	E4	Tangchi	LN	7	D6	Tangpeng	GD	21	C3
Taitouying	HEB	4	C7	Tangchi	HL	9	D2	Tangpu	ZJ	14	C5
(Taitung) Taidong	TW	17	D4	Tangchizi	LN	7	D8	Tangpu	JX	15	C2
				Tangchuan	FJ	16	D4	Tangqi	ZJ	14	B5
Taiwan Dao (Is.)	TW	43	E5	Tangcun	SD	10	D4	Tangqian	FJ	16	E5
Taiwan Strait	FJ	16	G4-E6	Tangcun	ZJ	14	C3	Tangqiu	HEB	4	F2
	TW	17	B2-A3	Tangcun	ZJ	14	C4	Tangquan	JS	12	A1
Taiwan Shan (Mts.)	TW	17	D3-B4	Tangcun	GD	21	A4	Tangquan	FJ	16	E3
Taixi	TW	17	C3	Tangcunxu	HN	20	F5	Tangra Yumco	XZ	34	C3
Taixi	FJ	16	D4	Tangdan	YN	33	B5	Tangshan	JS	11	D5
Tai Xian	JS	11	D6	Tangdaohe	HEB	4	C6	Tangshancheng	LN	7	D8
Taixing	JS	11	D6	(Tangdukou)	HN	20	E4				
Taiyang	ZJ	12	E2	Shaoyang				Tangshan	HEB	4	D6
Taiyangcun	SX	5	F2	Tang'erli	HEB	4	D4	Tangshi	JS	11	E6
Taiyanggou	HL	9	B3	Tangfang	HEB	4	D6	Tangtang	GD	23	G7
Taiyanghe	HB	19	D2	Tangfang	JX	15	E4	Tangtang	YN	33	B6
Taiyangmiao	NM	6	F10	Tanggangzi	LN	7	C6	Tangtian	HN	20	E6
Taiyangshan	NX	26	C3	Tanggarmo	QH	28	B7	Tangtianshi	HN	20	E4
Taiyang Shan	SN	25	G2	Tanggo	XZ	34	C5	Tangtou	SD	10	D5
Taiyi	SC	31	B3	Tanggor	SC	30	B4	Tangtou	GZ	32	C7
Taiyu	SN	25	F4	Tanggou	JS	11	C4	Tangtouxia	GD	21	B5
	SX	5	D3-4	Tanggu	TJ	3	D5	Tangwan	JX	15	C5
Taiyuan	SX	5	D4	Tangguantun	TJ	3	D4	Tangwan	HN	20	D3
Taiyuansi	HN	20	D5	Tanggulashan	QH	28	C3	Tangwanghe	HL	9	C5
Taiyue Shan	SX	5	E3-D4	(Tuotuoheyan)				Tangwang He	HL	9	D5
Taizhao	XZ	34	C5	Tanggula (Dangla)	QH	28	D2-4	Tangwang Shan	LN	38	C5
Taizhimiao	HN	20	D4	Shan (Mts.)				Tangwu	SD	10	C5
Taizhong(Taichung)	TW	17	B3		XZ	34	B3-5	Tangxi	ZJ	14	C4
				Tanggula (Dang La)	QH	28	D2	Tangxia	GD	23	H6
Taizhong(Taichung)	TW	17	B3	Shankou				Tangxia	ZJ	14	E5
(Fengyuan)					XZ	34	B4	Tangxia	HN	20	F6
(Taizhou) Linhai	ZJ	14	D6	Tang He	BJ	3	A3	Tangxia	GD	23	H7
				Tang He	HEB	4	E3	Tangxian	ZJ	14	C5
				Tang He	AH	13	C4	Tang Xian	HEB	4	E2
Taizhou Liedao	ZJ	14	D6	Tang He	HEN	18	E4	Tangxianzhen	HB	19	C6
Taizhou	JS	11	D5	Tanghekou	BJ	3	A3	Tangya	ZJ	14	C4
Taizhou Wan	ZJ	14	D6	Tanghe	HEN	18	E4	Tangyang	JS	11	D6
Taizi He	LN	7	C8	Tanghong	GX	24	D6	Tangyan He	SC	30	D7
Taizimiao	HN	20	C4	Tanghu	JX	15	E2	Tangyi	SD	10	C2
Taklimakan Shamo	XJ	29	D4-5	Tanghu	HEB	3	C1	Tangyin	JX	15	D4
				Tangji	JS	11	C5	Tangyin	HEN	18	B6
Talangkong	NM	9	B2	Tangjia	GD	21	B4	Tangyu	SN	25	G5
Talazhan	JL	8	D9	Tangjiagou	AH	13	E5	Tangyuan	HL	9	D5
Talian Dao	LN	7	E6	Tangjiagou	AH	13	F4	Tangzha	JS	11	D6
Taman Shan	TW	17	B4	Tangjiang	JX	15	F2	Tangzhuang	SD	10	E5

Tongdao Dongzu	HN	20	E2	Tonglushan	HB	19	D7	Toucheng	TW	17	B4
Zizhixian				Tonglu	ZJ	14	C4	Toudao	JL	8	F6
(Shuangjiang)				Tonglü Yunhe	JS	12	A5	Toudao Chuan	SN	25	C3-D4
Tongde	QH	28	C7	Tongmen	TW	17	C4	Toudaogou	JL	8	E10
Tong'erpu	LN	7	C7	Tongmu	JX	15	D1	Toudaohezi	SN	25	B5
Tongfosi	JL	8	E10	Tongmu	GX	24	C7	Toudaohu	NM	6	E3
Tongfupu	NX	26	B3	Tongmuxi	HN	20	D3	Toudao Jiang	JL	8	E8
Tonggou	JL	8	F6	Tongnan	HL	9	C3	Toudaokan	NX	26	A3
Tonggu	GD	23	I6	Tongnan	SC	30	C5	Toudaoqiao	NM	6	F10
Tongguan	YN	33	D4	Tongqiao	NX	26	B3	Toudaoying	HEB	3	A3
Tongguan	HN	20	C5	Tongqinzhai	SN	25	B6	Tou'erying	HEB	3	A2
Tongguan	SN	25	F6	(Tongquan) Malong	YN	33	C5	Toufen	TW	17	B3
(Wucun)								Tougong	GS	27	B2
Tongguanyi	SC	30	D6					Tou Guan	NX	26	B2
Tonggu Jiao	GD	45	E4	Tongren	QH	28	C8	Toulin	HL	9	D7
Tonggu	JX	15	C2	Tongren	GZ	32	C8	Toumen Shan	ZJ	14	D6
Tongguzbasti	XJ	29	D4	Tongshan	SX	5	F3	Toupai	GX	24	C8
Tonggu Zhang	GD	21	A6	Tongshan	JL	8	F8	Toupao	HEB	3	A2
Tonghaiji	AH	13	C5	Tongshan	JS	11	E4	Toupeng	ZJ	14	B5
Tonghaikou	HB	19	D6	Tongshan	AH	13	F4	Toutai	HL	9	E3
Tonghai	YN	33	C5	Tongshan	HB	19	E7	Touying	NX	26	D3
Tonghe	GX	24	D8	Tongshan	JS	11	B3	Touzha	NX	26	B3
Tonghe	HEN	18	E4	Tongshi	SD	10	D4	Touzhai	GS	26	D1
Tonghe	HL	9	E5	Tongshuping	JX	15	D2	Toxkan He	XJ	29	C3
Tong Hu	GD	21	B5	Tongtan	SC	31	D3	Tuanbaosi	HB	19	D2
Tonghua	SX	5	F2	Tongtian He (Zhi	QH	28	C4-D5	Tuanbi	SX	5	D5
Tonghua	SC	30	C4	Qu) (Riv.)				Tuancun	JX	15	D4
				Tongwan	GX	24	D7	Tuanfeng	HB	19	D7
Tonghua	JL	8	F6	Tongwaxiang	HEN	18	C6	Tuan He	HEN	18	D3-E3
Tonghua	JL	8	F6	Tongwei	GS	27	E7	Tuanjie	HL	9	D4
(Kuaidamao)				Tongxi	SC	31	C4	Tuankou	ZJ	14	B4
Tongji	SC	31	A1	Tong Xian	BJ	3	B3	Tuanlin	JL	8	E7
Tongjia	JX	15	C5	Tongxianchang	SC	31	B3	Tuanlin	HB	19	D5
Tongjia	SC	31	B3	Tongxiang	ZJ	14	B5	Tuannian	SC	31	C4
Tongjiachang	SC	31	C2	Tongxiao	TW	17	B3	Tuanpi	HB	19	D8
Tongjiadian	JL	8	C4	Tongxing	NM	6	D6	Tuanpo	TJ	3	D4
Tongjiang	HL	9	D4	Tongxing	SC	31	B4	Tuanshan	JL	8	C6
Tong Jiang	SC	30	C6	Tongxing	JS	11	C6	Tuanshansi	HB	19	E5
Tongjiangkou	LN	7	B7	Tongxingjie	JS	11	B5	Tuanwan	SD	10	C7
Tongjiangling	JX	15	B3	Tongxin	NX	26	D2	Tuanwang	SD	10	C7
Tongjiang	HL	9	D7	Tongxu	HEN	18	C6	Tuanxi	GZ	32	C6
Tongjiang	SC	30	C6	Tongyanghe	AH	13	E4	Tuban	SX	5	C2
Tongjiasi	SC	31	D3	Tongyang Yunhe	JS	11	D6	Tubo	GX	24	C7
Tongjing	SD	10	D5	Tongyi	NX	26	B3	Tuchang	TW	17	B4
Tongjing	JS	11	E4	Tongyu	SX	5	E5	Tuchang	GZ	32	E6
Tongjingzhen	SC	31	C5	Tongyu	ZJ	14	B5	Tucheng	HB	19	C3
Tongjunzhuang	BJ	3	B3	Tongyuan	JX	15	C4	Tucheng	GZ	32	B4
Tongken He	HL	9	D4	Tongyuanpu	LN	7	D7	Tucheng	GZ	32	D3
Tongkou	HEB	4	E3	Tongyu	JL	8	C4	Tuchengzi	HEB	4	B2
Tongle	HL	9	D4	(Kaitong)				Tuchengzi	HEB	4	B4
Tongli	JS	11	E6	Tongyu Yunhe	JS	11	C6	Tuchengzi	LN	7	D7
Tongliang	SC	30	D6	Tongzhaipu	HEN	18	E4	Tuchengzi	JL	8	C7
Tongliao	NM	6	D7	Tongzhong	HEN	18	E6	Tudian	ZJ	12	D4
Tongliao	NM	6	D7	Tongzhou	GZ	32	E6	Tudi'ao	GZ	32	B7
Tonglin	GZ	32	D7	Tongzi	SC	30	D6	Tudingzi	JL	8	D6
Tongling	GX	24	D7	Tongzicun	HN	20	C4	Tuditang	HB	19	D7
Tongling	AH	13	F4	Tongzi	GZ	32	B5	Tufang	FJ	16	E2
				Toson Hu	QH	28	B5	Tugao	GS	27	D7
Tongling	AH	13	F4	Tost	NM	6	D3	Tuguancun	YN	33	B4
Tongluo (Yanmu)	JS	12	D4	Toubei	JX	15	E4	Tuguancun	YN	33	C5

Tuhai He	SD	10	B4-5	(Tuotuoheyan) Tanggulashan	QH	28	C3	(Ulugqat) Wuqia	XJ	29	D2

Name	Prov	No	Grid	Name	Prov	No	Grid	Name	Prov	No	Grid
Wanbao	JL	8	C6	Wanghua	JX	15	D2	Wangtian	TW	17	B3
Wanchangchang	SC	31	C2	Wangji	JS	11	C3	Wangting	JS	11	E6
Wanda Shan	HL	9	E6-D7	Wangji	JS	11	C4	Wangtuan	HEB	4	F4
Wande	SD	10	C3	Wangji	HB	19	C5	Wangtuan	SD	10	B8
Wandi	SD	10	C7	Wangjiachang	HN	20	B4	Wangtuanji	AH	13	C3
Wandianzi	LN	7	C9	Wangjiadian	HL	9	D6	Wangtuanzhuang	NX	26	D2
Wandingzhen	YN	33	C3	Wangjiadian	HB	19	C6	Wangtuanzhuang	NX	26	D2
Wanfa	JL	8	B6	Wangjiajing	HEB	4	F3	Wangu	SC	31	B4
Wanfotang	BJ	3	B2	Wangjiangjing	ZJ	14	B5	Wanguzhen	SC	31	C4
Wanfu	LN	7	D6	Wangjiang	AH	13	F3	Wangwa	NX	26	D3
Wanfu	JX	15	D2	Wangjiaping	HN	20	E2	Wangwu	HEN	18	B4
Wanfu He	SD	10	D2-3	Wangjiaping	SN	25	D5	Wangwuqiao	HEN	18	E6
Wang'an	TW	17	C2	Wangjiapu	LN	7	D7	Wangwu Shan	SX	5	F4
Wang'anzhen	HEB	4	D2	Wangjiapu	JX	15	B3		HEN	18	B4
Wangben	JL	8	D4	Wangjiatan	HB	19	C3	Wangxian	HN	20	D6
Wangbi	SX	5	F4	Wangjiawan	HEB	3	B1	Wangxian	SX	5	F2
Wangbuzhuang	TJ	3	C4	Wangjiawan	SN	25	C5	Wangxian	JX	15	D3
Wangcang	SC	30	B6	Wangjiaxu	JX	15	C3	Wangxuzhuang	HEB	4	E5
(Fengjiaba)				Wangjiaying	HB	19	D1	Wangyangzhen	SC	31	C2
Wangcaoba	GZ	32	B6	Wangjiazhou	JX	15	C4	Wangyedian	NM	4	B6
Wangchang	SC	31	D2	Wangjiazhuang	YN	33	C5	Wangyin	SD	10	D3
Wangchenggang	JX	15	C3	Wangjie	YN	33	D4	(Wangying) Huaiyin	JS	11	C5
Wangcheng	HN	20	C5	Wangjing	HEB	3	D1				
(Gaotangling)				Wangkou	TJ	3	D3	Wangyingzi	HEB	3	A5
Wangchuan	FJ	16	E4	Wangkui	HL	9	D4	Wangyuanqiao	NX	26	B3
Wangcun	SD	10	C4	Wanglaorenji	AH	13	C2	Wangyukou	SX	5	F3
Wangcun	SD	10	C7	Wanglejing	NX	26	C4	Wangzhai	ZJ	14	D4
Wangcun	AH	13	G5	Wangling	HN	20	D6	Wangzhai	AH	13	B3
Wangcun	HN	20	C2	Wangliu	HEN	18	E7	Wangzhuang	SX	5	E3
Wangcun	SN	25	E6	Wanglong	GZ	32	B4	Wangzhuangbu	SX	5	B5
Wangcun	GS	26	E4	Wanglong	SC	31	D4	Wangzhuangji	JS	11	B4
Wangcun	AH	13	G4	Wangmao	GX	24	E7	Wangziguan	GS	27	F7
Wangcundian	SD	10	B3	Wangminbu	NX	26	E2	Wangzizhuang	SD	10	C3
Wangcunkou	ZJ	14	D3	Wangmo (Fuxing)	GZ	32	E5	Wanhedian	HB	19	B6
(Wangda) Zogang	XZ	34	C6	Wangmudu	JX	15	F2	Wanjiabu	JX	15	C3
				Wangou	JL	8	E7	Wanjialing	LN	7	E6
Wangdain	XZ	34	C4	Wangpan	HEB	3	D2	Wanjiamatou	TJ	3	D4
Wangdian	ZJ	14	B5	Wangpan Shan	ZJ	14	B6	Wanjiatun	LN	7	D3
Wangdian	GX	24	C4	Wangpan Yang	ZJ	14	B6	Wanjiazhai	SX	5	B3
Wangdu	HEB	4	E3	Wangpanzhen	SD	10	B4	Wanjinta	JL	8	C6
Wang'er	JX	15	C5	Wangping	HB	19	D2	Wanli	AH	13	E5
Wangfan	HEN	18	C3	Wangqi	JL	8	D7	Wanliang	JL	8	E8
Wangfeng	SD	10	C2	Wangqiao	HEN	18	C7	Wanlong	HL	9	E3
Wangfengqiao	SN	25	E6	Wangqiao	HB	19	E5	Wannian	JX	15	C5
Wangfu	LN	7	B5	Wangqingmen	LN	7	C9	(Chenying)			
Wangfu	JL	8	C6	Wangqingtuo	TJ	3	C4	Wanning	HI	21	D3
Wangfutai	NX	26	C3	Wangqing	JL	8	D10	(Wanping) Lugouqiao	BJ	3	B3
Wanggao	GX	24	C9	Wangqu	SN	25	F4	Wanqingsha	GD	23	H7
Wang Gaxun	QH	28	B6	Wangshi	AH	13	C3	Wanquan He	HI	21	D3
Wanggezhuang	SD	10	C7	Wangshi'ao	SN	25	E5	Wanquansi	HEB	3	A3
(Wanggezhuang)	SD	10	D6	Wangshiwan	HN	20	D5	Wanquan	HEB	4	C2
Jiaonan				Wangshu	HEB	4	F5	Wanrong	SX	5	F2
Wanggou	SD	10	D5	Wangsi	HEB	4	F4	(Xiedian)			
Wangguantun	SX	5	A5	Wangsi	GZ	32	D6	Wanshan	SC	31	B4
Wanghai Shan	LN	7	C5	Wangsitan	NX	26	C4	Wanshan Qundao	GD	21	B4-5
Wanghaotun	SD	10	D2	Wangsiying	SC	31	B1	Wanshan Tequ	GZ	32	C8
Wanghe	SX	5	E4	Wangtai	SD	10	C7	Wanshengchang	SC	30	D6
Wanghongpu	NX	26	B3	Wangtai	FJ	16	D3	Wan Shui	AH	13	F3
Wanghu	SD	10	D6	Wangtan	ZJ	14	C5	Wanshun	JL	8	C5
Wanghu	SX	5	B5	Wangtao	SX	5	E4	Wanshun	SC	31	C5

Wantan	HEN	18	C5	Weihuling	JL	8	D8	Weizha	NX	26	A3
Wantan	HB	19	D3	Weihu Ling	JL	8	D8	Weizhangzi	LN	7	D3
Wantang	YN	33	D5	Weijiadian	HB	19	C6	Weizheng	GD	23	G6
Wantouqiao	HN	20	E3	Weijiaqiao	SD	10	B4	Weizhou	NX	26	C3
Wanwei	GX	24	F6	Weijiatan	SX	5	C3	Weizhou	HEB	4	E2
Wan Xian (Shahezi)	SC	30	C7	Weijiaying	HEB	3	C2	(Weizhou) Wenchuan	SC	30	C4
Wan Xian	HEB	4	E3	Weijin	JL	8	E6				
				Weijingtang	JS	11	E6	Weizhou Dao	GX	24	F6
Wanxian	SC	30	C7	Weiling	HL	9	D5	Weizhouxu	GX	24	F7
Wanxian Zhan	HEB	4	E3	Weilinzhen	SN	25	F6	Weizi	LN	7	D7
Wanyang Shan	JX	15	E2	Weilu	SX	5	A4	Weiziyu	LN	7	C8
	HN	20	E6-7	Weiluo	GX	24	E6	Weizizhen	SX	5	E5
Wanyuan	SC	30	B7	Weima	SX	5	D5	Wen'an	HB	19	D4
Wanzai	GD	23	I7	Weimin	FJ	16	C3	Wen'an Wa	HEB	4	E4
Wanzai	JX	15	C2					Wen'an	HEB	4	E4
(Wanzhi) Wuhu	AH	13	E5	Weinan	SN	25	F5	Wenbu	NX	26	E2
Wanzhuang	HEB	4	D4	Weining	LN	7	C7	Wenchang	ZJ	14	C4
Waqên	SC	30	B4	Weining Yizu Huizu	GZ	32	D3	Wenchang	HI	21	D3
Warizhên	SC	30	D3	Miaozu Zizhixian				Wencheng	SX	5	E2
Warli	SC	30	D3	Weiqiao	JS	11	C4	Wencheng	ZJ	14	E5
Warzhong	SC	30	D3	Weiqiuji	HEN	18	B6	(Daxue)			
Watang	SX	5	C2	Weirong	GS	27	E7	Wenchuan	SC	30	C4
Watang	GX	24	E7	Weishan	HN	20	C4	(Weizhou)			
Wating	NX	26	E3	Weishan	ZJ	14	C5	Wenchun	HL	9	E5
Wawumiao	HEN	18	D4	Weishan Hu	SD	10	E4	Wencun	GD	23	I6
Wawutang	HN	20	E3	Weishan	SD	10	E4	Wendeng	SD	10	B9
Waxingzhen	HL	9	D4	(Xiazhen)				Wendi	GX	24	F8
Waxü	GS	27	E6	Weishan Yizu Huizu	YN	33	C4	Wendou	HB	19	E1
Waxxari	XJ	29	D5	Zizhixian				Wenfang	JX	15	C5
Wayao	BJ	3	B4	Weishanzhuang	BJ	3	C3	Wenfengzhen	GS	27	E7
Wayao	JS	11	B4	Weishi	HEN	18	C6	Weng'an	GZ	32	C6
Wayao	YN	33	C3	(Weishui) Jingxing	HEB	5	C6	(Yongyang)			
(Wayaobu) Zichang	SN	25	C5					Wengcheng	GD	21	A4
				Wei Shui	HN	20	C5	Wengdong	GZ	32	C8
Wayuan	HN	20	E5	(Weitang) Jiashan	ZJ	12	D5	Wenggulong	GZ	32	D7
Wazidian	HEB	4	B6					Wengjiabu	ZJ	12	E4
Wazijie	SN	25	E6	Weitian	FJ	16	C4	Wengjiang	HN	20	C6
Weibo	HEB	4	E3	Weiting	JS	11	E6	Weng Jiang	GD	21	A4-5
Weichang	HEB	4	B5	Weitou	FJ	16	F4	Wengong	SC	31	B2
(Zhuizishan)				Weitou Wan	FJ	16	F4	Wengshui	YN	33	A3
Weicheng	SC	30	E3	Weituo	SC	31	C4	Wengyang	ZJ	14	D5
Weicheng	GZ	32	D5	Weiwan	SD	10	C2	Wengyuan	GD	21	A5
Weicheng	SC	30	C5	Weiwan	SD	10	E2	(Longxian)			
Weichuan	HEN	18	C5	Weixi	SC	31	B5	Wen He	SD	10	C6
Weicun	JS	11	E5	Weixian	HEN	18	B6	Wen He	SD	10	D5
(Weidongmen) Qianjin	HL	9	D7	Wei Xian	HEB	4	G3	Wenheng	FJ	16	E2
Weidu	GX	24	D7	Wei Xian (Hanting)	SD	10	C6	Wenhua	SC	31	C3
	SD	10	C5-6	Wei Xian	HEB	4	G2	Wenjiadian	GZ	32	C6
Weifang	SD	10	C6	Weixin	GZ	32	C4	Wenjiadian	SD	10	B4
Weiganbao	HB	19	D2		HN	20	B4				
Weiguo	HL	9	C5	Weixinchang	YN	33	B6	Wenjiang	SC	30	C4
Weihai	SD	10	B9	Weixin (Zhaxi)	YN	33	B3	Wenjiao	HI	21	D3
Weihe	HL	9	E5	Weixi	XJ	29	C7	Wenjiashi	HN	20	C6
Wei He	HEB	4	G3	Weiya	JS	11	C4	Wenjiazhen	JX	15	C4
	SD	10	C2	Weiying	SX	5	B4	Wenjing	SC	31	A4
	HEN	18	B6	Weiyuanbu	YN	33	D4	Wenjing	YN	33	C4
Wei He	SN	25	F5	Weiyuan Jiang	HB	19	D8	Wenli	GX	24	E8
	GS	27	E8	Weiyuankou	LN	7	B8	Wenling	ZJ	14	D6
Wei He	SD	10	C6	Weiyuanpu	SC	30	D5	Wenlong	JX	15	G2
Weihui Qu	SN	25	F4	Weiyuan	GS	27	E7	Wenming	HN	20	F6

Wenmingpu	HN	20	E4	Wubu	SN	25	C6	Wufengxi	SC	31	B2
Wenping	GZ	32	B7	(Songjiachuan)				Wufeng	HB	19	D3
(Wenpingzhen)	YN	33	B5	Wuchagou	NM	6	C7	Wufosi	GS	27	D7
Ludian				Wuchang	HB	19	D7	Wufu	ZJ	12	E5
Wenqiao	JX	15	B4	Wuchang Hu	AH	13	F3	Wufu	FJ	16	C4
Wenqu	HEN	18	E3	Wuchang	HL	9	E4	Wufuchang	SC	31	D5
Wenquan	LN	7	D4	Wuchang	HB	19	D7	Wufuting	JX	15	E2
Wenquan	GD	23	G7	(Zhifang)				Wugang	JS	11	C5
Wenquan	QH	28	C6	Wucheng	SX	5	E2	Wugang	HN	20	E3
Wenquan	QH	28	D2	Wucheng	AH	13	G5	Wuge	FJ	16	E2
Wenquan	SC	30	C7	Wucheng	SX	5	B5	Wugong	HEB	4	E3
Wenquan	GZ	32	B6	Wucheng	SX	5	D3	Wugong	HEN	18	D5
Wenquan	GZ	32	C5	Wucheng	JX	15	B3	Wugong Shan	JX	15	D1-2
Wenquansi	LN	7	C8	Wucheng	HEN	18	D5		HN	20	E6-D6
Wenquantang	SD	10	B9	Wucheng	HEN	18	E5				
Wenquan(Arixang)	XJ	29	B4	Wucheng	SD	10	B2	Wugong Shan	JX	15	D2
				Wucheng	SD	10	B3	Wugong (Puji)	SN	25	F4
Wenquanzhen	HB	19	E7	Wucheng				Wugouying	HEN	18	D6
Wenren	HEB	4	E3	(Jiucheng)				Wuguan	SN	25	G6
Wenshang	SD	10	D3	Wuchuan (Duru)	GZ	32	B7	Wuguanhe	SN	25	G2
Wenshan	YN	33	D6	Wuchuan (Meilu)	GD	21	C3	Wuguanzhai	HEB	4	F3
				Wuchuan	NM	6	D4	Wuguzhang	SN	25	D3
				Wucun	GX	24	D4	Wuhai	NM	6	E3
				Wucun	SD	10	D4	(Haibowan)			
Wenshi	GX	24	B9	Wucun	HEN	18	B5				
Wenshui	GZ	32	B5	(Wucun) Tongguan	SN	25	F6	Wuhan	HB	19	D7
Wenshui	SX	5	D4					Wuhe	HL	9	E4
Wensu	XJ	29	C4	Wuda	NM	6	E3	Wuhe	AH	13	F3
Wentang	JX	15	B2	Wudabao	ZJ	14	E4	Wuhe	AH	13	C4
Wentang	JX	15	D2	Wuda Lian Chi	HL	9	C4	Wuhuanchi	LN	7	B5
Wentang Xia	SC	31	C5	(Wudan) Ongniud Qi	NM	6	D6	Wuhuang	SC	31	C3
Wenxi	ZJ	14	D5	Wudalianchi	HL	9	C4	Wuhua	GD	21	B5
Wen Xian	GS	27	F7	Wudang	GZ	32	D5	(Shuizhai)			
Wen Xian	HEN	18	C5	Wudang Shan	HB	19	B3	Wuhudong	NM	26	B4
Wenxi	SX	5	F3	Wudang Shan	HB	19	B4	Wuhu	AH	13	E5
Wenying	JX	15	F2	Wudao	LN	7	E5				
Wenyu	HEN	18	C3	Wudaogou	JL	8	D11	Wuhu (Wanzhi)	AH	13	E5
Wenyu He	SX	5	D3	Wudaogou	JL	8	E6	Wüjang	XZ	34	B1
Wenyu He	BJ	3	B3	Wudaogou	HL	9	B4	Wuji	HEB	4	G2
Wenzhenguan	SC	31	A1	Wudaojiang	JL	8	F7	Wuji	SD	10	B8
Wenzhou	ZJ	14	D5	Wudaoliang	QH	28	C3	Wuji	SD	10	D6
				Wudaoshui	HN	20	B2	Wuji	JS	11	B5
Wenzhou Wan	ZJ	14	E5	Wude	GX	24	E4	Wujia	HL	9	E4
Wenzhu	JX	15	D1	Wudian	AH	13	E2	Wujia	GX	24	F7
Wenzu	SD	10	C4	Wudian	HB	19	C5	Wujiachuan	GS	26	D1
Wofotang	HEB	3	D3	Wudian	AH	13	D4	Wujiadian	HEN	18	E5
Wohutun	JL	8	D4	Wuding He	SN	25	C6	Wujiagang	AH	13	D5
Woinbogoin	SC	30	B2	Wuding	YN	33	C5	Wujia He	NM	6	F10
Woken	HL	9	E6	Wudi	SD	10	B4	Wujiang	AH	13	E5
Woken He	HL	9	D6-E6	Wudong	SC	31	B6	Wujiang	JX	15	D3
Wolong	JL	8	E9	Wudu	ZJ	14	E3	Wujiang	GX	24	C8
Wolongshi	SC	30	C3	Wudu	JX	15	C6	Wu Jiang	SC	30	D6
Woluogu	HEB	3	C5	Wudu	SC	30	C5		GZ	32	C6
Woniushi	LN	7	B7					Wujiangdu	GZ	32	C5
Woniutu	HL	9	D2	Wuduhe	HB	19	C4	Wujiangpu	GS	27	C5
Wopi	JL	8	C6	Wuduizi	NX	26	B3	Wujiang	JS	11	E6
Woshi	HB	19	D5	Wudu	GS	27	F7	Wujiatang	FJ	16	C3
Woxi	HN	20	C3	Wufeng	LN	7	B6	Wujiazhan	JL	8	C6
Wu'anji	SD	10	D2	Wufeng	TW	17	C3	Wujiazhen	SC	31	C3
Wu'an	HEB	4	G2	Wufeng	TW	17	B3	Wujimi	HL	9	E4
Wubu	HEB	3	B1	Wufengpu	HN	20	E4	Wujing	SD	10	C5

Name	Prov.	Map	Grid
Wujing	GD	21	A5
Wujingfu	GD	21	B6
Wujin	JS	11	E5
Wuji	HEB	4	E2
Wukang	ZJ	14	B4
Wukeshu	JL	8	A4
Wukeshu	JL	8	C7
Wukou	HN	20	C6
Wulai	TW	17	B4
Wulajie	JL	8	C7
Wulanbulang	NM	6	F10
Wulang	XZ	34	C5
Wuleidao Wan	SD	10	C8
Wuli	QH	28	C3
Wuli	GX	24	E7
Wulian	SC	30	C5
Wulian Feng	YN	33	B5-A6
Wuliangdian	LN	7	C6
Wuliang Shan	YN	33	C4-D4
Wulian Shan	SD	41	C5
Wulian (Hongning)	SD	10	D6
Wuliba	SN	25	H3
Wuliba	SN	25	H4
Wulichuan	HEN	18	D3
Wulidian	HEN	18	E6
Wulie He	HEB	4	B5-6
Wuli Jiang	GX	24	E7-F7
Wulin	HL	9	E5
Wulin	GX	24	D8
Wuling	HEN	18	B6
Wuling	HN	20	F6
Wuling	GX	24	D6
Wuling Shan	HN	20	C2-B3
	GZ	32	C7-B8
Wuling Shan	HEB	4	C5
Wulingzhen	SC	30	C7
Wulipai	HN	20	F4
Wuliping	HB	19	E3
Wulipu	HB	19	D5
Wuliting	JX	15	G2
Wulongbei	LN	7	D8
Wulong He	SD	10	C7
(Wulongji) Huaibin	HEN	18	E7
Wulongpu	SN	25	C6
Wulongquan	HB	19	D7
Wulong	SC	30	D6
Wulubutie	NM	9	C3
Wuluo	GZ	32	B7
Wuluo	GZ	32	D7
Wumahe	HL	9	D5
Wumang Dao	LN	7	E7
Wumei Shan	JX	15	C2
Wumeng Shan	GZ	32	D2-3
	YN	33	B5-6
Wuming He	GX	24	D6
Wuming	GX	24	D6
Wunan Sha	JS	11	D7
Wuning Shui	JX	15	C2
Wuning	JX	15	B3
Wunüdian	HEN	18	C5
Wuping	FJ	16	E2
Wupo	SC	30	D4
Wuqi	TW	17	B3
Wuqia (Ulugqat)	XJ	29	D2
Wuqiang	HEN	18	C7
Wuqiang (Xiaofan)	HEB	4	E3
Wuqiao (Sangyuan)	HEB	4	F4
Wuqing (Yangcun)	TJ	3	C4
Wuqiu Yu	FJ	16	E5
Wuqi	SN	25	D4
Wurenqiao	HEB	4	E3
Wusha	AH	13	F4
Wusha	GZ	32	E3
Wushan	JS	12	B2
Wushan	AH	13	D4
Wushan	HB	19	B6
Wu Shan	HB	19	D3-C3
	SC	30	C7-8
Wushan	SC	30	C7
Wushan	GS	27	E7
Wushaoling	GS	27	D6
Wushe	TW	17	B4
Wusheng	ZJ	14	C4
Wusheng Guan	HEN	18	F6
	HB	19	C7
Wusheng	SC	30	C6
Wushi	JX	15	D4
Wushi	GD	21	A4
Wushi	GD	21	C2
Wushi	GX	24	E8
Wushibi	TW	17	B4
Wushi (Uqturpan)	XJ	29	C3
Wushu	JX	15	E2
Wu Shui	HN	20	D2
Wu Shui	HN	20	D3-E3
Wu Shui	HN	20	C2-3
Wu Shui	GD	21	A4
	SH	11	E7
Wusong	SH	11	E7
Wusong Jiang	SH	11	E7
Wusong Kou	SH	11	E7
Wusu	HN	20	C3
Wusuli	HL	9	A2
Wusuli Jiang	HL	9	D8
Wusuo	FJ	16	E2
Wuta	JS	12	B4
Wutai	XJ	29	B4
Wutai	HEN	18	D7
Wutai	SD	10	D4
Wutai Shan	SX	5	B5
Wutai Shan	SX	5	C4-B5
Wutai	SX	5	C5
Wutan	HN	20	C4
Wutang	GX	24	E6
Wutang	FJ	16	E5
Wutian	FJ	16	G3
Wutong	GX	24	B8
Wutong	SX	5	D3
Wutong	FJ	16	E4
Wutonghaolai	NM	7	B4
Wutonghe	HL	9	D6
Wutong He	HL	9	D6
Wutongqiao	SC	30	D4
Wutongshu	NX	26	B3
Wutongwozi Quan	XJ	29	C7
Wuwei	AH	13	E4
Wuwei (Liangzhou)	GS	27	D6
Wuxi	AH	12	C1
Wuxi	AH	12	D1
(Wuxi) Luxi	HN	20	C3
Wu Xia	HB	19	C3
	SC	30	C7-8
Wu Xian	JS	11	E6
Wuxiangpu	NX	26	B3
Wuxiangqi	ZJ	14	C6
Wuxiang (Duancun)	SX	5	E4
Wuxi Gang	ZJ	14	D3
Wuxing	ZJ	14	B5
Wuxiqiao	AH	13	F4
Wuxi	JS	11	E6
Wuxi	JS	11	E6
Wuxi	SC	30	C7
Wuxu	GX	24	E6
Wuxuan	GX	24	D7
Wuxue	HB	19	E8
Wuxun	JS	11	C6
Wuyan	ZJ	14	E5
Wuyang	SX	5	E5
(Wuyang) Zhenyuan	GZ	32	C7
Wuyang	JX	15	F3
Wuyang	HN	20	E3
Wuyang He	GZ	32	C7
Wuyang	HEN	18	D5
Wuyapao	HL	9	E5
Wuyi	AH	13	D5
Wuyiling	HL	9	C5
Wuying	HL	9	C5
Wuying	NX	26	D3
Wuyi Shan	JX	15	F4-E4
	FJ	16	E2-D2
Wuyi Shui	ZJ	14	D4
Wuyi	ZJ	14	D4
Wuyi	HEB	4	F3
Wuyongcun	HEB	3	C1
Wuyou	JS	11	C6
Wuyuancun	HEN	18	C3
Wuyuan	NM	6	D4
Wuyuan	JX	15	B5
(Wuyuanzhen) Haiyan	ZJ	14	B5

Name	Prov	No.	Grid
Wuyunqiao	JX	15	E2
Wuyur He	HL	9	D3
Wuzhai	ZJ	14	C4
Wuzhai	SX	5	C3
Wuzhan	HL	9	B3
Wuzhan	HL	9	E4
Wuzhen	ZJ	14	B5
Wuzhen	HB	19	C4
Wuzhen	SN	25	C5
Wuzhi Shan	HEB	4	C6
Wuzhi Shan	HI	21	D2
Wuzhi	HEN	18	B5
Wuzhong	NX	26	C3
Wuzhou	GX	24	D9
Wuzhu Zhou	GD	23	J6
Wuzong	JS	12	A5

X

Name	Prov	No.	Grid
Xabyaisamba	XZ	34	C6
Xagquka	XZ	34	C5
Xaidulla	XJ	29	D3
Xainza	XZ	34	C4
Xaitongmoin	XZ	34	C4
(Xamba) Hanggin Houqi	NM	6	D3
Xanagan Sum	NM	6	F10
Xangdoring	XZ	34	B2
Xang Qu	XZ	51	C4
Xarag	QH	28	B6
Xar Burd	NM	6	D3
Xar Moron	NM	6	F10
Xar Moron He	NM	6	D6
Xar'oi	QH	28	D7
Xayar	XJ	29	C4
Xebert	NM	6	C7
(Xêgar) Tingri	XZ	34	C3
Xia'ao	GX	24	C5
Xiaba	HB	19	B3
Xiabahe	HB	19	D8
Xiabaishi	FJ	16	D5
(Xiabancheng) Chengde	HEB	4	C6
Xiabaoping	HB	19	C4
Xiabuji	JX	15	C4
Xiacang	TJ	3	B4
Xiacaowan	JS	11	C4
Xiacengpu	HN	20	F4
Xiachabu	HB	19	D6
Xi'achao	HEB	4	B5
Xiachengzi	HL	9	E6
Xiachong	GD	21	B5
Xiachuan	SX	5	F4
Xiachuan Dao	GD	21	C4
Xiacun	JX	15	D2
(Xiacun) Rushan	SD	10	C8
Xiadachen Dao	ZJ	14	D6
Xiadanshui Xi	TW	43	E5
Xiadao	FJ	16	D4
Xiadian	SD	10	B7
Xiadian	SX	5	E4
Xiadian	SD	10	C6
Xiadian	HB	19	C7
Xiadian	HEB	4	D4
Xiadong	GS	27	B2
Xiafangqiao	ZJ	14	B5
Xiafangshen	LN	7	D6
Xiafeidi	LN	7	B8
Xiagang	JS	11	E6
Xiage	AH	13	E4
Xiagezhuang	SD	10	C7
Xiagou	SD	10	C3
Xiaguan	SX	5	B6
Xiaguan	ZJ	14	C6
Xiaguan	HEN	18	D3
(Xiaguan)Dali	YN	33	C4
Xiaguantun	SD	10	D3
Xiaguanying	GS	27	E7
Xiagui	SN	25	F5
Xiahecheng	SD	10	D6
Xiahe (Labrang)	GS	27	E6
Xiahu	FJ	16	D5
Xiahuaqiao	HN	20	E4
Xiahuayuan	HEB	4	C3
Xiajia	GX	24	C4
Xiajiang	GZ	32	E7
Xiajiang	JX	15	D3
Xiajiapu	LN	7	B8
Xiajin	SD	10	C2
Xiakou	ZJ	14	C3
Xiakou	ZJ	14	D3
Xiakou	HB	19	C4
Xiakou	NX	26	C3
Xiakou	SD	10	B3
Xialiang	SX	5	E5
Xialiushi	HN	20	D5
Xialiushui	NX	26	C2
Xialuhe	LN	7	D9
Xiamaguan	NX	26	C3
Xiamao	FJ	16	D3
Xiamaoshan	BJ	3	A3
Xiamatang	LN	7	C7
Xiamaya	XJ	29	C7
Xiamen Gang	FJ	16	F4
Xiamen	FJ	16	F4
Xianan	GX	24	C5
Xianbin Jiao	HI	22	D4
Xiancha	JX	15	B5
Xianchuankou	SN	25	D6
Xiancun	FJ	16	D5
Xiandi	GX	24	E8
Xiandu	FJ	16	E3
Xianduhe	SC	31	B5
Xian'e Jiao	HI	22	D3
Xianfeng	SC	31	D5
Xianfeng	HB	19	E2
Xiang'an	AH	13	E4
Xiangang	GD	23	H6
Xiangbei	GX	24	C6
Xiangbichang	SC	31	D2
Xiangcheng	SD	10	E4
Xiangcheng	JX	15	C3
Xiangchenggu	HEB	4	G3
Xiangcheng	SC	30	D2
Xiangcheng (Shuizhai)	HEN	18	D6
Xiangcheng	HEN	18	D5
Xiangdong	JX	15	D1
Xiangdu	GX	24	D4
Xiangfang	HL	9	E4
Xiangfan	HB	19	B5
Xiangfen (Shicun)	SX	5	F3
Xiangfuguan	JX	15	C3
Xianggongzhuang	SD	10	D5
Xiangguanji	AH	12	A1
Xianghe	SN	25	G6
Xiang He	AH	12	A1
Xiangheguan	HEN	18	D5
Xianghe	HEB	4	D5
Xianghongdian	AH	13	E3
Xianghongdian Sk.	AH	13	E3
Xianghu	JX	15	B5
Xianghua Ling	HN	20	F5
Xianghuang(Hobot Xar) Qi	NM	6	D5
Xianghuazhen	SH	12	B6
Xiangjia	ZJ	14	D3
Xiangjiahe	HB	19	C7
Xiang Jiang	HN	20	D5
	GX	24	B9-A9
Xiang Jiang	GZ	32	C6
Xiangjiangkou	HN	20	F4
Xiangjiaping	JX	15	C3
Xiangkou	AH	13	F3
Xianglan	HL	9	D5
Xiangling	SX	5	E3
Xianglinpu	HN	20	F4
Xiangning	SX	5	F2
Xiangongzhen	SN	25	F3
Xiangqi	GX	24	D8
Xiangquan	AH	12	B1
(Xiangquan He) Langqên Zangbo	XZ	34	C1-2
Xiangride	QH	28	C5
Xiangshan	AH	13	E5
Xiangshan	BJ	3	B3
Xiangshan	SC	31	B3
Xiangshan Gang	ZJ	14	C6
Xiangshan (Dancheng)	ZJ	14	C6

Name	Region	No.	Grid
Xiaojia	GD	23	I7
Xiaojiagang	HB	19	C6
Xiaojiahe	HL	9	D7
Xiaojiang	JX	15	F2
Xiaojiang	GD	21	A4
(Xiaojiang) Pubei	GX	24	E7
Xiaojiang	ZJ	14	E5
Xiao Jiang	SC	30	C7
Xiao Jiang	YN	33	B5
Xiaojiangbian	JX	15	D2
Xiaojiangkou	HN	20	E5
Xiaojianji	AH	13	C3
Xiaojiao	HEB	4	E1
Xiaojieji	NM	8	D2
Xiaojieling	HB	19	C8
Xiaojin	GS	27	E8
Xiaojin Chuan	SC	30	C4
Xiaojingzhuang	SX	5	B4
Xiaojin	SC	30	C4
Xiaoji Shan	ZJ	12	D6
Xiaojiu	HL	9	E4
Xiaolan	GD	21	B4
Xiaolan Yu	TW	17	E4
Xiaoliangshan	LN	7	B6
Xiaolin	ZJ	14	B6
Xiaolindian	HB	19	B6
Xiaoling	HL	9	E4
Xiaoling He	LN	7	C4
Xiaolipu	SD	10	C3
Xiaoliuji	SD	10	D2
Xiaoliuxiang	AH	13	C5
Xiaolizhuang	HEN	18	C5
Xiaolong	GX	24	C6
Xiaolongshan Dao (She Dao)	LN	7	F4
Xiaolou	GD	23	G7
Xiaolu	GS	26	D1
Xiaoluan He	HEB	4	A4-B4
Xiaolu Dao	LN	7	E7
Xiaomacun	GZ	32	B6
Xiaomaochang	GZ	32	D4
Xiaomei	ZJ	14	E3
Xiaomei Guan	JX	15	F2
	GD	21	A5
Xiaomengtong	YN	33	C3
Xiaomianzhen	SC	30	C6
Xiaomuhe	HL	9	D7
Xiaonanchuan	QH	28	C4
Xiaonangou	GS	26	D3
Xiaonanguan	HEB	4	B4
Xiaonanhai	SC	31	D5
Xiaopikou	SD	10	D2
Xiaoping	HN	20	C3
Xiaopingshan	GX	24	E8
Xiaopingyang	GX	24	D7
Xiaopu (Xiaobu)	JX	15	E3
Xiaopuzi	YN	33	B5
Xiao Qaidam	QH	28	B4
Xiao Qaidam Hu	QH	28	B4
Xiaoqiao	FJ	16	D4
Xiaoqiaozhen	SC	30	C6
Xiaoqin Dao	SD	10	A7
Xiaoqing He	SD	10	B4
Xiaoqiuzhen	SN	25	F4
Xiaoquandong	GS	27	B2
Xiaoquanzhen	SC	31	A2
Xiaoshakou	HB	19	E6
Xiaoshan	HEB	4	E5
Xiao Shan	HEN	18	C2-3
Xiaoshangqiao	HEN	18	D5
Xiaoshan	ZJ	14	B5
(Xiaoshi) Benxi	LN	7	C8
Xiaoshi	GD	23	G6
(Xiaoshi) Lu Xian	SC	31	D3
Xiaoshidian	HEN	18	D5
Xiaoshu	ZJ	14	B4
Xiao Shui	JX	15	D2
Xiao Shui	HN	20	E4-F4
Xiaoshuipu	HN	20	E5
Xiaoshun	ZJ	14	C4
Xiaosigou	HEB	4	C6
Xiaosiping	JL	8	E6
Xiaosong	JX	15	E4
Xiaosong	FJ	16	C4
Xiaosuan	SX	5	D2
Xiaosuangou	HEB	4	C2
Xiaosuifen He	HL	9	E6
Xiaosunzhuang	TJ	3	D4
Xiao Surmang	QH	28	D5
Xiaotang	GD	23	H6
Xiaotangshan	BJ	3	B3
Xiaotao	FJ	16	E3
Xiaotazi	LN	7	B7
Xiaotian	AH	13	E3
Xiaotianji	AH	13	D2
Xiaotun	LN	7	C7
Xiaowangjia Dao	LN	7	E7
Xiaowangmiao	ZJ	14	C6
Xiaowangying	AH	13	D5
Xiaowei	AH	13	C4
Xiaowutai Shan	HEB	4	D3
Xiaowu Zhan	HL	9	E6
Xiaoxi	AH	13	C4
Xiaoxi	JX	15	F3
Xiao Xi	ZJ	14	D4-5
Xiao Xian	AH	13	B3
Xiaoxiang Ling	SC	30	D4
Xiaoxiba	SC	30	C5
Xiaoxihe	AH	13	D4
Xiaoxingkai Hu	HL	39	B8
Xiaoxinqiao	JS	12	B3
(Xiaoxita) Yichang	HB	19	D4
Xiaoyan	HB	19	C4
Xiaoyangjie	YN	33	C5
Xiaoyangqi (Songling)	NM	9	B3
Xiaoyang Shan	ZJ	14	B7
Xiaoyaozhen	HEN	18	D6
(Xiaoyi) Gong Xian	HEN	18	C4
Xiaoyi	GX	24	E7
Xiaoyiji	AH	13	D4
Xiaoying	SD	10	B5
Xiaoyi	SX	5	D3
Xiaoyuan	HN	20	F6
Xiaoyuan	SC	31	C3
Xiaozhaiying	HEB	4	G2
Xiaozhan	TJ	3	D4
Xiaozhangzhuang	HEN	18	D5
Xiaozhi	SD	10	C3
Xiaozhongdian	YN	33	B3
Xiaozuo	FJ	16	F4
Xiapanshi	SX	5	D5
Xiapilin	GZ	32	E8
Xiaping	HB	19	D3
Xiapingyang	HEB	4	E2
Xiapu	JX	15	D2
Xiapu	HB	19	E7
Xiapu	FJ	16	D5
Xiaqi Dao	ZJ	14	C7
Xiaqiupu	SD	10	B6
Xiaruo	YN	33	B3
Xiashan	GZ	32	E4
Xiashankou	JX	15	D1
Xiashe	SX	5	B5
Xiashe	ZJ	12	D4
Xiashesi	HN	20	D5
Xiashi	GX	24	E4
(Xiashi) Haining	ZJ	14	B5
Xiashu	JS	11	D5
Xiashuitou	SX	5	B4
Xiasi	GZ	32	D6
Xiasi	GZ	32	E6
Xiasifen	GS	27	C6
Xiataizi	HEB	3	A5
Xiatang	HEN	18	D4
Xiatang	HN	20	E6
Xiatangji	AH	13	D4
Xiatianping	JL	8	E10
Xiatun	BJ	3	A2
Xiawa	NM	6	D7
Xiawan	GX	24	D8
Xiawei	SD	10	D5
Xiawentan	JX	15	F3
Xia Xian	SX	5	F3
Xiaxikou	FJ	16	D5
Xiaximian Shan	NM	38	B2
Xiaxinhe	JS	12	B3
Xiayang	FJ	16	E3
Xiayang	FJ	16	F2
Xiayang	FJ	16	D4
Xiaye	SX	5	E3
Xiayedi	XJ	29	B5
Xiaying	BJ	3	A4
Xiaying	TJ	3	B4
Xiaying	SD	10	B6
Xiaying	SN	25	F5
Xiaying	GX	24	D9

Name	Prov.	Map	Grid
(Xiayingpan) Luzhi Tequ	GZ	32	D4
Xiayi	HEN	18	C8
Xiayi Zhan	HEN	18	C8
Xiayukou	HN	20	B5
Xiayukou	SN	25	E6
Xiayunling	BJ	3	C2
Xiayuqiao	ZJ	14	B4
Xiazha	GD	23	I7
Xiazhai	FJ	16	F3
Xiazhai	SC	30	C3
Xiazhai	NX	26	E2
Xiazhang	SD	10	C3
Xiazhen	JX	15	C6
(Xiazhen) Weishan	SD	10	E4
Xiazhuang	SD	10	C6
Xiazhuang	SD	10	D5
(Xiazhuang) Linshu	SD	10	E5
Xiazhuang	HEN	18	E7
Xiazichang	GZ	32	C6
Xibaipo	HEB	4	E1
Xibali	HEB	3	A1
Xiban	SC	31	B4
Xibaoshui	HEB	4	E2
Xibaoyu	SX	5	C3
Xibaxa Qu	XZ	34	C5
Xibdê	SC	30	D2
Xibei	FJ	16	E3
Xibeicha	JL	8	D8
Xibeikou	HB	19	C4
Xibing	FJ	16	D5
Xibo He	NM	4	B6
Xibozi	BJ	3	B2
(Xibu) Dongshan	FJ	16	G3
Xibu	AH	13	E5
Xichahe	SN	25	G3
Xichang	GX	24	F6
Xichang	SC	30	E4
Xichang	SC	30	E4
Xiche	HN	20	B2
Xicheng	HEN	18	B7
(Xicheng) Yangyuan	HEB	4	C2
Xicheng	HL	9	C3
Xicheng Shan	SX	5	F4
Xichong	SC	30	C5
Xichou	YN	33	D6
Xi Chuan	GS	25	C2-D3
Xi Chuan	GS	26	D4
Xi Chuan	HEN	18	D3
Xichuan (Shangji)	HEN	18	D3
Xicun	JX	15	D2
Xidamiao	HEB	3	A5
Xidatan	NX	26	B3
Xide (Ganxiangying)	SC	30	D4
Xidian	ZJ	14	C6
Xiditou	TJ	3	C4
Xidongting Shan	JS	11	E6
Xidoupu	NM	6	D4
(Xidu) Hengyang	HN	20	E5
Xie Chi	SX	5	G3
(Xiedian) Wanrong	SX	5	F2
Xiefang	JX	15	F3
Xiegan	SD	10	D5
Xiehe	SC	31	C3
Xiehe	GZ	32	C5
Xie He	AH	13	C4
Xieji	HEN	18	C7
Xiejia	JL	8	E6
Xiejiachang	SC	31	B1
Xiejiaji	JS	11	D5
(Xiejiaji) Qingyun	SD	10	B4
Xiejiaqiao	ZJ	12	E4
Xiejiatan	JX	15	B4
Xiemachang	SC	31	C5
Xiemahe	HB	19	C4
Xiemating	SD	10	D4
Xiepu	ZJ	14	B6
Xieqiao	JS	11	D6
Xieqiao	ZJ	14	B5
Xieqiao	AH	13	D3
Xi'er	YN	33	C5
Xie Shan	JX	15	B4
Xie Shui	HN	20	B3-4
Xietan	JX	15	B3
Xietan	FJ	16	C5
Xietang	ZJ	12	E5
Xietang	ZJ	14	C4
Xietun	LN	7	C5
Xietun	LN	7	E5
Xiexian	SX	5	G2
Xieyang Dao	GX	24	G7
Xiezhuang	HEN	18	C5
Xifangcheng	SX	5	B5
Xifei He	AH	13	D3
Xifeng	HL	9	D7
Xifengkou	HEB	4	C6
Xifengling	HEN	18	C6
Xifeng	LN	7	B8
Xifeng (Yongjing)	GZ	32	C5
Xifeng	GS	27	E8
Xifo	LN	7	C6
Xifu	SD	10	C7
Xifuying	BJ	3	A3
(Xigang) Helan	NX	26	B3
Xigang	SD	10	E4
Xigangzi	HL	9	C4
Xi Ganqu	NX	26	B3
Xigazê	XZ	34	C4
Xi Golog	SC	30	C3
Xigong	GD	23	I8
Xigongyi	GS	26	E1
Xigou	SX	5	D5
Xigoucun	SX	5	E5
Xihan Shui	GS	27	F7
Xihaoping	HB	19	C3
Xihe	SD	10	C4
Xihe	SD	10	C7
Xihe	AH	13	F5
Xihe	SC	30	D4
Xihe	HB	19	C6
Xihe	SN	25	H4
Xi He	NM	6	D2
Xi He	LN	7	C5
Xi He	AH	13	G3
Xi He	JX	15	B4
Xi He	NX	26	D2
Xi He	SC	30	C5
Xi He	SC	30	C6
Xi He	SC	31	B1
Xihekou	SN	25	D5
Xihe	GS	27	E7
Xiheying	HEB	4	D2
Xihou	FJ	16	D3
Xihu	JX	15	B5
Xihu	TW	17	C3
Xi Hu (Lk.)	ZJ	12	E3
Xi Hu	HB	19	D7
(Xihuachi) Heshui	GS	27	E9
Xihuangcun	HEB	4	F2
Xihua	HEN	18	D6
Xiji	BJ	3	B4
Xiji	HL	9	D4
Xiji	SD	10	E4
Xijiang	JX	15	F3
Xi Jiang (Riv.)	GD	21	B3-4
Xijiaozi	SX	5	D3
Xijin	FJ	16	C4
Xijin	GX	24	E7
Xijing	SX	5	E5
Xijin Sk.	GX	24	E7
Xijir	QH	28	C2
Xijir Ulan Hu	QH	28	C2
Xijishui	GS	27	D6
Xijitan	NX	26	E2
Xiji	NX	26	E2
Xiji Yu	TW	17	C2
Xikeng	HB	19	E7
Xikeng	GD	21	B5
Xikou	NM	6	C7
Xikou	AH	13	F5
Xikou	AH	13	G5
Xikou	ZJ	14	B4
Xikou	ZJ	14	D3
Xikou	ZJ	14	D4
Xikou	JX	15	B2
Xikou	FJ	16	D2
Xikou	HN	20	B3
Xikou	HN	20	E2
Xikou	SC	31	B5

Name	Prov	No	Grid
Xikou	SC	31	B5
Xikouxu	FJ	16	E3
Xikuangshan	HN	20	D4
Xil	NM	6	D5
Xilai	SC	31	B1
Xilaizhen	JS	12	A4
Xilang He	JL	8	C8
Xilang He	JL	39	B5
Xilaotou Shan	NM	37	C8
Xileizi	HEB	3	C2
Xiliang Shan	AH	12	B1
Xiliangzi	QH	28	A3
Xiliao He (Riv.)	NM	6	D7
(Xiligou) Ulan	QH	28	B6
Xilin	HL	9	D5
Xiling	GD	23	G7
Xiling	GX	24	C8
Xilingjing	SX	5	C4
Xilingsi	HEN	18	C6
Xiling Xia	HB	19	D3
Xilinhe	HL	9	E6
Xilinhot	NM	6	D6
(Xilinji) Mohe	HL	9	A2
Xilin (Bada)	GX	24	C3
Xiliu	HEB	4	F3
Xiliuhe	HB	19	D6
Xiliushui	BJ	3	B3
Xiliyu	SN	25	C6
Xilong	SC	30	D4
Xiluga He	NM	4	A6
Xiluo	TW	17	C3
Ximafan	HB	19	D8
Ximahe	GZ	32	D6
Ximakou	HB	19	D6
Ximalin	HEB	4	C2
Ximayi Dao	LN	7	E5
Ximei	SC	31	B4
Ximeng Vazu Zizhixian	YN	33	D3
Ximiao	NM	6	D2
Ximing	SX	5	D4
Ximo	SX	5	G2
Ximucheng	LN	7	D6
(Xinan) Sanshui	GD	23	H6
Xinan	FJ	16	D5
Xinan	FJ	16	E3
Xin'an	SD	10	C7
Xin'an	HEB	4	D4
Xin'an	JL	8	C8
Xin'an	JL	8	D6
Xin'an	HL	9	C3
Xin'an	HL	9	E5
Xin'an	JS	11	E6
Xin'an	JS	12	B3
Xin'an	JX	15	E4
Xin'an	HN	20	B4

Name	Prov	No	Grid
Xin'an	GD	21	B5
Xinanban	FJ	16	F3
Xin'ancun	HEB	5	C6
Xin'andian	HEN	18	E6
Xin'andu	AH	13	F3
Xinanhe	HEB	4	E3
Xin'anji	HEN	18	D7
Xin'anjiang	ZJ	14	C4
Xin'an Jiang	AH	13	G5
	ZJ	14	C3
Xin'anjiang Sk.	ZJ	14	C3
Xin'ansuo	YN	33	D5
Xin'an	HEN	18	C4
Xin'anzhen	TJ	3	C4
(Xin'anzhen) Anxin	HEB	3	D2
Xin'anzhen	NM	6	D4
Xin'anzhen	JL	8	C4
(Xin'anzhen) Xinyi	JS	11	B4
(Xin'anzhen) Guannan	JS	11	B5
Xin'anzhuang	SD	10	B6
Xinba	JS	11	B5
Xinba	JS	12	A3
Xinbao'an	HEB	4	C3
Xin Barag Youqi (Altan Emel)	NM	6	B6
Xin Barag Zuoqi (Amgalang)	NM	6	B6
Xinbian He	AH	13	C4-5
Xinbin	GX	24	D6
Xinbin	LN	7	C9
Xinbo	HEB	4	A5
Xinbu	HEB	4	C2
Xinbu	TW	17	B4
Xincai	HEN	18	E6
Xincang	ZJ	12	D5
Xincang	ZJ	14	B5
Xinchang	JX	15	B5
Xinchang	HB	19	E5
Xinchang	HN	20	E2
Xinchang	SH	11	E7
Xinchang	SC	31	C2
Xinchang	SC	31	C6
Xinchang	GD	23	I6
Xinchang	ZJ	14	C5
Xincheng	TJ	3	D5
Xincheng	HEB	4	F3
Xincheng	SX	5	D4
Xincheng	HL	9	D6
Xincheng	HL	9	E6
Xincheng	JS	11	D5
Xincheng	JX	15	E2
Xincheng	JX	15	F2
Xincheng	TW	17	B4
Xincheng	HB	19	B6
Xincheng	HB	19	C7
Xincheng	NX	26	B3

Name	Prov	No	Grid
Xincheng	GS	26	E3
Xincheng	GS	27	C5
Xincheng	GS	27	E6
Xincheng	ZJ	14	B5
Xinchengbu	SN	25	C4
Xinchengpu	HEB	4	E2
Xincheng	GX	24	C6
Xincheng (Gaobeidian)	HEB	4	D3
Xinchengzi	BJ	3	A4
Xinchengzi,	LN	7	B7
Xinchengzi	XJ	29	B5
Xinchepaizi	SX	5	C3
Xincun	HI	21	D2
Xincun	GX	24	C7
Xincun	SC	31	C5
(Xincun) Dongchuan	YN	33	B5
Xincunji	AH	13	D2
Xindai	ZJ	14	B6
(Xindeng) Chengyang	ZJ	14	C4
Xindi	GX	24	D9
(Xindi) Honghu	HB	19	E6
Xindian	HEB	4	F2
Xindian	SD	10	B3
Xindian	SD	10	B4
Xindian	SD	10	B5
Xindian	SD	10	C5
Xindian	HL	9	E4
Xindian	YN	33	C5
Xindian	SX	5	E4
Xindian	JS	11	B4
Xindian	JX	15	D2
Xindian	FJ	16	F4
Xindian	TW	17	B4
Xindian	HEN	18	D4
Xindian	HEN	18	E4
Xindian	HB	19	E6
Xindian	GZ	32	D5
Xindianbu	AH	13	D3
Xindianping	HN	20	D2
Xindianzi	HEB	4	C6
Xindianzi	SC	30	C7
Xindongzhang	FJ	16	E5
Xindu	GX	24	C9
Xinduqiao	SC	30	C3
Xindu	SC	30	C5
Xin'ecun	HL	9	C4
Xinfan	SC	30	C5
Xinfeng	JS	12	A3
Xinfeng	JS	11	C6
Xinfeng	JS	11	D5
Xinfeng	AH	12	C1
Xinfeng	ZJ	14	B5
Xinfeng	JX	15	D4
Xinfeng	JX	15	D4
Xinfeng	GD	21	A6
Xinfeng	GX	24	E8
Xinfeng Jiang	GD	21	A5-B5
Xinfengjiang Sk.	GD	21	B5

Xinjin	LN	7	E5	Xinqiao	HN	20	D5	Xinxing	HI	21	D2
(Pulandian)				Xinqiao	GX	24	E8	Xinxing	HI	21	D3
Xinjin	SC	30	C4	Xinqiao	SC	31	C5	Xinxingchang	SC	31	A2
Xinjuntun	HEB	4	D5	Xinqiao He	FJ	16	E3	Xinxingji	AH	13	C3
Xinkaigang	JS	12	B5	Xinqiaozhen	SC	31	C1	Xinxing Jiang	GD	21	B4
Xinkaihe	LN	7	C6	Xinqing	HL	9	C5	Xinxing	GD	21	B4
Xinkai He	NM	8	C3	Xinqiu	LN	7	B5	Xinxu	FJ	16	F3
Xinkaitang	HN	20	B6	Xinqizhou	JX	15	C3	Xinxu	GD	23	H6
Xinkangzhen	HN	20	C5	Xinquan	FJ	16	E2	Xinxu	GD	23	H8
Xinkou	SX	5	C4	Xinshao	HN	20	D4	Xinxu	GX	24	B9
Xinkou	FJ	16	D3	(Niangxi)				Xinxu	GX	24	C7
Xinleitou	HEB	4	F3	Xinsheng	SC	31	A3	Xinxu	GX	24	C8
Xinle	HEB	4	E2	Xinsheng	JL	8	E7	Xinxu	GX	24	D4
(Dongchangshou)				Xinshengdian	SD	10	B3	Xinxu	GX	24	E8
Xinli	JL	8	B3	Xinshenggang	JS	12	A4	Xinxu	GX	24	E9
Xinli	JL	8	C7	Xinshi	JS	11	D6				
Xinliao Dao	GD	21	C3	Xinshi	ZJ	14	B5	Xinyang Gang	JS	11	C6
Xinlin	HL	9	B3	Xinshi	HN	20	C6	Xinyanggang Kou	JS	11	C6
Xinlincun	HL	9	D7	Xinshi	HN	20	D6	Xinyang	HEN	18	E6
Xinlipu	SC	31	B6	Xinshi	HN	20	E5	Xinyang	HEN	18	E6
Xinlitun	LN	7	C6	Xinshi	SC	31	A2	(Pingqiao)			
Xinlitun	HL	9	B4	(Xinshiba) Ganluo	SC	30	D4	Xinyangzhen	GS	27	E7
Xinliu	GZ	32	D7					Xinye	HEN	18	E4
Xinlizhuang	HEB	3	C3	Xinshicun	JS	11	B6	Xinyi	SX	5	D3
Xinlong	FJ	16	E5	Xinshizhen	SC	30	D4	Xinyi He	JS	11	B5
Xinlong	SC	30	C3	Xinshu He	SD	10	E5	Xinying	BJ	3	B3
Xinluhai	SC	30	C2		JS	11	B4-5	Xinying	HI	21	D2
Xinluwan	ZJ	14	D4	Xinshui He	SX	5	E2	Xinying	JX	15	C5
Xinmaqiao	AH	13	C4	Xinsi	GS	27	E7	(Xinying) Tainan	TW	17	C3
Xinmiao	JL	8	B5	Xinsui He	JS	11	C3-4				
Xinmiaozhen	SC	31	C5		AH	13	C5	Xinying	NX	26	D2
Xinmin	HL	9	C4	Xintai	SD	10	D4	Xinyi	GD	21	B3
Xinmin	SC	30	D4	Xintaizi	LN	7	B7	Xinyi	JS	11	B4
Xinmincun	NM	7	B4	Xintang	ZJ	12	C3	(Xin'anzhen)			
Xinminjie	SN	25	E6	Xintang	HB	19	D2	(Xinyuan) Tianjun	QH	28	B6
Xinminpu	GS	27	C3	Xintang	GD	21	B4				
Xinmintun	LN	7	C7	Xintankou	HB	19	D6	Xinyuan (Künes)	XJ	29	C4
Xinmin	LN	7	C6	Xintanpu	HB	19	E7				
Xinminzhen	SN	25	A6	Xintian	JX	15	D2	Xinyu	JX	15	D2
Xinminzhen	SC	31	B6	Xintian	JX	15	F3	Xinzao	GD	23	H7
Xinning	HN	20	E3	Xintianpu	HN	20	D4	Xinzhai	SD	10	C4
Xinpi	TW	17	D3	Xintian	HN	20	F5	Xinzhai	SD	10	C5
Xinpingbu	SX	5	A6	Xintongyang Yunhe	JS	11	D5-6	Xinzhai	HEB	4	D6
Xinping Yizu Daizu	YN	33	C4	Xintunchuan	GS	27	D6	Xinzhan	JL	8	C6
Zizhixian				Xinwen	SD	10	D4	Xinzhan	JL	8	D8
(Xinpu) Lianyungang	JS	11	B5	(Suncun)				Xinzhan	HL	9	E3
				Xinwo	ZJ	14	D5	Xinzhan	HEN	18	D6
Xinpu	SN	25	G2	Xinxian	HEB	4	F5	Xinzhan	GZ	32	B5
Xinpu	SN	25	G3	Xinxian	FJ	16	E5	Xinzhang	HEB	3	D3
Xinpu	NX	26	C2	Xinzhou	SX	5	C4	Xinzhangfang	NM	6	B7
Xinpuyan	ZJ	14	B6	Xin Xian	HEN	18	F6	Xinzhangzi	HEB	4	C5
Xinqiang	HN	20	B6					Xinzhelin	JX	15	B3
Xinqianhu	SD	10	B5					Xinzhen	SD	10	B5
Xinqiao	HEB	4	E3	Xinxiang	HEN	18	B5	Xinzhen	HEB	4	D4
Xinqiao	JS	12	B2	Xinxiang	HEN	18	B5	Xinzhen	HEN	18	B6
Xinqiao	FJ	16	C3	Xinxing	SD	10	C6	Xinzhen	SC	30	C6
Xinqiao	FJ	16	D3	Xinxing	JL	8	C3	Xinzheng	HEN	18	C5
Xinqiao	FJ	16	E2	Xinxing	JL	8	D10	Xinzhi	SX	5	E3
Xinqiao	FJ	16	E3	Xinxing	JL	8	E9	Xinzhi	JX	15	D2
Xinqiao	HEN	18	D6	Xinxing	JS	11	C6	Xinzhou	HI	21	D2

Name	Loc	Map	Grid
Xinzhou	GZ	32	C6
Xinzhou	HN	20	B4
Xinzhou	GD	21	C4
(Xinzhou) Dachang	GX	24	C5
Xinzhou	GZ	32	B6
Xinzhou	HB	19	D7
Xinzhuang	SD	10	B7
Xinzhuang	SD	10	C4
Xinzhuang[xi]	SD	10	D4
Xinzhuang	JS	11	E6
Xinzhuang[dong]	SD	10	D4
Xinzhuang	TW	17	A4
Xinzhuangji	NX	26	C3
Xinzhuangzi	HEB	4	C3
Xinzhuangzi	LN	7	C5
Xinzhuangzi	NX	26	C4
Xinzhu (Hsinchu)	TW	17	B3
Xinzhuzhen	SN	25	F5
Xinzuotang	GD	21	B5
Xiongcun	GX	24	B8
Xiongcun	JX	15	D5
Xiongdi Yu	FJ	16	G3
Xiong'er Shan	HEB	4	C2
Xiong'er Shan	HEN	18	D3-C3
Xiong'erzhai	BJ	3	B4
Xiongkou	HB	19	D5
Xionglu	AH	13	F5
Xiong Xian	HEB	4	E4
Xiongyuecheng	LN	7	D6
Xiongzhai	HEN	18	E6
Xipan	SX	5	C5
Xi Paozi	LN	7	B7
Xiping	SC	31	A3
(Xiping) Datong	SX	5	A5
Xiping	SX	5	F4
Xiping	FJ	16	E3
Xiping	HEN	18	D3
Xiping	ZJ	14	D4
Xiping	HEN	18	D5
Xipucun	HEB	4	C6
Xipuzhen	SC	31	B2
Xiqiao	JS	11	C5
Xiqiao Shan	GD	23	H6
Xiqin	FJ	16	D4
Xiqing Shan	GS	27	E5-6
	QH	28	C7
Xiqu	GS	27	C6
Xiquan	SX	5	D3
Xiquan Dao	FJ	16	D5
Xiquanjie	AH	13	D4
Xirongzhen	SC	31	D1
Xisa	YN	33	D4
Xisanshilidian	AH	13	D4
Xisantai	LN	7	E5
Xishan	JX	15	C3
Xi Shan	BJ	3	B2
Xishanbei	HEB	4	D3
Xishanqiao	JS	12	B1
(Xishanzui) Urad Qianqi	NM	6	D4
Xisha Qundao (Apg.)	HI	22	B2-3
Xishenba	SN	25	H2
Xishiqiao	JS	11	E6
Xishu	HEB	4	G1
(Xishuanghe) Kenli	SD	10	B5
Xi Shui	HB	19	D8
Xishui (Donghuang)	GZ	32	B5
Xishui	HB	19	D8
Xisipo	AH	13	C4
Xisipu	AH	13	C3
Xi Taijnar Hu	QH	28	B3
Xitan	FJ	16	G3
Xitang	ZJ	14	B5
Xitangchi	AH	13	E3
Xitiangezhuang	BJ	3	B3
Xitianmu Shan	ZJ	14	B4
Xitiao Xi	ZJ	14	B4
Xitieshan	QH	28	B4
Xiting	JS	11	D7
Xitou	JX	15	C3
Xitou	GD	21	C3
Xituozhen	SC	30	C7
Xiucaibu	JX	15	D3
Xiuguluan Shan	TW	17	C4
Xiuguluan Xi	TW	17	C4
Xi Ujimqin Qi (Bayan Ul Hot)	NM	6	C6
Xiuning	AH	13	G5
Xiuren	GX	24	C8
Xiu Shan	ZJ	14	B7
Xiushan	SC	30	D7
Xiushui	JL	8	C7
Xiu Shui	JX	15	B3
Xiushuihaizi	GZ	32	D2
Xiushui He	LN	7	B7
Xiushuihezi	LN	7	B7
Xiushui	JX	15	B2
Xiuwen	GZ	32	D5
Xiuwu	HEN	18	B5
Xiuxikou	HN	20	D3
Xiuyan	LN	7	D7
Xiuying	HI	21	C3
Xiwanbu	HEB	4	C2
Xiwangji	AH	13	D4
(Xiwanzi) Chongli	HEB	4	C3
Xiwei Tan	HI	22	D2
Xiwengzhuang	BJ	3	A3
Xiwu	ZJ	14	C6
Xiwu	QH	28	D5
Xiwujieqiao	JS	12	B4
Xixabangma Feng	XZ	34	C3
Xixi	FJ	16	D4
Xixi	HN	20	D3
Xi Xi	FJ	16	F3
Xi Xi	FJ	16	E4
Xi Xian	HEN	18	E6
Xi Xian	SX	5	E2
Xixiang	JX	15	C2
Xixiang	HEN	18	B4
Xixiang	GD	23	H8
Xixiang	SN	25	H3
Xixiaozhao	NM	6	F10
Xixiashu	JS	11	E5
Xixia	HEN	18	D3
Xixiaying	HEB	3	B5
Xixi He	SC	30	E4
Xixing	ZJ	14	B5
Xixing	SC	31	A4
Xiyan	SX	5	C5
Xiyan	HEB	3	D2
Xiyan	GX	24	D6
Xiyang	JL	8	D7
Xiyang	FJ	16	D4
Xiyang	FJ	16	E3
Xiyang Dao	FJ	16	D6
Xiyangji	AH	13	C3
Xiyang Jiang	GX	24	C3
	YN	33	C6
Xiyangjie	YN	33	D6
Xiyang	SX	5	D5
Xiyanshi	HN	20	E3
Xiyincun	HEB	4	F2
Xiyin Dao	FJ	16	D6
Xiying	SX	5	E5
Xiying	SD	10	C4
Xiyou	SD	10	B6
Xiyu	TW	17	C2
Xiyuan	HEB	3	D1
Xize	ZJ	14	C6
Xizhai	HB	19	E4
Xizhai	SX	5	D5
Xizhangdian	HB	19	C7
Xizhi Jiang	GD	21	B5
Xizhong Dao	LN	7	E5
Xizhou	ZJ	14	C6
Xizhou Shan	SX	5	C4-5
Xizhuangzhen	SN	25	E6
Xizi	NM	4	B7
Xobando	XZ	34	C5
Xoka	XZ	34	C5
Xorkol	XJ	29	D6
Xuanzhou	AH	13	F5
Xuande Qundao	HI	22	B3
Xuan'en	HB	19	D2
Xuanfeng	JX	15	D2
Xuangang	SX	5	C4
Xuanhan	SC	30	C6
Xuanhepu	NX	26	C2
Xuanhuadian	HB	19	C7
Xuanhua	HEB	4	C3
Xuanhui He	HEB	4	F4-5

Name	Prov	Map	Grid
Xuanjiabao	JS	11	D5
Xuantan	SC	31	D4
Xuanwei	GZ	32	D6
Xuanwei	YN	33	B6
Xuanwu	HEN	18	D7
Xuanzhou	HN	20	D5
Xuanzhuang	HEB	3	C5
Xubingshui	NX	26	C3
Xubu	SX	5	A5
Xuchang	SC	31	D2
Xuchang	HEN	18	C5
Xuchang	HEN	18	C5
Xucheng	SD	10	D3
Xucun	AH	13	F5
Xucun	ZJ	14	B5
Xucun	JX	15	B5
Xudai	ZJ	12	D5
Xudidong	GX	24	E8
Xuebu	JS	11	E5
Xuecheng(Lincheng)	SD	10	E4
Xuecheng	SC	30	C4
Xuedian	HEN	18	C5
Xuedian	HEN	18	C5
Xuedou Shan	ZJ	14	C6
Xuefang	SD	10	C7
Xuefeng Shan	HN	20	D3-C4
Xueguan	SX	5	E2
Xuehu	HEN	18	C8
Xuehua Shan	SX	5	G2
Xuejia	LN	7	C5
Xuejiadao	SD	10	D7
Xuejiaping	HB	19	C3
Xuejiaying	HEN	18	C2
Xuekengkou	AH	13	G5
Xuekou	ZJ	14	E5
Xuekulun	SX	5	B4
Xueping	HB	19	C4
Xue Shan	TW	17	B4
Xueshuiwen	HL	9	C5
Xueyanqiao	JS	11	E6
Xueyezhuang	SD	10	C4
Xuezhen	AH	13	E5
Xuezhuang	SD	10	D5
(Xugezhuang) Fengnan	HEB	4	D6
Xugong Dao	ZJ	12	D7
Xugongzhuang	HEN	18	C6
Xugou	SX	5	D4
Xugou	JS	11	B5
Xugu	HB	19	D7
Xuguanzhen	JS	11	E6
Xugui	QH	28	C4
(Xuguit) Yakeshi	NM	6	B7
Xuhe	AH	13	F3
Xuhui Qu	SN	25	G3
Xuji	AH	13	E3
Xujia	SC	31	A5
Xujiaba	GZ	32	C7
Xujiabu	JX	15	B4
Xujiadacun	SD	10	D6
Xujiadian	SD	10	B7
Xujiadong	HN	20	F6
Xujiadu	JX	15	C2
Xujiadu	YN	33	C5
Xujiamiao	SN	25	G3
Xu Jiang	JX	15	D4
Xujiaping	SN	25	G2
Xujiaqiao	AH	13	F3
Xujiataozi	NX	26	D2
Xujiatun	LN	7	D6
Xujiaweizi	HL	9	E3
Xukou	JS	12	C4
Xuling	AH	13	F3
Xuliu	JS	11	C4
(Xulun Hobot Qagan) Zhengxiangbai Qi	NM	6	D5
(Xulun Hoh) Zhenglan Qi	NM	6	D6
Xümatang	QH	28	D5
Xumeng	SD	10	D6
Xundian Huizu Yizu Zizhixian	YN	33	C5
Xungru	XZ	34	C3
Xunhe	HL	9	C5
Xun He	SN	25	G5
Xun He	HL	9	C4-5
Xunhua Salarzu Zizhixian	QH	28	C8
Xun Jiang	GX	24	B8
Xun Jiang (Riv.)	GX	24	D8
Xunjiansi	HB	19	C4
Xunjiansi	HB	19	C6
Xunjiansi	SN	25	F6
Xunjiansi	YN	33	D5
Xunjiansi	SN	25	C5
Xunjiaya	HB	19	C4
Xunke (Qike)	HL	9	C5
Xunkou	JX	15	D5
Xunle	GX	24	B6
Xunmukou	HEN	18	C6
Xunqiao	ZJ	14	D6
Xunshansuo	SD	10	B9
Xunwu Shui	JX	15	G3
	GD	21	A5
Xunwu	JX	15	G3
Xun Xian	HEN	18	B6
Xunyangba	SN	25	G4
Xunyang	SN	25	H5
Xunyi	SN	25	E4
Xunzhen	SX	5	B3
Xupingcun	NX	26	D2
Xupu	JS	11	E6
Xupu	HN	20	D3
Xur	QH	28	C4
Xusanwan	GS	27	C4
Xushe	JS	11	E5
Xushi	JS	11	E6
Xushi	FJ	16	C4
Xushui	HEN	18	C5
Xu Shui	HN	20	D3
Xushui He	SN	25	G3
Xushui	HEB	4	D3
Xutang	JS	11	B4
Xuwan	JX	15	D4
Xuwei	JS	11	B5
Xuwen	GD	21	C3
Xuyi	JS	11	C4
Xuyong (Yongning)	SC	30	D5
Xuzhen	HEN	18	B7
Xuzhou	JS	11	B3
Xuzhuang	SD	10	D4

Y

Name	Prov	Map	Grid
Ya'an	SC	30	D4
Yabrai Shan	NM	6	E2-D2
Yabrai Yanchang	NM	6	E2
Yabuli	HL	9	E5
(Yacha) Baisha	GD	21	D2
Yachang	GX	24	C4
Yacheng	FJ	16	D6
Yacheng	HI	21	D2
Yachi He	GZ	32	C5
Yadong	NM	6	B7
Yadong(Chomo)	XZ	34	D4
Ya'erya	SX	5	B4
Yafan	ZJ	14	C4
Yageying	HEB	4	F2
Yag Qu	QH	28	C4-D4
Yagra	XZ	34	C2
Yagradagzê Shan	QH	28	C4
Yahe	HL	9	E6
Yahongqiao	HEB	4	D5
Yajiang	SC	31	C6
Yajiangqiao	HN	20	D6
Yajiang	SC	30	C3
Yakeshi	NM	6	B7
Yakou	FJ	16	F4
Yaliji	HEB	4	G2
Yalong Jiang (Riv.)	SC	30	E3
Yalu	NM	6	B7
Yalu He	NM	6	C7
	HL	9	D2
Yalu Jiang	LN	7	D8
	JL	8	F7
Yalujiang Kou	LN	7	E8
Yamat	LN	7	C5
Ya Men	GD	21	B4
Yamenying	NM	8	D3
Yamenzhuang	QH	28	B7
Yamzho Yumco	XZ	34	C4
Yan'an	SN	25	D5

Yaocun	HEB	4	D3	(Yarkant) Shache	XJ	29	D3	Yeyungou	XJ	29	C5
Yaocun	SD	10	D3					Yezhuang	SX	5	C4
Yaocun	AH	13	F6	Yarkant He (Riv.)	XJ	29	D3-C4	Yi'an	SX	5	D3
Yaocun	HEN	18	A5	Yarlung Zangbo (Riv.)	XZ	34	C5	Yi'an	HL	9	D3
Yaodian	SN	25	D5	Jiang				Yiban	FJ	16	E4
Yaodian	GS	27	E8	Yarwa	SC	30	C2	Yibang	YN	33	D4
(Yaodu) Dongzhi	AH	13	F4	Yarzhong	XZ	34	C6	(Yibei) Minglun	GX	24	B6
Yaodu	SC	30	B5	Yashan	AH	13	F5				
Yaofupu	NX	26	B3	Yatan	AH	13	F3	Yibin	SC	30	D5
Yaogangxian	HN	20	F6	(Yatou) Rongcheng	SD	10	B9	Yibin	SC	30	D5
Yaogezhuang	SD	10	C6					Yibug Caka	XZ	34	B3
Yaogou	SD	10	C5	Yatunbu	HN	20	E2	Yibutan	SC	31	D2
Yaogou	AH	13	E4	Yawangkou	SD	10	C4				
Yaogou	NM	5	B3	Yawatongguzlangar	XJ	29	D4	Yichang Jiang	GX	24	D8-E9
Yaogu	GD	21	B4	Yaxi	GZ	32	C5	Yichang	HB	19	D4
Yaoguan	YN	33	C3					Yichang	HB	19	D4
Yaoguantun	HEB	4	E4	Yaxigang	JS	11	E5	(Xiaoxita)			
Yaojiaba	HN	20	D6	Yaxing	HI	21	D2	Yicheng	AH	13	E4
Yaojiadianzi	SD	10	D5	Yayao	GD	23	H7	Yicheng (Yixian)	SD	10	E4
Yaojiaji	HB	19	C7	Yayuan	JL	8	F7	Yicheng	HB	19	C5
Yao Jiang	ZJ	12	E5	Yazhou	GZ	32	E6	Yicheng	SX	5	F3
Yaojiaqiao	JS	12	A3	Yazhou	JS	11	D6	Yichexun	YN	33	B5
Yaojiashao	GZ	32	D5	Yazhuang	SD	10	C5	Yichuan	HEN	18	C4
Yaojie	GS	27	D6	Yazi	SD	10	B8	Yichuan	SN	25	D6
Yaokouji	AH	13	D3	Yazigang	HN	20	C5				
Yaoli	JX	15	B5	(Yebaishou) Jianping	LN	7	C3	Yichun	HL	9	D5
Yaolimiao	AH	13	E3								
Yaolin	JL	8	F7	Yecaowan	HEB	4	F2	Yichun	JX	15	D2
Yaoling	GD	21	A4	Yecheng (Kargilik)	XJ	29	D3	Yichun	JX	15	D2
Yaolingtou	AH	13	E3	Yellow Sea	SD	10	D7-9	Yidan	JL	8	D6
Yaolugou	LN	7	D3	Yecun	SN	25	G6	Yidao	SD	10	B7
Yaoluoping	AH	13	E3	Yehe	JL	8	E5	Yidian	SN	25	F3
Yaopi	HN	20	E6	Ye He	HEB	4	E2	Yidie	SX	5	D2
Yaopu	GZ	32	D4	Yeji	AH	13	E2	Yidouquan	SX	5	B6
Yaopu	LN	7	B6	Yejia	ZJ	12	E5	Yidun	SC	30	C2
Yaopu	AH	13	D5	Yejiaping	SN	25	G4	Yidushui	HN	20	E4
Yaoquanzi	GS	27	C3	Yejigang	HEN	18	C7	(Yidu) Zhicheng	HB	19	D4
Yao Sha	JS	11	C6	Yejituo	HEB	4	D6	(Yidu) Qingzhou	SD	10	C5
Yaoshan	NX	26	D3	Yeliguan	GS	27	E6	Yifeng	JX	15	C2
Yaoshang	HEB	4	C5	Yemachuan	GZ	32	C3	Yigang	GS	26	E2
Yaoshi	HN	20	D2	Yema Nanshan	GS	27	C2-3	Yigaolou	ZJ	12	D4
Yaotan	SC	31	C5	Yemaotai	LN	7	B6	Yigou	HEN	18	B6
Yaotou	SX	5	C2	Yema Shan	GS	27	C2-3	Yihe	SN	25	C6
Yaotou	SX	5	E2	Yematan	QH	28	B6	Yi He	HEN	18	C4
Yaotou	JX	15	E2	Yematan	QH	28	C6	Yi He	SD	10	D5
Yaotun	HL	9	C4	Yematu	JL	8	B2		JS	11	B4
Yaowan	JS	11	B4	Yengi'erik	XJ	29	D3	Yihezhuang	SD	10	B5
Yao Xian	SN	25	F5	Yengisar	XJ	29	C5	Yihuang Shui	JX	15	D4
Yaoxiaoling	HL	9	C4	Yengisar	XJ	29	D3	Yihuang	JX	15	D4
Yaoxiaozhuang	AH	13	E3	Yengisu	XJ	29	C5	Yijialing	HB	19	D5
Yaoxu	JX	15	D3	Yeniugou	QH	28	A6	Yijiangshan Dao	ZJ	14	D6
Yaozhai	GX	24	C5	Yeniugou	QH	28	C5	Yijiangzhen	AH	13	F5
Yaozhan	HL	9	B3	Yeping	JX	15	F4	Yijianpu	JL	8	C6
Yaozhen	SN	25	B6	Yesanguan	HB	19	D3	Yijiawan	HN	20	D6
Yaozitou	SX	5	B4	Yeshengpu	NX	26	B3	Yijing	SX	5	B3-4
(Yaqian) Yuexi	AH	13	F3	Ye Xian	HEN	18	D5	Yijinqiao	AH	13	F4
Yaqian	JX	15	C4	Ye Xian	SD	10	B6	Yijun	SN	25	E5
Yaqian	JX	15	E2	Yexie	SH	12	C5	Yiketian	NM	26	A2
Yaqueling	HB	19	D4	Yeyik	XJ	29	D4	Yikou [bei]	FJ	16	D3
Yaqueshui	HB	19	D2	Yeyuan	SD	10	C5	Yikou [nan]	FJ	16	D3

Yixi	GD	16	G2	Yongfengqu	XJ	29	C5	Yongren	YN	33	B4
(Yixian) Yicheng	SD	10	E4	Yongfeng	JX	15	D3	Yongshan	JX	15	B5
Yi Xian	LN	7	C5	Yongfu	FJ	16	E3	Yongshan	YN	33	A5
Yi Xian	HEB	4	D3	Yongfu	GX	24	C7	Yongshanzhuang	NM	6	F10
Yi Xian	AH	13	G4	Yonghan	GD	21	B4	Yongsheng	YN	33	B4
Yixiang	YN	33	D4	Yonghe	HEB	4	C6	Yongshou	SN	25	F4
Yixiken	HL	9	A3	Yonghe	HN	20	C6	(Jianjun)			
Yixingbu	TJ	3	C4	Yonghe	GD	21	A4	Yongshu Jiao	HI	22	D3
Yixing	JS	11	E5	Yongheguan	SX	5	E2	Yongshun	HN	20	B2
Yixu	FJ	16	D5	Yonghe	SX	5	E2	(Lingxi)			
Yixun He	HEB	4	B5	Yongjia	SC	31	C4	Yongsui	GX	24	A9
Yiyang	SD	10	C3	Yongjiabu	SX	5	A6	Yongtai	JX	15	D3
				Yong Jiang	ZJ	14	C6	Yongtai	SC	31	A2
Yiyang	HN	20	C5	Yong Jiang	GX	24	E6	Yongtai	FJ	16	E4
Yiyang	JX	15	C5	Yongjia	ZJ	14	D5	Yongxin	SC	31	D5
Yiyang	HEN	18	C4	Yongjiazhen	AH	12	C1	Yongxin	JL	8	E10
Yiyang	HN	20	C5	(Yongjing) Xifeng	GZ	32	C5	Yongxing	NM	6	F10
Yiyuankou	HEB	4	C7					Yongxing	JS	11	C5
Yiyuan (Nanma)	SD	10	C5	Yongjing	GS	27	E6	Yongxing	FJ	16	C4
Yizehe	GZ	32	C3	Yongji	JL	8	D7	Yongxing	HB	19	D6
Yizhang	HN	20	F5	(Kouqian)				Yongxing	SN	25	B6
Yizheng	JS	11	D5	Yongji (Zhaoyi)	SX	5	G2	Yongxing	SC	31	A2
Yolin Mod	NM	8	C3	Yongkang	AH	13	D4	Yongxing	SC	31	B4
Yong'an	HL	9	D4	Yongkang	YN	33	C3	Yongxing	SC	31	B5
Yong'an	HL	9	E6	Yongkangpu	NX	26	C2	Yongxing	SC	31	D4
Yong'an	SD	10	B5	Yongkang	ZJ	14	D5	Yongxing	GZ	32	C6
Yong'an	AH	13	C4	Yongle	HEB	3	C2	Yongxing	SC	31	A5
Yong'an	HN	20	F5	Yongle	GX	24	D4	Yongxing Dao	HI	22	B3
Yong'an	SC	31	D3	Yongledian	BJ	3	C3	Yongxingqiao	JX	15	D4
Yong'an	GZ	32	B6	Yongledian	SN	25	F4	Yongxing	HN	20	E6
Yong'anchang	SC	31	B2	Yongle Jiang	HN	20	E6	Yongxingzhen	SC	30	C5
Yong'an Guan	HN	20	F4	Yongle Qundao	HI	22	B2	Yongxin	JX	15	E2
	GX	24	B9	Yongling	LN	7	C8	Yongxiu	JX	15	B3
Yong'anshi	HN	20	C6	Yonglonghe	HB	19	D5	(Tujiabu)			
Yong'an Xi	ZJ	14	D5	Yongmao	JL	8	B3	Yongyang	JX	15	E2
Yong'an	FJ	16	E3	Yongnian	HEB	4	G2	(Yongyang) Weng'an	GZ	32	C6
Yongbi	HEB	4	F2	(Linmingguan)							
Yongchang	ZJ	14	C4	Yongning	BJ	3	A3	Yopurga	XJ	29	D3
Yongchang	JX	15	E2	Yongning	JL	8	D7	Youbu	ZJ	14	C4
Yongchang	GS	27	C5	Yongning	JS	11	D4	Youcheng	JX	15	B4
Yongcheng	HEN	18	D8	Yongning	FJ	16	F4	Youcun	JX	15	D3
				(Yongning) Xuyong	SC	30	D5	Youdunjie	JX	15	B4
Yongchuan	SC	30	D5					Youdunzi	QH	28	A2
Yongchun	FJ	16	E4	Yongning	GZ	32	E4	Youfang	HEB	4	F3
Yongcong	GZ	32	D8	Yongning	YN	33	B4	Youfang	JS	11	D5
Yongdeng Ansha	GD	22	D3	Yongning He	GS	25	F1-2	Youfanggou	SN	25	F2
Yongdeng	GS	27	D6	Yongning He	SC	32	B4	Youfangtai	SN	25	E5
Yongde	YN	33	C3	Yongningjian	LN	7	E5	Yougang	HN	20	B5
(Dedangzhen)				Yongning	NX	26	B3	Youguzhuang	TJ	3	B4
Yongdian	LN	7	D8	(Yanghe)				Youhao	HL	9	D5
Yongding He	BJ	3	C3	Yongning	GX	24	E6	Youji	AH	13	C4
	HEB	4	D4	(Pumiao)				Youjia	JX	15	D4
Yongding	FJ	16	F2	Yongping	JX	15	C5	Youjiabian	JX	15	D4
Yongding Xinhe	TJ	3	C4	Yongping	FJ	16	E2	You Jiang	GX	24	D5
Yongdingying	SC	30	E4	Yongping	SN	25	C5	Youjiatun	JL	8	C7
(Yongfeng)	HN	20	D5	Yongping	YN	33	C3	Youjiawan	HN	20	D4
Shuangfeng				Yongqiang	ZJ	14	E5	Youju	JX	15	C2
Yongfeng	SN	25	F5	Yongqing	SC	31	C3	Youlan	JX	15	C4
Yongfeng	SN	25	F6	Yongqing	HEB	4	D4	Youlan	GX	24	C7
Yongfengchang	SC	31	B6	Yongquan	ZJ	14	D6	Youli	GX	24	C4

Name	Prov	#	Grid
Youlin	SD	10	B5
Youma	GX	24	D8
Youmakou	GX	24	C8
Youquanzi	QH	28	A2
You Shan	JX	15	F2
	GD	21	A5
Youshashan	QH	28	A2
Youshui	JX	15	F3
You Shui	HN	20	C3
Youtian	JX	15	D2
Youtingpu	SC	31	C4
Youtingxu	HN	20	E4
Youxi	ZJ	14	D6
Youxi	HN	20	D4
Youxi	SC	30	D6
You Xi	FJ	16	D4
You Xian	HN	20	D6
Youxikou	FJ	16	D4
Youxi	FJ	16	D4
Youxizhen	SC	30	C6
Youyang	SC	30	D7
Youyi	HL	9	D6
Youyi Feng	XJ	29	A5
Youyiguan	GX	24	F4
Youyu	SX	5	A4
Youyu	SX	5	B4
(Liangjiayoufang)			
Youzai	SX	5	B5
Youzhagou	AH	12	C1
Youzhahe	HEN	18	F6
Youzhaping	GX	24	B8
Yuan'an	HB	19	C4
Yuanba	SN	25	H2
Yuanbao	HL	9	E5
Yuanbaoshan	NM	6	D6
Yuanbao Shan	GX	24	B7
Yuancun	HEN	18	A7
Yuandun	GS	27	D6
Yuanfang	HEN	18	C6
Yuangezhuang	SD	10	B8
Yuanhou	GZ	32	B4
(Yuanhouchang)			
(Yuanhouchang)	GZ	32	B4
Yuanhou			
Yuan Hu	HB	19	E8-9
Yuanhua	ZJ	12	D4
Yuanjiacun	SX	5	C3
Yuanjiahui	ZJ	12	D3
Yuan Jiang	YN	33	D4
Yuan Jiang (Riv.)	HN	20	C3
Yuanjiang Hanizu	YN	33	D4
Yizu Daizu			
Zizhixian			
Yuanjiang	HN	20	C5
(Yuanjiazhuang)	SN	25	G3
Foping			
Yuankeng	FJ	16	D3
Yuankou	GZ	32	D8
Yuanlang	GD	23	I8
Yuanli	TW	17	B3
Yuanlin	TW	17	C3
Yuanlin	NM	6	B7
Yuanling	HN	20	C3
Yuanmou	YN	33	C4
Yuanping	SX	5	C4
Yuanqiang	AH	13	C2
Yuanqiao	ZJ	14	D6
Yuanquan	SD	10	C5
Yuanqu	SX	5	F3
(Liuzhangzhen)			
Yuanshan	SC	30	C5
Yuanshanzi	GS	27	C4
Yuanshi	HEB	4	F2
Yuan Shui	JX	15	D2
Yuantan	HN	20	B6
Yuantan	AH	13	F3
Yuantan	HEN	18	E4
Yuantan	GD	21	B4
Yuantan	GZ	32	B5
Yuantian	SC	31	B1
Yuantongchang	HEB	4	F2
Yuantou	JX	15	E3
Yuantou	GX	24	C8
Yuantouzhu	JS	12	B4
Yuanwu	HEN	18	C5
Yuanxiang	HEN	18	C7
Yuanxiang	SX	5	D4
Yuanxiangzhen	JS	12	B2
Yuanyangqiao	SC	31	C5
Yuanyang	YN	33	D5
Yuanyang	HEN	18	B5
(Yangwu)			
Yuanyangzhen	GS	27	E7
Yuanyi	SC	30	C6
Yuanyongjing	YN	33	C4
Yuanzhuang	HEN	18	C4
Yuanzi He	SX	5	B4
Yucheng	ZJ	12	D5
Yucheng	SD	10	E3
Yucheng	SD	10	C3
Yucheng	HEN	18	C7
(Mamuji)			
Yuci	SX	5	D4
Yuci	SX	5	D4
Yucun	AH	13	F5
Yucun	ZJ	14	B4
Yudai He	SN	25	H2
Yudaokou	HEB	4	A4
Yudi Shan	NM	6	A7
	HL	9	A1
	JS	11	D7
Yudong	SC	31	D5
(Yudongxi) Ba	GS	26	E4
Yudu	SN	25	H3
Yuduba	JX	15	F3
Yudu	HEB	4	G2
Yuecheng	HEN	18	E6
Yuecheng	GD	21	B4
Yuecheng Ling	HN	20	F3-E3
	GX	24	B8-A8
Yuecheng Sk.	HEB	4	G1-2
Yuechi	SC	30	C6
Yuegezhuang	HEB	3	B5
Yuehedian	HEN	18	E5
Ynejiajing	NM	26	C1
Yuejin Qu	NX	26	C2
Yuejin Sk.	XJ	29	B5
Yuekou	JX	15	D4
Yuekou	HB	19	D6
(Yuelai) Huachuan	HL	9	D6
Yuelai	SC	30	C7
Yuelai	SC	31	B5
Yuelaichang	SC	30	D6
Yuele	GS	27	D8
Yueli	GX	24	B5
Yueliang Pao	JL	8	B4
Yuelongshi	HN	20	C6
Yuelu Shan	HN	20	C5
Yuemei	TW	17	C4
Yueqing Wan	ZJ	14	D6
Yueqing	ZJ	14	D5
Yu'erya	HEB	4	C6
Yueshan	AH	13	F3
Yueshan	HN	20	D5
Yuetian	HN	20	B6
Yuewang	JS	12	B5
Yue Xi	SC	31	D2
Yuexi He	SC	30	D4
Yuexi (Yaqian)	AH	13	F3
Yuexi	SC	30	D4
Yueyahu	NX	26	B3
(Yueyang) Gu Xian	SX	5	E3
Yueyang	HN	20	B6
Yuezhangji	AH	13	D3
Yuezhuang	SD	10	C5
Yuezi	JX	15	G3
Yufa	BJ	3	C3
Yufangwei	FJ	16	D3
Yufeng	SC	31	B3
Yufeng	SC	31	B4
Yufeng Shan	HEB	3	A1
Yufen He	SX	5	C3
Yugan	JX	15	C4
Yugong	HL	9	D6
Yugou	JS	11	C4
Yugou	AH	13	C4
Yuguan	HEB	4	D7
Yuguo	LN	7	C7
Yuhang	ZJ	14	B5
(Linping)			
Yuhe	HEN	18	B5
Yu He	SX	5	A5
Yuhebu	SN	25	C5
Yuhong	GX	24	C4
Yuhu	ZJ	14	E5
Yuhua	JS	11	C6
Yuhuan Dao	ZJ	14	D6
Yuhuang Ding	SD	10	C4

Yuxi	YN	33	C5	Zaoyuan	SD	10	C4	Zhaizi	HEB	4	F4
Yuya Ansha	HI	22	D3	Zaoyuan	SN	25	D5	Zhajiang	HN	20	D5
Yuyangguan	HB	19	D4	Zaoyuan	XJ	29	B5	Zhajin	JX	15	C2
Yuyang He	HB	19	D4	Zaoyuanpu	NX	26	C2	Zhajin Shui	JX	15	B2
Yuyao	ZJ	14	B6	Zaozhuang	SD	10	D4	Zhakou	HB	19	E5
Yuyi	JX	15	C4					Zhakou	GX	24	F7
Yuyingzi	HEB	3	A4	Zapug	XZ	34	B2	(Zhamo) Bomi (Bowo)	XZ	34	C5
Yuza	SC	30	C3	Zaqên	QH	28	D4				
Yuzaokou	SX	5	C5	Za Qu	QH	28	D5	Zhanang	XZ	34	C4
Yuzhang	GZ	32	E4	Zawa	QH	28	B7	Zhancheng	SD	10	B4
Yuzhen	HEN	18	C6	Zawa	XJ	29	D3	Zhandian	HB	19	C7
Yuzhong	GS	27	E7	Zayü	XZ	34	C6	Zhandian	HEN	18	B5
(Yuzhou) Chongqing	SC	30	D6	Zayü Qu	XZ	34	D6-C6	Zhan'erxiang	GS	27	F8
				Zayü　(Gyigang)	XZ	34	C6	Zhangbaiwan	HEB	4	C5
Yuzhuang	SX	5	C4	Zeguo	ZJ	14	D6	Zhangbaling	AH	13	D5
Yuzhuo Jiao	HI	22	B3	Zehe	GD	23	H6	Zhangba Ling	AH	42	B2-3
Yuzishan	BJ	3	B4	Zejiahu	HN	20	C2	Zhangbaotun	SD	10	B4
Yuzuizhen	SC	31	C5	Zêkog	QH	28	C7	Zhangbei	HEB	4	B2
				Zelinggou	QH	28	B5	Zhangcun	AH	13	C2
Z				Zêmdasam	SC	30	B3	Zhangcun	HEN	18	E3
				Zênda	SC	30	B1	Zhangcun	ZJ	14	B4
				Zengchong	GD	21	B4	Zhangcun	ZJ	14	C5
Zabqung	XZ	34	C3	Zengfeng Shan	JL	8	E9	Zhangcun	JX	15	C5
Zadoi	QH	28	D4	Zenggang	NX	26	B3	Zhangcun	JX	15	D4
(Zagunao) Li Xian	SC	30	C4	Zeng Jiang	GD	21	B4-5	Zhangcunyi	SN	25	E5
Za'gya Zangbo	XZ	34	B4	Zengmu Ansha	HI	22	E3	Zhangdang	LN	7	C8
Zaibian	GZ	32	E7	Zengsheng	JL	8	C6	(Zhangde) Anyang	HEN	18	A6
Zaima	GZ	32	D7	Zengtian	GD	21	A5				
Zaimiao	GX	24	E5	Zengtian	JX	15	D3	Zhangdeng	HEB	4	E3
Zaiyang	SC	30	D4	Zengwen Xi	TW	17	C3	Zhangdian	JS	11	D6
(Zalantun) Butha Qi	NM	6	B7	Zepu(Poskam)	XJ	29	D3	Zhangdian	SX	5	E4
				Zêtang	XZ	34	C4	Zhangdian	SX	5	F4
Zamtangdoima	SC	30	B3	Zetouji	SD	10	B8	Zhangdian	SX	5	G3
Zamtang	SC	30	B3	Zezhang	SX	5	F3	(Zhangdian) Zibo	SD	10	C5
(Gamda)				(Zhabdün) Zhongba	XZ	34	C3	Zhangdiyingzi	HL	9	B4
Zanda　(Toling)	XZ	34	C1					Zhangdu	AH	13	F5
Zangang	HEB	4	D4	Zhag'yab	XZ	34	C6	Zhangdu Hu	HB	19	D7
Zanggezhuang	SD	10	B7	Zhaiba	GZ	32	B5	Zhang'enpu	NX	26	C2
Zangguy	XJ	29	D3	Zhaidian	SX	5	F2	Zhangfang	BJ	3	C2
Zangji	HEN	18	E5	Zhaigang	GD	21	A4	Zhangfeng	YN	33	C2
Zangjiaqiao	HEB	4	E4	Zhaihao	GZ	32	D7	Zhangfengji	SD	10	D3
Zango	SC	30	C3	Zhaihe	HEN	18	E6	Zhanggang	JS	12	A3
Zangqênrong	SC	30	D2	Zhai He	HEN	18	E6	Zhanggang	HB	19	D5
Zanhuang	HEB	4	F2	Zhaijiasuo	GS	26	E2	Zhanggang	FJ	16	E5
Zaohe	JS	11	B4	Zhaike	NX	26	D3	Zhanggezhuang	BJ	3	B4
Zaoheshi	JX	15	E2	Zhaili	SD	10	B7	Zhanggezhuang	SD	10	C7
Zaohuli	SD	10	B4	Zhaili	SD	10	C4	Zhanggong	HEN	18	C7
Zaolin	SX	5	B5	Zhaili	FJ	16	C3	Zhanggongdu	JX	15	B3
Zaolin(Caolinxu)	JX	15	E2	Zhailing	HEB	4	B4	Zhangguan	SD	10	B3
Zaolinping	SN	25	C6	Zhaiqian	HN	20	F6	Zhangguandian	AH	13	D2
Zaoqiang	HEB	4	F3	Zhaiqiao	JS	11	E5	Zhangguang	AH	13	D4
Zaosheng	GS	27	E9	Zhaisha	GX	24	C7	Zhangguangcai Ling	JL	8	C9
Zaoshi	HB	19	D6	Zhaishang	SX	5	C3		HL	9	F4-E5
Zaoshi	HN	20	B4	Zhaishizhen	HN	20	E3	Zhangguizhuang	TJ	3	D4
Zaoshi	HN	20	E5	(Jiusuining)				Zhanggutai	LN	7	B6
Zaoxi	ZJ	14	B4	Zhaitang	BJ	3	B2	Zhang He	HEB	4	G2
Zaoyang	SN	25	H5	Zhaiwu	GD	23	H6	Zhang He	AH	12	D1
Zaoyang	HB	19	B5	Zhaixi	ZJ	14	C4	Zhanghedian	HEB	4	G2
Zaoyang Zhan	HB	19	B5	Zhaixidian	HEB	4	E2	Zhangheping	SN	25	H4
Zaoyuan	HEB	4	G3	Zhaixu	GX	24	E7	Zhanghuang	GX	24	E7

Zhanghuanggang	JS	12	A4	Zhangping	FJ	16	E3	Zhan He	HL	9	C4
Zhanghua (Changhua)	TW	17	B3	Zhangpu	JS	11	E6	Zhanhua	SD	10	B5
				Zhangpu	FJ	16	F3	(Fuguo)			
Zhanghuban	FJ	16	D4	Zhangqiangzhen	LN	7	B6	Zhanji	HEN	18	C7
Zhangji	AH	13	C2	Zhangqiao	AH	13	D4				
Zhangji	AH	13	D4	Zhangqiao	HEN	18	D6	Zhanjiang Gang	GD	21	C3
Zhangji	JS	11	B4	Zhangqiu	SD	10	C3	Zhanjiang	GD	21	C3
Zhangjiaba	JS	12	A3	Zhangqiu	SD	10	C4	Zhanjiaqiao	ZJ	12	D3
Zhangjiabang	HB	19	D8	(Mingshui)				Zhanshang	SX	5	D5
Zhangjiabian	GD	23	H7	Zhangsanying	HEB	4	B5	Zhanxi	JX	15	C3
Zhangjiabu	SD	10	B9	Zhangsanzhai	HEN	18	B6	Zhanyi	YN	33	C5
Zhangjiachuan Huizu	GS	27	E8	Zhangshanji	AH	13	D5	Zhanyu	JL	8	C3
Zizhixian				Zhangshanying	BJ	3	A2	Zhao'an Wan	FJ	16	G3
Zhangjiadian	JL	8	D10	Zhangshe	SD	10	C6	Zhao'an	FJ	16	G3
Zhangjiadian	AH	13	E3	Zhangshi	HEB	3	D2	Zhaobao	HEN	18	C5
Zhangjiadu	ZJ	14	D5	Zhangshi	HEN	18	C6	Zhaobei	SX	5	B6
Zhangjiafang	HN	20	C7	Zhangshudun	JX	15	C5	Zhaobeikou	HEB	4	E4
Zhangjiagang	JS	12	B4	Zhangshugang	HN	20	C5	Zhaobi	SX	5	D5
Zhangjiaji	HB	19	C5	Zhang Shui	JX	15	F2	Zhaobishan	NX	26	C2
Zhangjiajing	NX	26	D3	Zhang Shui	HB	19	C4	Zhaocheng	SX	5	E3
Zhangjiajuan	GS	27	B2	Zhang Shui	HB	19	C6	Zhaochuan	HEB	4	C3
				Zhangshuping	HB	19	C4	Zhaochuan	SN	25	G6
Zhangjiakou	HEB	4	C2	Zhangshuxia	HN	20	F5	Zhaocun	BJ	3	C3
Zhangjialing	JX	15	B4	(Zhangshuzhen)	JX	15	C3	Zhaocun	HEN	18	D4
Zhangjialou	SD	10	D6	Qingjiang				Zhaodong	HL	9	D3
Zhang Jiang	FJ	16	F3-G3	Zhangtaizi	LN	7	C7	(Zhaoge) Qi Xian	HEN	18	B6
(Zhangjiapan)	SN	25	C4	Zhangtao	HEN	18	E6	Zhaogezhuang	SD	10	C6
Jingbian				Zhangting	ZJ	14	B6	Zhaogezhuang	TJ	3	B4
Zhangjiaping	HN	20	C3	Zhangwan	FJ	16	D5	Zhaogezhuang	HEB	4	D6
Zhangjiashan	JX	15	C3	Zhangwei Xinhe	HEB	4	F4-5	Zhaogezhuang	SD	10	B7
Zhangjiatan	SN	25	D6		SD	10	B3	Zhaoguan	AH	13	E5
Zhangjiawan	BJ	3	B3	Zhangwu	ZJ	14	B4	Zhaoguang	HL	9	C4
Zhangjiawan	NX	26	D3	Zhangwu	LN	7	B6	Zhaoguanzhen	SD	10	C3
Zhangjiayingzi	LN	7	C3	Zhangxi	AH	13	F4	Zhaohe	HEN	18	D4
Zhangjiayuan	NX	26	D3	Zhangxi	ZJ	14	D5	Zhao He	HEN	18	E4
Zhangjiazhuang	HEB	4	D7	Zhangxia	SD	10	C3	Zhaohua	SC	30	B5
Zhangjiazhuang	SX	5	B3	Zhang	GS	27	E7	Zhaohuazhen	SC	31	D3
Zhangjiazhuang	SX	5	E3	Zhangxin	BJ	3	B3	Zhaoji	JS	11	B4
Zhangjicun	HEB	4	B2	Zhangxing	SD	10	B7	Zhaoji	AH	13	C3
Zhangjingqiao	JS	11	E6	Zhangyan	SH	11	F7	Zhaoji	HEN	18	E7
Zhangjinhe	HB	19	D5					Zhaojiachang	SC	30	C6
Zhangjunmu	HEN	18	C7	Zhangye	GS	27	C5	Zhaojiadian	HB	19	C4
Zhangla	SC	30	B4	Zhangyi	NX	26	E3	Zhaojiahe	NX	26	E3
Zhanglan	SX	5	D4	Zhangyuan	SX	5	E4	Zhaojiapeng	HEB	3	B1
Zhangli	SX	5	F3	Zhangzhen	ZJ	14	C5	Zhaojiapu	HEB	4	E5
Zhangliangdian	HEN	18	D5	Zhangzhou	FJ	16	F3	Zhaojiatun	LN	7	C5
Zhangling	SD	10	C6	Zhangzhu	JS	11	E5	Zhaojiazui	SD	10	B5
Zhangling	HL	9	A2	Zhangzhuang	SD	10	B3	Zhaojin	SN	25	E4
Zhanglou	JS	11	B3	Zhangzhuang	SD	10	C5	Zhaojue	SC	30	D4
Zhanglou	AH	13	D3	Zhangzhuang	SD	10	C5	Zhaojunmu	NM	6	F10
Zhanglu	SD	10	C2	Zhangzhuang	SD	10	D4	Zhaokang	SX	5	F3
Zhangmao	HEN	18	C3	Zhangzhuang	SD	10	D4	Zhaokua	YN	33	C5
Zhangmu	GX	24	C9	Zhangzhuang	HEN	18	E7	Zhaoling	HN	20	D6
Zhangmu	GX	24	D7	Zhangzhuang	JX	15	D2	Zhaoliqiao	HB	19	E6
Zhangmu	GX	24	E7	Zhangzi Dao	LN	7	E6	Zhaomiao	AH	13	C2
Zhangmuqiao	AH	13	E3	Zhangzihu	NM	26	C1	Zhaoniu He	SD	10	C3
Zhangmushi	HN	20	D5	Zhangzi	SX	5	E4	Zhaoping	GX	24	C8
Zhangmutou	GD	21	B5	Zhanhan Tan	GD	22	B3	Zhaoqiao	HEB	4	F3
Zhangouji	AH	13	D3	Zhanhe	HL	9	C4				
Zhangpeng	GD	23	H7	Zhanhe	YN	33	B4	Zhaoqing	GD	21	B4

Zhongzhou	GD	21	A4
Zhongzhuang	HEB	3	C1
Zhongzhuangpu	SX	5	B5
Zhouba	SC	31	D1
Zhoubuxu	JX	15	F2
Zhoucheng	NX	26	B3
Zhoucun	SX	5	F4
Zhoucun	SD	10	C4
Zhoudangfan	HEN	18	F6
Zhoudian	SD	10	C4
Zhouguan	HN	20	D4
Zhou He	TJ	3	B4
Zhou He	SC	30	C6
Zhou He	AH	13	E4
Zhouhu	JX	15	D2
Zhouji	AH	13	B3
Zhouji	AH	13	D2
Zhoujia	HL	9	E4
Zhoujia	ZJ	14	B4
Zhoujia	SC	31	B6
Zhoujiadian	HN	20	B4
Zhoujiagang	AH	13	D5
Zhoujiajian	SN	25	C5
Zhoujiajing	GS	27	C6
(Zhoujiaping) Nanzheng	SN	25	G2
Zhoujiatun	LN	7	C5
Zhoujiazhen	SC	31	B6
Zhoukoudianzhen	BJ	3	C2
Zhoukou	HEN	18	D6
Zhoulaozui	HB	19	D5
Zhouliangzhuang	TJ	3	C4
Zhoulichang	SC	30	D5
Zhoulu	GX	24	D5
Zhouning	FJ	16	C5
Zhoupeng	AH	13	D2
Zhoupo	SC	31	C2
Zhoupu	SH	11	E7
Zhouqin	GZ	32	E6
Zhouqingzhuang	HEB	3	D4
Zhouquan	ZJ	12	D4
Zhoushan Dao	ZJ	14	B7-C7
Zhoushan Qundao(Apg.)	ZJ	14	B7
Zhoushizhuang	SX	5	A5
Zhoushu	JS	12	C5
Zhoushuizi	LN	7	F5
Zhoutian	JX	15	B3
Zhoutian	JX	15	F3
Zhoutieqiao	JS	11	E5
Zhoutun	QH	28	C7
Zhouwangcun	AH	12	D1
Zhouwangmiao	ZJ	12	D4
Zhouwangpu	HN	20	D4
Zhouxiang	ZJ	14	B6
Zhouxin	GD	23	G6
Zhouxinzhen	JS	12	B4
Zhouying	SD	10	E4
Zhouzhai	AH	13	B3
Zhouzhi	SN	25	F4
Zhouzhuang	JS	11	D5
Zhouzhuang	JS	11	E6
Zhuaji	HL	9	C8
Zhuandian	HEN	18	E6
Zhuanghe	LN	7	E6
Zhuangjia Sha	JS	11	D7
Zhuanglang He	GS	27	D6
Zhuanglang	GS	27	E8
Zhuangli	SN	25	F5
Zhuanglicun	SX	5	C5
Zhuangmo	SX	5	C4
Zhuangmu	AH	13	D4
Zhuangqiao	ZJ	14	C6
Zhuangshi	ZJ	12	E6
Zhuangta	HN	20	B3
Zhuanjiao	SN	25	E4
Zhuanjing	SN	25	C3
Zhuanlu	HEB	3	D1
Zhuanqiao	SH	12	C5
Zhuantang	ZJ	14	B5
Zhubgyügoin	QH	28	D5
Zhubi Dao	HI	22	D3
Zhubuyuan	AH	13	E3
Zhucang	GZ	32	C6
Zhucang	GZ	32	D4
Zhucheng	SD	10	D6
Zhuchengzi	JL	8	C6
Zhucun	GD	23	G7
Zhu Dao	LN	7	E5
Zhudong	TW	17	B4
Zhudongshe	SX	5	C4
Zhudun	AH	13	F3
Zhufengzhen	AH	12	D2
Zhugan He	HEN	18	F6
Zhuganpu	HEN	18	E6
Zhugao	SC	31	B3
Zhugaotang	HN	20	D3
Zhuge	SD	10	D5
Zhuge	ZJ	14	C4
Zhugou	SD	10	C7
Zhugouzhen	HEN	18	E5
Zhugqu	GS	27	F7
Zhuguang Shan	JX	15	F1-E2
	HN	20	F6-7
Zhuguansi	HN	20	F5
Zhuguanzhai	SN	25	B6
Zhugusi	QH	28	B8
Zhuhai	GD	21	B4
Zhuhe	HB	19	E6
Zhuhe	HL	9	E5
Zhuhushan	JX	15	C4
(Zhuizishan) Weichang	HEB	4	B5
Zhuji	AH	13	D3
(Zhuji) Shangqiu	HEN	18	C7
Zhuji	SD	10	B8
Zhujiaba	SN	25	H3
Zhujia Chuan	SX	5	B3
Zhujiafang	LN	7	C6
Zhujia Jian	ZJ	14	C7
Zhujiajiao	SH	11	E7
Zhujiakeng	JX	15	C5
(Zhujiang) Jiangpu	JS	12	A1
Zhu Jiang (Riv.)	GD	23	H7
Zhujiang Kou	GD	21	C4-B4
Zhujiangqing	JX	15	D2
Zhujiaqiao	AH	12	D2
Zhujiatun	LN	7	C7
Zhujiawan	AH	13	D4
Zhujiawan	HB	19	D7
Zhujiayu	SX	5	E2
(Zhujing) Jinshan	SH	12	D5
Zhuji	ZJ	14	C5
Zhukeng	GD	21	B4
Zhukou	FJ	16	D3
Zhukou	HEN	18	C7
Zhulanbu	JX	15	F3
Zhuli	HEN	18	D6
Zhuliang	JX	15	D4
Zhuliao	GD	23	G7
Zhulin	JS	11	E5
Zhulin	HB	19	B6
Zhulin	YN	33	D6
Zhulinguan	SN	25	G6
Zhuliudian	SD	10	C5
Zhulong He	HEB	4	E3
Zhulongqiao	AH	13	D5
Zhuluke	LN	7	C3
Zhumadian	HEN	18	E6
Zhumaguan	ZJ	14	C4
Zhunan	TW	17	B3
Zhuogang	HB	19	D8
Zhuokeji	SC	30	C4
Zhuolan	TW	17	B3
Zhuolu	HEB	4	C3
Zhuoshui	SC	30	D7
Zhuoshui	GZ	32	B7
Zhuoshui Xi	TW	17	C3
Zhuotian	FJ	16	E2
Zhuozhou	HEB	4	D3
Zhuozhang Beiyuan	SX	5	E4-5
Zhuozhang He	SX	5	E5
Zhuozhang Nanyuan	SX	5	E5-4
Zhuozhang Xiyuan	SX	5	E4
Zhuozi Shan	NM	27	C8-B8
Zhuozi Shan	NM	37	E4
Zhuozi	NM	6	D5
Zhuping	GZ	32	C7
Zhuqi	FJ	16	D5
Zhuqi	TW	17	C3
Zhuqiao	SD	10	B7
Zhuqiao	JS	11	C5
Zhuqiao	SH	11	E7
Zhusha	GD	21	B3
Zhushan	JX	15	G2
Zhushan	TW	17	C3

Zhushanqiao	JX	15	D3
Zhushan	HB	19	B3
Zhushi	HEN	18	D5
Zhushui He	SD	10	D3
Zhutai	SD	10	C5
Zhutan	JX	15	C2
Zhutang	JS	11	E6
Zhutian	SD	10	D4
Zhutian	JX	15	C5
Zhuting	JX	15	D2
Zhuting	HN	20	D6
Zhutuo	SC	30	D5
Zhuwangpu	GS	27	C6
Zhuwo	BJ	3	B2
Zhuwu	SD	10	C8
Zhuxi	ZJ	14	D5
Zhuxi	ZJ	14	D3
Zhuxi	SC	31	C4
Zhuxiang	AH	13	D4
Zhuxianzhen	HEN	18	C6
Zhuxichang	JX	15	C2
Zhuxi	HB	19	B2
Zhuya	SD	10	C5
Zhuyang	SD	10	C4
Zhuyangguan	HEN	18	D3
Zhuyangxi	SC	31	D4
Zhuyangzhen	HEN	18	C2
Zhuyu	SC	30	B6
Zhuyu	HB	19	D6
Zhuyuan	SC	31	C2
Zhuyuan	YN	33	C5
Zhuyuanba	SC	30	B5
Zhuzeqiao	JS	11	E5
Zhuzhenji	JS	11	D4
Zhuzhoujiang	HN	20	E3
Zhuzhou	HN	20	D6
Zhuzhou (Lukou)	HN	20	D6
Zhuzhuang	SD	10	C2
Zhuzikou	HN	20	B5
Zibo (Zhangdian)	SD	10	C5
Zichang (Wayaobu)	SN	25	C5
Zichuan	SD	10	C4
Zigong	SC	30	D5
Zigui	HB	19	C3
Zihag	SC	30	D3
Zi He	SD	10	C5
Zihedian	SD	10	C5
Zihong	SX	5	D4
Zihukou	JX	15	C6
Zijiao	SD	10	B4
Zijin	HB	19	B4
Zijingguan	HEB	4	D3
Zijingguan	GZ	32	C7
Zijing Shan	SX	5	E3
Zijin Shan	JS	11	D4
Zijin	GD	21	B5
Zikoufang	FJ	16	D3
Zilaiqiao	AH	13	D5
Ziliang	GX	24	D8
Ziliangping	HN	20	A4
Zimenqiao	HN	20	D5
Zipingpu	SC	31	A1
Ziqiu	HB	19	D3
Zi Qu	QH	28	D5
Ziqudukou	QH	28	D4
Zirun	SX	5	B4
Zishan	HB	19	C5
Zishan	JX	15	F3
Zishi	SC	30	C4
Zishikou	HEB	3	C1
Zi Shui	HN	20	C4
Zitong He	SC	31	A3
Zitong	SC	30	C5
Ziwei	HEB	4	E3
Ziwu He	SN	25	G4
Ziwu Ling	SN	25	E4
	GS	27	E9
Ziwuzhen	SN	25	F4
Zixi	JX	15	C5
Zixi	HN	20	E4
Zixing	HN	20	F6
Zixiqiao	JX	15	D4
Zixi	JX	15	D5
Ziya He	TJ	3	D3
	HEB	4	E4
Ziyang	AH	13	C5
Ziyang	SC	30	C5
Ziyang	SN	25	H4
Ziya Xinhe	TJ	3	D4
Ziyuan	GX	24	A8
Ziyundong Shan	FJ	16	E3
Ziyun Miaozu Bouyeizu Zizhixian	GZ	32	E5
Zizhong	SC	30	D5
Zizhou (Shuanghuyu)	SN	25	C6
Zoco	XZ	34	B2
Zogang (Wangda)	XZ	34	C6
Zogqên	SC	30	B2
Zoigê	SC	30	B4
Zong'ai	SX	5	C5
(Zongga) Gyirong	XZ	34	C3
Zonggag	SC	30	C4
Zongjiafangzi	QH	28	B5
Zongjiangkou	GX	24	F7
Zongkou	HB	19	D5
Zongpu	AH	13	D4
Zongxoi	XZ	34	C4
Zongyang	AH	13	F4
Zongza	SC	30	D2
Zongzhai	GS	27	C4
Zoulang Nanshan	GS	27	C4
	QH	28	A6
Zouma	GX	24	C8
Zoumaping	HB	19	E3
Zoumayi	HEB	4	D2
Zouping	SD	10	C4
Zouqiao	JX	15	B3
Zoushi	HN	20	B4
Zouwu	SD	10	E4
Zou Xian	SD	10	D3
Zouxu	GX	24	D6
Zu'anzhen	SN	25	F4
(Zuitaizi) Kang Xian	GS	27	F7
(Zuitouzhen) Taibai	SN	25	F3
Zuli He	GS	27	D7-E7
Zulou	AH	13	B3
Zunhua	HEB	4	C5
Zunyi	GZ	32	C5
Zunyi (Nanbai)	GZ	32	C5
Zuo'an	JX	15	E2
Zuoba	AH	13	F3
Zuocheng	HEN	18	B6
Zuodeng	GX	24	D5
Zuogezhuang	HEB	3	D3
Zuohui	SX	5	E5
Zuo Jiang	GX	24	E5
Zuojiawu	HEB	3	B5
Zuojiazhen	JL	8	C7
Zuolonggou	SN	25	H4
Zuoquan	SX	5	D5
Zuoshan	SD	10	C6
Zuotan	GD	21	B5
Zuowei	HEB	4	C2
Zuoying	TW	17	D3
Zuoyun	SX	5	B4
Zuozhou	GX	24	E5
Zurong	GX	24	D4
Zuyangzhuang	HEB	4	F3

Pronunciation of Chinese Phonetic Alphabet
Noted with Approximate English Equivalents

Following is a Chinese phonetic alphabet table showing the alphabet pronunciation with approximate English equivalents. Spelling in the Wade system is in brackets for reference.

"**a**" (a), a vowel, as in far;

"**b**" (p), a consonant, as in be;

"**c**" (ts), a consonant, as "ts" in its; and "**ch**" (ch), a consonant, as "ch" in church, strongly aspirated;

"**d**" (t), a consonant, as in do;

"**e**" (e), a vowel, as "er" in her, the "r" being silent; but "**ie**", a diphthong, as in yes; and "**ei**", a diphthong, as in way;

"**f**" (f), a consonant, as in foot;

"**g**" (k), a consonant, as in go;

"**h**" (h), a consonant, as in her, strongly aspirated;

"**i**" (i), a vowel, two pronunciations:
1) as in eat;
2) as in sir in syllables beginning with the consonants c, ch, r, s, sh, z and zh;

"**j**" (ch), a consonant, as in jeep;

"**k**" (k), a consonant, as in kind, strongly aspirated;

"**l**" (l), a consonant, as in land;

"**m**" (m), a consonant, as in me;

"**n**" (n), a consonant, as in no;

"**o**" (o), a vowel, as "aw" in law;

"**p**" (p), a consonant, as in par, strongly aspirated;

"**q**" (ch), a consonant, as "ch" in cheek;

"**r**" (j), a consonant pronounced as "r" but not rolled, or like "z" in azure;

"**s**" (s, ss, sz), a consonant, as in sister; and "**sh**" (sh), a consonant, as "sh " in shore;

"**t**" (t), a consonant as in top, strongly aspirated;

"**u**" (u), a vowel, as in too, also as in the French "u" in "tu" or the German umlauted "u" in "Muenchen";

"**v**" (v), is used only to produce foreign and national minority words, and local dialects;

"**w**" (w), used as a semi-vowel in syllables beginning with "u" when not preceded by consonants, pronounced as in want;

"**x**" (hs), a consonant, as "sh" in she;

"**y**", used as a semi-vowel in syllables beginning with "i" or "u" when not preceded by consonants, pronounced as in yet;

"**z**" (ts, tz), a consonant, as in zero; and "**zh**" (ch), a consonant, as "j" in "jump".

Pronunciation of Chinese Phonetic Alphabet
Noted with International Phonetic Symbols

a [a]	g [k]	n [n]	sh [ʂ]	xu [ɕy]
b [p]	h [x]	ng [ŋ]	shi [ʂʅ]	xue [ɕyɛ]
c [tsʻ]	i [i]	o [o]	si [sʅ]	y [j]
ch [tʂʻ]	-ie [iɛ]	p [pʻ]	t [tʻ]	ye [jɛ]
chi [tʂʻʅ]	j [tɕ]	q [tɕʻ]	u [u]	yu [y]
ci [tsʻʅ]	ju [tɕy]	qu [tɕʻy]	ü [y]	yue [yɛ]
d [t]	jue [tɕyɛ]	que [tɕʻyɛ]	-üe [yɛ]	z [ts]
e [ə]	k [kʻ]	r [ʐ] [r]	v [v]	zh [tʂ]
er [ər]	l [l]	ri [ʐʅ]	w [w]	zhi [tʂʅ]
f [f]	m [m]	s [s]	x [ɕ]	zi [tsʅ]

Basic Geographic Terms in *Pinyin* (Chinese Phonetic Alphabet) and English

PINYIN	English	*PINYIN*	English
Ansha	shoal, reef	Qu	irrigation canal
Bandao	peninsula	Quan	spring
Bei	north	Qudao	irrigation canal
Changcheng	the Great Wall	Qundao	islands, archipelago
Chezhan	station	Qunjiao	reefs
Cunzhuang	village	Shadi	sands, sandy land
Da	greater, grand, big	Shamo	desert
Dao	island	Shan	mountain, mountains
Diqu	prefecture	Shandi	hilly land,
Dong	east		mountainous area
Dong	cave	Shanfeng	peak
Feng	peak, mount	Shang	upper
Fenhongqu	flood diversion area	Shankou	pass
Gang	harbor, port	Shanmai	mountains, range
Gaoyuan	plateau, highland	Shi	city
Gonglu	highway	Shui	river
Gongnongqu	industrial-agricultural	Shuidao	channel
	district	Shuiku (Sk.)	reservoir
Gongyuan	park	Si	temple, lamasery
Guan	pass	Tan	beach
Hai	sea	Tequ	special district
Haibin	seashore, beach	Tielu	railway
Haixia	strait, channel	Tiyuchang	stadium
He	river	Tiyuguan	gymnasium
Hou	rear, back	Wai	outer
Hu	lake	Wan	gulf, bay
Jiang	river	Wenhua guji	cultural and historical
Jianhe	distributary		site
Jiao	reef	Xi	west
Jiao	cape	Xi	stream, brook
Jie	street, avenue	Xia	gorge, valley
Jing	well	Xia	lower
Liedao	islands, archipelago	Xiagu	gorge, valley
Linchang	forestry center	Xian	county
Ling	mountain, ridge	Xiao	little, lesser, small
Linqu	forest district	Xingzhengqu	administrative district
Lu	road	Xuhongqu	flood storage area
Matou	dock	Yang	ocean
Meng	league	Yiji	relics
Miao	temple	You	right
Muchang	pasture-land	Yuchang	fishing ground
Nan	south	Yu	island
Nei	inner	Yunhe	canal
Nur	lake	Zhan	station
Pao, paozi	lake	Zhaoze	swamp, marsh
Pendi	basin	Zhen	town
Pingyuan	plain	Zhong	central
Po	lake	Zizhiqi	autonomous banner
Pubu	waterfall	Zizhixian	autonomous county
Qi	banner	Zizhizhou	autonomous prefecture
Qian	front	Zu	nationality, ethnic
Qiao	bridge		group
Qiuling	hills	Zuo	left

List of Abbreviations

Apg — Archipelago
A.Rgn — Autonomous Region
Bsn — Basin
Ch — Channel
Des — Desert
Gf — Gulf
Is — Island
Lk — Lake
Mt.Ar — Mountainous Area
Mts — Mountains
Pen — Peninsula
Pln — Plain
Plt — Plateau
Riv — River
Sk — Reservoir
Str — Strait
Wf — Waterfall

中华人民共和国地图集

（英文版）

中国地图出版社编制

外 文 出 版 社

中国地图出版社 出版

中国国际图书贸易总公司

（中国国际书店）发行

北京 399 信箱

1989 年　　　　第一版

ISBN 7-119-00560-X／K·36（外）

05000

12-E-2291D

本图上中国国界线系按照中国地图出版社
1980 年出版的《中华人民共和国地图》绘制。